Property of:

DISABILITY RIGHTS
INTERNATIONAL

202-296-0800 | info@driadvocacy.org

Eric,

Great to see you &
keep up the great work!
Best,
Peter

4-2-05

DISABILITY CIVIL RIGHTS LAW AND POLICY

By

Peter Blanck

Charles M. & Marion Kierscht Professor of Law
Director,
Law, Health Policy & Disability Center
University of Iowa

Eve Hill

Executive Director,
Western Law Center for Disability Rights
Visiting Associate Professor,
Loyola Law School

Charles D. Siegal

Partner,
Munger, Tolles & Olson LLP

Michael Waterstone

Assistant Professor,
University of Mississippi School of Law

HORNBOOK SERIES®

THOMSON
™
WEST

Mat #40124367

Hornbook Series, *WESTLAW* and West Group are trademarks registered in the U.S. Patent and Trademark Office.

© 2004 West, a Thomson business
      610 Opperman Drive
      P.O. Box 64526
      St. Paul, MN 55164–0526
      1–800–328–9352

Printed in the United States of America

ISBN 0–314–14514–1

TEXT IS PRINTED ON 10% POST CONSUMER RECYCLED PAPER

Dedication

To those individuals and advocates who have changed the world for the next generation of children with disabilities.

PB – for Wendy, Jason, Daniel, Albert and Caroline

EH – for John and the WLCDR

CDS – for Sandra and Anne

MW – for Julie, and my parents, Stuart and Judy

Preface

There have been dramatic legal and policy developments, and strong academic and practical interest, in the area of American and international disability civil rights law. This treatise presents a comprehensive examination of the development of disability rights law and policy in the United States, with additional commentary on international disability law.

The material in this treatise is placed in the context of disability civil rights law in general, and the law of the Americans with Disabilities Act (ADA) of 1990 in particular. The introduction by Paul Steven Miller eloquently states the simple message of disability civil rights and the ADA: independence, community integration, inclusion in society, and empowerment.

We begin the treatise in Part 1 with an examination of the basis of discrimination against people with disabilities, including the history of such discrimination and a review of studies that explore why people engage in this sort of discrimination. The treatise progresses through an examination of the federal laws that culminated in the passage of the ADA.

We next examine the debate in social science and economic literature dealing with the philosophy, appropriateness, and efficacy of laws like the ADA, as well as of the accommodation mandate defined by the statute. It is these public policy questions that are the ultimate queries: Do we need a law like the ADA, or should we, as some urge, rely on market forces to sort those with disabilities into jobs?

The definition of "disability" under the ADA and other laws, and the identification of those who have a covered disability are, to say the least, critical to any discussion of ADA law and policy. In Part 2, we explore the threshold question of how the ADA's definition of disability has been defined, interpreted, and studied, and what is required to achieve the social and economic equality for those with disabilities covered by the law.

In Part 3, the treatise presents extensive coverage of ADA employment discrimination issues and case law (Title I of the Act). The analysis includes review of issues associated with pre-employment interviews, job qualifications, medical examinations, and the constellation of issues associated with reasonable accommodations.

We proceed in Part 4 to address the ADA's requirements applicable to governmental and non-governmental actors (Title II of the Act), including issues related to the integration of people with disabilities into communities. We discuss among other topics Title II's statutory and regulatory scheme, the issue of whether Congress validly abrogated the states' sovereign immunity under Title II, and the elements of a Title II claim. We highlight several pressing Title II issues, such as access to voting and transportation.

We next turn in Part 5 to the law's requirements applicable to public accommodations under Title III of the statute. We review the scope of Title III coverage, prohibited conduct, effective communication, and the nature of reasonable modifications needed to achieve access to covered entities. We also address accessibility of buildings and other facilities.

In Part 6, the treatise provides an extensive review of the remedies available for the various ADA claims and the procedures required to pursue them, as well as alternative dispute resolution and mediation.

The treatise examines in Part 7 several state antidiscrimination laws, including recent amendments to those laws. We explore the similarities and differences between these laws and the ADA.

Looking farther beyond the United States, in Part 8 we review in detail international disability rights laws. The treatise examines the basics of international law, other states' approaches to disability civil rights, and existing initiatives by regional organizations and the United Nations.

The next parts of the treatise address applications of the ADA to emerging American law and policy. In Part 9, we examine the applicability of the ADA to employment, welfare, and health care policy – examining the ADA and the Workforce Investment Act, the Ticket to Work and Work Incentives Improvement Act, Medicaid and health insurance law, and genetic discrimination. We explore research seeking to understand the Act's real-world consequences: If unacceptably large numbers of individuals with disabilities are without jobs, will a law such as the ADA (or an even an amended ADA) bring about enhanced employment and economic independence? Or, will such a law only work to make employment more difficult for the disabled to find and to keep?

Finally, in Part 10 we explore the applicability of the ADA to technology law and policy, examining issues such as the relation of ADA accessibility requirements to the operation of private Internet sites, as well as the technology accessibility requirements of section 508 of the Rehabilitation Act.

In Part 10, we also examine the applicability of federal and state tax policies to the procurement and use of technology in the workplace, homes and elsewhere. Tax policy is reviewed as a tool for enhancing the employment of persons with disabilities, for instance, through federal provisions such as the "disabled access credit" and the small business tax deduction for expenses incurred making workplaces accessible.

The treatise contains an extensive appendix that sets out the ADA, the Civil Rights Act of 1991, and other relevant federal laws, as well as a representative state's – California's – antidiscrimination law. To complement the chapters of the treatise on other nations' laws, we also provide a list of constitutional and statutory enactments from those jurisdictions. Table of Cases and an Index are available to assist in the identification of particular topics.

This treatise is directed at legal practitioners and policymakers, disability advocates, researchers, law and graduate students taking disability and employment classes, and those who litigate disability civil rights cases. There has been substantial growth in this field that still is developing rapidly. Increasingly, there are courses taught at law and business schools and other undergraduate and graduate colleges focusing on disability studies and civil rights. We emphasize that the bodies of law we address are evolving rapidly. No week has failed to bring us new and often significant cases. Readers should bear in mind the morphing nature of the law when drawing on our analysis and the cases we cite.

We have tried to reflect our respective perspectives as law teachers and lawyers, social science researchers, non-profit legal advocates and policymakers, and practitioners working in the area of disability civil rights and labor law. The treatise has benefited greatly from input from many colleagues, leaders in the disability advocacy community, and others. As always, any errors are ours.

P.B
E.H
C.D.S.
M.W.

November, 2003

Acknowledgments

This project could not have been accomplished without the generous contributions of many individuals. Our editor, Louis Higgins, had the foresight and perseverance to support our work as West Publishing's first major treatment of disability civil rights law. Several of our colleagues read various drafts of the treatise and provided most helpful feedback including Michael Stein, James Schmeling, Helen Schartz, Jeff Schwartz, George Cochran, Jack Nowlin, Farish Percy, Paul Secunda, and Mercer Bullard.

Throughout the project, many members of the staffs at the University of Iowa's Law, Health Policy & Disability Center, the Western Law Center for Disability Rights at Loyola Law School, Munger, Tolles & Olson, LLP and the Mississippi School of Law provided outstanding editorial and technical assistance. William Myhill tirelessly lead a team of editors in Iowa. In Los Angeles, Sonia Arteaga shepherded innumerable drafts through the editing process. Extensive help in organizing, cite checking and proof reading the materials was provided by Kelly X. Zhu, Hansdeep Sahni (who compiled the international constitution and statute appendix), Liz Sturdevant, Stephanie McGraw, LeeAnn McCoy, Lara Rosen, Seana Fernandez, Frank Nicolosi, Nate Odem, Charlie Kierscht, Jamie Merchant, Jennifer Finch and Tim Harlan.

The work on the treatise was funded in part by grants to Peter Blanck from the U.S. Department of Education, National Institute on Disability and Rehabilitation Research, for (1) the Rehabilitation Research and Training Center (RRTC) on Workforce Investment and Employment Policy for Persons with Disabilities, Grant No. H133B980042-99, (2) "IT Works," Grant No. H133A011803, and (3) "Technology for Independence: A Community-Based Resource Center," Grant No. H133A021801; and by the Great Plains ADA and IT Center, the Nellie Ball Trust Research Fund, and The University of Iowa Law School Foundation.

Eve Hill's work on this treatise was funded in part by grants from Loyola Law School and the Pacific ADA and IT Center. Michael Waterstone's work on this treatise was supported in part by the Lamar Order of the University of Mississippi School of Law.

We thank Munger, Tolles & Olson, LLP for providing typically, but uniquely, generous support for one of their colleagues. And, at MTO, we single out Brenda Shurtleff — without her genius as a word processor/error finder/document organizer, all the drafts still would be scattered pieces of paper.

We would also like to thank those colleagues who provided us with advance drafts or hard to locate copies of their work, including Christine Jolls, J.J. Prescott, Patricia Thornton and Neil Lunt.

The views herein, of course, reflect only those of the authors and not any funding agency, university, law school or law firm.

Lastly, we thank our loving, wonderful and always patient life partners, who continue to live through "the next project."

WESTLAW® Overview

Disability Civil Rights Law and Policy offers a detailed and comprehensive treatment of legal principles and issues relating to disability civil rights law and policy. To supplement the information contained in this book, you can access Westlaw, a computer-assisted legal research service of West, a Thomson business. Westlaw contains a broad array of legal resources, including case law, statutes, expert commentary, current developments and various other types of information. You can access Westlaw via westlaw.com® at **www.westlaw.com**.

THE PUBLISHER

Summary of Contents

APPENDICES

Table of Contents

DISABILITY
CIVIL RIGHTS LAW
AND POLICY

FOREWORD
PAUL STEVEN MILLER[1]

This treatise presents a comprehensive treatment of disability civil rights laws, with particular analysis of the Americans with Disabilities Act of 1990 (ADA). The importance of this West volume to the community of persons with disabilities, their families and advocates, employers, government officials, lawyers, researchers and policymakers is evident in its extensive legal and interdisciplinary analysis of disability law and policy.

The treatise is a valuable tool to further the understanding of the civil rights and antidiscrimination protections set forth in disability law and policy in America and around the world. It is a neutral treatment of a subject that raises deep emotions and deep questions. Blanck, Hill, Siegal and Waterstone's achievement comes at an important time in the evolution of disability civil rights.

On one hand, people with disabilities and their advocates, courts, and policymakers are struggling with ways to interpret and apply the antidiscrimination provisions of the ADA to protect their civil rights in workplaces, schools, and public and governmental entities (see Treatise Part 2). This process is part of the ongoing evolution in thought about the civil rights of persons with disabilities from being recipients of charity after the Civil War, to recipients of corporate and governmental generosity, to a discreet and insular minority entitled to civil rights protections. Since 1990, when the ADA was passed, persons with disabilities have demanded treatment as respected, contributing and productive members of society with the full panoply of rights that other Americans possess.

On the other hand, the treatise appears at a time when civil rights, particularly disability civil rights, have been demonized and trivialized, questioned, narrowed, caricatured and "sound-bited," making the legal and political climate for these issues difficult, to say the least. This text is an antidote to unreasoned criticism of disability civil rights law, but it considers legitimate concerns of others — for example, academics who have studied the impact of the ADA on employment and contend it may have hurt as much as helped.

Disability as a Basis for Civil Rights

Disability civil rights laws owe much to the legacy of the race and gender civil rights movements. Those movements changed America forever, creating laws, regulations, business practices, and customs rooted in the universal principle that men and women, and members of racial, ethnic, and religious groups, must be treated equally. The response to

---

[1]   B.A., University of Pennsylvania, 1983; J.D. Harvard Law School, 1986.

discrimination by the federal and state governments springs from the seminal idea that all are equal before the law, and that differential treatment of individuals on the basis of race, national origin, gender, or religion, is impermissible.

People with disabilities largely were ignored by these political and legislative movements even as discriminatory barriers fell, society became more inclusive, and other groups, such as women and older workers, gained civil rights protections. Nearly forty years after the historic U.S. Supreme Court decision *Brown v. Board of Education* established that separate was not equal, and almost thirty years after the passage of the Civil Rights Act of 1964, Congress finally prohibited disability discrimination with the passage of the ADA.

On July 26, 1990, as he signed the Act into law on the South Lawn of the White House in front of a crowd of thousands of people with disabilities, President George Bush declared, "Let the shameful wall of exclusion finally come tumbling down." With the stroke of a pen, a new era in civil rights began.

The goal of disability civil rights laws is no different than those of other civil rights laws. These statutes seek to integrate people with disabilities into the mainstream of economic and social life. Importantly, the laws seek to achieve integration without paternalism or pity (as discussed in Part 1 of this treatise). Disability civil rights laws strive to remove arbitrary barriers in society that prevent persons with disabilities from living independent and dignified lives.

The ADA is based on a simple premise that disability is a natural part of the human experience that in no way diminishes the rights of individuals to live independently, pursue meaningful careers, make choices and enjoy full inclusion in the economic, political, cultural and educational life of American society.

Disability Civil Rights History

Notwithstanding its shared principles with other civil rights movements and laws, the disability movement that culminated in the ADA is rooted in a different history and context. With race, a public social revolution occurred in our living rooms, on our televisions, and in newspapers, convincing the nation that segregation was morally wrong, and that *separate* was not *equal*. That social revolution, lead by Dr. Martin Luther King, Jr. in the streets, and Thurgood Marshall in the courts, changed mainstream America and resulted in the sweeping civil rights legislation of the mid-1960s.

The disability experience was different. There was no visible social revolution that changed the hearts and minds of Americans. Rather, the ADA became law with little notice or public discourse.

Employers and businesses began to be regulated by the ADA without a public discussion about the obstacles confronting disabled people. Even today, due to the lack of context and public education, much of the public remains uninformed about the moral framework and philosophical underpinnings of the ADA. Too often, disability issues are analyzed in purely economic terms, rather than from the perspective of an individual's right to be free from discrimination, the right to participate in the economy, and the right to be fully integrated into the larger society (see Treatise Part 2).

Pre-ADA Disability Rights Legislation

Even though the ADA has become the most important piece of disability civil rights legislation, it was not the first law to address barriers facing disabled people. The 1960s and 1970s saw nascent and incremental efforts to address impediments that people with disabilities encountered.

As this treatise chronicles in Part 1, Congress began to address architectural obstacles in the Architectural Barriers Act of 1968. However, the reach of that law was restricted, as it applied only to federally-owned or leased buildings. Two years later, Congress passed the Urban Mass Transit Act, requiring new mass transit vehicles to be equipped with wheelchair lifts.

Congress acted again in 1973 on behalf of people with disabilities when it passed the Rehabilitation Act. Although broader in scope than any other disability law to date, its impact was limited because it only prohibited discrimination by the federal government itself, by federal contractors, or in programs or activities receiving federal financial assistance. The distinction between the federal response to disability discrimination and other forms of discrimination was stark.

Around this time, Congress introduced what eventually became known as the Individuals with Disabilities Education Act (IDEA). IDEA compelled the nation to provide an equal and appropriate education, in the mainstream, for America's children with disabilities. This Act gave children with disabilities access to the building blocks that would prepare them for full inclusion in society – basic education and interaction with non-disabled peers.

In 1988, Congress passed two new acts that were aimed at providing greater access for persons with disabilities. The Air Carrier Access Act guaranteed access to airline travel, while the Fair Housing Amendments Act prohibited housing discrimination against persons with disabilities and their families, and provided for the architectural accessibility, renovation, and modifications of some housing units.

Throughout this time, people with disabilities were organizing, becoming politically active, and demanding equal rights. The Independent Living Movement emerged, and it characterized disability not as a medical issue, but as a social, cultural and civil rights issue. It recognized the limitations and exclusions that people with disabilities face in the environment and the workplace as the arbitrary result of stigmatizing social policy and discrimination, rather than the product of physical or mental impairments. This analysis of the disability experience propelled disability policy in new directions.

The Americans with Disabilities Act

The ADA is a comprehensive law that prohibits discrimination against persons with disabilities in public and private employment (Part 3 of the treatise); in the delivery of public services (Treatise Part 4); in public transportation systems, through the development of accessible bus and subway systems (Part 4); in public accommodations (Part 5); and in telecommunications.

The ADA seeks to remove barriers in all aspects of a disabled person's life, and facilitate independence through assimilation and employment. The ADA is a comprehensive law because the problems of discrimination facing people with disabilities are multi-faceted and complex.

Although the ADA touches on many aspects of everyday life, its cornerstone is the prohibition of job discrimination because people achieve economic independence and social integration through employment (extensive discussion provided in Treatise Part 3). Disabled individuals' access to employment opportunities historically has been constricted as they suffer from destructive stereotypes about their alleged inabilities to do many jobs. The principle embodied in the ADA is simple – people in the workforce should be hired, promoted and judged based on their abilities, not on fears, myths, or stereotypes about physical or mental disability.

The ADA is a civil rights statute designed to aid and protect qualified people who want to work. The goal of the ADA is to keep people in jobs to permit and foster productive contributions to public and commercial enterprise. Unlike previous disability laws, it is not a benefits or welfare program, but an equal access law (see Treatise Part 9).

The message of the ADA is independence, empowerment and integration. The law has served as a groundbreaking vehicle for disabled people, causing historic changes in attitudes about disabled people that must continue to evolve so that this community can take its rightful place at society's table.

The ADA is a simple, but revolutionary law: Simple because the purpose of the law, like other civil rights laws, is to outlaw discrimination against disabled people. The ADA seeks to ensure that persons with disabilities are integrated without paternalism into the mainstream economic and social life of the community.

Yet the ADA is revolutionary in that it requires employers to make accommodations to enable qualified disabled workers to compete and succeed. The law creates an affirmative duty to accommodate within reason a worker's disability as long as such an accommodation does not create an undue hardship.

For people who need reasonable accommodations to perform the essential functions of their jobs, traditional "equal" treatment can be a barrier to employment. The ADA's requirement to provide reasonable accommodations to qualified individuals with disabilities means that employers must treat some employees differently to provide equal access to employment (see Treatise Part 3).

The ADA's contextual definitions of disability, reasonable accommodation, and undue hardship lie at the core of the statute's ability to respond to discrimination on an individualized basis (see Treatise Part 2). This flexibility embraced by the ADA is necessary to account for the range of covered disabilities, the variety of job functions, and the different resources of employers to provide for accommodations. Not every disability is manifested in the same way, and therefore, different accommodations require unique adjustments depending on the degree of limitation and the peculiarities of the job in question.

The ADA does not provide an all-inclusive list of disabilities that are covered by its provisions (see Treatise Part 2). Rather, the law's coverage is extended to individuals who fit within one of the three prongs of its definition of disability. The fluidity of this definition requires setting aside preconceived notions about disability, and evaluating each person's abilities and circumstances in an individualized way. Paradoxically, it is this flexibility and adaptability that sometimes is used by naysayers to criticize the ADA for failing to provide clear responses to all situations.

Critics have attacked the ADA for its lack of easy solutions and clear definitions of who is covered by the law and what is required as a reasonable accommodation. The drafters of the ADA purposefully required the courts to craft a jurisprudence that addresses the unique facts and circumstances of each situation. The contextual nature of disability does not allow for a one-size-fits-all approach, notwithstanding a legal system that values precedent and certainty (see Treatise Part 6, discussing ADA enforcement and remedies).

The ADA involves a fundamental expansion of democracy and the American dream to over 50 million people with disabilities. Inherent in such an expansion is the creation of new ways of thinking and practices of interaction. It should come as no surprise that not every question about the ADA has an answer that is codified. And yet, the principles underlying the law are universal, familiar, and provide the context for understanding the statute.

Despite Progress, Barriers Continue to Exist for People with Disabilities

The ADA and state disability laws are making progress in breaking down the discriminatory barriers facing persons with disabilities. Through enforcement, technical assistance and guidance by the federal government, compliance with the law is improving (see Treatise Part 6). According to the Census Bureau, approximately 800,000 more severely disabled individuals were working in 1994, two years after the ADA's employment provisions took effect, than in 1991. The ADA is working, and everyone, including business, is benefiting.

Yet the barriers to employment of persons with disabilities are pervasive. People with disabilities face bigotry and exclusion from the community. Stereotypes and arbitrary barriers continue to impede the integration of disabled people into the workplace. But facts should dispel fears. Studies consistently show that employees with disabilities perform as well on the job as non-disabled employees. In addition, the creativity and problem solving that is required of people who live with disabilities every day often is brought to bear on the work that they do. The reality is that the vast majority of reasonable accommodations are inexpensive and easy to implement. Still, with large numbers of persons with disabilities unemployed and underemployed, society has a responsibility to do better.

Changing Attitudes and Expectations About Disability

Resolving disputes involving disability issues requires an understanding of the text of the laws and the decisions that have applied them, as well as an appreciation for the social and historical context of the disability experience. Judges, lawyers, governments, businesses and employers, undergraduate and law students, researchers and policymakers must understand the disability experience, and all will benefit from the work of this treatise.

Due to more inclusive educational policies, an ever-growing number of individuals with disabilities are pursuing higher education, and more qualified individuals with disabilities will be entering the job market in the coming years. In addition, because of laws that provide disabled children with a mainstreamed and integrated education, a new generation of students without disabilities have the benefit of peers and classmates with disabilities to an extent that previous generations never experienced. The incoming workforce, therefore, will be more comfortable and experienced learning and working side-by-side with colleagues with disabilities than have previous generations.

Moreover, not only are greater numbers of people with disabilities educated and qualified for work, but people with disabilities are developing changed expectations about how they will be treated in the workplace and in society at large. The young people coming out of college today do not know a society without the ADA.

As Part 8 of the treatise shows, the ADA also has served as a model for other nations seeking to address disability discrimination within their borders. The ADA has reshaped environments for the better, and everyone, whether disabled or not, will benefit from its provisions.

Future of Disability Civil Rights

The goal of disability civil rights laws is to create an accessible playing field (see Treatise Parts 9 and 10 for examples). Our challenge, like the challenge of those who developed and implemented the civil rights jurisprudence of race, ethnicity, gender, religion and age, is to use these laws and statutes to make society more fair, open and just.

The ADA, along with other federal and state civil rights laws (for instance, state laws discussed in Treatise Part 7), is based on a simple and universal premise – that society should be welcoming and free of arbitrary barriers, and that people in the workplace should be hired, promoted and judged on their abilities, and not based on biases about their disabilities.

At bottom, this treatise closely and carefully articulates disability civil rights as being about safeguarding an individual's dignity. It is about ensuring that employers, businesses and public accommodations see an individual's ability – free from stereotypes, biases or preconceived notions about that person due to his or her disability.

As Justin Dart, Jr., the father of the disability civil rights movement, once stated,

> *Our forefathers and mothers came to this country because it offered unique legal guarantees of equal opportunity. They got rich, and America got rich. Every time we expanded our civil rights guarantees to include another oppressed minority, America got richer. America is not rich in spite of civil rights. America is rich because of civil rights.*

This is what disability civil rights and the ADA stand for. This is what must be the standard for America today. And, this is what must be the commitment of us all.

Part 1

Historical And Conceptual Foundations
Analysis

Chapter 1 INTRODUCTION

§ 1.1 Overview

This treatise examines the civil rights laws and policies affecting persons with disabilities, with primary focus on the Americans with Disabilities Act (ADA) of 1990. Analysis of evolving antidiscrimination laws and policies that affect the rights of persons of color, women, the elderly, or other groups is not new. What is relatively new is the study of laws, policies, and public attitudes about the civil rights of persons with disabilities.[1]

Throughout this treatise, we explore the ways in which public acceptance and inclusion of persons with disabilities into society is at least as much driven by political, economic, social, and attitudinal factors regarding conceptions of disability, as by law and policy themselves. Viewed in this way, an enriched analysis emerges of the historical forces

---

[1]   Throughout, we attempt to use "people first" language, focusing emphasis on the individual and not on the impairment or condition (e.g., persons with mental retardation). Sometimes, to reduce redundancy we deviate from this form.

affecting the civil rights movement of persons with disabilities in American society.

§ 1.2 American Conceptions Of Discrimination On The Basis Of Disability

A.   *Evolution Of Models For Societal Treatment Of Disability*

In the past thirty years, disability laws and policies have attracted widespread attention from policymakers, courts, legal academics, researchers, employers, and disability advocates.[2] The magnitude and tenor of the debate is not surprising. Since its passage in 1990, the ADA[3] has become America's prominent national policy statement affecting the lives of persons with disabilities. Despite the far-reaching implications of the ADA and related policy developments, analysis of the law and examination of its actual effects on persons with disabilities has been limited.

Moreover, to a remarkable degree, contemporary employment, health care, and governmental and rehabilitation programs for persons with disabilities still are modeled on outmoded and medicalized stereotypes about disabilities. These longstanding views date back to the birth of the Civil War pension system, which first linked the definition of disability to an inability to work and established physicians as the medical gatekeepers of disability benefits.[4] The medical model focused on the individual, whose disability was conceived as an infirmity that precluded full participation in the economy and society.

Historically, the medical model cast people with disabilities in a subordinate role in their encounters with doctors, rehabilitation professionals, governmental bureaucrats, and social workers who aimed to "help them" adjust to a society structured around the convenience and interests of the non-disabled. The medical model never questioned the

---

[2] For reviews, see Peter Blanck, The Economics of the Employment Provisions of the Americans with Disabilities Act: Part I–Workplace Accommodations, 46 DePaul L. Rev. 877 (1997); Peter Blanck & Mollie W. Marti, Attitudes, Behavior, and the Employment Provisions of the Americans with Disabilities Act, 42 Vill. L. Rev. 345 (1997).

[3] Americans with Disabilities Act of 1990, 42 U.S.C. § 12101 et seq. (2000).

[4] See generally Peter Blanck, Civil War Pensions and Disability, 62 Ohio St. L.J. 109, 112-16 (2001); Peter Blanck & Michael Millender, Before Disability Civil Rights: Civil War Pensions and the Politics of Disability in America, 52 Ala. L. Rev. 1, 1-50 (2000) (setting out this historical analysis, and from which this section draws; and acknowledgment to Michael Millender for helping to develop aspects of this discussion).

physical and social environment in which people with disabilities were forced to function. It countenanced their segregation and economic marginalization.[5] Because the medical model aimed to address the "needs" of people with disabilities rather than recognize their civil rights, it led to government policies that viewed assistance for people with disabilities as a form of either charity or welfare.

B.   *The Modern Disability Rights Movement*

The modern disability civil rights model began to influence government policy in the 1970s. The model conceptualized persons with disabilities as a minority group entitled to the same hard-won legal protections for equality that emerged from the struggles of African Americans and women. Proposing that disability is a social and cultural construct, the civil rights model focuses on the laws and practices that subordinate persons with disabilities. It insists that government secure the equality of persons with disabilities by eliminating the legal, physical, economic, and social barriers that preclude their equal involvement in society.

The civil rights model conceptualizes many barriers to full citizenship as being socially created, and therefore assigns society with some of the cost and responsibility of removing them. The emphasis is not on giving any group special treatment; rather, the issue involves balancing the scales. One commentator suggests:

> [T]he configurations of the existing environment confer enormous advantages on nondisabled persons. Machines have been designed to fit hands that can easily grip these objects, steps have been built for legs that bend at the knee .... Everything has been standardized for a model human being whose life is untouched by disability. All aspects of the built environment, including work sites, have been adapted for *someone*; the problem is that they have been adapted exclusively for the nondisabled majority.[6]

Although, until recently, federal policy continued to conceptualize disability from a medical perspective, people with disabilities as individuals and in organized groups began to challenge these stereotypes.

---

[5]   For a review, see Harlan Hahn, Accommodations and the ADA: Unreasonable Bias or Biased Reasoning?, 21 Berkeley J. Emp. & Lab. L. 166 (2000); see also Jonathan C. Drimmer, Cripples, Overcomers, and Civil Rights: Tracing the Evolution of Federal Legislation and Social Policy for People with Disabilities, 40 UCLA L. Rev. 1341 (1993) and Adam A. Milani, Living in the World: A New Look at the Disabled in the Law of Torts, 48 Cath. U. L. Rev. 323, 328-29 (1999).

[6]   Harlan Hahn, Equality and the Environment: The Interpretation of "Reasonable Accommodations" in the Americans with Disabilities Act, 17 J. Rehab. Admin. 101, 103 (1993).

Beginning in the 1970s, individuals with disabilities asserted their right to be independent in pursuing education and housing.[7] In New York, for example, an advocacy group for the rights of individuals with disabilities was formed in 1971 called "Disabled in Action."[8]

During this period, national disability policy began to integrate the concepts of the independent living philosophy. Title VII of the Rehabilitation Act of 1973 initiated funding for Centers for Independent Living (CILs). Not only did the CILs provide services *for* individuals with disabilities, but they were required to be operated *by* individuals with disabilities. Over the past decades, CILs have grown from ten centers in 1979 to over three hundred and fifty by the year 2002.[9]

The evolving policy of inclusion proceeded to foster federal and state laws from accessibility to voting and air travel, to independence in education and housing, culminating with passage of the ADA in 1990. In the ADA, Congress expressly recognized the minority status of people with disabilities, finding that:

> historically, society has tended to isolate and segregate individuals with disabilities, and, despite some improvements, such forms of discrimination against individuals with disabilities continue to be a serious and pervasive social problem;... [and that] individuals with disabilities are a discrete and insular minority who have been faced with restrictions and limitations, subjected to a history of purposeful unequal treatment, and relegated to a position of political powerlessness in our society....[10]

---

[7] See Joseph P. Shapiro, No Pity: People with Disabilities Forging a New Civil Rights Movement (1993) (reviewing the history of modern disability rights movement).

[8] For a review of the disability civil rights movement, see Nat'l Council on Disability, Achieving Independence: The Challenge for the 21st Century: A Decade of Progress in Disability Policy Setting an Agenda for the Future, http://www.ncd.gov/newsroom/publications/achieving.html (July 26, 1996).

[9] As of April 2002, there were 368 CILs, with approximately 207 satellite offices. Satellite offices are associated with CILs but typically are located elsewhere in the service area. See Dep'ts of Labor, Health, & Human Servs., Education, and Related Agency Appropriations for 2002, Hearing Before the U.S. House Appropriations Subcomm., 107th Cong. 2nd Sess., at 192 (2002) (statement of Kelly Buckland regarding reauthorization of the Rehabilitation Act of 1973).

[10] 42 U.S.C. § 12101(a) (2000).

§ 1.3 ADA Precursors

A.   *Early Statutes – Vocational Rehabilitation And Benefits*

The ADA was not drawn on a blank canvas. Federal laws addressing the rights of people with disabilities have been in existence since the first half of the 20th century. In scope and purpose, however, these laws were narrower than the ADA. These early laws generally established vocational or benefits programs that were supervised by professional medical and vocational personnel.[11] They were based on the medical model discussed above; that is, the idea that the presence of a disability separated an individual from the rest of society.

The early vocational laws were aimed at "rehabilitation." Their premise was that a person with a disability could achieve acceptance into the larger community by "overcoming" the disability and obtaining employment. In the aftermath of the First World War, in 1918, Congress enacted the Smith-Sears Act "[t]o provide for the vocational rehabilitation and return to civil employment of disabled persons discharged from the military or naval forces."[12]

The National Vocational Rehabilitation Act of 1920, the Smith-Fess Act, extended these vocational rehabilitation principles to civilians.[13] The "voc rehab" law attempted to "provide for the promotion of vocational rehabilitation of persons disabled in industry or in any legitimate occupation and their return to civilian employment ..." and offered services to people who, "by reason of a physical defect or infirmity, whether congenital or acquired by accident, injury, or disease, [are], or may be expected to be, totally or partially incapacitated for remunerative occupation."[14] The Randolph-Sheppard Act of 1938 subsequently created a federal program to employ qualified blind people as vendors on federal property.[15]

A second type of law conferred monetary and other benefits on certain groups of disabled persons. The Social Security Act of 1935 established a federal and state system of health services for "crippled"

---

[11]   See generally Drimmer, supra note 5 ; see also Milani, supra note 5, at 328-29.

[12]   Vocational Rehabilitation Acts of 1918, ch. 107, 40 Stat. 617, 617 (1918).

[13]   National Vocational Rehabilitation Act of 1920, ch. 219, Pub. L. No. 66-236, 41 Stat. 735 (1920) (codified as amended at 29 U.S.C. §§ 731-741 (repealed 1973, and reenacted in the Rehabilitation Act of 1973, Pub. L. No. 93-112, 87 Stat. 355 (codified at 29 U.S.C. §§ 701 et seq. (2000))).

[14]   Id.

[15]   Randolph-Sheppard Act of 1936, Pub. L. No. 74-732, ch. 638, 49 Stat. 1559 (1936) (codified as amended at 20 U.S.C. § 107 (2000)).

children.[16] In 1954, the Act was amended to provide monthly benefits for eligible workers who had become disabled.[17] In 1972, this Act again was amended to provide benefits to limited categories of disabled indigents.[18]

B.   *More Recent Statutes*

As part of the Civil Rights era of the 1960s, minority groups began to view equal access to society as a fundamental right. The federal statutes of this period, including the Civil Rights Act of 1964 and the Voting Rights Act of 1965, gave the federal government an increased role in protecting these rights.[19]

Starting slowly but progressively picking up steam, the disabled community started to view itself as a part of this larger struggle. As a result, the disability rights statutes of this period began to address the integration of people with disabilities into society as an issue of discrimination. These statutes increasingly required that society, as opposed to the individual with a disability, make changes to ensure access and integration. This approach draws closer to the ADA model.

1.   Architectural Barriers Act

The Architectural Barriers Act, passed in 1968, requires that new facilities built with federal funds be accessible to people with disabilities.[20] The Act charges the Administrator of General Services, the United States Postal Service, and the Secretaries of Housing and Urban Development and of Defense, in consultation with the Secretary of Health and Human Services, with developing accessibility standards for the design, construction, and alteration of their buildings and facilities.

The text of the Architectural Barriers Act contained no coherent vision of the rights of people with disabilities. The Act was limited in purpose and did not contain any enforcement provisions. Nevertheless, commentators generally have viewed this Act as an important first step in federal civil rights legislation for the disabled community.[21] This marked

---

[16]   Social Security Act of 1935, Pub. L. No. 74-271, ch. 531, 49 Stat. 620 (codified at 42 U.S.C. §§ 1381-83) (2000).

[17]   Social Security Amendments of 1954, Pub. L. No. 83-761, § 106, 68 Stat. 1052, 1080 (1954).

[18]   Social Security Amendments of 1972, Pub. L. No. 92-603, 86 Stat. 1329-1465 (codified at 42 U.S.C. §§ 1381-83 (2000)).

[19]   See 42 U.S.C. § 2000e (2000) (guaranteeing access to employment, education, and public accommodation); see also 42 U.S.C. §§ 1973, et seq. (guaranteeing access to political participation).

[20]   42 U.S.C. § 4151 (2000).

[21]   See Bob Dole, Are We Keeping America's Promises to People with Disabilities? – Commentary on Blanck, 79 Iowa L. Rev. 925-34 (1994); see also Drimmer, supra note 5, at 1376-79; Milani, supra note 5, at 332.

the first time that national policy was concerned with including, rather than excluding, people with disabilities in the mainstream.

The Barriers Act was the first law to acknowledge that people with disabilities had been overlooked in the construction of federal buildings. The law took the significant step of recognizing that people with disabilities have the right to use these buildings, even if the physical designs of the structures needed to be modified to vindicate that right. The idea that environmental change was a viable tool to combat inaccessibility and social isolation was developed and refined in later statutes.

2. Rehabilitation Act of 1973

Congressional efforts at a comprehensive federal disability rights statute intensified in the early 1970s. In 1972, Senator Hubert Humphrey and Congressman Charles Vanik independently proposed amending the Civil Rights Act of 1964 to include a prohibition on discrimination on the basis of disability in federally funded programs.[22] Both these bills died without hearings.

The next attempt was a proposed Rehabilitation Act of 1972.[23] This proposed Act began a shift away from the "vocational" roots of the earlier Vocational Rehabilitation Act. The Act would have required federal agencies to develop and implement affirmative action programs for the hiring, placement, and advancement of employees with disabilities, and created an enforcement agency to ensure compliance with the Architectural Barriers Act.[24]

Most importantly, the proposed 1972 Act contained a broad statement prohibiting discrimination in federally funded programs on the basis of disability.[25] Although President Nixon vetoed this Act, many of

---

[22] Senator Humphrey, for example, attempted to insert "physical or mental handicap" after "color" in the Civil Rights Act of 1964. See 118 Cong. Rec. 525 (1972). On January 20, 1972, while introducing his bill, Senator Humphrey stated:

> The time has come when we can no longer tolerate the invisibility of the handicapped in America .... I am insisting that the civil rights of 40 million Americans now be affirmed and effectively guaranteed by Congress .... The Federal Government must now take firm leadership to guarantee the rights of the handicapped.

Id.

[23] H.R. 8395, 92d Cong. (1972).

[24] Id. §§ 602-603.

[25] Id.

its provisions ultimately were retained in the passage of the Rehabilitation Act of 1973.

As originally passed, the primary focus of the Rehabilitation Act of 1973 was vocational training and rehabilitation.[26] The stated purpose of the Act was to "provide a statutory basis for the Rehabilitation Services Administration," an agency charged with carrying out the provisions of the Act, and to authorize various rehabilitation programs.[27]

The first four Titles of the 1973 Act, and the bulk of the Act's text, establish several incentive programs for states to receive federal grants. These funds are to meet the "current and future needs of handicapped individuals," authorize federal assistance on research relating to rehabilitation of individuals with disabilities, and provide evaluation mechanisms for these various programs.[28]

The final part of the original 1973 Act – Title V ("Miscellaneous") – contains the portions of the Rehabilitation Act which over time have had the greatest impact. Section 501 requires affirmative action and nondiscrimination in employment by federal agencies of the executive branch.[29] Section 502 established the Architectural and Transportation Barriers Compliance Board ("Access Board"), which is charged with ensuring compliance with the Architectural Barriers Act.[30]

---

[26]   Pub. L. No. 93-112; 87 Stat. 355 (1973).

[27]   Id. § 2 ("Declaration of Purpose").

[28]   See Title I, §§ 100-130 ("Vocational and Rehabilitation Services"); Title II, §§ 200-204 ("Research and Training"); Title III, §§ 300-306 ("Special Federal Responsibilities"); Title IV, §§ 400-407 ("Administration and Program and Project Evaluation").

[29]   29 U.S.C. § 791 (2000). Every department, agency, and instrumentality of the executive branch is required:

> [to] submit to the Commission [EEOC] and the Committee [Interagency Committee on Employees who are Individuals with Disabilities, also created by this Section] an affirmative action program plan for the hiring, placement, and advancement of individuals with disabilities .... Such plan shall include a description of the extent to which and methods whereby the special needs of employees who are individuals with disabilities are being met.

Id.

[30]   Id. § 502 (codified at 29 U.S.C. § 792).

Section 503 requires that to receive certain government contracts, entities must demonstrate that they are taking affirmative steps to employ people with disabilities.[31]

The enduring hallmark of the Rehabilitation Act, however, is Section 504. This Section provides:

> No otherwise qualified individual with a disability in the United States, as defined in Section 705(20), shall, solely by reason of her or his disability, be excluded from the participation in, be denied the benefits of, or be subjected to discrimination under any program or activity receiving Federal financial assistance.[32]

This sweeping language was the first explicit Congressional statement recognizing "discrimination" against people with disabilities.

The scheme of the original statute suggests that Congress may not have expected Section 504 to have a monumental impact. The conference and committee reports on the Rehabilitation Act paid virtually no attention to this provision.[33] The statutory definition of disability referenced in Section 504 was taken almost without change from the Vocational Rehabilitation Act of 1920.[34] It is tailored to employment situations, and therefore is ill-suited to support a larger antidiscrimination framework.

This background provided the impetus for two important modifications to Section 504 of the Rehabilitation Act of 1973. The first was a revised definition of "handicapped individual."

In the Rehabilitation Act Amendments of 1974, Congress defined a "handicapped" individual as one "who (A) has a physical or mental impairment which substantially limits one or more of such person's major

---

[31] Id. § 503 (codified at 29 U.S.C. § 793).

[32] Id. § 504 (codified at 29 U.S.C. § 794). This section is virtually unchanged from § 604 of the failed Rehabilitation Act of 1972.

[33] See Shapiro, supra note 7, at 65 (discussing work of sociologist Richard Scotch, who concluded that Congressional aides could not remember who had suggested adding this civil rights protection).

[34] The definition in § 705(20) of the Rehabilitation Act of 1973 is as follows:

> The term "handicapped individual" means any individual who (A) has a physical or mental disability which for such individual constitutes or result in a substantial hardship to employment and (B) can reasonably be expected to benefit in terms of employability from vocational rehabilitation services provided pursuant to titles I and III of this Act.

life activities; (B) has a record of such an impairment, or (C) is regarded as having such an impairment."[35]

This phrasing broke free of the earlier employment and rehabilitation-based roots of the original definition. The definition places less emphasis on an ability to cure or fix a disability, and instead, recognizes that perception of disability is important.[36] This is the definition the ADA eventually would use.[37]

The second area of development for the Rehabilitation Act was the interpreting regulations. The Department of Health, Education, and Welfare was charged with developing regulations for Section 504 of the Rehabilitation Act of 1973. It took five years to do so.[38] The Section 504 regulations introduced the concept of reasonable accommodation, which is the idea that some affirmative step, as opposed to strictly equal treatment, may be necessary to ensure equal access for people with disabilities to jobs, facilities, and programs.[39]

For example, the "Employment" section of the Section 504 regulations states:

> "A recipient [of federal funds] shall make reasonable accommodation to the known physical or mental limitations of an otherwise qualified handicapped applicant or employee unless the recipient can demonstrate that the accommodation would impose an undue hardship on the operation of its program or activity."[40]

The Section 504 regulations provide examples of reasonable accommodations, including altering facilities and modifying work schedules.[41]

---

[35] See Rehabilitation Act Amendments of 1974, § 111(a), Pub. L. No. 93-651, 89 Stat. 2 (1974) (codified at 29 U.S.C. § 705(20)(B)(i)-(iii)).

[36] See Drimmer, supra note 5, at 1386.

[37] See 42 U.S.C. § 12102(2) (2000).

[38] For discussion of the delay in promulgating these regulations, including a sit-in at the Department of Housing, Employment, and Welfare (HEW) Secretary's office, see Milani, supra note 5, at 334-35; Shapiro, supra note 7, at 65-70.

[39] A nuanced discussion of the role of the Rehabilitation Act in establishing the concept of accommodation is set forth infra in Section 2.1(B).

[40] 34 C.F.R. § 104.12(a) (2000). "Qualified handicapped person" is elsewhere defined in the regulations with respect to employment as "a handicapped person who, with reasonable accommodation, can perform the essential functions of the job in question." Id. § 104.3(l)(1).

[41] Id. § 104.12(b).

The Section 504 regulations' approach to facility access issues is similar. The regulations provide that "[n]o qualified handicapped person shall, because a recipient's facilities are inaccessible to or unusable by handicapped persons, be denied the benefits of, be excluded from participation in, or otherwise be subjected to discrimination under any program or activity ....".[42] This is commonly known as the "program access" requirement.

A recipient of federal funds does not have to make its facilities accessible; rather, accessibility is achieved when each program or activity within the facilities, viewed as a whole, is accessible.[43] Examples of steps to ensure program accessibility include redesigning equipment, reassigning classes to accessible buildings, and home visits.

Another issue covered by the Section 504 regulations is education. The regulations provide that recipients of federal funds that operate public or secondary schools *shall* provide a free appropriate public education to each qualified handicapped person, regardless of the nature or severity of the individual's handicap.[44]

Similarly, the regulations provide that qualified persons with disabilities may not be denied admission or be subjected to discrimination by postsecondary schools on the basis of disability.[45] A "qualified handicapped person" for the purposes of postsecondary and vocational education services is defined as "a handicapped person who meets the academic and technical standards requisite to admission or participation in the recipient's education program or activity."[46]

The Rehabilitation Act and its accompanying regulations frame the issues of employment, facility, and educational access for persons with a disability as a balancing test. Accommodation is desirable, so long as

---

[42] Id. § 104.21.

[43] Id. § 104.22.

[44] Id. § 104.33.

[45] Id. § 104.42. The regulations also contain equally strong language as to "treatment of students":

> No qualified handicapped student shall, on the basis of handicap, be excluded from participation in, be denied the benefits of, or otherwise be subjected to discrimination under any academic, research, occupational training, housing, health insurance, counseling, financial aid, physical education, athletics, recreation, transportation, other extracurricular, or other postsecondary education aid, benefits, or services ....

Id. § 104.43(a).

[46] 34 C.F.R. § 104.3(l)(3).

the methods of ensuring accessibility are reasonable. Although "reasonable" is not defined, a guiding principle is that a reasonable accommodation or modification does not require a change to the fundamental nature of the job, program, or facility. The early Rehabilitation Act cases reflected that struggle.

In *Alexander v. Choate*,[47] a class of Medicaid recipients argued that Tennessee's reduction of the number of inpatient hospital days paid for by Medicaid violated the Rehabilitation Act. Although the U.S. Supreme Court declined to find that this was a cognizable claim, it commented on the dangers inherent in interpreting Section 504 too broadly: "Any interpretation of § 504 must ... be responsive to two powerful but countervailing considerations – the need to give effect to the statutory objectives and the desire to keep § 504 within manageable bounds."[48]

In *Southeastern Community College v. Davis*,[49] a deaf woman tried to gain admission to a nurse's training program. At issue was the program's ability to impose physical qualifications for admission to its clinical training programs. The Supreme Court noted the difficulty of identifying the line between refusal to extend affirmative action and illegal discrimination, but ultimately concluded that "Section 504 imposes no requirement upon an educational institution to lower or to effect substantial modifications of standards to accommodate a handicapped person."[50]

The Rehabilitation Act of 1973 represented a significant step in defining and protecting the rights of individuals with disabilities insofar as federally funded entities were concerned. This is an important backdrop to the ADA.[51] Conceptually and doctrinally, these two statutes have a close relationship. Both are premised on the belief that people with disabilities have the right to be included in society, and that a denial of that right, including failure to make reasonable accommodations, constitutes discrimination.

The ADA concepts that courts have struggled with – reasonable accommodation, the definition of disability, and fundamental alteration – have their bases in the Rehabilitation Act. The ADA is explicit that

---

[47] Alexander v. Choate, 469 U.S. 287, 293 (1985).

[48] Id. at 299.

[49] Southeastern Cmty. Coll. v. Davis, 442 U.S. 397, 413 (1979).

[50] Id. at 412-13.

[51] One argument used to support the passage of the ADA was that it extended an existing federal statute into the private sector. See Nancy Lee Jones, Overview and Essential Requirements of the Americans with Disabilities Act, 64 Temp. L. Rev. 471, 475 (1991).

Rehabilitation Act regulations and case law are instructive to interpreting the ADA.[52]

In the years between the passage of the Rehabilitation Act and the ADA, several federal statutes began to extend the antidiscrimination principles of the Rehabilitation Act into different arenas.

3.   Education For All Handicapped Children Act of 1975 (Individuals With Disabilities Education Act)

In 1975, Congress passed the Education For All Handicapped Children Act.[53] This Act was an express recognition of the number and needs of children with disabilities in the public schools. Specifically, the Act noted that "there are more than eight million handicapped children in the United States today," the educational needs of which were not being met.[54]

The Act's purpose was to assure that children with disabilities have available to them a "free appropriate" public education which emphasizes special education and related services devoted to meet their unique needs.[55] The enforcement provisions and firm commitment to federal spending established in this Act are more aggressive and explicit than some of the later post-Rehabilitation Act statutes.

This Act eventually was amended to become the present-day Individuals with Disabilities Education Act ("IDEA").[56] To a greater extent than its predecessor, the IDEA reflects a modern approach to educational opportunities for students with disabilities. This includes a commitment to higher expectations, mainstreaming students where possible, and an increased federal role in ensuring equal educational opportunity for all students.[57]

IDEA requires public schools to make available to eligible children with disabilities a free public education in the least restrictive environment appropriate to their individual needs. The law requires public schools to develop appropriate Individualized Education Programs (IEPs) for each child, and provides certain procedures be followed in developing and implementing these IEPs.[58]

---

[52] 42 U.S.C. § 12201(a) (2000).

[53] Pub. L. No. 94-142, 89 Stat. 773 (1975).

[54] Id. § 3(b)(1)-(2).

[55] Id. § 3(c).

[56] 20 U.S.C. §§ 1400 et seq. (1997).

[57] See 20 U.S.C. § 1400-(c)(5)(A), (c)(5)(D), (c)(7)(A) (2000).

[58] Each student's IEP must be developed by a team of knowledgeable persons and reviewed annually. This team includes the child's teacher, parents, and if appropriate the child, and an agency representative who is qualified to provide or supervise the provision of special education. If the

4.   Voting Accessibility For The Elderly And
        Handicapped Act of 1984

In 1984, Congress passed the Voting Accessibility for the Elderly and Handicapped Act ("Voting Accessibility Act").[59]   With this Act, Congress sought to "promote the fundamental right to vote by improving access for handicapped and elderly individuals to registration facilities and polling places for Federal elections."[60]

The Voting Accessibility Act provided that the political subdivisions of the state that are responsible for conducting elections must ensure that polling places for federal elections are accessible to voters with disabilities.[61]   The Attorney General, or any person aggrieved by noncompliance with this Act, may bring a civil action to enforce its provisions.[62]

The Voting Accessibility Act demonstrates that during this time period, as Congress passed legislation on broad social issues, it was willing to consider and take action to protect the civil rights of people with disabilities. This Act has been criticized as weak, however, for providing no definition of "accessibility," and for leaving the means of compliance entirely to the states.[63] These weaknesses have generated momentum for additional federal legislation on this topic.[64]

---

parents disagree with the proposed IEP, they can request a due process hearing and a review from the State educational agency, and can appeal this decision to state or federal court. See id. §§ 1414, 1415.

[59]   42 U.S.C. §§ 1973ee et seq. (2000).

[60]   Id. § 1973ee.

[61]   Id. § 1973ee-1(a). There are exceptions. This section does not apply if the chief election officer of a State (1) determines there is an emergency; (2) determines that all polling places have been surveyed and no such accessible place is available; or (3) assures that any handicapped or elderly voter assigned to an inaccessible polling place upon request will be assigned to an alternative polling place, or provided with an alternative means for casting a ballot. Id. § 1973ee-1(b).

[62]   Id. § 1973ee-4.

[63]   See Michael E. Waterstone, Constitutional and Statutory Voting Rights for People with Disabilities, 14 Stan. L. & Pol'y Rev. 353, 358 (2003).

[64]   In October of 2002, with broad bi-partisan support, President Bush signed into law the Help America Vote Act, Pub. L. No. 107-252, 116 Stat. 1666 (2002). Among other things, this Act provides for accessible voting machines and a secret and independent ballot for voters with disabilities.

5. Air Carrier Access Act of 1986

Congress's next attempt to protect the rights of people with disabilities was the Air Carrier Access Act of 1986.[65] Like the Voting Accessibility Act, this Act focused on a single issue area – airline travel. The Act amended the Federal Aviation Act of 1958 to provide that prohibitions of discrimination by airline carriers applied to individuals with disabilities.

The Air Carrier Access Act's antidiscrimination provision paralleled Section 504 of the Rehabilitation Act. As originally passed, the Act provided that "[n]o air carrier may discriminate against any otherwise qualified handicapped individual, by reason of such handicap, in the provision of air transportation."[66] The Act also used the Rehabilitation Act's definition of "handicapped individual."[67]

6. Fair Housing Amendments Act of 1988

In 1988, Congress introduced a series of amendments to the Civil Rights Act of 1968, including a prohibition on housing discrimination against people with disabilities.[68] These amendments are known as the "Fair Housing Amendments Act of 1988."[69] Like the Voting Accessibility Act and the Air Carrier Access Act, the Fair Housing Amendments Act draws heavily on the approach and language of the Rehabilitation Act.[70]

---

[65] Pub. L. No. 99-435, 100 Stat. 1080 (1986).

[66] The language of the statute was later amended, without any substantive change to its meaning except to include foreign carriers. See 49 U.S.C. § 41705 (2000) ("In providing air transportation, an air carrier, including any foreign air carrier, may not discriminate against an otherwise qualified individual").

[67] See Pub. L. No. 99-435, 100 Stat. 1080 (1986) ("For the purposes of paragraph (1) of this subsection, the term 'handicapped individual' means any individual who has a physical or mental impairment that substantially limits one or more major life activities, has a record of such an impairment, or is regarded as having such an impairment."). As amended, the definition is the same. See 49 U.S.C. § 41705 (2000).

[68] See Pub. L. No. 100-430, 102 Stat. 1619 (1988).

[69] See 42 U.S.C. § 3601 et seq. (2000).

[70] This was intentional. The House Report on the 1988 Amendments states that:

> The Fair Housing Amendments Act, like Section 504 of the Rehabilitation Act of 1973, as amended, is a clear pronouncement of a national commitment to end the unnecessary exclusion of persons with handicaps from the American mainstream.

H.R. Rep., No. 100-171, at 18 (1988).

The Fair Housing Amendments Act makes it unlawful to discriminate in the sale or rental of housing, and the terms and conditions of such a sale or rental, on the basis of disability.[71] The Act has a broad scope. It protects not only a buyer or renter with a disability, but also a person with a disability who lives with the buyer or renter, or any other person associated with the buyer or renter.[72]

The concept of reasonable accommodation is integral to the Fair Housing Act's definition of discrimination. Discrimination includes:

(1) a refusal to permit an occupant with disability, at her own expense, from making "reasonable modifications" of the existing premises;

(2) a refusal to make reasonable accommodations in rules, policies, practices, or services; and

(3) a failure to construct multifamily dwellings, which contain four or more units, 30 months after September 13, 1988 so that specified portions of these facilities are accessible to individuals with disabilities.[73]

The Department of Housing and Urban Development (HUD), responsible for promulgating regulations pursuant to the new amendments, was cognizant of the difficulties in drawing lines as to what separates a "reasonable" accommodation or modification from one that is unreasonable. HUD offered its own interpretation that major costs or administrative burdens should not be imposed on landlords or sellers.[74]

---

[71] See 42 U.S.C. § 3604(f) (2000).

[72] Id.

[73] Id.

[74] A number of commentators were concerned that this language [reasonable accommodation] could be interpreted as requiring that housing providers provide a broad range of services to persons with handicaps that a housing provider does not normally provide as part of its housing. The Department wishes to stress that a housing provider is not required to provide supportive services, e.g., counseling, medical, or social services that fall outside the scope of the services that the housing provider offers to residents. A housing provider is required to make modifications in order to enable a qualified applicant with handicaps to live in the housing, but is not required to offer housing of a fundamentally different nature. The test is whether, with appropriate modifications, the applicant can live in the housing that the housing provider offers; not whether the applicant could benefit from some other type of housing that the housing provider does not offer.

See Implementation of Fair Housing Amendments of 1988, 54 Fed. Reg.

This Act, like the Air Carrier Access Act, began to extend disability discrimination law beyond federal or federally funded entities. The Civil Rights Act of 1968 applied to housing that received federal financial assistance, state and local government housing, *and* private housing.[75] The Fair Housing Amendments Act did not change this.[76] This movement into the private sphere was a significant step that was taken further with the eventual passage of the ADA.

3231, 3249 (Jan. 23, 1989).

[75] 42 U.S.C. § 3603.

[76] There are statutory exceptions. The "single-family homeowner" exemption applies to any single-family house sold or rented by an owner provided that the owner does not own more than three such houses at any one time, does not try to claim the exemption more than once every twenty-four months, does not own any interest in more than three single-family houses, and does not use a real estate agent in the transaction. Id. § 3603(b)(1). There is also a "four or less family residence" exception, which applies to rooms or units in dwellings containing living quarters occupied by no more than four families living independently of each other if the owner lives in one of the quarters. Id. § 3603(b)(2).

Chapter 2 THE ADA'S HISTORY AND PHILOSOPHY

§ 2.1 A Brief Guide To The ADA

The ADA has a preface section and five main parts. In the text of the statute, these five parts are referred to as "Subchapters." But they are commonly referred to as "Titles," and that is how we refer to them herein.

The preface contains two code sections. The first, § 12101, gives Congress's "Findings and Purposes."[1] Courts often have used this section as the best evidence of what Congress meant when it passed the ADA. This findings section identifies people with disabilities as "a discrete and insular minority who have been faced with restriction and limitations, subjected to a history of purposeful unequal treatment, and relegated to a position of political powerlessness in our society,"[2] states that "some 43,000,000 Americans have one or more physical or mental disabilities,"[3] and sets the nation's proper goals regarding individuals with disabilities as assuring "equality of opportunity, full participation, independent living, and economic self sufficiency."[4]

This section provides that the purpose of the chapter, among other things, is to "provide a clear and comprehensive national mandate for the elimination of discrimination against people with disabilities,"[5] and to ensure that the federal government plays a central role in enforcing these standards.[6]

The second code section sets forth certain definitions that apply throughout the rest of the Act.[7] This includes the definition of "disability," which we discuss in Part 2 of this treatise.

Next come the Act's five Titles. Title I deals with employment.[8] The general rule of discrimination it sets forth is that "no covered entity shall discriminate against a qualified individual with a disability because of the disability of such individual in regard to job application procedures, the hiring, advancement, or discharge of employees, employee compensation, job training, and other terms, conditions, and privileges of employment."[9] An employer does not need to take steps that create an

---

[1] 42 U.S.C. § 12101 (2000).

[2] Id. § 12101(a)(7).

[3] Id. § 12101(a)(1).

[4] Id. § 12101(a)(8).

[5] Id. § 12101(b)(1).

[6] Id. § 12101(b)(3).

[7] 42 U.S.C. § 12102.

[8] Id. §§ 12111-12117.

[9] Id. § 12112.

"undue hardship,"[10] or that create a situation where an employee is a significant risk to the health or safety of others in the workplace.[11] These and other employment issues under Title I, ranging from pre-hiring to termination, are explored in Part 3 of this treatise.

The next subchapter, Title II, covers discrimination by public entities.[12] Generally, this means discrimination by state or local governments.[13] This Title is in turn divided into two parts. Part A sets forth the general rule of non-discrimination by public entities. It provides that "no qualified individual with a disability shall, by reason of such disability, be excluded from participation in or be denied the benefits of the services, programs, or activities of a public entity, or be subjected to discrimination by any such entity."[14] Part B deals with discrimination by public entities in the context of public transportation. Title II in its entirety is discussed in Part 4 of this treatise.

The next subchapter is Title III.[15] This deals with discrimination in public accommodations and services operated by private entities. The general rule is that "[n]o individual shall be discriminated against on the basis of disability in the full and equal enjoyment of the goods, services, facilities, privileges, advantages, or accommodations of any place of public accommodation by any person who owns, leases (or leases to), or operates a place of public accommodation."[16] A public accommodation must make reasonable modifications in its policies, practices, and procedures, unless that entity can demonstrate that doing so would fundamentally alter the nature of its goods, services, or facilities.[17] Older facilities must remove architectural barriers if it is "readily achievable" to do so,[18] while facilities (or alterations) that post-date the ADA must be designed to be readily accessible to individuals with disabilities to the "maximum extent possible."[19] Title III is discussed in Part 5 of this treatise.

As a public law, the ADA contained a Title IV, entitled "Communications."[20] When the ADA became part of the United States Code, the Telecommunications section was codified elsewhere in the U.S.

---

10   Id. § 12111(10).
11   Id. §§ 12111(3), 12113 (a)-(b).
12   Id. §§ 12131-12181.
13   42 U.S.C. § 12131(1)(A).
14   Id. § 12132.
15   Id. §§ 12181-12189.
16   Id. § 12182(a).
17   Id. § 12182(b)(2)(A)(ii).
18   Id. § 12182(b)(2)(A)(iv).
19   42 U.S.C. § 12183(a)(2).
20   See Pub. L. No. 101-336, 104 Stat. 366 (July 26, 1990).

Code.[21] This section provides that manufacturers and providers of telecommunications equipment and services must ensure that their equipment and services are accessible to and useable by people with disabilities, if this is readily achievable.[22]

The final section, Title V of the public law (but Title IV in the U.S. Code), is entitled "Miscellaneous Provisions."[23] There are various significant provisions in this section that have aided courts in interpreting the ADA. For example, this section solidified the close relationship between the ADA and the Rehabilitation Act of 1973, by noting that nothing in the ADA is to be construed to provide a lesser standard of protection than the Rehabilitation Act.[24] This section also provides that states shall not be immune under the Eleventh Amendment for suits brought under the ADA.[25] These and other specific provisions in Title IV will be discussed throughout this treatise.

§ 2.2 ADA Background And Fundamentals

A.   *The Story Of The Passage Of The ADA*

The culmination of federal legislative efforts to establish and protect the rights of people with disabilities was the ADA. But the story of the ADA begins earlier than its passage in 1990.

In February 1986, the National Council on the Handicapped (later the National Council on Disability) released its report "Toward Independence: An Assessment of Federal Laws and Programs Affecting Persons with Disabilities – With Legislative Recommendations, a Report to the President and to the Congress of the United States" ("Toward Independence").[26]

---

[21]   47 U.S.C. § 255 (2000).

[22]   Id.

[23]   Id. §§ 12201-12213.

[24]   42 U.S.C. § 12201(a) (2000).

[25]   Id. § 12202. Although as will be discussed herein in Parts 3 and 4 of this treatise, the Supreme Court has held that Congress exceeded its authority by authorizing Title I suits for damages against states for discrimination in employment.

[26]   Nat'l Council on Disability, Toward Independence: An Assessment of Federal Laws and Programs Affecting Persons with Disabilities – With Legislative Recommendations, A Report to the President and to the Congress of the United States, www.ncd.gov/newsroom/publications/toward.html (Feb. 1986) [hereinafter Toward Independence]. The National Council on Disability is an independent Federal agency whose 15 members are appointed by the President and confirmed by the Senate. The Council was originally established under the Rehabilitation Act of 1973 as an advisory board to the Department of Education, but in 1984 it

The 15-member Council made three general conclusions:

(1) Approximately two-thirds of working-age persons with disabilities do not receive Social Security or other public assistance income;

(2) Federal disability programs reflect an overemphasis on income support and an under-emphasis of initiatives for equal opportunity, independence, prevention, and self-sufficiency;

(3) More emphasis should be given to Federal programs encouraging and assisting private sector efforts to promote opportunities and independence for individuals with disabilities.[27]

The Council emphasized the expense of disability governmental benefits programs and concluded that:

[The] "present and future costs of disability to the Nation are directly related to the degree of success we attain in reducing existing barriers, both structural and attitudinal, and in providing appropriate services to individuals with disabilities so that they may reach their full potential and become more independent and self-sufficient.[28]

The Council recommended changes to federal disability policy in ten issue areas:

Equal Opportunity Laws: The enactment of a comprehensive law requiring equal opportunity for individuals with disabilities, with broad coverage and setting clear, consistent, and enforceable standards prohibiting discrimination on the basis of handicap.

Employment: To increase employment among people with disabilities – a drastically underemployed segment of the population – several legislative changes, concerning the transition from school to work, supported employment, private sector initiatives, job training, job development, and placement.

Disincentives to Work under Social Security Laws: Ways in which provisions of existing Social Security laws serve to discourage and penalize people with disabilities if they seek to become employed and self supporting. In

---

was transformed into an independent agency. Nat'l Council on Disability, At a Glance, at http://www.ncd.gov/brochure.html (last modified Sept. 28, 2001).

[27] Toward Independence, supra note 26 ("Executive Summary").

[28] Id.

response to those work disincentives, corrective amendments to the problematic provisions.

Prevention of Disabilities: To promote prevention of disabilities and to assure that individuals with disabilities do not suffer unnecessary secondary disabilities or exacerbation of their impairments, the Federal Government mount a national program for the prevention of disabilities.

Transportation: Amendments to Federal transportation legislation to achieve the Nation's established policy that "disabled people have the same right to use public transportation as nondisabled persons." Proposals relate to urban mass transit, air transportation, intercity and interstate buses, and private vehicles.

Housing: To permit people with disabilities an opportunity to obtain appropriate housing, which is an important prerequisite to obtaining employment, living independently, and avoiding costly institutionalization. Provides recommendations designed to prohibit housing discrimination and to promote increased appropriate and accessible housing for persons with disabilities.

Community-Based Services for Independent Living: To achieve productivity and independence, people with disabilities require a range of support services according to the nature and degree of their disabilities. Measures, including amendments and funding support to promote availability of community-based services for independent living.

Educating Children with Disabilities: Legislative recommendations regarding educational opportunities for children with disabilities. These recommendations respond to: the need for special education and related services during infancy; the need to educate children with special needs in regular education facilities; and the need to assess progress made since the enactment of the Education for All Handicapped Children Act.

Personal Assistance: Attendant Services, Readers, and Interpreters: Because of the critical importance of such services in fostering independence and avoiding expensive institutionalization, a national commitment to developing a quality system of attendant services, readers, and interpreters.

Coordination: To ensure Federal and Federally supported disability-related programs be authorized and required to develop a joint plan for the systematic coordination of services and benefits.[29]

The Council's Report was a significant step. It set the stage for many of the same issues that even today are at the forefront of debates on disability civil rights.

Thus, the Council noted that "[v]arious estimates place the number of Americans with disabilities between 20 million and 50 million persons, with a figure of 35 or 36 million being the most commonly quoted estimate. A precise and reliable overall figure is not currently available ...."[30] As will be discussed infra in Part 2 of this treatise, the number of Americans with disabilities still has never been fully resolved. This continues to affect disability law and policy.

The Council described the two major approaches to the issue of defining disability as the "health conditions approach" and the "work disability approach." It found that neither approach was adequate.

The Council noted the health conditions approach as emphasizing "all conditions or limitations which impair the health or interfere with the normal functional abilities of an individual."[31] This approach produces high numbers of people with disabilities, because it includes conditions not typically viewed as disabling. For example, various respiratory, circulatory, digestive, skin, musculoskeletal conditions are included that are not typically categorized as disabilities.[32]

The work disability approach "focus[es] on individuals' reports that they have a condition that prevents them from working or limits their ability to work."[33] This emphasis over-estimates and under-estimates the number of people with disabilities, because individuals who are not working have a psychological incentive to classify themselves as having a work disability and because individuals with disabilities who are working are not counted.

The Council's Report articulated the idea that disability rights legislation was part of the larger civil rights movement in America. It determined that then-existing laws prohibiting disability discrimination were not as broad as those prohibiting discrimination on the basis of race, color, sex, religion, or national origin. Private employers, public

---

[29] Id.

[30] Id. ("The Population With Disabilities").

[31] Id.

[32] "Because of its focus on the medically oriented notions of health, the health conditions approach also does not provide adequate data on such conditions as learning disabilities and mental conditions." Id.

[33] Toward Independence, supra note 26.

accommodations, and housing were covered by other civil rights laws, but not by disability rights laws.[34]

As a result of these findings, the Council proposed the Americans with Disabilities Act of 1986.[35] The proposed legislation would extend to federal government, recipients of federal financial assistance, federal contractors, employers engaged in interstate commerce with fifteen or more employees, housing providers, public accommodations (as defined under Title II of the Civil Rights Act of 1964), interstate transportation, insurance providers, and state, county, and local governments.[36]

The Council's proposal identified a broad class of protected individuals. It recommended that there be no eligibility classification for coverage and that the law apply to "all situations in which a person is subjected to unfair or unnecessary exclusion or disadvantage because of some physical or mental impairment, perceived impairment, or history of impairment."[37] The proposal established a realm of prohibited conduct, including intentional and unintentional exclusion, segregation, and unequal treatment.

The proposal required reasonable accommodation and removal of architectural, transportation, and communication barriers. It called for an administrative federal enforcement mechanism and a private right of action if federal enforcement did not occur or at the conclusion of the federal process. Legal remedies included injunctive relief, monetary damages, attorneys' fees, back pay, fines, and termination of federal funding. The ADA of 1986 never became law. But "Toward Independence" formed the basis for what was to become the Americans with Disabilities Act of 1990.

The Council's second report, "On the Threshold of Independence" was submitted to the President and Congress in January of 1988 and included a proposed bill to implement the Council's recommendations.[38]

On April 28, 1988, fourteen co-sponsors introduced this bill in the Senate. The next day, thirty-four co-sponsors introduced it in the House of Representatives.[39] A joint congressional hearing was held on September 27, 1988, but the bills were not acted on by the 100th Congress

---

[34] Id. ("Analysis Of Federal Programs In Specific Topic Areas With Legislative Recommendations").

[35] Id.

[36] Id.

[37] Id.

[38] See generally, Nat'l Council on the Handicapped, On the Threshold of Independence (Andrea H. Farbman ed., 1988).

[39] Lowell Weicker, Jr., Historical Background of the Americans with Disabilities Act, 64 Temp. L. Rev. 387, 391 (1991).

before it adjourned.[40] The bill was modified in response to the information gathered in the congressional hearing and on May 9, 1989, the bill was reintroduced to the 101st Congress.[41]

The final bill passed the Senate by a vote of 91 to 6. It passed the House by a vote of 377 to 28. On the morning of July 26, 1990, on the south lawn of the White House, with 3,000 disability rights advocates, members of Congress and the Administration looking on, President George Bush signed the Americans with Disabilities Act into law. It was the largest signing ceremony in history.[42] President Bush described the ADA as

> [t]he world's first comprehensive declaration of the equality of people with disabilities, and evidence of America's leadership internationally in the cause of human rights. With today's signing of the landmark Americans with Disabilities Act, every man woman and child with a disability can now pass through the closed doors, into a bright new era of equality, independence, and freedom.[43]

B.   *Legislative History*

The ADA was the subject of numerous hearings, involving the testimony of hundreds of individuals, employers, and government representatives.[44]

Several books have been written about this legislative history,[45] and detailed treatment of all of its nuances is beyond the scope of this treatise. Here, we present several aspects of the legislative history that have been the source of much of the controversy of the ADA's subsequent interpretation by courts. First, we discuss the legislative history of the reasonable accommodation requirement, which is at heart of what makes

---

[40] Id.

[41] Id. The Senate version was S. 933, and the House version was H.R. 2273.

[42] See ADA Technical Assistance Ctrs., Historical Context of the Americans with Disabilities Act, at http://www.adata.org/whatsada-history.html (last visited Sept. 30, 2002).

[43] Id.

[44] Henry H. Perritt, Jr., 1 Americans with Disabilities Act Handbook §§ 2.2-2.3 (3rd ed. 1997) [hereinafter "Handbook"]. There are several useful compilations of this legislative history. See generally Legislative History of Public Law 101-336, The Americans with Disabilities Act, Prepared for the Committee on Education and Labor U.S. House of Representatives (U.S. Gov't Printing Office 1991); Arlene Mayerson, Americans with Disabilities Act Annotated: Legislative History, Regulations & Commentary (Clark Boardman Callaghan 1994).

[45] See supra note 44.

the ADA different from other federal disability discrimination statutes. Next, we discuss the wide variation in different parts of the ADA's legislative history, using the issue of mitigation in the definition of disability as an example. Finally, we outline major amendments that were made to the ADA as part of the committee process.

1. The Evolution and Legislative History of the Reasonable Accommodation Requirement

As discussed above, the ADA is a product of the civil rights movement. Its roots should be understood in the context of parallel developments in other areas of civil rights. In 1971, in *Griggs v. Duke Power Company*, the Supreme Court interpreted Title VII of the Civil Rights Act of 1964 to preclude facially neutral employment tests that disproportionately excluded African Americans.[46] Effect, even independent of intent, was deemed sufficient to trigger judicial involvement.

The extrapolation of the underlying argument to people with disabilities is manifest. Offering employment to everyone, without relation to disability is meaningless if the door to the work place is up a flight of stairs and the applicant uses a wheelchair. That fact, however, does not resolve how the legislature should deal with the dilemma — should governments pay for opening such doors or should private employers?

The phrase "reasonable accommodation" began percolating through another area of civil rights law shortly after Title VII was enacted, in 1964. Title VII provides that it is unlawful for an employer "to discriminate against any individual with respect to his compensation, terms, conditions, or privileges of employment, because of such individual's race, color, religion, sex, or national origin."[47]

The prohibition against discrimination based on religion inevitably raises accommodation issues: Is it discriminatory to force a person to work on a day on which her religion forbids working? Is it discriminatory to forbid a person from wearing certain garb that his religion requires?

The EEOC addressed these issues in a regulation in 1966, requiring employers to "accommodate to the reasonable religious needs of employees ... where such accommodation can be made without serious

---

[46] Griggs v. Duke Power Co., 401 U.S. 424, 431 (1971) ("The Act proscribes not only overt discrimination but also practices that are fair in form, but discriminatory in operation. The touchstone is business necessity. If an employment practice which operates to exclude Negroes cannot be shown to be related to job performance, the practice is prohibited.").

[47] Civil Rights Act of 1964, § 703(a)(1), 42. U.S.C. § 2000e-2(a)(1) (2000).

inconvenience to the conduct of the business."[48] A year later, it amended the guidelines to require employers to "make reasonable accommodations to the religious needs of employees and prospective employees where such accommodations can be made without undue hardships on the conduct of the employer's business."[49] Those themes – "reasonable accommodations" and "undue hardship" – echo in the ADA.

In 1977, the Supreme Court addressed the meaning of "reasonable accommodations" in *Trans World Airlines v. Hardison,* a case in which an employee alleged that his employer had discriminated against him by refusing to permit him not to work on Saturdays.[50] The court of appeals had suggested that the employer might have permitted the employee to work a four-day work week, replacing him on Saturday with supervisory or other personnel, or that the employer could have paid premium wages to others to induce them to work on Saturday.[51]

The Supreme Court rejected those alternatives:

> To require [the employer] to bear more than a *de minimis* cost in order to give Hardison Saturdays off is an undue hardship. Like abandonment of the seniority system, to require [the employer] to bear additional costs when no such costs are incurred to give other employees the days off that they want would involve unequal treatment of employees on the basis of their religion. By suggesting that [the employer] should incur certain costs in order to give Hardison Saturdays off, the Court of Appeals would in effect require [the employer] to finance an additional Saturday off and then to choose the employee who will enjoy it on the basis of his religious beliefs.[52]

The Court's opinion is mixed here. Is it saying solely that incurring more than *de minimis* additional costs would constitute undue hardship? Or, is it that incurring those costs would in effect favor one religion over another (or none)? To the extent the Court's interpretation of "undue hardship" is defined to cover anything more than *de minimis*, it would provide little play for the requirement of accommodations in the disability area. This is because typically at least some accommodations will require the expenditure of not insignificant funds.[53]

---

[48]   29 C.F.R. § 1605.1 (1967).

[49]   29 C.F.R. § 1605.2 (1968).

[50]   Trans World Airlines v. Hardison, 432 U.S. 63, 64 (1977).

[51]   Id. at 84.

[52]   Id.

[53]   See Nancy R. Mudrick, Employment Discrimination Laws for Disability: Utilization and Outcome, 549 Annals of the Am. Acad. of Pol. & Soc. Sci., 53, 57 (1997).

The *Hardison* limitation does not necessarily compel a similar result in the disability area, however. Accepting the *Hardison* Court's analysis, accommodating one religious group inevitably means giving it a preferential advantage over another religious group. This may implicate other concerns, such as first amendment freedom of religion issues. However, accommodating people with disabilities, having the practical effect of compensating them at a higher level, does not necessarily come at the expense of other employees, except to the extent that all salaries are reduced.[54]

This logic may explain why drafters of disability rights legislation and regulations were willing to adopt the reasonable accommodation formulation which the EEOC had used for religious discrimination. During the 1970s, at the federal and state levels, disability rights legislation deployed this reasonable accommodation/undue hardship model.

The regulations to Sections 503 and 504 of the Rehabilitation Act of 1973, issued by the Department of Health, Education, and Welfare in 1978, adopted the "reasonable accommodation" formulation previously used in the regulations adopted pursuant to the Civil Rights Act of 1964. However, the Rehabilitation Act regulations go further. They require recipients of federal funds to make "reasonable accommodation to the known physical or mental limitations of an otherwise qualified handicapped applicant or employee unless the recipient can demonstrate that the accommodation would impose an undue hardship on the operation of its program."[55]

Although the term reasonable accommodation was not new, the regulations avoid the *de minimis* trap of *Hardison* by defining a series of reasonable accommodations, such as making facilities accessible to people with disabilities, modifying work schedules or requiring assistive devices. By explicitly limiting the requirement of reasonable accommodations only to those situations where they would constitute an undue hardship, the regulations also require more than a *de minimis* effort by the recipient.

In *Southwestern Community College v. Davis*,[56] described earlier, the Supreme Court first interpreted the reach of Section 504. The Court held that the defendant nursing school had not discriminated against the hearing-impaired plaintiff because no program modifications would have permitted her to serve as a nurse.[57] Nonetheless, the Court recognized that

---

[54]   This assumes the employer simply cannot lower the pay of the disabled employee.

[55]   45 C.F.R. § 84.12(a) (2002).

[56]   Southwestern Cmty. Coll. v. Davis, 42 U.S. 397 (1979).

[57]   Id. at 412-13; see Chai Feldblum, The (R)evolution of Physical

Situations may arise where a refusal to modify an existing program might become unreasonable and discriminatory. Identification of those instances where a refusal to accommodate the needs of a disabled person amounts to discrimination against the handicapped continues to be an important responsibility of HEW.[58]

Thus, *Davis* sits on the cusp. The case is an exemplar of that body of civil rights law that goes no farther than requiring employers (or others) to treat all people without regard to the stereotyped characteristic, be it race, religion or disability. On the other hand, it explicitly understands that refusing to accommodate the needs of a person with a disability might itself amount to prohibited discrimination.

Perhaps inartfully, *Davis* did focus on the key issue that sets disability rights law apart from other branches of civil rights law. That is, treating qualified applicants or employees equally, without regard to whether they have a disability, will forever leave people with disabilities in a disadvantaged position. This is because certainly there are some factors that may affect their ability to participate equally in jobs, but which do not render them incapable of performing the key or essential functions of those jobs. The *Davis* court understood, in the words of Section 504, a "recognition by Congress of the distinction between the evenhanded treatment of qualified handicapped persons and affirmative efforts to overcome the disabilities caused by handicaps."[59]

Later, in *Alexander v. Choate*,[60] the Supreme Court read its earlier Davis decision to mean that "it appeared unlikely that [Davis] could benefit from *any* modifications that the relevant HEW regulations required and ... the further modifications Davis sought ... would have compromised the essential nature of the college's nursing program."[61] That interpretation expands the meaning of reasonable to include the universe of modifications that do not "compromise[ ] the essential nature" of a program.

Disability Antidiscrimination Law, 20 Mental & Physical Disability L. Rep. 613, 620 n.12 (1996) (pointing out that the plaintiff was only mildly hearing-impaired).

[58] Davis, 42 U.S. at 412-13.

[59] Id. at 406.

[60] Alexander v. Choate, 469 U.S. 287, 300 (1985).

[61] Id. Later courts and commentators, and eventually the Supreme Court itself, limited Davis. See, e.g., Camenish v. Univ. of Tex., 616 F.2d 127, 133 (5th Cir. 1980); Mark Martin, Accommodating the Handicapped: The Meaning of Discrimination Under Section 504 of the Rehabilitation Act, 55 N.Y.U. L. Rev. 881, 884-85 (1980); Donald Olenick, Accommodating the Handicapped: Rehabilitation Section 504 After Southeastern, 80 Colum. L. Rev. 171, 185 (1980).

The Rehabilitation Act regulations were not the only venue in which legislators were engrafting "reasonable accommodation" duties on civil rights laws. In 1973, California prohibited employment discrimination on the basis of "physical handicap" – later enlarged to "physical handicap, medical condition" – in its employment discrimination statute.[62]

The California Department of Fair Employment and Housing, which is responsible for enforcing the anti-employment discrimination provisions, adopted a regulation in 1980 that echoes the Rehabilitation Act § 504 regulation.[63] The regulation requires an employer to make "reasonable accommodation to the disability of any individual with a disability" if the employer knows of the disability and unless the employer can "demonstrate that the accommodation would impose an undue hardship."[64] Like the Section 504 regulations, California Section 7293.9 does not define reasonable accommodation but gives examples.[65]

In 1988, following a number of years of study,[66] Congress introduced legislation to prohibit discrimination against people with disabilities.[67] In these original bills, each defined reasonable accommodation and declared the failure or refusal to make reasonable accommodations to constitute discrimination.[68] Unlike the Rehabilitation Act and its state variants, these bills defined reasonable accommodation in terms of its goal – to provide "the equal opportunity to participate effectively in a particular program, activity, job or other opportunity."[69] Neither proposal had an undue hardship limitation.[70] Neither of the bills became law.

---

[62] Cal. Lab. Code § 1420, recodified as Cal. Gov't Code § 12940 (1999).

[63] Cal. Code Regs. tit. 2, § 7293.9 (1995).

[64] Id.

[65] See Fisher v. Sup. Ct., 223 Cal.Rptr 203, 205 (Cal. Ct. App. 1986) (reasonable accommodation required for medical condition – cancer). The phrase "reasonable accommodation" or similar ideas have also been interpreted in a variety of other settings, including the Individuals with Disabilities Education Act (20 U.S.C. § 1400 et seq. (2000); § 503 of the Rehabilitation Act (29 U.S.C. § 793 (2000), and the Developmental Disabilities Assistance and Bill of Rights Act (42 U.S.C. § 15001 et seq. (2000). See generally U.S. Comm'n on Civil Rights, Accommodating the Spectrum of Individual Abilities 104-06 (1983) [hereinafter Accommodating the Spectrum].

[66] See, e.g., Accommodating the Spectrum, supra note 65.

[67] See S. 2345, 100th Cong. (1988); H.R. 4498, 100th Cong. (1988).

[68] S. 2345, § 5(a)(3).

[69] See id. § 3(b)(5).

[70] One can argue that the theory of reasonable accommodation as

The proponents of the ADA focused on the *de minimis* or zero costs of many accommodations.[71] The legislative history of the bills that eventually became the ADA, which were introduced in the first session of the 101st Congress, reflect that concept.

During the Congressional consideration of the ADA, much of the testimony focused on the relative ease with which employers could accommodate people with disabilities. The Senate report cited the minimal costs of specific accommodations and noted that witnesses had explained that there would need to be more expensive accommodations, "[b]ut even costs for these accommodations are frequently exaggerated."[72] A number of supporters of legislation argued that employing people with disabilities would decrease the need for federal funding to support them and increase their tax revenues.[73]

ADA Title I, as proposed and eventually adopted, sets forth an inexact concept of reasonable accommodation. Reasonable accommodation is defined not teleologically, but to include "making existing facilities used by employees readily accessible to and useable by individuals with disabilities,"[74] and by listing a series of examples of accommodations.[75]

---

developed in federal and state statutes has been articulated from the wrong perspective. See Hahn, supra note 6, at 102. On this model, modifying the environment is simply to balance the scales properly, not to give additional assistance to people with disabilities.

[71] Accommodating the Spectrum, supra note 65, at 106-08.

[72] Sen. Comm. on Lab. & Human Res., S. Rep. No. 101-116, at 10 (1989); see also 135 Cong. Rec. S10,753 (daily ed. Sept. 7, 1989) (statement of Sen. Gore) ("by requiring only modifications that are readily achievable and providing that employers do not have to take actions that are unduly burdensome, the bill establishes flexible, workable and realistic obligations to eliminate discrimination against persons with disabilities").

[73] [W]e must bear the economic costs to our society when the
      disabled are prevented from fully participating in
      education, jobs, and community life. If the disabled are
      locked out of jobs, then society must bear the cost of
      maintaining these individuals and their families – families
      that otherwise would be self supporting and paying taxes.

136 Cong. Rec. H2447-448 (daily ed. May 17, 1990) (statement of Rep. Miller); id. H2438 (statement of Rep. Mineta) ("Sure, there are costs associated with this bill, but those costs are manageable. But the cost of not allowing disabled Americans to be full participants in our society will be much greater."); id. at H2,440 (statement of Rep. Fish) ("the bill does not put an undue burden on employers, businesses or the community at large. It strikes a balance.").

[74] 42 U.S.C. § 12111(9)(A) (2000).

[75] Id. § 12111(9)(B).

The drafters carried over language wholesale from the Section 504 regulations for pragmatic reasons: Congress was familiar with their effect and recipients of federal funds had been complying with the language since the late 1970s.[76] As do the Section 504 regulations, the ADA's definition of undue hardship functions as a limitation on Title I's reasonable accommodation requirement.[77]

As one of the drafters of the ADA has pointed out, the statutory definition of reasonableness creates an ambiguity. In the legislation introduced in 1988, "reasonable" meant effective. If the statute then imposed an undue hardship limitation, the logic of the statute would have been that an employer had to make an effective accommodation *up to* the undue hardship limit.[78]

The predominant way that reasonable is defined, however, is as a limitation on the extent to which one should act. Thus, rather than a description of the nature of the affirmative act, reasonableness and undue hardship appear as limitations on an employer's duty.[79]

In the Congressional debates on the ADA, the business community, and especially small businesses, argued against aspects of reasonable accommodations.[80] One opponent contended that the ADA entails "affirmative action ... requiring creative efforts to assure access rather than a legal standard against which to determine if an employer was guilty of discrimination."[81]

Opponents bolstered the "affirmative action" argument by suggesting that unlike other civil rights laws, the ADA would impose its

---

[76] See Feldblum, supra note 57, at 617.

[77] Title II, which deals with public accommodations, limits facilities modifications to those that are "readily achievable." 42 U.S.C. § 12182(b)(2)(A)(iv).

[78] See Feldblum, supra note 57, at 619.

[79] 136 Cong. Rec. H2,427-428 (daily ed. May 17, 1990) (statement of Rep. Owens) (noting that provisions of ADA "derive largely from § 504 of the Rehabilitation Act of 1973 and its implementing regulations, and the Civil Rights Act of 1964").

[80] E.g., Americans with Disabilities Act: Hearing on H.R. 101-45, Before the House Comm. on Small Bus., 101st Cong. 16-20 (1990) (statement of David Pinkus, Nat'l Small Bus. United), reprinted in Disability Law in the United States: A Legislative History of the Americans with Disabilities Act of 1990 (Pub. L. 101-33) 93 (Bernard D. Reams, Jr. et al., eds. 1992) [hereinafter Legislative History]; see also id. at 14 (statement of Kenneth Lewis, Nat'l Fed. of Indep. Bus.).

[81] See Civil Rights Act of 1990: Hearing on S. 2104, Before the House Comm. on Lab. & Human Res., 101st Cong. 206-14, 287, 290 (1990) (statement of Lawrence Z. Lorber, Am. Soc'y of Personnel Admin.).

costs on others.[82] They argued that the model for the ADA, Section 504 of the Rehabilitation Act, affects only government contractors, who presumably may build additional costs into their contracts.[83] They did not question the goal, but suggested that it was the government's duty to pay for it, either directly or through tax credits.[84]

To the business community, the open-ended nature of the ADA's central terms, such as "reasonable accommodation," "essential functions" and "undue hardship," amplified the problem of its potential costs.[85] This argument took two forms. First, businesses did not accept the *de minimis* projections.[86] They pointed out that for small businesses, an accumulation of "*de minimis*" costs can be painful.[87]

Second, opponents feared potential liability, based on assertedly unclear statutory language.[88] They testified that small businesses could not afford to hire counsel to advise them on their ADA duties.[89] Thus, they requested clearer guidelines, including monetary or percentage of income guidelines, on the reasonable accommodation mandate.[90] Along with these suggestions, they requested that businesses be given discretion in defining such concepts as essential job functions and that the ADA's effects be phased in over time.[91]

In the end, the ADA and its regulations addressed many such objections, giving substantial weight to an employer's definition of

---

[82] E.g. Legislative History, supra note 80, at 2, 84, 85 (statement of John J. Mottley III, Nat'l Fed. of Indep. Bus.).

[83] Id. at 4, 87.

[84] Legislative History, supra note 80, at 98-99 (statement of David Pinkus); id. at 78, 83 (statement of Joseph J. Dragonette, U.S. Chamber of Commerce).

[85] Legislative History, supra note 80, at 95 (statement of David Pinkus).

[86] E.g., id. at 5, 88 (statement of John J. Mottley III) (citing examples of $23/hour for sign language interpreter, $150-$700 to purchase a telecommunications device for the deaf [TDD] and $5000 to purchase a computer with speech synthesizer).

[87] Id. at 4, 87. These arguments tended to lump the costs of Title III (Public Services) accommodations with Title I (Employment) accommodations. See, e.g., id. at 5, 88; id. at 19 (statement of David Pinkus) (estimating that over $5 billion will be spent to renovate bathrooms to accommodate wheelchairs).

[88] Legislative History, supra note 80, at 86 (statement of Kenneth Lewis, Nat'l Fed. Indep. Bus.).

[89] Id. at 17 (statement of David Pinkus).

[90] E.g., id. at 92 (statement of Kenneth Lewis).

[91] E.g., id. at 76-84 (statement of Joseph J. Dragonette).

essential job functions.[92] In part to deal with liability concerns, Congress required the EEOC or analogous state agencies first to pass on employment discrimination claims.[93] However, the essential structure of the reasonable accommodation regime remained.

Many of the criticisms on the reasonable accommodation mandate were case specific and not empirically based. However, critics generally did not question the underlying assumption of proponents of the ADA that imposing an accommodation requirement on businesses would lead to higher employment levels for people with disabilities, other things being equal.

Today, the wisdom of these assumptions is the subject of debate. Thus, the question is raised whether the cost of accommodating qualified workers with disabilities affects their employment rates. In 1990, the data did not exist to study that question. In fact, it may not exist yet today. Economists and others have tried to answer the question with available data. Although the answer is far from conclusive, we discuss some of these analyses infra in § 2.3 of this Part, and also in Part 9.

2.   An Example of Mixed Signals in the Legislative History – Mitigating Measures

The ADA has a vast body of legislative history. One result is that courts have been able to point to divergent testimony on a given issue to demonstrate that the legislative intent of a particular provision or term is unclear and, therefore, subject to judicial interpretation. One example of this confusion has occurred in litigation over the definition of "mitigating measures."

As we will discuss infra in Part 2 of this treatise, the Supreme Court has ultimately weighed in on this issue and decided that individuals must be considered in their mitigated states in determining whether they are "disabled" in the meaning of the act.[94] We present this issue here not to show what the law is, but as an example of the mixed signals in the legislative history on any given topic.

In *Washington v. HCA Health Services*, the U.S. Court of Appeals for the Fifth Circuit noted that the Senate Report is inconsistent with the House Reports in its treatment of individuals with controlled disabilities.[95]

---

[92] 29 C.F.R. 1630.2(n)(3)(i)-(ii) (2003) (evidence includes, but is not limited to "the employer's judgment as to which functions are essential" and "[w]ritten job descriptions prepared before advertising or interviewing applicants for the job").

[93] 42 U.S.C. § 12117(a) (2000).

[94] See Sutton v. United Airlines, 527 U.S. 471 (1999).

[95] Wash. v. HCA Health Servs., 152 F.3d 464, 467-68 (5th Cir. 1998).

The House Education and Labor Committee Report explains that:

> Whether a person has a disability should be assessed
> without regard to the availability of mitigating measures,
> such as reasonable accommodations or auxiliary aids. For
> example, a person who is hard of hearing is substantially
> limited in the major life activity of hearing, even though the
> loss may be corrected through the use of a hearing aid.
> Likewise, persons with impairments, such as epilepsy or
> diabetes, which substantially limit a major life activity are
> covered under the first prong of the definition of disability,
> even if the effects of the impairment are controlled by
> medication.[96]

The House Judiciary Committee Report uses similar language to
describe the breadth and meaning of the first prong of the definition of
disability:

> The impairment should be assessed without considering
> whether mitigating measures, such as auxiliary aids or
> reasonable accommodations, would result in a less-than-
> substantial limitation. For example, a person with
> epilepsy, an impairment which substantially limits a major
> life activity, is covered under this test, even if the effects of
> the impairment which substantially limits a major life
> activity, is also covered, even if the hearing loss is corrected
> by the use of a hearing aid.[97]

These two House Reports indicate that individuals with epilepsy,
diabetes, or hearing impairment should be assessed without regard to
mitigating measures and, therefore, considered to be "disabled" under the
first prong.

By contrast, the Senate Labor and Human Resources Committee
Report, in addition to the statement that "whether a person has a
disability should be assessed without regard to the availability of
mitigating measures, such as reasonable accommodations or auxiliary
aids,"[98] describes the purpose of the third prong (i.e., "being regarded as
having such an impairment"[99]):

> Another important goal of the third prong of the definition
> is to ensure that persons with *medical conditions that are
> under control*, and that therefore do not currently limit
> major life activities, are not discriminated against on the

---

[96]   H.R. Rep. No. 101-485(II), at 52 (1990), reprinted in 1990
U.S.C.C.A.N. 303, 334.

[97]   Id. at 28, reprinted in 1990 U.S.C.C.A.N. 445, 451.

[98]   S. Rep. No. 101-116, at 23 (1989).

[99]   42 U.S.C. § 12102(2)(C) (2000).

basis of their medical conditions. [Examples include:] individuals with *controlled diabetes or epilepsy* ... [or individuals who] wear *hearing aids*....[100]

The Senate Report suggests that these individuals should be assessed for coverage by the law in their medicated state and thus are not disabled because they are not substantially limited in a major life activity. The Senate Report does, however, then state that these individuals may be compensated under the ADA if they are discriminated against because they are "regarded as" being disabled.

Unlike the Fifth Circuit, the First Circuit in *Arnold v. United Parcel Service*[101] stated that the "prong three" passage in the Senate Report is not inconsistent with that of the House Report, concluding that courts should focus on the untreated impairments. According to the First Circuit, "these passages may be easily squared by recognizing that an individual may have a 'disability' under prong one (having an impairment that substantially limits a major life activity) and prong three ('regarded as' having such an impairment) at the same time; one does not preclude the other. The ADA protects any individual with a 'disability' against both discrimination based on prong one and discrimination based on prong three."[102]

3. Significant Amendments in the Committee Process

As with any bill, amendments to the ADA were introduced throughout the committee process. The Senate Committee on Labor and Human Resources adopted three amendments. The Committee replaced punitive and compensatory damages with Title VII remedies (i.e., back pay, benefits, and injunctive relief); phased in the employment provisions (e.g., covering employers with 25 or more employees for the first two years, and employers with 15 or more employees later); and eliminated the prohibition against "anticipatory discrimination" (i.e., for individuals who believed they were about to be subjected to discrimination).[103] These amendments were to respond to concerns of the Bush administration.[104]

The House Committee on Education and Labor made amendments to the House bill on November 14, 1989, adopting the Senate's changes and making additional changes. The House bill:

excluded current users of illegal drugs from protection;

---

[100] S. Rep. No. 101-116, at 24 (1989) (emphasis added).
[101] Arnold v. United Parcel Serv., 136 F.3d 854, 860 (1st Cir. 1998).
[102] Id. at 860.
[103] H.R. Rep. No. 101-485(II), at 164 (1989) (minority views summarizing changes).
[104] Id.

limited employers' liability for contractors' discrimination to actions regarding the employer's own employees or applicants;

added consideration of site-specific factors to the determination of undue hardship;

clarified when an alteration to a facility would trigger accessibility requirements;

clarified that the Attorney General could not seek punitive damages on behalf of an aggrieved party;

replaced the term "potential places of employment" with "commercial facilities" for purposes of new construction;

required Federal agencies to develop coordination procedures;

required that plaintiffs filing public accommodations suits have reasonable grounds to sue;

authorized certification of state and local building codes by the Attorney General; and

allowed flexibility in applying accessibility requirements to historical buildings.[105]

The most controversial issue in committee was the damages provision. As of November 1989, a deal had been struck eliminating punitive and compensatory damages and incorporating by reference the remedies of Title VII. At that time, Title VII required Equal Employment Opportunity Commission (EEOC) conciliation as a prerequisite to a suit in federal court and limited remedies to back pay, benefits, and injunctive relief.

However, in early 1990, civil rights reform legislation was proposed that would have changed Title VII to allow direct access to courts, provide for jury trials, and permit compensatory and punitive damages.[106] The minority in the House, who had agreed reluctantly to the original deal, and the Bush administration, objected to the possibility of expanded remedies under the ADA.[107] Eventually, over the objections of the Bush administration, the parties relented, and an amendment to de-link the ADA from Title VII was voted down in the House, by a vote of 227 to 192.[108]

---

[105] Id. at 165-66.

[106] Perritt, supra note 44, at § 2.3.

[107] Id.

[108] Id.

In the Conference Committee, the changes were minor, and generally followed the House version of the bill. Regarding Title I, the Committee accepted the House definition of "essential functions," which required written job descriptions to be considered as evidence of essential functions and provided for consideration of the employer's judgment as to what job functions are essential.[109]

The Committee adopted the House's definition of "undue hardship."[110] It adopted the House's approach to direct threat, which expanded it to all threats to the health or safety of others, rather than just to contagious diseases.[111] The Committee adopted the House's clarification of the exclusion of current users of illegal drugs.[112]

Regarding Title II, the Committee adopted the House's structure, which split Title II's requirements into two subtitles – one covering general prohibitions and one covering public transportation.[113]

Regarding Title III, the Committee adopted the House's use of "commercial facilities" instead of "potential places of employment."[114] The Committee adopted the House list of factors for determining what barrier removal is "readily achievable," and providing more consideration for the resources of the individual facility.[115]

The Committee adopted the House's clarification that entities liable for violations of the Act include anyone who owns, leases (or leases to), or operates a place of public accommodation.[116] The Committee adopted the House definition of "direct threat" (the Senate version did not include a definition).[117] The Committee replaced the Senate's alterations provision, which applied to "major structural alterations," with the House's provision, applying to any alteration "that affects ... a primary function."[118]

Finally, the Committee adopted the House's remedies provision, which allowed anticipatory litigation only for an individual with "reasonable grounds" to believe he was about to be subject to discrimination.[119] The Committee adopted the House's clarification that

---

[109] H.R. Conf. Rep. No. 101-596, at 58 (1990).

[110] Id.

[111] Id. at 60.

[112] Id. at 63-65.

[113] Id. at 67.

[114] Id. at 75.

[115] H.R. Conf. Rep. No. 101-596, at 75-76.

[116] Id. at 76.

[117] Id. at 77.

[118] Id.

[119] Id. at 80.

the Attorney General was not authorized to seek punitive damages.[120] It adopted the House's grace period for compliance by small businesses, allowing them an additional six or twelve months, depending on size.[121]

Regarding Title V, the Committee adopted the House version of the exclusion of current users of illegal drugs. But it clarified that "[t]he provision is not intended to be limited to persons who use drugs on the day of, or within a matter of days or weeks before, the action in question. Rather, the provision is intended to apply to a person whose illegal use of drugs occurred recently enough to justify a reasonable belief that a person's drug use is current."[122]

The Committee adopted the House provision for use of alternative dispute resolution. It noted, however, that "[i]t is the intent of the conferees that the use of these alternative dispute resolution procedures is completely voluntary. Under no condition would an arbitration clause in a collective bargaining agreement or employment contract prevent an individual from pursuing their rights under the ADA."[123]

C. *Constitutional Basis*

Through the ADA, Congress attempted to exercise its full constitutional authority to prohibit and deter discrimination on the basis of disability.[124] To do this, Congress relied on the Equal Protection Clause of the Fourteenth Amendment to the Constitution,[125] and on the Interstate Commerce Clause.[126]

In exercising its authority pursuant to the Equal Protection Clause, Congress signaled a different approach than that taken by the U.S. Supreme Court. In several cases, the Supreme Court had indicated an unwillingness to treat people with disabilities as a group deserving of special, or "heightened" protection under the Equal Protection Clause.

The Supreme Court first addressed the protection afforded to people with disabilities under the Equal Protection Clause in 1927. In *Buck v. Bell*, the plaintiff challenged the constitutionality of a Virginia law requiring compulsory sterilization of people with mental retardation at the age of 18.[127] Although the Court held that the Virginia statute did not

---

[120] Id. at 80-81.

[121] H.R. Conf. Rep. No. 101-596, at 81.

[122] Id. at 87.

[123] Id. at 89.

[124] 42 U.S.C. § 12101(b)(4) (2000) ("It is the purpose of this chapter ... to invoke the full sweep of Congressional authority, including the power to enforce the fourteenth amendment and to regulate commerce ....").

[125] U.S. Const. amend. XIV, § 5.

[126] U.S. Const. art. I, § 8, cl. 3.

[127] Buck v. Bell, 274 U.S. 200, 205 (1927).

violate the Equal Protection Clause, it did not analyze the constitutional standard of review for disability-based discrimination.[128]

The *Buck* Court relied on the view, as articulated by Justice Oliver Wendell Holmes, of the limited societal responsibility for people with disabilities:

> We have seen more than once that the public welfare may call upon the best citizens for their lives. It would be strange if it could not call upon those who already sap the strength of the state for these lesser sacrifices, often not felt to be such by those concerned, in order to prevent our being swamped with incompetence. It is better for all the world, if instead of waiting to execute degenerate offspring for crime, or to let them starve for their imbecility, society can prevent those who are manifestly unfit from continuing their kind. The principle that sustains compulsory vaccination is broad enough to cover cutting the Fallopian tubes .... Three generations of imbeciles are enough.[129]

Whatever the standard, the Court considered the state's interest in preventing the birth of people with disabilities to be a significant or compelling enough reason to satisfy it.

The Court conducted a closer analysis of the constitutional standard of review in 1985, in the case of *City of Cleburne v. Cleburne Living Center*.[130] The City of Cleburne, Texas denied a special use permit for a group home of individuals with mental retardation.[131] The plaintiff challenged the zoning decision as violating the Equal Protection Clause because the decision was based purportedly on the mental retardation of the prospective residents.

This time the Court explicitly analyzed the appropriate standard of review. The Court found that a "heightened scrutiny" constitutional analysis was not necessary for disability discrimination because people with mental retardation:

- Are not a uniform, identifiable group because different degrees of mental retardation require different treatment;[132]

- Have special needs and of necessity must be treated differently from non-disabled people. The Court did not want to discourage special programs for people with mental

---

[128] Id. at 207.

[129] Id.

[130] City of Cleburne v. Cleburne Living Ctr., 473 U.S. 432 (1985).

[131] Id. at 436-37.

[132] Id. at 442-43.

retardation.[133] Thus, the Court believed that disability, unlike race, could not be presumed to be irrelevant to state interests;

- Are not politically powerless and have not faced a history of state prejudice, as evidenced by the state programs designed to benefit them;[134] and

- Are difficult to distinguish as a class of people from other groups, such as elderly people, people with physical disabilities, and people with mental illness. The Court was unwilling to start down a slippery slope that might result in these groups receiving heightened scrutiny.[135]

Instead, the Court found the "rational basis" review standard to be appropriate:

> To withstand equal protection review, legislation that distinguishes between the mentally retarded and others must be rationally related to a legitimate government purpose. This standard affords government the latitude necessary both to pursue policies designed to assist the retarded in realizing their full potential, and to freely and efficiently engage in activities that burden the retarded in what is essentially an incidental manner.[136]

However, the Court noted that people with disabilities, like other citizens, retain their substantive and fundamental constitutional rights, and cases involving those rights may be subject to a higher standard of review.[137]

Applying the rational basis test to the City's zoning decision at issue, the Court found that decision to be unconstitutional. The City's reasons for denying the permit – negative attitudes of neighboring property owners, the possibility of harassment from neighborhood junior high school students, the remote possibility of flooding, and the increased population density – were not legitimate rational bases for excluding the group home.[138]

Justices Marshall, Brennan, and Blackmun dissented, arguing that the rational basis standard discussion was dicta because it was not necessary to the outcome, as the zoning decision would have failed any constitutional standard. They argued that the Court was, in fact, applying a heightened scrutiny analysis. The dissenters believed

---

[133] Id. at 444.

[134] Id. at 445.

[135] Id. at 445-46.

[136] Cleburne Living Ctr., 473 U.S. at 446.

[137] Id. at 447.

[138] Id. at 448-50.

heightened scrutiny was justified by the importance of the right to establish a home and the history of segregation and discrimination against people with mental retardation.[139]

Disability advocates relied on this dissent to argue that heightened scrutiny, or at least "rational basis with teeth,"[140] should apply to disability discrimination.[141] However, the application of the rational basis test to disability discrimination was confirmed by the Court in *Board of Trustees of the University of Alabama v. Garrett*,[142] discussed infra in Parts 3 and 4 of the treatise.

D.   *Role Of Federal Agencies*

The ADA provided two roles for federal agencies: (1) development of regulations, and (2) enforcement.

1.   Regulations

The ADA charged several federal agencies with developing regulations. The Equal Employment Opportunity Commission (EEOC) was charged with issuing regulations interpreting and implementing the employment provisions under Title I of the ADA within one year of the ADA's enactment.[143]

The Department of Justice (DOJ) was charged with issuing regulations interpreting and implementing the state and local government requirements under Title II of the ADA within one year of enactment.[144]

The DOJ was required to issue regulations implementing the Title III requirements applicable to places of public accommodation.[145] However, the Department of Transportation (DOT) was charged with issuing regulations implementing the transportation requirements under Title II and Title III.[146]

The ADA required significant coordination between federal agencies. The DOJ's construction-related requirements and the DOT's requirements for accessible facilities and vehicles are required to be

---

[139] Id. at 461-62.

[140] Yeiter v. Sec'y of Health & Human Servs., 818 F.2d 8, 10 (6th Cir. 1987).

[141] Id.; see Heller v. Doe, 509 U.S. 312, 335-36 n.1 (1993) (Souter, J., dissenting); Stephen Mikochik, The Constitution and the Americans with Disabilities Act: Some First Impressions, 64 Temp. L. Rev. 619, 626-27 (1991).

[142] Bd. of Trs. of the Univ. of Alabama v. Garrett, 531 U.S. 356 (2001).

[143] 42 U.S.C. § 12116 (2000).

[144] Id. § 12134.

[145] Id. § 12186(b).

[146] Id. §§ 12149, 12186(a).

consistent with guidelines issued by the U.S. Architectural and Transportation Barriers Compliance Board ("Access Board").[147] The agencies responsible for regulation and enforcement were required to develop coordinated regulations and processes for handling complaints with the agencies responsible for enforcing the Rehabilitation Act.[148]

2. Enforcement

The ADA did not become effective on enactment in 1990. Instead, different titles of the ADA became effective after different periods. Title I became effective 24 months after enactment, or July 26, 1992, for employers with 25 or more employees. Title I became effective for smaller employers (with 15 or less employees) two years later, on July 26, 1994.[149]

The EEOC and the DOJ, as well as private individuals, were given enforcement authority, following the powers, remedies, and procedures of the Civil Rights Act of 1964.[150] Thus, individuals who believe they have faced employment discrimination must file a charge with the EEOC within 180 days of the violation. They must await a "right to sue" letter from the EEOC before they can pursue their claim in court. [151]

Title II of the ADA took effect on January 26, 1992.[152] The ADA provided for enforcing agencies to follow the enforcement procedures and remedies of Section 505 of the Rehabilitation Act of 1973.[153] Section 505, in turn, incorporates the procedures of Title VI of the Civil Rights Act of 1964.

Under Title VI of the Civil Rights Act, a federal agency that administers federal funding to the entity being challenged has jurisdiction to enforce the law, by seeking voluntary compliance, terminating federal funding through an administrative process, or referral to the DOJ for judicial enforcement. Because the ADA extended the disability discrimination prohibitions to non-federally funded state and local government programs, eight designated federal agencies were given

---

[147] Id. §§ 12134(c), 12186(c).

[148] Id. §§ 12117(b), 12134(b).

[149] 42 U.S.C. §§ 12111, 12111(5) (2000).

[150] Id. § 12117(a).

[151] Id. § 12117(a), § 2000e-5(e). That time period is extended to up to 300 days if the state has a law prohibiting the same conduct. See Bonilla v. Muebles J.J. Alvarez, Inc., 194 F.3d 275, 278 (1st Cir. 1999); see also Ebbert v. Daimler Chrysler Corp., 319 F.3d 103 (3d Cir. 2003) (holding that oral notice can be sufficient to start statutory period if it is as comprehensive as written notice).

[152] 28 C.F.R. pt. 35 app. B § 35.140 (2003) ("Employment Discrimination Prohibited").

[153] 42 U.S.C. § 12134(a).

jurisdiction over all programs of the *type* of program they fund (i.e., as opposed to programs they actually fund).[154]

The DOJ was given jurisdiction over any entities that did not fall within the jurisdiction of a designated agency.[155] When the federal agency actually funds the challenged entity, the agency must use the Section 504 process (including the possibility of funding termination), rather than the ADA process (which does not include the option of funding termination).[156]

Complaints under Title II must be filed with a federal agency within 180 days of the alleged violation.[157] However, unlike Title I, filing with a federal agency is not a prerequisite to a private suit.

The appropriate designated federal agency must accept all complete Title II complaints for investigation.[158] The designated agency must investigate, attempt informal resolution, and if resolution is not reached, issue a formal Letter of Findings to the public entity. The Letter

---

[154] Those agencies were:

Department of Agriculture: activities relating to farming and raising livestock;

Department of Education: activities relating to elementary, secondary, vocational, and higher education (other than health-related schools), and libraries;

Department of Health and Human Services: activities relating to provision of health care and social services, including health-related schools, social services providers, and preschool and daycare programs;

Department of Housing and Urban Development: activities relating to public housing;

Department of Interior: activities relating to lands and natural resources, including water and waste management, energy, historic and cultural preservation, and museums;

Department of Justice: activities relating to law enforcement, public safety, and administration of justice, commerce and industry, government support services (audit, personnel, etc.), and government functions not assigned to another designated agency;

Department of Labor: activities relating to labor and the work force;

Department of Transportation: activities relating to transportation.

28 C.F.R. pt. 35 app. A (1991) ("Section-by-Section Analysis, Subpart F").

[155] 28 C.F.R. pt. 35 app. B § 35.190(b)(6) (2003).

[156] 28 C.F.R. pt. 35 app. A ("Section-by-Section Analysis, Subpart F") (1991).

[157] 28 C.F.R. pt. 35 app. B § 35.170(b). The deadline is deemed to have been met if the complaint is filed with any federal agency within 180 days, even if that agency does not, in fact, have jurisdiction. Id.

[158] Id. § 35.171(c).

of Findings must include findings of fact and conclusions of law, remedies, and notice of the possibility of agency enforcement action and private enforcement.[159]

After issuance of a Letter of Findings, the designated agency must notify the DOJ of the finding and attempt to negotiate a written, enforceable voluntary compliance agreement with the entity.[160] If a voluntary compliance agreement is not reached, the designated agency must refer the matter to the DOJ for appropriate enforcement action.[161] The private complainant may pursue independent judicial enforcement at any time during this process, regardless of the federal agency's findings.[162]

Title III of the ADA became effective January 26, 1992.[163] However, businesses employing 25 or fewer employees and having gross receipts less than $1 million were given an additional six months, and businesses employing 10 or fewer employees and having receipts less than $500,000 were given an additional year.[164]

Title III adopted the remedies and procedures of Title II of the Civil Rights Act of 1964.[165] Title III gives the DOJ authority to investigate complaints and to conduct periodic compliance reviews in the absence of complaints.[166] If the DOJ believes an entity has engaged in a pattern or practice of discrimination or believes a violation raises an issue of public importance, the DOJ may file a civil action in federal court.[167]

§ 2.3 The Theory And Economics Of The Accommodation Principle

At the heart of the promise of the ADA and the controversy surrounding it is the requirement that employers make "reasonable accommodations" for qualified applicants or employees.[168] The explicit

---

[159] Id. § 35.172(a).

[160] Id. § 35.173.

[161] Id. § 35.174.

[162] Id. § 35.172(b).

[163] 42 U.S.C. § 12181(a) (2000).

[164] Id. § 12181(b).

[165] Id. § 12188(a)(1).

[166] Id. § 12188(b)(1)(A)(i).

[167] Id. § 12188(b)(1)(B).

[168] The requirement appears in a definitional section of Title I, § 102, 42 U.S.C. § 12112, which forbids a covered entity from discriminating against a qualified individual with a disability because of the disability. The word "discriminate" is defined to include "not making reasonable accommodations to the known physical or mental limitations of an otherwise qualified individual with a disability who is an applicant or employee," in the absence of "undue hardship on the operation of the

command that employers accept the burden of paying for accommodations – up to the undue hardship ceiling – arguably sets the ADA apart from other civil rights legislation and has created significant theoretical and practical disputes.

Theoretically, commentators have asked whether it is logical to impose on private entities the cost of achieving a societal goal and whether the method chosen is likely to achieve that goal. Practically, over a decade after Title I's effective date, investigators have reached various conclusions on whether it has been effective, or indeed whether it has impeded the employment of people with disabilities.

In theory it should be possible to measure the effects of the ADA on the employment of people with disabilities. One obvious test of the ADA should be whether it fulfills its goals: post-ADA are more people with disabilities employed in productive jobs than pre-ADA; post-ADA are workers with disabilities paid at comparable levels as workers without disabilities? Economists have been trying to study these questions, but there remain unresolved questions as to the proper analytic approach and as to interpretation of the results.

The Rehabilitation Act of 1973 imposed reasonable accommodation duties on the government and government contractors; the ADA extends those duties to private employers. The theory justifying the former does not necessarily work for the latter. Although the government may have aims beyond strictly maximizing its output, such as providing employment to those who might not otherwise find it, a private entity's overriding goal is to maximize its profits. To accomplish that, it presumably aims to operate in the most efficient manner.

This leads to two sets of questions regarding the impact of the accommodation mandate on the statutory goals of greater employment in integration. The first set asks whether, as a theoretical matter, requiring private entities to assume the burdens of integrating people with disabilities into the workforce likely is an effective way of achieving the policy goal.

The second question is whether in fact the ADA has achieved its goal of greater employment for people with disabilities. Despite a good deal of work, there appear to be no general answers to either of those questions.

Historically, anti-employment discrimination law in the United States has aimed at insuring that a person who fits a particular job is able to obtain that job, despite irrelevant personal features. A person's skin

---

business," or denying employment opportunities to such a job applicant or employee "if such denial is based on the need for such covered entity to make reasonable accommodations to the physical or mental impairments of the employee or applicant." Id. § 12112(d)(5).

color, gender, sexual orientation or religion generally have little bearing on the match between the person's skills and a particular job. Thus, the Civil Rights Act of 1964[169] and its later amendments forbid discrimination in employment. But they do not, except in the minimal sense of *Trans World Airlines v. Hardison*,[170] require recognition and amelioration based on protected characteristics.

In effect, such prohibitions insure that those irrelevant characteristics will not limit a person's employment opportunities.[171] To the extent these antidiscrimination laws focus employers' attentions on the actual fit between an employee and a job, they can be explained from an efficiency perspective.

Thus, they require employers properly to evaluate actual and potential employees without regard to irrelevant characteristics. In theory, this should lead to a workforce better able to perform the employers' tasks.[172] The antidiscrimination provisions in effect filters out irrelevant signals in the employment process and increases the employers' efficiency.

Least controversially, ADA Title I forbids discrimination against those "regarded as" having a disability. In that respect, it performs the same filtering function that traditional antidiscrimination law performs by removing misleading signals from the employers' information mix.

Title I also performs that function for people who actually have disabilities but who require no accommodations. Much research has shown that many people with disabilities require no, and often *de minimis* cost for, accommodations.[173] To this extent as well, the ADA should increase efficiency.

---

[169] Pub L. No. 88-352, 78 Stat. 241, 253-66 (codified as amended principally at 42 U.S.C. §§ 2000e-2000e-17 (2000)).

[170] Trans World Airlines v. Hardison, 432 U.S. 63 (1977).

[171] One commentator explains this concept by distinguishing among "contingent" equality (equality that depends upon the attitudes of third parties about a worker and not on her work), "intrinsic" equality (equality based upon the intrinsic ability of a person to perform a job) and "constructed" equality (equality created by legal dictates). John J. Donohue, III, Employment Discrimination Law in Perspective: Three Concepts of Equality, 92 Mich. L. Rev. 2583, 2585-86 (1994).

[172] See Pamela S. Karlen & George Rutherglen, Disabilities, Discrimination, and Reasonable Accommodation, 46 Duke L.J. 1, 23-24 (1996).

[173] In a study of accommodations for the U.S. Department of Labor, of workers with disabilities, only 22% received some form of accommodations of which half cost nothing and more than 2/3 cost less than $100, U.S. Dep't of Labor, A study of Accommodations Provided to Handicapped

The issue is more complex when accommodations have a non-zero, above *de minimis*, cost. Arguably, even in this situation, a number of factors could render the statutory requirement efficient.

In the first place, the cost of the accommodation could be less than the increased efficiency realized by hiring a specific employee. In addition, studies support the proposition that employees with disabilities tend to be more stable workers, have lower turnover, less absenteeism and lower accident risks.[174] This is not an unreasonable assumption in view of the fact that, once they have a job, people with disabilities may be less willing to lose that job to take another.

Certain accommodations also improve the productivity of other employees without disabilities. Ramps assist pregnant employees and accommodations involving technology often improve productivity for all workers as we discuss in treatise Part 10 infra. Moreover, there may be potential or actual employees with special skills that justify substantial accommodation expenses because others with similar skills are either hard to locate or rare in the labor force.[175]

Putting aside workers with unique skills and "spillover effects," any efficiency argument for hiring a group of people with disabilities assumes that there is not a parallel group of prospective employees with identical skills, who do not need to be accommodated. In general, that seems counterfactual.

Thus, as a purely theoretical matter, it would appear that one cannot use efficiency arguments to justify accommodation requirements.[176] That said, the issue is not purely one of theory: even in view of the minimal or zero costs of most accommodations, arguments based only on a theoretical pool of employees who require an employer to incur no additional costs arguably cannot answer the policy question.

Employees by Federal Contractors: Final Report (1982) (prepared by Berkeley Planning Associates (contract no. J-E 1-0009)); see Accommodating the Spectrum, supra note 65, at 106-07 & nn.24-29 (1983); see also Frederick C. Collignon, The Role of Reasonable Accommodation Employing Disabled Persons in Private Industry in Disability and the Labor Market 196, 215-16 (Monroe Berkowitz & M. Anne Hill, eds. 1986). However, other studies suggest this is overstated. See generally Thomas N. Chirikos, Will the Costs of Accommodating Workers with Disabilities Remain Low?, 17 Behav. Sci. & L. 93 (1999); Thomas N. Chirikos, The Economics of Employment, 69 Milbank Q. 150 (1991).

[174] Collignon, supra note 173, at 208 n.9.

[175] Of course, this expense is no different than the huge costs of "accommodating" film stars or corporate chief executives – it is part of the pay.

[176] See Karlen & Rutherglen, supra note 172, at 24-25.

Adopting a program of constructed equality assumes that an end other than efficiency has become the dominant policy goal.[177] Arguably, the ADA mandates such a program, at least in part, because people who require accommodations are not always economically equal to others from an employer's perspective.

Thus, one implicit assumption of requiring private enterprises to provide accommodation is that the costs of providing accommodations will be offset by the smaller government benefits paid to people with disabilities who will be employed and increased taxes from those workers (i.e., there will be a net gain).[178] A variant on this assumption is that it is more efficient to have individual employers "run" this social welfare program, so that even if there are net costs, they are smaller than if the government ran the program.

Yet another possible assumption is that a political decision has been made that costs and economic efficiency are dispensable (presumably within limits), if more people with disabilities are employed.

This accommodation requirement – an "accommodation mandate" in one commentator's terminology[179] – departs from prior conceptualizations of discrimination.[180] Under pre-ADA discrimination theory, in the absence of discrimination, individuals who are equally productive should receive the same compensation (i.e., wages, benefits, and other rewards). This definition of discrimination does not consider employer investments in making some, but not all, workers more productive than they otherwise would be. Under the ADA, an employer

---

[177] See Donohue, supra note 171, at 2609-10.

[178] Commentators have asked whether private entities should pay for accommodations in the first place or whether that should be left to the public sector. See e.g., Scott A. Moss & Daniel A. Malin, Public Funding for Disability Accommodations: A Rational Solution to Rational Discrimination in the Disabilities of the ADA, 33 Harv. C.R.-C.L. L. Rev. 197, 233 (1998); see also Sherwin Rosen, Disability Accommodation and the Labor Market, in Disability and Work: Incentives, Rights and Opportunities 27 (Carolyn L. Weaver ed., 1991) (arguing for governmental spending on education and work training, instead of accommodations).

[179] Christine Jolls, Accommodation Mandates, 53 Stan. L. Rev. 223 (2000).

[180] Robert L. Burgdorf, Jr., 'Substantially Limited' Protection from Disability Discrimination: The Special Treatment Model and Misconstructions of the Definition of Disability, 42 Vill. L. Rev., 409-509 (1997); S.A. Krenek, Beyond Reasonable Accommodation, 72 Texas L. Rev. 1969, 1996-98 (1994).

must make affirmative changes in response to a qualified individual's needs so they may perform essential job functions.[181]

In *U.S. Airways, Inc. v. Barnett*,[182] the Supreme Court summarized:

> [The ADA] seeks to diminish or to eliminate the stereotypical thought processes, the thoughtless actions, and the hostile reactions that far too often bar those with disabilities from participating fully in the Nation's life, including the workplace. These objectives demand unprejudiced thought and reasonable responsive reaction on the part of employers and fellow workers alike. They will *sometimes require affirmative conduct to promote entry of disabled people into the workforce. They do not, however, demand action beyond the realm of reasonable.*[183]

Moreover:

> The simple fact that an accommodation would provide a "preference" – in the sense that it would permit a worker with a disability to violate a rule that others must obey – cannot, *in and of itself*, automatically show that the accommodation is not "reasonable."[184]

But economics cannot be ignored completely.[185] Even if all

---

[181] See Jolls, supra note 179, at 231-32; Mark Kelman, Market Discrimination and Groups, 53 Stan. L. Rev. 833, 834-55 (2001).

[182] U.S. Airways, Inc. v. Barnett, 535 U.S. 391 (2002).

[183] Id. at 401 (citations omitted, emphasis added) (deciding that a job reassignment in violation of a company's seniority system would not be a "reasonable" accommodation.

[184] Id. at 398.

[185] There are also positive effects of accommodations. First, there are certain tax incentives. See infra treatise Part 9 for discussion. See also EEOC Facts About Disability-Related Tax Provisions: Disabled Access Tax Credit, at http://www.eeoc.gov/facts/fs-disab.html (last modified Jan. 15, 1997) (discussing 26 U.S.C. § 44, and Tax Deduction to Remove Architectural and Transportation Barriers to People with Disabilities and Elderly Individuals, 26 U.S.C. § 190, as applicable to the provision of accommodations by small businesses). Second, there is evidence that some accommodations boost profits. President's Committee on Employment of People with Disabilities, Job Accommodation Network (JAN) Reports (Oct.-Dec. 1994) (for every dollar invested in an effective accommodation, companies sampled realized an average of $50 in benefits). Finally, one should not overlook that corporate culture, in parallel with economic considerations, may motivate using accommodations. See Lisa Schur, Douglas Kruse & Peter Blanck,

employers follow the ADA to the letter, the argument may be made that because its requirements may raise employers' costs, they may lead to less overall employment and thus less employment of people with disabilities. Beyond that, any business that fails to provide accommodations to its employees has a price advantage over its competitors who do incur those costs.

Laws like the ADA are largely self-enforcing. Given the difficulties in enforcing any law as broadly applicable and as nuanced as the ADA, employers might not follow it to the letter and face no civil actions or governmental sanctions. Any real-world understanding of the ADA's impact must consider the effects of this differential compliance.[186]

Corporate Culture and the Employment of Persons with Disabilities, Behav. Sci. & L. (forthcoming 2004).

[186] There is an alternative way to view accommodations. If the "average" worker is viewed as unimpaired, the work environment can be expected to build on assumptions that workers have no limitations on their abilities to see, hear, walk, climb stairs, lift, grasp door knobs, write, speak, and so on. This environment becomes the baseline – *the* appropriate, efficient manner to order work given the perceived characteristics of the average individual in the labor market. Accommodations, thus, represent deviations from the presumptively efficient status quo necessitated by the appearance in the applicant pool, or in the workforce, of individuals with disabilities – individuals whose characteristics differ from those of the "model (able-bodied) worker" around whom the work environment was built. But this is one viewpoint. See Burgdorf, supra note 180, at 530; cf. Harlan Hahn, Equality and the Environment: The Interpretation of "Reasonable Accommodations" in the Americans with Disabilities Act, 17 J. Rehab. Admin. 101, 103 (1993).

Part 2

Definitional Issues
Analysis

Chapter 3 DISABILITY

§ 3.1 Overview

Much of the litigation under the ADA has focused on who is covered by the Act. The ADA protects primarily individuals with disabilities. A person is an individual with a disability if he or she falls into one of the following categories:

- An individual with an actual disability;[1]

- An individual with a record of a disability;[2] and

- An individual who is regarded or treated as if he or she has a disability ("regarded as").[3]

---

[1]   42 U.S.C. § 12102(2)(A) (2000).
[2]   Id. § 12102(2)(B).
[3]   Id. § 121022(C).

The definition of protected individuals appears only in the definitional section of the Act.[4] Therefore, the protected class does not vary among the five titles of the ADA. In addition to having a disability, to be protected under Titles I and II of the ADA, an individual must be a qualified individual with a disability.[5]

In addition to protecting individuals with disabilities, the ADA protects individuals from retaliation if they assert rights on behalf of individuals with disabilities or encourage or assist people with disabilities to assert their rights.[6] Finally, each title of the ADA specifies protection of individuals who associate with individuals with disabilities.[7]

The ADA definition of disability was taken directly from the definitions in Sections 501, 503, and 504 of the Rehabilitation Act of 1973 discussed supra.[8] Throughout nearly twenty years since the passage of the Rehabilitation Act, the regulatory agencies, courts, and even defendants applying the Act had taken a broad approach to the scope of coverage.[9] In fact, courts rarely even reviewed the definitional language.[10]

"Just as courts hearing employment discrimination cases under title VII never analyzed whether the plaintiff in a case was "really a woman," or "really black," courts hearing Section 504 cases rarely tarried long on the question of whether a plaintiff was "really a handicapped individual."[11] Rather, as with Title VII cases, courts hearing Section 504 cases tended to focus on the essential causation requirement: that is, had the plaintiff proven the alleged discriminatory action was taken solely *because of* his or her handicap."[12]

Advocates lobbying for the ADA believed any individual with a serious illness or with a non-trivial impairment would be covered.[13] However, courts applying the ADA have taken the opposite approach, focusing on the limits of the protected class and avoiding the causation issue.[14] As different courts (including, on more than one occasion, the Supreme Court) grapple with what it means to have a disability within

---

[4]   Id. § 12112(2).

[5]   Id. § 12111(8).

[6]   Id. § 12203.

[7]   Id. § 12112(b)(4); 28 C.F.R. §§ 35.130(g), 36.205 (2003).

[8]   29 U.S.C. § 705(9) (2000); Chai Feldblum, Definition of Disability Under the Federal Anti-Discrimination Law: What Happened? Why? And What Can We Do About It?, 21 Berkeley J. Emp. & Lab. L. 91, 91-92, 128-29 (2000).

[9]   Feldblum, supra note 8, at 91-92.

[10]   Id. at 92.

[11]   Id. at 106.

[12]   Id. (emphasis added).

[13]   Id. at 156-57.

[14]   Id.

the meaning of the statute, the interpretation of the definition of disability continues to evolve.

§ 3.2 Actual Disability

According to the text of the ADA, "disability" means, with respect to an individual, "(A) a physical or mental impairment that substantially limits one or more of the major life activities of such individual...."[15] There are three requirements within this definition:

- A physical or mental impairment;

- A substantial limitation; and

- A major life activity.

Each will be discussed in turn.

A. *Physical Or Mental Impairment*

A physical or mental impairment means an illness or injury, including anatomical loss, physiological or psychological disorders, mental illness, and cosmetic disfigurement.[16] Mere physical characteristics or personality traits, such as left-handedness, height, or short temper that are within the normal range do not constitute impairments.[17]

Conditions, such as pregnancy or advanced age, which are not the result of a physiological disorder, are not covered. However, medical conditions associated with pregnancy or age may be impairments.[18] Predisposition to illness is not an impairment.[19] However, some have argued that genetic conditions are covered, even before they manifest themselves with symptoms.[20]

Homosexuality, bisexuality, sexual behavior disorders, compulsive gambling, kleptomania, and pyromania are specifically excluded from coverage.[21] Drug and alcohol addiction are covered.[22] However,

---

[15] 42 U.S.C. § 12102(2) (2000).
[16] 28 C.F.R. § 36.104 (2003); 29 C.F.R. § 1630.2(h) (2003). The regulations implementing the ADA provide a list of impairments that is not intended to be exclusive.
[17] Equal Empl. Opportunity Comm'n, Title I Technical Assistance Manual § 2.2(a)(i), http://janweb.icdi.wvu.edu/links/ADAtam1.html (Oct. 29, 2002) [hereinafter TAM I].
[18] 29 C.F.R. pt. 1630, app., § 1630.2(h).
[19] Id.
[20] Paul Steven Miller, Is There a Pink Slip in My Genes? Genetic Discrimination in the Workplace, 3 J. Health Care L. & Pol'y 225, 237-38 (2000). See discussion infra at Chapter 9.
[21] 42 U.S.C. § 12211(1) (2000).

individuals who are currently using illegal drugs are specifically excluded from protection.[23] Casual drug use is not protected.[24] The question of whether an impairment exists is generally a question of law for the court to decide.[25]

The Supreme Court first addressed the definition of disability for purposes of disability discrimination in 1987 in *School Board of Nassau County v. Arline*.[26] This case involved an employment discrimination claim under Section 504 of the Rehabilitation Act.[27] Ms. Arline was an elementary school teacher with tuberculosis who was terminated by the school because of her illness.[28] The Court considered whether she was a person with a disability protected under the Rehabilitation Act.

In a 7-2 decision, the Court found that Ms. Arline was protected by the Act. The majority found that she had a physical impairment that substantially limited her major life activities by requiring hospitalization.[29] The Court found that the contagiousness of the disease did not preclude Ms. Arline from coverage.[30]

The school board argued that it had not fired her because of her diminished physical capabilities, but because of the contagious nature of tuberculosis. Thus, the school claimed, it had acted on the basis of the disease's effects on others, not its effects on Ms. Arline, and, therefore, had not discriminated on the basis of her disability. The Court rejected this distinction, relying on legislative history indicating that individuals were

---

[22] Id. § 12210; U.S. Dep't of Justice Title III Technical Assistance Manual § 2.3000, http://www.usdoj.gov/crt/ada/taman3.html (Nov. 1993) [hereinafter TAM III]; U.S. Dep't of Justice Title II Technical Assistance Manual § 2.3000 http://www.ada-infonet.org/ada-infonet/documents/titleII/ADA%20Title%20II%20Technical%20Assistance%20Manual.htm (last visited Oct. 9, 2003) [hereinafter TAM II].

[23] TAM II, supra note 22, at § 2.3000. "Current" drug use is use "that occurred recently enough to justify a reasonable belief that a person's drug use is current or that continuing use is a real and ongoing problem." Id. Raytheon v. Hernandez, 123 S.Ct. 1255 (Mem. 2003); Hernandez v. Hughes Missile Systems Co., 292 F.3d 1038, 1043 (9th Cir. 2002), cert. granted, Raytheon Co. v. Hernandez, 123 S.Ct. 1255 (Mem. 2003).

[24] TAM I, supra note 17, at § 2.2(b).

[25] Bristol v. Bd. of County Comm'rs of County of Clear Creek, 281 F.3d 1148, 1158-59 (10th Cir. 2002).

[26] School Bd. of Nassau County v. Arline, 480 U.S. 273, 281-85 (1987).

[27] 29 U.S.C. § 794 (2000).

[28] Arline, 480 U.S. at 276.

[29] Id. at 281.

[30] Id. at 282.

to be protected from discrimination based on their impairments' effect on themselves and on others.[31]

The Court remanded to the district court the question of whether Ms. Arline was qualified for her teaching job, including an assessment of the nature of the risk and the possibility of reasonable accommodation.[32] The Court thus made clear that the disability inquiry and the qualification/direct threat inquiry are two separate questions.

Justices Rehnquist and Scalia dissented, arguing that action taken on the basis of contagiousness is not disability discrimination.[33] Taken to its limit, this approach would mean that the only forms of prohibited discrimination would be those that rejected people with disabilities based on their own physical or mental limitations. This could leave employers free to discriminate against people with disabilities based on the morale of other employees or customers.

The Court next addressed the definition of disability and the issue of contagiousness under the ADA in the 1998 case of *Bragdon v. Abbott*.[34] In that case, a woman with asymptomatic HIV sought dental treatment for a cavity. The dentist refused to treat her in his office, offering, instead, to treat her in a hospital.[35]

The majority continued the *Arline* approach of not exempting contagious diseases from coverage and keeping the issues of qualification/direct threat separate from the issue of disability.[36] The Court found that HIV is an impairment from the moment of infection, even before it becomes symptomatic, because it causes immediate changes in the infected person's blood.[37] The Court relied on "the immediacy with which the virus begins to damage the infected person's white blood cells and the severity of the disease"[38] to find asymptomatic HIV to be a covered impairment.

The Court thus established a broad scope for the term "impairment" in the ADA. An impairment will be found whenever physiological or psychological changes result from an illness or injury. As a result, the question of whether a plaintiff has an impairment is rarely an issue in ADA case law.

---

[31]   Id. at 282-85 (including the impairment's effects on the attitudes of others). Notably, the Court's argument blends the "actual disability" and "regarded as" categories of coverage without acknowledging the distinction between the two. Feldblum, supra note 8 at 116-19.

[32]   Arline, 480 U.S. at 287-88.

[33]   Id. at 291-92.

[34]   Bragdon v. Abbott, 524 U.S. 624 (1998).

[35]   Id. at 629.

[36]   Id.

[37]   Bragdon, 524 U.S. at 632-37.

[38]   Id. at 638.

B.   *Substantially Limits*

There is no clear standard for when an impairment's limiting effect is substantial enough to merit ADA protection. To be *substantially* limited, an individual must be:

- Unable to perform a major life activity that the average person in the general population can perform; or

- Significantly restricted as to the condition, manner or duration under which an individual can perform a particular major life activity as compared to the condition, manner or duration under which the average person in the general population can perform that same major life activity.[39]

An impairment may interfere with the conditions (e.g., timing), manner (e.g., method or speed), or duration of a person's performance of an activity.[40] The impairment need not completely prevent the individual from engaging in the activity.[41] The individual's ability to perform the activity must be reduced in comparison to most people's, or the average person's, ability.[42] A mere difference in the method of accomplishing an activity does not amount to a substantial limitation.[43]

The factors to be considered in determining whether an impairment is substantially limiting include:

- The nature and severity of the impairment;

- The duration or expected duration of the impairment;

- The permanent or long-term impact or expected impact of the impairment.[44]

Short-term temporary impairments without long-term effects are unlikely to be considered substantial. "[T]emporary, non-chronic impairments of short duration, with little or no long term or permanent impact, are usually not disabilities. Such impairments may include, but

---

[39]   29 C.F.R. § 1630.2(j)(1)(i)-(ii) (2003).
[40]   TAM III, supra note 22, at § 2.4000; TAM II, supra note 22, at § 2.4000; TAM I, supra note 17, at § 2.2(a)(iii).
[41]   Bragdon, 524 U.S. at 641.
[42]   TAM III, supra note 22, at § 2.4000; TAM II, supra note 22, at § 2.4000; TAM I, supra note 17, at § 2.2(a)(iii).
[43]   Albertson's Inc. v. Kirkingburg, 527 U.S. 555, 565 (1999) (a person with monocular vision whose brain has developed coping mechanisms to adjust for depth perception is not disabled).
[44]   29 C.F.R. § 1630.2(j)(2)(i)-(iii).

are not limited to, broken limbs, sprained joints, concussions, appendicitis, and influenza."[45]

However, there is no bright line regarding the duration or expected duration necessary to be substantial.[46] Some courts have considered improvements in a person's condition subsequent to the discriminatory action to determine that an impairment was, in fact, temporary and not substantially limiting.[47] Hospitalization, alone, is not enough to make an impairment a substantial limitation.[48]

1. Individualized inquiry

The determination of whether an impairment substantially limits a person's major life activities is an *individualized* inquiry.[49] This is a factual inquiry that should generally be made by the trier of fact.[50] It examines the impairment's effect on the individual as of the time of the alleged discrimination, rather than relying on the general medical diagnosis or the average, general, or usual effect.[51] If a person has multiple impairments, their combined effect will be assessed in determining substantial limitation.[52] This individualized assessment

---

[45] Id. pt. 1630 app., § 1630.2(j). See also Sanders v. Arneson Products, Inc., 91 F.3d 1351, 1354 (9th Cir. 1996) (finding mental illness lasting less than four months not substantially limiting); Pollard v. High's of Baltimore, Inc., 281 F.3d 462, 469 (4th Cir. 2002) (9-month recovery from surgery is not substantial limitation).

[46] Id. pt. 1630 app., § 1630.2(j).

[47] Swanson v. Univ. of Cincinnati, 268 F.3d 307, 316 (6th Cir. 2001); Anyan v. N.Y. Life Ins. Co., 192 F.Supp.2d 228, 245 (S.D.N.Y. 2002).

[48] See Pollard, 281 F.3d at 467-68; Sorenson v. Univ. of Utah Hosp., 194 F.3d 1084, 1087 (10th Cir. 1999); Colwell v. Suffolk County Police Dep't, 158 F.3d 635, 645 (2d Cir. 1998); Burch v. Coca-Cola Co., 119 F.3d 305, 317 (5th Cir. 1997). Note that this contrasts with the Supreme Court's earlier approach under the Rehabilitation Act in *School Board of Nassau City. v. Arline*, where the Court noted that the plaintiff's hospitalization established a record of impairment. School Bd. of Nassau City. v. Arline, 480 U.S. 273, 281 (1987).

[49] But see Feldblum, supra note 8, at 151-52 (arguing that individualized assessment of substantial limitation was not foreseen or intended by the drafters of the ADA).

[50] Bristol v. Bd. of County Comm'rs of County of Clear Creek, 281 F.3d 1148, 1158-59 (10th Cir. 2002). However, courts frequently rule on the issue as a matter of law, finding that the plaintiff has failed to provide sufficient evidence to present to a jury.

[51] Id.

[52] TAM I, supra note 17, at § 2.2(a)(iii).

necessarily leads to different results for individuals with the same impairment.[53]

The Supreme Court in *Bragdon v. Abbott*[54] took up the issue of when an impairment's limiting effect is substantial. The divided Court found that Ms. Abbott's HIV substantially limited the major life activity of reproduction. The Court concluded that the risk of transmitting the disease to a fetus or sexual partner constitutes a limitation on the ability to reproduce.[55]

Thus, the Bragdon Court indicated that limitations external to the disabled individual may be taken into consideration. The Court also made clear that the impairment need not completely prevent the major life activity. In this case, the 8-25% risk of HIV transmission to a fetus was substantial enough.[56]

The Court considered whether the "substantial" inquiry should take into consideration personal choices as well as objective limitations. Because of the divisions within the majority, the Court did not provide a clear answer. The Court noted that Ms. Abbott had testified that the risk of transmission controlled her decision not to have a child, thus implying that the decision might have turned out differently if she had made the decision for other reasons or if she had chosen to ignore the risk and have a child.[57] However, the majority drew back from giving dispositive weight to the personal choice factor, stating that "[i]n the end, the disability definition does not turn on personal choice."[58]

The dissent relied heavily on the argument that the impairment must substantially limit an activity the plaintiff would otherwise have undertaken.[59] Most courts that have addressed the issue have followed that approach.[60]

---

[53] See Feldblum, supra note 8 at 150.

[54] Bragdon v. Abbott, 524 U.S. 624 (1998). See facts infra at text accompanying note 34.

[55] Bragdon, 524 U.S. at 641. Compare with Gutwaks v. Am. Airlines, 1999 WL 1611328, 4 (N.D. Tex. 1999) (court denies HIV positive man disability coverage under the ADA because although the Court in Bragdon recognized reproduction as a major life activity, Mr. Gutwaks admitted he did not ever desire to father children).

[56] Bragdon, 524 U.S. at 639-41.

[57] Id. at 641.

[58] Id.

[59] Id. at 658-59 (Rehnquist, J., dissenting).

[60] Banks v. Southwestern Bell Communications, Inc., 310 F.3d 398, 401 (5th Cir. 2002) (HIV positive man whose wife had already undergone surgery to prevent conception not disabled); Pimental v. Dartmouth-Hitchcock Clinic, 236 F.Supp.2d 177, 183 (D.N.H. 2002); Gutwaks, 1999

2.   Mitigation

In the ADA's legislative history, the House and Senate committees stated:

> Whether a person has a disability should be assessed without regard to the availability of mitigating measures, such as reasonable accommodations or auxiliary aids ... For example, a person who is hard of hearing is substantially limited in the major life activity of hearing, even though the loss may be corrected through the use of hearing aids. Likewise, persons with impairments such as epilepsy or diabetes, which substantially limit a major life activity are covered under the first prong of the definition of disability, even if the effects of the impairment are controlled by medication.[61]

However, "[i]n a series of cases regarding the ADA's definition of 'disability,' the [United States] Supreme Court has severely restricted the scope of the statute's protection."[62] The cases in which the Supreme Court first considered the substantial limitation requirement are *Sutton v. United Air Lines, Inc.*[63] and *Sutton's* companion cases, *Albertson's Inc. v. Kirkingburg*,[64] and *Murphy v. United Parcel Service, Inc.*[65]

In *Sutton*, twin sisters had vision worse than 20/200 in both eyes, but corrective lenses gave them 20/20 vision. United rejected them for positions as pilots based on a company requirement that pilots must have uncorrected vision of at least 20/100.

In *Albertson*'s, Mr. Kirkingburg was a truck driver who was blind in one eye. When the company discovered that he did not meet a federal vision guideline, it fired him without exploring the possibility of a waiver of the federal guideline.

In *Murphy*, the plaintiff was a mechanic with high blood pressure that was near normal when he took medication. His job required him to

---

WL 1611328 at 4. But see Roop v. Squadrito, 70 F.Supp.2d 868, 876 (N.D. Ind. 1999).

[61]   House Comm. on Educ. and Labor, H.R. Rep. 101-485, Pt. 2, at 50-53 (1990) (discussing breadth of the definition of disability); Senate Comm. on Labor and Hum. Res. S. Rep. 101-116, at 21-24 (1989).

[62]   Sharon Masling, Nat'l Council on Disability, The Americans with Disabilities Act Policy Brief Series: Righting the ADA, No. 7, The Impact of the Supreme Court's ADA Decisions on the Rights of Persons with Disabilities, Feb. 25, 2003, available at www.ncd.gov/newsroom/publications/decisionimpact.html (last visited July 31, 2003).

[63]   Sutton v. United Air Lines, Inc., 527 U.S. 471, 489 (1999).

[64]   Albertson's Inc. v. Kirkingburg, 527 U.S. 555, 564 (1999).

[65]   Murphy v. United Parcel Service, Inc., 527 U.S. 516, 518 (1999).

drive commercial vehicles and he was fired because the employer believed his high blood pressure would not meet a federal requirement.

This trilogy of cases raised the issue of whether mitigating measures should be taken into consideration when assessing whether a person's impairment is substantially limiting. Mitigating measures are measures, such as medication, equipment, or internal coping mechanisms, that reduce the effects of an impairment. In these cases, the Supreme Court has made clear that, when judging whether an individual is substantially limited for purposes of ADA protection, the individual's mitigating measures must be considered.[66]

Thus, the Sutton sisters are not covered by the ADA because their eyeglasses improve their vision to 20/20.[67] Mr. Murphy is not protected because, when medicated, his high blood pressure does not prevent him from functioning normally.[68] Mr. Kirkingburg may not be protected, despite having vision in only one eye, because his brain has developed subconscious adjustments to compensate for reduced depth perception.[69] The Court made clear that the side effects of medications and other mitigating measures should also be taken into account and could weigh in favor of finding a substantial limitation.[70]

The Court relied on three parts of the statute to support its conclusion: (1) the fact that the statute is written in the present indicative verb tense ("limits"), thus "requiring that a person be presently – not potentially or hypothetically – substantially limited;"[71] (2) the requirement of an individualized inquiry focusing on the actual effects on the particular individual, rather than general or speculative effects;[72] and (3) the statute's findings stating that there were approximately 43 million people with disabilities in the United States and the Court's belief that covering everyone who wears glasses would far exceed that number.[73] The Court's conclusion rejected the opposite analysis adopted by the

---

[66] Sutton, 527 U.S. at 487-89. Compare with Dahill v. Police Dep't of Boston, 748 N.E.2d 956, 961-962 (Mass. 2001) (holding that the Massachusetts antidiscrimination statute did not require consideration of any mitigating factors).

[67] Sutton, 527 U.S. at 487-89.

[68] Murphy, 527 U.S. at 519.

[69] Albertson's, 527 U.S. at 565-67.

[70] Id. at 565-66.

[71] Sutton, 527 U.S. at 482.

[72] Id. at 483-84.

[73] Id. at 484-87. See Feldblum, supra note 8, at 154 (indicating that the 43 million figure was not extensively researched or considered during the enactment of the ADA).

Department of Justice and the Equal Employment Opportunity Commission.[74]

In the Court's view, its analysis was compelled by the language of the statute. By adopting a limited concept of what it means to be disabled, the Court's has opened itself up to critique. Disability advocates contend that by narrowing the pool of people that, in the Court's view, Congress reached with the ADA, the Court demonstrates a particular view of disability and discrimination protections. The Court views people with disabilities as fundamentally different from the general population, rather than as part of the spectrum of ability levels within society. The Court also treats disability rights protections, not as a check on unfairness, justified by a history of prejudice, but as a type of affirmative action or charity intended only for a small group of individuals whose disabilities set them apart from the Court's view of the general population.[75]

Regardless of one's view of the propriety of the Court's analysis, it is undeniable that the *Sutton* trilogy will place a large category of potential plaintiffs outside of the ADA's protective sphere. The Court's analysis will prevent individuals with minor impairments from receiving accommodations, such as equipment or policy changes, in the workplace. It will allow a defendant to refuse to hire an individual solely because of his or her impairment, such as diabetes, but escape liability by arguing that the impairment does not arise to the level of a disability because the individual takes medication. It, thus, creates a gap in which individuals are considered (quite possibly unfairly) too impaired to work, but are not impaired enough to be protected from discrimination.

Courts now will be more frequently called upon to analyze whether a plaintiff's impairment significantly restricts him or her from engaging in a major life activity. Because the plaintiff bears the burden of proof on this issue, impairments that respond to medication, such as diabetes,[76] depression,[77] and epilepsy,[78] are difficult to establish as disabilities, often being ruled out on summary judgment.

---

[74] Sutton, 527 U.S. at 481-82.

[75] This approach reflects a belief that the societal assumptions about, and barriers to, people with disabilities are generally appropriate and that society's decision, through the ADA, to allow them to participate in society is a charitable act, rather than a civil right. This approach flows from the medical/charity model of disability discussed supra, treatise Part 1. Disability advocates would argue that society's assumptions about, and barriers to, people with disabilities are generally incorrect and unnecessary and that the disability rights laws are designed to redress unfairness, not to give people with disabilities a handout.

[76] See, e.g., Sepulveda v. Glickman, 167 F.Supp.2d 186, 191 (D. P.R. 2001); Anyan v. N.Y. Life Ins. Co., 192 F.Supp.2d 228, 244 (S.D.N.Y. 2002); but see Lawson v. CSX Transp., Inc., 245 F.3d 916, 929 (7th Cir.

The emphasis on mitigating measures can place plaintiffs in a difficult situation, particularly in employment cases. The plaintiff must prove that he or she is substantially enough impaired to constitute a person with a disability. However, if he or she succeeds in that burden, he or she must still prove that he or she was not so substantially impaired as to be unqualified for the job at issue. This is particularly difficult when the major life activity asserted is that of working.[79]

Even mitigation subsequent to the discriminatory action has been used by some courts as evidence that the impairment at the time of the discrimination was temporary.[80] Others have considered nonexistent mitigation when it was believed the plaintiff stopped mitigation without a good reason.[81] Generally, courts have assessed impairments as they actually existed at the time of the alleged discriminatory action, without speculation about the possibility of treatment.[82]

The mitigation assessment also makes it difficult for people with impairments to obtain reasonable accommodations necessary to implement possible mitigation (e.g., breaks or altered work schedules necessary for medication and other mitigating measure).[83] These people

---

2001) (treated diabetes may still limit ability to metabolize food; consider the discomfort and complexity of the mitigation; consider the effects of noncompliance with mitigation).

[77] Swanson v. Univ. of Cincinnati, 268 F.3d 307, 317 (6th Cir. 2001); Cooper v. Olin Corp., 246 F.3d 1083, 1091 (8th Cir. 2001); Spades v. City of Walnut Ridge, 186 F.3d 897, 900 (8th Cir. 1999); Robb v. Horizon Credit Union, 66 F.Supp.2d 913, 919 (C.D. Ill. 1999).

[78] Arnold v. City of Appleton, Wis., 97 F.Supp.2d 937, 949 (E.D. Wis. 2000).

[79] See discussion infra Section 3.2(B)(3).

[80] Swanson, 268 F.3d at 316 (because post-discrimination medication controlled plaintiff's depression, the impairment was temporary).

[81] Hein v. All American Plywood Co., 232 F.3d 482, 488 (6th Cir. 2000) (plaintiff not disabled because it was his own fault he failed to pick up prescription for mitigating medication); Tangires v. Johns Hopkins Hosp., 79 F.Supp.2d 587, 596 (D. Md. 2000) (plaintiff not disabled because she could control asthma with the proper medication. Plaintiff did not take the medication prescribed to her because she mistakenly believed it would affect another condition).

[82] Nawrot v. CPC Int'l, 277 F.3d 896, 904 (7th Cir. 2002); Finical v. Collections Unlimited, Inc., 65 F.Supp.2d 1032, 1037-1038 (D. Ariz. 1999) (plaintiff who chose not to wear hearing aids has a disability because disability should be assessed based on the person's condition at the time of the alleged discrimination).

[83] Orr v. Wal-Mart Stores, 297 F.3d 720, 724 (8th Cir. 2002) (pharmacy not required to close the pharmacy during the lunch hour to allow pharmacist with controlled diabetes to eat).

are in a Catch-22 situation because, to continue to do their jobs, they must receive accommodations. However, in order to be entitled to accommodations, they must stop their mitigating measures, rendering them unable to do the job. As discussed infra, the reasonable accommodation requirement does not appear to apply to people whose impairments are not substantially limiting, who are merely regarded as having disabilities, or who only have records of previous disabilities.[84] Some states, such as California, have amended their state laws to avoid the problems raised by the consideration of mitigating measures.[85]

Notably, whether or not the defendant's actions were actually based on a person's impairment has no bearing on whether that impairment will be considered a disability. Thus, the fact that an employer acted (even irrationally or unfairly) on the basis of a person's diabetes does not mean the person will have a claim. "[A]n employer is free to decide that certain physical characteristics or medical conditions that do not arise to the level of an impairment, such as one's height, build, or weight or singing voice, are preferable to others, just as it is free to decide that some limiting, but not substantially limiting impairments, make certain individuals less than ideally suited for a job."[86] Thus, a blanket exclusion of applicants based on physical characteristics will not be presumed to be discriminatory unless and until someone with a legally-defined disability is excluded because of it.

However, individuals with impairments that are judged not to substantially limit a major life activity still may proceed under the "regarded as" prong of the ADA definition.[87] Under the "regarded as" analysis discussed infra, the reasons for the defendant's actions can be considered.[88]

3. Substantial limitation on working

Working is specifically listed as a major life activity in the ADA regulations.[89] That major life activity was intended as a catch-all provision to cover those rare situations when a person's impairment affects *only* his or her capacity to work.[90] The Supreme Court has questioned whether it should be considered a major life activity at all.[91]

---

[84] See infra Part 3.

[85] See Cal. Gov. Code §§ 12926(i)(1)(A), 12926(k)(1)(B)(1) (2003) (limits shall be determined without regard to mitigating measures ... unless the mitigating measure itself limits a major life activity). See also infra Part 7 and Part 10.

[86] EEOC v. United Parcel Service, 306 F.3d 794, 804 (9th Cir. 2002).

[87] See discussion infra at Section 3.4.

[88] Id.

[89] 29 C.F.R. § 1630.2(i) (2003); 28 C.F.R. §§ 35.104, 36.104 (2003).

[90] 29 C.F.R. pt. 1630, app., § 1630.2(j).

[91] Toyota Motor Mfg., Ky., Inc. v. Williams, 534 U.S. 184, 198 (2002).

However, courts and parties continue to rely on the major life activity of working, often mistakenly, even in the face of more obviously impaired activities.[92]

Working is treated somewhat differently for purposes of substantial limitation than other major life activities. The ADA regulations provide that a person is substantially limited in working if he or she is "significantly restricted in the ability to perform either a *class* of jobs or a *broad range* of jobs in various classes as compared to the average person having comparable training, skills and abilities."[93]

In determining whether a person's limitation in working is substantial, a court will consider several factors:

- The geographical area to which the individual has reasonable access;

- The job from which the individual has been disqualified because of an impairment, and the number and types of jobs utilizing similar training, knowledge, skills or abilities, within that geographical area, from which the individual is also disqualified because of the impairment (class of jobs); and/or

- The job from which the individual has been disqualified because of an impairment, and the number and types of other jobs not utilizing similar training, knowledge, skills or abilities, within that geographical area, from which the individual is also disqualified because of the impairment (broad range of jobs in various classes).[94]

---

[92]   See, e.g., Mason v. United Air Lines, 274 F.3d 314, 317 (5th Cir. 2001) (relying on working instead of lifting); Mathieu v. Gopher News Co., 273 F.3d 769, 777 (8th Cir. 2001) (relying on working instead of lifting); Conant v. City of Hibbing, 271 F.3d 782, 785 (8th Cir. 2001) (relying on working instead of lifting); Thornton v. McClatchy Newspapers, Inc., 261 F.3d 789, 797 (9th Cir. 2001) (working instead of writing); Whitney v. Greenberg, Rosenblatt, Kull & Bitsoli, PC, 258 F.3d 30, 32 (1st Cir. 2001) (working instead of thinking or learning); Rhoads v. Fed. Deposit Ins. Corp., 257 F.3d 373, 390 (4th Cir. 2001) (working instead of breathing); Johnson v. Paradise Valley Unified Sch. Dist., 251 F.3d 1222, 1227 (9th Cir. 2001) (working instead of walking or standing).

[93]   29 C.F.R. § 1630.2(j)(3)(i) (2003). See also, Feldblum note 8, at 143 ("The resonance of the requirement that an individual be unable to work in a whole range of jobs no less, in order to meet the ADA's definition of disability reflects the staying power of the historical image of a 'disabled person' as a person who is unable to work and unable to function in society.").

[94]   29 C.F.R. § 1630.2(j)(3).

The regulation indicates that the ADA intended the limitation in working analysis not to be restricted to the type of jobs the plaintiff was seeking, but to consider a person substantially limited in working if she is prevented from performing a class of jobs in which she has no interest. Thus, a plaintiff who was turned down for a chef's job, could be considered substantially limited in working because of a lifting restriction that prevents him or her from performing heavy labor jobs. However, the courts have generally restricted themselves to the types of jobs being considered or pursued by the plaintiff.[95]

Determining what constitutes a class of jobs has been difficult for courts. Courts tend to rely on "[c]ommon job groupings within a particular industry."[96] Applying these concepts, courts have found that firefighting does not constitute a class of jobs.[97] However, public safety jobs may constitute a class of jobs.[98] Truck driving may constitute a class of jobs.[99] Courts have also tended to misread the requirement to demand limitation in a "broad class of jobs."[100] In fact, "broad class" is not required, but merely either a class or a "broad range."

This approach makes it difficult for plaintiffs to sustain a claim of substantial limitation in working, because they must then prove that they are qualified for the jobs from which they are being excluded. It is nearly a catch-22 for an individual to prove, first that her disability prevents her from doing a broad range of jobs that she is trained for, and later that her disability would not have prevented her from performing the job she was denied (i.e., that she was qualified).[101]

In addition, if the plaintiff found another job after being denied the disputed position, she will likely be held not to have been substantially limited in working.[102] On the other hand, if she fails to find a job and is,

---

[95] See, e.g., Murphy v. United Parcel Service, Inc., 527 U.S. 516 (1999) (finding plaintiff not substantially limited in working because there were many mechanic jobs he could do despite his high blood pressure, but failing to consider whether Plaintiff was substantially limited in working because he was precluded from jobs as a driver).

[96] DePaoli v. Abbott Labs, 140 F.3d 668, 673 (7th Cir. 1998).

[97] Bridges v. City of Bossier, 92 F.3d 329, 336 (5th Cir. 1996); Crocker v. City of Kenner, 2002 WL 31115255, *9 (E.D. La. 2002).

[98] Edge v. City of St. Paul, 2002 WL 31260012, 6 (D. Minn. 2002).

[99] Black v. Roadway Express, Inc., 297 F.3d 445, 454 n.12 (6th Cir. 2002); Best v. Shell Oil Co., 107 F.3d 544, 548 (7th Cir. 1997).

[100] See Cotter v. Ajilon Servs., Inc., 287 F.3d 593, 599 (6th Cir. 2002); Bristol v. Bd. of County Comm'rs of County of Clear Creek, 281 F.3d 1148, 1161 (10th Cir. 2002).

[101] Feldblum, supra note 8, at 145-46.

[102] Gutridge v. Clure, 153 F.3d 898, 901 (8th Cir. 1998) (computer technician with carpal tunnel syndrome who later secured a position that did not require lifting).

nonetheless, found not substantially limited in working, she may be held to have failed to mitigate damages.

Substantial limitation in working, as with other major life activities, is an individualized inquiry. However, many of the factors involved in working are external to the plaintiff and her condition, such as her skills, education, and work history and the health of the job market in the geographic area. Although the EEOC's guidance indicates that the individual inquiry was not intended to place an onerous evidentiary burden on plaintiffs,[103] courts have made clear that plaintiffs asserting a substantial limitation in working must prove specific facts about those factors.[104]

An individual need not be totally unable to work to be substantially limited. The EEOC Interpretive Guidance provides the following examples:

> [A]n individual who has a back condition that prevents the individual from performing any heavy labor job would be substantially limited in the major life activity of working because the individual's impairment eliminates his or her ability to perform a class of jobs. This would be so even if the individual were able to perform jobs in another class, e.g., the class of semi-skilled jobs. Similarly, suppose an individual has an allergy to a substance found in most high rise office buildings, but seldom found elsewhere, that makes breathing extremely difficult. Since this individual would be substantially limited in the ability to perform the broad range of jobs in various classes that are conducted in high rise office buildings within the geographical area to which he or she has reasonable access, he or she would be substantially limited in working.[105]

In *Toyota Motor Mfg., Kentucky, Inc. v. Williams,*[106] the Supreme Court emphasized the need to assess both work-related and non-work-related activities in determining whether a limitation is substantial.[107] The Supreme Court noted that the treatment of working, for purposes of finding substantial limitation, does not apply to other types of major life

---

[103] 29 C.F.R. pt. 1630, app., § 1630.2(j)(3) ("Rather the terms only require the presentation of evidence of general employment demographics and/or of recognized occupational classifications that indicate the approximate number of jobs (e.g., 'few,' 'many,' 'most') from which an individual would be excluded because of an impairment.").

[104] Gelabert-Ladenheim v. Am. Airlines, Inc., 252 F.3d 54, 58-60 (1st Cir. 2001).

[105] 29 C.F.R. pt. 1630, app., § 1630.2(j)(3).

[106] Toyota Motor Mfg., Ky., Inc. v. Williams, 534 U.S. 184 (2002).

[107] See discussion infra Section 3.2(C).

activities.[108] Thus, other major life activities do not need to be limited across a class or broad range of situations.

Some states have reacted to this limitation on coverage. For example, California has amended its disability rights laws to eliminate the requirement that a person be limited in a class or broad range of jobs. Under California law, it is sufficient if the individual is unable to perform in one job.[109] Through this and other efforts, California has taken the focus off the question of whether an individual has a disability and put it on whether the alleged discriminatory act was motivated by the disability.

4.   Effect of substantial limitation analysis

The current narrow interpretation of substantial limitation often leads to results in which discriminatory conduct is left unchallenged because the court cannot get past the preliminary requirement of coverage under the Act.[110]

As a result, commentators have suggested that "the Court's sweeping decisions have affected whole classes of individuals who Congress unequivocally intended to protect under the ADA ... The Supreme Court's narrow interpretation of the definition of disability validated and accelerated a line of cases in the lower courts restricting ADA coverage."[111]

These lower court rulings can be grouped into five categories:

1. Persons who use mitigating measures are not protected by the ADA.[112]

---

[108] Toyota Motor Mfg., 534 U.S. at 201.

[109] Cal. Gov. Code § 12926 (2003). See infra Part 7 and Part 10.

[110] ABA Commission on Mental and Physical Disability, Study Finds Employers Win Most ADA Title I Judicial and Administrative Complaints, 22 Mental and Physical Disability L. Rep. 403 (1998); Amy Albright, 2001 Employment Decisions Under the ADA – Survey Update, 26 Mental and Physical Disability L. Rep. 393 (2002) (survey results that defendants prevailed in over 95 percent of the ADA employment cases resolved in 2001); Masling, supra note 62.

[111] Masling, supra note 62.

[112] Id. (see generally EEOC v. Sara Lee, 237 F.3d 349 (4th Cir. 2001); Orr v. Wal-Mart Stores, 297 F.3d 720 (8th Cir. 2002); Chenoweth v. Hillsborough Co., 250 F.3d 1328, 1329 (11th Cir. 2001), cert. denied, 534 U.S. 1131 (2002); Taylor v. Nimock's Oil Co., 214 F.3d 957, 961 (8th Cir. 1999); Spades v. City of Walnut Ridge, 186 F.3d 897, 900 (8th Cir. 1999); EEOC v. R.J. Gallagher Co., 181 F.3d 645, 656 (5th Cir. 1999); Muller v. Costello, 187 F.3d 298, 314 (2d Cir. 1999); Saunders v. Baltimore Co., 163 F.Supp.2d 564 (D. Md. 2001); Gutwaks v. Am. Airlines, 1999 WL 1611328 (N.D. Tex. 1999); Todd v. Acad. Corp., 57 F.Supp.2d 448, 453-54 (S.D. Tex. 1999)).

2. Persons whose impairments could be mitigated by medication are not protected by the ADA.[113]

3. It is difficult for individuals to establish that they are substantially limited in the major life activity of working.[114]

4. Individuals must prove not only that they are substantially limited in major life activities, but that they are substantially limited in "activities central to daily life."[115]

5. It is almost impossible for individuals to establish that they fall within the "regarded as" prong of the ADA's definition of disability.[116]

The Supreme Court's definition cases have led to dismissal of many ADA claims on the grounds that litigants are not covered by the

---

[113] Masling, supra note 62; see generally Orr, 297 F.3d at 720; Hein v. All Am. Plywood Co., 232 F.3d 482 (6th Cir. 2000); Rose v. Home Depot, 186 F.Supp.2d 595 (D. Md. 2002); Hewitt v. Alcan Aluminum Corp., 185 F.Supp.2d 183 (N.D.N.Y. 2001); Spradley v. Custom Campers., Inc., 68 F.Supp.2d 1225 (D. Kan. 1999).

[114] Masling, supra note 62; see generally Duncan v. WMATA, 240 F.3d 1110 (D.C. Cir. 2001)(en banc); Broussard v. Univ. of Cal., 192 F.3d 1252 (9th Cir. 1999); Rhoads v. FDIC, 257 F.3d 373 (4th Cir. 2001); Whitson v. Union Boiler Co., 2002 WL 31205208 (6th Cir. 2002); Webb v. Clyde L. Choate Mental Health and Dev. Ctr., 230 F.3d 991 (7th Cir. 2000); Schneiker v. Fortis Ins. Co., 200 F.3d 1055 (7th Cir. 2000); Paul v. Wis. Dep't of Indus., 101 F.3d 456 (7th Cir. 1999).

[115] Masling, supra note 62; see generally Stedman v. Bizmart, 219 F.Supp.2d 1212 (N.D. Ala. 2002); Thornton v. McClatchy, 292 F.3d 1045 (9th Cir. 2002); Fultz v. City of Salem, 2002 WL 31051577 (9th Cir. 2002).

[116] Masling, supra note 62; see generally EEOC v. Rockwell Int'l Corp., 243 F.3d 1012 (7th Cir. 2001); EEOC v. Woodbridge, 263 F.3d 812 (8th Cir. 2001); Sorenson, supra note 48, 194 F.3d at 1084; Giordano v. City of New York, 274 F.3d 740 (2d Cir. 2001); Fultz v. City of Salem, 2002 WL 31051577 (9th Cir. 2002); Cooper v. Olin Corp., 246 F.3d 1083 (8th Cir. 2001); Steele v. Thiokel Corp., 241 F.3d 1248 (10th Cir, 2001); Krocka v. City of Chic., 203 F.3d 504, 507 (7th Cir. 2000); Doyal v. Okla. Heart, Inc., 213 F.3d 492 (10th Cir. 2000); Cash v. Samith, 231 F.3d 1301 (11th Cir. 2000); Kellogg v. Union Pac. R.R. Co., 233 F.3d 1083 (8th Cir. 2000); Syumbo v. Dyncorp Tech. Servs., Inc., 130 F.Supp.2d 771 (W.D. Va. 2001), aff'd Stumbo v. Dyncorp Procurement Systems, Inc., 17 Fed. Appx. 202 (4th Cir. 2001), cert. denied, 122 S.Ct. 1302 (2002); EEOC v. J.B. Hunt Transp., 128 F.Supp.2d 117 (N.D.N.Y. 2001); Arnold v. City of Appleton, 97 F.Supp.2d 937 (E.D. Wis. 2000); Piascyk v. City of New Haven, 64 F.Supp.2d 19 (D. Conn. 1999).

ADA.[117]   Moreover, the Supreme Court's definition cases "have had a chilling effect on individuals and attorneys considering filing ADA claims, which has resulted in fewer discrimination cases even ever being considered by the courts."[118]

Furthermore, the Supreme Court definition cases have had an impact on how the EEOC performs its work."[119]   As explained by Commission representatives,

- "After the issuance of the Sutton-Murphy-Kirkingburg trilogy, the General Counsel began submitting all ADA cases to the Commission for litigation authorization. Previously, the General Counsel exercised his own authority to authorize litigation of ADA cases, or delegated it to the Regional Attorneys... ."

- "We have always viewed 'regarded as being disabled' as a last resort for establishing coverage under the ADA, but we tend to rely on the theory even less, in part because of the proof element that the employer must regard the individual as being substantially limited in a major life activity, and evidence of this perception is difficult to obtain."

- "We have placed greater emphasis on a larger variety of major life activities to establish coverage under the ADA."

- "We are more reluctant to rely on 'working' as a major life activity, in both 'actual' and 'regarded as' cases, but due to increased difficulty in establishing a substantial limitation

---

[117] Masling, supra note 62 ("the Epilepsy Foundation has collected information showing that 'ADA claimants with epilepsy are generally not getting past the threshold question of whether their condition falls within the ADA's definition of disability. Indeed, of the cases of which we are aware, only two plaintiffs have successfully showed that they are disabled ....'")). See also id. ("private attorneys, who used to litigate the majority of ADA employment discrimination cases, are now reluctant to take these cases ... not-for-profit and publicly-funded attorneys find themselves reluctant – or at times unable – to take ADA cases as well ... some attorneys have stopped using the ADA altogether and only bring claims under state law.").

[118] Id. "Data from the Equal Employment Opportunity Commission (EEOC) shows that the number of ADA lawsuits filed by the EEOC decreased significantly after ...Sutton, Murphy and Kirkingburg [in 1999] and decreased again after [Williams in 2002]." Id.

[119] Id.

in other major life activities, we are frequently forced to assert 'working' as a major life activity."[120]

Finally, the Court's definition cases have impacted ADA enforcement by the U.S. Department of Justice.[121] As explained by representatives from the Civil Rights Division of the Department,

- "We are now making different decisions than we would have prior to the Sutton trilogy when deciding whether to open a complaint for investigation. It is more difficult to open an investigation when the complaint is from a person who is hard of hearing and whose hearing is ameliorated by hearing aids or when the complaint is from a person who has diabetes and uses insulin. Similar situations involve those whose physical conditions are controlled through medication (e.g., high blood pressure, epilepsy) or who have lost limbs (and may or may not use prosthetic devices.)"

- "We are unable to pursue some title I cases for people with depression who are treated with medication. For example, someone who uses Prozac and is not hired on that basis is not usually covered under the first prong of the definition or under the 'regarded as' prong."

- "We now have to spend additional time in developing matters into a case because of the need to develop a record of disability. In some cases we spend twice as much time and often have to go on site to develop a record that, despite the use of medication, a major life activity is substantially impaired... ."

- "Because of the *Sutton* cases, we now must engage in intrusive inquiries into the private lives of persons with disabilities who complain to us. We may have to look into debilitating side effects of medications [and make] minute inquiries into how someone carries out the activities of daily living, including intimate behaviors from toileting to sex. It seems incongruous and unjust for a person with a disability to have to reveal such detail about themselves merely to attend a concert or get a job."[122]

---

[120] Id. (see Correspondence from the EEOC to Masling, December 6, 2002).

[121] Masling, supra note 62.

[122] Masling, supra note 62 (see E-mail correspondence from the U.S. Dep't of Justice to Masling, December 5, 2002).

C. *Major Life Activity*

To be covered under the ADA, a person's impairment must substantially limit one or more major life activities. Major life activities include "functions such as caring for oneself, performing manual tasks, walking, seeing, hearing, speaking, breathing, learning and working."[123] This regulatory definition is not intended to be an exhaustive list.[124] Rather, major life activities are "those basic activities that the average person in the general population can perform with little or no difficulty.... Other major life activities include, but are not limited to, sitting, standing, lifting, reaching."[125] Whether an activity constitutes a major life activity is a question of law for the court.[126]

The Supreme Court in *Bragdon v. Abbott* provided that major life activities are not restricted to those that have "a public, economic, or daily character."[127] Thus, purely personal activities, such as reproduction, can be major life activities.[128] However, the activity must be of "comparative importance."[129]

The Court was less clear about whether the activity must be objectively important, i.e., to most people in the general population, or subjectively important, i.e., to the disabled individual personally. However, the Court's focus in *Bragdon* was on the general population and did not rely on evidence that Ms. Abbott personally considered reproduction important.[130] The *Bragdon* majority thus essentially required life activities to be of comparative importance to most people's lives.

Justices Rehnquist, Scalia, and Thomas, in dissent in *Bragdon*, took the position that a major life activity must be of importance both objectively to most people and subjectively to the particular individual. The requirement for subjective importance arises, they argued, from the statutory language requiring a "major life activity of such individual."[131] They believed reproduction failed on both accounts. First, it failed subjectively because there was insufficient evidence that Ms. Abbott

---

[123] 29 C.F.R. § 1630.2(i) (2003); 28 C.F.R. § 35.104 (2003) (defining "disability").

[124] 29 C.F.R. pt. 1630, app., § 1630.2(i).

[125] Id.

[126] Bristol v. Bd. of County Comm'rs of County of Clear Creek, 281 F.3d 1148, 1160 (10th Cir. 2002).

[127] Bragdon v. Abbott, 524 U.S. 624, 638 (1998).

[128] Id.

[129] Id. (quoting the lower court, Abbott v. Bragdon, 107 F.3d 934, 939, 940 (D. Me. 1997)).

[130] Id. at 638-49.

[131] Id. at 658-59 (Rehnquist, J., dissenting).

considered reproduction to be important to her own life.[132]   Second, it failed objectively because the dissenters insisted that a major life activity must be "repetitively performed and essential in the day-to-day existence of a normally functioning individual."[133]

Courts have used the major life activity factor extensively to rule out chronic illnesses as disabilities, such as hepatitis B, cancer, back pain, epilepsy, and asthma, because they do not disrupt a major life activity on a daily basis, but simply disrupt all major life activities for limited periods of time (e.g., during unconsciousness, hospitalization, treatment, or death).[134]

The more recent decision in *Toyota Motor Mfg., Kentucky, Inc. v. Williams*,[135] indicates that the dissenters' position has gained greater sway on the Court.   In *Toyota*, the plaintiff, Ms. Williams, had carpal tunnel syndrome, which prevented her from lifting more than 20 pounds, working with her arms raised, and doing repetitive wrist or elbow movements.   She worked doing paint inspection and assembly inspection at a Toyota factory.   Toyota added body auditing and surface repair to Williams' job.   To do these tasks, Williams had to hold her arms at shoulder height for several hours at a time.   Because her carpal tunnel syndrome bothered her, she requested to be reassigned to do only paint inspection and assembly inspection.   Toyota refused.   Williams was, therefore, placed under a no-work restriction and fired.

In that case, the Court addressed the boundaries of the major life activity of performing manual tasks.   A unanimous Court found that major life activities are those "activities that are of central importance to most people's daily life."[136]   The Court thus appears to have adopted the *Bragdon* dissenters' requirement that activities be "repetitively performed and essential in the day-to-day existence of a normally functioning individual."[137]   The Court went on to decide that performing manual tasks

---

[132] Id.

[133] Id. at 659-60.

[134] See generally Furnish v. SVI Sys., Inc., 270 F.3d 445 (7th Cir. 2001) (liver disease caused by hepatitis B); Whitney v. Greenberg, Rosenblatt, Kull & Bitsoli, PC, 258 F.3d 30 (1st Cir. 2001) (dementia caused by chemotherapy for cancer treatment); Rhoads v. Fed. Deposit Ins. Corp., 257 F.3d 373 (4th Cir. 2001) (asthma); Lebron-Torres v. Whitehall Lab., 251 F.3d 236 (1st Cir. 2001) (back pain); Chenoweth v. Hillsborough Cty., 250 F.3d 1328 (11th Cir. 2001) (epilepsy).

[135] Toyota Motor Mfg., Ky., Inc. v. Williams, 534 U.S. 184 (2002).

[136] Id. at 197.

[137] Bragdon v. Abbott, 524 U.S. 624, 660 (1998) (Rehnquist, J., dissenting).

could be a major life activity only if the tasks included were centrally important to most people's daily lives.[138]

The Court, therefore, confirmed that major life activities are not confined to those in the workplace, even when the case involves a workplace dispute.[139] Ms. Williams' disability must be judged according to "whether the claimant is unable to perform the variety of tasks central to most people's daily lives, not whether the claimant is unable to perform the tasks associated with her specific job."[140] The Court recognized that "the manual tasks unique to any particular job are not necessarily important parts of most people's lives."[141] Instead, "household chores, bathing, and brushing one's teeth are among the types of manual tasks of central importance to people's daily lives."[142]

The *Toyota* Court, therefore, required a weighing of the objectively important manual tasks Ms. Williams could and could not do.[143] No special weight or emphasis is to be placed at this stage on whether the impairment actually affects the activity from which the plaintiff is being excluded.

While the *Toyota* decision is arguably limited to the major activity of performing manual tasks, many courts that have addressed the issue have applied the requirement of "central importance to most people's daily lives" to other types of major life activities as well.[144]

D.   *Evolving Definitions Of Disability – A Research Dilemma*

The preceding discussion makes clear that we still are learning who falls within the ADA definition of disability. This has introduced confusion into the research process of quantifying the effects of the ADA on the labor force participation of people with disabilities.

Quite literally, the authors of these studies are trying to hit a moving target in defining disability. A primary difference between the research streams on the ADA and labor force participation of people with disabilities is how authors define and measure the concept of disability. In fact, how these researchers identify individuals with disabilities is

---

[138] Toyota Motor Mfg., 534 U.S. at 201.
[139] Id.
[140] Id. at 200-01.
[141] Id. at 201.
[142] Id. at 202.
[143] Id.
[144] See, e.g., Mahon v. Crowell, 295 F.3d 585, 590 (6th Cir. 2002) (lifting); Mack v. Great Dane Trailers, 308 F.3d 776, 781 (7th Cir. 2002) (lifting); Thornton v. McClatchy Newspapers, Inc., 292 F.3d 1045, 1045 (9th Cir. 2002) (typing).

fundamental to whether their findings are informative as to the impact of the ADA.

The answer, then, to the question whether the ADA has affected employment rates requires analysis of the *legally defined* group the ADA is meant to protect; the "ADA qualified disabled." No research conducted to date isolates this group. Studies have used measures of disability that deviate from the ADA's definition of disability. For example, many used the "health conditions approach," which looks at all limitations that impair the health of a person[145] and is much more inclusive than the ADA.

Others used the "work disability approach," which counts only people whose disability prevents them from working.[146] This approach is less inclusive than the ADA. By contrast, the ADA defines a person with disabilities as a person with "a physical or mental impairment that substantially limits one or more of the major life activities of such individual."[147] The greater the discrepancy between the group that the ADA protects and the group that policymakers or researchers identify as disabled (and that is compared to the group identified as nondisabled), the less that may be said about the ADA's effects.

In Part 9 of this treatise we discuss and critique the results of these research streams in more detail. We bring the issue up here to highlight the vital importance of the definition of disability, not only in the application of the ADA, but in its evaluation as a policy tool.

§ 3.3 Record Of A Disability

Individuals without a current disability, including those whose impairments are found to have been mitigated, can rely on the second prong of the disability definition – i.e., discrimination on the basis of a record of a disability.[148] According to the ADA's regulations, having a record of a disability means one "has a history of, or has been misclassified as having, a mental or physical impairment that substantially limits one or more major life activities."[149] This provision was intended to protect

---

[145] Nat'l Council on Disability, Toward Independence: An Assessment of Federal Laws and Programs Affecting Persons with Disabilities – With Legislative Recommendations, A Report to the President and to the Congress of the United States (Feb. 1986), www.ncd.gov/newsroom/publications/toward.html (last visited Aug. 20, 2003) [hereinafter Toward Independence].

[146] Id.

[147] 42 U.S.C. § 12102(2) (2000).

[148] Id. § 12102(2)(B).

[149] 29 C.F.R. § 1630.2(k) (2003).

"former cancer patients from discrimination based on their prior medical history" and to protect "individuals misclassified as learning disabled."[150]

To be protected, the record must be of an impairment that would substantially limit one or more of the individual's major life activities.[151] Thus, the former impairment must, itself, have been a legally-recognized disability.

This analysis requires courts to assess the somewhat esoteric question of whether the prior impairment substantially limited a major life activity. In doing so, courts use the same criteria as for an actual disability.[152] The fact that an individual has a record of being classified as disabled for some other purpose (e.g., disabled veteran status, disability retirement, social security, etc.) does not guarantee the individual will be considered to have a record of disability for ADA purposes,[153] because the definitions of disability for other purposes differ from the ADA definition.[154]

The fact that the plaintiff no longer has a disability often will argue against a finding that she had a record of a disability. This is because temporary impairments do not arise to the level of disabilities.[155] Thus, temporary hospital stays and recuperation periods, alone, generally will not be held to constitute a record of a disability.[156] However, lengthy hospital stays and frequent absences for medical treatment may be sufficient to constitute a record.[157]

In addition to demonstrating that she has a record of a disability, the plaintiff must prove that the defendant was aware of that record[158] and that it was the basis of the defendant's allegedly discriminatory action.

---

[150] 29 C.F.R. pt. 1630, app., § 1630.2(k); see also Dupre v. Charter Behavioral Health Sys. of Lafayette, Inc., 242 F.3d 610, 617 (5th Cir. 2001).

[151] TAM I, supra note 17, at § 2.2(b).

[152] Id.

[153] Id.

[154] But see Lawson v. CSX Transp. Inc., 245 F.3d 916, 927 (7th Cir. 2001) (receipt of SSI benefits is evidence of a record of inability to work).

[155] See supra text accompanying note 45. See also Rakity v. Dillon Cos., 302 F.3d 1152, 1160 (10th Cir. 2002).

[156] Sorenson v. Univ. of Utah Hosp., 194 F.3d 1084, 1086-1087 (10th Cir. 1999); Gutridge v. Clure, 153 F.3d 898, 901 (8th Cir. 1998); Colwell v. Suffolk County Police Dep't, 158 F.3d 635, 645-46 (2d Cir. 1998). But see McKenzie v. Dovala, 242 F.3d 967, 972 (10th Cir. 2001).

[157] EEOC v. R.J. Gallagher Co., 181 F.3d 645, 655 (5th Cir. 1999).

[158] Davidson v. Midelfort Clinic, Ltd., 133 F.3d 499, 510 n.8 (7th Cir. 1998).

§ 3.4 Regarded As Having A Disability

One of the main purposes of the ADA was to combat the long-held assumptions, prejudices, and stereotypes about disabilities that have unnecessarily kept people with disabilities out of the workplace and other aspects of society.[159] The final prong of the ADA's definition of disability is the "regarded as" prong. A person may be protected under the ADA if he is treated as having an impairment that substantially limits a major life activity.[160]

According to the ADA's interpretative regulations, the "regarded as" provision applies if an individual:

- Has a physical or mental impairment that does not substantially limit major life activities but is treated by a covered entity as constituting such limitation;

- Has a physical or mental impairment that substantially limits major life activities only as a result of the attitudes of others toward such impairment; or

- Has none of the impairments defined ... [above] but is treated by a covered entity as having a substantially limiting impairment.[161]

A. *Impairment That Does Not Substantially Limit*

An individual satisfies the first part of the "regarded as" definition if he has an impairment, but the impairment does not substantially limit a major life activity, and he is, nonetheless, treated as if that impairment is substantially limiting.[162]

The EEOC's Interpretative Guidance offers the following example:

[S]uppose an employee has controlled high blood pressure that is not substantially limiting. If an employer reassigns the individual to less strenuous work because of unsubstantiated fears that the individual will suffer a heart attack if he or she continues to perform strenuous work, the employer would be regarding the individual as disabled.[163]

The EEOC takes a broad approach to this situation, stating:

[I]f an individual can show that an employer or other covered entity made an employment decision because of a

---

[159] School Bd. of Nassau County v. Arline, 480 U.S. at 284-85; see also Arlene B. Mayerson, Restoring Regard for the "Regarded As" Prong: Giving Effect to Congressional Intent, 42 Vill. L. Rev. 587, 592 (1997).

[160] 42 U.S.C. § 12102(2)(C) (2000).

[161] 29 C.F.R. pt. 1630, app., § 1630.2(l) (2003).

[162] Id.

[163] Id.

perception of disability based on "myth, fear or stereotype," the individual will satisfy the 'regarded as' part of the definition of disability. If the employer cannot articulate a non-discriminatory reason for the employment action, an inference that the employer is acting on the basis of "myth, fear or stereotype" can be drawn.[164]

This approach allows a plaintiff to prove that the defendant acted based on the impairment and that the plaintiff was, in fact, qualified for the job. The theory is that it is reasonable to require that the defendant put forth a non-discriminatory reason for its actions, because the defendant has better access to that information than does the plaintiff.[165]

In practice, courts have applied the "regarded as" prong of the definition more narrowly than the EEOC approach.[166] Instead, in employment cases, for example, courts have required plaintiffs to demonstrate that their employers viewed them as unable to care for themselves (as opposed to the employers viewing their disability as having a detrimental effect on their job performance), or viewed the plaintiffs as being unable to work in a broad class of jobs (as opposed to not being able to perform their jobs).[167] Similarly, in Title III public accommodations cases, courts have required plaintiffs to show they were denied goods or services because the businesses viewed them as unable to perform a major life activity (as opposed to a belief that they could not enjoy or benefit from the denied good or service).[168]

The role of the "regarded as" prong of the definition of disability has become particularly important since the *Sutton* trilogy. As set forth above, these cases reduce the number of plaintiffs who will meet the ADA definition of actual disability. Such an individual's alternative argument

---

[164] Id. The Supreme Court in *Arline* took a similarly broad approach to the "regarded as" analysis. Arline, 480 U.S. at 284.

[165] See H.R. Rep. No. 101-485, pt. 3 at 30-31 (1990):

> In the employment context, if a person is disqualified on the basis of an actual or perceived physical or mental condition, and the employer can articulate no legitimate job-related reason for the rejection, a perceived concern about employing persons with disabilities would be inferred and the plaintiff could qualify for coverage under the "regarded as" test.

[166] See Feldblum, supra note 8, at 159.

[167] Id. at 157-60 (citing Ryan v. Grae & Rybicki, 135 F.3d 867 (2d Cir. 1998); Kocsis v. Multi-Care Mgmt., Inc., 97 F.3d 876, 885 (6th Cir. 1996); Ellison v. Software Spectrum, 85 F.3d 187, 192 (5th Cir. 1996); Chandler v. City of Dallas, 2 F.3d 1385, 1393 (5th Cir. 1993)).

[168] See id. at 157-60; see also Blubaugh v. Am. Contract Bridge League, 2001 WL 699656, 2001-2 Trade Cases P 73,337 (S.D. Ind. June 20, 2001).

is that his employer or potential employer regarded him as having a disability.

The Sutton sisters themselves made this argument. The Court declined to adopt a view of the "regarded as" prong that an employer who rejects an individual solely because of her impairment has treated that person as if she were disabled. Rather, the Court held that United did not regard the Suttons as being substantially limited in working because there was no evidence that United regarded the Suttons as being unable to work more than one job.[169] Similarly, in *Murphy v. United Parcel Service, Inc.*,[170] the Court found that UPS' refusal to allow Mr. Murphy to do his job because of his high blood pressure did not indicate that it regarded him as limited in working, but that it regarded him (incorrectly) as being unable to obtain a DOT health certification.[171]

The primary critique to this approach is that it places a premium on what was going on in an employer's head. This is an inherently difficult thing for a plaintiff to prove. This approach makes it difficult for plaintiffs to succeed, particularly if the court rules against them regarding actual disability on summary judgment. A court rarely will find that an employer thought a person was disabled if that court has already found that no reasonable jury could believe the plaintiff to be actually disabled.

This is especially the case when the major life activity is working. Not only must a plaintiff demonstrate that an employer thought he was disabled, he must also show that the employer thought that his disability would prevent him from performing a class or broad range of jobs. As it is safe to assume employers do not regularly consider the panoply of other jobs their employees could perform, and certainly do not often create direct evidence of such considerations, the plaintiff's task becomes even more difficult.[172]

In *Sutton*, the Court compounded the difficulty of this evidentiary burden by holding that an employer's refusal to hire an impaired

---

[169] Sutton v. United Air Lines, Inc., 527 U.S. 471, 493-94 (1999).

[170] Murphy v. United Parcel Service, Inc., 527 U.S. 516, 523-24 (1999).

[171] In fact, UPS simply *assumed* Mr. Murphy could not obtain a DOT certification, and that assumption was only one of a number of assumptions about high blood pressure's limitations on a variety of activities (e.g., that he could not safely perform strenuous activities). One could only speculate how the Court might have ruled if Mr. Murphy had relied on a life activity other than working.

[172] Cotter v. Ajilon Servs., Inc., 287 F.3d 593, 599 (6th Cir. 2002) ("Even though plaintiff's colitis substantially limited a major life activity, there was insufficient evidence that the plaintiff's impairment significantly restricted his ability to perform at least a wide range of jobs and there was not substantial evidence that the employer terminated the employee because of medical status.").

individual could not be considered as regarding him as substantially limited in working. Rather, a refusal to place an individual in a single job because of his impairment will be treated as evidence only of the employer's belief that the individual could not do that individual job, not a class or range of jobs.[173]

As counterintuitive as it might seem, there are instances where a plaintiff will have such proof. In *Edge v. City of St. Paul*,[174] the court found that the defendant's psychiatric exam indicated that the plaintiff was regarded as limited in the entire category of "public safety jobs" in general, rather than merely in the job of firefighter. Therefore, the plaintiff, who had depression, was able to pursue his claim.

The approach described above – making a plaintiff prove what an employer (or business owner) thought about his or her ability to perform a major life activity – can also be critiqued on the grounds that it divorces treatment from perception. It does not matter how the person was treated. Rather, the separate inquiry of how disabled the employer believed the employee to be is the focus.

This analysis erroneously equates the actual abilities of the plaintiff, which is what the court analyzes under the "actual disability" definition, and the defendant's myths, stereotypes and assumptions, which is the real issue under the "regarded as" definition. In analyzing the "regarded as" issue, the court should focus, not on the reality of the plaintiff's abilities, but on the assumptions among the defendant's employees and among the general society about individuals with disabilities and the particular disability at issue.

Several commentators have suggested that, from a policy perspective, the courts' approach is misguided, and that Congress intended the "regarded as" prong of the disability definition to have more bite.[175] Of course, other commentators disagree, and reject a broad interpretation of this part.[176]

B. *Impairment That Limits Because Of Attitudes Of Others*

The second way to be covered under the "regarded as" part of the disability definition is if a person has an impairment that is not functionally limiting, but is limiting because of attitudinal barriers. The EEOC's Interpretative Guidance gives the following example:

---

[173] Sutton, 527 U.S. at 491.

[174] 2002 WL 31260012, *4-5 (D. Minn. 2002).

[175] See Feldblum, supra note 8, at 159; see also Mayerson, supra note 159.

[176] See Samuel R. Bagenstos, Subordination, Stigma, and "Disability," 86 Va. L. Rev. 397 (2000).

[A]n individual may have a prominent facial scar or disfigurement, or may have a condition that periodically causes an involuntary jerk of the head but does not limit the individual's major life activities. If an employer discriminates against such an individual because of the negative reactions of customers, the employer would be regarding the individual as disabled and acting on the basis of that perceived disability.[177]

This part of the definition of disability has not given rise to much case law. It does, however, present a bit of a disconnect with the predilection of courts, as described above, to focus on actual disability.

This part of the definition makes clear that people can be protected, even if they have no limitation whatsoever. Moreover, it does not require the defendant to have believed the plaintiff had a limitation. Instead, it simply requires the defendant to have believed other people would object to the plaintiff because of his or her impairment.[178]

C.   *No Impairment*

The final piece of the "regarded as" definition protects individuals who have no impairment at all, but whom a covered entity believes has a substantially limiting impairment. The EEOC's Interpretative Guidance offers the following example:

This situation would occur, for example, if an employer discharged an employee in response to a rumor that the employee is infected with Human Immunodeficiency Virus (HIV). Even though the rumor is totally unfounded and the individual has no impairment at all, the individual is considered an individual with a disability because the employer perceived of this individual as being disabled.[179]

This part of the definition highlights the contrast between a broad interpretation and the narrow interpretation applied by many courts. The

---

[177] 29 C.F.R. pt. 1630, app., § 1630.2(l)(2).

[178] An overly strict interpretation may lead some courts to limit this coverage to situations where the defendant believes others will believe the plaintiff has a substantial limitation of a major life activity. For example, in *Deas v. River West*, 152 F.3d 471, 480 (5th Cir. 1998), a woman who disclosed to a prospective employer that she had seizures was later terminated because the employer believed she would not be able to safely and adequately fulfill her duties as an addiction technician. The Court concluded that the plaintiff had produced no evidence that would allow a trier of fact to conclude that she was substantially impaired, and upheld summary judgment. See also Huge v. Gen. Motors Corp., 2003 WL 1795691, *4 (6th Cir. 2003).

[179] 29 C.F.R. pt. 1630, app., § 1630.2(l)(3).

drafters of the ADA expected situations where persons with no impairments whatsoever would be protected from adverse action. One could point out the irony that, under the courts' current interpretation, persons with actual mitigated impairments can be categorically unprotected.

Chapter 4 OTHER PROTECTIONS

§ 4.1 Association

In addition to protecting people with disabilities from discriminatory actions, the ADA protects individuals, with and without disabilities, who are discriminated against because of their known association with an individual with a disability.[1] The protection is not limited to those with a familial relationship with an individual with a disability, but may include business, social, and other relationships as well.[2] The protection means that, if an entity denies service to an individual with a disability and his or her companions, the entity is liable to the disabled individual and, independently, the companions.[3]

Individuals are protected from exclusion, segregation, and denial of jobs or benefits, on the basis of their association with people with disabilities. However, they may not be entitled to reasonable accommodation, reasonable modification of policy, or auxiliary aids on the basis of association.[4] Thus, an employee with a spouse who has a disability would not be entitled to a modified work schedule to care for the spouse.[5]

Some courts confuse the ADA's association and retaliation provisions.[6] Associational discrimination occurs when an individual is discriminated against based on the status or actions of someone else who has a disability. Retaliation or coercion is discrimination based on one's own actions on behalf of an individual with a disability.[7]

To be protected from discrimination on the basis of association, the plaintiff must prove that she was qualified for the job, program, or service that she sought. The plaintiff must also prove that she was associated with a specific person or group with an actual disability or a record of a disability, or who is regarded as having a disability, and that the entity knew of the person's disability.[8] Therefore, the nondisabled plaintiff may

---

[1] 42 U.S.C. §§ 12112(b)(4), 12182(b)(1)(E) (2000); 29 C.F.R. § 1630.8 (2003); 28 C.F.R. §§ 35.130(g), § 36.205 (2003).

[2] 29 C.F.R. § 1630.8.

[3] U.S. Dep't of Justice Title III Technical Assistance Manual § 3.5000, http://www.usdoj.gov/crt/ada/taman3.html (Nov. 1993).

[4] 29 C.F.R. pt. 1630, app., § 1630.8.

[5] Id.

[6] See, e.g., Fogleman v. Mercy Hosp., Inc., 283 F.3d 561, 565 (3d Cir. 2002) (addressing an associational discrimination claim as a retaliation claim).

[7] Oliveras-Sifre v. P.R. Dep't of Health, 214 F.3d 23, 26 (1st Cir. 2000).

[8] Frelich v. Upper Chesapeake Health, Inc., 313 F.3d 205, 215 (4th Cir. 2002) (discrimination based on generalized advocacy for a type of individual is not sufficient); Oliveras-Sifre, 214 F.3d at 26.

have to prove that the associated individual's or group's impairment substantially limits a major life activity.[9]

§ 4.2 Retaliation

A. *General*

The ADA protects individuals with and without disabilities from retaliation or coercion for asserting disability rights.[10] The regulations provide:

> a. It is unlawful to discriminate against any individual because that individual has opposed any act or practice made unlawful by this part or because that individual made a charge, testified, assisted or participated in any manner in an investigation, proceeding, or hearing to enforce any provision contained in this part.

> b. It is unlawful to coerce, intimidate, threaten, harass or interfere with any individual in the exercise or enjoyment of, or because that individual aided or encouraged any other individual in the exercise of, any right granted or protected by this part.[11]

Illustrations of conduct prohibited by this section include, but are not limited to:

- Coercing an individual to deny or limit the benefits, services or advantages to which he or she is entitled under the Act ...;

- Threatening, intimidating, or interfering with an individual with a disability who is seeking to obtain or use the goods, services, facilities, privileges, advantages, or accommodations of a public accommodation;

- Intimidating or threatening any person because that person is assisting or encouraging an individual or group entitled to claim the rights granted or protected by the Act ...; or

---

[9]   See MX Group, Inc. v. City of Covington, 293 F.3d 326, 336-42 (6th Cir. 2002).

[10]   42 U.S.C. § 12203 (2000) ("No person shall discriminate against any individual because such individual has opposed any act or practice made unlawful by this chapter or because such individual made a charge, testified, assisted, or participated in any manner in an investigation, proceeding, or hearing under this chapter."); 29 C.F.R. § 1630.12 (2003); 28 C.F.R. §§ 35.134, 36.206 (2003).

[11]   29 C.F.R. § 1630.12; see also 28 C.F.R. §§ 35.134, 36.206.

- Retaliating against any person because that person has participated in any investigation or action to enforce the Act ....[12]

To succeed in a claim for retaliation in employment, a "plaintiff must show: '(1) protected employee activity; (2) adverse action by the employer either after or contemporaneous with the employee's protected activity; and (3) a causal connection between the employee's protected activity and the employer's adverse action.'"[13]

Protection from retaliation does not depend on the ultimate outcome of the enforcement action being pursued.[14] Therefore, the individual claiming retaliation does not have to have been legally correct that the action she opposed was illegal. She simply must have a good faith reasonable belief that she was asserting covered rights.[15] However, to be protected activity, the individual's actions must have been asserting possible ADA violations. Merely advocating on behalf of individuals with disabilities for non-civil-rights matters will not be protected from retaliation.[16]

The retaliation and coercion provisions are not limited in their application to covered public entities, public accommodations, and employers. Rather, private individuals are prohibited from retaliation or coercion as well.[17]

Courts disagree about whether a plaintiff may assert a retaliation claim for protected conduct she was not, personally, engaged in.[18] In *Fogleman v. Mercy Hosp., Inc.*, the plaintiff alleged that he was fired from his job with the defendant because his father had filed an ADA claim against the defendant.[19]

---

[12] 28 C.F.R. § 36.206(c).

[13] Fogleman v. Mercy Hosp., Inc., 283 F.3d 561, 567-68 (3d Cir. 2002) (quoting Krouse v. American Sterilizer Co., 126 F.3d 494, 500 (3d Cir. 1997)).

[14] 28 C.F.R. § 35.134, app. A; id. § 36.206, app. B.

[15] Fogleman, 283 F.3d at 565; Frelich v. Upper Chesapeake Health, Inc., 313 F.3d 205, 216-17 (4th Cir. 2002); Weissman v. Dawn Joy Fashions, Inc., 214 F.3d 224, 234 (2d Cir. 2000).

[16] Oliveras-Sifre v. P.R. Dep't of Health, 214 F.3d 23, 27 (1st Cir. 2000).

[17] 28 C.F.R. § 35.134, app. A; id. § 36.206, app. B. See also Shotz v. City of Plantation, Fla., 2003 WL 22071566 (11th Cir. 2003).

[18] See Smith v. Riceland Foods, Inc., 151 F.3d 813, 819 (8th Cir. 1998) (plaintiff cannot assert retaliation for someone else's protected conduct); Holt v. JTM Indus., Inc., 89 F.3d 1224, 1227 (5th Cir. 1996) (same). But see EEOC v. Nalbanian Sales, Inc., 36 F.Supp.2d 1206, 1212 (E.D. Cal. 1998) (plaintiff may assert retaliation for someone else's conduct); De Medina v. Reinhardt, 444 F.Supp. 573, 580 (D.D.C. 1978) (same).

[19] Fogleman, 283 F.3d at 565-66.

The text of the EEOC regulation refers to protected activity by "that individual,"[20] thus indicating that a plaintiff may only assert a retaliation claim if he was retaliated against because of his own protected actions (or his own actions to assist protected individuals). However, the Third Circuit noted that this literal reading of the regulation is at odds with the policies animating those provisions. The anti-retaliation provisions recognize that enforcement of the antidiscrimination laws depends in large part on employees to initiate administrative and judicial proceedings. An employer who retaliates against the friends and relatives of employees who initiate antidiscrimination proceedings will deter employees from exercising their protected rights.

As the Seventh Circuit observed, "To retaliate against a man by hurting a member of his family is an ancient method of revenge, and is not unknown in the field of labor relations."[21] Allowing employers to retaliate via friends and family would be in significant tension with the purpose of the anti-retaliation provisions, which are intended to promote the reporting of discriminatory conduct in the workplace.[22]

In spite of these policy arguments, the *Fogelman* Court followed the strict language of the regulations and held that an individual may only pursue a retaliation claim if the retaliatory action was based on her own protected activities.[23] Thus, if an individual is retaliated against because of the protected actions of an associate, she may not have a retaliation claim.[24]

The *Fogleman* court also found that there is a retaliation cause of action for adverse actions taken because the covered entity believed, incorrectly, that the plaintiff was engaging or assisting in protected conduct.[25] The court determined that the employer's subjective reason for the discriminatory action is the important factor, not whether that reason was factually correct.[26]

B.   *Evidence And Burdens Of Proof*

Title I provides a cause of action for an employee who is subjected to an adverse employment action in retaliation for making an employment

---

[20]   29 C.F.R. § 1630.12(a) (2003).

[21]   NLRB v. Advertisers Mfg. Co., 823 F.2d 1086, 1088 (7th Cir. 1987).

[22]   Fogleman, 283 F.3d at 568-69.

[23]   Id. at 569-70.

[24]   However, in somewhat strained reasoning, the Third Circuit also found that the coercion provision of the regulation provides broader coverage, and allows assertion of a claim based on adverse action taken because of someone else's protected activity. Id. at 570-71. The issue before this court would more appropriately have been addressed as an association claim. See supra text accompanying note 7.

[25]   Fogleman, 283 F.3d at 571-72.

[26]   Id.

discrimination claim under the ADA.[27]   An employee can bring a retaliation action even if she fails to establish that she is disabled within the meaning of the ADA.[28]

As with other federal civil rights statutes, courts have grappled with what evidence a plaintiff needs to demonstrate a prohibited retaliatory animus. Some courts have held that temporal proximity between the protected activity and termination is sufficient to establish a causal link.[29]

Other courts have applied a "pretext" theory. For an employee to prevail under the pretext theory, she must show: "(1) protected employee activity [e.g., filing a Title I claim with the EEOC]; (2) adverse action by the employer either after or contemporaneous with the employee's protected activity; and (3) a causal connection between the employee's protected activity and the employer's adverse action."[30]

If the plaintiff can establish these three elements, the burden then shifts to the employer to prove a legitimate, non-retaliatory reason for the adverse employment action.[31] If the employer proffers such a reason, the burden then shifts back to the plaintiff to prove that "retaliatory animus played a role in the employer's decision making process and that it had a determinative effect on the outcome of that process."[32]

In *Stone v. City of Indianapolis Public Utilities Division*,[33] the Seventh Circuit outlined another, slightly different evidentiary procedure for a Title I employment discrimination retaliation claim. The first step is for the plaintiff to present direct evidence that she engaged in protected activity, and as a result suffered an adverse employment action.[34] If the employer does not contradict this evidence, the plaintiff is entitled to summary judgment.

If the employer rebuts plaintiff's evidence, the case proceeds to trial unless the employer adduces uncontradicted evidence that the adverse employment action would have been taken against the plaintiff regardless of retaliatory motive. In that case, the employer is entitled to

---

[27]   See Shellenberger v. Summit Bancorp, 318 F.3d 183, 188 (3d Cir. 2003) (employee had filed Title I employment discrimination claim with EEOC).

[28]   Id.

[29]   Id. at 189.

[30]   Id. This follows the *McDonnell Douglas* framework established in racial discrimination cases. The larger application of *McDonnell Douglas* to ADA Title I cases is discussed infra in treatise Part 3.

[31]   Id.

[32]   Id.

[33]   Stone v. City of Indianapolis Pub. Utilities Div., 281 F.3d 640 (7th Cir. 2002).

[34]   Id. at 644.

summary judgment because it has established that the plaintiff was not harmed by the retaliation.[35]

According to the Seventh Circuit, "mere temporal proximity between the filing of the charge of discrimination and the action alleged to have been taken in retaliation for that filing will rarely be sufficient in and of itself to create a triable issue."[36]

---

[35] Id.
[36] Id.

Chapter 5 QUALIFIED

In addition to being a person with a disability, to be protected under Title I or Title II of the ADA, a person must be qualified.[1] Title III does not contain a qualification requirement. The Title I and II qualification standard requires the plaintiff be able to meet the essential eligibility requirements of the job, program, or service at issue, with or without reasonable accommodations or reasonable modifications.[2] The plaintiff bears the burden of proving she is qualified for the position.[3]

§ 5.1 Prerequisites

The first step in the qualification inquiry is whether the person meets the nondiscriminatory prerequisites for the position or program, such as educational background, experience, skills, or licenses.[4] To be considered nondiscriminatory in the employment context, these prerequisites must be job-related and consistent with business necessity.[5] In the context of government programs, they must be "necessary for the provision of the service, program or activity being offered."[6]

In *Albertson's, Inc. v. Kirkingburg*,[7] the Supreme Court analyzed the qualification standard in the employment context. Mr. Kirkingburg worked as a truck driver for Albertson's. Kirkingburg had amblyopia, meaning he essentially could only see out of one eye. After nearly two years on the job, the employer discovered that Kirkingburg did not meet a U.S. Department of Transportation ("DOT") visual acuity standard requiring 20/40 vision in each eye.

Kirkingburg applied for a waiver from the DOT of the vision requirement, but Albertson's insisted on applying the basic DOT standard and fired him. After he was granted a waiver from DOT, Albertson's refused to re-hire him. The Supreme Court held that Kirkingburg was not

---

[1]   42 U.S.C. § 12112(a) (2000). Qualification is also a requirement for an association claim under Title I, but not under Title II or Title III. See 29 C.F.R. § 1630.8 (2003); 28 C.F.R. § 35.130(g) (2002); id. § 36.205.

[2]   28 C.F.R. § 35.104 (2003); 29 C.F.R. § 1630.2(m) (2003).

[3]   Cleveland v. Pol'y Mgmt. Sys. Corp., 526 U.S. 795, 806 (1999).

[4]   29 C.F.R. pt. 1630, app., § 1630.2(m).

[5]   42 U.S.C. § 12113(a).

[6]   28 C.F.R. § 35.130(8).

[7]   Albertson's, Inc. v. Kirkingburg, 527 U.S. 555 (1999). See also National Council on Disability, The Supreme Court's Kirkingburg Decision and the Impact of Federal Safety Regulations in ADA Cases, Policy Briefing Paper, http://www.ncd.gov/newsroom/publications/safetyregs.html (Oct. 21, 2003) (examining intersection of ADA with safety standards imposed under other federal laws).

qualified for the job because he could not meet the basic DOT visual acuity standard.[8]

The Court found that Albertson's was entitled to rely on the DOT visual acuity standard. Albertson's was not independently required to assess whether the standard was, in fact, essential to the job of driving a truck.[9]

The Court further held that the DOT's issuance of a waiver to Kirkingburg did not change the analysis for the employer's purposes. Albertson's was entitled to rely on the basic DOT standard and not the DOT waiver. The Court found that the waiver program was simply a method for DOT to gather information about whether the visual acuity standards were unnecessarily strict. Because the waiver program did not undermine or alter the acuity standard, the employer was entitled to rely on the underlying standard and not participate in the DOT's "experimental waiver."[10]

§ 5.2 Essential Requirements

Under Title I, qualification means the person can perform the essential functions of the job at issue with or without reasonable accommodations.[11] The essential functions of the job are "the fundamental duties of the employment position.... The term 'essential functions' does not include the marginal functions of the position."[12]

A job function may be considered essential for any of several reasons, including but not limited to the following:

(i)   The function may be essential because the reason the position exists is to perform that function;

(ii)   The function may be essential because of the limited number of employees available among whom the performance of that job function can be distributed; and/or

---

[8]   In dicta, the Court also held that he may not be a person with a disability at all, because the coping mechanisms his body had adopted to compensate for his vision impairment were mitigating measures under Sutton, which mean his vision impairment may not substantially limit a major life activity. Id. at 562-67.

[9]   Kirkingburg's safe operation of a truck for nearly two years would likely have been evidence that the DOT standard, was not, in fact, necessary to the performance of the job. Id. at 567.

[10]   Id. at 577.

[11]   29 C.F.R. pt. 1630, app., § 1630.2(m) (2003).

[12]   Id. § 1630.2(n)(1).

(iii)   The function may be highly specialized so that the incumbent in the position is hired for his or her expertise or ability to perform the particular function.[13]

Any one of these factors or combination of factors may make a function an essential one. The number of employees to whom a job function can be distributed can be important either because there is a small workforce at a given company in comparison to the work load, or because the work load fluctuates and it is essential to have all employees do multiple tasks during peak work periods.[14]

The essential functions analysis is a factual one.[15] Evidence may include:

(i)   The employer's judgment as to which functions are essential;

(ii)   Written job descriptions prepared before advertising or interviewing applicants for the job;

(iii)   The amount of time spent on the job performing the function;

(iv)   The consequences of not requiring the incumbent to perform the function;

(v)   The terms of a collective bargaining agreement;

(vi)   The work experience of past incumbents in the job; and/or,

(vii)   The current work experience of incumbents in similar jobs.[16]

An employer is not required to modify its production standards. Therefore, production standards, such as the ability to type a certain number of words per minute or accomplish a certain number of tasks in a day, will not be subject to judicial scrutiny regarding whether those standards are actually essential. The EEOC Intepretative Guidance provides:

However, if an employer does require [such a production standard] it will have to show that it actually imposes such requirements on its employees in fact, and not simply on paper. [I]f it is alleged that the employer intentionally selected the particular level of production to exclude

---

[13] Id. § 1630.2(n)(2).
[14] 29 C.F.R. pt. 1630, app., § 1630.2(n).
[15] Id.
[16] Id. § 1630.2(n)(3).

individuals with disabilities, the employer may have to offer a legitimate, nondiscriminatory reason for its selection.[17]

As noted, the individual may be qualified because she can perform the essential functions if she is given reasonable accommodations. Thus, the qualification standard often incorporates the central question of whether the employer is required to accommodate the individual.

Some circuit courts have held that a former employee is not qualified if she is on long-term disability leave because she could no longer perform the essential functions of her job. Thus, the employee could not challenge a discriminatory long-term disability insurance policy.[18] However, most circuits have rejected that approach, finding that the employee earned the insurance benefit while she still was qualified for her job.[19]

Under Title II, qualification means the person "meets the essential eligibility requirements for the receipt of services or the participation in programs or activities provided by a public entity," with or without reasonable modification to rules, policies or practices, the removal of architectural barriers, or the provision of auxiliary aids and services.[20] The essential eligibility requirements for a program may fall anywhere on the spectrum, from programs that require a request for services, to programs that require proof of residency within the government providing the service, to programs requiring proof of low income status.

For many services, programs, or activities that public entities offer, the only "essential eligibility requirement" is a desire to participate. In *Concerned Parents To Save Dreher Park Center v. City of West Palm Beach*, the City of West Palm Beach had stopped offering several recreational programs, including programs that previously had been structured for people with disabilities.[21] In considering whether the plaintiffs (various individuals with disabilities and associations of parents and volunteers) were "qualified individuals with disabilities," the court held that the only "essential eligibility requirement" of a city's recreational

---

[17]   Id. pt. 1630, app., § 1630.2(n); 29 C.F.R. § 1630.2(n)(3)

[18]   See Weyer v. Twentieth Century Fox Film Corp., 198 F.3d 1104, 1110 (9th Cir. 2000); EEOC v. CAN Ins. Cos., 96 F.3d 1039, 1045 (7th Cir. 1996).

[19]   Johnson v. K-Mart Corp., 273 F.3d 1035, 1036-49 (11th Cir. 2001); Ford v. Schering-Plough Corp., 145 F.3d 601, 608 (3d Cir. 1998), cert. denied, 525 U.S. 1093 (1999); Castellano v. City of N.Y., 142 F.3d 58, 68 (2d Cir. 1998), cert. denied, 525 U.S. 820 (1998). Cf. Robinson v. Shell Oil Co., 519 U.S. 337 (1997) (Title VII of the Civil Rights Act covers former employees).

[20]   28 C.F.R. § 35.104 (2002).

[21]   Concerned Parents to Save Dreher Park Center v. City of West Palm Beach, 846 F.Supp. 986, 989 (S.D. Fla. 1994).

program is a request for benefits of the program.[22] The regulations promulgated by the DOJ recognize that oftentimes this will be the case.[23]

An individual may be qualified only if policies are reasonably modified, auxiliary aids are provided, or physical barriers are removed.[24] Therefore, the qualification analysis often includes an analysis of the defendant's obligations to reasonably modify policies, provide auxiliary aids, or remove architectural barriers. The defenses to these obligations are that the requested changes would constitute a fundamental alteration of the public program or a direct threat to the health or safety of others. Therefore, the plaintiff's burden of proving qualification often leads directly to the defendant's burden of proving fundamental alteration or direct threat.[25]

In *Southeastern Community College v. Davis*,[26] the Supreme Court explored the balance between qualification and modification of eligibility standards under Section 504 of the Rehabilitation Act. In this case, Ms. Davis had a significant hearing impairment which, even with hearing aids, made it difficult for her to understand spoken language. She had to rely on reading lips.

Davis applied to the nursing school clinical program at Southeastern Community College. The college denied her application because of her hearing impairment. She requested several modifications of the program to accommodate her hearing impairment, including providing individual supervision by faculty members when she interacted with patients, and dispensing with the curriculum requirement of several

---

[22] Id. at 990.

[23] See 28 C.F.R. Pt 35, app. A, § 35.104 Text C (The "essential eligibility requirements" for participation in some activities covered under this part may be minimal. For example, most public entities provide information about their operations as a public service to anyone who requests it. In such situations, the only "eligibility requirement" for receipt of such information would be the request for it.).

[24] Id.

[25] Orr v. Wal-Mart Stores, 297 F.3d 720, 725 n.5 (8th Cir. 2002). The court stated:

> Had Orr established a prima facie case of actual disability under the ADA, Wal-Mart could have raised threat-to-self defense. Wal-Mart could have argued that, accepting Orr's contentions at face value, working in a single-pharmacist pharmacy, which did not provide for uninterrupted meal breaks, posed a direct threat to Orr's health and that Wal-Mart was justified in not continuing his employment.

[26] Southeastern Community College v. Davis, 442 U.S. 397 (1979).

clinical courses because she would not be able to gain the benefit of those courses due to her hearing impairment.[27]

The Court stated that "[a]n otherwise qualified person is one who is able to meet all of a program's requirements in spite of his handicap."[28] The Court rejected the plaintiff's argument that "'otherwise qualified' persons protected by § 504 include those who would be able to meet the requirements of a particular program in every respect except as to limitations imposed by their handicap."[29]

Thus, the *Davis* Court refused to require covered entities to lower their qualification standards if there was a legitimate policy underlying the standards. Instead, entities may take disabilities into account in determining whether a person is qualified.

The Court found that the modifications requested by Davis were a fundamental alteration of the nursing program. The purpose of the nursing program was to train persons to serve the nursing profession in all customary ways. With the requested modifications to the curriculum, Davis would not be trained to perform all the duties of a registered nurse – she only would be qualified to perform some of the customary duties.

Because Davis would not be receiving the functional equivalent of the degree provided to other students, the changes would fundamentally alter the nursing program.[30] The Court did not closely examine the school's allegation that this purpose was necessary or that the current curriculum was necessary to achieve that purpose. Rather, it deferred to the school's expertise.

In *Alexander v. Choate*,[31] the Supreme Court shifted away from the *Davis* principle of absolute deference to an entity's eligibility criteria. The Court wrote:

> The balance struck in *Davis* requires that an otherwise qualified handicapped individual must be provided with meaningful access to the benefit that the grantee offers. The benefit itself, of course, cannot be defined in a way that effectively denies otherwise qualified handicapped

---

27 Id. at 407-08. See also Doherty v. S. Coll. of Optometry, 862 F.2d 570, 575 (6th Cir. 1988) (school not required to waive a clinical proficiency requirement on the use of several instruments for a student with a vision and neurological impairment).

28 Davis, 442 U.S. at 406.

29 Id.

30 Id. at 409-11. "Section 504 imposes no requirement upon an educational institution to lower or to effect substantial modifications of standards to accommodate a handicapped person." Id. at 413.

31 Alexander v. Choate, 469 U.S. 287 (1985).

individuals the meaningful access to which they are entitled; to assure meaningful access, reasonable accommodations in the grantee's program or benefit may have to be made.[32]

Thus, the Court made clear that courts can examine whether an entity's eligibility criteria are, in fact, necessary to its program and not an attempt to exclude individuals with disabilities. Moreover, the Court determined that some changes to an entity's program will constitute reasonable modifications required to ensure that otherwise qualified individuals are not excluded because of disability barriers that can be overcome.[33]

The courts also have rejected "broad judicial deference resembling that associated with the 'rational basis' test."[34] However, they will generally accord deference to the standards of an entity, provided the entity establishes some non-discriminatory justification for the standards.[35]

Medical schools have been the source of several significant cases reviewing the appropriateness of academic standards. Many medical schools require graduates to be prepared to perform all the customary duties of the job (e.g., nurse, optometrist, physician) for which students are being trained. Thus, the school's standards are allowed to require more breadth of education than might be strictly necessary for someone who planned to pursue only a particular field.

These reasons lie beneath the Court's decision in *Davis* that Southeastern Community College was allowed to require Ms. Davis to participate in clinical courses, even though she might never plan to practice in a clinical setting. Similarly, in *Doherty v. Southern College of Optometry*,[36] the school was not required to modify its requirement of proficiency with certain machines to accommodate a student's vision impairment, even though many optometrists do not use those machines. In *Ohio Civil Rights Commission v. Case Western Reserve University*,[37] the defendant school did not have to provide one-on-one tutoring, redesign

---

[32]   Id. at 301.

[33]   Strathie v. Dept. of Transp., 716 F.2d 227, 231 (3d Cir 1983); see also Wynne v. Tufts Univ. Sch. of Med., 932 F.2d 19, 24-25 (1st Cir. 1991) (school is required to consider alternative methods of testing other than multiple choice tests for a student with dyslexia).

[34]   Wynne, 932 F.2d at 25; Strathie, 716 F.2d at 231.

[35]   Zukle v. Regents of the Univ. of Cal., 166 F.3d 1041, 1047-48 (9th Cir. 1999).

[36]   Doherty v. S. Coll. of Optometry, 862 F.2d 570, 575 (6th Cir. 1988).

[37]   Ohio Civil Rights Comm'n v. Case Western Reserve Univ., 76 Ohio St. 3d 168 (Ohio 1996).

lectures, and assign students to describe observations to a blind student, even though the student planned to practice only psychiatry.

However, admissions decisions must not be based on assumptions about the possible difficulties a disabled student may have finding a job or patients. In *Pushkin v. Regents of the University of Colorado*,[38] the possibility that future patients might object to treatment by a psychiatrist who uses a wheelchair was not a basis for excluding a student from a residency program. The discriminatory attitudes of future clients or employers are not a proper basis for discriminatory qualification standards.

§ 5.3 Estoppel

Can an individual with a disability be estopped from claiming she is qualified if she has made contradictory statements about her capabilities. Because applications for some benefits require the applicant to certify that she is unable to work, some defendants have argued that those statements should automatically estop individuals from claiming that they were qualified for positions from which they were excluded. The Supreme Court rejected this bright-line rule in *Cleveland v. Policy Management Systems Corp.*[39]

In that case, Ms. Cleveland lost her job because she had had a stroke. Cleveland applied for Social Security Disability Insurance (SSDI) benefits, then filed suit claiming her employer had discriminated against her on the basis of her disability by failing to provide her reasonable accommodations. In the application for SSDI benefits, Cleveland was asked the following questions:

> Are you presently working? (If so, you are ineligible)
>
> Do you have a "severe impairment," i.e. one that "significantly limits" your ability to do basic work activities? (If not, you are ineligible)
>
> Does your impairment "mee[t] or equa[l]" an impairment on a specific (and fairly lengthy) SSA list? (If so, you are eligible without more)
>
> If your impairment does not meet or equal a listed impairment, can you perform your "past relevant work?" (If so, you are ineligible)
>
> If your impairment does not meet or equal a listed impairment and you cannot perform your "past relevant work," then can you perform other jobs that exist in

---

[38] Pushkin v. Regents of the Univ. of Colo., 658 F.2d 1372 (10th Cir. 1981).

[39] Cleveland v. Pol'y Mgmt. Sys. Corp., 526 U.S. 795, 806-07 (1999).

significant numbers in the national economy? (If not, you are eligible)[40]

The Court found that SSDI's simplified analysis of disability was not the same as the ADA analysis, particularly because SSDI does not consider the possibility of reasonable accommodation.[41] Therefore, the Court rejected any presumption that an application for, or receipt of, SSDI benefits would necessarily preclude an ADA claim.[42] However, a plaintiff must be prepared to prove that any assertion in a benefits application that she is "unable to work" is not contradictory to her ADA claim's assertion that she was qualified for a job. "[43]

In this case, Cleveland argued that her benefits application and her ADA claim were not contradictory because the SSDI claim did not consider reasonable accommodations (which were denied by her employer but to which she claimed she was entitled under the ADA), and the SSDI statements were accurate at the time they were made because the employer had denied her reasonable accommodation.[44] The Court agreed and remanded the case for further proceedings.[45]

---

[40] Id at 804 (citations omitted).

[41] Id. at 802-03.

[42] Id. at 805.

[43] Id. at 806 ("An ADA plaintiff cannot simply ignore the apparent contradiction that arises out of an earlier SSDI total disability claim. Rather, she must proffer a sufficient explanation.").

[44] Id. at 807.

[45] Id.

Part 3

Employment Discrimination: ADA Title I
Analysis

Chapter 6   OBJECTS OF TITLE I

§ 6.1   Overview

Perhaps the most heavily litigated provisions of the ADA have been the employment sections. They impose comprehensive – from application to termination – obligations on covered employers.

Many of the ADA's restrictions may seem counter-intuitive to employers, such as the limitations on pre-employment questioning of applicants, or the need in some circumstances to accommodate an applicant's or employee's disability by restructuring her job or creating another position. Some of the restrictions may run contrary to the prevailing employment at will doctrine that gives substantial discretion to employers. As the number of interpretive issues that have reached the Supreme Court indicates, some believe that the statute suffers from ambiguities.

In this Part we first address the question of which entities are covered under Title I as "employers" and "employees." Next, we turn to the types of inquiries and medical examinations employers may demand. Distinct but related restrictions apply to the pre-employment setting, the post-conditional-offer setting, and the working environment.

We consider the permissible range of an employer's inquiries and medical examinations when an employee returns to work after incurring or being perceived as having incurred the onset of a disability. One recurring question in the early days of the ADA was legal standing; may a job applicant or employee who does not have a disability bring an ADA claim if the employer asks impermissible questions and may that person seek a remedy?

A covered entity has an obligation to reasonably accommodate a qualified person with a disability. We review this obligation in a number of contexts, including those in which an employee requests reassignment and in which an employee must be disciplined. We then briefly delve into wrongful termination law. The Part concludes with a review of the defenses to Title I claims, and the increasing relevance and treatment of expert testimony in Title I cases.

As with much of the Act's interpretation, disputes over the legitimate scope of inquiries and examinations and the degree to which employers must accommodate employees often are fact-specific. Courts may rely on the pragmatics of a situation and this may result in deferring to the employer's judgment of an employee's ability to perform essential functions. Or, it may result in skepticism that a particular examination was simply a proxy to exclude persons with (or with perceived) disabilities from the workplace.

§ 6.2 Covered Entities

The basic non-discrimination provision of Title I provides:

> No covered entity shall discriminate against a qualified individual with a disability because of the disability of such individual in regard to job application procedures, the hiring, advancement, or discharge of employees, employee compensation, job training, and other terms, conditions, and privileges of employment.[1]

A. *Definition Of Employer*

Under Title I, a "covered entity" is defined as "an employer, employment agency, labor organization, or joint labor-management committee."[2] An "employer" is defined as:

> A person engaged in an industry affecting commerce who has 15 or more employees for each working day in each of 20 or more calendar weeks in the current or preceding calendar year, and any agent of such person.[3]

An employer does not include the United States, a corporation wholly owned by the United States, an Indian tribe, or a private membership club (other than a labor organization) that is exempt from taxation under section 501(c) of Title 26 of the Internal Revenue Code of 1986.[4]

The EEOC's Interpretive Guidance on Title I establishes that the term "employer" is to be given the same meaning as under the Civil Rights Act of 1964.[5] The definition of employer in Title I parallels that used in

---

[1]   42 U.S.C. § 12112(a) (2000).

[2]   Id. § 12111(2).

[3]   Id. § 12111(5)(A).

[4]   Id. § 12111(5)(B)(i).

[5]   56 Fed. Reg. 35, 740 (1991) (codified at 29 C.F.R. pt 1630 app., § 1630.2 (a)-(f)). The EEOC is the agency designated to administer and enforce ADA Title I. 42 U.S.A. §§ 12116-17. The EEOC's interpretive

Title VII and in the Age Discrimination in Employment Act of 1967 ("ADEA").[6] Courts have applied the same standards of individual liability to these statutes.[7]

B.   *Definition Of Employee*

Title I defines employers (and therefore covered entities) in terms of having the requisite number of employees. The statutory definition of "employee" is: "an individual employed by an employer." This definition does not offer much guidance, and the Supreme Court recently characterized it as "a mere 'minimal' definition that is 'completely circular and explains nothing.'"[8]

Confusion often arises regarding the question of how courts should treat an individual who is a shareholder or director of a professional corporation. Are these individuals "employees" for the purposes of the statute? Under the ADA and other federal civil rights statutes, the circuit courts have split on this issue. Some courts have focused on the "economic realties," such as management, control, and ownership, and reasoned that shareholders and directors are more akin to partners and not employees.[9]

Yet, other courts have held differently, suggesting that the use of the corporate form, including a professional corporation, "precludes any examination designed to determine whether the entity is in fact a partnership."[10] In classifying shareholders, directors, and partners as employees, these courts have reasoned that allowing corporations to evade civil rights laws by classifying workers as "partners" or "directors" is unfair.[11]

The Supreme Court recently addressed this conflict in views among the circuits. In *Clackamas Gastroenterology Associates, P.C. v. Wells*,[12] the plaintiff worked for the clinic as a bookkeeper, and brought an

---

guidance uses the terms "employer" or "other covered entity" interchangeably to refer to covered entities subject to Title I.

[6]   See Williams v. Banning, 72 F.3d 552, 553-554 (7th Cir. 1995).

[7]   See, e.g., EEOC v. AIC Sec. Investigations, Ltd., 55 F.3d 1276 (7th Cir. 1995) (comparing the ADA, ADEA, and Title VII); Miller v. Maxwell's Int'l, Inc., 991 F.2d 583, 587 (9th Cir. 1993) (comparing ADEA and Title VII).

[8]   Clackamas Gastroenterology Assocs., P.C. v. Wells, 123 S.Ct. 1673, 1677 (2003) (quoting Nationwide Mut. Ins. Co. v. Darden, 503 U.S. 318, 323 (1992)).

[9]   See EEOC v. Dowd & Dowd, Ltd., 736 F.2d 1177, 1178 (1984) (Title VII case).

[10]   See Hyland v. New Haven Radiology Ass'n., P.C., 794 F.2d 793, 798 (2d Cir. 1986).

[11]   Id.

[12]   Clackamas, 123 S.Ct. at 1673.

action under Title I for disability discrimination. The issue of whether the clinic was a covered entity for purposes of Title I turned on whether its four physician-shareholders (who also constituted the clinic's board of directors) counted as "employees."

To decide this issue, the Court looked to the common law for guidance. The Court reasoned that in defining the traditional master-servant common-law relationship, the key element was control. The Court thereby adopted the definition of "employee" in the Equal Employment Opportunity Commission's ("EEOC") Compliance Manual, which also focuses on the common-law touchstone of control.[13]

Under the EEOC standard, each of six factors is relevant to the inquiry of whether a shareholder-director is an employee for purposes of analysis under the ADA:

1. Whether the organization can hire or fire the individual or set the rules and regulations of the individual's work.

2. Whether and, if so, to what extent, the organization supervises the individual's work.

3. Whether the individual reports to someone higher in the organization.

4. Whether and, if so, to what extent, the individual is able to influence the organization.

5. Whether the parties intended that the individual be an employee, as expressed in written agreements or contracts.

6. Whether the individual shares in the profits, losses, and liabilities of the organization.[14]

The Court held that the district court's findings, when considered in light of the EEOC's standard, weighed in favor of a conclusion that the director-shareholder physicians were not employees, because they controlled the clinic, they shared in profits, and they were personally liable for malpractice claims.[15]

The dissent criticized the majority's emphasis on the control element, and noted that sheltering shareholder-directors from the ADA ran contrary to the broad purposes of the ADA.[16] This decision affects

---

[13]   Id. at 1680.

[14]   Id. (citing Equal Emp. Opportunity Comm'n, Compliance Man. § 605.0009 (2000)).

[15]   See Clackamas, 123 S.Ct. at 1681. The Court ultimately remanded the case back to the Court of Appeals to consider the record in light of the EEOC standard.

[16]   See id at 1681-82 (Ginsburg, J., dissenting); see also Nathan Odem & Peter Blanck, Physician-shareholder Practice Groups and ADA

coverage determinations under the Civil Rights Act of 1964 and other employment anti-discrimination laws (e.g., the ADEA), which have language similar to ADA Title I.[17]

C. *Jurisdictional Versus Merits Analysis Of Covered Entity*

What is the effect of *not* naming a covered entity as a defendant? In other words, is the ADA's requirement that there be discrimination by a "covered entity" who is an "employer" jurisdictional, or is it instead a merits issue?

There currently is a split in the Courts of Appeals on this issue. Some courts have held that a district court lacks subject matter jurisdiction over an ADA claim lodged against a defendant that is neither an employer, employment agency, labor organization, nor a joint labor-management committee as those terms are defined in the ADA.[18] However, others have held that the question of whether a defendant is a covered entity is not jurisdictional, but merits related.[19]

D. *States As Employers* – **Board of Trustees of the University of Alabama v. Garrett**

Many individuals are employed by the state, or state agencies. However, states are treated differently for ADA Title I purposes than are private employers.

In *Board of Trustees of the University of Alabama v. Garrett*,[20] the Court held that, pursuant to the Eleventh Amendment, a state is immune to suits for money damages under ADA Title I. The Court held that Congress had not found a sufficient pattern of unconstitutional discrimination against people with disabilities in the specific area of state

---

Compliance, 28 Spine 3, 309-313 (2003) (discussing other implications of Clackamas).

[17] See, e.g., EEOC v. Dowd & Dowd, Ltd., 736 F.2d 1177, 1178 (7th Cir. 1984) (shareholders of a professional corporation are not employees under Title VII of the Civil Rights Act of 1964).

[18] See Jones v. Am. Postal Workers Union, 192 F.3d 417, 423 (4th Cir. 1999); see also Scarfo v. Ginsberg, 175 F.3d 957, 961 (11th Cir. 1999); Armbuster v. Quinn, 711 F.2d 1332, 1335 (6th Cir. 1983); Woodward v. Va. Bd. of Bar Examiners, 598 F.2d 1345, 1346 (4th Cir. 1979).

[19] See Sharpe v. Jefferson Distrib. Co., 148 F.3d 676, 677-78 (7th Cir. 1998), abrogated on other grounds by Papa v. Katy Indus., Inc. 166 F.3d 937, 939-40 (7th Cir. 1999); see also EEOC v. St. Francis Xavier Parochial Sch., 117 F.3d 621, 623-24 (D.C. Cir. 1997).

[20] Bd. of Trs. of the Univ. of Ala. v. Garrett, 531 U.S. 356, 374 (2001). The larger implications of the *Garrett* decision, and its application to ADA Title II in the case of *Tennessee v. Lane*, 123 S.Ct. 2622 (2003), are explored infra in Part 4.

employment. Therefore, Congress's abrogation of the states' Eleventh Amendment sovereign immunity was invalid. Moreover, Congress' actions in Title I as applied to states, prohibiting discrimination and requiring reasonable accommodation, were not a congruent and proportional remedy to the harms it did find.

Ultimately, although they could not sue the state for damages under the ADA, the Garrett plaintiffs were not without relief. On remand, the Eleventh Circuit held that they could sue the state of Alabama for damages under the Rehabilitation Act of 1973.[21] The court held that the state, and by implication its agencies, waived its sovereign immunity by accepting federal funds.[22]

E. *Title I Covered Employers: Illustrations*

1. Temporary employment agencies and staffing firms

Increasingly in the workplace, employers are using temporary or "contingent" workers to fill employment functions. Contingent workers lie outside an employer's core work force and include those whose jobs are structured to last only a limited period of time, are sporadic, or differ in any way from the norm of full-time, long-term employment.[23] Typically, staffing firms, temporary employment agencies, and contract firms hire and pay contingent workers,[24] and control their employment conditions.

There are at least two questions regarding the application of Title I to contingent workers. First, are contingent workers "employees" within the meaning of Title I, or are they independent contractors? Second, if they are employees, who is their employer for the purposes of the ADA – the staffing firm, or the company using the staffing firm for its employment needs?

---

[21] See Garrett v. Univ. of Ala., 2003 WL 22097772 (11th Cir. 2003).

[22] Id.

[23] See U.S. Equal Emp. Opportunity Commission, Enforcement Guidance: Application of EEOC Laws to Contingent Workers Placed by Temporary Employment Agencies and Other Staffing Firms (Notice No. 915,002), at 8 FEP Man. (BNA) 405:7551 (Dec. 3, 1997), available at http://www.eeoc.gov/docs/conting.html [hereinafter Contingent Workers]. Recent statistics show that the temporary help industry currently employs more than 2.3 million individuals, representing a 100% increase since 1991. Id. (citing statistics compiled by National Association of Temporary and Staffing Services).

[24] See id; see also Peter Blanck & Patrick Steele, The Emerging Role of the Staffing Industry in the Employment of Persons with Disabilities: A Case Report on Manpower Inc. 6 (1998), http://disability.law.uiowa.edu/lhpdc/publications/documents/blancketaldocs/Manpower_Report.pdf.

Is the staffing firm worker an employee within the meaning of the ADA, or an independent contractor? If the worker is an independent contractor, the ADA does not apply.[25] The EEOC Guidance states that the worker qualifies as an "employee" in the great majority of circumstances.[26]

However, the label alone is not determinative. Rather, the crucial issue arises in regard to whether the staffing firm, its client, or its worker, has the right to control the means and manner of work performance.[27] This is an individual inquiry that must be done on a case-by-case basis.

The individual likely will be viewed as an employee if the firm/client has the right to control where, when, and how the worker performs the job; the work does not require a high level of skill or expertise; the firm/client furnishes the tools, materials, and equipment; the work is performed on the premises of the firm/client; there is a continuing relationship between the worker and the firm/client; and the firm/client sets the hours of work and the duration of the job.

Once the determination is made that the worker is an employee, the question must follow: who is the "employer?" Is it the staffing firm, its client, or both? Often, throughout the duration of the employment, both qualify, yet the key object is to find out which entity exercises control over the worker's employment. The same questions discussed above are relevant to this inquiry.

In addressing the relationship between a staffing firm and its workers, the EEOC Guidance states that this relationship generally qualifies as an employer-employee relationship "because the firm typically hires the worker, determines when and where the worker should report to work, pays the wages, is itself in business, withholds taxes and social security, provides workers' compensation coverage, and has the right to discharge the worker."[28] In limited circumstances, in which, for example, the client firm puts its employees on the staffing firm's payroll solely to transfer the responsibility of administering wages and insurance benefits, the staffing firm still can qualify as an employer despite its lack of adequate control.[29]

If the client exercises supervisory control over the worker, the client can be the employer together with the staffing firm (or independently of it).[30] For example, while the staffing firm could pay the

---

[25] Lerohl v. Friends of Minn. Sinfonia, 322 F.3d 486, 489 (2003).

[26] See Contingent Workers, supra note 23.

[27] Id.

[28] Id.

[29] See Astrowsky v. First Portland Mortgage Corp., 887 F.Supp. 332, 337 (D. Me. 1995) (ADEA case).

[30] See, e.g., Poff v. Prudential Ins. Co. of Am., 882 F.Supp. 1534, 1536 (E.D. Pa. 1995).

worker a salary based on the number of hours worked for the client, as well as withhold taxes and provide workers' compensation coverage, the client could set the hours and terms of work, use its equipment on its premises, and report the worker's performance to the staffing agency. In this scenario, the staffing firm and its client likely qualify as joint employers because each have the right to exercise control over the terms of the worker's employment. Of course, either entity would need the requisite number of employees to be a covered entity under Title I.[31]

An entity also may be liable for the actions of companies with which it contracts, if those actions have the effect of discriminating against the entity's employees. Therefore, an employer may be liable for the discriminatory acts of its employment agency, labor union, provider of employee benefits, or trainer on its behalf. When it has known or should have known of the discrimination and failed to take prompt corrective measures, the employer may be liable even without having actively participated in the discriminatory policy or practice of the contractor.[32]

2.   Single and multiple employers

Sometimes, a court must decide whether to treat two entities as a single employer for the purpose of aggregating the number of employees to meet the numerosity requirement of Title I. The Courts of Appeals have applied at least two different tests to resolve this issue.

The Sixth Circuit has applied an "integrated enterprise" test. In *Swallows v. Barnes & Noble Book Stores, Inc.*, plaintiffs were allegedly discharged from their jobs at the state university bookstore because of their age and disability.[33] The defendant, a national bookstore chain, had contracted with the state university to operate and manage the store. Plaintiffs settled their claims with the defendant but appealed the dismissal of their action against the state.

In holding that the state was not a covered entity, the *Swallows* court framed the issue as whether the state and the bookstore were an integrated enterprise. The court considered the interrelation of operations and common management, labor relations, ownership, and financial control.[34] Although no single factor was dispositive, the Sixth Circuit placed particular importance on labor relations.

---

[31]   Id. (noting that a respondent must count each employee from the day that the employment relationship begins until the day that it ends, regardless of whether the employee is present at work or on leave on each working day; a client of a staffing firm must count each worker assigned to it from the first day of the job assignment until the last day).

[32]   See Contingent Workers, supra note 23.

[33]   Swallows v. Barnes & Noble Book Stores, Inc., 128 F.3d 990, 994 (6th Cir. 1997).

[34]   Id.

In *Papa v. Kathy Industries, Inc.*, the Seventh Circuit took a different approach in determining affiliate liability for age and disability discrimination. The court viewed the factors enunciated in the integrated enterprise test to be vague.[35] Instead, the court adopted a test that requires that a plaintiff show either that the conditions for "piercing the corporate veil" are present, the enterprise split itself into different entities (with fewer than the statutory minimum number of employees) for the purpose of avoiding Title I liability, or the parent corporation directed the discriminatory act against the employee of the subsidiary.[36] The court reasoned that this restrictive test was consistent with Congress's statutory purpose of sparing small firms the expense of antidiscrimination laws.

3.   Extraterritorial application of Title I

As discussed in Part 6 infra, the remedies available under the ADA are based on the remedies established under Title VII of the Civil Rights Act. Until 1991, the Supreme Court had limited the reach of Title VII of the Civil Rights Act (and thereby the remedies of ADA Title I) to American citizens and aliens working in the United States.[37] Congress enacted the Civil Rights Act of 1991 (and amended Title VII) to provide increased extraterritorial reach. The 1991 Act expands Title VII's definition of "employee" to include United States citizens employed abroad.[38] This coverage is limited to corporations that are controlled by United States employers.[39]

---

[35]   Papa v. Kathy Indus., Inc., 166 F.3d 937, 940-41 (7th Cir. 1999).

[36]   Id. The Seventh Circuit later applied this new test in *Worth v. Tyer*, 276 F.3d 249, 260 (7th Cir. 2001), and in *Breece v. AmeriCare Living Centers*, 2002 WL 31132308 (S.D. Ind. Sept. 25, 2002).

[37]   See EEOC v. Arabian Am. Oil Co., 499 U.S. 244, 257-59 (1991) (Title VII does not have an extraterritorial application to the employment of American citizens abroad by United States firms). This decision was superceded by Civil Rights Act of 1991, Pub. L. No. 102-166, § 109(a) (1991) (codified as amended at 42 U.S.C. § 2000e(f) (2000)). However, the 1991 amendments to Title VII did not overrule the Supreme Court's determination that Title VII is inapplicable to aliens employed outside the United States. See Shekoyan v. Sibley Int'l Corp., 217 F.Supp.2d 59, 64-65 (D.D.C. 2002) (discussing these issues).

[38]   42 U.S.C. § 2000e(f) ("With respect to employment in a foreign county, such term [employee] includes an individual who is a citizen of the United States."). In addition, Congress explicitly precluded Title VII's extraterritorial scope from covering aliens. Id. § 2000e-1 ("This subchapter shall not apply to an employer with respect to the employment of aliens outside any State....").

[39]   See id. § 2000e-1(c).

In the ADA, Congress qualified Title I's extraterritorial application in two additional ways. First, with respect to an employee in a workplace in a foreign country, actions that would otherwise constitute discrimination would not be unlawful if compliance with Title I would cause the covered entity to violate the law of the foreign country in which the workplace is located.[40]

Second, Title I does not apply to foreign operations of a foreign corporation unless the foreign corporation is controlled by a U.S. employer.[41] Where an American employer controls a corporation whose place of incorporation is a foreign country, an action in which the corporation has engaged that constitutes discrimination under Title I is imputed to the employer.[42] "Control" of a foreign corporation is determined by factors related to the interrelation of operations and common management, labor relations and financial control.[43]

At least one Court of Appeal has determined that the ADEA (and by implication, Title I of the ADA's pre-employment provisions) does not extend coverage to foreign nationals who apply in foreign countries for jobs in the United States.[44] However, Title I protects a qualified foreign national with a disability who is legally employed in the United States from discrimination during the course of his employment.[45]

This last principle is demonstrated in the case of *Torrico v. IBM, Corp.*,[46] wherein the plaintiff-employee was a non-U.S. citizen who worked in New York as the general manager of an American telecommunications corporation. Torrico traveled frequently to Latin America and agreed to a three-year temporary rotational assignment to Chile. He was subsequently terminated while on medical leave for autoimmune disease.

The district court found that a non-U.S. citizen employee is entitled to Title I protections when asserting a claim with respect to employment in the United States, rather than in a foreign country.[47] However, whether a non-U.S. citizen who is on a temporary assignment in a foreign country is "employed" in the United States depends on factors such as the terms and intent of the employment negotiated, the job duties and reporting relationship, the duration of the employment assignments

---

[40] Id. § 12112(c)(1).

[41] Id. § 12112(c)(2).

[42] Id.

[43] Id.

[44] See Reyes-Gaona v. N.C. Growers Ass'n, 250 F.3d 861, 866-67 (4th Cir. 2001).

[45] Id. at 867 (Motz J., concurring).

[46] Torrico v. IBM, Corp., 213 F.Supp.2d 390, 393 (S.D.N.Y. 2002).

[47] Id. at 403.

in various locations, and where the allegedly discriminatory conduct occurred.[48]

4. Religious entities as employers

Title I does not prohibit a religious corporation, association, educational institution, or society from giving preference in employment to individuals of a particular religion. This employment must include, however, the performance of work connected with the activities of the religious entity.[49]

A religious organization may require as a condition of employment that job applicants and employees conform to the religious tenets of the organization.[50] Nevertheless, a religious entity may not discriminate against a qualified individual, who satisfies the permitted religious criteria, because of her disability.[51]

5. Employers under Section 504 of the Rehabilitation Act

Like Title I of the ADA, Section 504 of the Rehabilitation Act provides a private right of action to qualified individuals with disabilities who have been subjected to employment discrimination. The Rehabilitation Act defines a covered entity as a "program or activity," including the operations of a corporation, partnership, private organization, or a sole proprietorship, as long as federal assistance is provided to the entity engaged in the covered business activities.[52]

Until the passage of the ADA, there was no issue of there being a requirement under the Rehabilitation Act that an employer have any requisite number of employees. But in 1992, Congress amended the Rehabilitation Act to provide that in employment discrimination cases, the standards to determine a violation of the Rehabilitation Act are the same as those applied under the ADA.[53]

Thus far, the only Court to squarely consider the issue has concluded that, although the Rehabilitation Act incorporates Title I's substantive standards for determining conduct volatile to the Act, it does not incorporate the ADA's definition of covered entity.[54] Therefore, there is no requirement under the Rehabilitation Act that a employer have 15

---

[48] Id. at 400.

[49] 42 U.S.C. § 12113(c) (2000).

[50] Id.

[51] 29 C.F.R. pt. 1630 app., § 1630.16(a) (2002).

[52] 29 U.S.C. § 794(b)(3)(A)(ii) (2000).

[53] Id. § 794(d).

[54] Schrader v. Ray, 296 F.3d 968, 975 (10th Cir. 2002).

employees.[55] But other courts have indicated they would decided the other way.[56]

6. Indirect employment relationships

Can a plaintiff sue an employer with whom she only has an indirect employment relationship? What if, for example, the plaintiff's primary employer has contracted with a third-party to regulate and administer some aspect of that plaintiff's employment? Can the plaintiff sue the third party for disability discrimination?

Although there is no hard and fast answer to this question, courts have generally allowed such suits, despite there being no direct employment relationship, if the third party has a significant amount of control over the employment function at issue. In this way, it is a parallel inquiry to the coverage for workers of "temporary employment agencies and staffing firms" discussion supra.

In *Carparts Distribution Center, Inc. v. Automotive Wholesaler's Ass'n New England Inc.*,[57] the plaintiff was an employee (and sole shareholder, president, and chief executive director) of Carparts, an automotive parts wholesaler distributor. Carparts was a participant in a self-funded medical reimbursement plan offered by the defendants. Plaintiff, who had AIDS, submitted numerous claims for payment for illnesses that were AIDS-related. The plaintiff alleged that with knowledge of his illness, defendants amended the Plan to limit benefits for AIDS-related illnesses.

To bring a claim for disability discrimination, the plaintiff had to show that defendants were his employers for purposes of the ADA. The defendant argued that it could not be a covered entity for purposes of Title I because the plaintiff was not one of its employees. In denying the defendant's motion to dismiss, the Court held that the defendant could be plaintiff's employer (even though the plaintiff was not defendant's

---

[55] Id. at 972-975.

[56] See Hiler v. Brown, 177 F.3d 542, 547 (6th Cir. 1999) (assuming, without deciding, that Rehabilitation Act's incorporation of ADA standards extends to definition of employer, including requirement of 15 employees).

[57] Carparts Distribution Center, Inc. v. Automotive Wholesaler's Ass'n New England Inc., 37 F.3d 13 (1st Cir. 1994). For a review, see Peter Blanck, et al., AIDS-Related Benefits Equation: Soaring Costs Times Soaring Needs Divided by Federal Law, in 2 Mealey's Litigation Reports: Americans with Disabilities Act 20-28 (1994). *Carparts* also is discussed as a Title III case, see infra Part 5.

employee) because the defendant could have exercised "significant control" over aspects central to plaintiff's employment.[58]

The *Carparts* court suggested that defendants could have assumed responsibility for providing health care insurance for Carparts' employees. The Court also said persuasive factors would include: whether defendants had the authority to determine the level of benefits provided to Carparts employees; whether alternative health plans were available to Carparts employees through their employment; and whether Carparts shared the administrative responsibilities that resulted from its employees.[59] *Carparts* stands for the proposition that an entity may be considered an employer when it acts as an agent of a Title I covered entity by administering important aspects of employment, such as health insurance services and benefits.[60]

Although courts have reached different conclusions as to whether a particular "indirect" employer is a covered entity, they have consistently focused on the third-party's control over a key employment function as the most important factor to consider. In *Bloom v. Bexar*, the plaintiff was hired as a court reporter by a state district court judge.[61] In holding that Bexar County was not a covered entity for plaintiff's purposes, the Court reasoned that the state legislature had exclusively vested the right to control the means and manner of a court reporter's performance in the state district court (controlled by the state, not the county).[62]

Similarly, in *United States v. New York State Department of Motor Vehicles*, a school bus company refused to rehire an individual with a missing limb as a bus driver.[63] Plaintiff named four defendants as his "employer" for purposes of Title I – the bus company, the school district, the New York Department of Motor Vehicles ("DMV") and the New York State Department of Education ("SED"). The latter two state agencies had regulations barring the operation of a bus by an individual missing a limb and the contract between the bus company and the school district incorporated those regulations.

---

[58] Mealey's Litigation Reports, supra note 57, at 21. The First Circuit remanded to the District Court to allow the plaintiff to develop the proper factual record.

[59] Id. at 17.

[60] Id. The Court also suggested that an entity may be covered under Title I when it significantly affects access of an individual with a disability to employment opportunities. Id. at 12, 18.

[61] Bloom v. Bexar County, 130 F.3d 722, 725 (5th Cir. 1997) (although Bloom was a Title VII case, the holding applies by implication to the ADA).

[62] Id. at 724.

[63] United States v. N.Y. State Dep't of Motor Vehicles, 82 F.Supp.2d 42, 43 (E.D.N.Y. 2000).

In a separate decision, the bus company was found liable as plaintiff's employer.[64] The question remained which of the remaining three defendants (the school district, DMV, and SED) were covered entities and employers for the purposes of plaintiff's Title I claim?

The district court stated the general rule as being that "a [d]efendant that does not have a direct relationship with a plaintiff may nonetheless be liable under ... the ADA for its discriminatory acts if it interferes with the plaintiff's employment opportunities with a third party and the defendant controls access to those opportunities."[65] The court held that the school district was a covered entity and plaintiff's employer for the purposes of Title I because the contract between the school district and the bus company provided the district sufficient control over the plaintiff's employment.[66]

The court also held that the state defendants – the DMV and the SED – also exercised sufficient control over plaintiff's employment to be considered covered entities and his employers for purposes of Title I.[67] Nevertheless, the court held that these state agencies ultimately could not be considered his employers under an indirect employment theory because their actions were regulatory in nature, taken in exercise of the state's police power.[68] According to the court, when regulating pursuant to its police power, the state is acting as a sovereign and not as employer.

There is a line as to how far the "interference theory" can go – that is, when a non-direct employer can be liable under the ADA if it interferes with plaintiff's employment prospects and controls access to those employment opportunities. In *Satterfield v. Tennessee,*[69] a state employer contracted with a private company to perform pre-employment physical examinations. The doctor employed by the private company found that plaintiff was not physically qualified for the position. The Sixth Circuit held that the private company and the doctor were not covered under Title

---

[64]   See EEOC v. Amboy Bus Co., 96-CV-5451.

[65]   N.Y. State Dep't of Motor Vehicles, 82 F.Supp.2d at 46.

[66]   Id. at 49. But the court went on to hold that there was insufficient evidence of causation for the school district to be liable for employment discrimination, because the evidence indicated that the bus company failed to rehire plaintiff because of the DMV regulations, not because of the contract between the school district and the bus company. Id. at 56.

[67]   Id. at 49.

[68]   Id. at 51-53; see also George v. N.J. Bd. of Veterinary Med. Exam'rs, 635 F.Supp. 953, 955 (D. N.J. 1985), aff'd, 794 F.2d 113 (3d Cir. 1986) ("where a governmental organization is exercising its police power, the control it exerts over a person's access to the job market does not render the governmental organization an 'employer' or 'employment agency' within the meaning of Title VII").

[69]   Satterfield v. Tennessee, 295 F.3d 611, 619 (6th Cir. 2002).

I as employers because they did not have direct control over plaintiff's employment opportunities. Ultimately, the state employer made the final decision in regard to plaintiff's employment.

7. Supervisors and other employees

Title I only covers employers. Individuals that are not employers are not covered entities and therefore not subject to liability.[70] Supervisors and other employees generally are not personally and individually liable under Title VII of the Civil Rights Act (and by extension the ADA).[71] Although an employee's supervisor is not personally liable for discriminatory actions,[72] that supervisor's actions may give rise to respondeat superior liability.[73]

8. Labor organizations

Congress incorporated Title VII's definition of labor organization into Title I:[74]

> Any organization of any kind, any agency, or employee representation committee, group, association, or plan so engaged in which employees participate and which exists for the purpose, in whole or in part, of dealing with employers concerning grievances, labor disputes, wages, rates of pay, hours, or other terms or conditions of employment, and any conference, general committee, joint or system board, or joint council so engaged which is subordinate to a national or international labor organization.[75]

A labor organization is engaged in an industry affecting commerce, when it maintains a hiring office or has 15 or more members and either:

> (1) is the certified representative of employees under the provisions of the National Labor Relation Act ..., or the Railway Labor Act...;
>
> (2) although not certified, is a national or international labor organization or a local labor organization recognized

---

[70] See Ostrach v. Regents of the Univ. of Cal., 957 F.Supp. 196, 200 (E.D. Cal. 1997); Lund v. J.C. Penny Outlet, 911 F.Supp. 442, 445 (D. Nev. 1996); Hardwick v. Curtis Trailers Inc., 896 F.Supp. 1037, 1038-39 (D. Or. 1995); Gallo v. Bd. of Regents of Univ. of Cal., 916 F.Supp. 1005, 1009-10 (S.D. Cal. 1995).

[71] Greenlaw v. Garrett, 59 F.3d 994, 1001 (9th Cir. 1995).

[72] Miller v. Maxwell's Int'l, Inc., 991 F.2d 583, 587 (9th Cir. 1993).

[73] Stern v. Ca. St. Archives, 982 F.Supp. 690, 692 (E.D. Cal. 1997).

[74] 42 U.S.C. § 12111(2) (2000).

[75] Id. § 2000e(d).

or acting as the representative of employees of an employer or employers engaged in an industry affecting commerce; or

(3) has chartered a local labor organization or subsidiary body which is representing or actively seeking to represent employees of employers within the paragraph (1) or (2);

(4) has been chartered by a labor organization representing or actively seeking to represent employees within the meaning of paragraph (1) or (2) as the local or subordinate body through which such employees may enjoy membership or become affiliated with such labor organization; or

(5) is a conference, general committee, joint system board, or joint council subordinate to a national or international labor organization, which includes a labor organization in an industry affecting commerce within the meaning of any of the preceding paragraphs of this subsection.[76]

Title I adopts the definition of an "industry affecting commerce"[77] as an "activity, business, or industry in commerce or in which a labor dispute would hinder or obstruct commerce or the free flow of commerce and includes ... any governmental industry, business or activity."[78] A federal district court lacks subject matter jurisdiction over a Title I employment discrimination claim against a defendant that is not a labor organization as defined in the ADA.

In *Jones v. American Postal Workers Union*, the Fourth Circuit confronted the issue of whether a labor organization that represents federal employees is a covered entity under the ADA.[79] Although the court viewed the ADA as ambiguous on this point, it deferred to the EEOC's interpretation of § 2000e(d) of Title VII, holding that where a labor organization representing federal employees exists for the purpose of negotiating with the United States or its agencies concerning grievances and labor disputes, it is engaged in an "industry affecting commerce" and is covered by Title VII and, by implication, the ADA.[80]

9.   Federal agency as employer

As used in Title I, the term employer does not include "the United States or a corporation wholly owned by the government of the United States."[81] A suit against a federal agency or against an officer of a federal

---

[76]   Id. § 2000e(e).

[77]   Id. § 12111(7).

[78]   Id. § 20000e(h).

[79]   Jones v. Am. Postal Workers Union, 192 F.3d 417, 426 (4th Cir. 1999).

[80]   Id. at 427-28.

[81]   42 U.S.C. § 12111(5)(B)(i) (2000).

agency in her official capacity constitutes a suit against the United States, and is not permitted under the ADA.[82]

In *Whaley v. United States*, the plaintiff, a former employee of the Central Intelligence Agency, alleged a violation of the ADA by the defendant, the United States of America, acting through the Central Intelligence Agency, the Director of the Central Intelligence Agency, and Mutual of Omaha Insurance Company, for offering and approving an employee insurance plan that contained a twenty-year limit on the payment of disability benefits as a result of a mental disorder.[83] The court dismissed plaintiff's Title I claim for lack of subject matter jurisdiction with respect to the claim against the federal defendants (the United States of America, acting through the Central Intelligence Agency, and the Director of the Central Intelligence Agency).

§ 6.3 Hiring, Discipline And Benefits

A. *Hiring*

Employers are prohibited from discriminating against people with disabilities in their hiring practices. Thus, an employer may not adopt qualification standards that unnecessarily exclude people with disabilities.[84] Qualification standards based on disability, such as vision or hearing, lifting or walking ability, must be job-related and consistent with business necessity.[85] Thus, they must be narrowly tailored to reflect the actual essential functions of the job. In addition, the employer must be prepared to provide reasonable accommodations for people who can do

---

[82] See, e.g., Kemer v. Johnson, 900 F.Supp. 677, 681 (S.D.N.Y. 1995), aff'd, 101 F.3d 683 (2d Cir. 1996), cert. denied, 519 U.S. 985 (1996).

[83] Whaley v. United States, 82 F.Supp.2d 1060, 1061 (D. Neb. 2000). Because the ADA only provides for employer liability, not individual liability, an ADA plaintiff cannot circumvent this rule by naming the director of a federal agency in his individual capacity. See id. at 1061 n.1; see also Mason v. Stallings, 82 F.3d 1007, 1009 (11th Cir. 1996); U.S. EEOC v. AIC Sec. Investigations, Ltd., 55 F.3d 1276, 1279-82 (7th Cir. 1995).

[84] "Discrimination" includes:

> using qualification standards, employment tests or other selection criteria that screen out or tend to screen out an individual with a disability or a class of individuals with disabilities unless the standard, test or other selection criteria, as used by the covered entity, is shown to be job-related for the position in question and is consistent with business necessity.

42 U.S.C. § 12112(b)(6).

[85] Id.; see also infra Section 9.1.

the job but do not meet the restriction. The safer practice, rather than relying on physical or mental attributes, focuses on the ability to do the tasks required by the job. Thus, instead of a requirement that an emergency medial technician be able to lift 200 pounds, the qualification standard should be the ability to move a 200-pound patient. The latter standard would not disqualify an individual with a prosthetic arm, who, although she could not lift a 200-pound weight, could maneuver a 200-pound person.[86]

B. *Discipline*

A disability does not immunize an employee for behavior and performance-based discipline, as long as the discipline also is applied uniformly to non-disabled employees.[87] An employer with no knowledge of an employee's disability may apply its usual behavior, performance, and discipline standards. A request for accommodation made after disciplinary action is taken does not raise a defense to the initial discipline. Rather, accommodation requests generally are only effective prospectively. Thus, if an employer undertakes discipline after refusing to provide reasonable accommodation, an ADA claim may arise.

C. *Benefits And Privileges Of Employment*

Title I requires employers to provide accommodations to qualified employees with disabilities so that they may enjoy the same terms, benefits and privileges of employment as those comparable employees without disabilities.[88] Employment benefits and privileges may include employer-sponsored job training or in-service programs. This also may include access to electronic bulletin boards and Internet services, company credit unions, cafeterias, auditoriums, transportation, and social functions.

---

[86] See, e.g., Gillen v. Fallon Ambulance Serv., Inc., 283 F.3d 11, 28 (1st Cir. 2001).

[87] U.S. EEOC, Enforcement Guidance on the Americans with Disabilities Act and Psychiatric Disabilities, at http://www.eeoc.gov/docs/psych.html (March 25, 1997). An employer may enforce a workplace behavior standard:

> provided that the workplace conduct standard is job-related for the position in question and is consistent with business necessity. ...An employer must make reasonable accommodation to enable an otherwise qualified individual with a disability to meet such a conduct standard in the future, barring undue hardship. Because reasonable accommodation is always prospective, however, an employer is not required to excuse past misconduct.

Id. at Questions 30 & 31.

[88] See 29 C.F.R. pt. 1630 app., § 1630.9 (2002).

However, many courts have found that Title I generally does not require an employer to ensure that insurance benefits treat people with disabilities equally.[89] This question has arisen primarily in the context of long-term disability insurance policies that cap the coverage for mental disabilities, but not physical disabilities. Title I generally does not require employers to alter their insurance benefit plans for employees working part-time as an accommodation to their disability.[90] Thus, an employer may provide health benefits only to full time workers, even if this requirement results in reduction in benefits for workers with disabilities who are accommodated with part-time schedules.[91]

---

[89] See EEOC v. Aramark Corp., Inc., 208 F.3d 266, 268-69 (D.C. Cir. 2000) (Title I "safe harbor" provision, 42 U.S.C. § 12201(c)(3) (2000), exempts insurance plans that pre-exist the ADA); Weyer v. Twentieth Century Fox Film Corp., 196 F.3d 1092, 1101-02 (10th Cir. 1999) (employee on disability leave is not qualified because she cannot perform essential functions, therefore, she cannot challenge long-term disability insurance policy); Lewis v. KMart Corp., 180 F.3d 166, 170 (4th Cir. 1999), cert. denied, 528 U.S. 1136 (distinctions within insurance policy are not employment discrimination because all employees are offered access to the same plan); Kimber v. Thiokol Corp., 196 F.3d 1092, 1101-02 (10th Cir. 1999) (same); Ford v. Schering-Plaugh Corp., 145 F.3d 601, 608-10 (3d Cir. 1998), cert. denied, 525 U.S. 1093 (1999); Parker v. Metro. Life Ins. Co., 121 F.3d 1006, 1015-19 (6th Cir. 1997) (en banc), cert. denied, 522 U.S. 1084 (1998); EEOC v. CAN Ins. Cos., 96 F.3d 1039, 1044-45 (7th Cir. 1996) (employee cannot perform essential job function and cannot challenge insurance policy when on disability leave). But see Johnson v. KMart Corp., 273 F.3d 1035, 1048-59 (11th Cir. 2001) (long-term disability policy that provides less coverage for mental disability is discriminatory unless covered by safe harbor provision).

[90] See, e.g., Tenbrink v. Fed. Home Loan Bank, 920 F.Supp. 1156, 1162 (D. Kan. 1996).

[91] For a review, see Bonnie P. Tucker, Insurance and the ADA, 46 DePaul L. Rev. 915, 916-17 (1997).

Chapter 7 EXAMINATIONS AND INQUIRIES

In section 12112(a), the ADA prohibits discrimination in employment on the basis of disability. Section 12112(d) expands the generic prohibition to include certain kinds of inquiries as employment discrimination.[1]

The restrictions on inquiries and examinations at different phases of employment serve distinct purposes:

- *Pre-employment* (§ 12112(d)(2)): The potential employer may not try to learn if the applicant has a disability. This provision is prophylactic, allowing individuals with a disability "a fair opportunity to be judged on their qualifications, 'to get past that initial barrier' where an employment judgment may be unfairly based on disabilities rather than abilities."[2]

- *Post-conditional offer* – before start of employment (§ 12112(d)(3)): At this point, an employer already has made an offer and decided the potential employee meets the job's requirements. The employer may require an examination if all employees – or a least all employees performing similar tasks – must take it. The examination is subject to rigid confidentiality restrictions and it is used to determine if the employee can perform essential job functions. At this stage, the employer may determine if an employee can perform the job's essential functions.

- *During course of employment* (§ 12112(d)(4)): An employer may not make inquiries or require a medical examination "unless such examination or inquiry is shown to be job-related and consistent with business necessity." Employees also may submit to voluntary examinations as part of employee health plans.

Each of these limitations can raise difficult questions for employers. What are the position's essential functions? How must the examination be validated? What is a medical examination? How broadly can questions explore applicants' abilities? What is the proper scope of an examination if an applicant reveals she has a disability and requests an accommodation? What precautions must an employer take to protect the privacy of information? The EEOC has developed guidelines for proper inquiries, to which courts often refer, although they are not obliged to adhere to them.[3]

---

[1] See 42 U.S.C. §§ 12112(d)(2)-(4) (2000).

[2] Harris v. Harris & Hart, Inc., 206 F.3d 838, 841 (9th Cir. 2000) (quoting 135 Cong. Rec. 10,768 (daily ed. Sept. 7 1989) (statement of Sen. Harkin)).

[3] U.S. Equal Emp. Opportunity Comm'n, Enforcement Guidance on Disability-Related Inquiries and Medical Examinations of Employees

These provisions also have the effect of extending the Act's reach beyond people with disabilities. The point of the pre-employment restriction in particular is to forefend certain kinds of questions, so arguably anyone asked such a question may be entitled to relief. This has lead into a thicket of legal standing issues, which we will explore.

§ 7.1 Permissible Scope Of Inquiries And Examinations

A. *Pre-Employment*

The general pre-employment rule is that an employer may not attempt to find out if an applicant has a disability. But an employer can try to ascertain if the applicant can perform tasks that will be important to the job. As set forth in the statute:

> (A) Prohibited examination or inquiry
> Except as provided in paragraph (3), a covered entity shall not conduct a medical examination or make inquiries of a job applicant as to whether such applicant is an individual with a disability or as to the nature or severity of such disability.

> (B) Acceptable inquiry
> A covered entity may make pre-employment inquiries into the ability of an applicant to perform job-related functions.

The standard to ascertain whether an inquiry is "disability-related" is whether it is "a question (or series of questions) that is likely to elicit information about a disability."[4] This standard is the same pre- and post-offer. The scope of permitted questions increases, however, if the applicant volunteers information about a disability, has an obvious disability, or requests an accommodation.

1. No known disability or requested accommodation

In most cases, the employer will not know if the applicant has a disability. The ADA functions to ensure that the employer cannot consider the applicant's possible hidden disability before evaluating an applicant's non-medical qualifications.[5] In this way, the ADA channels employers' questioning of job applicants to their abilities, rather than their disabilities.

There are two types of behaviors in which employers are not permitted to engage at the pre-offer stage. First, they cannot ask

---

Under the Americans with Disabilities Act, http://www.eeoc.gov/docs/guidance-inquiries.html (Sept. 27, 2000) [hereinafter Inquiries and Medical Examinations].

[4] Id.

[5] Id.

disability-related questions, whether direct ("do you have a disability?") or indirect ("have you ever taken the medication AZT?").[6] However, an employer may ask questions to which there are many possible answers, only some of which are disability-related (e.g., "do you have an arrest or conviction record?" or "can you meet our attendance policy?").[7]

An exception to this rule occurs when the questions relate to the essential functions of the job. Under the express language of § 12112(d)(2)(B), employers may ask whether an applicant can perform essential job functions. Courts may defer to an employer's judgment, but an applicant may nonetheless attack the functions as inessential or marginal. In such a circumstance wherein a doubt arises regarding a particular function, it is useful for the employer to validate the inquiry, for instance, by showing that there is a meaningful relation between success in the job and ability to perform the function.

If the essential functions include lifting objects of a certain weight, the employer may ask about lifting objects of a certain weight. The questions may include not merely the intellectual and physical functions, but also the psychological functions. For example, if the job requires working in a small, enclosed space, such as a narrow tunnel, the employer may ask whether an applicant can do so.[8] Such an inquiry must be limited to seeking information about *current* abilities (not past histories). Any such inquiry also must be carefully tailored to allow for reasonable

---

[6] Id.

[7] Id. The prohibition extends to questions, such as the use of prescription drugs, which might imply the existence of a disability. See Griffin v. Steeltek, Inc., 160 F.3d 591, 594 (10th Cir. 1998), cert. denied, 119 S.Ct. 1455 (1999) (on its application for employment, employer unlawfully asked: "Have you received workers' compensation or disability payments? If yes, describe."); cf. Krocka v. Bransfield, 969 F.Supp. 1073, 1079 (N.D. Ill. 1997) (police department implemented a policy of monitoring employees taking psychotropic medication); Roe v. Cheyenne Mountain Conference Resort, Inc., 920 F.Supp. 1153, 1154-55 (D. Colo. 1996), aff'd in pertinent part, 124 F.3d 1221, 1226 (10th Cir. 1997) (current employee; employer had a policy of requiring all employees to report every drug, including legal prescription drugs). However, because a person who currently uses illegal drugs is not considered disabled within the Act, questions about current illegal drug use are not forbidden and drug tests are permitted. 42 U.S.C. § 12114(a) (2000); 29 C.F.R. pt. 1630 app, § 1630.3(a) (2002).

[8] Grenier v. Cyanimid Plastics, Inc., 70 F.3d 667, 675 (1st Cir. 1995) (citing Voytek v. Univ. of Cal., No. C-9203465 EFL, 1994 WL 478805, at *15 (N.D. Cal., Aug. 25, 1994) (employee legally denied re-employment after period of disability where he "could not continue to perform all of the tasks assigned to him," due in part to "the ongoing conflict with his supervisor").

accommodation. Thus, "do you have any condition that limits your ability to perform this job" is impermissible, while "do you have any condition that currently prevents you from performing the essential functions of this job, with or without reasonable accommodation" may be acceptable.

There are, however, other inquiries that, though less traditional, are still acceptable under Title I. For example, an employer may perform general fitness or agility tests, psychological tests, tests that evaluate an employee's ability to read labels or distinguish objects as part of a demonstration of the ability to perform actual job functions and polygraph examinations (where permitted by law).[9] Assuming these tests are not interpreted to be medical in nature, their acceptability relies on the employer's ability to prove that they are job-related; an employer may not ask about the applicant's ability to perform functions that are not essential to the job.[10]

The other type of prohibited behavior relates to specific medical examinations. Generally, until the employer makes a "conditional offer" – an offer that may be conditioned on the applicant's passing a physical examination administered to all prospective employees,[11] the employer may not require medical examinations. The theory behind disallowing medical examinations in the pre-offer context is identical to that behind disability-related questions: such examinations tend to prematurely reveal

---

[9] See Inquiries and Medical Examinations, supra note 3. Employers who administer personality tests prior to hiring face the possibility that the test will be construed as a medical examination. See Gregory R. Vetter, Comment, Is a Personality Test a Pre-Job-Offer Medical Examination Under the ADA?, 93 Nw. U. L. Rev. 597, 638-639 (1999). The EEOC permits psychological testing as long as it is not a medical examination under the EEOC guidelines. See Inquiries and Medical Examinations, supra note 3, at 14. For example, an industrial psychologist could evaluate whether an applicant for a sales job could deal with rejection or whether the applicant for a managerial job is detail-oriented. The analysis depends on a number of factors, including whether a health care professional administers or interprets it. Id. Compare Barnes v. Cochran, 944 F.Supp. 897, 905 (S.D. Fla. 1996) (psychological evaluation administered by licensed psychologist was a medical examination) with Thompson v. Borg-Warner Protective Servs. Corp., 1996 WL 162990, at *6 (N.D. Cal. Mar. 11, 1996) (psychological evaluation not administered or interpreted by health care professional was not a medical examination) and Varnagis v. City of Chi., 1997 WL 361150 (N.D. Ill. June 20, 1997) (discovery permitted to determine if psychological evaluation is a medical examination).

[10] Gillen v. Falcon Ambulance Serv., 283 F.3d 11, 27 (1st Cir. 2002) (post conditional-offer; evidence conflicting whether ability to lift 70 pounds essential function).

[11] See 42 U.S.C. § 12112(d)(3) (2000).

disabilities that may not be related to an applicant's ability to perform a job with or without reasonable accommodation.

Of course, there is a fine line between what constitutes a "medical examination," and what is a permissible inquiry that tests job-related functions. For example, consider a case where an employer requires an applicant to lift a thirty-pound box and carry it twenty feet. The EEOC Guidance suggests that this is not a medical examination; rather, it is "a test of whether the applicant can perform the task."[12] Generally, the distinction between acceptable "inquiries" and prohibited "medical examinations" turns on the nature of the procedure: a medical examination is a "procedure or test that seeks information about an individual's physical or mental impairments or health."[13]

2.   Known disability or requested accommodation

There are two situations in which an applicant might have a "known disability." These are if the applicant has an obvious disability, or if the applicant has voluntarily disclosed a hidden disability. An applicant also might voluntarily disclose to a potential employer that she might need a reasonable accommodation to perform a job. Any one of these three events broadens the range of permissible questions that an employer may ask.

In the first two situations, an employer may ask if the applicant needs a reasonable accommodation to perform the job, and what type of reasonable accommodation that might be. If an applicant with a visual impairment applies for a job involving computer work, the employer may ask whether he will need reasonable accommodation to perform the

---

[12] See U.S. Equal Emp. Opportunity Commission, Enforcement Guidance: Application of EEOC Laws to Contingent Workers Placed by Temporary Employment Agencies and Other Staffing Firms (Notice No. 915,002), at 8 FEP Man. (BNA) 405:7551 (Dec. 3, 1997), available at http://www.eeoc.gov/docs/conting.html [hereinafter Contingent Workers]. In this scenario, for this to be a permissible inquiry, carrying a thirty-pound weight would need to be an essential part of the job.

[13] Id. The EEOC looks to:

> (1) whether the test is administered by a health care professional; (2) whether the test is interpreted by a health care professional; (3) whether the test is designed to reveal an impairment or physical or mental health; (4) whether the test is invasive; (5) whether the test measures an employee's performance of a task or measures his/her physiological responses to performing the task; (6) whether the test normally is given in a medical setting; and, (7) whether medical equipment is used.

Inquiries and Medical Examinations, supra note 3.

functions of the job. If the applicant answers "no," this ends the inquiry, although the employer may ask the applicant to describe or demonstrate performance. If the applicant answers "yes," the employer may ask questions about the type of accommodation ("What will you need?" or "Do you need a particular brand of software?").[14] Similarly, if the applicant requests an accommodation, the employer may inquire about the accommodation but not the underlying disability.[15]

The theory behind the courts' and the EEOC's permitting expanded inquires in the case of a known disability is drawn from the larger purposes of the Act. The primary goal of the ADA's employment provisions is to prevent the unnecessary or stigmatizing discovery of hidden disabilities. No violence is done to this purpose when an applicant has a known disability and the scope of questioning is thus broadened.[16]

The underlying notion is that revelation of this information should be useful to both the applicant and the employer. And, when the employer requests more information than the employee can provide, "inquiries" may broaden beyond simply asking the applicant questions.[17]

B.   *Post-Conditional Offer And Course Of Employment*

After an employer makes an employee an offer, the range of permissible behavior by an employer again broadens. At this point, the

---

[14]   This hypothetical is taken from the Contingent Workers, supra note 12.

[15]   Id.

[16]   EEOC guidance indicates:

> [W]here an applicant has an obvious disability, and the employer has a reasonable belief that s/he will need a reasonable accommodation to perform specific job functions, the employer may ask whether the applicant needs a reasonable accommodation and, if so, what type of accommodation. These same two questions may be asked when an individual voluntarily discloses a nonvisible disability or voluntarily tells the employer that s/he will need a reasonable accommodation to perform a job.

Inquiries and Medical Examinations, supra note 3; see also Equal Emp. Opportunity Comm'n, Reasonable Accommodation and Undue Hardship Under the ADA , 8 Fair Emp. Prac. Man. (BNA) 405:7601, 7611 (1999); Psychiatric Disabilities and the ADA, 8 Fair Emp. Prac. Man. (BNA) 405:7461, 7467-68 (1997); Enforcement Guidance on Pre-employment Inquiries Under the Americans with Disabilities Act, 8 Fair Emp. Prac. Man. (BNA) 405:7191, 7193-94 (1995).

[17]   See Grenier v. Cyanimid Plastics, Inc., 70 F.3d 667, 673 (1st Cir. 1995); cf. Brumley v. Pena, 62 F.3d 277, 280 (8th Cir. 1995) (similar result under Rehabilitation Act of 1973).

employer may ask disability-related questions and perform medical examinations that need not be job-related.[18]

A job offer may be conditioned on the results of post-offer disability-related questions or medical examinations. But, if an individual does not get the job because these questions or examinations reveal a disability, the employer must show that the exclusionary criteria are job-related and consistent with business necessity.[19]

If an employer elects to ask disability-related questions or require medical examinations after a job offer, it must make sure that all entering employees in the same job category are subjected to the examination or inquiry. The medical information obtained must be kept confidential.[20]

1.   What constitutes a "job offer?"

The EEOC defines a job offer as one made after the employer "has evaluated all relevant non-medical information which it reasonably could have obtained and analyzed prior to giving the offer."[21] But if the employer can show that it was not reasonable to obtain all non-medical information at the pre-offer stage, an offer still can be enough to move the parties into the post-offer stage.

For example, it may be too costly for a law enforcement employer wishing to administer a polygraph examination to administer both a pre-offer examination asking non-disability related questions, and a post-offer examination asking disability-related questions.[22] Or, an applicant might request that a reference not be contacted until after a conditional offer is made.[23]

Job offers do not have to be limited to current vacancies. An employer may give offers to fill current vacancies or reasonably anticipated openings.[24] An employer even can give offers in increase of

---

[18]   Contingent Workers, supra note 12.

[19]   42 U.S.C. § 12112(b) (2000); 29 C.F.R. pt. 1630 app., §§ 1630.10, 1630.14(b)(3) (2003).

[20]   42 U.S.C. § 12112(d)(3); 29 C.F.R. § 1630.14(b)(1)-(2).

[21]   See Equal Emp. Opportunity Comm'n, ADA Enforcement Guidance: Preemployment Disability-Related Questions and Medical Examinations, http://www.eeoc.gov/docs/preemp.html (Oct. 10, 1995).

[22]   Id.

[23]   Id.

[24]   Id.

this number when it can show that it needs more offers to fill vacancies or reasonably anticipated openings.[25]

2. Post-offer medical examinations and inquiries

After an employer makes a conditional offer, it may require a medical examination if all entering employees are subjected to the examination regardless of disability and the exam is subject to restrictive confidentiality rules.[26]

Though Title I does not explicitly state what an employer may properly review in such a medical examination, courts have nonetheless stated that the scope of the examination is unlimited.[27] The statute provides some ways that the information may be used.

The employer may use the examination to tailor accommodations[28] and also may alert safety personnel to a disability.[29] Unlike the pre-offer stage, a post-offer medical examination may be used to determine whether the employee can safely perform the essential functions of the job. In *Gillen v. Falcon Ambulance Service, Inc.*,[30] the First Circuit assumed without deciding that a post-conditional-offer medical examination was permissible when designed to determine whether the plaintiff (a genetic amputee with one functioning hand) could lift a specified weight.[31]

Nevertheless, the results of such examinations or inquiries may not be used in a way that is inconsistent with the ADA's purposes.[32] Once the offer has been given, it is presumed – subject to later refutation – that the applicant is a qualified individual. Employers may not use post-offer responses or examinations to screen people out unless the results

---

[25] Id. An example is if the employer can demonstrate that a certain percentage of the applicant pool will likely be disqualified or withdraw from the pool.

[26] 42 U.S.C. § 12112(d)(3) (2000).

[27] "The Act 'imposes no restrictions on the scope of entrance examinations; it only guarantees the confidentiality of the information gathered ... and restricts the use to which an employer may put the information.'" Garrison v. Baker Hughes Oil Field Operations, Inc., 287 F.3d 955, 962 (10th Cir. 2002) (quoting Norman-Bloodsaw v. Lawrence Berkeley Lab., 135 F.3d 1260, 1273 (9th Cir. 1998)).

[28] 42 U.S.C. § 12112(d)(3)(B)(i).

[29] Id. § 12112(d)(3)(B)(ii).

[30] Gillen v. Falcon Ambulance Serv., Inc., 283 F.3d 11, 33 (1st Cir. 2002).

[31] See also Barnes v. Cochran, 944 F.Supp. 897, 901-02 (S.D. Fla. 1996) (pre-employment psychological examination for sheriff deputy position that reveal psychological problems used to disqualify plaintiff).

[32] See 42 U.S.C. § 12112(d)(3)(C) ("the results of such examination [may be] used only in accordance with this subchapter").

demonstrate a direct threat or an inability to perform the job's essential functions that cannot be accommodated.

The scheme of permitting inquiries only at the post-offer stage of the process mitigates the problems of proof that arise when a person is forced to reveal a disability before an offer is made. At that stage, absent an admission by the employer, the applicant will not know whether her exclusion was due to her disability or her qualifications.

3. Course of employment and return to work

The restrictions on an employer's ability to make disability-related inquiries or require medical examinations continue after the person is hired.[33] As in the pre-offer and post-conditional-offer contexts, the prohibitions are tempered by practicalities.

Once again, the basic rule applies that employers may not ask questions seeking information that reveals disabilities.[34] However, if the inquiry is "job-related and consistent with business necessity," it is permissible.[35] The Second Circuit has articulated the standard:

> [I]n proving a business necessity, an employer must show more than that its inquiry is consistent with "mere expediency." An employer cannot simply demonstrate that an inquiry is convenient or beneficial to its business. Instead, the employer must first show that the asserted "business necessity" is vital to the business. For example, business necessities may include ensuring that the workplace is safe and secure or cutting down on egregious absenteeism. The employer must also show that the examination or inquiry genuinely serves the asserted business necessity and that the request is no broader or more intrusive than necessary. The employer need not show that the examination or inquiry is the only way of achieving a business necessity, but the examination or

---

[33] 42 U.S.C. § 12112(d)(4).

[34] Conroy v. N.Y. State Dep't of Correctional Servs., 333 F.3d 88 (2d Cir. 2003), aff'g in part and remanding Fountain v. N.Y. St. Dep't of Correctional Servs., 190 F.Supp.2d 335, 338 (N.D.N.Y. 2002) (question is "whether inquiry would be likely to require employees to disclose their disabilities or perceived disabilities").

[35] An objective test, rather than the employer's subjective belief, determines whether an inquiry is consistent with business necessity. Tice v. Cent. Area Transp. Auth., 247 F.3d 506, 518 (3d Cir. 2001) (citing Taylor v. Pathmark Stores, Inc., 177 F.3d 180, 193 (3d Cir. 1999)); Fitzpatrick v. City of Atlanta, 2 F.3d 1112, 1119 n.6 (11th Cir. 1993).

inquiry must be a reasonably effective method of achieving the employer's goal.[36]

The EEOC's regulations clarify that an employer can seek to determine if the employee can perform essential job functions,[37] if the employer has an objective reasonable belief that the employee has a disability that may interfere with job performance. The legitimate reasons for requiring a medical exam for an employee are

> (1) when an employee is having difficulty performing his or her job effectively; (2) when an employee becomes disabled on the job or wishes to return to work after suffering an illness; (3) if an employee requests an accommodation; and (4) if medical examination, screening, and monitoring is required by other laws.[38]

A disability-related leave gives rise to an objective basis to question the employee's ability to perform. Therefore, when an employee returns to work after a medical leave, the employer may demand an examination[39] or a medical release stating that the employee can safely perform the job's essential functions.[40] However, an employer may not require a "general diagnosis," which may reveal a disability.[41] An inquiry

---

[36] Conroy, 333 F.3d at 97-98.

[37] 29 C.F.R. pt. 1630, app. § 1630.14(c) (2003); see also Covelli v. Nat'l Fuel Gas Dist., 2002 WL 31422862, at *1 (2d Cir. Oct. 29, 2002) (court noting in dicta that employer may require medical examination to determine if employee who had previously claimed to be injured could perform essential functions); Tice, 247 F.3d at 517-18 (based on employer's knowledge of employee's condition and employee's own doctor's failure to justify return to work, request for independent medical examination justified); Reichmann v. Cutler-Hammer, Inc., 183 F.Supp.2d 1292, 1297 (D. Kan. 2001); Ocasio v. Fed. Express Corp., 977 F.Supp. 106, 110-11 (D.P.R. 1977) (employee seeking to return to work after auto accidents failed to present sufficient evidence to enable employer to evaluate whether she could perform essential functions).

[38] EEOC v. Prevo's Family Market, Inc., 135 F.3d 1089, 1103 (6th Cir. 1998); see also Chai R. Feldblum, Medical Examinations and Inquiries Under the Americans with Disabilities Act: A View from the Inside, 64 Temp. L. Rev. 521, 543 (1991).

[39] Grenier v. Cyanimid Plastics, Inc., 70 F.3d 667, 669 (1st Cir. 1995); White v. City of Boston, 7 Mass. L. Rptr. 232, 1997 WL 416586, at *2-3 (Mass. Super. Jul. 22 1997).

[40] Grenier, 70 F.3d 667.

[41] Conroy, 333 F.3d at 95-96; see also Roe v. Cheyenne Mountain Conference Resort, 920 F.Supp. 1153, 1154-55 (D. Colo. 1996), aff'd in pertinent part, 124 F.3d 1221 (10th Cir. 1997).

also is permitted when a worker with a known disability is sent out from a union's hiring hall.[42]

The courts have applied these principles in a variety of cases:

- A court granted summary judgment against an employer with a sick leave policy that required an employee returning to work after a leave of any duration to present a doctor's certificate with a diagnosis. The inquiry was prohibited, because it might have revealed a disability[43] and was too broad to be justified by business necessity.[44] On appeal, the Second Circuit found a question of fact about the "business necessity" of the inquiry.[45]

- An employer properly requested that an employee, returning to work after suffering severe depression, provide a release permitting her doctor to give the employer more information. The employee's refusal caused a breakdown in the interactive accommodation process, such that the employer could not be liable for failing to accommodate the employee.[46] The court affirmed a summary judgment in favor of the defendant.

---

[42] Harris v. Harris & Hart, Inc., 206 F.3d 838, 843 (9th Cir. 2000).

[43] The court analogized to asking about all an employee's prescription medications, which was found improper in *Roe*, 124 F.3d at 1230-31.

[44] Fountain v. N.Y. St. Dep't of Correctional Servs., 190 F.Supp.2d 335, 340 (N.D.N.Y. 2002).

[45] Conroy, 333 F.3d at 97-98.

[46] Beck v. Univ. of Wis. Bd. of Regents, 75 F.3d 1130, 1135-37 (7th Cir. 1995); see also Conrad v. Bd. of Johnson County Comm'rs, 237 F.Supp.2d 1204, 1231-36 (D. Kan. 2002) (defendant county properly required "fitness for duty evaluation and psychiatric testing" of prenatal nurse for high-risk patients, who worked too many hours and required subordinated to do the same, sent long memo complaining of "virtually every aspect of the Health Department's operations," sent a "bizarre and inappropriate" e-mail stating: "I am asking the 'force' to release everyone of us from the 'chains that bind' and 'the walls that keep our Spirits apart'" and spoke in an extremely rapid and "scattered" manner); Donofrio v. N.Y. Times, 2001 WL 1663314, at *8 (S.D.N.Y. Aug. 24, 2001) (employer reasonably requested independent medical examination after employee's unexplained three-week absence and contact by employee's doctor stating employee was suffering from mental disorder; employee's refusal obstructed interactive process); Swanson v. Allstate Ins. Co., 102 F.Supp.2d 949, 975-78 (N.D. Ill. 2000) (employee's psychiatrist's evaluation, stating employee was not disabled, conflicted with employer's psychiatrist's evaluation of employee, which found severe psychological disorders; employee refused

- The court denied summary judgment to an employer where the employee challenged the scope of an inquiry. The employer had requested that the employee, who had returned from a lengthy sick leave the previous month, to submit to an independent medical examination to see if she could resume a job she had previously held. The employer's knowledge of the employee's heath problems and the fact that she had returned to work earlier than her doctor recommended justified the examination,[47] but did not justify the breadth of the inquiry, which requested all medications.[48]

- A court upheld an employer's requirement that all correctional officers fill out biannually a "Disclosure of Disability Form," which asked the employees to check if they had one of six disabilities – "(1) visual; (2) hearing; (3) speech; (4) physical; (5) learning; and (6) other."[49] Although this inquiry seems intended to discover whether the employee has a disability, not whether he can perform the essential functions of the job, the court found that the employee had failed to rebut the employer's statement that the purpose of the inquiries was to "gather information to be used in setting post assignments and establishing reasonable accommodations, which are job-related purposes that are consistent with business necessity."[50] However, the employee had not refused an assignment before the inquiry, and had not asked for accommodations.

- An employer may require a fitness for duty examination where an employee suffers an on-the-job injury.[51]

§ 7.2 Confidentiality Of Information

If an employer administers any type of medical test or inquiry, the employer must treat the results as confidential medical records. The statute tightly controls how this information can be used, and who has access to the information:

---

employer's request for second independent medical examination, thereby thwarting interactive process).

[47] Reichmann v. Cutler-Hammer, Inc., 95 F.Supp.2d 1171, 1175-76 (D. Kan. 2001).

[48] Id. at 1186-87.

[49] Martin v. Kansas, 190 F.3d 1120, 1124 (10th Cir. 1999).

[50] Id. at 1134.

[51] Tice v. Cent. Area Transp. Auth., 247 F.3d 506, 517-518 (3d Cir. 2001); Wade v. Knoxville Utils. Bd., 259 F.3d 452, 462 (6th Cir. 2001).

[I]nformation obtained regarding the medical condition or history of the applicant [must be] collected and maintained on separate forms and in separate medical files and is treated as a confidential medical record, except that – (i) supervisors and managers may be informed regarding necessary restrictions on the work or duties of the employee and necessary accommodations; (ii) first aid and safety personnel may be informed, when appropriate, if the disability might require emergency treatment; and (iii) government officials investigating compliance with this chapter shall be provided relevant information on request ...[52]

Not complying with these record-keeping restrictions is a per se violation of the Act. In contrast to § 12112(d)(3)(C), which requires the results of medical examinations to be "used only in accordance with the subchapter," § 12112(d)(3)(B) mandates that information be protected in the same manner as medical records. Employers thus assume a function similar to medical providers and medical information therefore may not be kept in personnel files.[53] The analysis of the consequences of breaches of the mandates should be understood on those terms and on the understanding of privacy violations.[54] A plaintiff might show emotional distress (with the proof problems entailed therein), as well as more strictly economic consequences.[55]

This requirement for confidentiality may give rise to tensions in the context of reasonable accommodations, when other employees seek an explanation for the "special" treatment of the disabled employee. The ADA is clear that such pressures do not justify the employer revealing an employee's disability, for that decision is to be made by the employee with the disability.

---

[52] 42 U.S.C. § 12112(d)(3)(B) (2000), also incorporated into § 12112(d)(4).

[53] 29 C.F.R. pt. 1630 app., § 1630.14 (2003).

[54] Employers, or employees involved in human resources, may view medical records confidentiality as among their less important tasks and may thus be less than completely diligent in insuring the confidentiality of those records.

[55] Cf. Doe v. U.S. Postal Serv., 317 F.3d 339, 344-45 (D.C. Cir. 2003) (summary judgment in favor of employer reversed where employee show release of medical information in violation of Rehabilitation Act §§ 501(g) and 504(d), 29 U.S.C. § 791(g) and 794(d), that incorporate ADA's confidentiality provisions); but see Tice, 247 F.3d at 519-20 (plaintiff failed to go beyond "bare allegations" of emotional distress in opposition to summary judgment motion).

§ 7.3 Rights Of People Without Disabilities To Bring Inquiry/Examination Claims – Standing

What happens if a job applicant without a disability is asked an improper question – for example, one designed to find a disability, answers truthfully, and is refused the job for "other" reasons?[56] Or, in the post-conditional-offer context, if an employee misrepresents her medical history and the employer improperly uses the misrepresentation as a reason for not hiring.[57] May such an aggrieved person sue for violation of the ADA?

The broader context of the inquiry sometimes is formulated as a standing question. As set forth in *Lujan v. Defenders of Wildlife*,[58] the plaintiff must pass a three-part test: (1) "injury in fact – an invasion of a legally protected interest which is (a) concrete and particularized, and (b) actual or imminent, not conjectural or hypothetical;"[59] (2) "a causal connection between the injury and the conduct complained of – the injury has to be fairly ... trace[able] to the challenged action of the defendant, and not ... th[e] result [of] the independent action of some third party not before the court;"[60] (3) "[i]t must be likely, as opposed to merely speculative, that the injury will be redressed by a favorable decision."[61]

There may be no injury in fact, when the forbidden inquiry has not caused an applicant to lose a job. In *Armstrong v. Turner Industries, Ltd.*,[62] the Fifth Circuit found that an improper inquiry, without more, does not constitute an injury to support damages liability. Thus, the plaintiff, who was not hired based on false answers rather than a discriminatory motive, could not state a claim for damages.[63]

Alternatively, the court may frame the issue in terms of whether the plaintiff must prove disability status as part of his claim.[64] (Of course,

---

[56] E.g., Griffin v. Steeltek, Inc., 160 F.3d 591, 593-95 (10th Cir. 1998), cert. denied, 119 S.Ct. 1455 (1999).

[57] E.g., Garrison v. Baker Hughes Oil Field Operations, Inc., 287 F.3d 955, 960-961 (10th Cir. 2002).

[58] Lujan v. Defenders of Wildlife, 504 U.S. 555, 560 (1992).

[59] Id. (citations and internal quotation marks omitted).

[60] Id. (citation and internal quotation marks omitted).

[61] Id. at 561 (citation and internal quotation marks omitted).

[62] Armstrong v. Turner Indus., Ltd., 950 F.Supp. 162, 166-68 (M.D. La. 1996), aff'd on other grounds, 131 F.3d 554, 561 (5th Cir. 1998).

[63] See also Cossette v. Minn. Power & Light, 188 F.3d 964, 971 (8th Cir. 1999).

[64] E.g., Griffin v. Steeltek, Inc., 160 F.3d 591, 594 (10th Cir. 1998), cert. denied, 119 S.Ct. 1455 (1999) (plaintiff need not be disabled to bring claim under § 12112(d)(2)(A), distinguishing Armstrong, 950 F.Supp. at 167-68,

that question may be cast in standing terminology: does the plaintiff have a "legally protected interest?") The confusion stems from the statutory language. While the ADA's general prohibition on discrimination in section 12112 protects "a qualified individual with a disability," section 12112(d)(2)(A), which addresses inquiries, focuses on "job applicant[s]."[65]

Some courts conclude that individuals without disabilities may not bring claims for unlawful medical examinations or inquiries.[66] However, the majority of courts have come out the other way. These courts recognize that the statute expressly uses different terms in different sections. Based on this, and to give effect to the policies underlying the ADA, these courts have held that individuals without disabilities may bring claims for unlawful medical examinations or inquiries.[67]

---

and dealing with question of proving whether one is a person with a disability as an element of the cause of action).

[65] 42 U.S.C. § 12112(d)(2) (2000).

[66] Armstrong, 950 F.Supp. at 166-68.

[67] Conroy v. N.Y. St. Dep't of Correctional Servs., 333 F.3d 88, 94-94 (2d Cir. 2003); Cossette, 188 F.3d at 969-70; Fredenburg v. Contra Costa County Dep't of Health Servs., 172 F.3d 1176, 1182 (9th Cir. 1999) (requiring plaintiffs to prove that they are persons with disabilities to challenge a medical examination would render § 12112(d)(4)(A) of the ADA "nugatory"; thus, plaintiffs need not prove that they are qualified individuals with a disability to bring claims challenging the scope of medical examinations under the ADA); Karraker v. Rent-A-Center, Inc., 239 F.Supp.2d 828, 834-36 (C.D. Ill. 2003); Roe v. Cheyenne Mountain Conference Resort, Inc., 920 F.Supp. 1153, 1154-55 (D. Colo. 1996), aff'd in pertinent part, 124 F.3d 1221, 1234 (10th Cir. 1997) (non-disabled employee could bring claim under § 12112(d)(4)); Mack v. Johnstown Am. Corp., 1999 WL 304276, at *5 (W.D. Pa. 1999); see also Garrison v. Baker Hughes Oil Field Operations, Inc., 287 F.3d 955, 961 (10th Cir. 2002) ("§§ 12112(d)(3)(A) and (B) claims arise out of an employer's post-offer hiring practices and are not related to an entering employee's disability status", although § 12112(d)(3)(C) claim must be based on "use [of] collected medical information to discriminate on the basis of disability;" "plaintiff need only 'prove injury flowing from' the statutory violation rather than injury from discrimination based on a disability" to recover compensatory damages under § 12112(d)(3)); but see Tice v. Cent. Area Transp. Auth., 247 F.3d 506, 516-17 (3d Cir. 2001) (declining to reach issue); Watson v. City of Miami Beach, 177 F.3d 932, 935 (11th Cir. 1999) (same); Armstrong v. Turner Indus., Ltd., 141 F.3d 554, 559 (5th Cir. 1998) (same). See Natalie R. Azinger, Too Healthy To Sue Under the ADA? The Controversy Over Pre-Offer Medical Inquiries and Tests, 25 Iowa J. Corp. L. 193, 204-207 (1999). But see William D. Wickard, The New Americans Without a Disability Act: The Surprisingly Successful

This extension certainly seems well reasoned. In addition to the statutory interpretation argument, applying certain Title I protections to people without disabilities would have a prophylactic effect, and prevent employers from using prohibited inquiries or medical examinations in all circumstances. As the Tenth Circuit has pointed out, it would be incongruous for a statute that prevents inquiries into whether a person has a disability to require a claimant to prove that he had a disability to avail himself of the protection of the statute.[68] Such a requirement would, as a practical matter, gut the rule – making it clear to every employer that anyone who objects to the question must be a person with a disability. Congress aimed in the ADA to protect people with diseases such as cancer, who "may object merely to being identified, independent of the consequences," because of the stigmatizing effect.[69]

The few courts that have reached the opposite conclusion rely on the fact that § 12112(a) forbids only discrimination against "a qualified individual with a disability," and § 12112(d)(1) refers back to that earlier section.[70] However, that argument assumes that the statute protects only against disability discrimination and inquiries that could result in that discrimination.

The majority analysis has other implications. If an employer makes an impermissible pre-offer inquiry and the applicant does not answer or misrepresents her health history, may the employer subsequently discipline or dismiss the employee on the basis of the original misrepresentation? The courts have not addressed this issue, but allowing the employer to punish the employee would appear to immunize the employer from its own illegal actions.

Plight of the Non-Disabled Plaintiff Under the ADA, 61 U. Pitt. L. Rev. 1023, 1049-50 (2000).

[68] Griffin, 160 F.3d at 594; Fountain v. N.Y. St. Dep't of Correctional Servs., 190 F.Supp.2d 335, 335-38 (N.D.N.Y. 2002). In Garrison, the court held that, because § 12112(d)(3)(C) states "the results of such examination are used only in accordance with this subchapter," 287 F.3d at 960, "to recover under subsection 12112(d)(3)(C) a plaintiff must show the employer used collected medical information to discriminate on the basis of disability." Id. at 961 n.4. Thus, while a nondisabled applicant will have a cause of action to challenge the inquiry, he may have difficulty demonstrating a compensable injury.

[69] See H.R. Rep. No. 101-485(2), at 22-23 (1990), reprinted in 1990 U.S.C.C.A. 303, 357-58.

[70] See Armstrong, 950 F.Supp. at 166-68.

Chapter 8 REASONABLE ACCOMMODATION

§ 8.1 Overview And Illustrations

The conceptual foundation of accommodation for purposes of ADA Title I was introduced in Part 1 of this treatise and will be elaborated upon in this chapter. An employee is not a "qualified" person with a disability for purposes of Title I if he cannot perform the essential job functions with or without a reasonable accommodation.[1]

A. *Statutory Definitions*

Discrimination under Title I includes a covered entity:

> (5)(A) not making reasonable accommodations to the known physical or mental limitations of an otherwise qualified individual with a disability who is an applicant or employee, unless such covered entity can demonstrate that the accommodation would impose an undue hardship on the operation of the business of such covered entity; or

> (B) denying employment opportunities to a job applicant or employee who is an otherwise qualified individual with a disability, if such denial is based on the need of such covered entity to make reasonable accommodation to the physical or mental impairments of the employee or applicant;[2]

Title I defines reasonable accommodation to include:

> (A) making existing facilities used by employees readily accessible to and usable by individuals with disabilities; and

> (B) job restructuring, part-time or modified work schedules, reassignment to a vacant position, acquisition or modification of equipment or devices, appropriate adjustment or modifications of examinations, training materials or policies, the provision of qualified readers or interpreters, and other similar accommodations for individuals with disabilities.[3]

ADA Title IV also provides:

---

[1] See 42 U.S.C. 12111(8) (2000); 29 C.F.R. pt. 1630 app, § 1630.1(c)(2) (2003) (noting that reasonable accommodation and undue hardship requirements supercede state or local disability antidiscrimination laws to the extent that they offer less protection than the ADA).

[2] 42 U.S.C. § 12112(b)(5)(A-B); id. (noting that accommodation does not include providing personal use items needed to accomplish daily activities off the job, such as a prosthetic limb, a wheelchair, eyeglasses, or hearing aids).

[3] Id. § 12111(9).

Nothing in this chapter should be construed to require an individual with a disability to accept an accommodation, aid, service, opportunity, or benefit which such individual chooses not to accept.[4]

B.   *EEOC Regulations*

The EEOC Title I regulations provide guidance on the concept of "reasonable accommodation" and include under their definition:[5]

(i) Modifications or adjustments to a job application process that enable a qualified applicant with a disability to be considered for the position such qualified applicant desires; or

(ii) Modifications or adjustments to the work environment, or to the manner or circumstances under which the position held or desired is customarily performed, that enable a qualified individual with a disability to perform the essential functions of that position; or

(iii) Modifications or adjustments that enable a covered entity's employee with a disability to enjoy equal benefits and privileges of employment as are enjoyed by its other similarly situated employees without disabilities.

According to EEOC guidance, there are three categories of accommodation: those (1) required to ensure equal opportunity in the job application process; (2) that enable the qualified employee with a disability to perform the essential job functions; and (3) that enable the qualified employee with a disability to enjoy equal benefits and privileges of employment.[6]

The concept underlying reasonable accommodation is that an employer must be prepared to change the way an employee with a disability performs a job. The employer need not change the result of the job (e.g., a certain number of items produced), but may need to change the means of accomplishing the result (e.g., the employee sits while producing, instead of standing). Such accommodations are made informally on a regular basis, at least when they impose no costs on the employer. The ADA extends this informal process to those changes that impose some burdens on the employer.

One may describe an accommodation as a case-by-case modification or adjustment to a workplace process or environment that makes it possible for a qualified person with a disability to perform essential job functions.[7] Possible accommodations virtually are unlimited.

---

4   Id. § 12201(d).

5   29 C.F.R. §§ 1630.2(o)(1), 1630.9.

6   Id., pt. 1630, app., §§ 1630.2(o)(1), 1630.9.

7   For general interpretive guidance from the EEOC, see the Regulations to Implement the Equal Employment Provisions of the Americans with

Accommodations may include physical modifications to a workspace, flexible scheduling of duties, or provision of equipment, assistive technologies, or job training to aid in job performance.[8] A covered employer discriminates against a qualified person with a disability when it refuses to make a reasonable accommodation that does not cause that employer an undue hardship.

A discrimination claim premised on a failure to reasonably accommodate does not require that an employer's action be motivated by a discriminatory animus directed at the person with a disability.[9] The statute provides that the failure to provide a reasonable accommodation for a qualified individual is actionable discrimination.[10] An employer who has knowledge of an individual's disability but does not provide reasonable accommodations violates Title I, regardless of intent.[11] Accommodations are required at the application and interview stages, as well as on the job.

C. *Failure To Accommodate Claim: Summary*

As illustrated below in detail, to survive a motion for summary judgment on a failure to accommodate claim, a plaintiff typically must show:[12]

- evidence that he is a qualified individual with a disability within the meaning of Title I;[13]

Disabilities Act, 29 C.F.R. pt. 1630 app.; 67 Fed. Reg. 61,757 (Oct. 1, 2002); see also Equal Emp. Opportunity Comm'n, Reasonable Accommodation and Undue Hardship Under the ADA , 8 Fair Emp. Prac. Man. (BNA) 405:7601 (1999) [hereinafter Reasonable Accommodation and Undue Hardship].

[8] See Vande Zande v. St. of Wis. Dept. of Admin., 44 F.3d 538, 542 (7th Cir. 1995) (citations omitted) (noting that reasonable accommodations "is not a legal novelty").

[9] Higgins v. New Balance Athletic Shoe, Inc., 194 F.3d 252, 263-64 (1st Cir. 1999).

[10] Id.; see also Bultemeyer v. Fort Wayne Cmty. Schs., 100 F.3d 1281, 1283-84 (7th Cir. 1996).

[11] See Higgins, 194 F.3d at 264 (noting that the McDonnell Douglas burden shifting scheme therefore is inapposite in respect to failure to accommodate claims (citing Pond v. Michelin N. Am., Inc., 183 F.3d 592, 597 n.5 (7th Cir. 1999); Bultemeyer, 100 F.3d at 1283-84)).

[12] For a summary, see Higgins, 194 F.3d at 264 (citing Kralik v. Durbin, 130 F.3d 76, 78 (3d Cir. 1997); Lyons v. Legal Aid Soc'y, 68 F.3d 1512, 1515 (2d Cir. 1995)).

[13] The accommodation request for an individual's impairment typically is not considered when assessing whether that individual is substantially limited in the major life activity of working. See Black v. Roadway

- he works (or worked) for an employer covered by Title I;

- the employer, despite knowledge of the employee's disability, did not reasonably accommodate the employee; and,

- the employer's failure to accommodate adversely affected plaintiff's employment.

D.   *Accommodation Illustrations*

Neither the statute nor the EEOC regulations provide a bright-line definition of reasonable accommodation.[14]   The EEOC defines a workplace modification as feasible if it "seems reasonable on its face, i.e., ordinarily or in the run of cases,"[15] or if it is feasible and plausible to effectively meet the needs of a qualified person with a disability.[16]

Several alternative scenarios introduce what Title I may require of employers facing two hypothetical job applicants, one disabled under the ADA and one not, in the context of the accommodation process.

Scenario 1: The applicants are identical in terms of education and experience, and each holds necessary licenses and other prerequisites for the position.   The disabled individual can perform (essential and non-essential) job functions without accommodation.   The employer under these circumstances is free to choose the non-disabled applicant, as long as the choice is not based on the other applicant's disability.

Scenario 2: The non-disabled applicant has more education and experience than the disabled individual, who can perform (essential and non-essential) job functions without accommodation. Here, the employer again is free to choose the non-disabled applicant.

Express, Inc., 297 F.3d 445, 451 (6th Cir. 2002) (citing Mondzelewski v. Pathmark Stores, Inc., 162 F.3d 778, 786 (3d Cir. 1998)) (noting a trial court must assess whether a plaintiff is disabled in the major life activity of working without considering the possible mitigating effects of accommodations that may be provided by other relevant and similar employers; in Black, in the case of an individual with a leg impairment, the provision of trucks with cruise control as an accommodation made by other trucking companies was not relevant to determining the case at issue).

[14] See 29 C.F.R. pt. 1630 app., § 1630.2(o)(2) (2003).   For general examples, see Equal Emp. Opportunity Comm'n, The Americans with Disabilities Act: A Primer for Small Business, at http://www.eeoc.gov/ada/adahandbook.html#types (last modified Sept. 10, 2002) [hereinafter EEOC Primer].

[15] Equal Emp. Opportunity Comm'n, ADA Technical Assistance Manual Addendum, at http://www.eeoc.gov/docs/adamanual_add.html (Oct. 29, 2002) (citing U.S. Airways, Inc. v. Barnett, 535 U.S. 391, 401-02 (2002)).

[16] Id.

Scenario 3: The disabled applicant has more education and experience than the non-disabled individual, and does not require accommodation to perform the essential job functions. Here, an employer hiring the non-disabled individual would be violating Title I.

Scenario 4: The disabled applicant has more education and experience than the non-disabled individual, and requires that accommodations be made to perform essential job functions. Here, an employer violates Title I if it refuses to make reasonable accommodations (unless they impose an "undue hardship"), or if it refuses to hire the disabled applicant because of the need to make accommodations.

Empirical evidence suggests that on average, employers facing scenario 1 make hiring decisions without considering individuals' disabilities.[17] The evidence suggests that employers facing scenario 3 hire those persons with disabilities who can perform essential and non-essential job functions, as well as those whose abilities outweigh the costs associated with the employee being unable to perform non-essential functions.[18] Employers facing scenario 4 generally hire only those persons with disabilities whose accommodations pose small costs, or whose wages can be reduced to offset whatever accommodation costs are incurred.[19]

Illustrative examples of accommodation principles in the case law follow.

1.   Workplace attendance, schedule modifications

Workplace attendance (including work schedule modifications) may be an essential job requirement, thereby not subject to reasonable accommodation.[20]   In *Vande Zande v. Wisconsin Department of*

---

[17] See Peter Blanck, The Economics of the Employment Provisions of the Americans with Disabilities Act, in Employment, Disability, and the Americans with Disabilities Act 201, 212 (Peter Blanck, ed., Nw. Univ. Press 2000).

[18] Id. at 213-18.

[19] Id.

[20] Amadio v. Ford Motor Co., 238 F.3d 919, 927 (7th Cir. 2001). The Seventh Circuit has consistently found that plaintiffs who have poor attendance records do not qualify for protection under the ADA. Id. (citing Jovanovic v. In-Sink-Erator Div. of Emerson Elec. Co., 201 F.3d 894, 900 (7th Cir. 2000) (employee missing twenty-four days in past twelve months not qualified); Waggoner v. Olin Corp., 169 F.3d 481, 485 (7th Cir. 1999) (employee missing 5 1/2 months of work, and showing up late or not at all for forty days in a fourteen-month period, not qualified); Corder v. Lucent Techs., Inc., 162 F.3d 924, 928 (7th Cir. 1998) (employee missing eighteen months of work not qualified); Nowak v. St. Rita High Sch., 142 F.3d 999, 1003-04 (7th Cir. 1998) (employee missing eighteen months of work not qualified)).

Administration,[21] the Seventh Circuit held that regular attendance may be required of clerical worker positions as an essential job function. Cases subsequent to *Vande Zande* have held regular attendance as an essential job function in the positions of teacher,[22] account representative,[23] production employee,[24] and plant equipment repairman.[25]

Nevertheless, workplace attendance at the work site is not a per se essential function of every employment position. The requirement that an employee be in workplace attendance is particularly apparent in factory or manufacturing positions "where the work must be done on the employer's premises; maintenance and production functions cannot be performed if the employee is not at work."[26] However, a short medical leave (e.g., one-week), a leave in combination with leave time under the Family Medical Leave Act (FMLA, up to 12 weeks leave), or an insignificant work schedule change that does not affect worker productivity may be a reasonable accommodation in many circumstances.[27]

A leave of absence from work poses a different scenario, and depending on the circumstances, may or may not be a reasonable accommodation. The Eleventh Circuit has held that an indefinite leave of absence is not a reasonable accommodation. In *Wood v. Green*,[28] the Eleventh Circuit concluded that a reasonable accommodation was an accommodation that enables the employee to perform the essential functions of his job presently or in the immediate future.[29] Wood did not seek an accommodation that would allow him to continue his work presently; rather, he sought an indeterminate leave of absence that would allow him to work at a future, indefinite time.[30] Because the ADA covers those individuals who "can perform the essential functions of their jobs presently or in the immediate future," the Eleventh Circuit concluded that Wood was not a qualified individual under the ADA.[31]

---

[21]   Vande Zande v. St. of Wis. Dept. of Admin., 44 F.3d 538, 544 (7th Cir. 1995).

[22]   Nowak, 142 F.3d at 1004.

[23]   Corder, 162 F.3d at 928.

[24]   Waggoner, 169 F.3d at 485.

[25]   Jovanovic, 201 F.3d at 900.

[26]   Amadio v. Ford Motor Co., 238 F.3d 919, 927 (7th Cir. 2001) (quoting Jovanovic, 201 F.3d at 900).

[27]   Id. at 928.

[28]   Wood v. Green, No. 02-12971, 2003 WL 1090412 (11th Cir. Mar. 13, 2003).

[29]   Id. at *3.

[30]   Id. at *4.

[31]   Id.

The length of a requested leave also will affect whether the leave constitutes an undue burden for the employer regarding the expense of replacement workers, the difficulty of shifting tasks, or the difficulty of planning.

2. Home work

Courts generally have taken the position that working at home full time is not a reasonable accommodation. In *Vande Zande*, for example, a woman who was a paraplegic prone to pressure ulcers requested that the company provide her with a desktop computer, and allow her to work full-time at home during an eight week recovery period.[32] The Seventh Circuit held that this request was unreasonable.

The *Vande Zande* court reasoned the employee's job involved teamwork under supervision, and this could not be accomplished at home without substantially diminishing the quality of the employee's performance. Similarly, in *Rauen v. United States Tobacco Manufacturing*,[33] the Seventh Circuit held that a request for a complete home office was unreasonable. The court based this holding on the fact that the employee's job required immediate resolution of issues raised on the spur of the moment.

The prevalent view is that an employer is not required to accommodate an individual with a disability by allowing that person to work at home full time, alone and without supervision.[34] The rationale derives from the notion that an employee who requires significant supervision cannot be adequately supervised at home, and that the quality or productivity of such an employee's work thus may decline significantly.

Time will tell if, as home office technology improves, and working from home becomes more popular, this general rule will hold firm. The D.C. Circuit already has concluded that a request to work at home full time is a reasonable accommodation in the case of a computer programmer who could do his job at home without loss of productivity.[35]

---

[32] Vande Zande v. St. of Wis. Dept. of Admin., 44 F.3d 538, 544-45 (7th Cir. 1995).

[33] Rauen v. U.S. Tobacco Mfg., No. 01-3973, 2003 WL 262477, at *1 (7th Cir. Feb. 10, 2003).

[34] Vande Zande, 44 F.3d at 545; see also Tyndall v. Nat'l Educ. Ctrs., Inc., 31 F.3d 209, 212 (4th Cir. 1994).

[35] See Langdon v. Dep't of Health and Human Servs., 959 F.2d 1053, 1060-61 (D.C. Cir. 1992) (cited in accord in Buckingham v. United States, 998 F.2d 735, 740 (9th Cir. 1993)); see also Carr v. Reno, 23 F.3d 525 (D.C. Cir. 1994).

3. Job reassignment – generally

Title I specifically refers to job reassignment as a reasonable accommodation option. However, the task of explaining what this means, as well as sketching out the parameters of what is required, has fallen largely to the courts.

An employee who develops a disability after being employed may be entitled to reassignment if he cannot perform the essential functions of his current job and be accommodated in his current job. Applicants, as opposed to employees, are not entitled to reassignment and an employer may not require reassignment if a reasonable accommodation is available to allow the employee to do his current job.

An employer may attempt to accommodate an employee by placing him in another position, suggested either by the employee or employer. To be considered a reasonable accommodation, the new job duties must be comparable and not entail a substantial cut in pay.

In using job reassignment as an accommodation, the employer is free to first consider lateral moves to other jobs that are equivalent. An employer may consider a job reassignment to "lesser jobs" that constitute a demotion as an accommodation only if there are no equivalent positions available.[36]

The Seventh Circuit has held that Title I's job reassignment provision (putting aside for the moment the presence of a collective bargaining or seniority agreement, as discussed below) requires an employer to consider the feasibility of reassigning a qualified worker to a different job where the disability is not an impediment to the performance of essential job tasks.[37]

According to the EEOC, reassignment does not involve simply allowing the disabled employee to apply and compete for the open position, but rather transferring said employee to the open position.[38] But nevertheless, the Seventh Circuit has held that the reassignment

---

[36]   Dilley v. SuperValu, Inc., 296 F.3d 958, 964 (10th Cir. 2002).

[37]   EEOC v. Humiston-Keeling, Inc., 227 F.3d 1024, 1028 (7th Cir. 2000).

[38]   Equal Emp. Opportunity Comm'n, Title I Technical Assistance Manual (EEOC-M-1A) No. 24 (1992)); Equal Emp. Opportunity Comm'n, Enforcement Guidance: Reasonable Accommodation and Undue Burden under the Americans with Disabilities Act, Question 29, http://www.eeoc.gov/docs/accommodation.html#reassignment   (Oct.   17,   2002) ("Reassignment means that the employee gets the vacant position if s/he is qualified for it.   Otherwise, reassignment would be of little value and would not be implemented as Congress intended.").

obligation does not require the employer to reject better qualified applicants for the vacant position.[39]

Lastly, an employer is not required to "reassign" an employee with a disability to a promotion to satisfy the duty of accommodation.[40]

4. Job reassignment – collective bargaining or seniority agreement

The job reassignment option is constrained when it would require an employer to violate its bona fide seniority system or the terms of its collective bargaining agreement.[41]

In general, Title I does not require an employer to violate its legitimate seniority provisions to accommodate a qualified employee with a disability. The Supreme Court, in *U.S. Airways v. Barnett*, held such an accommodation to be presumed unreasonable where the seniority or collective bargaining agreement contains bona fide seniority provisions.[42] The Court held that reassignment to another job in direct violation of a company seniority system is unreasonable as a matter of law, absent a special showing by plaintiff to the contrary.[43]

---

[39] Humiston-Keeling, 227 F.3d at 1028.

[40] Id.

[41] Dilley v. SuperValu, Inc., 296 F.3d 958, 963 (10th Cir. 2002) (citing Aldrich v. Boeing Co., 146 F.3d 1265, 1272 n.5 (10th Cir. 1998) ("[H]ad Boeing transferred Aldrich to any of the last three disputed jobs... it would have violated the seniority provisions of the collective bargaining agreement."); Milton v. Scrivner, Inc., 53 F.3d 1118, 1125 (10th Cir. 1995) ("[P]laintiffs' collective bargaining agreement prohibits their transfer to any other job because plaintiffs lack the requisite seniority.")).

[42] See U.S. Airways, Inc. v. Barnett, 535 U.S. 391, 394 (2002) ("[T]o show that a requested accommodation conflicts with the rules of a seniority system is ordinarily to show that the accommodation is not 'reasonable.'") In so holding, the Court followed the lead of many of the Courts of Appeals. See Willis v. Pacific Mar. Ass'n, 236 F.3d 1160, 1166 (9th Cir. 2001) (holding that "the per se rule that we adopt today for this circuit is only applicable where there is a direct conflict between the proposed accommodation and the collectively-bargained seniority rights of other employees"); id. at 1164 (citing other federal circuits in accord: Davis v. Fla. Power & Light Co., 205 F.3d 1301, 1307 (11th Cir. 2000); Feliciano v. Rhode Island, 160 F.3d 780, 787 (1st Cir. 1998); Cassidy v. Detroit Edison Co., 138 F.3d 629, 634 (6th Cir. 1998); Kralik v. Durbin, 130 F.3d 76, 81-83 (3d Cir. 1997); Foreman v. Babcock & Wilcox Co., 117 F.3d 800, 810 (5th Cir. 1997); Eckles v. Consol. Rail Corp., 94 F.3d 1041, 1051 (7th Cir. 1996); Benson v. Northwest Airlines, Inc., 62 F.3d 1108, 1114 (8th Cir. 1995); Milton v. Scrivner, Inc., 53 F.3d 1118, 1125 (10th Cir. 1995)).

[43] Barnett, 535 U.S. at 406.

Thus, a showing that the accommodation of reassignment would violate the rules of a seniority system typically warrants summary judgment for the employer, "unless there is more."[44] According to the Court, the plaintiff bears the burden of showing that special circumstances surrounding the case demonstrate the reasonableness of the assignment.[45] Once the plaintiff has made this showing, the employer then must show evidence of case-specific circumstances that demonstrate undue hardship.

The *Barnett* decision, however, is limited to an actual, as opposed to a potential, violation of a seniority system. In *Dilley v. SuperValu*,[46] the employer SuperValu did not contend that the plaintiff lacked the seniority to be placed in a non-lifting driver position at the company, but that the seniority system would be violated if a more senior employee subsequently requested the plaintiff's new reassigned position, and the employer left the plaintiff in that position.[47] The Tenth Circuit held that the *Barnett* rule does not apply in such situations, wherein only potential violations of the seniority system exist.

5.   Company policies, discipline and termination

The case law under the ADA has not developed a comfortable balance between the ADA's reasonable accommodation standard and an employer's ability to enforce company policies, discipline, and termination decisions. Were it possible to establish a general "rule" or common approach that unifies the ADA's and employers' policies, it would most likely maintain that the ADA's reasonable accommodation standard does not require an employer to abandon "legitimate and non-discriminatory" company policies.[48] But, of course, this "rule" only can go so far in deciding the hard cases.

---

44   Id.

45   Id. at 406 (noting that special circumstances may exist where an employer retains the right to alter, or has altered, the seniority system unilaterally, therefore making a single exception to the seniority system to accommodate a disabled employee may be required).

46   Dilley v. SuperValu, Inc., 296 F.3d 958, 963-64 (10th Cir. 2002).

47   Id. (noting that SuperValu's witness testified that Dilley ranked fifth out of forty-two drivers in seniority; and the jury could have concluded that the prospect of Dilley's displacement by a more senior driver was remote).

48   See, e.g., EEOC v. Sara Lee Corp., 237 F.3d 349, 354 (4th Cir. 2001); id. (citing in accord Burns v. Coca-Cola Enters., 222 F.3d 247, 257 (6th Cir. 2000) ("Employers are not required to ... violate other employees' rights under a collective bargaining agreement or other non-discriminatory policy in order to accommodate a disabled individual."); Cravens v. Blue Cross and Blue Shield of Kansas City, 214 F.3d 1011,

The Supreme Court dealt with this tension in *Barnett*. There, it held that, in the run of cases, a company's seniority system trumps a conflicting accommodation demand. Sometimes, therefore, a requested accommodation may violate a "disability-neutral" workplace rule, such as a seniority rule, and provide the job applicant or employee with a disability accommodation with "treatment that other workers could not receive."[49]

But the Court was clear that asking for a difference in treatment in the face of a "neutral" rule would not always make an accommodation unreasonable. If that were not the rule, the Court concluded:

> Neutral office assignment rules would automatically prevent the accommodation of an employee whose disability-imposed limitations require him to work on the ground floor. Neutral "break-from-work" rules would automatically prevent the accommodation of an individual who needs additional breaks from work, perhaps to permit medical visits. Neutral furniture budget rules would automatically prevent the accommodation of an individual who needs a different kind of chair or desk.[50]

To be sure, the ADA is not a license for "insubordination in the workplace."[51] Despite a covered disability and a request for a reasonable accommodation, an employee may be disciplined or terminated for behavior that is not consistent with a normal workplace, such as, for

---

1020 (8th Cir. 2000) ("[T]he employer is generally not required to transfer a disabled employee if such reassignment would violate ... a legitimate, non-discriminatory policy of the employer.") (internal quotations omitted); Aka v. Wash. Hosp. Ctr., 156 F.3d 1284, 1305 (D.C. Cir. 1998) (en banc) ("An employer is not required to reassign a disabled employee in circumstances when such a transfer would violate a legitimate, nondiscriminatory policy of the employer.") (internal quotations omitted); Daugherty v. City of El Paso, 56 F.3d 695, 700 (5th Cir. 1995) ("[W]e do not read the ADA as requiring affirmative action in favor of individuals with disabilities, in the sense of requiring that disabled persons be given priority in hiring or reassignment over those who are not disabled.")).

[49] U.S. Airways, Inc. v. Barnett, 535 U.S. 391, 397 (2002).

[50] Id. Most employers have neutral rules governing the kinds of actions most needed to reasonably accommodate a worker with a disability. See 42 U.S.C. § 12111(9)(b) (2000) (setting forth examples such as "job restructuring," "part-time or modified work schedules," "acquisition or modification of equipment or devices," "and other similar accommodations").

[51] See Reed v. Le Page Bakeries, 141 F.3d 667, 668 (7th Cir. 1998).

example, threatening behavior toward co-workers or supervisors.[52] Similarly, an employee with alcoholism may be terminated for related behavior that is unacceptable in the workplace, even when that behavior is a result of alcoholism.[53] Employers are allowed to have drug and alcohol free workplaces.[54]

However, it would be incorrect to suggest that employment policies and rules – even non-discriminatory ones – are not completely subject to the reasonable accommodation requirement. The EEOC guidance indicates that modifying workplace rules for a qualified employee with a disability often is considered a reasonable accommodation. The Guidance suggests that allowing an employee with a psychiatric impairment more frequent breaks during the work day, but not more break time in the aggregate, may be a reasonable and cost-effective accommodation.[55] The Guidance also suggests that although the reasonable accommodation requirement does not require an employer to provide an employee with a new supervisor, it may require an alteration of supervisory methods.[56]

Moreover, certain facially valid company employment policies may be invalid as applied under the ADA. In *Hernandez v. Hughes Missile*

---

[52] See id. (upholding termination of employee with bipolar disorder after employee threatened supervisor).

[53] For example, recently Larry Eustachy, the former head basketball coach at the Iowa State, generated some publicity after he was photographed at a college party holding a beer can while kissing and being kissed by young women on the cheek. During the time period in which his job status was uncertain as a result of this conduct, Eustachy revealed that he was being treated for alcoholism. Some suggested that if it could be shown the effects of the alcoholism caused Eustachy to violate his contract, it would be possible that the ADA would protect him from the University terminating his employment. Others, including one of the authors of this treatise, disagreed. See Sports Illustrated.com, Fighting for His Job: Despite AD's Action, Eustachy Trying to Keep ISU Post (May 2, 2003), http://sportsillustrated.cnn.com/basketball/college/news/2003/05/01/eustachy_update_ap/.

[54] See U.S. Equal Emp. Opportunity Comm'n, Enforcement Guidance on Disability-Related Inquiries and Medical Examinations of Employees Under the Americans with Disabilities Act, http://www.eeoc.gov/docs/guidance-inquiries.html (Sept. 27, 2000) [hereinafter Inquiries and Medical Examinations].

[55] Equal Emp. Opportunity Comm'n, Enforcement Guidance on the Americans with Disabilities Act and Psychiatric Disabilities, at http://www.eeoc.gov/docs/psych.html (Mar. 25, 1997) [hereinafter Psychiatric Disabilities].

[56] Id.

Systems Co.,[57] the plaintiff worked as a technician for Hughes.[58] During his employment, he was addicted to drugs and alcohol, and eventually tested positive for cocaine. The plaintiff was given the option to resign in lieu of termination, which he chose to do.[59] Hernandez did not challenge the legality of this action on the basis of his then-current drug use.

Two years later, Hernandez applied to be rehired with Hughes, attaching a letter from his counselor to his application. His counselor indicated Hernandez had been attending AA and staying sober. Hughes declined to rehire the plaintiff based on an unwritten policy of not rehiring former employees whose employment had ended due to termination or resignation in lieu of termination.[60] The Ninth Circuit found this facially neutral policy could be discriminatory if Hughes regarded Hernandez as being disabled – by virtue of being a previous drug and alcohol user – at the time it failed to rehire him.[61] The Ninth Circuit found that Hughes had an obligation to determine the underlying reason for the plaintiff's resignation and to accommodate him by modifying its no-rehire policy if the original reason was disability-related.

The Supreme Court has granted certiorari in this case.[62] The analysis is clearer when the emotional elements, such as the involvement of drug use, is absent. Let us apply the analysis to a less inflammatory hypothetical case, such as that of an individual with Tourette Syndrome who worked as a sales associate for a store. Assume he was terminated because his disability prevented him from interacting with customers appropriately. If, after successfully seeking treatment for his disability, he seeks re-hiring, may the store apply its general rule against hiring former employees who were fired, or must it reasonably accommodate him by waiving the general rule?

The Ninth Circuit's analysis would require the employer to change the rule to avoid regarding the employee as disabled. As a policy matter, allowing the employer to rely on its previous disability-based decision, although legal, inappropriately perpetuates the effects of the disability. The Ninth Circuit likely would require the employer to review the employee's record, determine if the termination was disability-based, and, if so, waive the no-rehire rule.

However, this approach arguably conflicts with other requirements of the ADA. If the store has complied with its

---

[57] Hernandez v. Hughes Missile Sys. Co., 298 F.3d 1030, 1034 (9th Cir. 2002).

[58] Id. at 1032.

[59] Id.

[60] Id.

[61] Id. at 1036.

[62] See Raytheon Co. v. Hernandez, 123 S.Ct. 1255 (2003).

confidentiality obligations, there will be no reference to the employee's disability in his personnel file.[63] Therefore, it will be difficult to ascertain whether the termination was disability-related. Moreover, requiring this effort to discover an applicant's disability conflicts with the purpose of the ADA's prohibition on pre-employment inquiries.[64] The ADA intends for hidden disabilities to remain hidden.

Seen from this perspective, the Supreme Court may decide the *Hernandez* case for either party. However, given the burden the Ninth Circuit's approach places on employers, and the affirmative advantage it would give disabled applicants over non-disabled ones, the Court is likely to reverse the Ninth Circuit.

6.   Job rotation

Most courts have held that it is not a reasonable accommodation to require an employer to create new jobs tailored to an employee with a disability.[65] Where an employer shows a business purpose in rotating its manual workers through positions on its assembly line, an employee with a disability will be considered not "otherwise qualified" if she is unable to perform one or more of the individual positions.[66]

The unreasonableness of a proposed accommodation that compromises an employer's job rotation scheme is magnified where that system is the employer's norm and serves a legitimate business purpose. It is ordinarily not discriminatory (nor a pretext to avoid ADA obligations) when an employer's mandatory job rotation system is used to reduce the risk of injury caused by long-term repetition of particular motions.

Similarly, it would not necessarily violate Title I for an employer to require that every worker be qualified to perform each essential task on a production line. This is particularly true where job rotation is shown to facilitate production tasks by making it easier for the employer to substitute among workers when injury occurs, when some take leave or are absent, or during peak production periods when employees must perform all tasks.[67]

---

[63] 29 C.F.R. § 1630.14 (2003).

[64] 42 U.S.C. § 12112(a)(2) (2000).

[65] Watson v. Lithonia Lighting, 304 F.3d 749, 751 (7th Cir. 2002) (citing in accord Mays v. Principi, 301 F.3d 866 (7th Cir. 2002); Hansen v. Henderson, 233 F.3d 521, 523-24 (7th Cir. 2000)).

[66] Id. (citing 42 U.S.C. § 12112(b)(5)(A)).

[67] Id; see also Barnard v. ADM Milling Co., Inc., 987 F.Supp. 1337, 1343 (D. Kan. 1997) (accommodation which results in other employees having to work longer hours or to work harder in the same time is not reasonable and therefore not required).

7. "Light duty" positions

An employer may need to establish a pool of light duty positions as an accommodation.[68] Historically, the primary function of light duty work is to enable an injured employee to continue to work after injury.

The ADA does not require an employer who establishes light duty positions for employees with disabilities (for instance, recovering from a workplace injury) to maintain these positions indefinitely. This may be particularly true when an employee's "recovery" period has ended without restoration to original health and work capabilities.[69]

8. Equipment modifications/computer technology/accessible materials

Purchasing equipment or modifying existing equipment is a form of accommodation when it enables the job applicant or employee with a disability to perform essential job functions. Whether involving acquisition or modification of equipment or provision of other workplace changes, an equipment modification is not required where it would prevent the employee from conducting an essential job function.[70]

As an example, the ability to contact the public by telephone would be an essential job function for many occupations. An accommodation would be to provide the employee with access to a TTY system to call a relay service operator (who then places the telephone call and relays the conversation between the parties).

New technology has revolutionized the range of available accommodations.[71] This has become especially significant with the growing prevalence of computers in the everyday workplace. Computer technologies accommodate for the physical limitations inherent in some disabilities – for example, while people without finger dexterity can use voice-recognition software to run a computer, people with vision impairments may use software to make their computers read documents

---

[68] See Hendricks-Robinson v. Excel Corp., 154 F.3d 685, 696 (7th Cir. 1998)); Dalton v. Subaru-Isuzu Auto., Inc., 141 F.3d 667, 680 (7th Cir. 1998).

[69] Dalton, 141 F.3d at 680.

[70] Gilbert v. Frank, 949 F.2d 637, 643 (2d Cir. 1991).

[71] See generally David Klein et al., Electronic Doors to Education: Study of High School Website Accessibility in Iowa, 21 Behav. Sci. & L. 27 (2003); Heather Ritchie & Peter Blanck, The Promise of the Internet for Disability: A Study of Online Services and Web Site Accessibility of Centers for Independent Living Web Sites, 20 Behav. Sci. & L. 5 (2003); Kevin Schartz et al., Employment of Persons with Disabilities in Information Technology Jobs: for Individuals with Disabilities: Literature Review for "IT Works," 20 Behav. Sci. & L. 637 (2002).

aloud, and those with severe speech impairments may use software that allows them to "speak" through the computer by using a keyboard.[72]

Apart from accommodations provided by technologies, computers play a role in increasing the productivity levels of people with disabilities.[73] Among people with spinal cord injuries (SCIs), for instance, those using computers prior to the SCI had more rapid returns to work.[74]

Another potential accommodation would be the distribution of work-related materials (written or otherwise) in an alternative format such as an electronic file, Braille — one could even have a co-worker read or explain written materials.[75]

9.　　Provision of services such as interpreters, job coaches

The EEOC's Interpretative Guidance endorses the reasonable accommodations of sign interpreters, video describers, or other such aids for qualified applicants or employees with sensory impairments. The EEOC also endorses as an accommodation "supported employment" strategies that include providing a temporary job coach to assist a qualified individual with a cognitive disability, absent undue hardship.[76]

The EEOC provides an example of an employee with mental retardation who is qualified for the position and may obtain a job coach as an accommodation. This strategy can help the worker learn and maintain essential job tasks.[77]

---

[72]　See, e.g., Abledata, Welcome to ABLEDATA, the Premier Source for Information on Assistive Technology!, at http://www.abledata.com (last visited Sept. 22, 2003).

[73]　See, e.g., Peter Blanck et al., Calibrating the Impact of the ADA's Employment Provisions, 14 Stan. L. & Pol'y Rev. 267, 284 (2003).

[74]　Doug Kruse & Alan Krueger, Nat'l Bureau of Econ. Research, Labor Market Effects of Spinal Cord Injuries in the Dawn of the Computer Age Working Paper No. 5302, http://www.nber.org/papers/w5302.pdf (Oct. 1995). Despite the positive effects of computer use on the employment and earnings of people with SCI, they still are less likely than other workers to be computer users and receive computer training following the injury. See Doug Kruse et al., Computer Use, Computer Training, and Employment Outcomes Among People with Spinal Cord Injuries, 21 Spine, 891, 891-896 (1996).

[75]　For other examples, see EEOC Primer, supra note 14.

[76]　Psychiatric Disabilities, supra note 55; see also Peter Blanck, The Americans with Disabilities Act and the Emerging Workforce: Employment of People with Mental Retardation 46-47 (1998) (discussing job coaching as a reasonable accommodation).

[77]　See EEOC Primer, supra note 14.

In *EEOC v. Hertz*,[78] a court ruled that, for a Hertz employee with mental retardation, a temporary job coach providing job training might be a reasonable accommodation.[79] However, the court found that the provision of a full-time job coach who provides more than training (e.g., performs essential job functions) is not an accommodation within reason because the employee is, by definition, not a qualified individual.[80]

§ 8.2 The Process

A. *The Request*

To be eligible for an accommodation, an employee must make his disability known to the employer and request an accommodation.[81] Reasonable accommodations must be provided to qualified job applicants and employees whether they work part-time or full-time, or are

---

[78] EEOC v. Hertz, 1998 WL 5694, at *2 (E.D. Mich., Jan. 6, 1998) (noting that supported employment, which applies "to a wide variety of programs to assist individuals with severe disabilities in both competitive and non-competitive employment, is not synonymous with reasonable accommodation" (quoting 29 C.F.R. pt. 1630, app. § 1630.9)).

[79] See Miami Univ. v. Ohio Civil Rights Comm'n, 726 N.E.2d 1032, 1043 (Ohio App. 12 Dist., 1999) (accommodation of job coach was reasonable for plaintiff with mental retardation who did not require job coaching beyond the first week or so in any of her previous jobs).

[80] Hertz, 1998 WL 5694, at *5 (citing Ricks v. Xerox Corp., 877 F.Supp. 1477 (D. Kan. 1995) (an employee's request for a full-time "helper" to assist in the performance of the essential functions of his job was unreasonable as a matter of law); Gilbert v. Frank, 949 F.2d 637, 643 (2d Cir. 1991) (not reasonable to have two people performing the same tasks normally performed by one)).

[81] Reed v. LePage Bakeries, Inc., 244 F.3d 254, 258-61 (1st Cir. 2001). The request need not be phrased in terms of "reasonable modification" or any other particular language. The employee need not identify the particular change needed. However, the employee must identify her disability and its affect on her job performance. The accommodation request must be "sufficiently direct and specific," giving notice that she needs a "special accommodation." Wynne v. Tufts Univ., 976 F.2d 791, 795 (1st Cir. 1992) (quoting Nathanson v. Med. Coll. of Pa., 926 F.2d 1368, 1381 (3d Cir. 1991)). At a minimum, the request must explain how the proposed accommodation is linked to some disability. "The employer has no duty to divine the need for a special accommodation where the employee merely makes a mundane request for a change at the workplace." See Reasonable Accommodation and Undue Hardship, supra note 7, at A.9, Example B (1999) (request for new office chair because current one is "uncomfortable" does not provide sufficient notice that accommodation is needed due to a disability).

probationary employees.[82] The accommodation requirement places a particular burden on an individual with a hidden and non-obvious impairment to disclose the claimed disability and request the employer to provide an accommodation.[83]

An employee need not make the accommodation request before accepting the job or when she first begins the job. She may attempt to work without accommodation and only request accommodation if she finds she cannot perform the job without it. However, she may face normal discipline for any performance failures prior to the request.[84]

Generally, an employer may not instigate the reasonable accommodation process itself or impose accommodations on an employee.

---

[82] U.S. Equal Emp. Opportunity Commission, Enforcement Guidance: Application of EEOC Laws to Contingent Workers Placed by Temporary Employment Agencies and Other Staffing Firms (Notice No. 915,002), at 8 FEP Man. (BNA) 405:7551 (Dec. 3, 1997), available at http://www.eeoc.gov/docs/conting.html (discussing accommodation requirements for contingent workers).

[83] But it is still a process that places obligations on both parties. See Bultemeyer v. Fort Wayne Cmty. Schs., 100 F.3d 1281, 1285 (7th Cir. 1996) ("properly participating in the interactive process means that an employer cannot expect an employee to read its mind and know that he or she must specifically say 'I want a reasonable accommodation,' particularly when the employee has a mental illness."). Moreover, "[t]he employer has to meet the employee half-way, and if it appears that the employee may need an accommodation but doesn't know how to ask for it, the employer should do what it can to help." Id.

[84] See EEOC Enforcement Guidance: Reasonable Accommodation and Undue Hardship Under the Americans with Disabilities Act, at Question 4, http://www.eeoc.gov/docs/accommodation.html (Oct. 17, 2002). Generally, an applicant or employee can request an accommodation at any time. The ADA

> does not preclude an employee with a disability from requesting a reasonable accommodation because s/he did not ask for one when applying for a job or after receiving a job offer. Rather, an individual with a disability should request a reasonable accommodation when s/he knows that there is a workplace barrier that is preventing him/her, due to a disability, from effectively competing for a position, performing a job, or gaining equal access to a benefit of employment. As a practical matter, it may be in an employee's interest to request a reasonable accommodation before performance suffers or conduct problems occur.

Id.

An employee is not required to use particular language when requesting an accommodation. There are no magic words; an employee need only "inform the employer of the need for an adjustment due to a medical condition."[85]

Once an accommodation request is made, an employer generally may not disclose to co-workers or others that an employee is receiving a reasonable accommodation.[86] The exceptions to the ADA confidentiality requirements include the following: supervisors and managers may be told about restrictions on the work duties of the employee and about necessary accommodations; safety personnel may be informed; and government officials investigating ADA compliance may be provided appropriate information.[87]

In addition, a plaintiff likely will lose on a failure to accommodate claim if he does not request accommodation until after termination.[88] Similarly, an employee cannot dictate exactly which reasonable accommodation he wants. An employer is not obligated to provide the specific accommodation requested or preferred by the applicant or employee, but only a reasonable accommodation.[89] In *Webster v. Methodist Occupational Health Ctrs., Inc.*,[90] the Seventh Circuit concluded that an employee cannot refuse all accommodations during the interactive process, suggest a different accommodation after dismissal, and then claim the employer has a duty to consider that accommodation.

---

[85] Barnett v. U.S. Airways, Inc., 228 F.3d 1105, 1114 n.5, 1115 (9th Cir. 2000) (en banc).

[86] See 42 U.S.C. § 12112(d)(3)(B), (d)(4)(C) (2000); 29 C.F.R. § 1630.14(b)(1) (2003).

[87] In addition, the EEOC has interpreted Title I to allow employers to disclose medical information in accordance with state workers' compensation laws and for insurance purposes. See 29 C.F.R. § 1630.14(b); see also Enforcement Guidance on Pre-employment Inquiries Under the Americans with Disabilities Act, 8 Fair Emp. Prac. Man. (BNA) 405:7191, 7193-94 (1995).

[88] Amadio v. Ford Motor Co., 238 F.3d 919, 929 (7th Cir. 2001) (concluding that an employee cannot wait until after dismissal to inform an employer of his disability and then request an accommodation for the first time).

[89] See Zivkovic v. S. Cal. Edison Co., 302 F.3d 1080, 1089 (9th Cir. 2002); EEOC v. Yellow Freight Sys. Inc., 253 F.3d 943, 951 (7th Cir. 2001) (en banc); Barnett, 228 F.3d at 1115 (requiring the selected accommodation to be reasonable and effective).

[90] Webster v. Methodist Occupational Health Ctrs., Inc., 141 F.3d 1236, 1238 (7th Cir. 1998).

B.   *Interactive Process*

Once the accommodation request is made, the ADA requires a consultative "interactive process." In this process, the employer retains the right to choose the accommodation according to its reasonable effectiveness and the employee's good faith opportunity to participate in the process.

At this point, an employer may request supporting documentation of the disability from an appropriate professional, such as a doctor or rehabilitation counselor, in furtherance of the consultative process.[91]

The EEOC regulations note that the interactive process should "identify the precise limitations resulting from the disability and potential reasonable accommodations that could overcome those limitations."[92]

The EEOC's implementing regulations state: "To determine the appropriate reasonable accommodation it may be necessary for the covered entity to initiate an informed, interactive process with the qualified individual with a disability in need of the accommodation."[93] Furthermore, the employer must make a reasonable effort to determine the appropriate accommodation. The reasonable accommodation is best determined through a flexible, interactive process that involves the employer and the disabled employee.[94]

The interactive process requires direct and good faith communication between the employer and the qualified individual, consideration of the request, and an offer of an accommodation that is reasonable and effective.[95]

Most federal courts of appeal have endorsed the interactive process.[96] In *Mengine v. Runyon*,[97] for instance, the Third Circuit explained that the process furthers the purposes of the ADA because employers typically do not know the job abilities of qualified individuals

---

[91]   See Vinson v. Thomas, 288 F.3d 1145, 1153 (9th Cir. 2002); Grenier v. Cyanamid Plastics, Inc., 70 F.3d 667, 674 (1st Cir. 1995) (citing Inquiries and Medical Examinations, supra note 54).

[92]   29 C.F.R. § 1630.2(o)(3) (2003).

[93]   Id. § 1630.2(o)(3).

[94]   Id. § 1630.9.

[95]   Id. §§ 1630.2(o)(3); 1630.9.

[96]   See U.S. Airways, Inc. v. Barnett, 535 U.S. 391, 407 (2002) (Stevens, J., concurring) (noting that the Ninth Circuit's holding with respect to interactive process was "correct" and "is untouched by the Court's opinion").

[97]   Mengine v. Runyon, 114 F.3d 415, 420 (3d Cir. 1997).

with disabilities, and an applicant or worker may not be aware of the available employment opportunities or job requirements.[98]

An employer who does not engage in the interactive process proceeds at its peril, and the evidentiary deck will be stacked against it. The Ninth Circuit has held that a failure to participate in the interactive process may preclude an employer from obtaining summary judgment on an ADA failure to accommodate claim.[99]

The EEOC recognizes that, as part of this process, an employer may be forced to disclose confidential medical information about its job applicants or employees with disabilities to supervisors and managers when necessary for the development of an effective accommodation.[100]

The interactive *process* is just that, a process. The Ninth Circuit has held that the duty to accommodate is an ongoing duty that is "not exhausted by one effort."[101] In *Humphrey v. Memorial Hospitals Association*, the court stated the goal of the accommodation process:

> [T]he employer's obligation to engage in the interactive process extends beyond the first attempt at accommodation and continues when the employee asks for a different accommodation or where the employer is aware that the initial accommodation is failing and further accommodation is needed. This rule fosters the framework of cooperative problem-solving contemplated by the ADA, by encouraging employers to seek to find accommodations that really work, and by avoiding the creation of a perverse incentive for employees to request the most drastic and burdensome

---

[98]   Lovejoy-Wilson v. NOCO Motor Fuel, Inc., 263 F.3d 208, 218-19 (2d Cir. 2001) ("[t]he ADA envisions an 'interactive process' by which employers and employees work together to assess whether an employee's disability can be reasonably accommodated." Jackan v. N.Y. St. Dep't of Lab., 205 F.3d 562, 566 (2d Cir. 2000) (citing Beck v. Univ. of Wis. Bd. of Regents, 75 F.3d 1130, 1135 (7th Cir. 1996); 29 C.F.R. § 1630.2(o)(3)).

[99]   See Barnett v. U.S. Airways, Inc., 228 F.3d 1105, 1112 (9th Cir. 2000) (en banc), vacated on other grounds, 535 U.S. 391, 407 (2002). Similarly, California law provides that an employer's failure to engage in the interactive process, alone, constitutes a violation. Cal. Gov. Code 12926(e) (2003).

[100] EEOC Primer, supra note 14.

[101] Humphrey v. Mem'l Hosps. Ass'n, 239 F.3d 1128, 1138 (9th Cir. 2001) (citing McAlindin v. County of San Diego, 192 F.3d 1226, 1237 (9th Cir. 1999), amended, 201 F.3d 1211 (9th Cir. 1999), cert. denied, 530 U.S. 1243 (2000)).

accommodation possible out of fear that a lesser accommodation might be ineffective.[102]

C.   *Accommodation For "Regarded As" Disability*

On its face, Title I's reasonable accommodation requirement does not distinguish between the rights of those individuals with actual disabilities and those individuals who are "regarded as" having a disability or have a "record" of disability. But do employers have a duty to accommodate employees who do not actually have a covered disability but fall into one of the latter two categories?

The majority rule is that they do not. This view holds that an employer need only accommodate actual disabilities.[103] In *Weber v. Strippit*, the Eighth Circuit concluded:

> The reasonable accommodation requirement is easily applied in a case of an actual disability. … The reasonable accommodation requirement makes considerably less sense in the perceived disability context. Imposing liability on employers who fail to accommodate non-disabled employees who are simply regarded as disabled would lead to bizarre results.[104]

This approach leaves individuals with mitigated impairments that do not "substantially limit" them under the *Sutton* test with no recourse. In order to mitigate their conditions, they may need accommodations, such as breaks on which to take medication or meals, but they will not be entitled to accommodation as long as they are using the mitigating measure.   Only when they actually miss a dose, suffer the health consequences and become substantially limited, will they be entitled to accommodation. People with conditions that can be mitigated often face a

---

[102] Id.

[103] Weber v. Strippit, Inc., 186 F.3d 907, 915 (8th Cir. 1999).   For additional discussion, see Mack v. Great Dane Trailers, 2002 WL 31367863, at *5 n.2 (7th Cir. 2002) (stating that although plaintiff may have been able to perform particular work with accommodations – e.g., being excused from tasks requiring heavy lifting – accommodation is not required if the employee is not covered by the statute – therefore employer's failure to accommodate does not suggest that it necessarily regarded plaintiff as disabled; but not deciding whether there is any duty to accommodate an employee who is not actually disabled but is regarded as disabled).

[104] Weber, 186 F.3d at 916. In accord, "regarded as" disabled plaintiffs are not entitled to reasonable accommodations. Workman v. Frito-Lay, Inc., 165 F.3d 460, 467 (6th Cir. 1999); Newberry v. E. Tex. St. Univ., 161 F.3d 276, 280 (5th Cir 1998).

Catch-22 in which they must stop using their mitigation to be entitled to use it.[105]

The First Circuit has endorsed the possibility of accommodation for a regarded as plaintiff in certain circumstances (e.g., employer's knowledge of employee's heart attack).[106] The court reasoned that the language of Title I does not distinguish between "regarded as" disabled plaintiffs and actually disabled plaintiffs in defining who is a qualified individual.[107]

The court also reasoned that the Act's legislative history supports the conclusion that Congress wanted "regarded as" plaintiffs with impairments to be entitled to accommodations. Under this view, the employer's obligation to engage in the "interactive process" is triggered when the employer regards an employee who has requested an accommodation as disabled.[108]

§ 8.3 Undue Hardship

A common critique of Title I is that accommodations for qualified individuals create economic hardships that are costly and burdensome for employers. The statutory mechanism for dealing with this criticism is the "undue hardship" defense.

Employers only are required to make accommodations that do not impose undue hardships on them.[109] An undue hardship is a significant difficulty or expense when considered in light of various factors (discussed

---

[105] In fact, some courts would not even allow that desperate approach. In *Hein v. All American Plywood Co., Inc.*, 232 F.3d 482 (6th Cir. 2000), the court ruled against a plaintiff on an accommodation claim because he did not take his medication. Id. at 488.

[106] Katz v. City Metal Co., Inc., 87 F.3d 26, 33-34 (1st Cir. 1996).

[107] Nevertheless, see Barker v. Int'l Paper Co., 993 F.Supp. 10, 14 (D. Me. 1998) (individuals with a relationship or association with a person with a disability typically are not entitled to receive reasonable accommodation (citing Den Hartog v. Wasatch Acad., 129 F.3d 1076, 1084 (10th Cir. 1997))).

[108] For a detailed analysis, see Jacques v. DiMarzio, Inc., 200 F.Supp.2d 151, 166-67 (E.D.N.Y. 2002); id. (citing H.R. Rep. 101-485(III), 1990 U.S.C.C.A.N. 445, 453 and School Bd. of Nassau County v. Arline, 480 U.S. 273, 284 (1987). Arline held "that a [teacher] suffering from the contagious disease of tuberculosis can be a handicapped person within the meaning of § 504 of the Rehabilitation Act of 1973" and entitled to reasonable accommodation. Arline, 480 U.S. at 289.

[109] Morton v. United Parcel Serv., Inc., 272 F.3d 1249, 1257 (9th Cir. 2001) (citing 42 U.S.C. § 12112(b)(5)(A)).

below). The undue hardship analysis is "a fact-intensive inquiry, rarely suitable for resolution on summary judgment."[110]

Undue hardship is an affirmative defense that must be raised and proved by the employer. The degree of the difficulty of accommodation, central to the undue hardship analysis, will turn on evidence regarding the accommodation expense, compared to the firm's size and resources.[111] When determining undue hardship in the application and interview stage of employment, only the cost of providing the accommodation in the application or interview, not the cost for the full course of employment, may be considered. For example, providing a sign language interpreter every day of work may be an undue hardship, whereas providing an interpreter for an interview may not. At that interview, the applicant then may explain that she will not need an interpreter every day on the job.

An employer may not claim undue hardship based on other employees' or customers' fears or prejudices. Also, undue hardship may not be based on the view that an accommodation might have a negative impact on the morale of co-workers.[112]

A.   *Statutory Definition*

Title I defines undue hardship in detailed but inexact terms. The definition is:

(A) In general

The term "undue hardship" means an action requiring significant difficulty or expense, when considered in light of the factors set forth in subparagraph (B).

(B) Factors to be considered

In determining whether an accommodation would impose an undue hardship on a covered entity, factors to be considered include:

(i) the nature and cost of the accommodation needed under this chapter;

(ii) the overall financial resources of the facility or facilities involved in the provision of the reasonable accommodation; the number of persons employed at such facility; the effect on expenses and resources, or the impact otherwise of such accommodation upon the operation of the facility;

---

[110] Id.

[111] Lovejoy-Wilson v. NOCO Motor Fuel, Inc., 263 F.3d 208, 221 (2d Cir. 2001).

[112] See 29 C.F.R. pt. 1630, app., § 1630.15(d) (2003).

(iii) the overall financial resources of the covered entity; the overall size of the business of a covered entity with respect to the number of its employees; the number, type, and location of its facilities; and

(iv) the type of operation or operations of the covered entity, including the composition, structure, and functions of the workforce of such entity; the geographic separateness, administrative, or fiscal relationship of the facility or facilities in question to the covered entity.

B.   *EEOC Regulations*

The EEOC regulations expand on the statutory definition. They define undue hardship in regard to accommodation as:

(1)... significant difficulty or expense incurred by a covered entity, when considered in light of the factors set forth in paragraph (p)(2) of this section.

(2) Factors to be considered. In determining whether an accommodation would impose an undue hardship on a covered entity, factors to be considered include:

(i)   The nature and net cost of the accommodation needed under this part, taking into consideration the availability of tax credits and deductions, and/or outside funding;

(ii) The overall financial resources of the facility or facilities involved in the provision of the reasonable accommodation, the number of persons employed at such facility, and the effect on expenses and resources;

(iii) The overall financial resources of the covered entity, the overall size of the business of the covered entity with respect to the number of its employees, and the number, type and location of its facilities;

(iv) The type of operation or operations of the covered entity, including the composition, structure and functions of the workforce of such entity, and the geographic separateness and administrative or fiscal relationship of the facility or facilities in question to the covered entity; and

(v) The impact of the accommodation upon the operation of the facility, including the impact on the ability of other employees to perform their duties and the impact on the facility's ability to conduct business.

§ 8.4 Burdens Of Production And Proof

A. *Relationship Between Reasonable Accommodation And Undue Hardship*

In many ways, reasonable accommodation and undue hardship are flipsides of the same coin. For the most part, an accommodation will be reasonable as long as it does not cause an undue hardship on the employer (and no other affirmative defense applies). Courts have created a judicial model that gives structure to this by allocating the burdens of proof differently as to reasonable accommodation and undue hardship. [113]

Federal courts of appeal generally have concluded that the qualified applicant or employee bears the burden of production to show that an accommodation is possible.[114] When a plaintiff produces evidence "sufficient to make a facial showing that accommodation is possible, the burden of production shifts to the employer to present evidence of its inability to accommodate."[115] Where an employer does not engage in the interactive process, the burden of proof shifts from the employee to the employer concerning the availability of an accommodation.[116]

Ordinarily, a plaintiff cannot pursue a claim for failure to accommodate without showing that an accommodation within reason existed. This is where the interactive process, discussed above, becomes important from an evidentiary perspective. A plaintiff likely will lose a claim where he causes a breakdown of interactive process, for example, by

---

[113] For a full discussion of this issue, see Reed v. LePage Bakeries, Inc., 244 F.3d 254, 258-61 (1st Cir. 2001).

[114] See, e.g., Shaprio v. Township of Lakewood, 292 F.3d 356, 358-60 (2002) (citing Jackan v. N.Y. State Dep't of Lab., 205 F.3d 562, 567 (2d Cir. 2000) ("[A] plaintiff seeking to hold the employer liable for failing to transfer her to a vacant position as a reasonable accommodation must demonstrate that there was a vacant position into which she might have been transferred."); Smith v. Midland Brake, Inc., 180 F.3d 1154, 1174 (10th Cir. 1999) (en banc) ("Even if Midland Brake failed to fulfill its interactive obligations to help secure a reassignment position, Smith will not be entitled to recovery unless he can also show that a reasonable accommodation was possible and would have led to a reassignment position."); Willis v. Conopco, Inc., 108 F.3d 282, 285 (11th Cir. 1997) ("[W]here a plaintiff cannot demonstrate 'reasonable accommodation,' the employer's lack of investigation into reasonable accommodation is unimportant.").

[115] White v. York Int'l Corp., 45 F.3d 357, 361 (10th Cir. 1995) (citation omitted).

[116] Mays v. Principi, 301 F.3d 866, 870 (7th Cir. 2002).

refusing to release necessary medical records.[117]   Where an employee cannot document the existence of an accommodation because the employer did not engage in the interactive process, "the fault in the failure to make the accommodation available would be the employer's...."[118]

A qualified job applicant or employee is not required to initiate the interactive process where employer has said it will not engage in the process.[119] The majority view is that failure of an employer to engage in the interactive process does not itself give rise to per se liability under Title I, although for summary judgment purposes such failure often is considered evidence that the employer acted in bad faith.[120]

In *Mays v. Principi*, Judge Posner summarizes one view of the interactive process:

> The purpose of the consultative process is to find a reasonable accommodation for the particular disabled employee, and if she proves that ... there was no consultative process, suspicion arises that the reason her disability was not accommodated was not that she turned down a reasonable accommodation but that the employer failed to explain her options to her and thus did not make it "available" to her in a practical sense. The burden shifts to the employer to produce some evidence that even if he failed to consult or "interact" with her, soliciting her suggestions for a reasonable accommodation, etc., he offered her such an accommodation with sufficient clarity to make the accommodation available to her in a practical sense, so that her rejecting it was her own fault.[121]

---

[117] See Beck v. Univ. of Wis. Bd. of Regents, 75 F.3d 1130, 1136-37 (7th Cir. 1996) (summary judgment for employer affirmed where employee caused breakdown of interactive process).

[118] Mays, 301 F.3d at 870 (citing Emerson v. N. Sts. Power Co., 256 F.3d 506, 515 (7th Cir. 2001); Ozlowski v. Henderson, 237 F.3d 837, 840 (7th Cir. 2001)).

[119] See, e.g., Davoll v. Webb, 194 F.3d 1116, 1132-33 (10th Cir. 1999).

[120] See, e.g., Ballard v. Rubin, 284 F.3d 957, 960 (8th Cir. 2002) (citing Taylor v. Phoenixville Sch. Dist., 174 F.3d 142, 165 (3d Cir. 1999).

[121] See Mays, 301 F.3d at 870-71 stating that:

> The principal significance of the consultative process is not that the employee is likely to come up with a reasonable accommodation if only she is consulted, but that she is quite likely to turn it down and either quit or sue unless the employer explains why he can't do more to enable her to work despite her disability. That can be presumed from the employer's failure to consult but he can meet the

In accord with this view, the Seventh and other Circuits have followed a burden-shifting consequence of the employer's failure to engage in the interactive process.[122] Yet, when no reasonable accommodation is possible, the failure to engage in the interactive process is harmless.[123]

In contrast, the Ninth Circuit has come closer to adopting a view that an employer's failure to engage in the interactive process in and of itself constitutes a violation of the ADA. In *Barnett v. U.S. Airways, Inc.*, the court held that when a job applicant or employee requests an accommodation (or an employer recognizes the employee's need for an accommodation but the employee cannot or does not request it because of a disability) the employer *must* engage in an interactive process to determine any possible reasonable accommodation.[124]

The First Circuit, alternatively, resolves the consequences of a failure by an employer to engage in the interactive process on a case-by-case basis. It maintains that although there may be situations in which failure to engage in the process constitutes a violation, the omission is not considered if the trial record "forecloses a finding that the plaintiff could perform the duties of the job, with or without reasonable accommodation," that is, is not a qualified individual with a disability.[125]

The defendant then bears the burden to show that the accommodation would impose an undue hardship.[126] However, courts of appeal have varied in their interpretation of whether Title I imposes the same evidentiary burdens on the disabled plaintiff requesting accommodation as on the defendant employer.

The approach of the First, Second, Third, Eighth and Tenth Circuits shifts the burden of persuasion from plaintiff to defendant, such that the burden of identifying an accommodation is one of production.[127]

---

presumption with evidence that he said enough to avoid being blamed for her failure to accept his offer.

[122] Id. at 871 (citing Shapiro v. Township of Lakewood, 292 F.3d 356, 359-60 (2002); Frazier v. Simmons, 254 F.3d 1247, 1261 (10th Cir. 2001); cf. Lucas v. W.W. Grainger, Inc., 257 F.3d 1249, 1256 n.2 (11th Cir. 2001)).

[123] Id. (citing, e.g., Kvorjak v. Maine, 259 F.3d 48, 53 (1st Cir. 2001)).

[124] Barnett v. U.S. Airways, Inc., 228 F.3d 1105, 1112 (9th Cir. 2000) (en banc), vacated on other grounds, 535 U.S. 391, 407 (2002).

[125] Kvorjak, 259 F.3d at 53.

[126] See 42 U.S.C. § 12112(b)(5)(A) (2000).

[127] Reed v. LePage Bakeries, Inc., 244 F.3d 254, 258-59 (1st Cir. 2001) (citing Borkowski v. Valley Cent. Sch. Dist., 63 F.3d 131, 138 (2d Cir. 1995); Walton v. Mental Health Assoc., 168 F.3d 661, 670 (3d Cir. 1999); Fjellestad v. Pizza Hut, 188 F.3d 944, 950 (8th Cir. 1999); Benson v. Northwest Airlines, Inc., 62 F.3d 1108, 1112 (8th Cir. 1995); White v. York Int'l Corp., 45 F.3d 357, 361 (10th Cir. 1995)).

In this approach, the "plaintiff's burden is not a heavy one."[128] The plaintiff must show a plausible and reasonable accommodation (e.g., where the costs on its face do not clearly exceed its benefits). If the plaintiff then meets its burden of showing that an accommodation is available, plausible and reasonable, the burden then shifts to the defendant.

An alternative approach has been adopted by the D.C. Circuit,[129] and the Fifth, Sixth, and Seventh Circuits. These circuits place the burden on the plaintiff to prove by a preponderance of the evidence that the accommodation is reasonable.[130] The plaintiff must make a facial showing of reasonableness (e.g., proportionality to costs). The defendant then must show undue burden with careful consideration that the costs involved are excessive.[131]

But the burden-shifting paradigm does not go all the way in defining the relationship between reasonable accommodation and undue burden. As the First Circuit has stated in *Reed*, some courts "are reluctant to examine the relationship between "reasonable accommodation" and "undue hardship" as one of shifting burdens.[132] "The

---

[128] Id. at 258.

[129] See Barth v. Gelb, 2 F.3d 1180, 1186 (D.C. Cir. 1993) (Rehabilitation Act case finding that the burden remains with the plaintiff to prove his case "by a preponderance of the evidence").

[130] Hoskins v. Oakland Cty. Sheriff's Dep't, 227 F.3d 719, 728 (6th Cir. 2000); Willis v. Conopco, Inc., 108 F.3d 282, 285-86 (11th Cir. 1997); Riel v. Elec. Data Sys. Corp., 99 F.3d 678, 682-83 (5th Cir. 1996); Monette v. Elec. Data Sys. Corp., 90 F.3d 1173, 1183, n.10, 1186 n.12 (6th Cir. 1996); Vande Zande v. Wis. Dep't of Admin., 44 F.3d 538, 542- 43 (7th Cir. 1995).

[131] See Vande Zande, 44 F.3d at 542.

[132] Reed, 244 F.3d at 258-59; see also id. at 259 n.3 stating:

> The burden-shifting model was introduced into employment law in order to allow indirect proof of the often elusive "intent" to discriminate. See Higgins v. New Balance Athletic Shoe, Inc., 194 F.3d 252, 264 (1st Cir. 1999). Thus, burden shifting allows a plaintiff to make a small showing of discrimination, whereupon the employer must articulate a non-discriminatory reason for its actions, and if that reason proves to be untrue, then an inference of discrimination may be warranted. See McDonnell Douglas Corp. v. Green, 411 U.S. 792, 802-04, 93 S.Ct. 1817, 36 L.Ed.2d 668 (1973) .... By contrast, whether a requested accommodation is reasonable or whether it imposes an undue hardship are questions typically proved through direct, objective evidence. Accordingly, we have already held that the *McDonnell Douglas* model does not apply to

real issue is the quantum of proof needed to show reasonable accommodation vis-à-vis the quantum of proof needed to show undue hardship."[133]

In *Reed,* the First Circuit rejected the position of the EEOC that a plaintiff need only show that the accommodation would effectively enable her to perform essential job functions and that a defendant then must show that the accommodation would be too costly or difficult.[134] Said differently, the "reasonable" element is not proven by the lack of undue hardship, but by effectiveness. The First Circuit required that a plaintiff demonstrate more to show that her requested accommodation is "reasonable," because Title I limits the plaintiff's accommodation request only to those within reason of difficulty or expense.

The majority view is that to prove "reasonable accommodation," a plaintiff needs to show that the accommodation would enable her to perform essential job functions, and that, facially, it is feasible for the employer to implement the accommodation in the circumstances.[135]

If a plaintiff succeeds in this showing, the defendant must show that the accommodation is not "as feasible as it appears but rather that there are further costs to be considered, certain devils in the details."[136] Given the inexactness of the burdens of proof for accommodation and hardship, counsel typically "errs on the side of offering proof beyond what their burdens require."[137]

ADA discrimination claims based on failure to reasonably accommodate. Higgins, 194 F.3d at 264.

[133] Reed, 244 F.3d at 259.

[134] Id.

[135] Id.

[136] Id. at 259-60. Noting that where the costs of an accommodation are obvious, plaintiff's burden and defendant's burden may be similar. The burdens will differ when the costs of an accommodation are not evident on the face of things, but rather are better known to the employer. Cf. Barnett v. U.S. Airways, Inc., 228 F.3d 1105, 1113 (9th Cir. 2000) (finding employer's "superior knowledge" as to certain matters relevant to determining extent of parties' burdens). For example, an employee's proposal that her work area be modified might be facially reasonable, but the employer may still show that, given the particular limitations on its financial resources, or other hidden costs, such accommodation imposes an undue hardship. Id. (citing 42 U.S.C. § 12111(10)(B).

[137] Reed, 244 F.3d at 260.

B. *Disparate Treatment – Application Of* McDonnell Douglas Corp. *And* Price Waterhouse

Above, we have discussed the evidentiary burden-shifting scheme when a Title I plaintiff attempts to prove her case. Here, we discuss an additional evidentiary twist that must be considered in a limited number of ADA cases.

Broadly speaking, under Title VII of the Civil Rights Act (prohibiting employment discrimination on the basis of race, color, religion, sex, or national origin)[138] and ADA Title I, a plaintiff may proceed under one of two discrimination theories. A plaintiff may either show that she was intentionally treated differently on the basis of a prohibited characteristic (for purposes of the ADA, disability, or for Title VII, race, color, religion, sex, or national origin). This is referred to as a "disparate treatment" claim. Or plaintiff may argue that the effect of a facially non-discriminatory, or "neutral" rule, had a greater statistical impact on the member of the plaintiff's protected group. This is referred to as a "disparate impact" claim, and as will be discussed below, often is used in connection with class action lawsuits.[139]

Proving intentional discrimination in a disparate treatment theory often is difficult; typically, there is no "smoking gun" document to show intent. To give structure to the plaintiff's burden of proof in this situation, courts have used a burden-shifting scheme set out in *McDonnell Douglas Corp. v. Green*.[140]

Under the *McDonnell Douglas* analysis, the plaintiff must establish a prima facie case of discrimination. The burden then shifts to the defendant to present a legitimate, nondiscriminatory reason for the challenged employment action. The burden then shifts back to the plaintiff to demonstrate that the defendant's proffered reason is a pretext for discrimination. This *McDonnell Douglas* framework has been applied to disparate treatment ADA Title I cases.[141]

However, if the employer admits that disability played a prominent part in the decision, or the plaintiff has other direct evidence of discrimination based on disability, the *McDonnell Douglas* framework

---

[138] 42 U.S.C. § 2000e (2000).

[139] See Harold S. Lewis, Jr. & Elizabeth J. Norman, Employment Discrimination Law and Practice, 115 (West Group 2001).

[140] McDonnell Douglas Corp. v. Green, 411 U.S. 792 (1973).

[141] See Hardy v. S.F. Phosphates Ltd. Co., 185 F.3d 1076, 1079 (10th Cir. 1999); see also Kiel v. Select Artificials, Inc., 169 F.3d 1131, 1135-36 (8th Cir. 1999); Skomsky v. Speedway Superamerica, LLC, 267 F.Supp.2d 995, 998 (D. Minn. 2003).

typically is not used[142] Where an employer's reason for a non-hire or other adverse action is that the action was not based disability per se, but rather, for example, on hiring a more qualified individual, the usual evidentiary approach for resolving the issue is through the ADA's "qualified individual" analysis, not the *McDonnell Douglas* framework.

This distinction is demonstrated in *Davidson v. America Online, Inc.*[143] In this case, America Online's ("AOL") Call Center in the Philippines only was set up to handle non-voicemail communications.[144] The admitted effect of this was that people with deafness were not considered for employment at AOL.[145] Davidson, who had unsuccessfully applied for a job with AOL, brought a ADA Title I claim.

AOL argued that the reason it did not hire Davidson was not because he was deaf, but rather because he was unable to perform the jobs available for hire, that is, voicemail positions.[146] AOL therefore suggested that the *McDonnell Douglas* framework was appropriate, and that Davidson should have to counter AOL's proffered non-discriminatory reason.[147]

The court disagreed with AOL. In the court's view, defendant's "non-discriminatory" reason was linked to plaintiff's disability.[148] The court viewed the defendant essentially as arguing that Davidson was not a "qualified individual" with a disability, and therefore the *McDonnell Douglas* framework was inappropriate and unnecessary.[149]

Sometimes, in ADA Title I and Title VII cases, legitimate and illegitimate reasons motivated the employment action. These are referred to as "mixed motive" cases. The Supreme Court discussed the evidentiary burden used in these cases in the Title VII case of *Price Waterhouse v. Hopkins*.[150]

The *Price Waterhouse* Court found that the employer had an affirmative defense that it would have taken the same action regardless of race or gender. However, the Court was divided on the question whether

---

[142] Morgan v. Hilti, Inc., 108 F.3d 1319, 1323 n.3 (10th Cir. 1995), citing White v. York Int'l Corp., 45 F.3d 357, 361 n.6 (10th Cir. 1995).

[143] Davidson v. Am. Online, Inc., 337 F.3d 1179 (10th Cir. 2003).

[144] Id. at 1182.

[145] Id.

[146] Id. at 1189.

[147] Id.

[148] Id. ("In other words, AOL's explanation for its action established that it relied on Davidson's disability when it refused to hire him.").

[149] Davidson v. Am. Online, 337 F.3d at 1189.

[150] Price Waterhouse v. Hopkins, 490 U.S. 228, 269-70 (1989).

the burden should shift to the defense.[151] Justice O'Connor's concurring opinion provided a standard that was widely followed, finding that the burden should shift to the defense only if the plaintiff showed, by *direct evidence*, that the illegitimate consideration was a substantial factor in the employment action.[152]

Congress, in the Civil Rights Act of 1991, disagreed with the Court's *Price Waterhouse* analysis and provided that Title VII would be violated if an illegitimate consideration was "a motivating factor for any employment practice, even though other factors also motivated the practice."[153] Congress went on to provide that, if the employer proves it would have taken the same action in the absence of the impermissible factor, that affirmative defense would limit the remedies available to declaratory and injunctive relief. However, under this approach, the employer would not avoid liability.[154]

The Civil Rights Act of 1991 only expressly applies to employment actions on the basis of race, color, religion, sex, or national origin. It is unclear that, as a strictly textual matter, the amendments embodied in the 1991 Act apply to employment claims for disability discrimination under the ADA. Courts have applied *Price Waterhouse*, and not the changes embodied in the 1991 Act, to ADEA cases.[155] Nevertheless, in the ADA context, the vast majority of courts have applied the framework set forth in the 1991 Civil Rights Act (motivating, as opposed to substantial factor, and no liability affirmative defense for same action) and not *Price Waterhouse*.[156]

After 1991, the courts were divided as to whether a plaintiff's proof of an impermissible factor must be by *direct*, as opposed to

---

[151] Desert Palace, Inc. v. Costa, 123 S.Ct. 2148, 2150-51 (2003) (citing the concurring opinions of Justices White and O'Connor in Price Waterhouse, 490 U.S. at 244 and 261). The *Price Waterhouse* plurality would have shifted the burden to the defense if the plaintiff showed gender was a motivating factor, Price Waterhouse, 490 U.S. at 258, while Justice White would have shifted the burden only if gender were a substantial factor. Id. at 259 (White, J., concurring).

[152] Id. at 2151 (O'Connor, J., concurring).

[153] 42 U.S.C. § 2000e-2(m) (2000).

[154] Id. § 2000e-5(g)(2)(B). Relief would also include costs and attorneys' fees. Id.

[155] See Miller v. Cigna Corporation, 47 F.3d 586 (3d Cir. 1995); see also Lewis v. Young Men's Christian Ass'n, 208 F.3d 1303.

[156] See, e.g., Foster v. Arthur Anderson, LLP, 168 F.3d 1029, 1033-34 (7th Cir. 1999); Doane v. City of Omaha, 115 F.3d 624, 629 (9th Cir. 1997); Pedigo v. P.A.M. Transp., Inc., 60 F.3d 1300, 1301-02 (8th Cir. 1995); Katz v. City Metal Co., 87 F.3d 26, 33 (1st Cir. 1996); Buchanan v. City of San Antonio, 85 F.3d 196, 200 (5th Cir. 1996).

circumstantial, evidence to shift the burden under the *Price Waterhouse* analysis.[157]

In *Desert Palace, Inc. v. Costa*, the Supreme Court found that Congress did not intend to impose a heightened standard on plaintiffs and that circumstantial evidence is appropriate for civil rights cases. Therefore, it held that direct evidence of discrimination is not required to shift the burden of proof to the defendant in a mixed-motive discrimination case.[158] Rather, "a plaintiff need only present sufficient evidence for a reasonable jury to conclude, by a preponderance of the evidence, that 'race, color, religion, sex, or national origin was a motivating factor for any employment practice.'"[159]

After *Desert Palace*, the *Price Waterhouse* and *McDonnell Douglas* burden-shifting analyses will be applicable in far fewer ADA and other Title VII cases. This is because circumstantial evidence that an employment action was based on disability will be sufficient to shift the burden of proof to the defense, and increasing the likelihood of surviving a summary judgment motion.[160]

C.   *Disparate Impact – ADA Title I Class Actions*

At times, ADA Title I plaintiffs have attempted to proceed on a disparate impact class action theory. These plaintiffs have argued that a given employer's policy or practice (for example, a hiring or firing policy) is an adverse employment action on the employer's disabled employees or applicants. By and large, the class action strategy has not been successful in ADA Title I cases.[161]

---

[157] Desert Palace, Inc., 123 S.Ct. at 2151-52; see, e.g., Mohr v. Dustrol, Inc., 306 F.3d 636, 640-41 (8th Cir. 2002); Fernandes v. Costa Bros. Masonry, Inc., 199 F.3d 572, 580 (1st Cir. 1999); Trotter v. Bd. of Tr. Univ. of Ala., 91 F.3d 1449, 1453-54 (11th Cir. 1996); Fuller v. Phipps, 67 F.3d 1137, 1142 (4th Cir. 1995); see also Costa v. Desert Palace, Inc., 299 F.3d 838 (9th Cir. 2002), cert. granted, 123 S.Ct. 2148.

[158] Desert Palace, Inc., 123 S.Ct. at 2155.

[159] Id. (quoting 42 U.S.C. §2000e-2(m)); see also Dare v. Wal-Mart Stores, Inc. 267 F.Supp.2d 987, 989 (D. Minn. 2003).

[160] See Dare, 267 F.Supp.2d 987 at 990-993 (challenging the false dichotomy established in *McDonnell Douglas* and applying the "same decision test" in a single-motive, rather than mixed-motive, case); Skomsky v. SuperAmerica, LLC, 267 F.Supp.2d 995, 1000 (D. Minn. 2003).

[161] This is in contrast to access cases under Title II or Title III, where the class action procedure has been more of a viable tool. See Barden v. City of Sacramento, 292 F.3d 1073 (9th Cir. 2002) (Title II); see also Colorado Cross-Disability Coalition v. Taco Bell Corp., 184 F.R.D. 354 (D. Colo. 1999) (Title III).

To certify a class in federal court, the class representatives must show that the requirements of Federal Rule of Civil Procedure 23(a) are met. This includes a showing that (1) the class is so numerous that joinder of all members is impracticable; (2) there are questions of law or fact common to the class; (3) the claims or defenses of the representative parties are typical of the claims or defenses of the class, and (4) the representative parties will fairly and adequately protect the interest of the class.[162]

Because the ADA and its interpreting regulations require an individualized analysis of a plaintiff's disability, potential reasonable accommodations, and employer's defenses, courts have been hesitant to find that a class representatives' claims are typical of and common to the class.[163]

An example of this is found in the case of *Lintemuth v. Saturn Corporation*.[164] Six employees with different disabilities sued an auto manufacturer, claiming that the manufacturer discriminated against them in violation of Title I by using placement procedures that did not reasonably accommodate their known medical conditions.[165] In holding that the proposed class representatives could not establish the typicality needed for a class to be certified, the court reasoned:

> The variance in the named plaintiffs' personal characteristics, coupled with the individualized, case-by-case analysis required by the ADA, renders the proposed representatives in this action unable to establish the necessary elements of the claims of the class in the course of establishing their own. Furthermore, the highly personal nature of each representative's disability also subjects their claims to unique defenses under the ADA which are significant enough to destroy typicality.[166]

However, some courts have held that ADA Title I class actions are appropriate vehicles to challenge employment policies. In *Hendricks-*

---

[162] See Fed. R. Civ. P. 23(a). The class representative also must show that the class should be certified pursuant to one of the three categories set forth in Fed. R. Civ. P. 23(b).

[163] See David T. Wiley, If You Can't Fight 'Em, Join 'Em: Class Actions Under Title I of the Americans With Disabilities Act, 13 Labor Lawyer 197 (1997); see also Lintemuth v. Saturn Corp., 1994 WL 760811 (M.D. Tenn. 1994); Chandler v. City of Dallas, 2 F.3d 1385, 1396 (5th Cir. 1993) (Rehabilitation Act); Davoll v. Webb, 160 F.R.D. 142, 143 (D. Colo 1995).

[164] Lintemuth v. Saturn Corp., 1994 WL 760811 (M.D. Tenn. 1994).

[165] Id. at *3.

[166] Id. at *4.

Robinson v. Excel Corporation,[167] a group of employees challenged their employer's medical leave policy. The employees proposed a class of "all ... employees ... whom Excel perceives to have permanent medical restrictions and who were placed on medical layoff pursuant to Excel's medical layoff policy...."[168] The court held that "we see no reason why a case which challenges a *policy* cannot proceed as a class action under the ADA."[169] Because plaintiffs were not seeking to support their claims by reference to their respective injuries and defenses, but merely sought to attack the policy, the court held that there was typicality.[170]

---

[167] Hendricks-Robinson v. Excel Corporation, 164 F.R.D. 667 (C.D. Illinois 1996).

[168] Id. at 669.

[169] Id. at 670 (emphasis in original).

[170] Id. See also Wilson v. Pennsylvania State Police Dep't, 1995 WL 422750 (E.D. Pa. 1995) (certifying a class of plaintiffs who challenged the Pennsylvania State Police Department's employment policy against applicants with poor eyesight as violative of the ADA).

Chapter 9 TITLE I DEFENSES BASED ON QUALIFICATIONS STANDARDS

Congress acknowledged in the ADA that discrimination takes many forms, including paternalism and stereotyping.[1] An insidious aspect of this type of discrimination is the assumption that people with disabilities are not competent to make informed and safe life choices in the employment context.[2] In the ADA, Congress addressed discrimination resulting from over-protective qualification rules and policies, as well as intentional discrimination, that relegated individuals with disabilities to lesser and inferior jobs and foreclosed their employment opportunities.[3]

However, Title I permits certain employer defenses to a charge of discrimination based on qualification standards that are job-related and consistent with business necessity.[4] One of those defenses is the requirement that an employee not pose a "direct threat" to others in the workplace.[5] Direct threat is "a significant risk to the health or safety of others that cannot be eliminated by reasonable accommodation."[6]

Employer assessment of the direct threat to the employee historically served as a reason for the unwarranted exclusion – well meaning or otherwise – of qualified individuals from work. The ADA tightens the reins on what an employer may consider on this point. Employers only may consider health or safety to the extent an individual's condition or behavior imperils health or safety in the workplace, or the

---

[1] See H.R. Rep. No. 101-485, pt. 2, at 74 (1990), reprinted in 1990 U.S.C.C.A.N. 303, 356.

[2] The myth is apparent in employment given employers' assumption that many persons with disabilities are likely to be injured and thereby enhance exposure to tort liability. See Peter Blanck & Glen Pransky, Workers with Disabilities, 14 Occupational Med. 581, 587 (1999).

[3] H.R. Rep. No. 101-485, pt. 2, at 28-29 (1990), reprinted in 1990 U.S.C.C.A.N. 303, 310-11. For a review of the disability policy framework, see Peter Blanck & Helen Schartz, Towards Reaching a National Employment Policy for Persons with Disabilities, in Emerging Workforce Issues: W.I.A., Ticket to Work, and Partnerships 1-10 (R. McConnell ed., Switzer Seminar Monograph Series, Nat'l Rehab. Ass'n 2001).

[4] 42 U.S.C. § 12113(a) (2000).

[5] Id. § 12113(b).

[6] Id. § 12111(3). As will be discussed below, although Title I does not define direct threat as a risk to self, the EEOC subsequently issued regulations that expanded the direct threat defense to include a "significant risk of substantial harm to the ... individual" that cannot be addressed by accommodation. See 29 C.F.R. § 1630.2(r) (2003).

individual fails to meet specific health or safety standards imposed by government authorities, such as OSHA workplace requirements.[7]

Under Title I, the direct threat defense does not arise as part of the plaintiff's showing that he is a "qualified individual."[8] Rather, the issue arises as part of a defense by the employer that the job applicant does not meet necessary qualification standards.[9]

Qualification standards are "personal and professional attributes including skill, experience, education, physical, medical, safety and other requirements" necessary for an individual to be eligible for the position.[10] Congress placed the evidentiary burden on the employer to demonstrate that such qualification standards are job-related and necessary to business functioning.[11] With respect to business necessity and direct threat, the employer often will have superior information and knowledge about workplace requirements and operations.

§ 9.1 Direct Threat Defense To Others And To Self

The direct threat to others defense is a subset of the qualifications defense, specifically carved out by Congress to meet the health and safety aspects of the more general defense.[12] The statute provides that "'qualification standards' may include a requirement that an individual shall not pose a direct threat to the health or safety of other individuals in

---

[7]   See Albertson's Inc. v. Kirkingburg, 527 U.S. 555, 557 (1999).

[8]   See, e.g., 42 U.S.C. § 12111(8). In others words, health and safety factors are not a required aspect of the plaintiff's title I showing that he is a qualified individual.

[9]   Id. §§ 12112(b)(6), 12113(a).

[10]   See 29 C.F.R. § 1630.2(q); 42 U.S.C. § 12113(a). In general, health and safety considerations are a critical component of the Act's tiered analysis, but are not to be confused with essential job functions or qualifications, except in limited circumstances. There are instances where essential functions implicate issues of safety; for instance, a firefighter who could not "carry an unconscious adult out of a burning building," 29 C.F.R. § 1630.2(n), would not be qualified to perform the essential functions of the position and would be unsafe. In such instances, the essential functions are not analyzed in terms of safety but, rather, the inability to perform job tasks.

[11]   See 42 U.S.C. § 12112(b)(6) ("unless" the standard is "job related ... [and] consistent with business necessity ..."); see also id. § 12113(a); H.R. Rep. No. 101-485, pt. 3, at 42 (1990), reprinted in 1990 U.S.C.C.A.N. 445, 465 ("[A] facially neutral qualification standard, employment test or other selection criterion that has a discriminatory effect on persons with disabilities ... would be discriminatory unless the employer can demonstrate that it is job related and required by business necessity.").

[12]   42 U.S.C. § 12113(a-b) (2000).

the workplace.[13]   The EEOC subsequently issued regulations that expanded the direct threat defense beyond the language of the statute to include a significant risk of harm to *the individual* or others that cannot be addressed by reasonable accommodation.[14]

In *Chevron U.S.A. v. Echazabal*,[15] the Supreme Court considered the validity of these regulations.

§ 9.2 *Chevron v. Echazabal*

In this case, Echazabal was denied employment by Chevron because Chevron believed the job would exacerbate his Hepatitis. Echazabal argued that the EEOC's threat-to-self defense was not present in the language of the ADA, was contrary to a plain and natural reading of the Act, and was inconsistent with the expressed intent of Congress.[16] The threat-to-self defense, Chevron contended, properly allows employers to decide the degree of risk an individual with a disability can and should accept in performing his job.   The district court granted summary judgment in favor of Chevron.

The Ninth Circuit reversed, holding that the direct threat defense contained in the ADA did not permit employers to exclude from employment qualified individuals with disabilities who pose a risk only to themselves and not others; and that the risk that the job posed to Echazabal's own health did not affect whether he was a qualified individual for purposes of the Act.[17]   The Supreme Court granted Chevron's petition for certiorari.

A unanimous Supreme Court rejected Echazabal's arguments, and upheld the EEOC direct threat-to-self regulations. The Court ruled that Title I allows employers to decide whether qualified people with disabilities should be excluded from the workplace based on the employer's conclusion that they create a direct threat of harm solely to themselves.

---

[13]   Id. § 12113(b).

[14]   29 C.F.R. §§ 1630.2(r), 1630.15(b)(2) (2003).

[15]   Chevron U.S.A. v. Echazabal, 536 U.S. 73, 74 (2002).

[16]   Id.

[17]   Echazabal v. Chevron U.S.A., Inc., 226 F.3d 1063, 1072 (9th Cir. 2000).

A.   *Deference To EEOC Direct Threat-To-Self Defense Regulations*

The statutory standard provided that qualification standards "may include a requirement that an individual shall not pose a direct threat to the health or safety of other individuals in the workplace."[18]

The EEOC's regulation, however, allows an employer to screen out an individual with a disability not only for risks that he would pose to others in the workplace, but also for risks on the job to his own health or safety.[19]

The Court concluded that Congress included the harm-to-others provision merely as one example of a legitimate qualification standard that may be job-related and consistent with business necessity. These "defensive categories," it reasoned, were intended to allow the EEOC reasonable discretion in establishing permissible qualification standards.[20] Because Congress has not spoken equivocally on threats to a worker's own health, the Court concluded that the EEOC regulation survives under the agency deference rule in Chevron.[21]

However, the Court noted that its decision did not mean that Title I's defense provisions placed no limit on EEOC rulemaking, as some regulations are precluded by the Act's specification that the direct threat defense does not include "indirect" threats of "insignificant" harm."[22]

---

[18]   The Court notes the EEOC's rule interpreting the Rehabilitation Act of 1973, 87 Stat. 357 (as amended at 29 U.S.C. § 701 et seq.), and that like the ADA, the Rehabilitation Act does not specify covered threats to self that particular employment might pose. 42 U.S.C. § 12113(b) (2000).

[19]   Echazabal, 536 U.S. at 78-79 ("qualification standard" may include that an individual not pose a direct threat to the health or safety of the individual or others in the workplace (citing 29 C.F.R. § 1630.15(b)(2))).

[20]   Id. at 80 ("discretion is confirmed" by the provision that qualification standards within the limits of job relation and business necessity "may include" "a veto on those who would directly threaten others in the workplace"). A second reason was that the Court saw no basis for the view that Congress, in specifying a threat-to-others defense, intended not to cover others whose safety could be considered inside and outside the workplace.

[21]   Echazabal, 536 U.S. at 86.

[22]   The Court notes that the defense is a "direct" threat of "significant" harm, 42 U.S.C. §§ 12113(b), 12111(3), intended to forbid qualifications that screen out by reference to general categories pretextually applied. See Echazabal, 536 U.S. at 80 n.3.

B. Direct Threat-To-Self Defense As Job-Related And Consistent With Business Necessity

As mentioned, under the ADA, the direct threat defense is part of qualification standards that are "job-related and consistent with business necessity."[23] Chevron contended that the threat-to-self defense is job-related and necessary to "avoid time lost to sickness, excessive turnover from medical retirement or death, litigation under state tort law, and the risk of violating the national Occupational Safety and Health Act of 1970 ("OSHA")."[24]

The Supreme Court focused primarily on the concern with OSHA[25] in upholding the EEOC direct threat-to-self regulation.[26] The Court noted that the intent of OSHA is to assure "safe and healthful working conditions," and for an employer to furnish a "place of employment which is free from recognized hazards that are causing or are likely to cause death or serious physical harm to his employees."

Although the Court acknowledged that it is not clear whether an employer would be liable under OSHA for hiring an individual with a disability who consented to the particular dangers of a job,[27] it reasoned that:

> there is no denying that the employer would be asking for trouble: his decision to hire would put Congress's policy in the ADA, a disabled individual's right to operate on equal terms within the workplace, at loggerheads with the competing policy of OSHA, to ensure the safety of "each" and "every" worker.[28]

---

23   42 U.S.C. § 12113(a).

24   Echazabal, 536 U.S. at 84.

25   29 U.S.C. § 651 et seq. (2000).

26   Echazabal argued that there was no known instance of OSHA enforcement, or even threatened enforcement, against an employer who relied on the ADA to hire a worker willing to accept a risk to himself from his disability on the job." Echazabal, 536 U.S. at 84.

27   See 29 U.S.C. §§ 651(b), 654(a)(1) (2000).

28   Echazabal, 536 U.S. at 85. The Court rejected "Echazabal's contention that the Act's legislative history is to the contrary." Id. at 86 n.5. It noted comments in the ADA's legislative history that "decry paternalism in general terms." Id. (citing, e.g., H.R. Rep. No. 101-485, pt. 2, p. 72 (1990), reprinted in U.S.C.C.A.N. 303, 354 ("It is critical that paternalistic concerns for the disabled person's own safety not be used to disqualify an otherwise qualified applicant.")). However, the Court concluded that those comments express only the general point that such justifications are rooted in generalities and misperceptions about disabilities. Id. (citing, e.g., H.R. Rep. No. 101-485, at 74, reprinted in 1990 U.S.C.C.A.N. at 356

In the Court's view then, the EEOC's direct threat-to-self guidance is a reasonable balance between OSHA's objectives of workplace safety and the ADA's rejection of employer paternalism.[29] As the Court held:

> [T]he EEOC has taken this to mean that Congress was not aiming at an employer's refusal to place disabled workers at a specifically demonstrated risk, but was trying to get at refusals to give an even break to classes of disabled people, while claiming to act for their own good in reliance on untested and pretextual stereotypes.[30]

The Court concluded that the EEOC's regulation "disallows just this sort of sham protection, through demands for a particularized enquiry into the harms the employee would probably face."[31]

The Court then proceeded to uphold the EEOC's regulations on direct threat and to reaffirm its previous holding in *Bragdon v. Abbott* that the:

(1)   direct threat determination must be based on an individualized assessment of a demonstrable current, significant risk of substantial harm while performing the essential functions of the particular job;

("Generalized fear about risks from the employment environment, such as exacerbation of the disability caused by stress, cannot be used by an employer to disqualify a person with a disability.")). The Court rejected Echazabal's analogy to its Title VII decisions in which employers adopted rules that excluded women from jobs that were seen as too risky. Id. (citing Auto. Workers v. Johnson Controls, Inc., 499 U.S. 187, 202 (1991); Dothard v. Rawlinson, 433 U.S. 321, 335 (1977). The Court distinguished those cases as involving blanket paternalistic judgments based on the category of gender, and not on individualized risk assessments. Id.

[29] Id. at 85 (noting that Congress viewed the paternalism, see § 12101(a)(5), in "overprotective rules and policies" as a form of discrimination under the ADA). But see Orr v. Wal-Mart Stores, Inc., 297 F.3d 720 (8th Cir. 2002). *Orr* is a post-*Echazabal* case holding that a Wal-Mart pharmacist who was a diabetic did not have an actual disability that presently and substantially limited a major life activity, and therefore, he was not disabled under the ADA. Id. at 725. The Eighth Circuit went on to note in dicta that, had the plaintiff established a prima facie case of actual disability under Title I, Wal-Mart could have raised the threat-to-self defense that working in a single-pharmacist pharmacy, which did not provide for uninterrupted meal breaks, posed a direct threat to plaintiff's health and that Wal-Mart was justified in not continuing his employment. Id at 725 n.5 (citing Echazabal, 536 U.S. 73).

[30] Echazabal, 536 U.S. at 85.

[31] Id. at 86.

(2)   risk cannot be eliminated or reduced to below the level of a direct threat with reasonable accommodation;[32] and,

(3)   determination as to whether the risk exists must be grounded in current medical knowledge and/or the best available objective evidence.[33]

In sum, the Court found that the EEOC acted within reason "when it saw a difference between rejecting workplace paternalism and ignoring specific and documented risks to the employee himself, even if the employee would take his chances for the sake of getting a job."[34] The Court did not decide the parameters of an impairment that would allow an employer to disqualify a job applicant or employee with a disability, as the trial court must make this determination on a case-by-case basis.

C.   *Remand To The Ninth Circuit*

The question considered on remand by the Ninth Circuit was whether Chevron's decision to exclude Echazabal, because he allegedly posed a direct threat to himself, was based on an individualized inquiry and reasonable medical judgment as required by the ADA and EEOC regulations.[35]

The EEOC regulations (upheld in *Chevron*) set forth the following four factors for determining whether a direct threat exists: (1) the potential duration of the threat; (2) the nature and severity of the threat; (3) the likelihood that the threat will occur; and (4) the imminence of the

---

[32]   There is dispute over whether Echazabal requested, and Chevron or Irwin Industries could have made, a reasonable accommodation to enable him to work at the plant. On remand to the Ninth Circuit, Echazabal argued that Chevron failed to prove that reasonable accommodation was not viable, including the possibility of medical monitoring and protective devices. Appellant's Post-Remand Supplemental Reply Brief, 2002 WL 32102832, at *14.

[33]   Echazabal, 536 U.S. at 86 (citing 29 C.F.R. § 1630.2(r)); see also Kapche v. City of San Antonio, 304 F.3d 493, 494-95 (5th Cir. 2002) (post-Chevron v. Echazabal case discussing ADA direct threat defense and individualized inquiry requirement). Id. at 495 (remanding the case to the district court for a "determination whether today there exists new or improved technology ... that could now permit insulin-dependent diabetic drivers in general, and Kapche in particular, to operate a vehicle safely").

[34]   Echazabal, 536 U.S. at 86.

[35]   Echazabal v. Chevron U.S.A., Inc., 336 F.3d 1023, 1026 (9th Cir. 2002) (stating that "the only remaining issue on remand is whether Chevron has met the requirements for assertion of the direct threat defense."). See also Echazabal v. Chevron, Supplemental Brief of the Equal Employment Opportunity Commission as Amicus Curiae, U.S. Court of Appeals for the Ninth Circuit, Docket No. 98-55551 (Aug. 8, 2002), at 1-2 (arguing same).

threat.[36]   The Supreme Court considered this approach reasonable because it supported a particularized analysis of the harms to the employee.[37]   On remand, Echazabal, and the EEOC as amicus curiae, contended that the Ninth Circuit should reverse the district court's grant of summary judgment to Chevron because no such individualized assessment was made.

Before excluding Echazabal as a direct threat, they argued that Chevron was required to show that it had made an individualized assessment of his current ability to perform essential job functions. This evaluation was required to have been derived from current medical knowledge and objective evidence.[38]   They argued that the district court had committed a reversible error in holding that Chevron's direct threat determination process (i.e., its reliance on the medical opinions of physicians unschooled in the areas of hepatitis/liver disease and toxicology) sufficient under the ADA.[39]   They contended the company needed to review the level and degree of toxicity of the actual exposures to which Echazabal was in fact exposed, an evaluation they argue Chevron did not conduct.

For several reasons, the Ninth Circuit determined that Chevron had not met its burden of proving direct threat:

> 1) Chevron's doctors were not trained in liver disease, while the plaintiff's doctors, who reached the opposite conclusion, were specialists;
>
> 2) One of Chevron's doctors did not support the direct threat conclusion;
>
> 3) Doctor's recommendations against employment were insufficient when they were not based on specific information about the chemicals Echazabal would encounter and the levels of exposure;

---

[36]   Id; see also 29 C.F.R. pt. 1630 app., § 1630.2(r) (EEOC Interpretive Guidance stating that direct threat consideration "must rely on objective factual evidence").

[37]   Echazabal, 536 U.S. at 86.

[38]   Echazabal, 336 F.3d at 1033 (citing 29 C.F.R. § 1630.2(r)).

[39]   See EEOC Supplemental Brief as Amicus Curiae, supra note 35, at 4 (arguing that "Chevron needed to obtain and consider more objective and accurate information about Echazabal's liver function, ..."); Chevron v. Echazabal, Appellant's Post-Remand Supplemental Opening Brief, U.S. Court of Appeals for the Ninth Circuit, Docket No. 98-55551 (Aug. 27, 2002), at 12-13 (arguing same).

4) Chevron gave no weight to Echazabal's 20 years of work without injury.[40]

Because the direct threat analysis is an objective one, not based on what Chevron believed, the court was willing to consider the plaintiff's expert medical evidence even though they were not presented at the time Chevron made its hiring decision.

§ 9.3 The Role Of Experts In Title I Cases

Crucial issues in ADA cases include whether a plaintiff has the physical or mental capabilities to perform the essential job requirements with or without reasonable accommodation, or whether a plaintiff is a direct threat to himself or others in the workplace. As in other cases, both sides of an ADA case typically will have an expert opine on these issues, and how the judge and/or jury treats this testimony often is outcome-determinative.

These types of issues usually involve testimony by medical doctors and there are several interesting variations in how the court will receive this testimony. The primary question is whether a court itself will weigh conflicting medical testimony, or merely ensure that the employer considered a certain acceptable threshold level of medical evidence?

If a court does itself weigh conflicting testimony, there are other questions. How does a court weigh the competing testimony of an employer's doctor against the testimony of the physician of an employee's choice? What about the relative merits of a doctor who is a specialist in a given field as opposed to a treating physician?

To discharge its burden under a direct threat defense, for example, an employer must show that it made its decision based on "reasonable medical judgment that relies on the most current medical knowledge and/or on the best available objective evidence."[41] How current or specific does the medical knowledge have to be?

In the case of *Echazabal v. Chevron USA, Inc.*, the Ninth Circuit addressed many of these issues.[42] As discussed supra, Chevron terminated Echazabal's employment when it determined that, as a result of his liver disease, he created a direct threat to himself through his work at an oil refinery. The District Court granted summary judgment in favor of Chevron, holding that the EEOC's "direct threat to self" regulations were valid, and that Chevron had made out this defense as a matter of law. On remand from the Supreme Court,[43] the Ninth Circuit had to

---

[40] Echazabal, 336 F.3d at 1032.

[41] 29 C.F.R. § 1630.2(r).

[42] Echazabal, 336 F.3d 1023.

[43] Originally, the Ninth Circuit reversed the District Court, holding that the EEOC's "direct threat to self" regulations were invalid. See Echazabal

consider whether there were material issues of fact as to whether Chevron had made out its affirmative defense.

Chevron submitted testimony from its medical doctors who examined Echazabal and found that his liver was not functioning normally. These doctors recommended that Echazabal therefore not be exposed to chemicals that could be toxic to his liver.[44] Neither of Chevron's doctors had special training in liver disease.[45]

Echazabal's examining doctors, who were specialists in toxicology and liver disease, disagreed with Chevron's doctors.[46] They found that tests revealed that Echazabal's liver was functioning properly, and that there was no "medical or scientific evidence" supporting a finding that Echazabal's chemical exposures from working as a plant helper or in the refinery coker unit would present an appreciable or clinically significant risk.[47] In light of Echazabal's experts' testimony, the Ninth Circuit held that summary judgment was inappropriate because a jury could conclude that Chevron failed to rely on the most current medical knowledge and on the best available objective evidence.[48]

The Ninth Circuit's opinion in *Echazabal* stands for the proposition that an employer who relies only on its medical professionals, who are not experts in the relevant field and who only offer generalized conclusions about possible harms, cannot receive summary judgment on a direct threat defense.[49] A court will inquire into what it considers to be the basis for the medical opinion. Because the individualized inquiry requirement is the same for the determination of whether a plaintiff can perform the essential elements of a given job, this holding could extend in that direction as well.

Other courts have not taken as stringent an approach as to what quality of expert testimony will be sufficient for an employer to meet his

---

v. Chevron U.S.A., Inc., 226 F.3d 1063, 1075 (9th Cir. 2000). The Supreme Court then reversed the Ninth Circuit, holding that the EEOC's regulations were valid, and remanded the case back to the Ninth Circuit. See Chevron U.S.A. v. Echazabal, 536 U.S. 73, 87 (2002).

[44] Echazabal, 336 F.3d at 1029.

[45] Id.

[46] These opinions were not offered, nor were they considered by Chevron, at the time Chevron made its determination.

[47] Echazabal, 336 F.3d at 1029.

[48] Id. at 1028-29.

[49] This is the strongest statement of the potential *Echazabal* rule. The dissent in *Echazabal* argues that Chevron did consider the opinion of Echazabal's treating physician, and that physician's opinion was that Echazabal should avoid the type of position that he was employed in. Id at 1037-1040.

burden by showing that an employee is a direct threat to himself or others in the workplace (or, correspondingly, for an employee to show that he can perform the essential functions of a job with or without reasonable accommodation). As pointed out in dissent in *Echazabal*,[50] the Ninth Circuit's majority opinion on remand could penalize an employer who has made a good faith attempt (by utilizing the opinion of its own trained professionals) to comply with the law. The dissent argues that the Ninth Circuit's rule effectively requires an employer to second-guess its own doctors, and be responsible for making the "correct" decision in light of conflicting medical opinions.

To safeguard against these concerns, other courts have required less of an employer to prove their direct threat defense as a matter of law. Under this view, a court's role is to make sure that an employer has considered sufficient medical evidence specific to the individual, but *not* to itself weigh the medical evidence.

For example, in *Knapp v. Northwestern University*, a student was barred from participation in intercollegiate basketball because of a heart defect.[51] The student brought suit under the Rehabilitation Act, seeking an injunction that would allow him to play. In discussing whether the student was an "otherwise qualified individual" within the meaning of the Rehabilitation Act, the court considered evidence as to the player's risk of injury or death if he played (if the risk was severe enough, he could not be a "qualified individual.").

The university considered the medical opinion of its team doctor in making the determination that the risk was significant. In spite of a conflicting opinion by Knapp's testifying doctor, the court held that the university had satisfied its evidentiary burden. The Seventh Circuit held that it was the province of the employer decision-maker, not the courts, to weigh conflicting evidence and decide which medical professional's opinion on which to base its decision. The court's role was limited to making sure the university considered individualized, medically acceptable evidence.[52]

Time will tell if *Echazabal* is followed widely, and whether courts will rigorously inquire into the propriety of the employer's medical decisions before granting an employer summary judgment. At a minimum, though, some courts will inquire deeper into what type of medical information an employer considers before making a summary judgment determination.

---

[50] Id. at 1035-38.

[51] Knapp v. Nw. Univ., 101 F.3d 473, 477 (7th Cir. 1996).

[52] Id. at 485.

Part 4

Access To Public Services: ADA Title II
Analysis

Chapter 10 STATUTORY BACKGROUND

ADA Title II requires that the services, programs, and activities of public entities be accessible to people with disabilities. Before the ADA was enacted, the Rehabilitation Act of 1973 prohibited some public entities from discriminating on the basis of disability.[1] This protection, however, was limited to public entities that received federal financial assistance.

---

[1]   29 U.S.C. § 794 (1973) ("No otherwise qualified individual with a disability in the United States ... shall, solely by reason of his or her disability, be excluded from the participation in, or be denied the benefits of, or be subjected to discrimination under any program or activity receiving Federal financial assistance.").

A primary purpose of Title II was to extend the existing prohibition on discrimination to state and local government entities, regardless of whether they received federal financial assistance.[2] Title II is therefore the least revolutionary of the major titles of the ADA.

Nevertheless, the implementation of Title II has not been without controversy. Like the other titles of the law, courts have grappled with questions concerning what entities should be covered, what proactive steps covered entities must take, and what exactly constitutes discrimination. These issues, and others, will be explored in this Part.

§ 10.1 Statutory And Regulatory Scheme

ADA Title II is divided into two main sections. Part A, entitled "Prohibition Against Discrimination And Other Generally Applicable Provisions," sets forth the general definitions and prohibitions against discrimination by public entities. The two major terms for the purposes of Title II, "public entity" and "qualified individual with a disability," are defined as follows:

(1)   Public entity

The term "public entity" means –

(A)   any State or local government;

(B)   any department, agency, special purpose district, or other instrumentality of a State or States or local government; and

(C)   the National Railroad Passenger Corporation, and any commuter authority (as defined in Section 24102(4) of Title 49).

(2)   Qualified individual with a disability

The term "qualified individual with a disability" means an individual with a disability who, with or without reasonable modifications to rules, policies, or practices, the removal of

---

[2]   E.g., S. Rep. No. 101-116, at 44 (1989); see also H.R. Rep. No. 101-485(II), at 84 (1990), reprinted in 1990 U.S.C.C.A.N. 303, 336, stating:

The first purpose [of Title II] is to make applicable the prohibition against discrimination on the basis of disability, currently set out in regulations implementing section 504 of the Rehabilitation Act of 1973, to all programs, activities, and services provided or made available by state and local governments or instrumentalities or agencies thereto, regardless of whether or not such entities receive Federal financial assistance.

architectural, communication, or transportation barriers, or the provision of auxiliary aids and services, meets the essential eligibility requirements for the receipt of services or the participation in programs or activities provided by a public entity.[3]

Title II's discrimination provision reads:

Subject to the provisions of this subchapter, no qualified individual with a disability shall, by reason of such disability, be excluded from participation in or be denied the benefits of the services, programs, or activities of a public entity, or be subjected to discrimination by any such entity.[4]

Part A of Title II contains an extensive regulatory scheme. The law requires the Attorney General to promulgate regulations implementing Part A.[5] The regulations can be found in Section 35 of Title 28 of the Code of Federal Regulations.[6] The regulations are intentionally patterned after, and to be interpreted consistently with, the regulations written pursuant to the Rehabilitation Act of 1973.[7]

Part B, entitled "Actions Applicable To Public Transportation Provided By Public Entities Considered Discriminatory," addresses the specialized issue of discrimination in public transportation. One purpose of Title II is to clarify and extend the Rehabilitation Act's requirements for public transportation entities, regardless of whether they receive federal aid.[8]

Part B is divided into two Subparts: "Subpart I – Public Transportation Other Than by Aircraft or Certain Rail Provisions," and "Subpart II – Public Transportation by Intercity and Commuter Rail."

---

[3]   42 U.S.C. § 12131 (2000) ("Definitions").

[4]   Id. § 12132 ("Discrimination").

[5]   See id. § 12134 ("Regulations").

[6]   28 C.F.R. §§ 35.101-35.190 (2002).

[7]   42 U.S.C. § 12134(b) (providing that these regulations "shall be consistent" with various sets of regulations that had been promulgated by the Department of Health, Education, and Welfare and the Department of Justice pursuant to the Rehabilitation Act). See 28 C.F.R. § 35.103 ("Relationship to other laws").

[8]   Anna L. Georgiou, Numby's Legacy – A Challenge to Local Autonomy: Regulating the Sitting of Group Homes in New York, 26 Fordham Urb. L.J. 209, 232 n.118 (citing S. Rep. No. 116, 101st Cong., 1st Sess. § 44 (1989)) ("The second purpose [of Title II] is to clarify the requirements of section 504 for public transportation entities that receive Federal aid, and to extend coverage to all public entities that provide public transportation, whether or not such entities receive Federal aid.").

The Subparts describe in detail the compliance requirements for public entities in the context of public transportation. Section 12132 provides a general prohibition on discrimination. Part B also has an extensive regulatory scheme, which the statute directs will be promulgated by the U.S. Department of Transportation.[9]

§ 10.2 Federalism And Title II – Did Congress Validly Abrogate The States' Sovereign Immunity?

Title II prohibits discrimination by state and local governmental entities. It also established compliance obligations toward this end.

The ADA's Findings and Purposes state the Congressional finding that discrimination against individuals with disabilities persists in such critical areas as education, transportation, communication, recreation, institutionalization, health services, voting, and access to public services.[10] In reaching this conclusion, Congress received testimony from individuals who documented accounts of state-sponsored discrimination in voting, education, licensing, and other public services.[11]

---

[9] See 42 U.S.C. §§ 12149, 12164 (2000).

[10] See id. § 12101(a)(3).

[11] See, e.g., Americans with Disabilities Act of 1988: Oversight Hearing on H.R. 4498, Before the House Comm. Subcomm. on Select Educ. of the House Comm. on Educ. and Lab., 100th Cong. 50 (1998) (statement of Ilona Durkin, Conn. Traumatic Brain Injury Ass'n) ("State agencies discriminate against people with traumatic brain injury because of their disability"); id. at 32 (statement of Eric L. Griffin, V.P. External Affairs, Nat'l Council on Indep. Living) (reading from the disability diary of Gloria Grabert, who while attending a college reunion "was unable to attend several events because of barriers such as stairs"); id. at 40-41 (statement of Emeka Nwojke, Assistant Dir., Northeast Indep. Living Program) (describing barriers in attempting to gain access to courtroom); id. at 46 (statement of Bonnie O'Day, Exec. Dir., Indep. Ctr. of Hampton Roads, Norfolk, Va.) (describing the death of an individual at a state university who was forced to traverse a dangerous grassy area because an intersection did not have a curb cut); id. at 48 (statement of Ellen Telker, Attorney at Law, Milford, Conn.) (explaining that state and local municipalities do not make materials available to a person who is unable to read print and that at least one courthouse in Connecticut did not have tactile markings in the elevators); id. at 73 (statement of Melissa Marshall, Exec. Dir., Disabilities Network of E. Conn.) (describing her experience with an inaccessible multi-building campus of a state university law school); id. at 88 (statement of Eileen Healy Horndt, Exec. Dir., Independence Northwest) (some state commissions on the deaf and hearing impaired are considering whether or not they can continue to provide interpreting services when they are unable to charge for these

A. *Recent Trends In Federalism Cases*

Recently, the U.S. Supreme Court has addressed the question of whether Congress exceeded its constitutional authority in abrogating or limiting states' sovereign immunity in civil rights statutes such as the ADA. The Eleventh Amendment to the Constitution, as interpreted by the Court, provides that states generally are immune from suits by citizens for monetary damages.[12]

In certain circumstances, however, Congress may abrogate states' sovereign immunity pursuant to Section 5 of the 14th Amendment.[13] Yet, in a recent line of cases, the Court has taken a narrow view of when such action is appropriate.

---

services); id. at 130 (statement of Barbara Waters) (asked to leave a state college as a result of her epileptic seizures); id. at 194 (statement of Denise Karuth, Chair, Mass. Coalition of Citizens with Disabilities) (due to inability to read a photo-reduced score had to drop a required theory course at a state university); id. at 156 (statement of Linda Mills) (explained difficulties in obtaining driver's license). Legislative History of Public Law 101-336, the Americans with Disabilities Act, Committee Print prepared for the House Education and Labor Committee, 101st Cong., Vol. 3 (Dec. 1990); WL A & P ADA Comm. Print 1990 (28B), at 1186-1187; Americans with Disabilities Act of 1989: Hearing on H.R. 2273 Before the Subcomm. on Select Educ. of the House Comm. on Educ. and Lab., 101st Cong. 65 (1989) (statement of Rick Edwards, Program Consultant of the Office of Vocational Rehab.) (state code provides for issuance of handicapped placards but handicapped spaces are filled with abusers); WL A & P Hearings S. 2273, at *63-64; and Americans with Disabilities Act of 1989; Hearings Before the Committee on Labor and Human Resources and the Senate Subcommittee on the Handicapped, 101st Cong. 101-156 (Sept. 20, 1989) (statement of Laura Oftedahl) (describing barriers to accessing information from public agencies in Braille, large-print, recorded, or computer-accessible form); WL A & P ADA Comm. Print 1990(28C), at *3075-3079.

[12]   U.S. Const. amend. XI ("The judicial power of the United States shall not be construed to extend to any suit in law or equity, commenced or prosecuted against one of the United States by citizens of another state, or by citizens or subjects of any foreign state."); see Seminole Tribe of Fla. v. Florida, 517 U.S. 44 (1996).

[13]   See U.S. Const. amend. XIV, § 1 ("No State shall make or enforce any law which shall abridge the privileges or immunities of citizens of the United States; nor shall any State deprive any person of life, liberty, or property, without due process of law; *nor deny to any person within its jurisdiction the equal protection of the laws.*") (emphasis added); id. § 5 ("The Congress shall have power to enforce, by appropriate legislation, the provisions of this article.").

In *City of Boerne v. Flores*, the Court struck down the Religious Freedom Restoration Act, holding that Congress only may use its Section 5 powers to provide *remedies* for constitutional rights recognized by the Courts.[14] The Court held that Congress may not create new constitutional rights or expand the scope of existing rights. Moreover, legislation passed pursuant to Congress's Section 5 powers must be "congruent and proportional" to the constitutional wrong to be prevented.

Similarly, in *Kimel v. Florida Board of Regents*, the Court held that the Age Discrimination in Employment Act (ADEA) was not a valid exercise of Congress's Section 5 power to enforce the 14th Amendment.[15] Thus, Congress exceeded its constitutional authority and could not abrogate states' immunity from suit. The Court held that there was not a documented constitutional wrong that Congress was attempting to remedy, because there was insufficient evidence of a pattern of unconstitutional discrimination on the part of states on the basis of age.[16]

Similarly, in *Florida Prepaid Postsecondary Education Expense Board v. College Savings Bank*,[17] the Court struck down the Patent and Plant Variety Protection Remedy Clarification Act, a federal statute authorizing private persons to sue a state for patent infringement. The Court again held that Congress had exceeded its constitutional authority in abrogating the states' immunity because it had not identified a pattern of patent infringement by the states.[18]

More recently, and arguably in contrast to its prior rulings in the area, in *Nevada Department of Human Resources v. Hibbs*, the Court ruled that state employees may recover money damages in federal court in the event of a state's failure to comply with the Family and Medical Leave Act (FMLA).[19] Here, the Court was satisfied that Congress, in passing the FMLA, had acted to correct and deter documented constitutional wrongs.

Dubbed by some as the "new federalism," this line of jurisprudence has generated controversy and commentary. Some commentators believe that the Court has restored the proper balance between federal legislation and state sovereignty.[20] Others argue that this line of cases is unfounded

---

[14] City of Boerne v. Flores, 521 U.S. 507 (1997).

[15] Kimel v. Fla. Bd. of Regents, 528 U.S. 62 (2000).

[16] Id. at 88-89.

[17] Florida Prepaid Postsecondary Educ. Exp. Bd. v. Coll. Sav. Bank, 527 U.S. 627 (1999).

[18] Id. at 640.

[19] Nev. Dep't of Human Res. v. Hibbs, 123 S.Ct. 1972 (2003).

[20] See Roderick M. Hills Jr., The Eleventh Amendment As Curb on Bureaucratic Power, 53 Stan. L. Rev. 1225 (2001) (arguing that the Rehnquist Court's Eleventh Amendment jurisprudence serves the public interest by maintaining a damages/injunction distinction which serves as

and the product of an activist court.[21] Critics contend that the Court has exceeded its role in limiting Congressional efforts to legislate pursuant to the Fourteenth Amendment.[22]

The ADA has played a prominent role in the development of this recent Eleventh Amendment jurisprudence. It is clear that Congress' intent in ADA Title II is to abrogate the states' sovereign immunity; it says as much.[23] The question for purposes of constitutional analysis is whether Congress has the power to do so.

---

a check on federal agencies); see also Ann Woolhandler, Old Property, New Property, and Sovereign Immunity, 75 Notre Dame L. Rev. 919, 920 (2000).

[21] See States' Rights Muddle, Wash. Post, May 28, 2003, at A18; see also Evan H. Caminker, "Appropriate" Means-Ends Constraints on Section 5 Powers, 53 Stan. L. Rev. 1127, 1129 (2001); Vicki C. Jackson, Principle and Compromise in Constitutional Adjudication: The Eleventh Amendment and State Sovereign Immunity, 75 Notre Dame L. Rev. 953, 953 (2000) ("The Court's Eleventh Amendment jurisprudence and sovereign immunity case law deserves the condemnation and resistance of scholars."); National Council on Disability, Tennessee v. Lane: The Legal Issues and the Implications for People with Disabilities, Policy Briefing Paper, http://www.ncd.gov/newsroom/publications/legalissues.html (Sept. 4, 2003) [hereinafter NCD Policy Briefing Paper].

[22] For a recent treatment of this subject, see John T. Noonan, Jr., Narrowing the Nation's Power: The Supreme Court Sides with the States (Univ. of Cal. Press 2002). Judge Noonan offers a powerful critique of the Supreme Court's recent jurisprudence. His thesis is that the Supreme Court has unjustifiably elevated state sovereign immunity to a constitutional principle, and in so doing, transferred power from Congress to itself. Judge Noonan also criticizes the "proportionality and congruence" tests that the Court has used to strike down these federal statutes.

[23] See 42 U.S.C. § 12202 (2000). Section 12202 provides:

A State shall not be immune under the eleventh amendment to the Constitution of the United States from an action in Federal or State court of competent jurisdiction for a violation of this chapter. In any action against a State for a violation of the requirements of this chapter, remedies (including remedies both at law and in equity) are available for such a violation to the same extent as such remedies are available for such a violation in an action against any public or private entity other than a State.

Four years after *City of Boerne*, in *Board of Trustees of the University of Alabama v. Garrett*,[24] the Court held that, pursuant to the Eleventh Amendment, a state is immune to suits for money damages under ADA Title I.

The Court's reasoning in *Garrett* can be summarized as follows: To abrogate the states' Eleventh Amendment sovereign immunity pursuant to Section 5 of the Fourteenth Amendment, Congress must find sufficient proof of a pattern of unconstitutional discrimination against people with disabilities in the specific area of state employment.

As discussed in Part 2, supra, the Supreme Court had previously held in *City of Cleburne v. Cleburne Living Center, Inc.* that people with disabilities do not invoke a heightened scrutiny analysis under the Equal Protection Clause.[25] Instead, states are free to discriminate on the basis of disability whenever it is *rational* to do so (a rational basis standard). To find that there was a pattern of unconstitutional wrongs, the Court in *Garrett* held that Congress would have needed to find a pattern of states irrationally discriminating against people with disabilities in employment.

The *Garrett* Court held that Congress failed to demonstrate such a pattern when it passed the ADA. Moreover, Congress' actions in Title I as applied to states, prohibiting discrimination and requiring reasonable accommodation, were not a congruent and proportional remedy to the harms it did find.[26]

B. *Title II Under Review* – Tennessee v. Lane

In *Garrett*, the Court declined to decide whether Congress validly abrogated sovereign immunity in enacting ADA Title II.[27] The lower courts have split on this issue.[28]

---

[24] Bd. of Trs. of the Univ. of Ala. v. Garrett, 531 U.S. 356, 374 (2001).

[25] City of Cleburne v. Cleburne Living Ctr., Inc., 473 U.S. 432 (1985).

[26] For a critique of the Court's decision in Garrett, see Noonan, supra note 22, at 113-19. Among other things, Judge Noonan takes issue with what he believes is the Court's improper weighing of the evidence before Congress when it passed the ADA. As the appendix to Justice Breyer's dissent made clear, Congress found many instances of state-sponsored discrimination. And although most of these did not demonstrate discrimination in employment, Judge Noonan argues that Congress is not a court of law, and should be allowed to draw inferences and conclusions from the type of testimony and evidence it reviewed.

[27] Garrett, 531 U.S. at 360 n.1.

[28] For cases holding that the Eleventh Amendment does not preclude monetary damages against states under Title II, see Popovich v. Cuyahoga County Ct. of Common Pleas, 276 F.3d 808 (6th Cir. 2002) (Due Process Clause); Shaboon v. Duncan, 252 F.3d 722 (5th Cir. 2001); Wroncy v. Or.

During its 2003-2004 term, however, the Supreme Court will resolve this issue. In some fundamental ways, ADA Title II is different from the other statutes that the Court has considered in the area of Eleventh Amendment jurisprudence. Title II addresses *access to* government service, and goes to the heart of the federalism debate. Should the Court rule that Title II's remedies exceeded Congress' constitutional authority to abrogate states' sovereign immunity, its practical reach will be curtailed. In this scenario, Title II would be limited to prospective injunctive relief against states and to suits for damages against local governments.[29]

The Court was set to decide this issue in the case of *Medical Board of California v. Hason.* The case involved the state of California's denial of Dr. Hason's application for license to practice medicine on the grounds of mental illness.

The Court accepted certiorari on the question: "Does the Eleventh Amendment bar suit under Title II of the ADA against the California Medical Board for denial of medical license based on the applicant's

---

Dep't of Transp., 2001 WL 474550 (9th Cir. 2000); ProjectLife, Inc. v. Glendening, 139 F.Supp.2d 703 (D. Md. 2001); Navedo v. Maloney, 172 F.Supp.2d 276 (D. Mass. 2001); Bowers v. NCAA, 171 F.Supp.2d 389 (D. N.J. 2001); Bartlett v. N.Y. St. Bd. of Law Exam's, 2001 WL 930792 (S.D.N.Y. 2001); Jones v. Pa. Dep't of Welfare Bureau of Blindness and Visual Servs., 164 F.Supp.2d 490 (E.D. Pa. 2001). For cases holding that Title II does not validly abrogate the states sovereign immunity, see Angel v. Commonwealth of Kentucky, 314 F.3d 262 (6th Cir. 2002); Wessel v. Glendening, 306 F.3d 203 (4th Cir. 2002); Garcia v. S.U.N.Y. Health Sci. Ctr. of Brooklyn, 280 F.3d 98 (2d Cir. 2001); Thompson v. Colorado, 258 F.3d 1241 (10th Cir. 2001); Reickenbacker v. Foster, 274 F.3d 974 (5th Cir. 2001); Neiberger v. Hawkins, 150 F.Supp.2d 1118 (D. Colo. 2001); Doe v. Div. of Youth and Family Servs., 148 F.Supp.2d 462 (D. N. J. 2001); Frederick L. v. Dep't of Pub. Welfare, 157 F.Supp.2d 509 (E.D. Pa. 2001).

[29] As will be discussed below, this form of relief would be allowed pursuant to the doctrine of Ex Parte Young, 209 U.S. 123 (1908). In this instance, the question of what entities are "arms of the state" for Eleventh Amendment purposes would take on increased significance. See, e.g., Fresenius Med. Care Cardiovascular Res., Inc., v. P.R. and the Caribbean Cardiovascular Ctr. Corp., 322 F.3d 56 (1st Cir. 2003) (holding that hospital was not an arm of the state and therefore not entitled to Eleventh Amendment immunity). Prospective injunctive relief is also permissible under an entirely different constitutional provision – the Commerce Clause. See U.S. Const., Art. I, § 8 (giving Congress the power to regulate "commerce among the several states"). For a discussion of how that separate power might be limited under recent Supreme Court decisions, see NCD Policy Briefing Paper, supra note 21, at 7, n.13.

mental illness?" However, the state withdrew its petition prior to oral argument, and the writ of certiorari was dismissed. [30]

During its 2003-2004 term, the Court again accepted *certiorari* in a case that will begin to settle this issue. In *Tennessee v. Lane*,[31] two persons with disabilities – a defendant in a traffic case and a court reporter – sued under Title II to vindicate their fundamental right of access to the courts.

The facts in *Lane* are compelling. The plaintiffs claim that they were excluded from courthouses and court proceedings through an inability to access the physical facilities. One of the plaintiffs, George Lane, crawled up two flights of steps to attend his state court hearing in a building that lacked an elevator. He decided not to make the same attempt when called for a second hearing, and notified the judge that he was downstairs. The judge had him arrested and jailed for failure to appear in court.[32]

The other plaintiff, Beverly Jones works as a certified court reporter in Tennessee. She claimed that her work opportunities were limited because courthouses in Tennessee are physically inaccessible to her. She identified twenty-five counties in Tennessee that she claims were inaccessible at the time of her complaint. Her requests for accommodations were met without success.[33]

Like the respective states in *Hason* and *Garrett* (i.e., California and Alabama), the state of Tennessee moved to dismiss Lane's complaint on the grounds that Congress did not validly abrogated Tennessee's sovereign immunity under Title II. Unlike the *Garrett* and *Hason* cases, the *Lane* plaintiffs argued that their claims were based on the Due Process Clause of the 14th Amendment, *not* the Equal Protection Clause.

The state of Tennessee responded in two ways: it argued, first, that the plaintiffs' claims did not allege due process violations,[34] and second, that even if there were due process violations, Title II's abrogation of sovereign immunity was invalid.

The District Court agreed with Tennessee, and granted the state's motion to dismiss. The Sixth Circuit reversed. The appeals court held

---

[30]   Med. Bd. of Cal. v. Hason, 123 S.Ct. 1179 (2003).

[31]   Tennessee v. Lane, 123 S.Ct. 2622 (2003).

[32]   See 26(12) Rep. on Disability Programs 91 (June 26, 2003).

[33]   Id.

[34]   Lane v. Tennessee, 315 F.3d 680, 682 (6th Cir. 2003). For example, one of plaintiff Jones's claims is that because of her disability she cannot get into many courtrooms for jobs. This may fall short of being a protected due process right.

that the right to access the courts was among the fundamental rights guaranteed by the Due Process Clause of the Fourteenth Amendment.[35]

The Sixth Circuit followed its earlier holding in *Popovich v. Cuyahoga County Court of Common Pleas*.[36] Here, the court ruled that, although the Eleventh Amendment barred claims under Title II on equal protection protections, it did not do so as to plaintiffs' due process claims.[37]

The Sixth Circuit reasoned that before enacting Title II, Congress received evidence of the pervasive physical barriers in government buildings, including courthouses and courtrooms. Congress concluded these barriers had the effect of denying people with disabilities the opportunity to exercise their rights guaranteed by the Due Process Clause.[38]

The appeals court held that Title II was appropriate legislation to prevent states from unduly burdening these constitutional rights. Because the district court had granted the state's motion to dismiss without developing a factual record as to whether the plaintiffs' claims were due process violations, the court reversed and remanded the case for such a determination.[39]

The Supreme Court's acceptance of *certiorari* in *Lane* will serve to resolve this pressing issue. It is unclear whether the use of a due process theory, as opposed to an equal protection theory, will result in a different outcome.

The Sixth Circuit in *Lane* suggests that a criminal defendant's right to access courts should invoke a heightened scrutiny analysis under the Due Process Clause. The use of a due process theory may prove to be a crucial distinction from the equal protection theory pursued in *Garrett*.

Again, in *Garrett*, the Court held that Congress would have to have found sufficient evidence of a pattern of unconstitutional discrimination judged under a *rational basis* standard – under *Cleburne*,

---

[35] See id. at 682. The court noted that the Due Process Clause has been interpreted to provide the accused a right to be present at all stages of the trial where his absence might frustrate the fairness of proceedings. Id. (citing Faretta v. California, 422 US 806, 819 n.15 (1975)). The court also noted that parties in civil litigation have an analogous due process right to be present in the courtroom and to meaningfully participate in the process. Id. (citing Popovich v. Cuyahoga County Ct. of Common Pleas, 276 F.3d 808 (6th Cir. 2002)).

[36] Popovich v. Cuyahoga County Ct. of Common Pleas, 276 F.3d 808 (6th Cir. 2002).

[37] Lane, 315 F.3d at 682.

[38] Id.

[39] Id. at 683.

people with disabilities are not a protected class entitled to heightened scrutiny under the Equal Protection Clause. The *Lane* Due Process theory skirts the protected class issue that led to the *Garrett* plaintiffs' downfall. This is because access to the courts is a fundamental right guaranteed to all citizens under the Due Process Clause, and thereby subject to strict scrutiny analysis.

However, the crucial issue in *Garrett* – the modicum of proof and the level of specificity that Congress needs before legislating to remedy a pattern of unconstitutional discrimination by states – likely is no different for the Due Process Clause than for the Equal Protection Clause. This leads commentators, including one of the authors of this treatise, to predict that the Court will follow its decision in *Garrett* and hold that Title II's damages provisions against state officials violate the Eleventh Amendment.[40] Such a decision will direct the future impact of the ADA and related federal civil rights statutes.[41]

C.   *Other Immunities As Defenses In Title II Cases*

Thus far, we have discussed scenarios where an individual sues a state for a violation of Title II seeking money damages. In these cases, the individual typically names a state official in his official capacity, which is interpreted as a suit against the state.[42] A state therefore may raise its Eleventh Amendment sovereign immunity as a defense, as discussed above.

However, when a claim is made against a state officer in his official capacity and only requests the remedy of prospective injunctive relief, there is an exception to the sovereign immunity rule. Under the doctrine of *Ex Parte Young*,[43] the Eleventh Amendment is no bar to "federal jurisdiction over a suit against a state official when that suit seeks only prospective injunctive relief in order to 'end a continuing violation of federal law.'"[44]

---

[40]   See 26(12) Rep. on Disability Programs 91 (June 26, 2003) (views of Peter Blanck).

[41]   For an alternative view that Congress has the ability to abrogate the states' 11th Amendment immunity pursuant to the Privileges or Immunities Clause, see William J. Rich, Taking "Privileges or Immunities" Seriously: A Call to Expand the Constitutional Canon, 87 Minn. L. Rev. 153 (2002). For a further discussion of the ramifications of this decision on the lives of people with disabilities, see NCD Policy Briefing Paper, supra note 21.

[42]   See Hafer v. Melo, 502 U.S. 21 (1991).

[43]   Ex Parte Young, 209 U.S. 123 (1908).

[44]   Seminole Tribe of Fla. v. Florida, 517 U.S. 44, 73 (1996) (quoting Green v. Mansour, 474 U.S. 64, 68 (1985)).

The *Ex Parte Young* doctrine rests on the premise that "a suit against a state official to enjoin an ongoing violation of federal law is not a suit against the State."[45] This rule generally holds even when the relief sought has a substantial ancillary effect on the state treasury.[46]

In *Armstrong v. Wilson*,[47] a class of inmates with various disabilities claimed that the state prison system violated Title II by not providing adequate evacuation plans for prisoners with disabilities. They also claimed that the range of vocational programs for disabled inmates was more limited than those for non-disabled prisoners.[48] Note that we discuss below that in *Pennsylvania Department of Corrections v. Yeskey* the Court determined that state prisons were "public entities" for the purposes of the statute.[49]

In *Armstrong v. Wilson*, the plaintiffs named the state prison officials in their official capacities, and sought only prospective injunctive relief. The Ninth Circuit held that even though the plaintiffs in essence were asking for wide-ranging, wholesale institutional reforms, their claims fell squarely within the *Ex Parte Young* exception to Eleventh Amendment sovereign immunity.[50]

Other courts have held that the ADA and Rehabilitation Act of 1973 allow plaintiffs to sue state officials in their individual capacities for money damages in certain circumstances.[51] In these cases, however, the state officers typically raise the defense of *qualified immunity* (also referred to as *good faith immunity*).

This defense provides immunity from liability to government officials engaged in discretionary government activities unless their conduct violates "clearly established statutory or constitutional rights."[52] The right must be established such that a reasonable official would have understood that his behavior violated that right.[53]

---

[45] Idaho v. Coeur d'Alene Tribe, 521 U.S. 261, 295 (1997).

[46] Papasan v. Allain, 478 U.S. 265, 278 (1986).

[47] Armstrong v. Wilson, 124 F.3d 1019 (9th Cir. 1997).

[48] Id. at 1021.

[49] Pa. Dep't of Corrections v. Yeskey, 524 U.S. 207 (1998)

[50] Id. at 1025-26. The issue of whether injunctive relief could be justified under the Commerce Clause is a separate one. See supra note 29.

[51] See Shotz v. City of Plantation, Fla., 2003 WL 2207156 (11th Cir. 2003) (Title II of ADA); see also Lee v. Trs. of Dartmouth Coll., 958 F.Supp. 37, 45 (D.N.H. 1997).

[52] Harlow v. Fitzgerald, 457 U.S. 800, 818 (1982).

[53] See Summar v. Bennett, 157 F.3d 1054, 1058 (6th Cir. 1998).

An example of this principle in the ADA and Rehabilitation Act contexts can be found in *Key v. Grayson*.[54] A prisoner brought actions under Title II and the Rehabilitation Act for damages against officials of the state department of corrections in their individual capacities. The prisoner claimed that the officials discriminated against him because of his hearing impairment. He was not allowed to participate in his sex offender therapy because he needed an interpreter, which the prison officials claimed would have violated the confidentiality of the therapy sessions.[55]

The defendants raised the qualified immunity defense, on the grounds that at the date the alleged discrimination occurred (1996), the Court had not yet determined that the ADA and Rehabilitation Act applied to prisoners.[56] The Sixth Circuit agreed, and the defendants therefore were afforded qualified immunity.[57]

D. *The Rehabilitation Act of 1973*

Section 504 of the Rehabilitation Act, the other federal statute that prohibits state discrimination against people with disabilities, has not been immune to questions related to its proper reach. Generally, the applicable Eleventh Amendment jurisprudence has tracked the ADA cases. Presently, there is a split among the courts of appeals as to whether a plaintiff may bring suit against a state for money damages under the Rehabilitation Act.

In *Reickenbacker v. Foster*, the Fifth Circuit held that the Rehabilitation Act did not represent a valid exercise of Congress's power under Section 5 of the Fourteenth Amendment, despite a clear Congressional intent to abrogate the states' sovereign immunity.[58] But in *Miranda B. v. Kitzhaber*, the Ninth Circuit held that with the Rehabilitation Act, Congress validly abrogated the states' sovereign immunity.[59]

---

[54] Key v. Grayson, 179 F.3d 996 (6th Cir. 1999).

[55] Id. at 998.

[56] Id. at 1000. As discussed below, this issue was later resolved, in favor of coverage, by the Supreme Court in *Pennsylvania Department of Corrections v. Yeskey*, 524 U.S. 207 (1998).

[57] See Grayson, 179 F.3d at 1001. See also Gorman v. Bartch, 152 F.3d 907 (8th Cir. 1998).

[58] Reickenbacker v. Foster, 274 F.3d 974, 983 (5th Cir. 2001). This case also involved Title II of the ADA. The court's reasoning followed the Supreme Court's decision in *Garrett*. The court held that Title II's and Section 504's affirmative accommodation obligation exceeded that imposed by the Constitution.

[59] Miranda B. v. Kitzhaber, 328 F.3d 1181, 1186 (9th Cir. 2003). This case also involved Title II of the ADA.

The Rehabilitation Act contains a unique wrinkle on this issue. It is settled that, even if Congress does not validly abrogate state sovereign immunity using its Section 5 powers, a state may voluntarily waive its sovereign immunity by consenting to a suit.[60] For example, a state can choose to waive its immunity in exchange for some "gratuity" (i.e., funds) from Congress,[61] or because it for other reasons wishes to submit itself to federal jurisdiction.[62]

Some courts have held that by accepting federal funds under the Rehabilitation Act, states consent to suit in federal court and waive their Eleventh Amendment sovereign immunity.[63] Ultimately, this may be the ground on which the *Garrett* plaintiffs obtain relief. The Eleventh Circuit has ruled that plaintiffs' case against various Alabama state agencies for employment discrimination, which the Supreme Court held could not proceed under ADA Title I,[64] may proceed under the Rehabilitation Act.[65] The court held that the state, and by implication its agencies, waived its sovereign immunity by accepting federal funds.[66]

Other courts have rejected this theory. These courts, relying on the Supreme Court's guidance that waiver and consent to suit must be "voluntary," have held that states could not have voluntarily waived sovereign immunity by accepting Rehabilitation Act funds during a period when they believed Congress had already abrogated their immunity under the law.[67] The Supreme Court may act in the near future to resolve this circuit split.

---

[60] See Coll. Sav. Bank v. Fla. Prepaid Postsecondary Educ. Expense Bd., 527 U.S. 666, 670 (1999).

[61] Id. at 686.

[62] For example, in the wake of *Board of Trustees of the University of Alabama v. Garrett*, 531 U.S. 356, 374 (2001), several states have waived their sovereign immunity to suits under Title I of the ADA. See discussion in Part 7 of this treatise, infra.

[63] See Clark v. Cal. Dep't of Corrections, 123 F.3d 1267, 1271 (9th Cir. 1997); see also A.W. v. Jersey City Pub. Sch., 2003 WL 21962952 (3d Cir. 2003); Miranda B., 328 F.3d at 1186.

[64] See Garrett, 531 U.S. at 374.

[65] See Garrett v. Univ. of Ala., 2003 WL 22097772 (11th Cir. 2003).

[66] Id.

[67] See Miller v. Tex. Tech Univ. Health Sci. Ctr., 330 F.3d 691, 695 (5th Cir. 2003) ("What looks like a hard but plain choice in retrospect – accept funds and thereby waive sovereign immunity – at the time was in fact an easy and carefree choice for Tech – accept funds without consequence, because [§ 504] appeared already to have abrogated Tech's immunity."). This case will be reheard en banc. See Miller v. Tex. Tech Univ. Health Sci. Ctr., 342 F.3d 563 (2003).

There is an additional layer of complexity relating to whether Rehabilitation Act suits can proceed against a state in *state* court. In *Robinson v. Kansas*,[68] the Tenth Circuit held that Kansas waived its sovereign immunity and consented to suit under the Rehabilitation Act in federal court.[69] However, in *Purvis v. Williams*,[70] the Supreme Court of Kansas reached the opposite conclusion as to Rehabilitation Act suits for money damages in state courts. The high state court held that Kansas's sovereign immunity – which it had not waived by accepting federal funds – precluded suit in Kansas's state courts under the Rehabilitation Act for money damages.[71]

A separate sub-issue is whether the acceptance of federal money requires an institution or even a state as a whole to refrain from discrimination, or whether only the specific program or agency funded has that obligation.[72] Federal regulations have been issued to clarify that there is broad coverage for institutions that receive federal funds.[73]

---

[68] Robinson v. Kansas, 295 F.3d 1183 (10th Cir. 2002).

[69] Id.

[70] Purvis v. Williams, 73 P.3d 740 (2003).

[71] Id. at 751.

[72] See, e.g., Cureton v. NCAA, 198 F.3d 107 (3d Cir. 1999) (holding that the disparate-impact regulations promulgated under Title VI are program specific, and the NCAA was not subject to Title VI based on funds received by affiliated youth enrichment program).

[73] See generally "Nondiscrimination on the Basis of Race, Color, National Origin, Handicap, or Age in Programs or Activities Receiving Federal Financial Assistance; Final Rule," 68 Fed. Reg. 51,334 (Aug. 26, 2003).

Chapter 11 COVERAGE

§ 11.1 Introduction

Title II applies to the services, programs, and activities that are offered by public entities.

A. *"Public Entity"*

As a threshold matter, the text of the statute unambiguously defines "public entities" as state and local governments.[1] The question has arisen, however, as to what "instrumentalities" of state and local governments fall within Title II's ambit.

In *Pennsylvania Department of Corrections v. Yeskey*, the Supreme Court considered whether state prisons were "public entities" for the purposes of the ADA.[2] The case involved a state prison inmate who claimed that he was denied admission to a prison boot camp program due to a history of hypertension in violation of Title II. The State argued that state prisons were not covered under Title II of the ADA.

Justice Scalia, writing for a unanimous Court, held that the statute's language unambiguously included state prisons.[3] Other courts have held that public entities include state universities,[4] state and municipal courts,[5] state bars and board of law examiners,[6] local police departments,[7] city planning and zoning boards,[8] high school athletic associations,[9] state judicial nominating commissions,[10] and state pension

---

[1] 42 U.S.C. § 12131(1)(A) (2000).

[2] Pa. Dep't of Corrections v. Yeskey, 524 U.S. 207 (1998).

[3] Id. at 209; see also Randolph v. Rodgers, 980 F.Supp. 1051 (E.D. Mo. 1997); Saunders v. Horn, 959 F.Supp. 689 (E.D. Pa. 1996).

[4] See Coleman v. Zatechka, 824 F.Supp. 1360 (D. Neb. 1993); see also Bowers v. Nat'l Collegiate Athletic Ass'n, 9 F.Supp.2d 460 (D. N.J. 1998); Darian v. Univ. of Mass. Boston, 980 F.Supp. 77 (D. Mass. 1997).

[5] See Galloway v. Sup. Ct. of District of Columbia, 816 F.Supp. 12 (D. D.C. 1993); see also Soto v. City of Newark, 72 F.Supp.2d 489 (D. N.J. 1999); People v. Caldwell, 603 N.Y.S.2d 713 (N.Y. City Crim. Ct. 1993).

[6] See Petition of Rubenstein, 637 A.2d 1131 (Del. 1994); see also Ware v. Wyo. Bd. of Law Exam's, 973 F.Supp. 1339 (D. Wyo. 1997), affirmed, 161 F.3d 19 (10th Cir. 1998); State ex rel. Okla. Bar Ass'n v. Busch, 919 P.2d 1114 (Okla. 1996).

[7] See Gorman v. Bartch, 152 F.3d 907 (8th Cir. 1998).

[8] See Innovative Health Sys., Inc. v. City of White Plains, 117 F.3d 37 (2d Cir. 1997).

[9] See Cruz ex. rel. Cruz v. Pa. Interscholastic Athletic Ass'n, Inc., 157 F.Supp.2d 485 (E.D. Pa. 2001); see also Johnson v. Fla. High Sch. Activities Ass'n, 899 F.Supp. 579 (M.D. Fla. 1995).

funds.[11] Note, however, that courts have declined to classify federal agencies or private groups as public entities for the purposes of Title II.[12]

According to the Department of Justice, factors to be considered in determining whether an entity is a public entity include:

(1) Whether the entity is operated with public funds;

(2) Whether the entity's employees are considered government employees;

(3) Whether the entity receives significant assistance from the government by provision of property or equipment; and

(4) Whether the entity is governed by an independent board selected by members of a private organization or a board elected by the voters or appointed by elected officials.[13]

Sometimes, a state will establish an entity that then becomes run as a public corporation. In *Fresnius Medical Care Cardiovascular Resources, Inc. v. Puerto Rico*,[14] the First Circuit had to determine whether a special purpose hospital that was state established but currently a public corporation was a "public entity." In holding that the hospital was a public entity, the court applied the two-part analysis set forth by the Supreme Court in *Hess v. Port Auth. Trans-Hudson Corp.*[15]

The *Fresnius* court first examined whether the state had "clearly structured the entity to share its sovereignty."[16] If the answer to that

---

[10] See Doe v. Judicial Nominating Comm'n for Fifteenth Judicial Cir. of Fla., 906 F.Supp. 1534 (S.D. Fla. 1995).

[11] See Piquard v. City of E. Peoria, 887 F.Supp. 1106 (C.D. Ill. 1995).

[12] See Isle Royale Boaters Ass'n v. Norton, 154 F.Supp.2d 1098 (W.D. Mich. 2001) (National Park Service, as unit of federal government, not "public entity" for purposes of Title II); see also Zingher v. Yacavone, 30 F.Supp.2d 446 (D. Vt. 1997) (U.S. Department of Education and Secretary of Department of Education were not "public entities" for purposes of Title II); Ellis v. Morehouse Sch. of Med., 925 F.Supp. 1529 (N.D. Ga. 1996).

[13] U.S. Dep't of Justice, Title II Technical Assistance Manual § 2.3000, http://www.usdoj.gov/crt/ada/taman3.html (Nov. 1993) [hereinafter TAM II].

[14] Fresenius Med. Care Cardiovascular Res., Inc. v. P.R. and the Caribbean Cardiovascular Ctr. Corp., 322 F.3d 56, 75 (1st Cir. 2003).

[15] Hess v. Port Auth. Trans-Hudson Corp., 513 U.S. 30 (1994).

[16] Among the factors the court considered in this analysis were: the extent of state control in matters such as appointment of board members,

question is clear, it ends the analysis. If the answer to that question is unclear, the court examines whether the state treasury is liable for damages caused by the entity.

In this case, the First Circuit found the first question did not resolve the issue. The court then concluded, under the second part of the test, that the hospital was not an arm of the state because the state was not obligated on the debt of the hospital.[17]

Of course, if a defendant is found not to be an arm of the state, that defendant may be sued under a different title of the ADA. In *Savage v. Glendale Union High School*,[18] a terminated employee sued the school district claiming disability discrimination in violation of Title I. The school district attempted to claim Eleventh Amendment sovereign immunity. The court held that the school district was not an arm of the state, and therefore not entitled to sovereign immunity.[19]

B.   *Service, Program, Or Activity*

1.   The general rule – broad construction

Title II applies to "services, programs, and activities" of public entities.[20] At various times, litigants have attempted to use this language to limit the functions of a public entity that fall within Title II's ambit. By and large, this has not been a successful strategy.

In *Pennsylvania Department of Corrections v. Yeskey*, discussed earlier, the state of Pennsylvania argued that state prisons did not provide "services, programs, or activities" as those terms are commonly understood.[21] Justice Scalia, writing for a unanimous Court, rejected this argument and took a broad view of what services, programs or activities could be.

Lower courts have done the same. In *Bay Area Addiction Research Treatment, Inc. v. City of Antioch*, the city argued that zoning

---

veto of board action, and defining board responsibilities; the legislative history regarding the characterization of the entity and state courts' characterization of the entity; whether the entities functions were readily classifiable as state, local, or non-governmental functions; and whether the state was legally responsible for the entity's debts. Hess, 513 U.S. at 44; Fresenuis, 322 F.3d at 65 n.7.

[17]   Fresenius, 322 F.3d at 68-72.

[18]   Savage v. Glendale Union High Sch., 2003 WL 22087572 (9th Cir. 2003).

[19]   Id. at *2.

[20]   See 42 U.S.C. § 12132 (2000).

[21]   See Pa. Dep't of Corrections v. Yeskey, 524 U.S. 206, 212 (1998).

was not a service, program, or activity for purposes of the statute.[22] In rejecting this argument, the Ninth Circuit noted that the Rehabilitation Act defined "program or activity" to include "all of the operations of" a qualifying local government.[23] This is important because Congress instructed that the ADA be interpreted consistently with the Rehabilitation Act.

The *Bay Area* court was reluctant to take a narrow view of "service, program, or activity." It reasoned that Congress had intended to sweep broadly with the ADA, and had analogized the plight of people with disabilities to that of "discrete and insular minorities."[24]

The Ninth Circuit noted that the ADA's legislative history supported a broad view of "service, program, or activity."[25] The court pointed out that the Report of the House Committee on Education and Labor stated as much:

> The Committee has chosen not to list all the types of actions that are included within the term "discrimination," as was done in titles I and III, because this title essentially simply extends the anti-discrimination prohibition embodied in section 504 to all actions of state and local governments.[26]

Finally, the *Bay Area* court noted that in the Department of Justice Regulations, the preamble to § 12132 notes that "Title II applies to

---

[22]   See Bay Area Addiction Research Treatment, Inc. v. City of Antioch, 179 F.3d 725, 731 (9th Cir. 1999).

[23]   Id. (citing 29 U.S.C. § 794(b)(1)(A)).

[24]   See Bay Area, 179 F.3d at 731 ("This sweeping language ... strongly suggests that § 12132 should not be construed to allow the creation of spheres in which public entities may discriminate on the basis of an individual's disability."); see also United States v. Carolene Prods., Inc., 304 U.S. 144, 153 n.4 (1938) ("[P]rejudice against discrete and insular minorities may be a special condition, which tends seriously to curtail the operation of those political processes ordinarily to be relied upon to protect minorities, and which may call for a correspondingly more searching judicial inquiry.").

[25]   Bay Area, 179 F.3d at 731.

[26]   Id. at 731-2 (citing H.R. Rep. No. 101-485(II), at 84 (1990), reprinted in U.S.C.C.A.N. 303, 367). The court also noted that the House bill's general prohibition against discrimination won out over the Senate bill's enumeration of general and specific prohibitions against discrimination. Id. at 732 ("In other words, Congress specifically rejected an approach that could have left room for exceptions to § 12132's prohibition on discrimination by public entities.").

anything a public entity does."[27] The court concluded that zoning was a covered "service, program, or activity" for purposes of Title II.[28]

Similarly, in *Barden v. City of Sacramento*, at issue was whether sidewalks were a service, program, or activity within the meaning of Title II.[29] Following the same analysis as the court in *Bay Area*, the *Barden* Court chose to view any public function, or anything the state or city does, as a service, program, or activity.[30] To rule otherwise, and to distinguish which public functions are services, programs, or activities, and which are not, "would disintegrate into needless 'hair splitting arguments.'"[31]

Other courts have followed substantially similar logic in holding that various state and local government functions, including farmers' practices of burning wheat stubble,[32] meetings at state courthouses,[33] voting,[34] municipal wedding ceremonies,[35] use of telephones in prisons,[36] and Lamaze classes in hospitals[37] are services, programs, or activities within the meaning of Title II.

There are limits, however. Courts have held that incarceration or sleeping in one's prison cell[38] and cable television reception for inmates[39] are not services, programs, or activities for Title II purposes.

---

[27] Id. at 732 (citing 28 C.F.R. pt. 35, app. A, at 438).

[28] Id. The court never addressed the issue of whether it was a program, a service, or an activity. Most other courts have similarly declined to pigeonhole the function at issue into one of these three boxes.

[29] Barden v. City of Sacramento, 292 F.3d 1073 (9th Cir. 2002).

[30] Id. at 1076 ("In keeping with our precedent, maintaining public sidewalks is a normal function of a city and 'without a doubt something that the [City] does'.") (citations omitted).

[31] Id. (citing Innovative Health Sys., Inc. v. City of White Plains, 117 F.3d 37, 45 (2d Cir. 1997)). The Supreme Court denied certiorari in Barden. See City of Sacramento, Cal. v. Barden, 123 S.Ct. 2639 (2003).

[32] Save Our Summers v. Wash. St. Dep't of Ecology, 132 F.Supp.2d 896 (E.D. Wash. 1999).

[33] Layton v. Elder, 143 F.3d 469, 471 (8th Cir. 1998).

[34] Lightbourn v. County of El Paso, Tex., 118 F.3d 421 (5th Cir. 1997).

[35] Soto v. City of Newark, 72 F.Supp.2d 489, 493-94 (D. N.J. 1999).

[36] Niece v. Fitzner, 922 F.Supp. 1208, 1217 (E.D. Mich. 1996).

[37] Bravin v. Mount Sinai Med. Ctr., 186 F.R.D. 293, 304-05 (S.D.N.Y. 1999).

[38] Bryant v. Madigan, 84 F.3d 246, 249 (7th Cir. 1996).

[39] Aswegan v. Bruhl, 113 F.3d 109, 110 (8th Cir. 1997).

2.   Employment under Title II

There is one significant open issue concerning the scope of "service, program, or activity." It concerns employment. The regulations promulgated by the Attorney General provide that Title II applies to employment: "No qualified individual with a disability shall, on the basis of disability, be subjected to discrimination in employment under any service, program, or activity conducted by a public entity."[40] Legislative history suggests that Congress intended Title II, as well as Title I, to reach employment.[41]

Accordingly, some courts have entertained employment discrimination claims under Title II. In *Bledsoe v. Palm Beach City Soil & Water Conservation District*, the plaintiff brought a Title II claim after he was terminated when his employer failed to accommodate his disability.[42] The district court focused on the words "services, programs, or activities," and found that "understood as a whole, [these words] focus on a public entity's outputs rather than inputs."[43] The court concluded that because employment was not directly tied to a service, program, or activity, employment actions fell outside of Title II.[44]

The Eleventh Circuit rejected this analysis, reasoning that the district court had ignored the final clause of § 12132, which protects qualified individuals with a disability from being "subjected to discrimination by any such entity."[45] The court held that this language did not limit the ADA's coverage "to conduct that occurs in the 'programs, services, or activities' of [a public entity]. Rather, it is a catch-all phrase that prohibits all discrimination by a public entity, regardless of the context."[46]

The court also reasoned that the DOJ regulations, the Rehabilitation Act precedent, and the legislative history of the ADA compelled such a conclusion.[47] Other courts have followed this analysis,

---

[40]   28 C.F.R. § 35.140(a) (2003).

[41]   H.R. Rep. No. 101-485(III), at 84 (1990).

[42]   Bledsoe v. Palm Beach City Soil & Water Conservation Dist., 133 F.3d 816 (11th Cir. 1998).

[43]   See Bledsoe v. Palm Beach Soil and Water Conservation Dist., 942 F.Supp. 1439, 1443 (S.D. Fla. 1996).

[44]   Id.

[45]   Bledsoe, 133 F.3d at 821.

[46]   Id. at 822 (citing Innovative Health Sys., Inc. v. City of White Plains, 117 F.3d 37, 44-45 (2d Cir. 1997)).

[47]   Id.

and held that employment discrimination claims can be properly brought under Title II.[48]

Because Title II, unlike Title I, is not limited to public employers with 25 or more employees, this approach substantially expands the non-discrimination obligations of government entities. It also releases government employees from the procedural prerequisites of Title I (e.g., filing with the EEOC).

Other courts, however, have viewed the "services, programs, or activities" language as a limiting factor, and reasoned that employment does not fall within this language. In *Zimmerman v. State of Oregon Department of Justice*,[49] the Ninth Circuit reasoned that the first clause of § 12132 (i.e., the services, programs, or activities clause) is linked to the second clause (i.e., the more general discrimination clause). Because obtaining or retaining a job is not the receipt of services, and employment is not a program or activity, the court held that employment could not be covered under Title II.[50]

In reaching this conclusion, the court considered the overall structure of the ADA, reasoning that if Title II were construed to include employment claims it would make Title I redundant as to public employees and would eviscerate the procedural requirements of Title I for these employees.[51] The court therefore rejected the DOJ regulations,

---

[48] See, e.g., Doe v. Univ. of Md. Med. Sys. Corp., 50 F.3d 1261, 1264-65 (4th Cir. 1995); Downs v. Mass. Bay Transp. Auth., 13 F.Supp.2d 130 (D. Mass. 1998); Dominguez v. City of Council Bluffs, Iowa, 974 F.Supp. 732, 736-37 (S.D. Iowa 1997); Hernandez v. City of Hartford, 959 F.Supp. 125, 133 (D. Conn. 1997); Wagner v. Tex. A&M Univ., 939 F.Supp. 1297 (S.D. Tex. 1996); Davoll v. Webb, 943 F.Supp. 1289, 1297 (D. Colo. 1996); Graboski v. Guiliani, 937 F.Supp. 258, 267-69 (S.D.N.Y. 1996); Silk v. City of Chi., No. 95C0143, 1996 WL 312074, at *11 (N.D. Ill. June 7, 1996); Lundstedt v. City of Miami, 1995 WL 852443, at *8 (S.D. Fla. Oct. 11, 1995); Bruton v. Southeastern Pa. Transp. Auth., Civ.A.No. 94-CV-3111, 1994 WL 470277, at *2 (E.D. Pa. Aug. 19, 1994); Ethridge v. State of Alabama, 847 F.Supp. 903, 905-06 (M.D. Ala. 1993); Eisfelder v. Mich. Dep't of Natural Res., 847 F.Supp. 78, 83 (W.D. Mich. 1993); Finley v. Giacobbe, 827 F.Supp. 215, 219-20 (S.D.N.Y. 1993); Petersen v. Univ. of Wis. Bd. of Regents, 818 F.Supp. 1276, 1278 (W.D. Wis. 1993); Bell v. Ret. Bd. of Firemen's Annuity & Benefit Fund, No. 92C5197, 1993 WL 398612, at *5 (N.D. Ill. Oct. 6, 1993).

[49] Zimmerman v. St. of Or. Dep't of Justice, 170 F.3d 1169, 1176-77 (9th Cir. 1999).

[50] Id. at 1176.

[51] Id.

holding that they were entitled to no deference under *Chevron U.S.A. Inc. v. Natural Resources Defense Council.*[52]

This issue takes on importance after the Supreme Court's decision in *Garrett*. At this point, Title II offers the only option for qualified individuals with disabilities who are state employees to seek damages under the ADA for employment related discrimination on the basis of disability. Although this point may be moot after *Tennessee v. Lane* (discussed supra this Part) is decided, as it stands now, whether state employees may pursue ADA claims for employment discrimination depends on the jurisdiction in which the claim is brought.

§ 11.2 Elements Of Title II Claim

We turn next to what a plaintiff must show to make out a claim under ADA Title II. Because of the close relationship between Title II and the Rehabilitation Act, generally this showing is the same for both statutes.[53]

Under both statutes, courts have required a plaintiff to show that:

(1) he or she is a qualified individual with a disability;

(2) he or she was either excluded from participation in or denied the benefits of the some public entity's services, programs, or activities or was otherwise discriminated against; and

(3) such exclusion, denial of benefits, or discrimination was by reason of the plaintiff's disability.[54]

The various issues involved in interpreting and testing the limits of these requirements are discussed below.

§ 11.3 "Qualified Person With A Disability"

To bring a claim for discrimination under Title II, a plaintiff must demonstrate that she is a "qualified person with a disability" for purposes of the title. This means that the plaintiff is an individual with a disability who can meet the essential eligibility requirements with or without reasonable modification.[55]

---

[52] Chevron U.S.A. Inc. v. Natural Res. Def. Council, 467 U.S. 837 (1984).

[53] See Doe v. Univ. of Md. Med. Sys. Corp., 50 F.3d 1261, 1264-65 (4th Cir. 1995).

[54] See Parker v. Universidad de P.R., 225 F.3d 1, 5 (1st Cir. 2000); see also Layton v. Elder, 143 F.3d 469, 472 (9th Cir. 1998); Lightbourn v. County of El Paso, Tex., 118 F.3d 421, 428 (5th Cir. 1997); Doe, 50 F.3d at 1265.

[55] See discussion supra Part 2 (regarding "qualified individual").

This definition and concept was derived from the Rehabilitation Act and its implementing regulations.[56] The key parts of this definition are: individual with a disability, essential eligibility requirements, and reasonable modification. The definition of disability is constant throughout the ADA, and therefore the discussion of disability in Part 2 supra applies here. The concept of reasonable modification is discussed below.

A full discussion of "essential eligibility requirements" also is presented in Part 2, supra. But there are some unique wrinkles on this issue, in the Title II context, that merit discussion.

Unlike employment situations, for many services, programs, or activities that public entities offer, the only "essential eligibility requirement" is a desire to participate. In *Concerned Parents To Save Dreher Park Center v. City of West Palm Beach*,[57] the City stopped offering recreational programs that had been structured for people with disabilities. In considering whether the plaintiffs were "qualified individuals with disabilities," the court held that the only "essential eligibility requirement" of a city's recreational program is a request for benefits of the program.[58] As discussed supra in Part 2, the DOJ regulations recognize that often this will be the case.[59]

Sometimes, even under Title II, the determination of an "essential eligibility requirement" is more difficult, and triggers the question of what rules or policies are proper subjects of a request for reasonable accommodation. What about the case where a public entity has a threshold rule for participation, but if the rule is waived so that a person with a disability can participate, the purposes behind the rule are altered?

One well-litigated example of this issue involves age eligibility rules in high school athletics. Many high school athletic associations have requirements that high school athletes be below a certain age, or that athletes only may participate in high school athletics for a certain number

---

[56] See H.R. Rep. No. 101-485(III), at 49 (1990), reprinted in 1990 U.S.C.C.A.N., 445, 472 ("This section defines the term 'qualified individual with a disability.' This definition is derived from the regulations implementing Section 504 of the Rehabilitation Act of 1973 [45 C.F.R. 84.3(k)].").

[57] Concerned Parents to Save Dreher Park Ctr. v. City of W. Palm Beach, 846 F.Supp. 986, 989 (S.D. Fla. 1994)(discussed supra Part 2).

[58] Id. at 990.

[59] See 28 C.F.R. pt 35, app. A, § 35.104 ("The 'essential eligibility requirements' for participation in some activities covered under this part may be minimal. For example, most public entities provide information about their operations as a public service to anyone who requests it. In such situations, the only 'eligibility requirement' for receipt of such information would be the request for it.").

of semesters. The purposes behind these rules are to keep competition level (so that significantly older and more physically mature children do not skew the balance), to reduce the risk of injury, and to discourage parents from holding back their children in school so that the children have a competitive advantage over their younger peers.

This issue has come up where a child with a learning disability has been held back in school, and therefore is too old to participate in high school athletics. Are the age requirements "essential eligibility" criteria, such that these students cannot participate? Courts have split on this issue.

In *Sandison v. Michigan High School Athletic Association*,[60] the Sixth Circuit held that the age rule was "essential," and no reasonable modification would allow the plaintiff to meet the rule. The plaintiff could not be made younger, and it would be unreasonable to force the association to decide on a case-by-case basis whether the rule should or could be waived.[61]

Likewise, in *McPherson v. Michigan High School Athletic Association*,[62] the Sixth Circuit found that making a determination on a case-by-case basis whether to waive an eight semester high school athletic eligibility rule would require too much of an administrative and financial burden. Therefore, the court would not entertain the plaintiff's argument that as applied to him, one individual waiver was not unreasonable.

In *Pottgen v. Missouri High School State Activities Ass'n*,[63] the Eighth Circuit reviewed the importance of an age requirement to a high school baseball program, and found that the requirement was "essential" because it was necessary for the provision of the activity being offered. The court declined to conduct an individualized inquiry to determine whether the rule's purposes would be harmed by waiving the rule in this individual case.[64]

Other courts would require more of a public entity to show a given requirement is essential. In *Pottgen*, the dissent suggested that the ADA

---

[60] Sandison v. Mich. High Sch. Athletic Ass'n, 64 F.3d 1026 (6th Cir. 1995). Although the discussion of the "essential eligibility" criteria under the ADA was under Title III of the ADA (the court declined to consider Sandison's Title II claim), the Court also analyzed the issue for purposes of Rehabilitation Act.

[61] Id. at 1035. See also Reaves v. Mills, 904 F.Supp. 120 (W.D.N.Y. 1995).

[62] McPherson v. Mich. High Sch. Athletic Ass'n, 119 F.3d 453 (6th Cir. 1997).

[63] Pottgen v. Mo. High Sch. St. Activities Ass'n., 40 F.3d 926, 930 (8th Cir. 1994).

[64] Id. at 931.

required an individualized assessment in every case.[65] This rule could not be essential if waiving it in the case of this plaintiff would not violate any purpose behind the rule. In *Washington v. Indiana High School Athletic Ass'n*,[66] the Seventh Circuit adopted the approach of the *Pottgen* dissent, and held that the rule was not "essential" if modifying the rule for this particular athlete caused no competitive advantage or safety threat.

§ 11.4 Not Excluding, Denying, Or Discriminating – Affirmative Responsibilities Of Public Entities

To have a viable Title II claim, a plaintiff must demonstrate that she was either excluded from participation in or denied the benefits of some public entity's services, programs, or activities, or was otherwise discriminated against.[67]

Perhaps more than in any other title, the regulations offer extensive guidance on what that means, and in some cases require that public entities make proactive changes. The regulations provide that by one year after their effective date, every public entity must complete a self-evaluation of their "services, policies, and practices," and develop a transition plan to make any necessary modifications.[68]

The regulations, discussed below, explain the steps public entities must take to ensure that their various programs, services, and activities are accessible. The regulations set out a range of accommodations that must be made; that is, the DOJ has determined that not making these particular modifications constitutes discrimination.

In the "General prohibitions against discrimination" section, the regulations set out a list of activities that a public entity may *not* do on the basis of disability in providing benefits or services:

> (i) Deny a qualified individual with a disability the opportunity to participate in or benefit from the aid, benefit, or service;
>
> (ii) Afford a qualified individual with a disability an opportunity to participate in or benefit from the aid, benefit, or service that is not equal to that afforded others;
>
> (iii) Provide a qualified individual with a disability with an aid, benefit, or service that is not as effective in affording equal opportunity to obtain the same result, to gain the

---

[65] See id. at 931-33 (Arnold, J., dissenting).

[66] Washington v. Ind. High Sch. Athletic Ass'n, 181 F.3d 840, 852 (7th Cir. 1999).

[67] 42 U.S.C. § 12132 (2000).

[68] 28 C.F.R. § 35.105 (2003).

same benefit, or to reach the same level of achievement as that provided to others;

(iv)   Provide different or separate aids, benefits, or services to individuals with disabilities or to any class of individuals with disabilities than is provided to others unless such action is necessary to provide qualified individuals with disabilities with aids, benefits, or services that are as effective as those provided to others;

(v)   Aid or perpetuate discrimination against a qualified individual with a disability by providing significant assistance to an agency, organization, or person that discriminates on the basis of disability in providing any aid, benefit, or service to beneficiaries of the public entity's program;

(vi)   Deny a qualified individual with a disability the opportunity to participate as a member of planning or advisory boards;

(vii)   Otherwise limit a qualified individual with a disability in the enjoyment of any right, privilege, advantage, or opportunity enjoyed by others receiving the aid, benefit, or service.[69]

Conceptually, it is useful to think about the affirmative responsibilities of public entities in five areas:

(a)   making reasonable modifications to policies, practices, and procedures;

(b)   administering services, programs, or activities in the most integrated setting appropriate to the needs of qualified individuals with disabilities;

(c)   modifications to facilities;

(d)   communications modifications, and

(e)   accommodations in transportation.

We discuss each of these in turn. We then examine the issue of voting as an example of public entities' affirmative responsibilities.

A.   *Reasonable Modifications To Policies, Practices, And Procedures*

The Title II regulations provide that a public entity must reasonably modify policies, practices or procedures when necessary to allow participation by a person with a disability. Analytically, this is similar to the reasonable accommodation requirement of Title I.

---

[69]   28 C.F.R. § 35.130 (2003).

The regulations set the outer limits of reasonable accommodations. Consistent with *Southeastern Community College v. Davis*,[70] and other Rehabilitation Act precedent, the regulations provide that reasonable modifications must be made *unless* the public entity can demonstrate that making the modifications would fundamentally alter the nature of the program, service, or activity.[71]

Although the reasonable modification requirement of Title II does not include an undue hardship defense, the courts have read undue hardship into the fundamental alteration defense. Thus, courts determining whether a modification will constitute a fundamental alteration consider whether the change will cause an undue financial or administrative burden on the entity.[72]

Even if a given program, service, or activity has an essential eligibility requirement, the plaintiff still can be a "qualified individual with a disability" if she can meet that requirement with or without "reasonable modifications to rules, policies, or practices, the removal of architectural, communication, or transportation barriers, or the provisions of auxiliary aids and services."[73]

These two terms – "essential eligibility requirements" and "reasonable modification" – are related. As discussed, courts have split on the issue of whether the waiver of an essential eligibility requirement in a given case can in and of itself be a reasonable modification.

The concept of reasonable modifications for Title II purposes has its roots in the Rehabilitation Act. In *School Board of Nassau County v. Arline*, a Rehabilitation Act case discussed supra in Part 2, the Supreme Court stated an "accommodation is not reasonable if it either imposes 'undue financial and administrative burdens' on a grantee, or requires 'a fundamental alteration in the nature of [the] program."[74] Substantial modifications do not have to be made.

Thus, in *McGuinness v. University of New Mexico School of Medicine*, a medical student demonstrated disability by virtue of test anxiety.[75] He attempted to prove he was a "qualified individual with a disability," claiming that he could meet the essential eligibility criteria for the program if the University would modify its testing practices to advance him to the next level. The court held this was a substantial modification, and therefore he was not a qualified person with a disability.

---

[70] Southeastern Cmty. Coll. v. Davis, 442 U.S. 397 (1979).

[71] 28 C.F.R. § 35.130(b)(7) (2003).

[72] E.g., Olmstead v. Zimring, 527 U.S. 581, 597, 603-04 (1999).

[73] 42 U.S.C. § 12131(2) (2000).

[74] School Bd. of Nassau County v. Arline, 480 U.S. 273, 287 n.17 (1987).

[75] McGuinness v. Univ. of N.M. Sch. of Med., 170 F.3d 974 (10th Cir. 1998).

B.   *Integration*

The regulations provide that public entities must administer services, programs, or activities in the most integrated setting appropriate to the needs of qualified individuals with disabilities.[76] In *Olmstead v. Zimring*, the Supreme Court considered the interplay between this integration mandate and the "fundamental alteration" limit on reasonable accommodation.

In *Olmstead*, two women with mental retardation and psychiatric conditions brought suit under Title II, claiming that the state of Georgia had discriminated against them by keeping them in institutionalized settings instead of community placements that were more appropriate for their needs.[77] The State's professionals had determined that community-based settings would be more appropriate for the women, but none were available.[78]

The Court held that this unjustified institutional isolation constituted discrimination within the meaning of Title II.[79] This was because "institutional placement of persons who can handle and benefit from community settings perpetuates unwarranted assumptions that persons so isolated are incapable or unworthy of participating in community life," and "confinement in an institution severely diminishes the everyday life activities of individuals, including family relations, social contacts, work options, economic independence, educational advancement, and cultural enrichment."[80]

However, the Court recognized that the duty to accommodate was not absolute. In deciding whether this accommodation would fundamentally alter the state's mental health treatment program, the proper inquiry was *not* the cost of accommodating these two plaintiffs weighted against the states' overall mental health budget.

Rather, the Court directed the lower court to consider the larger picture: "[s]ensibly construed, the fundamental-alteration component of the reasonable modifications regulation would allow the State to show that, in the allocation of available resources, immediate relief for the plaintiffs would be inequitable, given the responsibility the State has

---

[76]   28 C.F.R. § 35.130(d).

[77]   Olmstead v. L.C. ex rel. Zimring, 527 U.S. 581 (1999); see also Helen L., 46 F.3d 325 (3d Cir. 1995) (holding that a Pennsylvania program requiring that a disabled individual receive required care services in a segregated setting, instead of in nursing home, violates ADA).

[78]   Olmstead, 527 U.S. at 602-03.

[79]   Id. at 600-01.

[80]   Id.

undertaken for the care and treatment of a large and diverse population of persons with mental disabilities."[81]

At least one U.S. Court of Appeal has held that to have standing to bring an *Olmstead* claim, a plaintiff does not have to currently be in an institutionalized setting. In *Fisher v. Oklahoma Health Care Authority*,[82] a group of participants in a community-based Medicaid program challenged a decision by the State of Oklahoma to cease providing unlimited, medically-necessary prescription benefits for program participants. The plaintiffs claimed that placing them at risk of premature institutionalization in nursing homes was violative of *Olmstead* integration mandate.

The state of Oklahoma argued that because the plaintiffs were not currently institutionalized, they could not bring an *Olmstead* claim.[83] The Tenth Circuit, noting that there was nothing in the text of the statute nor in the *Olmstead* decision supporting such an interpretation, disagreed.[84]

While the integration mandate is important, it is not absolute. The regulations and case law are particularly sensitive to integration concerns working *against* the creation of programs tailored to particular types of individuals with disabilities.

This was the issue in *Easley by Easley v. Snider*.[85] The state of Pennsylvania had a program whereby individuals with physical disabilities could receive home assistance to enable them to live at home, instead of institutions.[86] A prerequisite for this program was that the individual be "mentally alert."[87] The *Easley* plaintiffs, who had intellectual disabilities, requested a modification of the mental alertness requirement to allow a surrogate to supervise the assistant.

The Third Circuit court found that "mental alertness" was an essential eligibility requirement, and that any modification (i.e., use of surrogates) would "change the entire focus of the program."[88] The court concluded that the Rehabilitation Act case law protected the ability of a public entity to offer a service to a certain class of people with disabilities

---

[81] Id. at 604.

[82] Fisher v. Okla. Health Care Auth., 335 F.3d 1175 (10th Cir. 2003).

[83] Id. at 1181.

[84] Id. at 1181-82.

[85] Easley by Easley v. Snider, 36 F.3d 297 (3d Cir. 1994).

[86] Id. at 299.

[87] Id. at 300.

[88] Id. at 305.

and not extend it to everyone, and that the ADA regulations supported this view.[89]

In July of 2001, President George W. Bush entered an Executive Order reinforcing the *Olmstead* decision, and providing guidance to the Attorney General, the Secretaries of Health and Human Services, Education, Labor, and Housing and Urban Development, and the Commissioner of the Social Security Administration in its implementation.[90] As part of the administration's "New Freedom" initiative, the Centers for Medicare and Medicaid Services distributed over $120 million in grants in 2001 and 2002 to help states increase community based integration for people with disabilities.[91]

However, years after the *Olmstead* decision, states are facing a lack of coordinated community-based services and a shortfall of funds in carrying out the integration mandate. One reason is what is referred to as an "institutional bias," which results in institutions receiving a disproportionate share of Medicaid funding and which is the primary source of funding for long-term care.[92] An increased emphasis on community alternatives also causes concern on the part of some state employees, as state-funded institutions serve as a key economic force in some areas.[93]

---

[89] Id. at 305 (citing Traynor v. Turnage, 485 U.S. 535, 548 (1987) ("[t]here is nothing in the Rehabilitation Act that requires any benefit extended to one category of handicapped persons also be extended to all other categories of handicapped persons.")); id. at 301 (citing 28 C.F.R. § 35.130(c) ("Nothing in this part prohibits a public entity from providing benefits, services, or advantages to individuals with disabilities, or to a particular class of individuals with disabilities beyond those required by this part.") and 28 C.F.R. pt. 35, app. A, § 35.130 ("State and local governments may provide special benefits, beyond those required by non-discrimination requirements of this part that are limited to individuals with disabilities or a particular class of individuals with disabilities, without thereby incurring additional obligations to persons without disabilities or to other classes of persons with disabilities.")).

[90] Exec. Order No. 13,217, 66 F.R. 33155 (June 18, 2001) ("Community-Based Alternatives for Individuals with Disabilities").

[91] See Johanna M. Donlin, Moving Ahead with Olmstead: To Comply with the Americans with Disabilities Act, States Are Working Hard to Find Community Placements for People with Disabilities, 29 St. Legislatures 28 (Mar. 1, 2003), 2003 WL 8909235. Part 9 of the treatise infra describes in detail the applicability of the ADA to health and welfare programs.

[92] Id. See also infra Part 9 (discussing the applicability of the ADA to Social Security programs).

[93] Id.

C.   *Facilities Modification*

Title II applies to a public entity's physical structures. Courts have interpreted this reach to include, among other things, city buildings,[94] botanical gardens on the premises of a state university,[95] publicly owned sporting arenas and theatres,[96] and recently, city sidewalks.[97]

The regulations speak in terms of physical structures as "facilities," which are defined as:

> all or any portion of buildings, structures, sites, complexes, equipment, rolling stock or other conveyances, roads, walks, passageways, parking lots, or other real or personal property, including the site where the building, property, structure, or equipment is located.[98]

The regulations' prohibition of discrimination in facility access is patterned after the Title II general discrimination provision:

> [N]o qualified individual with a disability shall, because a public entity's facilities are inaccessible to or unusable by individuals with disabilities, be excluded from participation in, or be denied the benefits of the services, programs, or activities of a public entity, or be subjected to discrimination by any public entity.[99]

Therefore, textually, facilities serve two functions. They may themselves be "programs, services, or activities" within the meaning of the statutory text,[100] or conduits (e.g., websites) to other "programs, services, or activities" public entities may offer.[101]

The regulations set forth the "program access" standards for facilities. What a public entity must do to ensure "program access" to its facilities varies according to whether the facility is an "existing" facility, a new facility, or a facility that has been altered.

---

[94] See Johnson v. City of Saline, 151 F.3d 564 (6th Cir. 1998).

[95] See Parker v. Universidad de P.R., 225 F.3d 1 (1st Cir. 2000).

[96] See Ass'n for Disabled Ams., Inc. v. City of Orlando, 153 F.Supp.2d 1310 (M.D. Fla. 2001).

[97] See Barden v. City of Sacramento, 292 F.3d 1073 (9th Cir. 2002).

[98] 28 C.F.R. § 35.104 (2003).

[99] Id. § 35.149.

[100] See Barden, 292 F.3d at 1074 (holding that sidewalks are a "service, program, or activity" of the City within the meaning of Title II).

[101] See infra Part 10 (discussing the applicability of the ADA to Internet websites).

1.   Existing facilities

The regulations provide that each service, program, or activity conducted by a public entity, when viewed in its entirety, must be readily accessible to and useable by individuals with disabilities.[102] This does not mean, however, that each existing facility must be physically accessible to and usable by individuals with disabilities.[103]

In ensuring program access in existing facilities, a public entity does not have to take action that will result in fundamental alteration in the nature of a service, program, or activity, or cause an undue financial or administrative burden.[104] The public entity has the burden of showing that compliance with the program access standard would result in such alteration or burden.[105] The decision that compliance would result in such an alteration or burden must be made by the head of the public entity, in writing.[106]

The regulations allow public entities latitude in determining how to make existing facilities meet the program access standard for existing facilities.   Structural changes are not required necessarily.[107]   The regulations suggest alternatives, such as redesign of equipment, reassignment of services to accessible buildings (either permanently or on request), assignment of aids to beneficiaries, and home visits.[108] Preference should be given to methods that offer the most integrated setting appropriate.[109]

If a public entity chooses structural modifications, there are additional regulations which the public entity must comply. These include transition plans for public entities with 50 or more employees, setting forth the steps necessary to achieve program access.[110] The necessary structural changes were to be completed by January 26, 1995.[111]

If the public entity has responsibility over streets, roads, or walkways, the transition plan must include a schedule for installing curb cuts.[112] The plan must identify physical obstacles that limit program accessibility, describe the methods to make facilities accessible, specify a

---

[102]   28 C.F.R. § 35.150(a) (2003).
[103]   Id. § 35.150(a)(1).
[104]   Id. § 35.150(a)(3).
[105]   Id.
[106]   Id.
[107]   Id. § 35.150(b).
[108]   28 C.F.R. § 35.150(b) (2003).
[109]   Id.
[110]   Id. § 35.150(d)(1).
[111]   Id. § 35.150(c).
[112]   Id. § 35.150(d)(2).

schedule for compliance, and indicate the official responsible for implementation.[113]

An example of the ADA applied to existing facilities is the case of *Parker v. Universidad de Puerto Rico.*[114] The plaintiff was a visitor to the state university's botanical gardens who suffered injuries when his wheelchair overturned on a garden path. The First Circuit reasoned that the University was obligated to ensure that the botanical garden "when viewed in its entirety" was accessible to individuals with disabilities.[115]

Because the University held open the gardens as a place for group convocations, it had a duty under Title II to ensure that persons with disabilities could travel to and from the botanical gardens using safe walkways, ramps, and curbcuts.[116] Every passageway did not have to be accessible, but at least one did, absent an undue burden or fundamental alteration defense.[117] Ultimately, the Court of Appeals remanded the case to the district court for a determination of this issue.[118]

Notably, a program must be accessible "when viewed in its entirety." Therefore, if a government program offers identical services at more than one facility, not every facility must be accessible. In order to allow some facilities to remain unchanged, the alternative facilities must offer equivalent services in terms of type of service, hours of operation, convenience, and quality.

2. New or modified facilities

The regulations create a different set of responsibilities for public entities for construction of new facilities and alterations of existing facilities. For new construction, the regulations provide:

> Each facility or part of a facility constructed by, on behalf of, or for the use of a public entity shall be designed and constructed in such manner that the facility or part of the facility is readily accessible to and usable by individuals with disabilities, if the construction was commenced after January 26, 1992. [119]

For alterations of existing facilities, the regulations provide:

> Each facility or part of a facility altered by, on behalf of, or for the use of a public entity in a manner that affects or

---

[113] Id. § 35.150(d)(3).

[114] Parker v. Universidad de P.R., 225 F.3d 1 (1st Cir. 2000).

[115] Id. at 6.

[116] Id. at 7.

[117] Id.

[118] Id. at 8.

[119] 28 C.F.R. § 35.151(a) (2003).

could affect the usability of the facility or part of the facility shall, to the maximum extent feasible, be altered in such manner that the altered portion of the facility is readily accessible to and useable by individuals with disabilities, if the alteration was commended after January 26, 1992. [120]

Public entities must choose between two sets of accessibility standards for the construction or alteration of facilities. The first is the Uniform Federal Accessibility Standards (UFAS). The second is the Americans with Disabilities Act Accessibility Guidelines for Buildings and Facilities (ADAAG).[121]

In contrast to the regulations governing existing facilities (where entities are exempted from making fundamental alterations and bearing undue financial burdens), the regulations for new construction and alteration are more stringent. There is no "undue burden" provision, with the regulations stating facilities "shall" be accessible.[122]

There has been litigation over what constitutes an alteration of an existing facility, thus triggering the need to comply with the accessibility standards. As set forth in the regulations, the test is whether the modification affects the usability of the facility. Normal maintenance is not an alteration unless it affects the usability of the facility.[123]

In *Kinney v. Yerusalim*, the issue was whether resurfacing city streets constituted an "alteration" within the scope of the regulations.[124] The Third Circuit noted that the purpose of the alteration standard was that "if an alteration renders a street more 'usable' to those presently using it, such increased utility must also be made fully accessible to the disabled through the installation of curb ramps."[125]

The court took a broad view of "usability," and reasoned that resurfacing a street affects it in ways that are integral to its purpose.[126] Therefore, resurfacing was an "alteration," and when a public entity resurfaced its streets, it needed to construct curb ramps.[127]

---

[120] Id. § 35.151(b).

[121] Id. § 35.151(c). The Uniform Federal Accessibility Standards are found at appendix A to 41 C.F.R. part 101-19.6, and the ADA Accessibility Guidelines (ADAAGs) are found at appendix A to 28 C.F.R. part 36.

[122] See Kinney v. Yerusalim, 9 F.3d 1067, 1071 (3d Cir. 1993).

[123] See generally 28 C.F.R. pt. 36, app. A (2003).

[124] Kinney, 9 F.3d at 1071.

[125] Id. at 1072-73.

[126] Id.

[127] See 28 C.F.R. § 35.151(e) ("Newly constructed or altered streets, roads, and highways must contain curb ramps or other sloped areas at any

Similarly, in *Civic Association of the Deaf of New York City, Inc. v. Giuliani*,[128] the court held that changing over from one emergency call box system to another constituted an alteration of public facilities.

D.   *Effective Communication*

Like the program access standard, Title II's communications provisions have a statutory and regulatory component. Title II's definition of qualified person with a disability links the "provision of auxiliary aids and services" to the concept of reasonable accommodations. The Title II regulations have a separate section devoted to "Communication" which makes clear that communication is an integral part of a public entities' responsibilities under Title II.

Title II's communication regulations and the case law interpreting them stand for the proposition that a public entity must offer *effective* communication alternatives. The "General" provision in the regulations dealing with communications states: "A public entity shall take appropriate steps to ensure that communications with applicants, participants, and members of the public with disabilities are as effective as communications with others."[129]

The regulations further provide that auxiliary aids and services be furnished when necessary to afford an individual with a disability an equal opportunity to participate in and enjoy the programs, services, or activities of the public entity.[130] The effective communication obligation is owed to people with hearing, speech, and vision disabilities.

In terms of types of auxiliary aids and services, a public entity is to give primary consideration to the requests of individuals with disabilities.[131]   Auxiliary aids and services for people with hearing

---

intersection having curbs or other barriers to entry from a street level pedestrian walkway.").

[128] See Civic Ass'n of the Deaf of N.Y. City, Inc. v. Giuliani, 970 F.Supp. 352, 359 (S.D.N.Y. 1997). But see Molloy v. Metro. Trans. Auth., 94 F.3d 808, 811-12 (2d Cir. 1996) (holding that a staff reduction plan whereby human ticket clerks were replaced with ticket vending machines was not "alteration" within meaning of Title II's transportation regulations).

[129] 28 C.F.R. § 35.160(a) (2003).   See also infra Part 10 (discussing communication technology and the ADA).

[130] Id. § 35.160(b)(1).

[131] Id. § 35.160(b)(2).   There are specific provisions relating to TDD's and telephone emergency services. See id. § 35.161 ("Where a public entity communicates by telephone with applicants and beneficiaries, TDD's or equally effective telecommunication systems shall be used to communicate with individuals with impaired hearing or speech."); id. § 35.162 ("Telephone emergency services, including 911 services, shall provide direct access to individuals who use TDD's and computer modems.").

impairments include qualified interpreters, notetakers, written materials, amplifiers, captioning, TTYs and others.[132] For people with vision impairments they include qualified readers, taped text, Braille, large print, assistance locating items, and others.[133] For people with speech disabilities they include TTYs, computer terminals, speech synthesizers, communication boards, and others.[134] The regulations provide that a public entity does not need to take any action that it can demonstrate would result in a fundamental alteration or an undue financial and administrative burden.[135]

Generally, the case law has shown that above all else, communication must be effective. One example of a court requiring a public entity to take steps to ensure effective accommodation is found in *Soto v. City of Newark*.[136] Plaintiffs were hearing-impaired individuals getting married at the Newark Municipal Court. They requested that the city provide a sign language interpreter at their wedding so that they might understand the marriage proceedings. The city refused.

The court, following the regulations, held that without an interpreter, plaintiffs could not participate or benefit from the wedding service in a manner equal to that afforded to others, because they could not hear the vows or understand the judge.[137] The city therefore had failed to provide an effective means of communication.[138]

Similarly, in *Aikins v. St. Helena Hospital*, the court held that a hospital must "effectively" communicate with a patient's hearing-impaired spouse.[139] The court framed the inquiry in functional terms, noting that the attending doctor had the wrong impression as to what the spouse had told him.[140]

What about the situation where an accommodation is "effective," but not equal to the access that non-disabled participants in the program receive? In *Spurlock v. Simmons*, a prisoner with hearing and speech

---

[132] TAM II, supra note 13, at § 7.1000.

[133] Id.

[134] Id.

[135] See 28 C.F.R. § 35.164 (2003). The public entity has the burden of proving undue burden or fundamental alteration, and the decision must be made by the head of the public agency in writing.

[136] Soto v. City of Newark, 72 F.Supp.2d 489 (D. N.J. 1999).

[137] Id. at 494.

[138] Id.

[139] Aikins v. St. Helena Hosp., 843 F.Supp. 1329, 1336 (N.D. Cal. 1994).

[140] Id. at 1336; see also Hanson v. Sangamon County Sheriff's Dep't, 991 F.Supp. 1059 (C.D. Ill. 1998) (holding that a hearing impaired arrestee, who claimed that the sheriff's department failed to provide him with adequate means for communication, stated claim under Title II of ADA).

impairments brought a claim under Title II, arguing that other prisoners got unlimited use of the public telephones, while he was forced to use a TDD telephone in a special office in limited intervals.[141] The court found that the prisoner's access was "meaningful," and was not troubled that his use was not proportionate with other prisoners.[142]

A final issue involves the scope of a public entity's responsibility to make the particular requested communication accommodation. Generally, provided that the accommodation that is offered is effective, courts have not been swayed by a request for a specific type of accommodation.

In *Petersen v. Hastings Public Schools*, plaintiffs with hearing impairments brought a Title II claim challenging the school district's decision to educate students by use of a sign language system that was different than that used in their homes.[143] The Eighth Circuit, while noting that the regulations provide that primary consideration be given to the expressed accommodation choice made by the person with a disability, nevertheless held that the sign language system that was employed was an "effective" means of communication, and that there was no ADA violation.[144]

Similarly, in *Dobard v. San Francisco Bay Area Rapid Transit ("BART") District*, the plaintiff requested a computer aided transcription auxiliary aid so that he could participate fully in a BART board meeting.[145] The court granted defendants' motion to dismiss, holding that the ADA gave BART discretion as to how to achieve accessibility, and that the use of the best or most advanced technology was not required.[146]

E. *Transportation*

Title II has a separate part dedicated to nondiscrimination in transportation provided by public entities. Transportation was an area where the ADA's framers recognized an existing pattern of discrimination and inequity.

The ADA explicitly states that "[d]iscrimination against individuals with disabilities persists in such critical areas as ...

---

[141] Spurlock v. Simmons, 88 F.Supp.2d 1189, 1192 (D. Kan. 2000)

[142] Id. at 1196.

[143] Petersen v. Hastings Pub. Sch., 31 F.3d 705 (8th Cir. 1994).

[144] Id. at 709.

[145] Dobard v. S.F. Bay Area Rapid Transit ("BART") Dist., 1993 WL 372256, at *1 (N.D. Cal.).

[146] Id. at *3. See also Rosen v. Montgomery County Md., 121 F.3d 154 (4th Cir. 1997) (holding that a county was not required to provide a drunk driving arrestee who was deaf with an interpreter so that he could participate in a particular alcohol education program that he desired, when an accessible program was available).

transportation"[147] and "[i]ndividuals with disabilities continually encounter various forms of discrimination, including ... transportation ... barriers."[148] The debates on ADA passage suggest that the framers viewed transportation as crucial in unlocking other opportunities that the ADA would help create.[149]

Public transportation is especially important to people with disabilities because the evidence suggests that they are more reliant on public transportation than the general population.[150] The legal and policy tensions specific to transportation issues are a microcosm of the entire Act. These issues include mainstreaming of existing transportation to accommodate people with disabilities versus paratransit (i.e., transportation services usually performed by vans that are provided separate from mass transit's normal operations), and whether there should be a "threshold" or "necessary" level of spending on mass transportation options for people with disabilities.

1.   Pre-ADA statutes and regulations

As with the rest of the ADA, the law's transportation provisions were not drawn on a blank slate. There is a history of federal legislation aimed at improving public transportation options and accessibility for people with disabilities. One court dubbed the pre-ADA federal statutory and regulatory scheme a "welter of statutory provisions."[151]

The first relevant federal statute was the Urban Mass Transportation Act of 1964, amended by Congress in the Urban Mass

---

[147] 42 U.S.C. § 12101(a)(3) (2000).

[148] Id. § 12101(a)(5).

[149] See S. Rep. No. 101-116, at 11 (1989) ("Several witnesses [asked] ... why don't people with disabilities frequent places of public accommodations and stores? ... The third reason is architectural, communication, and transportation barriers."); 135 Cong. Rec. S10792 (daily ed. Sept. 7, 1989) (statement of Sen. Biden) ("Too many persons with impaired mobility have been blocked from taking part in a variety of opportunities, because simple physical access has not been provided."); 136 Cong. Rec. H2438 (daily ed. May 17, 1990) (statement of Rep. Mineta) ("[D]isabled Americans are ready, willing and able, to use their talents, skills, and energy in communities across the country; but today many wait for full access to our transportation systems.").

[150] See Bonnie P. Tucker, The Americans With Disabilities Act: An Overview, 1989 U. Ill. L. Rev. 923, 934 (1989).

[151] Ams. Disabled for Accessible Pub. Transp. ("ADAPT") v. Skinner, 881 F.2d 1184, 1186 (3d Cir. 1989). This case contains an excellent discussion of the pre-ADA legislative landscape from which much of the ensuing discussion is drawn.

Transportation Assistance Act in 1970.[152] This Act originally provided for federal financial assistance to local transit operators, and the 1970 amendments declared a national policy that:

> elderly and handicapped persons have the same right as other persons to utilize mass transportation facilities and services; that special efforts shall be made in the planning and design of mass transportation facilities and services so that the availability to elderly and handicapped persons of mass transportation which they can effectively utilize will be assured.[153]

The next federal statute was Section 504 of the Rehabilitation Act of 1973. Congress then enacted Section 165(b) of the Federal-Aid Highway Act of 1973, which provided that:

> [t]he Secretary of Transportation shall require that projects receiving Federal financial assistance ... shall be planned, designed, constructed, and operated to allow effective utilization by elderly and handicapped persons who, by reason of illness, injury, age, congenital malfunction, or other permanent or temporary incapacity or disability ... are unable without special facilities or special planning or design to utilize such facilities and services effectively .... The Secretary shall not approve any program or project to which this section applies which does not comply with the provisions of this subsection requiring access to public mass transportation facilities, equipment, and services for elderly or handicapped persons.[154]

These broad mandates needed fleshing out, and several sets of regulations followed. The Department of Transportation promulgated its initial regulations in 1976.[155] Then-President Ford issued an executive order directing the Department of Health and Human Services ("HEW") to coordinate implementation of the non-discriminatory policy announced in Section 504 of the Rehabilitation Act.[156]

In 1978, HEW issued its guidelines, drawing a careful line between mainstreaming and paratransit. The following year the DOT promulgated another set of regulations in compliance with the HEW

---

[152] 49 U.S.C. § 1612(a) (1970).

[153] Id.

[154] 23 U.S.C. § 142 (2000).

[155] See 41 Fed. Reg. 18,234 (Apr. 30, 1976) (requiring local planners to make "special efforts in planning public mass transportation facilities and services that can effectively be utilized by elderly and handicapped persons.").

[156] Exec. Order No. 11,914, 41 Fed. Reg. 17,871 (Apr. 28, 1976).

guidelines. These regulations came down firmly on the side of mainstreaming and required across-the-board alterations to ensure that transportation facilities were accessible to persons with disabilities, including retrofitting existing systems.[157]

The regulations were immediately challenged in *American Public Transportation Association (APTA) v. Lewis*.[158] The D.C. Circuit found that compliance would require extensive modifications to existing systems and impose heavy financial burdens on local transit authorities, and invalidated the retrofitting regulations.[159] Following several sets of interim regulations and legislative and judicial prodding,[160] the DOT

---

[157] 44 Fed. Reg. 31,442 (May 31, 1979); see also ADAPT v. Skinner, 881 F.2d 1184, 1188 (3d Cir. 1989).

[158] Am. Pub. Tranp. Ass'n (APTA) v. Lewis, 655 F.2d 1272 (D.C. Cir. 1981).

[159] Id. at 1278.

[160] For a discussion of the several rounds of interim regulations, see ADAPT, 881 F.2d at 1188-90. Briefly stated, the DOT first promulgated interim regulations in 1981. See 46 Fed. Reg. 37,448 (July 20, 1981). These regulations gave local transit authorities nearly complete control in formulating accessibility strategies. They could opt whether (1) to make their buses accessible by installing wheelchair lifts; (2) to establish a paratransit system; or (3) to establish a mixed system. These regulations also contained a safe harbor, whereby transit operators could be relieved of their obligation to provide transportation services to people with disabilities as long as they spent 3½% of their federal money on such services. In January of 1982, DOT announced a notice of proposed rulemaking, to consider whether the safe harbor provision provided insufficient guidance. Congress moved the process along by passing the Surface Transportation Act of 1982, requiring the DOT to issue regulations to establish minimum criteria for the provision of services to people with disabilities. 49 U.S.C. § 1612(d) (1988). As part of the passage of the Surface Transportation Act, Senator Cranston criticized the 1981 interim regulations as "a total abdication of Federal responsibility for protecting handicapped persons from discrimination and inadequate services." 128 Cong. Rec. 30,822-24 (1982). In response, the DOT published a second notice of proposed rulemaking to replace the 1981 Interim Regulations. See 48 Fed. Reg. 40,684 (Sept. 8, 1983). These proposed regulations continued to allow local transit systems to select how they would provide for the transportation needs of people with disabilities, but established six service criteria that special transit systems were required to meet. In Maine Association of Handicapped Persons v. Dole, 623 F.Supp. 920, 926 (D. Me. 1985), the court criticized the Secretary's "unimaginably leisurely pace" in promulgating final regulations, and ordered that final regulations be issued.

promulgated final regulations in 1986.[161]

The final regulations provided that local transit authorities could make their mass transportation systems accessible to people with disabilities in one of three ways: accessible buses, paratransit, and a combination of the two.[162] The regulations set minimum service criteria for each of the available options, including those addressing nondiscriminatory eligibility criteria, maximum response time, restrictions or priorities based on trip purpose, comparable fares to those for the general public, comparable hours and days of service, and comparable service area.[163]

The regulations contained a "safe harbor" provision, whereby transit systems were not required to spend more than 3% of operating costs on service for people with disabilities, even if, as a result, they did not meet the DOT's minimum service criteria.[164]

These regulations were challenged by a group of organizations representing people with disabilities in *ADAPT v. Skinner*.[165] The plaintiffs specifically challenged the local option and safe harbor provisions of the regulations.

The Third Circuit rejected the plaintiffs' first argument that the local option rule violated a statutory mandate of "mainstreaming," because the court found no "mainstreaming" requirement in the relevant statutes (Rehabilitation Act, Urban Mass Transportation Act, Surface Transportation Act, and Federal-Aid Highway Act).[166] The court, however, invalidated the safe-harbor provision as arbitrary and capricious, holding that "under the safe harbor provision, cities could deny to the disabled the minimum quality of service mandated by the Congress with impunity."[167]

After *ADAPT*, many transit systems sought to make their buses accessible to people with disabilities.[168] However, members of Congress,

---

[161] See 51 Fed. Reg. 18,994 (May 3, 1986).

[162] See ADAPT, 881 F.2d at 1189.

[163] See 49 C.F.R. § 27.95 (1989) (no longer in force).

[164] See 49 C.F.R. § 27.97(b) (1989) (no longer in force); see also ADAPT, 881 F.2d at 1190.

[165] ADAPT, 881 F.2d at 1184.

[166] Id. at 1191.

[167] Id. at 1201.

[168] See Michael Lewyn, "Thou Shalt Not Put A Stumbling Block Before The Blind": The Americans with Disabilities Act and Public Transportation for the Disabled, 52 Hastings L.J. 1037, 1064 (2001) (citing H.R. Rep. No. 101-485, pt. I, at 24 (1990) and Paul Stephen Dempsey, The Civil Rights of the Handicapped in Transportation: The Americans with

as well as advocates for people with disabilities, believed that more robust protection was necessary, in part to protect a larger universe of people with disabilities.[169] The ADA followed.

2.   ADA transportation provisions

Title II has an entire part dedicated to discrimination in public transportation.[170]   This evidences recognition by Congress of the importance of transportation to achieve the ADA's other goals, and of the history of overbroad and under-enforced transportation statutes discussed above.

The Act's transportation provisions generally should be thought of as an explanation of how public entities must comply with Title II's general discrimination prohibition in their capacity as providers of public transportation.[171]

Disabilities Act and Related Legislation, 19 Transp.L.J. 309, 317 (1991), for the proposition that by 1990, 35% of America's buses, and half of all newly acquired buses, were accessible to the disabled).

[169] See H.R. Rep. No. 101-485, pt. IV, at 24 ("17 years of experience with [the Rehabilitation Act] ... have demonstrated the need for further legislative action in this area."); see also H.R. Rep. No. 101-485, pt. II, at 37 ("Witnesses testified about the need to pursue a multi-modal approach to ensuring access for people with disabilities which provides that ... paratransit is made accessible for those who cannot use the fixed route accessible vehicles."). The House Report stated:

> The House Education and Labor Committee found that paratransit was often inadequate for the following reasons, among others; the need to make reservation in advance often conflicts with one's work schedule or interests in going out to restaurants and the like; the cost of rides when used frequently is often exorbitant; limitations on time of day and the number of days that the paratransit operates; waiting time; restrictions on use by guests and nondisabled companions who are excluded from accompanying the person with a disability; the expense to the public agency; and restrictions on eligibility placed on use by social service agencies.").

H.R. Rep. No. 101-485, pt. I, at 38.

[170] See Title II, Part B, "Actions Applicable to Public Transportation Provided By Public Entities Considered Discriminatory."   42 U.S.C. §§ 12141-12165 (2000).

[171] See 42 U.S.C. 12132 ("Subject to the provisions of this subchapter, no qualified individual with a disability shall, by reason of such disability, be excluded from participation in or be denied the benefits of the services,

<blockquote>a. *Subpart I – trains, cabs, buses, and other paratransit*</blockquote>

The first "subpart" of Title II's transportation provisions covers "public transportation other than by aircraft or certain rail operations." This excludes air travel, which is covered by the Air Carrier Access Act,[172] and "intercity and commuter rail" operations, which are covered in the second transportation subpart. This subpart covers fixed route systems (e.g., buses and rails that run on fixed schedules), paratransit, and demand response systems (e.g., any system, such as taxicab service, that is not a fixed route).

<blockquote>i. Fixed route systems</blockquote>

Section 12142 deals with accessibility of "fixed route systems," which are defined elsewhere as "a system of providing designated public transportation on which a vehicle is operated along a prescribed route according to a fixed schedule."[173] This may be buses or rails that run on regular schedules.

Transit systems must purchase and lease vehicles (buses, rapid rail vehicles, and other vehicles) that are "readily accessible to and usable by individuals with disabilities, including individuals who use wheelchairs."[174] Otherwise, they have discriminated.[175]

Transit systems may not purchase and lease used vehicles that are inaccessible unless they have demonstrated "good faith efforts" to purchase or lease a used accessible vehicle.[176] Again, failure to do so constitutes discrimination.[177] It also is discriminatory for transit systems to "remanufacture" (i.e., extend a vehicle's usable life for 5 years or more) without, to the maximum extent possible, making the vehicle readily accessible to and usable by people with disabilities.[178] The same applies

---

programs, or activities of a public entity, or be subjected to discrimination by any such entity.").

[172] 49 U.S.C. § 41705 (2000).

[173] 42 U.S.C. § 12141(3).

[174] Id. § 12142(a).

[175] Id.

[176] Id. § 12141(b). In explaining "good faith," the regulations provide that transit providers may not purchase inaccessible vehicles merely because accessible vehicles are more expensive. The agency must show it conducted a nationwide search for an accessible vehicle, and "good faith efforts [may] involve buying fewer accessible buses in preference to more inaccessible buses." 49 C.F.R. pt. 37, app. D, § 37.73 (2002).

[177] Id.

[178] 42 U.S.C. § 12142(c) (2000). The term remanufacture does not include engine overhaul and the like. See 49 C.F.R. pt. 37, app. D, § 37.75 (2000).

to the purchase or lease of remanufactured vehicles.[179]   There is an exception for historic vehicles.[180]

Section 12143 deals with accessibility for paratransit as a complement to fixed route systems.   The general rule is that it is considered discrimination for a public entity that operates a fixed route system (i.e., other than a system which provides solely commuter bus service) to fail to provide paratransit and other special transportation services to individuals with disabilities, including individuals who use wheelchairs. The level of service must be one which:

> (1)   is comparable to the level of designated public transportation services provided to individuals without disabilities using such system; or

> (2)   in the case of response time, is comparable, to the extent practicable, to the level of designated public transportation services provided to individuals without disabilities using such system.[181]

This section provides the Secretary of Transportation specific directives on issuing regulations. In accordance with these directives, the regulations require public entities to provide paratransit to individuals with disabilities whether or not they need the assistance of other people to use paratransit, and to one other individual to ride with the person with a disability (and for additional people if this will not take space away from other people with disabilities).[182]

In addition, the regulations provide an undue financial burden defense for public entities.[183]   Also, under the regulations each public entity that operates a fixed route system, after holding a public hearing, must submit a plan to the Secretary of Transportation, which is to be updated annually, for providing compliant services.[184] Failure to abide by these regulations constitutes discrimination.[185]

In *Liberty Resources, Inc. v. Southeastern Pennsylvania Transportation Authority (Septa)*, the court considered whether Septa's paratransit system met the requirements of Section 12143 and its accompanying regulations.[186] Under Septa's system, five percent of total

---

[179]   42 U.S.C. § 12142(c)(1)(B).

[180]   Id. § 12142(c)(2).

[181]   Id. § 12143(a).

[182]   Id. § 12143(c).

[183]   Id. § 12143(c)(4).

[184]   Id. § 12143(c)(7).

[185]   42 U.S.C. § 12143(e).

[186] Liberty Res., Inc. v. Southeastern Pa. Trans. Auth. ("Septa"), 155 F.Supp.2d 242 (2001).

trip requests resulted in "capacity" trip denials (i.e., Septa was unable to schedule rides within a requested two hour interval because the available seats were taken by prior reservations).[187]

The court construed Section 12143 to require that the level of paratransit service be comparable to fixed route service and the response time be comparable to fixed route service to the extent practicable.[188] It acknowledged that such a comparison is difficult and presents an "apple to oranges" comparison,[189] but ultimately found that the Septa system was *not* comparable, and therefore violated the ADA.[190] Here, approximately 30 patrons per day were denied next-day service, and Septa provided no safety net for these passengers.[191]

The court found that the system developed by Septa did not attempt to provide rides to one hundred percent of ADA-eligible callers, and was premised on the belief that not all disabled riders would be granted rides.[192] Septa did not request a waiver based on the undue hardship exception.[193]

How accessible does service have to be? How often can mistakes happen before there is an ADA violation? The Ninth Circuit considered these questions in *Midgett v. Tri-County Metropolitan Transportation District*.[194]

In *Midgett*, the plaintiff brought a claim against the Transportation District, alleging that it had discriminated against him in

---

[187] Id. at 245.

[188] Id. at 253.

[189] Id. at 257. The court, quoting 56 Fed. Reg. 45,584, 45,608 (Sept. 6, 1991) stated:

> Certainly no system administrator tells ... a [non-disabled] passenger that he can forget about traveling that day because he has already ridden the bus 20 times that month or that he needs to work his way to the top of a waiting list before he can elbow his way onto a train. If the administrator of a paratransit system tells a similar story to a passenger, it is not a story about a comparable system. Capacity constraint mechanisms of this kind are incompatible with a comparable paratransit system, and the rule will continue to prohibit them.

[190] Septa, 155 F.Supp.2d at 257-58.

[191] Id. at 257.

[192] Id.

[193] Id.

[194] Midgett v. Tri-County Metro. Trans. Dist., 254 F.3d 846 (9th Cir. 2001).

violation of Title II. He had attempted to ride a bus on a particularly cold day, and the lift had malfunctioned because of the low temperatures.[195] This repeated itself on a different bus, although eventually the plaintiff was able to find a bus with a functioning lift.[196] He submitted a declaration that he had experienced problems with buses on several days, and other declarations from similarly situated people who had experienced multiple failures.[197] The court reviewed the DOT's regulations which did not "contemplate perfect service," and held that on these facts an injunction requiring systemic changes was not warranted.[198]

ii.   Demand responsive systems

Section 12144 takes a similar approach for "demand response systems," which are defined as "any system of providing designated public transportation which is not a fixed route system."[199] An example would be a city-owned taxi-cab service.

This section provides that a public entity operating a demand responsive system must buy or lease only accessible vehicles.[200] Otherwise, they have discriminated.[201] The exception is when the demand responsive system, when viewed in its entirety, "provides a level of service to such individuals [with disabilities] equivalent to the level of service such system provides to individuals without disabilities."[202] There is no paratransit requirement for demand responsive systems.

iii.   Transportation facilities

The facilities modification issue, discussed above, has a statutory basis as far as transportation facilities. Similar to the regulations promulgated under the first part of Title II, the statute provides different standards for new and existing transportation facilities.

It is discriminatory to construct a new facility "unless such facility is readily accessible to and usable by individuals with disabilities, including individuals who use wheelchairs."[203] Altered areas also must be accessible and entities must spend additional money on making the path

---

[195] Id. at 847.

[196] Id.

[197] Id. at 848.

[198] Id. at 849-50. But see Cupolo v. Bay Area Rapid Transit, 5 F.Supp.2d 1078, 1083-84 (N.D. Cal. 1997) (holding that systemic failures with elevators in key stations warranted injunction under Title II).

[199] 42 U.S.C. § 12141(1) (2000).

[200] Id. § 12144.

[201] Id.

[202] Id.

[203] 42 U.S.C. § 12146.

of travel to the altered area accessible if it is a primary function area.[204] Moreover, public entities discriminate if they make alterations to public transit facilities in a manner that does not, to the maximum extent feasible, make the altered portions of the facilities useable and readily accessible to people with disabilities.[205]

Section 12148 provides that transportation programs and activities operated in existing facilities must be conducted so that, when viewed in their entirety, the program or activity is readily accessible to and usable by individuals with disabilities.[206] This section sets forth a "one car per train rule": if a light or rapid rail system has two or more vehicles, at least one vehicle per train must be accessible.[207]

b.   Subpart II – intercity and commuter rail

The second "subpart" of the ADA's transportation provisions covers rail service that is dedicated to commuters and that runs between cities.[208]   Like subpart I, the statute details specific acts that are "discriminatory," and many of these prohibited acts echo the first subpart.

Commuter service and intercity rail are required to provide one accessible car per train, and public entities operating such systems must purchase accessible new cars to meet that standard.[209]   For commuter service and intercity rail, the statute goes into detail as to what is required (i.e., so as not to be discriminatory) in each car.   This includes entrance, exit, and restroom accessibility for single level passenger coaches for individuals who use wheelchairs;[210] rules for single level and bi-level dining cars;[211] required wheelchair spaces and storage facilities for

---

[204] 49 C.F.R. § 37.43 (2002).

[205] 42 U.S.C. § 12147. The Secretary is supposed to identify "key" rapid and light rail and commuter rail transportation stations. For these key stations, the special rule is that they must be accessible by July 26, 1993 (with possible extensions). Id.; 49 C.F.R. §§ 37.47(c)(1), 37.51. This necessarily implies that non-"key" stations can be closed even if this inconveniences people with disabilities. See Hassan v. Slater, 41 F.Supp.2d 343 (E.D.N.Y. 1999). Intercity rail stations are required to be accessible by January 2010. 49 C.F.R. § 37.55.

[206] 42 U.S.C. § 12148.   The exception is that public entities are not required to make structural changes in order to make existing facilities accessible to individuals who use wheelchairs, unless they would be required to do so under § 12147(a) or (b). Id. See also 49 C.F.R. § 37.61.

[207] 42 U.S.C. § 12148. There is an exception for historic trains. Id. § 12148(b)(1).

[208] See id. § 12161.

[209] See id. §§ 12162 (a)(1), a(2)(A), (b)(1), b(2)(A).

[210] Id. §§ 12162 (a)(2)(B), b(2)(B).

[211] Id. §§ 12162(a)(2)(C)-(D), (a)(4).

single level cars;[212] "remanufactured" cars;[213] and station accessibility.[214] The commuter rail transportation section has more detail on accessibility standards for new and existing stations.[215]

In *Wray v. National Railroad Passenger Corp.*, two disabled passengers brought suit against Amtrak.[216] These passengers had attempted to sit in a wheelchair accessible Amtrak train, but were removed from their seats to make room for other disabled passengers who had reserved their disabled-accessible seats beforehand.[217]

The court held for Amtrak, reasoning that the ADA did not grant plaintiffs a right to sit in the disabled section when there were other disabled passengers who had made advance reservations.[218] Although the court pointed out that the one-car-per-train rule "might be worthy of review" because it does not address the number of seats which must be accessible, the court held that Amtrak's reservation system was a reasonable response to the problem of excess demand.[219]

3.   Reflections on the ADA's transportation provisions

As evident from the foregoing discussion, the ADA's transportation provisions are some of the most, if not the most, detailed in the statute. At no other point in the statute do we see explicit provisions of comparable specificity: bathroom accessibility in station cars, provisions for types of eating facilities in rail cars, and so on.

Also, nowhere else does the statute spell out so precisely what constitutes discrimination. This is, at least in part, an explicit recognition on the part of the framers of the crucial nature of transportation.[220] This

---

[212] 42 U.S.C. § 12162(a)(3) (2000).

[213] Id. § 12162(d).

[214] Id. § 12162(e). Similar to subpart I, there is a new/existing station dichotomy. New stations must be accessible. Existing stations for intercity rail transportation, and "key" stations in commuter rail transportation, must be made accessible as soon as practicable, but not later than July 26, 2010. Alterations must be made with accessibility in mind.

[215] Id.

[216] Wray v. Nat'l R.R. Passenger Corp., 10 F.Supp.2d 1036 (E.D. Wis. 1998).

[217] Id. at 1040.

[218] Id.

[219] Id.

[220] See e.g., H.R. Rep. No. 485(II), at 37 (1990), reprinted in 1990 U.S.C.C.A.N. 303, 319 ("Transportation is the linchpin which enable people with disabilities to be integrated and mainstreamed into society."); see also id. (observing that testimony of the Executive Director of

specificity should be judged against the backdrop of the pre-ADA transportation related statutes, whose failure had been attributed to a lack of clear guidance.[221]

Has this specificity helped? To be sure, there are fewer reported cases dealing with public transportation than the rest of Title II, and most of the ADA.[222] However, some suggest that the ADA's transportation provisions fail to adequately protect the transportation needs of the disabled.[223]

Nevertheless, it is inescapable that the ADA's transportation provisions provide public entities more guidance than operators of other public functions like voting and public education. It is worth keeping in mind this principle as future modifications and amendments to the ADA are debated and adopted.

F.   *Antidiscrimination Mandate – Voting*

The above sections describe the major categories of a public entity's affirmative responsibilities under Title II. These are not hermetically sealed categories, and any given issue may be thought of as implicating several of these requirements. For example, voting. When administering the program, service, or activity of voting, a public entity must make reasonable modifications to its policies, practices, and procedures. It has to administer these services in the most integrated setting appropriate.

The application of voting to the ADA is a complicated, important, and timely issue with which courts and commentators have grappled.[224]

President's Committee on Employment of People with Disabilities was similar: "inaccessible transportation has been identified as the major barrier, second only to discriminatory attitudes."); H.R. Rep. No. 485(IV), at 25 (1990), reprinted in 1990 U.S.C.C.A.N. 512, 514 (Committee on Energy and Commerce noted that: "[Transportation] is a veritable lifeline to the economic and social benefits that our Nation offers its citizens .... For this reason, the National Council on Disability has declared that 'accessible transportation is a critical component of a national policy that promotes self-reliance and self-sufficiency of people with disabilities.'").

[221] See, e.g., ADAPT v. Skinner, 881 F.2d 1184, 1186 (3d Cir. 1989).

[222] At press time, the annotations to the United States Code included only nine reported cases dealing with transportation issues. An independent Westlaw search found no more.

[223] See generally Lewyn, supra note 168.

[224] See e.g., Nelson v. Miller, 170 F.3d 641, 649-53 (6th Cir. 1999); Lightbourn v. City of El Paso, 118 F.3d 421 (5th Cir. 1997); New York v. County of Schoharie, 82 F.Supp.2d 19, 21 (N.D.N.Y. 2001); Symposium, The End of the Beginning For Election Reform, 9 Geo. J. on Poverty L. & Pol'y 285, 336-56 (2002); Michael Waterstone, Constitutional and

It is reasonably clear that Congress considered voting when it enacted the ADA, and that voting is covered by Title II's program access standard.[225] Voting programs, services, and activities, viewed in their entirety, must be readily accessible to people with disabilities, unless to do so would result in a fundamental alteration or cause an undue financial or administrative burden. However, unlike the transportation provisions discussed above, neither Title II nor its implementing regulations offer much guidance on what this actually means.

One common method that most states have adopted to expand voting opportunities for people with disabilities is to offer "curbside voting." This is a procedure whereby a polling place worker brings a voting machine curbside for voters whose disability precludes them from entering the polling place. This procedure does not, in and of itself, provide accessible voting machines. Blind individuals, for example, vote with third-party assistance.

Some commentators have suggested that curbside voting and voting with third-party assistance are "cheapened" forms of the voting experience that do not provide the same dignity, privacy, and independence as voting in secret and in private with accessible voting machines.[226] An argument could be made that Title II requires more. The Title II regulations draw a connection between "different" and "discrimination."[227] Thus, a different voting experience (not voting secretly and independently) could constitute discrimination in violation of Title II.

However, courts generally have not been receptive to this argument. In *Lightbourn v. County of El Paso*, a group of mobility- and vision-impaired Texas voters argued that El Paso discriminated against them in violation of Title II by providing inaccessible polling places and voting apparatus that only allowed blind individuals to vote with third-party assistance.[228] The court rejected this argument on the grounds that the Secretary of Elections did not have a duty or responsibility to prevent the claimed violations.

Statutory Voting Rights for People with Disabilities, 14 Stan. L. & Pol'y Rev. 353, 358-361 (2003); US Gen. Accounting Office, Voters with Disabilities – Access to Polling Places and Alternative Voting Methods 7, http://www.gao.gov/new.items/d02107.pdf (Oct. 2001) [hereinafter GAO Study]; Kay Schriner & Andrew I. Batavia, The Americans with Disabilities Act: Does it Secure the Fundamental Right to Vote?, 29 Pol'y Stud. J. 663 (2001).

[225] See Waterstone, supra note **224**, at 360 nn.51 & 52.

[226] Id. at 360; Schriner & Batavia, supra note 224.

[227] See 28 C.F.R. § 35.150 (2003).

[228] Lightbourn v. County of El Paso, 118 F.3d 421, 426-27 (5th Cir. 1997).

Similarly, in *Nelson v. Miller*, a class of blind voters argued that Michigan violated Title II by not providing machines with which blind voters could mark ballots without third-party assistance.[229] The Sixth Circuit disagreed, holding that the Michigan Constitution did not guarantee a secret vote, and therefore Michigan had not denied its visually-impaired citizens a right it had given to its other citizens.[230]

Congress, perhaps prompted by the lamentations of commentators that the ADA has had limited effectiveness in creating social change with regard to the right to vote,[231] has responded. In 2002, Congress passed the Help America Vote Act, which for the first time offered a federal guarantee of a secret and independent right to vote for people with disabilities.[232] Time will tell how successful this statute is in its implementation.

§ 11.5 By Reason Of Disability – Intentional Discrimination Versus Disparate Impact

Title II's discrimination provision provides that "no qualified individual with a disability shall, *by reason of such disability*, be excluded from participation in or be denied the benefits of services, programs, or activities of the public entity, or be subjected to discrimination by any such entity."[233] Does this impute an "intentional discrimination" standard on Title II claims, analogous to claims under the Equal Protection Clause of the Fourteenth Amendment?[234] As a general matter, it does not.

In *Alexander v. Choate*, the Supreme Court rejected the contention that Section 504 of the Rehabilitation Act only reached purposeful discrimination against persons with disabilities.[235] The Court indicated that there is strong support in the legislative history for the proposition that the Rehabilitation Act was not intended to prohibit solely intentional discrimination: "[d]iscrimination against the handicapped was perceived by Congress to most often the product, not of invidious animus, but rather of thoughtlessness and indifference – of benign neglect."[236]

The Court noted that "much of the conduct that Congress sought to alter in passing the Rehabilitation Act would be difficult if not

---

[229] Nelson v. Miller, 170 F.3d 641, 649-53 (6th Cir. 1999).

[230] Id.

[231] See Schriner & Batavia, supra note 224; see also GAO Study, supra note 224, at 14.

[232] Pub. L. No. 107-252, 116 Stat. 1666 (2002) (signed into law on Oct. 29, 2002).

[233] 42 U.S.C. § 12132 (2000) (emphasis added).

[234] See, e.g., Washington v. Davis, 426 U.S. 229 (1976).

[235] Alexander v. Choate, 469 U.S. 287 (1985).

[236] Id. at 295.

impossible to reach were the Act construed to proscribe only conduct fueled by a discriminatory intent."[237]

For the most part, courts have imparted this principle whole-cloth to the ADA, and held that a plaintiff need not prove impermissible intent under either Section 504 of the Rehabilitation Act or Title II of the ADA.[238] Courts have offered guidance on what a plaintiff must show to demonstrate that he was discriminated against "by reason of such disability" for purposes of the Rehabilitation Act and Title II.

In *Washington v. Indiana High School Athletic Association*, the Seventh Circuit stated:

> Discrimination under both acts may be established by evidence that (1) the defendant intentionally acted on the basis of disability, (2) the defendant refused to provide a reasonable accommodation, or (3) the defendant's rule disproportionably impacts disabled people.[239]

The court noted that proving discriminatory intent through refusal to accommodate had been approved for purposes of the Rehabilitation Act in *Southeastern Community College v. Davis*.[240]

An example of discriminatory intent proved through discriminatory effect can be found in *Henrietta D. v. Giuliani*.[241] The plaintiffs challenged New York's provision of social welfare benefits to persons with HIV and related illnesses. Plaintiffs offered proof that under existing New York law, they were not receiving adequate services. Although there was no proof of a discriminatory intent on the part of the

---

[237] Id. at 296-97.

[238] See Washington v. Ind. High Sch. Athletic Ass'n, 181 F.3d 840, 846-47 (7th Cir. 1999); see also McPherson v. Mich. High Sch. Athletic Ass'n, 119 F.3d 453, 460 (6th Cir. 1997); Crowder v. Kitagawa, 81 F.3d 1480, 1483-84 (9th Cir. 1996); Norcross v. Sneed, 755 F.2d 113, 117 n.4 (8th Cir. 1985); Pushkin v. Regents of the Univ. of Colo., 658 F.2d 1372, 1385 (10th Cir. 1981); Prewitt v. U.S. Postal Serv., 662 F.2d 292, 306 (5th Cir. 1981).

[239] See Washington, 181 F.3d at 847 (adopting the Seventh Circuit analysis in McPherson, 119 F.3d at 460).

[240] Southeastern Cmty. Coll. v. Davis, 442 U.S. 397 (1979).

[241] Henrietta D. v. Giuliani, 119 F.Supp.2d 181 (E.D.N.Y. 2000); see also Helen L. v. Didario, 46 F.3d 325, 335 (3d Cir. 1995) ("Because the ADA evolved from an attempt to remedy the effects of 'benign neglect' resulting from the 'invisibility' of the disabled, Congress could not have intended to limit the Act's protections and prohibitions to circumstances involving deliberate discrimination."); Tyler v. City of Manhattan, 857 F.Supp. 800, 817 (D. Kan. 1994).

New York legislature, the court held the disparate impact was sufficient to prove a Title II violation. [242]

Although intentional discrimination generally is not required to make out a Title II claim, a plaintiff may have to demonstrate deliberate discrimination to receive a compensatory damage award. In *Ferguson v. City of Phoenix*,[243] the Ninth Circuit held that a Title II plaintiff could not receive compensatory damages without showing discriminatory intent.[244] In its ruling, the Ninth Circuit relied on Fifth and Eleventh Circuit decisions that concluded compensatory damages were unavailable for unintentional violations of the Rehabilitation Act.[245]

Not requiring deliberate discrimination seems the preferred result, and more in line with Rehabilitation Act case law and the legislative history of Title II.[246] But in close cases, some courts have moved toward requiring a higher standard of discriminatory intent.

Ironically, this approach also has its genesis in *Alexander v. Choate*,[247] the same case establishing that the Rehabilitation Act applies to more than just intentional discrimination. This case involved a policy decision to reduce hospital stays from twenty days to fourteen days. The plaintiffs in that case were people with disabilities who claimed that, because of their disabilities, they were more likely to need twenty days of hospital care than people without disabilities.

Therefore, the plaintiffs argued, the policy had a disparate impact on people with disabilities in violation of the ADA. While assuming that the Rehabilitation Act reached "at least some conduct that has an unjustifiable disparate impact upon the handicapped,"[248] the Court rejected the notion that this showing of a disparate impact was enough to state a claim under Section 504.[249]

The Court concluded that Tennessee's facially neutral reduction of in-patient hospitalization coverage was not the sort of disparate impact cognizable as discrimination under the Rehabilitation Act. The Court found that the Rehabilitation Act "seeks to assure evenhanded treatment

---

[242] Henrietta D., 119 F.Supp.2d at 209.

[243] Ferguson v. City of Phoenix, 157 F.3d 668 (3d Cir. 1998).

[244] Id. at 676.

[245] Wood v. President and Trs. of Spring Hill Coll., 978 F.2d 1214 (11th Cir. 1992); Carter v. Orleans Parish Pub. Schs., 725 F.2d 261 (5th Cir. 1984).

[246] See, e.g., Comm. Print, vol. I, 101st Cong., 2d Sess., at 302 (1990) ("Discrimination against people with disabilities results from actions or inactions that discriminate by effect as well as by intent and design.").

[247] Alexander v. Choate, 469 U.S. 287 (1985).

[248] See id. at 299.

[249] Id.

and the opportunity for handicapped individuals to participate in and benefit from programs."[250] The Court found that, at least "when the same benefit is meaningfully and equally offered to them," people with disabilities cannot demand better service based on their disabilities.[251]

A limited number of courts have interpreted *Alexander* to mean that if a rule is "neutral," it does not discriminate on the basis of disability, but instead on some other non-prohibited criteria. For example, in *Sandison v. Michigan High School Athletic Association* discussed supra in this Part, a student with a learning disability who had been held back in school challenged a high school association's "age-rule" that declared 19-year old students ineligible to compete.[252] The Sixth Circuit found that this was a "neutral" rule and therefore did not discriminate against the student because of his disability, but rather because of his age.[253] This case has not been widely followed.

Most courts have read *Alexander* to hold no more than that neutral rules are discriminatory if they deny meaningful access to people with disabilities to government services. For example, in *Crowder v. Kitagawa*,[254] a class of blind persons with guide dogs challenged a Hawaii law that imposed a 120-day quarantine on all animals brought into the state. The Ninth Circuit found that the quarantine, though facially neutral, "burdens visually-impaired persons in a manner different and greater than it burdens others" because of plaintiffs' "unique dependence upon guide dogs."[255]

The court concluded that the quarantine "effectively denies ... *meaningful access* to state services, programs and activities while such services, programs and activities remain open and easily accessible by others. The quarantine, therefore, discriminates against the plaintiffs by reason of their disability."[256]

---

[250] Id. at 288.

[251] Id. at 308.

[252] Sandison v. Mich. High Sch. Athletic Ass'n, 64 F.3d 1026, 1036 (6th Cir. 1995).

[253] Id.

[254] Crowder v. Kitagawa, 81 F.3d 1480, 1481 (9th Cir. 1996).

[255] Id. at 1484.

[256] Id. (emphasis added).

Part 5

Access To Public Accommodations: ADA Title III
Analysis

Chapter 12 COVERED ENTITIES

Title III extends the ADA's antidiscrimination mandate to places of public accommodation and commercial facilities. Title III therefore is broader in scope than Title II, which essentially extended the existing

Rehabilitation Act to additional public entities (i.e., not only those receiving federal financial assistance). The goal of Title III is to integrate people with disabilities into the mainstream of American life.

The overarching requirement of Title III is as follows:

> No individual shall be discriminated against on the basis of disability in the full and equal enjoyment of the goods, services, facilities, privileges, advantages, or accommodations of any place of public accommodation by any private entity who owns, leases (or leases to) or operates a place of public accommodation.[1]

The premise of Title III is straightforward: places of public accommodation are barred from discriminating against people with disabilities in their use of facilities and the provision of goods and services. To this extent, Title III parallels Title II of the Civil Rights Act of 1964.[2]

However, discrimination under Title III is defined broadly to include failure to make reasonable modifications of policies, practices and procedures, failure to ensure effective communication, and failure to take steps to make facilities physically accessible. The defenses to a charge of discrimination rely on concepts of undue burden, fundamental alteration, and readily achievable.

Title III's scope has generated controversy in the case law and commentary. In some ways, Title III has provided more questions than answers. What entities are covered as Title III public accommodations? Which party bears the evidentiary burdens in the various phases of the Title III legal analysis? Are there types of public accommodations (for example, professional sports competitions or professional licensing exams) that contain stringent and tightly controlled requirements so that *any* program modification is fundamentally transforming? These and other questions are discussed in this Part.

§ 12.1 Places Of Public Accommodation And Commercial Facilities

A. *General*

Title III covers "places of public accommodation" and "commercial facilities." Public accommodations consist of twelve specified categories of businesses that affect commerce:

> (A) an inn, hotel, motel, or other *place of lodging*, except for an establishment located within a building that contains not more than five rooms for rent or hire and that is

---

1   42 U.S.C. § 12182 (2000).

2   Id. § 2000a.

actually occupied by the proprietor of such establishment as the residence of such proprietor;

(B) a restaurant, bar, or other *establishment serving food or drink*;

(C) a motion picture house, theater, concert hall, stadium, or other *place of exhibition or entertainment*;

(D) an auditorium, convention center, lecture hall, or other *place of public gathering*;

(E) a bakery, grocery store, clothing store, hardware store, shopping center, or other *sales or rental establishment* [wholesale establishments that sell to the public are included, but wholesale establishments that sell exclusively to other businesses are not[3]];

(F) a Laundromat, dry-cleaner, bank, barber shop, beauty shop, travel service, shoe repair service, funeral parlor, gas station, office of an accountant or lawyer, pharmacy, insurance office, professional office of a health care provider, hospital, or other *service establishment*;

(G) a terminal, depot, or other station used for *specified public transportation* [air travel is not included in the definition of specified public transportation];

(H) a museum, library, gallery, or other *place of public display or collection*;

(I) a park, zoo, amusement park, or other *place of recreation*;

(J) a nursery, elementary, secondary, undergraduate, or postgraduate private school, or other *place of education*;

(K) a day care center, senior citizen center, homeless shelter, food bank, adoption agency, or other *social service center establishment*; and

(L) a gymnasium, health spa, bowling alley, golf course, or other *place of exercise or recreation*.[4]

The twelve categories are exhaustive, but the examples therein are not.[5] If a business does not fit into one of the twelve categories, it is

---

[3] 28 C.F.R. pt. 36, app. B, § 36.104 (2003); see Torres v. AT&T Broadband, LLC, 158 F.Supp.2d 1035, 1038 (N.D. Cal. 2001) (digital cable television system is not a place of public accommodation).

[4] 42 U.S.C. § 12181(7) (2000).

[5] 28 C.F.R. § 36.104 (2003).

not a place of public accommodation.[6] Thus, warehouses, factories, or office buildings where only employees are permitted are not places of public accommodation.[7]

Similarly, private airports, which do not fall in one of the twelve categories, are not places of public accommodation.[8] Instead, they are considered "commercial facilities"[9] if they are intended for nonresidential use.[10] As described in subsequent chapters, public accommodations are subject to the nondiscrimination obligations of Title III, while commercial facilities are subject only to the requirements for new construction and alterations.[11]

---

[6] U.S. Dep't of Justice, Title III Technical Assistance Manual § 1.2000 [hereinafter TAM III], http://www.usdoj.gov/crt/ada/taman3.html (Nov. 1993).

[7] Indep. Living Res. v. Or. Arena Corp., 982 F.Supp. 698, 758-59 (D. Or. 1997); TAM III, supra note 6, § 1.3000; see also 28 C.F.R. § 36.104.

[8] Title III TAM, supra note 6, § 1.3100; see also 28 C.F.R. § 36.104.

[9] Commercial facilities do not include rail vehicles, or facilities covered or specifically exempted, by the Fair Housing Act (e.g., residential dwelling units, or owner-occupied rooming houses occupied by four or fewer families). TAM III, supra note 6, § 1.3100. By contrast, an entity covered by the Fair Housing Act may be a place of public accommodation. For example, a homeless shelter that allows stays ranging from overnight to long-term may be a place of lodging covered by Title III and a residential facility covered by the Fair Housing Act. Id. § 1.2000.

[10] 42 U.S.C. § 12181(2) (2000).

[11] [T]he bill originally introduced into Congress included all of what is now § 12182 and § 12183 in the same section, and made no distinction between public accommodations and commercial facilities; that is, all of the species of discrimination described in §§ 12182(b), 12183(a) applied without exception to both types of buildings. ... Congress separated § 12182 and § 12183 in the final bill in order to make a distinction between public accommodations and commercial facilities that would make the application of Title III to commercial facilities more limited than the application of Title III to public accommodations (i.e., the discrimination described in § 12182(b) applies only to public accommodations, whereas the discrimination described in § 12183(a), "design and construct" discrimination, applies to both public accommodations and commercial facilities).

Lonberg v. Sanborn Theaters Inc., 259 F.3d 1029, 1035 n.7 (9th Cir. 2001) (citations omitted).

A single facility may contain public accommodations and commercial facilities.[12] In addition, a single entity may operate a public accommodation and a commercial facility. However, policies or decisions made in the commercial facility that affect the public accommodation must comply with Title III.[13]

B. *Residential Facilities*

Title III does not cover residential facilities.[14] However, sometimes it is difficult to distinguish between a residential facility and a place of public accommodation. Common areas within residential facilities that are open to the public (e.g., not restricted to residents and their guests) may be considered Title III public accommodations.[15]

Similarly, sales or rental offices within a residential facility or within a model home may be places of public accommodation covered by Title III.[16] A vacation timeshare may be a place of public accommodation if its operation resembles that of a hotel or other place of transient lodging. In this example, factors to be considered include:

> Whether the timeshare offers short-term ownership interests (e.g., 1 week or less);

> The nature of the ownership interest conveyed (e.g., fee simple);

> The degree of restriction placed on ownership; and

> The extent to which the operation resembles that of a hotel (e.g., central registration, reservations, and services).[17]

Areas of a private home that are used as a place of public accommodation will be covered under Title III.[18] Therefore, a home that houses a daycare facility or a physician's office will be covered under Title III, at least in those areas used for the public accommodation or used for residential and public activities.[19]

---

[12] TAM III, supra note 6, § 1.3000 (e.g., stores within a private airport are public accommodations, even thought the airport itself is a commercial facility). See also Johnson v. Gambrinus Co./Spoetzl Brewery, 116 F.3d 1052, 1057 (5th Cir. 1997) (public areas of brewery are public accommodations, while non-public areas are commercial facilities).

[13] TAM III, supra note 6, § 1.2000.

[14] Id. at 4.

[15] Id.

[16] Id.

[17] Id. at 4-5.

[18] 28 C.F.R. pt. 36, app. B., § 36.207 (2003).

[19] Id. § 36.104.

C. *Responsible Parties*

Title III regulates the conduct of a private[20] entity that owns, leases (or leases to) or operates a place of public accommodation or commercial facility.[21] Therefore, landlords, tenants, and operators of public accommodations are responsible for ensuring compliance with Title III. These entities may contractually allocate responsibility among themselves for complying with particular responsibilities. However, such an allocation is effective only between the parties and each party remains fully liable to an individual with a disability who encounters discrimination at the public accommodation.[22]

Nevertheless, to be responsible under Title III, an individual or entity must have some ability to control the place of public accommodation. Thus, in *Aikins v. St. Helena Hospital*,[23] a doctor who worked as an independent contractor, and who did not control the relevant operations or policies of the hospital, was not liable under Title III for the hospital's actions.[24]

In *Neff v. American Dairy Queen Corp.*,[25] the Fifth Circuit dealt with the analogous issue of whether a franchisor, rather than solely the franchisee, "operates" a franchise for purposes of Title III coverage. The court held that the proper inquiry is whether the franchisor controls the relevant aspects of franchise operation; for example, in this case, the decision to make architectural modifications to ensure building accessibility under Title III.[26]

D. *Protected Individuals*

In some cases, simultaneous questions have arisen as to whether an individual was an employee covered under Title I, a member of the public covered under Title III, or some other category without protection of

---

[20] A private entity is defined as an entity other than a public entity (as defined in section 201(1)). 42 U.S.C. § 12181(6) (2000). Therefore, Title II and Title III are mutually exclusive, as no single entity can be both public (Title II) and private (Title III).

[21] Id. § 12182(a).

[22] TAM III, supra note 6, § 1.2000.

[23] Aikins v. St. Helena Hosp., 843 F.Supp. 1329 (N.D. Cal. 1994).

[24] Id. at 1335. But see Howe v. Hull, 874 F.Supp. 779, 787-788 (N.D. Ohio 1994) (doctor was "operator" of hospital because he had role in admitting patients).

[25] Neff v. Am. Dairy Queen Corp., 58 F.3d 1063 (5th Cir. 1995).

[26] Id. at 1068; see also Pona v. Cecil Shitaker's, Inc., 155 F.3d 1034, 1036 (8th Cir. 1998) (restaurant franchisor could not be held liable to customer who was asked to leave restaurant because she had service dog because franchisor did not reserve right under franchise agreement to control entry to restaurant).

the ADA. As a general matter, the courts have been careful to ensure that individuals are not denied coverage under both Title I and Title III.

Thus, a physician is covered under Title III for the purposes of accommodations in hospital privileges, because his independent contractor status does not bring him within Title I's employment protections.[27] It is less clear, however, whether a physician who is an employee of a hospital covered under Title I also may assert her Title III rights.[28]

Because Title III does not include an employee size limitation for coverage of public accommodations and commercial facilities, it may apply to entities that are not covered under Title I of the ADA (i.e., to entities with less than 15 employees). There is some concern, therefore, that Title III provides employees of small businesses ADA rights they would not otherwise have under Title I.

The superior rule is that the distinction between access to the public aspects of a business and access to the employment aspects of a business should be maintained. For example, an employee of a small bakery (with 7 employees) who uses a wheelchair may be able to assert that the bakery must remove a step at the main public entrance pursuant to Title III, if it is readily achievable to do so. However, the same employee may not be able to require accessibility modifications to the employee-only work areas of the bakery, which would be covered only under Title I.

Some defendants have tried to restrict who is considered the "public" for purposes of determining a public accommodation. For instance, the argument is made that certain individuals, such as college students, theatre performers, or competitors in sports contests, are not protected by Title III because they are not clients nor customers. Nor are they employees subject to the requirements of Title I.

This argument attempts to exempt from coverage areas that are restricted for the use of certain designated individuals (e.g., locker rooms, playing fields, and class rooms). Under this theory, only the general public (e.g., spectators of a football game, but not athletes) would be able to assert rights or have legal standing under Title III.

In *PGA Tour Inc., v. Martin*,[29] the U.S. Supreme Court found that, for the purposes of Title III, sports competitors are clients or customers of a place of public accommodation. The Court found that players in

---

[27] Menkowitz v. Pottstown Mem'l Med. Ctr., 154 F.3d 113, 122-23 (3d Cir. 1998).

[28] See DeWyer v. Temple Univ., 11 A.D. Cases 800, 20 NDLR 50, 2001 WL 115461, at *3 (E.D. Pa. 2001) (employee can assert employment-related rights under Title I, not Title III. It is also possible for an employee to assert Title III for non-employment related rights).

[29] PGA Tour, Inc. v. Martin, 532 U.S. 661, 679-680 (2001).

competitive sports, such as those on the PGA Tour, are members of the general public. Indeed, they constitute a sub-group of the general public who have paid a fee and met a qualification standard.[30] Therefore, the playing areas, rules of play, and so on are subject to the Title III requirements for places of public accommodation.

E. *Physical Structures*

There is a split among the federal circuit courts regarding whether an entity may be a place of public accommodation when it does not occupy a physical "place" that is open to the public. The issue has arisen in the context of insurance offices and considers whether insurance policies, as opposed to the physical insurance offices themselves, are subject to Title III requirements. As discussed infra in Part 10, the issue also has arisen in the context of the applicability of Title III to private Internet sites.

In *Carparts Distribution Center v. Automotive Wholesaler's Association of New England*,[31] the First Circuit considered whether a disability insurance policy that capped payments for AIDS-related treatment at $25,000, but allowed $1 million in payments for other illnesses, was covered under Title III.

In its analysis, the court relied first on the fact that the plain language of Title III did not require a physical structure for purposes of coverage.[32] In addition, the court relied on public policy concerns to find that it would not be rational to conclude, as would occur in the case of travel agents, that entities are covered when their customers come to their offices, but not when their customers access the same services by phone, mail, or the Internet.[33] However, the court acknowledged that Title III was ambiguous on the issue, and concluded that it would decide only that there was a "possibility" that Title III covered the substance of insurance policies and not only the place where they are issued.

Most other circuits, on the other hand, have found that Title III does not cover the substance of an insurance plan.[34] The Sixth Circuit, in *Parker v. Metropolitan Life Insurance Co.*,[35] found that "a public

---

[30] Id. at 679-80; see also Indep. Living Res. v. Or. Arena Corp., 982 F.Supp. 698, 759 (D. Or. 1997) (executive seats in the Rose Garden Arena were subject to the ADA, although they were not open to the general public).

[31] Carparts Distribution Ctr., Inc. v. Automotive Wholesaler's Ass'n of New England, 37 F.3d 12 (1st Cir. 1994).

[32] Id. at 19.

[33] Id.

[34] See Weyer v. Twentieth Century Fox Film Corp., 198 F.3d 1104, 1115 (9th Cir. 2000); Ford v. Schering-Plough Corp., 145 F.3d 601, 612-13 (3d Cir. 1998).

[35] Parker v. Metro. Life Ins. Co., 121 F.3d 1006 (6th Cir. 1997).

accommodation is a physical place."[36]   Therefore, an insurance policy offered, not in an insurance office but through an employer, is not covered by Title III.   The fact that Metropolitan Life Insurance did operate insurance offices did not change the analysis because the plaintiff in the case did not obtain her policy through such an office.[37] The court treated the insurance company as a wholesaler, selling to another business, rather than a retailer selling to the public and, therefore, found that Title III did not cover its services.[38]

Courts also have interpreted the requirement of a "place" of public accommodation to require a nexus with a physical location, even if the discrimination does not occur in the physical place.   Thus, a telephone qualification test for a television game show is covered under Title III, and therefore must be accessible to players with manual dexterity disabilities, because the telephone contest has a direct relationship to the actual physical place of the game show (i.e., the television studio).[39]

Thus, "the fact that the plaintiffs in this suit were screened out by an automated telephone system, rather than by an admission policy administered at the studio door, is of no consequence under the statute; eligibility criteria are frequently administered off-site − for example, through the mail or over the telephone."[40] By extension, court have held that Internet stores may not be places of public accommodation, unless there is a significant nexus with a physical place of public accommodation.[41]

§ 12.2 Insurance

In addition to the question of whether the substance of insurance policies, as opposed to only physical insurance offices, is covered under Title III because of the requirement of a physical "place," the courts have struggled with other aspects of the coverage of insurance.

On the substance issue, the Sixth Circuit found that Title III did not require a place of public accommodation to stock accessible goods, such

---

[36]   Id. at 1010.

[37]   Id. at 1011.

[38]   Id. at 1011-12.

[39]   Rendon v. Valleycrest Prods., Ltd., 294 F.3d 1279, 1283 (11th Cir. 2002).

[40]   Id. at 1286.

[41]   Access Now, Inc. v. Southwest Airlines Co., 227 F.Supp.2d 1312, 1321 (S.D. Fla. 2002) (nexus to an airline is not sufficient because airlines are not places of public accommodation); Noah v. AOL Time Warner Inc., 261 F.Supp.2d 532, 540 (E.D. Va. 2003) (America Online internet chat rooms are not places of public accommodation).

as Braille books.[42] Therefore, the court held that, like bookstores, insurance companies are not required to offer for sale accessible goods (i.e., in this case "nondiscriminatory" insurance policies).[43]

The Sixth Circuit treated insurance companies who sell policies to employers like wholesalers who sell to retail stores. Therefore, because wholesalers do not sell to the general public, Title III does not cover them under the Sixth Circuit's analysis.[44]

By contrast, the Second Circuit held that the substance of insurance policies is covered under Title III.[45] The Second Circuit found that "an entity covered by Title III is not only obligated by the statute to provide disabled persons with physical access, but is also prohibited from refusing to sell them its merchandise by reason of discrimination against their disability."[46] The court relied, in part on the "safe harbor" provision of Title V of the ADA, which provides –

> Titles I through IV of this Act shall not be construed to prohibit or restrict:
>
> (1) an insurer, hospital or medical service company, health maintenance organization, or any agent, or entity that administers benefit plans, or similar organizations from underwriting risks, classifying risks, or administering such risks that are based on or not inconsistent with State law; or
>
> (2) a person or organization covered by this Act from establishing, sponsoring, observing or administering the terms of a bona fide benefit plan that are based on underwriting risks, classifying risks, or administering such risks that are based on or not inconsistent with State law; or
>
> (3) a person or organization covered by this Act from establishing, sponsoring, observing or administering the terms of a bona fide benefit plan that is not subject to State laws that regulate insurance.

---

[42] Parker, 121 F.3d at 1012.

[43] Id. at 1012-13; see also McNeil v. Time Ins. Co., 205 F.3d 179, 187 (5th Cir. 2000).

[44] Parker, 121 F.3d at 1011-12 (the Sixth Circuit also held that the ADA does not prohibit discrimination between different disabilities; e.g., treating mental and physical disabilities differently).

[45] Pallozzi v. Allstate Life Ins. Co., 198 F.3d 28, 33 (2d Cir. 2000) (Allstate refused to issue a life insurance policy to a couple because of their mental disabilities).

[46] Id. at 33.

Paragraphs (1), (2), and (3) shall not be used as a subterfuge to evade the purposes of titles I and III.[47]

According to the Second Circuit:

> If the ADA were not intended to reach insurance underwriting under any circumstances, there would be no need for a safe harbor provision exempting underwriting practices that are consistent with state law.... And, in any event, the subterfuge clause suggests that, notwithstanding compliance with state law, Titles I and III do apply to insurance practices where conformity with state law is used as a subterfuge to evade their purposes. Considering the net effect of these provisions, it seems clear to us that Title III was intended by Congress to apply to insurance underwriting.[48]

The First Circuit, in *Carparts*,[49] and the Sixth Circuit, in *Parker*,[50] do not deal persuasively with Title V's "safe harbor" provision. The First Circuit did not decide whether the safe harbor provision indicated that, but for that requirement, insurance policies would have been covered or whether that provision was added in caution to resolve possible uncertainty in the statutory language.[51] The Sixth Circuit merely cited the provision in a footnote without comment.[52] In a separate decision, the Fifth Circuit at least raised the issue, but decided "it would be oxymoronic to interpret the 'safe harbor' [provision] for the insurance industry as ensuring more regulation of that same industry."[53]

Although the analyses vary, most circuits, except the First and Second, have not applied the provisions of Title III to the substance of insurance policies, under one or more of several theories:

> Only policies bought at a physical office will be covered;

> Only policies bought directly, as opposed to through an employer, will be covered (i.e., insurance companies as wholesalers);

> Title III is limited to "access" to places, and it does not cover "content" of the goods or services offered (i.e., insurance

---

[47]   42 U.S.C. § 12201(c) (2000).

[48]   Pallozzi, 198 F.3d at 32.

[49]   Carparts Distribution Ctr., Inc. v. Automotive Wholesaler's Ass'n of New England, 37 F.3d 12, 20 (1st Cir. 1994).

[50]   Parker v. Metro. Life Ins. Co., 121 F.3d 1006, 1012 n.6 (6th Cir. 1997).

[51]   Carparts, 37 F.3d at 20.

[52]   Parker, 121 F.3d at 1012 n.6.

[53]   McNeil v. Time Ins. Co., 205 F.3d 179, 187 n.10 (5th Cir. 2000).

companies, like bookstores, are not required to sell accessible goods (e.g., Braille books));

Title V's "safe harbor" provision would exempt insurance policies, even if they were otherwise covered under Title III.

An additional question in applying Title III to insurance coverage is whether doing so would run afoul of the McCarran-Ferguson Act. That law provides that "no Act of Congress shall be construed to invalidate, impair, or supercede any law enacted by any State for the purpose of regulating the business of insurance ... unless such Act specifically relates to the business of insurance."[54] The question of whether this Act precludes application of Title III to insurance policies has generated a split among the federal circuits that have considered the issue.[55]

§ 12.3 Examinations And Courses

Title III covers private entities that offer certain examinations or courses:

Any person that offers examinations or courses related to applications, licensing, certification, or credentialing for secondary or postsecondary education, professional, or trade purposes shall offer such examinations or courses in a place and manner accessible to persons with disabilities or offer alternative accessible arrangements for such individuals.[56]

The requirements for providers of examinations and courses are similar, but not identical, to the public accommodations requirements of Title III. These requirements apply to providers of examinations and courses, regardless of whether or not they qualify for treatment as places of public accommodation.

---

[54]   15 U.S.C. § 1012(b) (2000).

[55]   Compare Ford v. Schering-Plough Corp., 145 F.3d 601, 612 (3d Cir. 1998) (holding that because the term "insurance" does not appear in the "Findings and Purposes" section of the ADA, the ADA does not relate to the business of insurance) and Doe v. Mutual of Omaha Ins. Co., 179 F.3d 557, 563-64 (7th Cir. 1999) (holding that although the ADA can be construed as prohibiting insurance companies from refusing to insure disabled individuals, the ADA cannot be interpreted to govern rate and coverage issues) with Pallozzi v. Allstate Life Ins. Co., 198 F.3d 28, 34-35 (2d Cir. 1999) (holding that because § 12201(c) relates to insurance and Title III defines public accommodation to include insurance offices which offer the "good and service" of insurance policies, the ADA can apply to insurance policies).

[56]   42 U.S.C. § 12189 (2000).

At the district court level, courts have grappled with the effects of this section on various types of tests and exams, such as bar exams,[57] medical licensing exams,[58] and law school admissions exams.[59]

In *Doe v. National Board of Medical Examiners*,[60] the Third Circuit addressed the National Board of Medical Examiners' practice of "flagging" examinations on which it granted accommodations that it deemed made such scores non-comparable with other test-takers (for example, providing extra time to students with learning disabilities or alternative formats to blind and deaf students). The court first held that these types of challenges were properly considered under 42 U.S.C. § 12189 (Title III's section on examinations and courses), as opposed to the more general antidiscrimination provisions in § 12182.

The plaintiff argued that because he would be discriminated against (stigmatized) when his examination was "flagged," the Board did not offer the exam in a manner that was "accessible" to people with disabilities. The court rejected this argument, concluding that he had not proven that he would face discrimination when his exam was flagged, and that he had not shown that the Board was incorrect in terming his scores incomparable.

§ 12.4 Exempt Entities

Religious entities and private clubs are exempt from the requirements of Title III, including the nondiscrimination and construction requirements.[61] A religious entity is one controlled by a religious organization; the term refers not only to places of worship, but also to facilities that, but for religious ownership, would be places of public

---

[57] See Ellen S. v. Fla. Bd. of Bar Exam'rs, 859 F.Supp. 1489, 1490-91 (S.D. Fla. 1994) (challenging questions on Florida state bar application); Argen v. N.Y. St. Bd. of Law Exam'rs, 860 F.Supp. 84, 90-91 (W.D.N.Y. 1994) (denying special accommodation on bar exam because of failure to prove learning disability); Pazer v. N.Y. State Bd. of Law Exam'rs, 849 F.Supp. 284, 285 (S.D.N.Y. 1994) (detailing visually disabled person's claim for accommodation in taking bar exam); D'Amico v. N.Y. State Bd. of Law Exam'rs, 813 F.Supp. 217, 218 (W.D.N.Y. 1993) (reviewing visually-impaired individual's claim for preliminary injunction seeking accommodations in taking bar exam).

[58] Biank v. Nat'l Bd. of Med. Exam'rs, 130 F.Supp.2d 986, 989 (N.D. Ill. 2000) (national medical examination board, as a private entity offering examinations related to licensing of physicians, was subject to ADA requirements).

[59] Agranoff v. Law Sch. Admission Council, 97 F.Supp.2d 86, 87 (D. Mass. 1999) (applying Title III to law school admission exam).

[60] Doe v. Nat'l Bd. of Med. Exam'rs, 199 F.3d 146, 148 (3d Cir. 1999).

[61] 42 U.S.C. § 12187 (2000).

accommodation, such as hospitals, schools, and day care facilities.[62] The existence of a lay board of directors does not mean the entity is not a religious entity. "The test is a factual one – whether the church or other religious organization controls the operations [of the entity]."[63]

The religious entity exemption applies to all activities of the religious entity. However, it does not extend to activities of non-religious entities because they are associated with a religious entity or located on a religious entity's facility. Thus, a private day care provider who leases space in a religious facility is not exempt from Title III, as long as the space is not a place of worship, a lease exists, and consideration is paid.[64]

Private clubs are exempt from Title III[65] and are defined as those clubs exempted from coverage under Title II of the Civil Rights Act of 1964. Factors to determine whether a private entity constitutes an exempt private club include:

> Whether members exercise a high degree of control over club operations;

> Whether the membership process is highly selective;

> Whether substantial membership fees are charged; and

> Whether the entity is operated on a non-profit basis.

The club must not have been founded to avoid compliance with federal civil rights laws.[66] A private club loses its exemption to the extent it allows nonmembers to use the facility as a place of public accommodation.[67]

§ 12.5 Relationship To Title II

Title III is limited to private entities, defined as those that are not public entities within the meaning of Title II of the ADA.[68] Therefore, no entity may be covered both by Titles II and III. However, there are situations in which private and public entities are closely related.

Because public entities are prohibited from discriminating through contract, a state or local government that contracts with a private entity for the provision of a service to the public must ensure that the service complies with Title II. The private entity, itself, may be covered by

---

62 TAM III, supra note 6, § 1.5000.
63 28 C.F.R. pt. 36, app. B, § 36.104 (2003).
64 Id.
65 42 U.S.C. § 12187.
66 TAM III, supra note 6, § 1.6000.
67 Id.
68 42 U.S.C. § 12181(6).

Title III or may not be covered by the ADA, for instance if the public entity contracts with a religious organization.

Regardless of the private entity's separate obligations, the public entity must ensure (for instance, by contract) that the service complies with Title II.[69] In determining whether an undue burden is present in such an instance, the private entity will be judged according to its own resources. However, the public entity will be judged by its own, likely more substantial resources. Therefore, a public entity must be prepared to make its resources available to the private entity to ensure compliance with Title II. These same principals apply when public and private entities act jointly.[70]

---

[69] TAM III, supra note 6, § 1.7000.
[70] Id.

Chapter 13 PROHIBITED CONDUCT

§ 13.1 General

Title III provides general and specific prohibitions on discriminatory conduct. General discrimination prohibited under Title III includes:

- Denial of participation
- Participation in unequal benefit
- Providing a separate benefit when separation is not necessary
- Failure to ensure that people with disabilities receive goods or services in the most integrated setting appropriate to their needs
- Denying an individual with a disability the opportunity to participate in an integrated benefit because of the availability of a separate benefit
- Using contractual or administrative methods that have the effect of discriminating or that perpetuate the discrimination of others who are subject to common control
- Discrimination on the basis of association with a person with a known disability[1]

Specific types of discrimination under Title III include:

- Discriminatory eligibility criteria
- Failure to make reasonable modifications of policy, practice, or procedure when necessary to permit a person with a disability to benefit from a place of public accommodation
- Failure to ensure effective communication through the provision of auxiliary aids
- Failure to remove architectural barriers to access when it is readily achievable to do so[2]

A place of public accommodation may not assess any charge to a person with a disability for any action, aid, or service required by the ADA, even to cover the actual costs of the action, aid, or service.[3] Rather, the cost of compliance must be considered an overhead expense.

---

[1]   42 U.S.C. § 12182(b)(1).

[2]   Id. § 12182(b)(2).

[3]   28 C.F.R. § 36.301(c) (2003).

§ 13.2 Denial Of Participation

Section 12182(b)(1)(A)(i) provides:

It shall be discriminatory to subject an individual or class of individuals on the basis of a disability or disabilities of such individual or class, directly, or through contractual, licensing, or other arrangements, to a denial of the opportunity of the individual or class to participate in or benefit from the goods, services, facilities, privileges, advantages, or accommodations of an entity.[4]

This prohibition tracks those protections set out in the Civil Rights Act of 1964. Although this provision appears clear, it is difficult sometimes to determine whether an individual is being excluded from a facility because of her disability. Of course, an individual may not be excluded simply because of the existence of a disability, as periodically happens to individuals with mental illnesses, for example. Such exclusions are presumptuously based on prejudice and incorrect assumptions about people with disabilities.

However, a person also cannot be excluded on the basis of the effects of her disability. Thus, a person with Tourette's Syndrome may not be excluded from a store because she blurts out words or phrases. The store owner's argument that he is excluding the person because of her behavior (which purportedly keeps away or scares other customers), and not her disability, would not succeed where the behavior is a direct result of the disability. Instead, the store owner must demonstrate that the person's disability-related behavior fundamentally interferes with the operation of the store and cannot be accommodated.

§ 13.3 Unequal Participation

Under Title III:

It shall be discriminatory to afford an individual or class of individuals, on the basis of a disability or disabilities of such individual or class, directly, or through contractual, licensing, or other arrangements with the opportunity to participate in or benefit from a good, service, facility, privilege, advantage, or accommodation that is not equal to that afforded to other individuals.[5]

This requirement does not guarantee that an individual with a disability will achieve an identical result as a non-disabled individual.

---

[4]   42 U.S.C. § 12182(b)(1)(A)(i) (2000); 28 C.F.R. § 36.202(a).

[5]   42 U.S.C. § 12182; 28 C.F.R. § 35.202(b).

However, she must be given an equal opportunity to benefit.[6] Thus, for example, a person who uses a wheelchair cannot be excluded from an exercise class because she cannot do all the exercises and derive the same benefit as participants without disabilities.[7]

§ 13.4 Separate Benefit

According to Title III:

It shall be discriminatory to provide an individual or class of individuals, on the basis of a disability or disabilities of such individual or class, directly, or through contractual, licensing, or other arrangements with a good, service, facility, privilege, advantage, or accommodation that is different or separate from that provided to other individuals, unless such action is necessary to provide the individual or class of individuals with a good, service, facility, privilege, advantage, or accommodation, or other opportunity that is as effective as that provided to others.[8]

The primary goal of this provision is to integrate people with disabilities into "mainstream" society.[9] This goal is established for several reasons:

(1) prejudice is based largely on unfamiliarity and fear, which is reduced through interaction with people with disabilities;

(2) incorrect stereotypes and assumptions are discredited through interaction with people with disabilities;

(3) "special" programs for people with disabilities often are the first things to be eliminated when budget or other cuts are proposed; and

(4) because the "special" accessible program is used infrequently, equipment tends to be lost or not maintained, and staff forget how to provide the accessible service.

Separate or "special" programs for people with disabilities are permitted when they are necessary to provide individuals with an equal opportunity to benefit from the program.[10] The program must be designed to meet the needs of individuals with disabilities. Thus, in the above

---

[6]   U.S. Dep't of Justice, Title III Technical Assistance Manual § 3.3000 [hereinafter TAM III], http://www.usdoj.gov/crt/ada/taman3.html (Nov. 1993).

[7]   Id. § 3.3000, illus. 2.

[8]   42 U.S.C. § 12182(b)(1)(A)(iii) (2000); 28 C.F.R. § 36.202(c) (2003).

[9]   TAM III, supra note 6, § 3.4000.

[10]   Id. § 3.4100.

example, a special exercise class designed with exercises for people who use wheelchairs may be permitted. However, a person who uses a wheelchair may not be segregated into a separate class that was substantively the same as the regular class.

If a separate program is provided, people with disabilities must be allowed to participate in the regular program if they choose to do so.[11] Therefore, even if a gym offers a special exercise class designed for people with disabilities, an individual who uses a wheelchair may decide to participate in the regular class. In fact, the gym may have to reasonably modify the regular class to meet the needs of the individual.[12]

§ 13.5 Eligibility Criteria

Title III prohibits:

the imposition or application of eligibility criteria that screen out or tend to screen out an individual with a disability or any class of individuals with disabilities from fully and equally enjoying any goods, services, facilities, privileges, advantages, or accommodations, unless such criteria can be shown to be necessary for the provision of the goods, services, facilities, privileges, advantages, or accommodations being offered.[13]

Examples of eligibility criteria include those that affect only people with disabilities, such as a rule requiring blind people to bring traveling companions along on trips. They also include those criteria that affect everyone, but that screen out people with disabilities because of their disabilities, such as a strength requirement for participation as a volunteer at a summer camp. To the extent that such standards screen out, or tend to screen out, people with disabilities, they are permissible only when necessary for the provision of the goods or services at issue.

Legitimate safety requirements are permissible if they are necessary for operation of the program or service. However, such safety requirements may not be based on assumptions, speculation, stereotypes, or generalizations.[14]

Thus, a white water rafting company may not exclude people who use wheelchairs on the assumption that they cannot swim. Although a requirement for swimming ability may be legitimate, wheelchair users who can swim must be permitted to participate. Furthermore, for this to

---

[11] Id. § 3.4200.

[12] Id. § 3.4300 (availability of the special program will be a factor in determining modifications required to the regular program, if the special program is appropriate to the needs of the individual with a disability).

[13] 42 U.S.C. § 12182(b)(2)(A)(i) (2000); 28 C.F.R. § 36.301(a) (2003).

[14] 28 C.F.R. § 36.301(b) (2003).

be considered a legitimate requirement, the swimming ability of all participants, with and without disabilities, must be assessed.

Generally, courts have been deferential to higher education providers' determinations of essential eligibility criteria and educational requirements. For example, in *Southeastern Community College v. Davis*,[15] a Rehabilitation Act case discussed supra, the Supreme Court deferred to the school's determination that its mission was to "train persons who could serve the nursing profession in all customary ways."[16] The school was not required to alter that mission to admit a student who's hearing impairment would prevent her from participating as a nurse in clinical settings.[17]

§ 13.6 Reasonable Modifications

In addition to prohibiting direct discrimination, Title III provides that discrimination includes:

> a failure to make reasonable modifications in policies, practices, or procedures, when such modifications are necessary to afford such goods, services, facilities, privileges, advantages, or accommodations to individuals with disabilities, unless the entity can demonstrate that making such modifications would fundamentally alter the nature of such goods, services, facilities, privileges, advantages, or accommodations.[18]

A reasonable modification, like a reasonable accommodation in the employment context, can be any change to the way a good or service is provided.[19] A common form of reasonable modification involves the case of

---

[15] Southeastern Comty. Coll. v. Davis, 442 U.S. 397 (1979).

[16] Id. at 413.

[17] Id. This case is instructive in its analysis of the potential reasonable modification of exempting the applicant from clinical courses and its conclusion that such a change would be a fundamental alteration because it would defeat the school's mission.

[18] 42 U.S.C. § 12182(b)(2)(a) (ii) (2000); 28 C.F.R. § 36.302(a) (2003).

[19] See, e.g., PGA Tour, Inc. v. Martin, 532 U.S. 661, 690 (2001) (allowing use of a golf cart in a tournament that prohibits carts); Dudley v. Hannaford Bros. Co., 190 F.Supp.2d 69, 77 (D. Me. 2002) (reconsidering a cashier's determination that a customer is drunk when the customer has a disability that can mimic drunkenness); Matthews v. Nat'l Collegiate Athletic Ass'n, 179 F.Supp.2d 1209, 1227 (E.D. Wa. 2001) (a reduction of academic eligibility requirements for participation in sports for a student with learning disability that prevents him from meeting the requirements); Burriola v. Greater Toledo YMCA, 133 F.Supp.2d 1034, 1040 (N.D. Ohio 2001) (allowing parents to provide a one-on-one aide in order to enable a child with autism to participate in a daycare program);

a grocery store's no-pets policy. A store with such a policy must modify it to allow a person with a service animal to access the store's goods and services.

However, the reasonable modification requirement may be broader. Examples required by the courts include:

Accepting a state-issued ID card in lieu of a driver's license for paying by check for a person whose disability prevents driving.[20]

Reconsidering a cashier's determination that a customer is drunk when the customer has a disability that can mimic drunkenness.[21]

An alteration of academic eligibility requirements for participation in sports for a student whose learning disability prevents him from meeting certain requirements.[22]

Allowing use of a golf cart in a tournament that usually prohibits carts.[23]

Allowing parents to provide a one-on-one aide in order to enable a child with autism to participate in a daycare program.[24] And,

Allowing a woman to use the men's dressing room when her personal assistant is male.[25]

A.   *Note On Service Animals*

A service animal is any animal that has been individually trained to provide a service related to a person's disability.[26] While guide dogs for blind people are a well-known type of service animal, a service animal need not be a dog and need not work for a blind person. Dogs and other animals provide services to individuals with hearing impairments, seizure

---

Anderson v. Ross Stores, 2000 WL 1585269, at *2 (N.D. Cal. 2000) (allowing a woman to use the men's dressing room when her personal assistant is male); U.S. v. Venture Stores, Inc., 1994 WL 86068, at *1 (N.D. Ill. 1994) (accepting a state-issued ID card in lieu of a driver's license for paying by check for a person who's disability prevents driving).

[20] Venture Stores, Inc., 1994 WL 86068, at *1.

[21] Dudley, 190 F.Supp.2d at 77.

[22] Matthews, 179 F.Supp.2d at 1227.

[23] Martin, 532 U.S. at 690.

[24] Burriola, 133 F.Supp.2d at 1040.

[25] Anderson, 2000 WL 1585269, at *2.

[26] TAM III, supra note 6, § 4.2300.

disorders, mobility impairments, manual dexterity impairments, and other disabilities.

The key to determining whether an animal is a service animal is its training. Service animals need not be certified[27] and need not wear special identification or equipment. A service animal need not have attended specific or accredited training; its disabled owner may instead train it at home. A typical pet, or "companion animal," is not considered a service animal when it is not trained to provide a relevant support service. Therefore, a "therapeutic pet" or "companion animal" will generally not be considered a service animal under Title III.[28]

The care and supervision of a service animal is the responsibility of the individual with a disability.[29] Similarly, the behavior of the service animal is the responsibility of its owner. A service animal may be excluded if it misbehaves and interferes with the operation of the business, but not solely on a fear that it might misbehave.

A business may impose limitations on the admittance of service animals if those limitations respond to legitimate safety or health risks. Thus, a hospital may ban a service animal from an emergency treatment room.[30] Similarly, a brewery tour may prohibit a service animal from areas where it would pose a clear risk of food contamination.[31]

B. *Specialties*

A place of public accommodation need not change its specialty to accommodate a person with a disability. Thus, if a person with a disability is seeking a service outside the business' area of specialization, the business appropriately may refer the individual elsewhere, if it would do the same for a customer without a disability.[32] The Title III regulation provides the example of medical specialties:

> A health care provider may refer an individual with a disability to another provider, if that individual is seeking, or requires, treatment or services outside of the referring provider's area of specialization, and if the referring

---

[27] Id.

[28] Department of Justice letter from John R. Dunne, Assistant Attorney General, Civil Rights Division to Honorable Martin Frost, July 31, 1992, http://www.usdoj.gov:80/crt/foia/tal146.txt. State law may provide more protection.

[29] 28 C.F.R. pt. 36, app. B, § 36.302(c)(2).

[30] Pool v. Riverside Health Serv., Inc., 1995 WL 519129, at *4, 12 A.D.D. 143, 7 NDLR 118 (D. Kan. 1995).

[31] Johnson v. Grambrinus Co./Spoetzl Brewery, 116 F.3d 1052, 1064 (5th Cir. 1997).

[32] 28 C.F.R. § 36.302(b)(1) (2003).

provider would make a similar referral for an individual without a disability who seeks or requires the same treatment or services. A physician who specializes in treating only a particular condition cannot refuse to treat an individual with a disability for that condition, but is not required to treat the individual for a different condition.[33]

A public accommodation also is not required to alter its inventory to carry accessible goods.[34] Thus, a video store need not carry captioned videos, and a grocery store need not sell diabetic foods.[35] However, a public accommodation may be required to special order accessible goods if it regularly makes such orders on request for other goods not in its inventory and if it can obtain the accessible goods from its usual suppliers without significant hardship.[36]

C.   *Burdens Of Proof*

The legal burden of proof analysis in Title III reasonable modification cases is similar to the burden of proof analysis in Title I reasonable accommodation cases.[37]

> The plaintiff has the burden of proving that a modification was requested and that the requested modification was reasonable. The plaintiff meets this burden by introducing evidence that the requested modification is reasonable in the general sense, that is, reasonable in the run of cases. While the defendant may introduce evidence indicating that the plaintiff's requested modification is not reasonable in the run of cases, the plaintiff bears the ultimate burden of proof on the issue....

> If the plaintiff meets this burden, the defendant must make the requested modification unless the defendant pleads and meets its burden of proving that the requested modification would fundamentally alter the nature of the public accommodation. The type of evidence that satisfies this burden focuses on the specifics of the plaintiff's or defendant's circumstances and not on the general nature of the accommodation. Under the statutory framework, such evidence is relevant only to a fundamental alteration defense and not relevant to the plaintiff's burden to show

---

[33] Id. § 36.302(b)(2); see also infra Chapter 27 (discussion of Ticket to Work Program and Employment Network provider services).

[34] Id. § 36.307(a).

[35] Id. § 36.307(c).

[36] Id. § 36.307(b).

[37] Johnson v. Gambrinus Co./Spoetzl Brewery, 116 F.3d 1052, 1059 (5th Cir. 1997).

that the requested modification is reasonable in the run of cases.[38]

This burden shifting analysis may change, however, where a defendant offers an alternative modification to the one requested by the plaintiff.[39] Because the statute prohibits a "failure to make reasonable modifications," a defendant may prevail by offering a reasonable modification that differs from the one proposed by the plaintiff, as long as the defendant's proposal is effective to remedy the accessibility issue.

D.   *Reasonable*

Unlike Title I's accommodation requirement, Title III'se reasonable modification requirement does not provide for an "undue hardship" defense. However, courts generally have incorporated undue hardship elements into the reasonableness determination in plaintiff's prima facie case.

According to the Second Circuit, "the determination of whether a particular modification is reasonable ... considers, among other factors, the effectiveness of the modification in light of the nature of the disability in question and the cost to the organization that would implement it."[40]

A Title III entity does not have to provide participants with disabilities with personal devices, such as prescription eyeglasses or hearing aids, or services of a personal nature, such as eating, toileting, and dressing assistance.[41]

E.   *Fundamental Alteration*

The defense to the reasonable modification requirement is that the requested modification would fundamentally alter the nature of the goods or services being provided.[42]

The Supreme Court addressed the application of the fundamental alteration defense in *PGA Tour, Inc. v. Martin.*[43] Casey Martin, a

---

[38] Id. at 1059-60; see also Dahlberg v. Avis Rent A Car Sys., Inc., 92 F.Supp.2d 1091, 1105-06 (D. Colo. 2000).

[39] Johnson, 116 F.3d at 1059 n.5.

[40] Staron v. McDonald's Corp., 51 F.3d 353, 356 (2d Cir. 1995); see also Larsen v. Carnival Corp., Inc. 242 F.Supp.2d 1333, 1342-43 (S.D. Fla. 2003); Roberts v. KinderCare Learning Ctrs., Inc., 86 F.3d 844, 846 (8th Cir. 1996) (treating reasonable modification case like an effective communication case and borrowing the undue burden defense to find that it would constitute an undue burden to require a day care center to provide part time one-on-one personal assistance for a client child).

[41] 28 C.F.R. § 36.306 (2003).

[42] 42 U.S.C. § 12182(b)(2)(a)(ii) (2000).

[43] PGA Tour, Inc. v. Martin, 532 U.S. 661 (2001).

professional golfer, has Klippel-Trenauney-Weber Syndrome, which is a degenerative circulatory disorder that obstructs the flow of blood from his right leg to his heart. The disease causes severe pain when Martin walks, and walking creates a significant risk of hemorrhaging, blood clots, and bone fractures.[44]

Martin entered the PGA's "Q school," a three-stage qualifying tournament for the PGA Tour. During the first two stages of qualification, players were permitted to use golf carts on the courses. As a result, Martin was able to play without any change to the rules of the games and he succeeded in both stages.[45] In the final stage of the competition, golf carts were not permitted. Instead, golfers were required to walk all 18 holes of the course. Martin's disability prevented this and he requested a waiver of the walking rule.[46] When the request was denied, Martin filed suit, claiming his request for a waiver was a reasonable modification required by Title III.

The PGA Tour conceded that a golf cart was necessary for Martin to participate in the tour, but argued that the requested modification would fundamentally alter the nature of the event.[47] The Court addressed three different ways in which a modification could constitute a fundamental alteration:

(1) by altering "such an essential aspect of the game of golf that it would be unacceptable even if it affected all competitors equally";[48]

(2) by giving the individual with a disability an unfair advantage over the other players;[49] or

(3) by imposing administrative burdens on the operator of a place of public accommodation.[50]

The Court found that none of those possible alterations arose to the level of a permissible defense in this case.[51]

---

[44] Id. at 668.

[45] Id. at 669.

[46] Id.

[47] Martin, 532 U.S. at 682.

[48] Id.

[49] Id. at 682-83.

[50] Id. at 690-91.

[51] For a discussion of the extension of this principle to other professional sports, and for factors that courts should consider in determining whether requested rule changes in sports will "fundamentally alter" the sport, see Michael Waterstone, "Let's Be Reasonable Here: Why the ADA Will Not Ruin Professional Sports," 2000 BYU L. Rev. 1489, 1506-1510 (2000).

1. Alteration of essential element

The *Martin* Court stated that one example of the first type of fundamental alteration would be changing the diameter of the hole from three inches to six inches.[52] The Court found that "from early on, the essence of the game [of golf] has been shot-making – using clubs to cause a ball to progress from the teeing ground to a hole some distance away with as few strokes as possible."[53]

A review of the Rules of Golf revealed no prohibition on use of a cart. Based on that fact, and that the PGA's rules allowed carts in other tournaments, the Court rejected the argument that allowing carts would fundamentally change an essential aspect of the game.[54]

2. Unfair advantage

The Court addressed whether allowing Mr. Martin to use a cart would give him an unfair advantage. The PGA argued that changing an outcome-affecting rule would violate the principal of comparing different competitors under identical substantive rules.[55] The PGA argued that the walking rule "inject[ed] an element of fatigue into the skill of shot-making."[56]

The Court rejected that argument for two reasons. First, it disagreed that it was essential that all players compete under exactly the same conditions and it disagreed that the PGA's rules guaranteed that an individual's talent would be the sole determinant of the outcome.[57] Instead, changes in weather may alter conditions for players and luck may be as outcome-affecting as fatigue. Given the impossibility of ensuring identical conditions for all players and ensuring that skill would be the only outcome-determinative factor, the Court believed requiring a waiver of the walking rule was not unreasonable.[58]

More importantly, the Court challenged the factual basis of the PGA's argument that the walking rule injected an element of fatigue into the competition. Medical testimony indicated that fatigue from the exercise of walking a golf course slowly and intermittently, with rest periods and refreshments, was not a serious factor in tournament play.[59]

---

[52]   Martin, 532 U.S. at 682.

[53]   Id. at 683.

[54]   Id. at 683-86.

[55]   Id. at 686.

[56]   Id.

[57]   Martin, 532 U.S. at 686-87.

[58]   Id.

[59]   Id. at 687.

The Court noted that most golfers would choose to walk, even if they had the option of using a cart.[60]

Finally, the Court found that, even if fatigue were an outcome-affecting factor, the PGA would have to assess whether Martin's use of a cart would, in fact, make him less fatigued than a non-disabled golfer without a cart.[61] Before the PGA could refuse a modification, it would have to conduct an individualized assessment to determine whether, given the extent of Martin's disability, it would be unfair to the other players to allow him to use a cart.

The evidence was uncontested that Martin would be as fatigued by the amount of walking he would have to do, even with a cart, as a non-disabled golfer would be without a cart.[62] "The purpose of the walking rule was therefore not compromised in the slightest by allowing Martin to use a cart. A modification that provides an exception to a peripheral tournament rule without impairing its purpose cannot be said to 'fundamentally alter' the tournament."[63]

3. Administrative burden

Finally, the *Martin* Court noted that "[t]he ADA admittedly imposes some administrative burdens on the operators of places of public accommodation that could be avoided by strictly adhering to general rules and policies that are entirely fair with respect to the able-bodied but that may indiscriminately preclude access by qualified persons with disabilities."[64]

However, the Court believed the PGA's description of the burden was overstated, given that they had received only two requests for carts in three years.[65] Significantly, the Court stated that, "surely, in a case of this kind, Congress intended that an entity like the PGA not only give individualized attention to the handful of requests that it might receive from talented but disabled athletes for a modification or waiver of a rule to allow them access to the competition, but also carefully weigh the purpose, as well as the letter, of the rule before determining that no accommodation would be tolerable."[66]

The Court made clear that the mere existence of a rule does not mean that any modification will be a fundamental alteration. Instead, the rule itself must be essential and the purpose and the letter of the rule

---

[60] Id. at 687-88.

[61] Id. at 688-89.

[62] Id. at 690.

[63] Martin, 532 U.S. at 690.

[64] Id.

[65] Id. at 691 n.53.

[66] Id. at 690-91.

must be significantly undermined for a modification to be considered a fundamental alteration.

F. *Direct Threat*

Title III provides an affirmative defense in situations where providing a modification would pose a direct threat to the health or safety of others.[67] As opposed to Title I, the direct threat defense under Title III currently applies only where the individual poses a direct threat to the health or safety of others (i.e., not to self as was found in the *Echazabal* case described in Part 3).[68] The statute defines "direct threat" as "a significant risk to the health or safety of others that cannot be eliminated by a modification of policies, practices, or procedures or by the provision of auxiliary aids or services.[69]

The ADA regulations provide that the direct threat determination should be based on individualized assessment and must be based on reasonable judgment that relies on current medical knowledge or on the best available objective evidence. It must consider the nature, duration, and severity of the risk, the probability that the potential injury actually will occur, and whether modifications will mitigate the risk.[70]

In *Bragdon v. Abbott*,[71] a dentist refused to fill a cavity for a patient with HIV in his office, and the patient sued under Title III. Ms. Abbott, the patient, prevailed at the trial and Court of Appeals. The Supreme Court stated that the relevant risk assessment must be based on medical or other objective evidence, and not simply on that covered entity's good-faith belief that a significant risk existed.

The Supreme Court vacated and remanded to the Court of Appeals to consider the direct threat issue in light of that standard. On remand, the First Circuit held that the dentist's performance of a cavity-filling procedure did not pose a "direct threat" to him.[72]

In *Montalvo v. Radcliffe*,[73] a post-*Bragdon* application, the Fourth Circuit applied the direct threat analysis to a child with AIDS who wanted to participate in a karate class. The court first assessed the nature of the threat. It found that the child's disease did constitute a direct threat

---

[67] 42 U.S.C. § 12113 (2000). This defense applies to all Title III requirements, not just reasonable modifications, but it arises frequently in the reasonable modification context.

[68] 28 C.F.R. § 36.208 (2003). Although courts may extend the defense to cover threats to self, as they have under Title I.

[69] 42 U.S.C. § 12113 (2000).

[70] 28 C.F.R. pt. 36, app. B, § 36.208.

[71] Bragdon v. Abbott, 524 U.S. 624 (1998).

[72] Bragdon v. Abbott, 163 F.3d 87, 90 (1st Cir. 1998).

[73] Montalvo v. Radcliffe, 167 F.3d 873, 874 (4th Cir. 1999).

because the type of karate taught in the class "emphasized sparring, attack drills, and continuous body interaction with the result that the participants frequently sustained bloody injuries, such as nose bleeds, cuts inside the mouth, and external abrasions."[74] The evidence indicated that the blood from such injuries was extremely likely to come in contact with other students' skin.

The court went on to assess whether a reasonable modification was available to reduce the threat. It concluded that the parents' proposed modification to the class (e.g., softening the teaching style of the program) constituted a fundamental alteration that would not be required and that the modification of requiring participants to use gloves and eye protection would be ineffective.[75]

§ 13.7 Effective Communication

A. *General*

Title III, like Title II, requires covered entities to communicate effectively with individuals with hearing, vision, and speech disabilities.[76]

Discrimination under Title III includes:

a failure to take such steps as may be necessary to ensure that no individual with a disability is excluded, denied services, segregated or otherwise treated differently than other individuals because of the absence of auxiliary aids and services, unless the entity can demonstrate that taking such steps would fundamentally alter the nature of the good, service, facility, privilege, advantage, or accommodation being offered or would result in an undue burden.[77]

According to the regulations implementing Title III, a public accommodation must provide auxiliary aids and services in order to meet the standard of "effective communication."[78] Auxiliary aids and services include:

(1) Qualified interpreters, note-takers, computer-aided transcription services, written materials, telephone handset amplifiers, assistive listening devices, assistive listening systems, telephones compatible with hearing aids, closed

---

[74] Id. at 877.

[75] Id. at 879.

[76] TAM III, supra note 6, § 4.3100. Non-communication-related disabilities are not entitled to auxiliary aids or services, but are entitled to reasonable modifications of policies, practices and procedures.

[77] 42 U.S.C. § 12188 (2000); 28 C.F.R. pt. 36, app. B, § 36.303(a) (2003).

[78] Id. § 36.303(c).

caption decoders, open and closed captioning, telecommunications devices for deaf persons (TDDs), videotext displays, or other effective methods of making aurally delivered materials available to individuals with hearing impairments;

(2) Qualified readers, taped texts, audio recordings, Brailled materials, large print materials, or other effective methods of making visually delivered materials available to individuals with visual impairments;

(3) Acquisition or modification of equipment or devices; and

(4) Other similar services and actions.[79]

Most auxiliary aids disputes have arisen in the context of deaf patients' requests for sign language interpreters for medical visits or procedures. Under Title III, the major obstacle to pursuit of such cases by deaf individuals is the requirement of standing.

Title III does not authorize compensatory damages. Therefore, plaintiffs are limited to seeking injunctive relief. To have standing before a court to seek injunctive relief, an individual with a disability must "demonstrate a 'real and immediate threat' of repeated future harm."[80]

In *Aikins v. St. Helena Hospital*,[81] the plaintiff's mere allegation that she was a deaf woman who lived part of the year close to a particular hospital that failed to provide a sign language interpreter previously was not sufficient to demonstrate that she was likely to use the hospital again or that the hospital was likely to discriminate against her again.[82] On the other hand, a plaintiff who desires to visit the same health care provider in the future likely would have standing to bring a claim of discrimination under Title III.[83]

Plaintiffs, nevertheless, may independently pursue such access claims against medical providers under Section 504 of the Rehabilitation Act,[84] which provides similar requirements and allows monetary damages. If a medical care provider accepts federal financial assistance, such as Medicaid funds, it will be a covered entity under the Rehabilitation Act,

---

[79] Id. § 36.303(b).

[80] Aikins v. St. Helena Hosp., 843 F.Supp. 1329, 1333 (N.D. Cal. 1994).

[81] Id.

[82] Id. at 1333-34 (the court granted leave to amend the complaint to allege sufficient facts to demonstrate standing, and Aikins was found to have standing on remand; see Aikins v. St. Helena Hosp., 10 A.D.D. 544, 6 NDLR Plaintiff 129 (N.D. Cal. 1994)).

[83] Majocha v. Turner, 166 F.Supp.2d 316, 324-25 (W.D. Penn. 2001).

[84] 29 U.S.C. § 794 (2000); see Proctor v. Prince George's Hosp. Ctr., 32 F.Supp.2d 820, 826 (D. Md. 1998).

even if the deaf individual complaining of discrimination is not a Medicaid patient.[85]

A question that frequently arises in auxiliary aid cases is what type of aid is required, and who gets to make that decision. The place of public accommodation has the final decision-making authority, as long as its choice ensures that the communication is effective.[86]

The type of aid that will be effective depends on the language ability of the individual with a disability and on the length and complexity of the communication at issue. While a simple conversation, such as a question about a book in a bookstore, may be conducted using handwritten notes, a complex conversation, such as a medical visit concerning the possibility of surgery, may require a sign language interpreter.[87]

An individual who was born deaf and has spoken only American Sign Language (ASL) his entire life is likely to have difficulty understanding complex notes in English, which differs from ASL.[88] On the other hand, a deaf person probably cannot insist on a licensed or certified interpreter, but simply on one that is capable of interpreting the information at hand.[89]

Note that effective communication is not presumed because the medical care has been provided or because the outcome would not have improved had an interpreter been provided.[90] It is not sufficient that a deaf patient eventually received an interpreter and retroactively understood what procedures had been performed. "The real inquiry is whether equal opportunity was provided *during* the course of Plaintiff's treatment."[91] Every incident will be considered individually.[92] The communication provided to the plaintiff should be compared with the communication provided to hearing individuals in similar circumstances.[93]

Courts have reached different conclusions about whether Title III requires movie theatres to provide films that are accessible to people with hearing impairments through captioning. The Department of Justice

---

[85] Davis v. Flexman, 109 F.Supp.2d 776, 786 (S.D. Ohio 1999).

[86] TAM III, supra note 6, § 4.3200.

[87] Majocha, 166 F.Supp.2d at 321-23.

[88] Id. at 317.

[89] Alvarez v. N.Y. City Health & Hosps. Corp., 220 WL 1585637, at *3 (S.D.N.Y. 2002).

[90] Aikins v. St. Helena Hosp., 843 F.Supp. 1329, 1338 (N.D. Cal. 1994).

[91] Proctor v. Prince George's Hosp. Ctr., 32 F.Supp.2d 820, 827 (D. Md. 1998).

[92] Id.

[93] Falls v. Prince George's Hosp. Ctr., 1999 WL 33485550, at *8 (D. Md. 1999).

commentary on the issue provides that movie theaters are not required to present open-captioned films.[94]

Relying on that language, an Oregon district court found that movie theatres are not required to provide either open captioning or rear-window captioning of films, which hearing patrons cannot view.[95] The court treated movie films like a store's inventory and relied on the Department of Justice's statement that public accommodations are not required to change their inventory to provide accessible goods, such as Braille books or captioned videotapes.[96]

However, a Washington, D.C. district court reached the opposite conclusion.[97] That court relied on the statutory language, which does not address captioning, and minimized the importance of the Department of Justice comment about open captioning, finding that

> [w]hen the ADA was signed into law in 1990, only open-captioning of theatrical films was in use at that time and there were not yet any systems available for providing closed captions in theatres.... Therefore, the isolated statement that open captioning of films in movie theatres was not required in 1990 cannot be interpreted to mean that Defendants cannot now be expected and required to provide closed captioning of films in their movie theatres.[98]

That court went on to conclude that movie theatres are not like bookstores, in that they are providing the service of showing movies, rather than goods. Therefore, requiring them to show captioned movies would not constitute requiring them to change their inventory.[99]

In addition, the screening of closed-captioned films would not fundamentally alter the service, because deaf moviegoers can see the captions without changing how other patrons see the films.[100] Nor did the fact that most films are not yet compatible with rear-window captioning

---

94 28 C.F.R. pt. 36, app. B, § 36.303 (2003).

95 Cornilles v. Regal Cinemas, Inc., 2002 WL 31440885, at *7 (D. Or. 2002).

96 Id. at *6.

97 Ball v. AMC Entm't, Inc., 246 F.Supp.2d 17, 19 (D.D.C. 2003).

98 Id. at 22.

99 Id. at 24-25.

100 Id. at 20. Rear-window captioning projects captions below the movie screen. The captions are seen by deaf viewers on individual clear plastic screens. The captions do not appear on the movie screen for other viewers. The individual clear plastic screens do not interfere with other patrons' view.

(RWC) serve as a defense, as "requiring installation of RWC does not require exhibition of all RWC-compatible films."[101]

The court deferred the question of whether installing rear-window captioning technology would constitute an undue burden. It noted that the plaintiffs only were seeking installation in twenty screens, not all the defendants' screens, and that tax benefits would be available.[102]

B.   *Note On Interpreters*

The ADA refers to "qualified interpreters." An interpreter need not meet any particular licensing or certification standard to be qualified.[103]   A qualified interpreter "is able to interpret effectively, accurately and impartially both receptively and expressively, using any necessary specialized vocabulary."[104]

To ensure impartiality, public accommodations generally should avoid using relatives or other interested parties as interpreters. "In certain circumstances, notwithstanding that the family member or friend is able to interpret or is a certified interpreter, the family member or friend may not be qualified to render the necessary interpretation because of factors such as emotional or personal involvement or considerations of confidentiality that may adversely affect the ability to interpret 'effectively, accurately, and impartially.'"[105]

The presence of a professional interpreter does not interfere with the confidentiality of a communication between a health care provider or attorney and a patient or client.[106]

C.   *TTYs And Closed Caption Decoders*

TTYs or TDDs (telecommunication devices for the deaf) generally are not required in businesses, either to receive calls from individuals with disabilities or to allow customers with disabilities to place outgoing calls.[107]   However, if allowing clients or customers to make outgoing calls

---

[101] Id. at 25.

[102] Id. at 26.

[103] Alvarez v. N.Y. City Health & Hosps. Corp., 220 WL 1585637, at *4 (S.D.N.Y. 2002).

[104] 28 C.F.R. pt. 36, app. B, § 36.104 (2003).

[105] Id. § 36.104.

[106] Certified interpreters must comply with a code of ethics that ensures that assignment-related information is kept confidential. See Registry of Interpreters for the Deaf, RID's Code of Ethics, http://www.rid.org/coe.html (last visited Sept. 23, 2003).

[107] TAM III, supra note 6, § 4.3410.

is more than incidental to the business, then a TTY will be required.[108] For that reason, hotels and hospitals must make TTYs available.[109]

Most businesses also are not required to ensure that their televisions offer closed captioning. However, hotels and hospitals that provide televisions must provide closed captioning.[110]

D. *Undue Burden*

The effective communication requirement is balanced by a defense that the requested auxiliary aid would impose an undue burden on the covered entity.

Undue burden means significant difficulty or expense. In determining whether an action would result in an undue burden, several factors to be considered include:

(1) The nature and cost of the action needed under this part;

(2) The overall financial resources of the site or sites involved in the action;

(3) The number of persons employed at the site; the effect on expenses and resources; legitimate safety requirements that are necessary for safe operation, including crime prevention measures; or the impact otherwise of the action upon the operation of the site;

(4) The geographic separateness, and the administrative or fiscal relationship of the site or sites in question to any parent corporation or entity;

(5) If applicable, the overall financial resources of any parent corporation or entity; the overall size of the parent corporation or entity with respect to the number of its employees; the number, type, and location of its facilities; and

(6) If applicable, the type of operation or operations of any parent corporation or entity, including the composition, structure, and functions or the workforce of the parent corporation or entity.[111]

---

[108] Id. at § 4.3420.

[109] Id.

[110] 28 C.F.R. pt. 36, app. B, § 36.303(e) (2003).

[111] Id. § 36.104.

The undue burden standard in Title III is defined in the same manner as in Title I. However, it is significantly greater than the "readily achievable" standard for architectural barriers under Title III.[112]

Courts also have recognized administrative burdens, such as the difficulty of scheduling an interpreter for a medical emergency or for a physician who does not keep to a regular schedule.[113]

§ 13.8 Architectural Barriers

Unlike previous civil rights laws, the drafters of the ADA had to contend with the fact that overcoming traditional discriminatory attitudes alone would not be sufficient to bring people with disabilities into mainstream society. Rather, societal prejudice had been "built" into our environment. The assumption of building design always had been that people with disabilities would stay home. This surely would be a self-fulfilling assumption unless changes were to be made in existing buildings and those designed in the future.

Because of the expense of retrofitting existing buildings to make them accessible, the drafters of the ADA reached a compromise that provides for a gradual approach to facility accessibility.

A. *Existing Facilities*

1. Barrier removal

In facilities existing before January 26, 1993, Title III requires architectural barriers to access to be removed "where such removal is readily achievable, i.e., easily accomplishable and able to be carried out without much difficulty or expense."[114] The regulation provides examples of barrier removal steps.[115]

---

[112] TAM III, supra note 6, § 4.3600.

[113] Proctor v. St. George's Hosp. Ctr., 32 F.Supp.2d 820, 828 n.5 (D. Md. 1998).

[114] 28 C.F.R. § 36.304(a) (2003).

[115] Examples of steps to remove barriers include, but are not limited to, the following actions:
    (1) Installing ramps;
    (2) Making curb cuts in sidewalks and entrances;
    (3) Repositioning shelves;
    (4) Rearranging tables, chairs, vending machines, display racks, and other furniture;
    (5) Repositioning telephones;
    (6) Adding raised markings on elevator control buttons;
    (7) Installing flashing alarm lights;
    (8) Widening doors;
    (9) Installing offset hinges to widen doorways;

In deciding which barriers to remove, a public accommodation must prioritize according to the significance of the barrier to the disabled person's attempt to access the goods and services of the public accommodation. Thus, the first priority includes access to, and into, the facility from sidewalks, parking areas, and public transportation. Elements to be addressed under this first priority include parking, entrances, and curbs, among others.

The second priority level includes access to the goods and services of the public accommodation. Elements to be addressed include aisles, shelves, signage, doorways, and so on.

The third priority includes restroom access and involves elements such as toilet stalls, dispensers, grab bars, and mirrors. The final priority includes any other barriers to access to the goods and services of the public accommodation.[116]

The standard for changes to meet the barrier removal obligation is the same as for altered elements. The changes generally must comply with the requirements of altered accessible elements set out in the ADA Accessibility Guidelines ("ADAAG").[117] The entity may take measures that do not comply fully, provided that they nevertheless increase access; but this is permissible only when total compliance with the appropriate ADA Standard prevents the measure from being readily achievable.[118]

---

(10) Eliminating a turnstile or providing an alternative accessible path;
(11) Installing accessible door hardware;
(12) Installing grab bars in toilet stalls;
(13) Rearranging toilet partitions to increase maneuvering space;
(14) Insulating lavatory pipes under sinks to prevent burns;
(15) Installing a raised toilet seat;
(16) Installing a full-length bathroom mirror;
(17) Repositioning the paper towel dispenser in a bathroom;
(18) Creating designated accessible parking spaces;
(19) Installing an accessible paper cup dispenser at an existing inaccessible water fountain;
(20) Removing high pile, low density carpeting; or
(21) Installing vehicle hand controls.

Id. § 36.304(b).

[116] Id. § 36.304(c).

[117] Id. § 36.304(d)(1). Those standards are set out in 28 C.F.R. §§ 36.402, 36.404, and 36.405, and in 28 C.F.R. pt. 36, app. A.

[118] 28 C.F.R. pt. 36, app. B, § 36.304(d)(2).

Examples of barrier removal include widening aisles to less than the generally-required 36 inches, or installing a ramp steeper than 1:12 (i.e., one foot of rise for every 12 feet of run). "No measure shall be taken, however, that poses a significant risk to the health or safety of individuals with disabilities or others."[119] In this regard, the Title III regulations address portable ramps. The regulations emphasize that portable ramps should be used only when installation of a permanent ramp would not be readily achievable.[120]

"Readily achievable" is a lesser standard than the "undue burden" defense to the provision of auxiliary aids or the "undue hardship" defense of Title I.[121] The determination of achievability depends on a case-by-case analysis of the same factors involved in the "undue burden" defense.[122] Courts have applied these factors to reach varied conclusions.

---

[119] Id.

[120] Id. § 36.304(e).

[121] TAM III, supra note 6, § 4.4200.

[122] Colo. Cross-Disability Coalition v. Hermanson Family Ltd., 264 F.3d 999, 1009 (10th Cir. 2001). "[D]etermining whether an action is readily achievable" may include consideration of the following:

> (1) The nature and cost of the action needed under this part;
>
> (2) The overall financial resources of the site or sites involved in the action; the number of persons employed at the site; the effect on expenses and resources; legitimate safety requirements that are necessary for safe operation, including crime prevention measures; or the impact otherwise of the action upon the operation of the site;
>
> (3) The geographic separateness, and the administrative or fiscal relationship of the site or sites in question to any parent corporation or entity;
>
> (4) If applicable, the overall financial resources of any parent corporation or entity; the overall size of the parent corporation or entity with respect to the number of its employees; the number, type, and location of its facilities; and
>
> (5) If applicable, the type of operation or operations of any parent corporation or entity, including the composition, structure, and functions or the workforce of the parent corporation or entity.

28 C.F.R. § 36.104.

In *Alford v. City of Cannon Beach*,[123] the court found that the cost of the needed alterations must be compared with the gross profits of the business, rather than the net profits.[124] It was determined to be a question of fact whether an $8,344 expense was readily achievable when compared with $308,000 in gross profits.[125]

In *Parr v. L & L Drive-Inn Restaurant*,[126] the court found that installation of an accessible parking space was not readily achievable because, although it was inexpensive, it would require the business not only to lose a parking space in a small parking lot that it shared with other businesses, but also to violate a local parking ordinance.[127]

The Title III regulations provide specific requirements for barrier removal in existing assembly areas.[128] Such a facility must, to the extent it is readily achievable:

> (i) Provide a reasonable number of wheelchair seating spaces and seats with removable aisle-side armrests; and (ii) Locate the wheelchair seating spaces so that they – (A) are dispersed throughout the seating area; (B) Provide lines of sight and choice of admission prices comparable to those for members of the general public; (C) Adjoin an accessible route that also serves as a means of egress in case of emergency; and (D) Permit individuals who use to sit with family members or other companions.[129]

2. Limits

There are additional limits on the readily achievable standard. Even if it is readily achievable to do so, entities are not required to remove barriers, if doing so would exceed the requirements of the ADAAG for alterations or new construction.[130]

A covered entity does not have to rearrange removable features if doing so would result in "a significant loss of selling or serving space."[131]

---

[123] Alford v. City of Cannon Beach, 2002 WL 31439173, at *1 (D. Or. 2002).

[124] Id. at *9.

[125] Id.

[126] Parr v. L & L Drive-Inn Restaurant, 96 F.Supp.2d 1065 (D. Haw. 2000).

[127] Id. at 1088-89.

[128] 28 C.F.R. § 36.104.

[129] Id. § 36.308.

[130] Id. § 36.304(g).

[131] Id. § 36.304(f).

Courts have interpreted this as a limitation on the removal of permanent features as well as "removable" ones.[132] This is a case-by-case analysis.

In *Guzman v. Denny's, Inc.*, the court did not find that the reduction of a restaurant's storage space by one quarter to one third constituted a significant loss as a matter of law.[133] In *Alford*, the court found that, as a matter of law, a loss of over 41 percent of a shop's inventory and retail space made a proposed alteration not readily achievable.[134]

A contested issue in barrier removal has been whether department stores have to provide 36-inch aisles between "self-service" racks or shelves of clothing and other goods. *Lieber v. Macy's West, Inc.*[135] is instructive on this question.

In considering whether providing more space would reduce stock and result in a corresponding reduction in sales, one court found that any study of the issue would have to consider the extent to which shoppers would be more likely to shop at the store were the environment more spacious and comfortable.[136] It also would have to consider the extent to which the store could keep non-displayed merchandise in stock rooms.[137]

In *Lieber*, Macy's did not demonstrate a significant loss of selling space and, therefore, was not excused from installing accessible aisles between racks.[138] However, the court found that 36-inch aisles were required by the ADAAG only for fixed racks, and that the California building code only applied its aisle width requirement to "circulation aisles," which differ from the aisles where customers browse among the merchandise.

Therefore, the *Lieber* court found that the space between removable racks had to be wider, but not necessarily 36 inches wide.[139] The court rejected Macy's argument that its vendors would object to increased space between racks, finding that "the ADA clearly prohibits Macy's from maintaining access barriers that discriminate against patrons with disabilities through contractual arrangements with vendors."[140]

---

[132] Guzman v. Denny's, Inc., 40 F.Supp.2d 930, 936 n.4 (S.D. Ohio 1999).

[133] Id.

[134] Alford v. City of Cannon Beach, 2002 WL 31439173, at *10 (D. Or. 2002).

[135] Lieber v. Macy's West, Inc., 80 F.Supp.2d 1065, 1067 (N.D. Cal. 1999).

[136] Id. at 1071.

[137] Id. at 1072.

[138] Id. at 1078.

[139] Id. at 1078-79.

[140] Id. at 1081.

Landlord-tenant responsibility further comes into play when determining what barrier removal is readily achievable. Generally, "a contract assigning responsibility for [ADA] compliance to one party [to a lease] does not insulate the other party from liability."[141]

However, in *Alford*, the court found that, although both landlord and tenant are responsible for barrier removal, the tenants could not make alterations to those common areas for access purposes without the landlord's permission unless the lease had authorized them to do so. "While it is generally accepted that a landlord cannot unreasonably withhold permission under such a term,..." the fact that the lessor was not a party to the action made it impossible for the court to decide that the needed alterations were readily achievable and the court granted summary judgment in favor of the tenants.[142]

3. Burden of proof

Title III does not specify which party must bear the burden of proving that barrier removal is or is not readily achievable. It does indicate, however, that the burden is not exclusively on the plaintiff: "where an entity can demonstrate that the removal of a barrier under clause (iv) is not readily achievable," it must use alternative readily achievable methods to make its goods and services accessible.[143]

The one court that has analyzed the issue fully determined that readily achievable is an affirmative defense to be proved by the defendant.[144] The plaintiff must produce evidence "tending to show that the suggested method of barrier removal is readily achievable under the particular circumstances. If Plaintiff does so, Defendant then bears the ultimate burden of persuasion that barrier removal is not readily achievable."[145]

---

[141] Botosan v. Fitzhugh, 13 F.Supp.2d 1047, 1054 (S.D. Cal. 1998).

[142] Alford v. City of Cannon Beach, 2002 WL 31439173, at *15-16 (D. Or. 2002).

[143] 42 U.S.C. § 12182(b)(2)(A)(v) (2000).

[144] Colo. Cross-Disability Coalition v. Hermanson Family Ltd., 264 F.3d 999, 1002-06 (10th Cir. 2001); see also Parr v. L & L Drive-Inn Restaurant, 96 F.Supp.2d 1065, 1085 (D. Haw. 2000).

[145] Colo. Cross-Disability Coalition, 264 F.2d at 1002-03; cf. Lieber v. Macy's West, Inc., 80 F.Supp.2d 1065, 1077 (N.D. Cal. 1999) ("Plaintiffs bear the burden of establishing the existence of access barriers .... Plaintiffs also bear the burden of putting forward reasonable modifications. The burden then shifts to Macy's to show that the requested modifications would fundamentally alter the nature of its public accommodation.").

The plaintiff must do more than speculate, however. In *Colorado Cross-Disability Coalition v. Hermanson Family Ltd.*,[146] the court affirmed a judgment as a matter of law against the plaintiff, finding that:

> Plaintiff introduced evidence regarding only speculative concepts of ramp installation, rather than evidence that a specific design was readily achievable. For instance, Plaintiff failed to present any evidence to establish the likelihood that the City of Denver would approve a proposed modification to the historical building. Plaintiff also failed to provide any precise cost estimates regarding the proposed modification. Perhaps most importantly, Plaintiff's expert testimony failed to demonstrate that under the particular circumstances installing a ramp would be readily achievable. Instead, expert Winter provided speculative conceptual ideas, rather than a specific design which would be easily accomplishable and able to be carried out without much difficulty or expense.[147]

4. Standing

A plaintiff challenging a public accommodation's failure to remove architectural barriers must have standing to bring the claim.[148] Because Title III allows only injunctive relief, she must demonstrate "a real and immediate threat of future harm."[149] In the case of access to a place of public accommodation, the threat may be demonstrated by a history of past patronage, the plaintiff's expressed intent to return, and factors indicating likelihood of return.[150]

A plaintiff may have standing to challenge barriers she did not actually encounter, if she learned of them through expert testimony and if she was on notice that the defendant did not intend to remove the barriers.[151] However, a plaintiff may not have standing to challenge barriers that are not related to her particular disability.[152]

Therefore, a person with a mobility impairment may not have standing to sue a restaurant to install Braille signage to provide

---

[146] Colo. Cross-Disability Coalition, 264 F.3d at 999.

[147] Id. at 1009.

[148] Parr v. L & L Drive-Inn Restaurant, 96 F.Supp.2d 1065, 1079 (D. Haw. 2000); see also ch. 25, § 25.3.A.2.

[149] Parr , 96 F.Supp.2d at 1079.

[150] Id. (other factors include patronage of other restaurants in the same chain and whether the restaurant's location is within a reasonable distance from the plaintiff's home).

[151] Id. at 1081-82.

[152] Id. at 1082-83.

accessibility for people with vision impairments.[153] In addition, a plaintiff may not have standing to challenge barriers at facilities she has not visited, unless she has actual notice of the existence of those barriers.[154]

> ### 5.   Alternatives to barrier removal

If removal of a barrier or barriers is not readily achievable, a place of public accommodation still must attempt to make its goods and services accessible to people with disabilities through alternative methods that are readily achievable.[155]   Examples of alternatives to barrier removal include:

> (1) Providing curb service or home delivery;
>
> (2) Retrieving merchandise from inaccessible shelves or racks;
>
> (3) Relocating activities to accessible locations."[156]

The entity that undertakes these steps as alternatives to barrier removal may not charge the person with a disability for them, as that would constitute a prohibited surcharge for the costs of compliance.[157] Thus, if a grocery store is inaccessible and offers home delivery for a fee, it must offer the home delivery without charge to people whose disabilities prevent them from accessing the store. However, if the store is physically accessible, it may charge for home delivery to people with and without disabilities.

B.   *Alterations*

The ADA takes a gradual approach to facility accessibility. Alterations must be accessible, plus certain alterations trigger an obligation to make pathways and amenities accessible. In this way, as building updates and renovations are made, inaccessible spaces will be made accessible as part of the normal course of renovations, and paths to and from the main spaces, as well as amenities, will be made accessible.

Title III entities making alterations or renovations to existing facilities for other than barrier removal purposes must "make such alterations ... in such a manner that, to the maximum extent feasible, the altered portions of the facility are readily accessible to and usable by individuals with disabilities, including individuals who use wheelchairs...."[158] This requirement applies to alterations that began

---

[153] Id.

[154] Clark v. McDonald's Corp., 213 F.R.D. 198, 229-230 (D. N.J. 2003) (citing Moreno v. G&M Oil Co., 88 F.Supp.2d 1116, 1117 (C.D. Cal. 2000)).

[155] 28 C.F.R. § 36.305 (2003).

[156] Id. § 36.305(b).

[157] Id. § 36.301(c); see supra Section 19.1.

[158] 42 U.S.C. § 12147(a) (2000).

after January 26, 1992.[159] Both public accommodations and commercial facilities[160] must comply with the requirements for alterations.[161] Alterations that make a facility less accessible than before the alteration are not permitted.[162] Alterations generally must comply with the ADAAG standards for new construction.[163]

1. What constitutes an alteration

An alteration covered by Title III is "a change to a place of public accommodation or a commercial facility that affects or could affect the usability of the building or facility or any part thereof."[164] Additions are treated as alterations.[165]

Examples of alterations include:

> remodeling, renovation, rehabilitation, reconstruction, historic restoration, changes or rearrangement in structural parts or elements, and changes or rearrangement in the plan configuration of walls and full-height partitions. Normal maintenance, reroofing, painting or wallpapering, asbestos removal, or changes to mechanical and electrical systems are not alterations unless they affect the usability of the building or facility.[166]

A "facility" is defined broadly as "all or any portion of buildings, structures, sites, complexes, equipment, rolling stock or other conveyances, roads, walks, passageways, parking lots, or other real or personal property, including the site where the building, property, structure, or equipment is located."[167] Therefore, changes to equipment, such as rail ticket vending machines[168] and emergency alarm boxes[169] have been treated as alterations required to be made accessible. In addition, resurfacing of streets is considered an alteration requiring

---

[159] 28 C.F.R. § 36.402(a)(1) (2003).

[160] See generally TAM III, supra note 6.

[161] 28 C.F.R. § 36.402(a).

[162] Id. pt. 36, app. A, ADAAG, § 4.1.6(a).

[163] Id. § 36.406(a).

[164] Id. § 36.402(b).

[165] Id. pt. 36, app. A, § 4.1.5.

[166] Id. § 36.402(b).

[167] Id. § 36.104.

[168] Molloy v. Metro. Transp. Auth., 94 F.3d 808, 812 (2d Cir. 1996). Although this is a Title II case, the same principles apply to alterations under Title II and Title III.

[169] Civic Ass'n of the Deaf of N.Y. City v. Giuliani, 970 F.Supp. 352, 359 (S.D.N.Y. 1997).

accessibility (e.g., the provision of sidewalk curb-cuts),[170] making clear that the accessibility requirement is not limited to major alterations.

An alteration is covered if it affects or could affect the usability of the altered facility. Thus, according to one court, the installation of pizza ovens at concession stands did not trigger an obligation to make the service counters accessible, because the ovens did not affect the patrons' ability to use the concession stands.[171]

Title III addresses the need to make accessibility alterations to historic buildings. Historic buildings are not exempted from compliance. Instead, alterations to historic buildings[172] generally are required to comply with the ADAAG, including the path of travel requirement, unless providing access will threaten or destroy the historic significance of the building.[173] When compliance with the ADAAG alterations standards threaten the historic significance of the building, ADAAG provides alternative requirements.[174]

2.   Path of travel

In addition to making any altered element accessible, a public accommodation or commercial facility has additional obligations whenever it undertakes an alteration that affects or could affect the usability of an area that contains a primary function.[175] A primary function is "a major activity for which the facility is intended."[176]

---

[170] Kinney v. Yerusalim, 9 F.3d 1067, 1072-73 (3d Cir. 1993).

[171] Ass'n for Disabled Ams. v. City of Orlando, 153 F.Supp.2d 1310, 1320 (M.D. Fla. 2001).

[172] Historic buildings are those listed or eligible for listing on the National Register of Historic Places under the National Historic Preservation Act or designated as historic under state or local law. 28 C.F.R. § 36.405(a) (2003).

[173] Id. § 36.405(b); id. pt. 36, app. A, § 4.1.7 (providing procedures for determination of threat to historic significance).

[174] Id. pt. 36, app. A, § 4.1.6.

[175] Id. § 36.403(a).

[176] Id. § 36.403(b). Examples include:

> the customer service lobby of a bank, the dining area of a cafeteria, the meeting rooms in a conference center, as well as offices and other work areas in which the activities of the [entity] are carried out. Mechanical rooms, boiler rooms, supply storage rooms, employee lounges or locker rooms, janitorial closets, entrances, corridors, and restrooms are not areas containing a primary function.

Id. Alterations to primary function areas include:

When a primary function area is altered, the covered entity must dedicate an additional 20 percent[177] of the overall cost of the alteration to ensure that the path of travel to the altered area and the restrooms, telephones, and drinking fountains that serve the altered area, are accessible.[178] A path of travel is a pedestrian passage by means of which the altered area may be approached, entered, and exited, and which connects the altered area with an exterior approach, an entrance to the facility, and other parts of the facility."[179] In deciding which accessibility features to improve in a path of travel, entities must prioritize as follows:

(1) accessible entrance;

(2) accessible route to the altered area;

(3) accessible restroom(s);

(4) accessible telephones;

(5) accessible drinking fountains;

(6) parking, storage, alarms, and other elements.[180]

An entity cannot avoid the "path of travel" obligation by doing a series of small alterations where 20 percent of the cost would not be enough to accomplish access to the path of travel. The costs of any alterations where no path of travel changes were made in a three-year period may be combined when determining the 20 percent figure.[181]

It is sometimes difficult to determine what alteration costs should be included in determining the 20 percent figure, particularly when remodeling and barrier removal are being undertaken together. Essentially, the expenses of barrier removal (e.g., changes being made solely to make the facility accessible) are not considered in determining the cost of the alteration for purposes of the 20 percent disproportionality figure.

(i) Remodeling merchandise display areas or employee work areas in a department store; (ii) Replacing an inaccessible floor surface in the customer service or employee work areas of a bank; (iii) Redesigning the assembly line area of a factory; or (iv) Installing a computer center in an accounting firm.

28 C.F.R. § 36.403(c)(1).

[177] Id. § 36.403(f).

[178] Id. § 36.403(a).

[179] Id. § 36.403(e).

[180] Id. § 36.403(g)(2).

[181] Id. § 36.403(h)(2)(i).

3. Technically infeasible

Alterations and path of travel alterations only have to be made accessible "to the maximum extent feasible."[182] Put another way, accessibility modifications that are technically infeasible do not have to be made. This is a fairly narrow exception "where the nature of the existing facility makes it virtually impossible to comply fully with applicable accessibility standards."[183] The fact that adding accessibility features increases the cost of the alteration does not make it technically infeasible.[184] Rather, technical infeasibility is demonstrated when accessibility would require removal of an essential structural element.[185]

If it is technically infeasible to comply with the ADAAG new construction standards, ADAAG provides fall-back standards for alterations.[186] Only when compliance with those reduced standards is technically infeasible is the entity allowed to use a lesser standard.

4. Statute of limitations

Title III does not address the question of when the statute of limitations runs on a challenge to an inaccessible alteration. Plaintiffs argue typically that failure to comply with the ADA requirements is an ongoing violation and the statute of limitations should begin to run whenever an individual with a disability actually encounters the inaccessible feature. This argument has merit, as a plaintiff probably does not have standing to challenge a barrier until he has actually encountered it.[187] However, one court has held that the statute of limitations should run from the date of the alteration's completion.[188]

C. *New Construction*

Buildings constructed for first occupancy after January 26, 1993 must be fully accessible in accordance with the ADAAG standards.[189] Unlike Title II entities, places of public accommodation and commercial facilities do not have the option of using the Uniform Federal Accessibility Standards ("UFAS").

The exception to full compliance with ADAAG occurs when the entity can demonstrate that full compliance is structurally

---

[182] 28 C.F.R. § 36.402(c).

[183] Id.

[184] TAM III, supra note 6, § 6.1000.

[185] Id. Illus. 1.

[186] 28 C.F.R. pt. 36, app. A, § 4.1.6.

[187] Moreno v. G&M Oil Co., 88 F.Supp.2d 1116, 1117 (C.D. Cal. 2000).

[188] Speciner v. Nationsbank, N.A., 215 F.Supp.2d 622, 634-35 (D. Md. 2002) (applying a three-year statute of limitations).

[189] 28 C.F.R. § 36.401 (2003).

impracticable.[190] Structural impracticability will be found "only in those rare circumstances when the unique characteristics of terrain prevent the incorporation of accessibility features."[191]

1. ADAAG

The ADA Accessibility Guidelines provide general, scoping (i.e., how many of each element must be accessible), and technical (i.e., what an accessible element looks like) standards. The general provisions, including definitions, are in ADAAG sections 1-3.

The scoping provisions are at sections 4.1.1-4.1.7, while the technical standards are in sections 4.2-4.35. Additional scoping and technical standards for particular types of facilities are provided in:

Section 5 for restaurants and cafeterias,

Section 6 for medical facilities,

Section 7 for business and mercantile facilities,

Section 8 for libraries,

Section 9 for transient lodging,

Section 10 for transportation facilities,

Section 11 (proposed) for judicial, legislative and regulatory facilities, and

Section 12 (proposed) for detention facilities.

Proposed standards for residential facilities and for public rights of way have been reserved.[192] An appendix provides supplemental information about accessibility standards.

The ADAAG allows departures from particular technical and scoping requirements if other designs and technologies will provide substantially equivalent or greater access to and usability of the facility.[193] Means of equivalent facilitation are acceptable only if they are at least as accessible as the ADAAG standards.

---

[190] Id. § 36.401(c).

[191] Id.

[192] 28 C.F.R. pt. 36, app. A, §§ 11-12. The proposed sections have been adopted by the U.S. Architectural and Transportation Barriers Compliance Board ("Access Board"), but have not been approved by the U.S. Department of Justice and, therefore, are not in effect at the time of printing. A proposed section for recreational facilities is under consideration by the Access Board. See Summaries of Accessibility Guidelines for Recreation Facilities, at http://www.access-board.gov/recreation/guides/index.htm (June 2003).

[193] 28 C.F.R. pt. 36, app. A, § 2.2.

2. Lines of sight

Some of the most hotly contested issues in new construction have involved entertainment venues, such as stadiums and movie theatres, and have focused on the issue of whether people who use wheelchairs are entitled to seats where they can see over people who stand in the rows in front of them. This is referred to as a "line of sight over standing spectators." The issue arises from ADAAG section 4.33.3, which provides:

> Wheelchair areas shall be an integral part of any fixed seating plan and shall be provided so as to provide people with physical disabilities a choice of admission prices and lines of sight comparable to those for members of the general public. ... When the seating capacity exceeds 300, wheelchair spaces shall be provided in more than one location.[194]

Plaintiffs and the U.S. Department of Justice have interpreted this section to require that in large (>300 seat) venues, wheelchair seating be dispersed in all price ranges available to nondisabled people.[195] They also interpret the section to require that, in venues where spectators can be expected to stand (e.g., sports arenas, rock concerts), wheelchair seating must provide lines of sight over the shoulders and between the heads of standing spectators in front of the wheelchair seating.[196]

Because the DOJ's interpretation has been released informally, rather than through formal rulemaking, courts have had to grapple with the issue.[197] The courts have split on the resolution. In *Paralyzed Veterans of America v. D.C. Arena L.P.*, the District of Columbia Circuit upheld the district court's decision that an arena that provided lines of sight over standees for 70 percent of its wheelchair seats was in accordance with the ADA regulations.[198]

In so holding, the court noted that the Department of Justice's recent compliance manual took the position that ADAAG § 4.33.3 required wheelchair seats to have sight lines over standing patrons. Moreover, although this was not the same as an actual "regulation" so requiring, the sight line issue was not so substantive a rule that, as a matter of

---

[194] Id. § 4.33.3.

[195] See Disability Rights Section, U.S. Dep't of Justice, Accessible Stadiums 1, http://www.usdoj.gov/crt/ada/stadium.pdf (last visited Oct. 9, 2003).

[196] Id. at 2.

[197] For a discussion of the history of the Department's interpretation, see Paralyzed Veterans of Am. v. Ellerbe Becket Architects & Eng'rs, P.C., 950 F.Supp. 393, 395-396 (D.D.C. 1996).

[198] Paralyzed Veterans of Am. v. D.C. Arena L.P., 117 F.3d 579, 589 (D.C. Cir. 1997).

administrative law, the DOJ could not clarify it without formally revising and inviting comments.[199]

The Third Circuit, in *Caruso v. Blockbuster-Sony Music Entertainment Centre*, disagreed.[200] In that case, the court held that the ADA regulations did not address the issue of sightlines over standing spectators. The court concluded that ADAAG § 4.33.3 meant only that

> if a facility's seating plan provides members of the general public with different lines of sight to the field or stage (e.g., lines of sight at a baseball game from behind the plate, on either side of the diamond, and from the outfield bleachers), it must also provide wheelchair users with a comparable opportunity to view the field or stage from a variety of angles.[201]

Another contested issue regarding ADAAG § 4.33.3 is that of whether wheelchair seating in stadium-style movie theatres must offer choices of position within the theatre and whether it has to be integrated into the stadium seating section of the theatre.

In *Lara v. Cinemark USA, Inc.*,[202] the Fifth Circuit held that § 4.33.3 did not require viewing angles that are as comfortable as those offered to the general public. Therefore, Cinemark theatres were permitted to put wheelchair seats at the bottom of the theatres, forcing patrons in wheelchairs to crane their necks uncomfortably to see the screen.

In *United States v. Hoyts Cinemas Corp.*, the Massachusetts district court disagreed, finding that "to comply with the 'integral part' and the comparable 'lines of sight' requirements of § 4.33.3," there must be wheelchair-accessible seats somewhere in the stadium section, and that the rear of the stadium section is acceptable so long as it is a truly integrated part of the stadium section.[203] The Central District of California also has found that stadium-style movie seating must include wheelchair accessible seats in the stadium section of the theatre.[204]

---

[199] Id. at 586.

[200] Caruso v. Blockbuster-Sony Music Entm't Ctr., 193 F.3d 730, 736-737 (3d Cir. 1999).

[201] Id. at 732.

[202] Lara v. Cinemark USA, Inc., 207 F.3d 783, 788-789 (5th Cir. 2000); see also Meineker v. Hoyts Cinemas Corp., 216 F.Supp.2d 14, 18 (N.D.N.Y. 2002).

[203] United States v. Hoyts Cinemas Corp., 256 F.Supp.2d 73, 90-91 (D. Mass. 2003).

[204] United States v. Am. Multi-Cinema, Inc., 232 F.Supp.2d 1092, 1112 (C.D. Cal. 2002).

In *Oregon Paralyzed Veterans of America v. Regal Cinemas, Inc.,*[205] the Ninth Circuit reversed a district court's award of summary judgment to the defendant theater owners. The district court had followed the reasoning of the Fifth Circuit in *Lara.* The Ninth Circuit found the Department of Justice's interpretation of ADAAG § 4.33.3 that comparable viewing angles for wheelchair users were required, reasonable and, therefore, entitled to deference.[206]

3. Responsible parties

Title III's new construction requirements make it a violation to "design and construct facilities" in contravention of the ADAAG.[207] This raises the possibility that architects and designers, as well as owners, lessors, and operators could be liable for new construction violations.

However, the Ninth Circuit has found that architects are not covered under Title III. In *Lonberg v. Sanborn Theaters, Inc.,* the Ninth Circuit rejected the approach adopted by some district courts of asserting liability against a party with a "significant degree of control" over the design and construction process.[208] The court limited liability to owners, lessees, lessors, and operators of places of public accommodation.

One court has found that a franchisor may be liable for new construction violations when it has the authority to control the process and has, in fact, exercised that control.[209] However, in the absence of an exercise of control or actual knowledge of the noncompliance, the franchisor would not be considered liable.[210]

D. *Relation To Building Codes*

The ADA requirements for new construction and alterations do not necessarily coincide with state or local building codes. They are based, in part, on the American National Standards Institute (ANSI) document A117.1-1980.[211]

Many building codes contain accessibility requirements. Due to principles of federal supremacy, the ADA standards override state or local building codes that directly conflict with their own and result in a lower

---

[205] Or. Paralyzed Veterans of Am. v. Regal Cinemas, Inc., 339 F.3d 1126, 1127 (9th Cir. 2003).

[206] Id. at 1132.

[207] 42 U.S.C. § 12146 (2000).

[208] Lonberg v. Sanborn Theaters, Inc., 259 F.3d 1029, 1036 (9th Cir. 2001).

[209] United States v. Days Inns of Am., Inc., 151 F.3d 822, 827 (8th Cir. 1998).

[210] Id.

[211] 28 C.F.R. pt. 36, app. A, § 1 (2003).

standard of accessibility. This separation of the two codes results in some confusion among owners, builders, and building officials.

Building officials have authority to enforce only their state or local building code. They are not authorized to enforce the ADA standards. Therefore, approval by a state or local building official will not insulate a building owner from liability under the ADA. A variance from a local accessibility requirement will not have any bearing on an ADA challenge.

Nor is there any federal cadre of ADA building inspectors. Building code enforcement is done pre-construction, by reviewing plans and physically inspecting progress. ADA enforcement, on the other hand, occurs after construction has been completed and a problem is encountered.

Recognizing that accessibility corrections are easier and less costly to accomplish before construction is completed, the ADA includes provisions for state and local building codes to be "certified" as equivalent to the ADA. If a building code is certified, builders can be more assured that a local building inspection is taking ADA requirements into account.

Although a local variance will have no bearing on ADA liability, a certified building code will give rise to a rebuttable presumption that a builder that has complied with her local code also has complied with the ADA.[212] A state or local government must submit its code for review by the Department of Justice to be certified.[213]

---

[212] Id. § 36.602.
[213] Id. § 36.603-608.

Part 6

Enforcement And Remedies
Analysis

Chapter 14 INTRODUCTION TO ENFORCEMENT PROCEDURES

§ 14.1 Overview

Not wanting to depart markedly from existing legislation, the drafters of the ADA tried to adopt other available statutes for the ADA's enforcement and remediation provisions. The business community, which was used to dealing with the EEOC and coordinate state agencies, concurred. In response, Congress constructed the ADA's enforcement mechanisms from the preexisting structures in the Rehabilitation Act of 1973 and the Civil Rights Act of 1964, as amended.[1] However, the ADA covers a broader swath of territory than those acts, from employment to telecommunications to public accommodations. It thus utilizes a range of procedures to achieve a range of remedies. Since it tries to be the model of a modern civil rights act, it also provides for alternative dispute resolution (ADR), both arbitration and mediation. The result is a complex – some would say confusing – set of remedies and procedures.

§ 14.2 Relation To Civil Rights Act

Each of the titles of the ADA contains a range of remedies keyed to the entities upon which the Act imposes obligations. In turn, each of those remedies refers to analogous provisions in the Civil Rights Act of 1964.

- The remedies for employment discrimination in violation of Title I are those provided in Title VII of the Civil Rights Act.[2] Cases interpreting other statutes that rest on Title VII, such as the Age Discrimination in Employment Act (ADEA)[3] thus inform the interpretation of the ADA. The remedies include the traditional equitable remedies for

---

[1] Chai R. Feldblum, Medical Examinations and Inquiries Under the Americans with Disabilities Act: A View from the Inside, 64 Temp. L. Rev. 521, 521-23 (1991).

[2] 42 U.S.C. § 12117 (2000) (citing sections 705, 706, 707, 709 and 710 of the Civil Rights Act of 1964, 42 U.S.C. §§ 2000e-4, 2000e-5, 2000e-6, 2000e-8 and 2000e-9).

[3] 29 U.S.C. § 621, et seq. (2000).

employment discrimination: back pay, front pay, reinstatement and attorneys' fees. They also include both compensatory damages, such as for emotional distress, and, upon a showing of "malice or ... reckless indifference to the federally protected rights of an aggrieved individual," punitive damages.

- The remedies for violations of the public services provisions of Title II are the same as those in Section 505 of the Rehabilitation Act, which in turn are drawn from Title VI of the Civil Rights Act of 1964.[4] These include compensatory damages, injunctive relief, and attorneys' fees.

- The remedies for violations of the public accommodation provisions of Title III are those set forth in Title II of the Civil Rights Act of 1964.[5] Those actions are limited to injunctive relief and attorneys' fees.

The ADA likewise parcels out enforcement responsibilities broadly. Both the EEOC and the Attorney General are granted power to investigate and enforce various titles of the ADA. The EEOC may investigate Titles I[6] and II[7] and may enforce Title I;[8] the Attorney General has the ability to investigate and seek relief for alleged denials of rights under Titles II[9] and III.[10] Individuals, of course, may bring their own actions.[11] Other agencies have roles to play, including the Department of Transportation for parts of Titles II and III. However, most frequently, "enforcement" is the work of private individuals seeking private relief. Even here, the backward linkages to the Civil Rights Act engender inconsistency. Under Title I, but not Titles II and III, individuals must exhaust administrative remedies.

---

[4] 42 U.S.C. § 12133 (adopting remedies of section 505 of the Rehabilitation Act of 1973, 29 U.S.C. § 794a, which in turn adopts section 717 of the Civil Rights Act, 42 U.S.C. § 2000e-16).

[5] Id. § 12188 (adopting remedies of section 204(2) of the Civil Rights Act of 1964, 42 U.S.C. § 2000a-3(a)).

[6] Id. § 12117 (referring to 42 U.S.C. § 2000e-5 (EEOC)).

[7] Id. § 12133 (referring to 29 U.S.C. § 794a, which refers to 42 U.S.C. § 2000e-16 (EEOC)).

[8] Id. § 12117 (referring to 42 U.S.C. § 2000e-6 (EEOC)).

[9] Id. § 12133 (referring to 29 U.S.C. § 794a, which refers to 42 U.S.C. § 2000e-5 (EEOC and Dep't of Justice)).

[10] 42 U.S.C. § 12188(b) (referring to 42 U.S.C. § 2000a-3(a) (Dep't of Justice)).

[11] Id. § 12117 (Title I: implicitly referring to 42 U.S.C. § 2000e-5(f)(2)), § 12133 (Title II: referring to 29 U.S.C. § 794a, which refers to 42 U.S.C. § 2000e-16(d), which refers to 42 U.S.C. § 2000e-5), § 12188(a) (Title III: referring to 42 U.S.C. § 2000a-3(a)).

The Title I procedures contain further complications. States that have equivalent civil rights protections have the first opportunity to respond to employment discrimination complaints. Only after a "deferral period" may the EEOC act and only after the EEOC determines not to pursue a case itself, or not to refer it to the Department of Justice, can an individual sue.

In an effort to streamline the process, the EEOC has developed a process for nonbinding mediation.[12] We will address this in section 20.1 below. In parallel, many employers insert mandatory arbitration provisions in their employment contracts, to preclude resort to judicial fora. The applicability, scope and enforceability of those provisions, which affect important statutory rights, has been the subject of litigation and are discussed in section 20.2 below.

---

[12] Equal Emp. Opportunity Comm'n, Mediation, at http://www.eeoc.gov/mediate/index.html (last modified Mar. 24, 2003).

Chapter 15 TITLE I – EMPLOYMENT DISCRIMINATION

§ 15.1 Introduction

An individual who perceives that he has been the subject of disability-based employment discrimination by a private entity may seek relief under Title I of the ADA. The Act makes available – and forces the individual to use – the procedures and remedies of Title VII of the Civil Rights Act of 1964, as amended. In particular, section 107(a) of the ADA provides as follows:

> The powers, remedies, and procedures set forth in sections 705, 706, 707, 709, and 710 of the Civil Rights Act of 1964 (42 U.S.C. 2000e-4, 2000e-5, 2000e-6, 2000e-8, and 2000e-9) shall be the powers, remedies, and procedures this title provides to the Commission, to the Attorney General, or to any person alleging discrimination on the basis of disability in violation of any provision of this Act, or regulations promulgated under section 106, concerning employment.[1]

That Act lays out a detailed set of procedures, as well as available remedies.

§ 15.2 Procedure

A. *Administrative Exhaustion*

A person who believes he has been discriminated against on the basis of disability must first file an administrative claim.[2] The claim must articulate the basis of the discrimination claim.[3] The law sets out a detailed time sequence for filing claims.

---

[1] 42 U.S.C. § 12117(a) (2000); see Jacob A. Stein, Stein on Personal Injury Damages, § 5:9 (3d ed. 1997).

[2] 42 U.S.C. § 2000e-5(e); id. § 12117(a); Love v. Pullman Co., 404 U.S. 522, 523 (1972) ("A person claiming to be aggrieved by a violation of Title VII of the Civil Rights Act of 1964 may not maintain a suit for redress in federal district court until he has first unsuccessfully pursued certain avenues of potential administrative relief."); Maynard v. Pneumatic Products Corp., 256 F.3d 1259, 1262 (11th Cir. 2001); Zillyette v. Capital One Fin. Corp., 179 F.3d 1337, 1339 (11th Cir. 1999) ("It is settled law that, under the ADA, plaintiffs must comply with the same procedural requirements to sue as exist under Title VII of the Civil Rights Act of 1964.").

[3] Failure to state a basis may preclude a later suit on that ground. See Ferrero v. Henderson, 244 F.Supp.2d 821, 830 (S.D. Ohio 2002) (Rehabilitation Act plaintiff's administrative claim asserted on physical impairment, while plaintiff's suit alleged discrimination of the basis of a

The first time limit is the time to file a claim with the appropriate administrative agency. The basic rule is that a claim must be filed with the EEOC within 180 days of the "alleged unlawful employment practice."[4] However, where the complainant has instituted proceedings "with a State or local agency with authority to grant or seek relief from such practice or to institute criminal proceedings with respect thereto" the complainant has 300 days after the alleged unlawful employment practice or 30 days after receiving notice that the state or local agency has terminated proceedings, whichever is earlier, to file with the EEOC.[5]

The Civil Rights Act requires exhaustion of state, as well as federal, administrative remedies and does not permit a claimant to file a claim with the EEOC until 60 days after the claimant has instituted proceedings under state or local law, unless those proceedings were terminated before 60 days had passed.[6] Thus, federal jurisdiction is deferred during the 60-day period of state jurisdiction.

States with appropriate state or local agencies that are able to grant relief from discriminatory employment practices are known as "deferral states" and the agencies are known as "deferral agencies." The reason for the deferral is "to give state agencies a prior opportunity to consider discrimination complaints" and "to ensure expedition in the filing and handling of those complaints."[7] When a complainant first files charges in the EEOC, rather than the appropriate state agency, the EEOC is required to notify the state or local agencies in deferral states and provide them a reasonable time, at least 60 days, to act under state or local law.[8]

A deferral state may enter into a "work sharing agreement" (WSA) with the EEOC.[9] Under a WSA,[10] a deferral state may waive its period of

---

mental impairment; court ordered plaintiff to show cause why her claim should not be dismissed for failure to exhaust).

[4]   42 U.S.C. § 2000e-5(e).

[5]   Id. § 2000e-5(e)(1).

[6]   Id. § 2000e-5(c).

[7]   Love, 404 U.S. at 526; see also 42 U.S.C. § 2000e-4(g)(1) (the EEOC "shall have power to cooperate with and, with their consent, utilize regional, State, local, and other agencies, both public and private, and individuals."); id. § 2000e-8(b) (the EEOC "may enter into written agreements with such State or local agencies and such agreements may include provisions under which the Commission shall ... relieve any person or class of persons in such State or locality from requirements imposed under this Section").

[8]   42 U.S.C. § 2000e-5(d).

[9]   Puryear v. County of Roanoke, 214 F.3d 514, 517-18 (4th Cir. 2000). WSAs are authorized by 42 U.S.C. § 2000e-8(b). The states with WSAs are: Alaska, Arizona, California, Colorado, Connecticut, Delaware,

exclusive jurisdiction, thus terminating its proceedings within the meaning of § 2000e-5(c).[11] If the WSA so provides, filing with the EEOC constitutes the filing with the State or local agency. In that event, the state or local administrative proceeding is deemed exhausted by filing with the EEOC.[12]

B.   *Administrative Limitations Periods*

The pre-suit administrative process contains rigid timelines. The complainant must file a charge with the EEOC "within 180 days after the

---

Florida, Georgia, Hawaii, Idaho, Illinois, Indiana, Iowa, Kansas, Kentucky, Louisiana, Maine, Maryland, Massachusetts, Michigan, Minnesota, Missouri, Montana, Nebraska, Nevada, New Hampshire, New Jersey, New Mexico, New York, North Carolina, North Dakota, Ohio, Oklahoma, Oregon, Pennsylvania, Puerto Rico, Rhode Island, South Carolina, South Dakota, Tennessee, Texas, U.S. Virgin Islands, Utah, Vermont, Virginia, Washington, Washington, DC, West Virginia, Wisconsin, Wyoming.

[10] Most circuits have approved worksharing agreements. Puryear, 214 F.3d at 521 (citing Trevino-Barton v. Pittsburgh Nat'l Bank, 919 F.2d 874, 879-80 (3d Cir. 1990) (concluding that where WSA entitled plaintiff to file her charge only with the EEOC, giving her the benefit of her EEOC filing favors upholding her right to proceed before the court and does not sacrifice any significant rights of the employer or the state agency)); Griffin v. City of Dallas, 26 F.3d 610, 612-13 (5th Cir. 1994) (state proceedings instituted for purposes of §§ 706(c) and (e) when EEOC received the complaint, based on WSA designating the EEOC as the state agency's agent for purposes of receiving charges, with state's waiver of its exclusive jurisdiction period); Worthington v. Union Pac. R.R., 948 F.2d 477, 482 (8th Cir. 1991) (EEOC constructively received the charge on the day it was filed with a state agency, by WSA's provisions that agencies acted as each others' agents, with self-executing waiver of exclusive state proceedings); Sofferin v. Am. Airlines, Inc., 923 F.2d 552, 556-59 (7th Cir. 1991) (holding that under a WSA with a self-executing waiver, a filing with the EEOC simultaneously initiates and terminates state proceedings); Marlowe v. Bottarelli, 938 F.2d 807, 814 (7th Cir. 1991) (same); Green v. L.A. County Superintendent of Sch., 883 F.2d 1472, 1479-80 (9th Cir. 1989) (a filing with state agency deemed to be a filing with EEOC, by the self-executing clause of the WSA); Griffin v. Air Prods. & Chems., Inc., 883 F.2d 940, 943 (11th Cir. 1989) (WSA between EEOC and state agency created an instantaneous "constructive termination" of state agency's proceedings).

[11] EEOC v. Commercial Office Prods. Co., 486 U.S. 107, 114-15 (1988).

[12] It is the plaintiff's burden to prove the existence and terms of the WSA. See Maynard v. Pneumatic Products Corp., 256 F.3d 1259, 1264 (11th Cir. 2001) (plaintiff's failure to introduce WSA into the record permitted defendant to prevail on summary judgment).

alleged unlawful employment practice."[13] As noted, the Civil Rights Act expands the time limit for filing in the event the person previously has instituted a proceeding with a state or local agency to 300 days from the alleged unlawful employment practice or 30 days from the date the complainant received notice that the state or local agency had terminated its proceeding under state or local law, whichever is first.[14] The complainant must serve the claim on the opposing party within ten days of filing.[15]

The existence of two jurisdictional possibilities can and does create confusion. For example, a person may not be aware of local agencies' role and may file a charge initially with the EEOC. If there is a WSA between the EEOC and the appropriate state or local agency, the filing will be timely. However, in the absence of such an agreement, if the EEOC takes some time to act, the complainant may not have time to file a charge with the state agency, then return to the EEOC before the EEOC filing time runs out. [16]

As with any statute of limitation, parties often dispute when an action "accrues," here, when the violation occurred. In general, the violation occurs when the employee receives notice of it, for example, a discharge, demotion or failure to hire.[17] However, the violation may include acts before the 180/300 day period. [18] But the failure to remedy a preexisting violation is not itself a violation.[19]

1.   [The former] continuing violation doctrine

The courts had developed the continuing violation doctrine to permit employees to bring claims encompassing acts of discrimination that occurred outside the limitations period. The elements of the doctrine

---

13   42 U.S.C. § 2000e-5(e)(1) (2000).

14   Id. § 2000e-5(e)(1).

15   Id.

16   Melendez-Arroyo v. Cutler-Hammer de P.R. Co., Inc., 273 F.3d 30, 37 (1st Cir. 2001); Boos v. Runyon, 201 F.3d 178, 185 (2d Cir. 2000); Bravo Perazza v. Commonwealth of P.R., 218 F.Supp.2d 176, 179-80 (D.P.R. 2002).

17   "The 300-day limit ... begins to run when the defendant has taken the action that injures the plaintiff and when the plaintiff knows [he] has been injured ... 'not when [plaintiff] determines that the injury was unlawful.'" Sharp v. United Airlines, Inc., 236 F.3d 368, 372 (7th Cir. 2001) (quoting Thelen v. Marc's Big Boy Corp., 64 F.3d 264, 267 (7th Cir. 1995)) (citation omitted).

18   E.g., Jones v. United Parcel Serv., 2002 WL 1268050, at *2 (D. Del. May 23, 2002) (last day of wrongful denial of accommodations).

19   Minter v. CSX Transp., Inc, 2002 WL 99734, at *3 (N.D. Ill. Jan. 25, 2002) (refusal to undo discriminatory act not itself discrimination).

varied by jurisdiction.[20] A number of courts followed the Fifth Circuit's decision in *Berry v. Board of Supervisors of L.S.U.*, which limited the continuing violation doctrine to situations involving three factors.[21] First, the acts outside and inside the period must have been the same type of discrimination.[22] Second, the acts must have recurred with some frequency.[23] Finally, the acts must have had a degree of permanence, so the employee understood that further conciliation with the employer would not resolve them.[24] It was not sufficient if only the effects of the

---

[20] Compare Williams v. Owens-Ill., Inc., 665 F.2d 918, 924 (9th Cir. 1982) (systematic policy of discrimination that continues into statutory period) with Moskowitz v. Trs. of Purdue Univ., 5 F.3d 279, 281-82 (7th Cir. 1993) (equitable tolling basis for doctrine) and with Berry v. Bd. of Supervisors of La. St. Univ., 715 F.2d 971, 981 (5th Cir. 1983) (multiple-factor inquiry, including equitable tolling)). These cases are discussed in *Richards v. CH2M Hill, Inc.*, 29 P.3d 175 (2001), in the context of an alleged California Fair Employment and Housing Act claim for disability discrimination. See also Place v. Abbott Labs., 215 F.3d 803, 807, 808 (7th Cir. 2000) (The courts have recognized three types of continuing violations: (1) "where the exact day of the violation is difficult to pinpoint because the employer's decisionmaking process takes place over a period of time"; (2) "where the employer has a systematic, openly espoused policy alleged to be discriminatory"; and (3) "where the employer's discriminatory conduct is so covert that its discriminatory character is not immediately apparent.") (citing Selan v. Kiley, 969 F.2d 560, 565 (7th Cir. 1992)) and Williams, 665 F.2d at 924 (continuing violation theory does not apply where discriminatory policy has no impact on complainant during limitations period).

[21] Filipovic v. K & R Exp. Sys., Inc., 176 F.3d 390, 396 (7th Cir. 1999); Bullington v. United Air Lines, Inc., 186 F.3d 1301, 1311 (10th Cir. 1999); Sabree v. United Bhd. of Carpenters & Joiners, 921 F.2d 396, 402 (1st Cir. 1990); Hendrix v. City of Yazoo City, Miss., 911 F.2d 1102, 1104 (5th Cir. 1990); Roberts v. Gadsden Mem'l Hosp., 835 F.2d 793 (11th Cir. 1988); Berry, 715 F.2d at 981.

[22] Berry, 715 F.2d at 981.

[23] Id.; see also Lambert v. Genesee Hosp., 10 F.3d 46, 53 (2d Cir. 1993) ("multiple incidents of discrimination, even similar ones, that are not the result of a discriminatory policy or mechanism do not amount to a continuing violation"; no continuing violation in one unremedied discriminatory act). Multiple acts of discrimination against the same individual or others may not constitute such a policy or practice. Gallo v. Eaton Corp., 122 F.Supp. 2d 293, 301-02 (D. Conn. 2000) (300 day period expired).

[24] Berry, 715 F.2d at 981; see also EEOC v. N. Gibson Sch. Corp., 266 F.3d 607, 617 (7th Cir. 2001) ("[T]he continuing violation doctrine does not apply when a time-barred incident cannot be linked with an incident that

policy continue into the period.[25]   The factors were non-exclusive and could be weighed differently in different factual settings.[26]   But if the facts justifying the doctrine were established, the charging party might be able to obtain relief for acts before the filing period.[27]

In *National Railroad Passenger Corp. v. Morgan*,[28] the Supreme Court rejected the continuing violation doctrine in race discrimination and retaliation cases under Title VII, although it kept it alive for hostile environment race discrimination cases. The Court looked to the language of Title VII and held, "A discrete retaliatory or discriminatory act 'occurred' on the day that it 'happened.' A party, therefore, must file a charge within either 180 or 300 days of the date of the act or lose the ability to recover for it."[29] Courts have interpreted *Morgan* to mean that repeated refusals to grant accommodations, which occur outside the 300-day period, are time-barred, even if done pursuant to a discriminatory policy.[30]

---

occurred with the statutory period or when the time-barred incident alone should have triggered the plaintiff's awareness that his rights had been violated.") (citing Simpson v. Borg-Warner Auto., Inc., 196 F.3d 873, 875-76 n.1 (7th Cir. 1999)).

[25]   United Air Lines, Inc. v. Evans, 431 U.S. 553, 558 (1977) (violation must continue into filing period, not merely effects of the violation); Harris v. City of N.Y., 186 F.3d 243, 250 (2d Cir. 1999) ("continuing violation cannot be established merely because the claimant continues to feel the effects of a time-barred discriminatory act").

[26]   Gallo, 122 F.Supp.2d at 302-03 (repeated failure to provide accommodation not a continuing violation); see id. at 302 n.3 (citing additional cases).

[27]   Van Zant v. KLM Royal Dutch Airlines, 80 F.3d 708, 713 (2d Cir. 1996).

[28]   Nat'l R.R. Passenger Corp. v. Morgan, 536 U.S. 101 (2002).

[29]   Id. at 110.

[30]   See Cherosky v. Henderson, 330 F.3d 1243, 1247 (9th Cir. 2003) (Rehabilitation Act claim alleging failure to permit use of respirators). The plaintiffs' "assertion that this series of discrete acts flows from a company-wide, or systematic, discriminatory practice will not succeed in establishing the employer's liability for acts occurring outside the limitations period because the Supreme Court has determined that each incident of discrimination constitutes a separate actionable unlawful employment practice." Id. at 1247 (quoting Lyons v. England, 307 F.3d 1092, 1107 (9th Cir. 2002)); see also Elmenayer v. ABF Freight Sys., Inc., 318 F.3d 130, 134-35 (2d Cir. 2003) (repeated refusals to accommodate employee's religious needs by permitting rescheduling of work time constituted discrete violations).

2.   Equitable grounds for relief

The filing requirements of Title VII are not jurisdictional and thus may be extended upon a proper showing.[31] First, they may be equitably tolled.[32] The EEOC's Guidance lists four reasons for equitable tolling:[33] (1) No reason to suspect discrimination at the time of the disputed event[34]; (2) mental incapacity[35]; (3) misleading information or mishandling of charge by the EEOC or FEPA[36]; and (4) timely filing in the wrong forum, as long as the charging party diligently pursued the action.[37]

Second, the employer may be estopped from raising the limitation period. Standard grounds for estoppel include a promise not to raise the period,[38] a threat of retaliation,[39] failure to post notices informing

---

[31] See generally U.S. Equal Emp. Opportunity Comm'n, EEOC Compliance Manual, http://www.eeoc.gov/docs/threshold.html (last visited Oct. 6, 2003).

[32] Morgan, 536 U.S. at 122 (explicitly leaving open the possibility of "equitable doctrines that may toll or limit the time period").

[33] EEOC Compliance Manual, supra note 31, at 2-IV(D)(1).

[34] Cada v. Baxter Healthcare Corp., 920 F.2d 446, 450-51 (7th Cir. 1990) (where terminated older worker had no reason to suspect discrimination until younger worker replaced him, he could be given reasonable period of time to file charge), cert. denied, 501 U.S. 1261 (1991). But see Washburn v. Sauer-Sundstrand, Inc., 909 F.Supp. 554, 559 (N.D. Ill. 1995) (plaintiff alleged that he had not known that he had a claim until learning that he had been discharged, rather than merely suspended, upon receiving an arbitration decision; the court found that plaintiff failed to exercise due diligence because he could have obtained this information from union representatives who brought his grievance).

[35] But see Hood v. Sears Roebuck & Co., 168 F.3d 231, 233 (5th Cir. 1999) (mental incapacity did not prevent plaintiff from pursuing her legal rights where she retained counsel before expiration of filing period).

[36] E.g., Anderson v. Unisys Corp., 47 F.3d 302, 307 (8th Cir. 1995) (misleading letter from Minnesota Department of Human Resources justified equitable tolling), cert. denied, 516 U.S. 913 (1995); Bracey v. Helene Curtis, Inc., 780 F.Supp. 568, 570 (N.D. Ill. 1992); Sarsha v. Sears, Roebuck & Co., 747 F.Supp. 454, 456 (N.D. Ill. 1990) (tolling appropriate where state agency improperly rejected charge on jurisdictional grounds).

[37] Oshiver v. Levin, Fishbein, Sedran, & Berman, 38 F.3d 1380, 1387 (3d Cir. 1994).

[38] Cada, 920 F.2d at 450-51.

[39] Felty v. Graves-Humphreys Co., 785 F.2d 516, 519-20 (4th Cir. 1986) (limitations period extended by such time as employer's misconduct effectively operates to delay employee's effort to enforce his/her rights; individual was cautioned that he would be subject to "instant dismissal"

employees of their rights,[40] concealment of the discriminatory act,[41] and a promise to provide relief.[42] Although the EEOC lists the above grounds, there may be other circumstances in which an estoppel might arise.

Third, the employer may waive the bar of the period. Waiver is the intentional relinquishment of a known right.[43] The most obvious example occurs when the employer informs the employee that it will not use the passage of time against the employee. [44]

C. *EEOC Procedures*

The EEOC has been given the authority to issue regulations regarding Title I.[45] The EEOC's administrative process for pursuing ADA

---

and loss of "generous severance package" if he discussed his pending termination with anyone).

[40] EEOC v. Ky. St. Police Dep't, 80 F.3d 1086, 1096 (6th Cir. 1996) (where employer failed to post required EEO notices and employee was unaware of his rights, ADEA filing period may be extended; filing period begins to run when charging party retains lawyer or obtains actual knowledge of his ADEA rights).

[41] Rhodes v. Guiberson Oil Tools Div., 927 F.2d 876, 880-81 (5th Cir. 1991) (time frame should be extended under equitable estoppel theory where employer misrepresented facts relating to discharge by indicating that employee was being terminated due to reduction in force and would consider rehiring him, and failed to disclose that it was replacing him with younger individual at lower salary).

[42] See Currier v. Radio Free Europe/Radio Liberty, Inc., 159 F.3d 1363, 1368 (D.C. Cir. 1998) ("an employer's affirmatively misleading statements that a grievance will be resolved in the employee's favor can establish an equitable estoppel").

[43] Coll. Savings Bank v. Fla. Prepaid Postsecondary Educ. Expense Bd., 527 U.S. 666, 680-82 (1999) ("The classic description of an effective waiver of a constitutional right is the 'intentional relinquishment or abandonment of a known right or privilege.'") (citations omitted).

[44] Leake v. Univ. of Cincinnati, 605 F.2d 255, 259 (6th Cir. 1979) (filing period should be extended because plaintiff and defendant agreed not to use time spent to investigate complaint to prejudice complainant with respect to time limitations).

[45] 42 U.S.C. § 12116 (2000). The EEOC's Procedural Regulations are in 29 C.F.R. pt. 1601 (2003). The regulations in 29 C.F.R. pt. 37 (2000) set forth procedures for resolving conflicts of jurisdiction that might arise when complaints are filed under both Title I of the ADA and section 504 of the Rehabilitation Act. Id. § 37.2(a). Part 37 also covers complaints that fall within the overlapping jurisdiction of Titles I and II (and not section 504) and complaints that fall within Title II. Id. § 37.2(2). And it covers complaints that fall solely within section 504 or Title I is filed with the EEOC or the section 504 entity.

claims follows that of other discrimination claims. The EEOC assigns an investigator to the case and the investigator may seek information from the employer. The EEOC may obtain documents from the entity against which a charge is made.[46] It will determine whether "there is reasonable cause to believe that an unlawful employment practice has occurred or is occurring."[47] If it finds reasonable cause, it must attempt to conciliate the matter with the employer.[48] It may not file a suit without first going through the conciliation process. If it successfully conciliates the matter, it may dismiss the claim.[49] During this process, it may ask the parties if they will mediate the dispute. Eventually, if the EEOC does not resolve the matter, it either will issue a "determination that reasonable cause exists to believe that an unlawful employment practice has occurred or is occurring under title VII or the ADA"[50] or find there is "not reasonable cause to believe that an unlawful employment practice has occurred or is occurring as to all issues addressed in the determination" and issue a "right to sue letter."[51]

The Commission has 30 days after a charge is filed or after the end of a period of reference to a deferral agency to obtain an acceptable conciliation agreement.[52] Failing that, the Commission may bring a civil action against the respondent, unless the respondent is a government, governmental agency, or political subdivision.[53] In that case, the Commission "shall" refer that matter to the Attorney General who may bring a civil action against the respondent.[54] Only a relatively minor number of claims result in civil actions by the EEOC or the Attorney General.

The EEOC's ability to pursue a remedy for discrimination is independent of an individual's rights, even when the EEOC is seeking the same remedy an individual would seek. In *EEOC v. Waffle House, Inc.*,[55] the charging party had entered into an arbitration agreement with the respondent. The EEOC filed an enforcement action in the United States district court, seeking damages and injunctive relief. The respondent moved to stay the case pending arbitration. The district court denied the

---

[46]   42 U.S.C. § 2000e-8(b). For the scope of the EEOC's authority see EEOC v. Dillon Co., Inc., 310 F.3d 1271, 1274-75 (10th Cir. 2002).

[47]   29 C.F.R. § 1601.24 (2003).

[48]   Id.; 42 U.S.C. § 2000e-5(b).

[49]   29 C.F.R. § 1601.20.

[50]   Id. § 1601.21.

[51]   Id. § 1601.19.

[52]   42 U.S.C. § 2000e-5(f)(1).

[53]   29 C.F.R. § 1601.27.

[54]   Id.

[55]   EEOC v. Waffle House, Inc., 534 U.S. 279 (2002).

motion; the court of appeals affirmed as to the injunctive relief, but reversed as to damages, finding that to let the EEOC seek damages on behalf of the charging party would violate the policy of the Federal Arbitration Act.[56]   Noting that the EEOC was not a party to the arbitration agreement[57] and that the EEOC controls its claim once it files,[58] the Supreme Court reversed. It held that refusing to permit the EEOC to sue for damages failed to account for the EEOC's statutory authority to seek appropriate relief and that the court of appeals's "compromise" was illogical, because even injunctive relief could help the individual.[59]

    If the Commission dismisses the charge or, if within 180 days from the filing of the charge or the expiration of the reference period, whichever is later, neither the EEOC nor the Attorney General has filed a civil action against the employer, the EEOC or the Attorney General must notify the complainant. After 180 days, at the request of the charging party, the EEOC must issue a right to sue letter.[60]

    In by far the majority of cases with potentially meritorious claims, the EEOC does not itself pursue the investigation, but issues a "right to sue" letter to the complainant.[61]   The right to sue letter, in that circumstance, constitutes exhaustion of the complainant's administrative remedies.[62]   Within 90 days of receipt of the right to sue letter, the complainant may herself bring a civil action against the respondent.[63]

---

[56]   9 U.S.C. § 1 et seq. (2000); EEOC v. Waffle House, Inc., 193 F.3d 805, 812 (4th Cir. 1999).

[57]   Waffle House, 534 U.S. at 290.

[58]   Id. at 291.

[59]   Id at 292-96.

[60]   29 C.F.R. § 1601.28 (2003).

[61]   In 2002, the EEOC reported receiving 15,964 charges, of which it settled 9.1%, found 60.3% had no reasonable cause and issued a right to sue letter, found 8.4% had reasonable cause which can lead to conciliation, administratively closed 17.7%, and noted a withdrawal of benefits in 4.4%. U.S. Equal Emp. Opportunity Comm'n, Americans with Disabilities Act of 1990 (ADA) Charges FY 1992-FY 2002, http://www.eeoc.gov/stats/ada-charges.html (last modified Feb. 6, 2003).

[62]   "Exhaustion occurs when the plaintiff files a timely charge with the EEOC and receives a statutory notice of right to sue." Dao v. Auchan Hypermarket, 96 F.3d 787, 788-89 (5th Cir. 1996); see also Taylor v. Books A Million, Inc., 296 F.3d 376, 378-79 (5th Cir. 2002); Williams v. Little Rock Mun. Water Works, 21 F.3d 218, 222 (8th Cir. 1994). Nevertheless, the completion of that two-step process constitutes exhaustion only as to those allegations set forth in the EEOC charge and those claims that are reasonably related to such allegations. See id. ("A plaintiff will be deemed

§ 15.3 Remedies

The default remedy under the ADA for intentional discrimination is equitable – enjoining the respondent from continuing to engage in the unlawful employment action and ordering reinstatement or hiring, as the case may be.[64] As an adjunct to reinstatement or hiring, the court may order back pay or other appropriate equitable relief.[65] The time period for back pay is limited to two years.[66] In the event reinstatement is not appropriate, the court may order front pay.[67] The Civil Rights Act imposes monetary limitations on damage awards, depending on the size of the employer.[68]

In addition, an injured party may receive other compensatory damage pursuant to 42 U.S.C. § 1981a, including damages for "future pecuniary losses, emotional pain, suffering, inconvenience, mental anguish, loss of enjoyment of life, and other non-pecuniary losses."[69] Section 1981a also authorizes punitive damages, when the respondent acts with "malice or with reckless indifference to the federally protected rights of an aggrieved individual."[70] As Justice Stevens has written:

> In enacting the Civil Rights Act of 1991 (1991 Act), Congress established a three-tiered system of remedies for a broad range of discriminatory conduct, including violations of Title VII of the Civil Rights Act of 1964, 42 U.S.C. § 2000e et seq., as well as some violations of the Americans with Disabilities Act of 1990 (ADA), 42 U.S.C. § 12101 et seq. (1994 ed. and Supp. III). Equitable remedies are available for disparate impact violations; compensatory

---

to have exhausted administrative remedies as to allegations contained in a judicial complaint that are like or reasonably related to the substance of charges timely brought before the EEOC."); Faibisch v. Univ. of Minn., 304 F.3d 797, 803 (8th Cir. 2002) (same; Title VII claim).

[63] 42 U.S.C. § 2000e-5(f)(1) (2000); Taylor, 296 F.3d at 379. The Third Circuit has held that the 90-day period is interpreted as an ordinary statute of limitations, such that the EEOC's interpretation of it is not entitled to heightened deference. Ebbert v. DaimlerChrysler Corp., 319 F.3d 103, 114 (3d Cir. 2003).

[64] 42 U.S.C. § 2000e-5(g)(1).

[65] Id.

[66] Id.

[67] Salitros v. Chrysler Corp., 306 F.3d 562, 572 (8th Cir. 2002).

[68] Damages for employment discrimination are not available from a state under Title I of the ADA, because of the 11th Amendment. Bd. of Trs. of the Univ. of Ala. v. Garrett, 531 U.S. 356, 360 (2001).

[69] 42 U.S.C. § 1981a-(b)(3).

[70] Id. § 1981a-(b)(1).

damages for intentional disparate treatment; and punitive damages for intentional discrimination "with malice or with reckless indifference to the federally protected rights of an aggrieved individual." § 1981a(b)(1).[71]

A.   *Equitable Remedies*

1.   Injunctive relief – reinstatement

The ADA's remedies for employment discrimination are those of Title VII. The favored remedy under Title VII, as can be seen from the language of the Act, is equitable relief – ordering the reinstatement or hiring of the aggrieved individual.[72] In the ADA context, reinstatement or hiring often will mean making a reasonable accommodation to the complaining individual's disability.[73]

Reinstatement must, of course, be actual reinstatement. In a case where reinstatement was "illusory" because the employer's continued harassment of the employee damaged the employee physically and psychologically, reinstatement was ineffective.[74] Because the remedy is equitable, it is within the discretion of the trial court.[75] On appeal, it is thus unlikely that the trial court's determination not to order reinstatement of an employee will be reversed.

2.   Back pay; front pay

Back pay and front pay are equitable remedies in this context, and are within the discretion of the trial court,[76] but each serves a distinct purpose. Back pay provides a remedy for the time when the aggrieved party was not employed, but should have been. Front pay, on the other hand, is a surrogate for hiring or reinstatement. The entitlement to and computation of each entails somewhat different factors.

---

[71]   Kolstad v. Am. Dental Ass'n, 527 U.S. 526, 547-58 (1999) (Stevens, J., concurring and dissenting).

[72]   Salitros, 306 F.3d at 572; Davoll v. Webb, 194 F.3d 1116, 1144 n.19 (10th Cir. 1999). If the job no longer exists, reinstatement is not required. Shea v. Tisch, 870 F.2d 786, 788-90 (1st Cir. 1989).

[73]   Dilley v. Supervalue, Inc., 296 F.3d 958, 963-64 (10th Cir. 2002).

[74]   Salitros, 306 F.3d at 572; Mathieu v. Gopher News Co., 273 F.3d 769, 778 (8th Cir. 2001); Criado v. IBM Corp., 145 F.3d 437, 446 (1st Cir. 1998).

[75]   Mathieu, 273 F.3d at 778 (citing Newhouse v. McCormick & Co., Inc., 110 F.3d 635, 641 (8th Cir. 1997) (denying reinstatement because of hostility between employee and employer)).

[76]   Moysis v. DTG Datanet, 278 F.3d 819, 829 (8th Cir. 2002) (front pay equitable remedy within court's discretion).

a. *Back pay*

Back "pay" is somewhat of a misnomer, because back pay can include a range of benefits in addition to pay that the complainant would have received. Those include: (1) pay at the rate the complainant would have been paid; (2) overtime if the complainant can show that he would have worked overtime; (3) prejudgment interest on the back pay award;[77] (4) the amount of contributions to pension plans and the accumulated growth thereon.[78]

The back pay award may take into account any of the plaintiff's mitigating activities or the lack thereof. For example, if the plaintiff could have obtained other employment, that may be used to reduce back pay.[79] Because back pay replaces time when an employee would have been working, if the employee would not have been working for part of that period, for example, if the employee were on an extended sick leave, back pay would not be awarded for the period.[80]

b. *Front pay*

Front pay, unlike back pay, is a secondary remedy, designed for situations in which hiring or reinstatement are unavailable.[81] Where

---

[77] McKnight v. Gen. Motors Corp., 973 F.2d 1366, 1372 (7th Cir. 1992).

[78] Best v. Shell Oil Co., 4 F.Supp.2d 770, 772-74 (N.D. Ill. 1998).

[79] Carr v. Fort Morgan Sch. Dist., 4 F.Supp.2d 989, 996-97 (D. Colo. 1998).

[80] Flowers v. Komatsu Mining Sys., Inc., 165 F.3d 554, 557-58 (7th Cir. 1999).

[81] In Pollard v. E.I. du Pont de Nemours & Co., 532 U.S. 843 (2001), a sex discrimination case under Title VII, the Supreme Court noted the similarity between 42 U.S.C. § 2000e-5(g)(1) and section 10(c) of the National Labor Relations Act, 29 U.S.C. 160(c). It wrote:

> In applying § 10(c) of the NLRA, the Board consistently had made awards of what it called "backpay" up to the date the employee was reinstated or returned to the position he should have been in had the violation of the NLRA not occurred, even if such event occurred after judgment. ...In the Title VII context, this form of "backpay" occurring after the date of judgment is known today as "front pay."

Id. at 849. See also Quint v. A.E. Staley Mfg. Co., 172 F.3d 1, 15-16 (1st Cir. 1999) ("[R]einstatement is the 'overarching preference' among all equitable remedies under the ADA, as it most efficiently furthers 'the dual goals of providing full coverage for the plaintiff and of deterring such conduct by employers in the future.'") (quoting Selgas v. Am. Airlines, Inc., 104 F.3d 9, 12 (1st Cir. 1997)).

reinstatement (or instatement) would be inappropriate either because the requested position no longer exists or because of provable hostility between co-workers and the plaintiff, an award of front pay will take its place. Because of its equitable status, courts have broad discretion in awarding front pay. Where, for example, the employee has obtained a new job and the other elements of the award are sufficient, a court may properly limit or deny front pay.[82] Nor is it unusual for courts to impose limits that might seem arbitrary on the length of time used to compute the front pay.[83] On the other hand, courts have permitted the period of front pay to extend the employee's projected retirement date.[84]

Unlike back pay, the calculation of front pay has an inherent uncertainty. (Of course, this does not distinguish it from other forward-looking damages.) Courts look to a number of factors:

> Courts are able to alleviate the uncertainty of future damages by taking into account a discharged employee's duty to mitigate, "the availability of employment opportunities, the period within which one by reasonable efforts may be re-employed, the employee's work and life expectancy, the discount tables to determine the present value of future damages and other factors that are pertinent on prospective damages awards.' ... *E.E.O.C. v. Prudential Federal Savings and Loan Assoc.*, 763 F.2d at 1172-1173 (citations omitted).[85]

In addition to front pay (or, in some cases, as part of it[86]), courts may order other benefits that an employee would be entitled to. They may include the monetary equivalent of essentially anything that an employee might earn during her future tenure.[87]

---

[82] Moysis v. DTG Datanet, 278 F.3d 819, 829 (8th Cir. 2002).

[83] See Criado v. IBM Corp., 145 F.3d 437, 445 (1st Cir. 1998) (front pay limited to 6 months); Best, 4 F.Supp.2d at 774-76 (front pay limited to 9 months, because plaintiff could work and back pay was substantial).

[84] Mathieu v. Gopher News Co., 273 F.3d 769, 779 (8th Cir. 2001).

[85] Carr v. Fort Morgan Sch. Dist., 4 F.Supp.2d 989, 995 (D. Colo. 1998) (but instatement ordered because "there was little evidence to suggest that the relations between the parties were actually so strained that insurmountable hostility would prevent plaintiff from performing teaching duties in the district").

[86] Davoll v. Webb, 194 F.3d 1116, 1144 (10th Cir. 1999).

[87] See Downes v. Volkswagen of Am., Inc., 41 F.3d 1132, 1142 & n.8 (7th Cir. 1994) (front pay in Age Discrimination in Employment Act case may include pension benefits and car usage); Best v. Shell Oil Co., 4 F.Supp.2d 770, 776 (N.D. Ill. 1998); Marlborough v. Am. Steel Foundries, No. 95 C 3151, 1995 WL 765275, at *13 (N.D. Ill. Dec. 26, 1995) (front pay in Age

c.   *Limitations on back and front pay –*
       mitigation

The Fifth Circuit has held that because the back pay remedy is equitable, there is a duty to mitigate.[88] The burden of proof on mitigation typically falls upon the defendant employer, which must demonstrate (1) the availability of substantially equivalent jobs, and (2) the absence of reasonable diligence by the former employee.[89]   However, where the employer demonstrates that the employee sought no jobs, the court may remove from the employer the burden of showing that there were no substantially equivalent jobs in the geographic area.[90] Therefore, where a plaintiff fails to produce sufficient evidence of his attempts to mitigate, a court may be justified in exercising its discretion to deny a back pay award in its entirety.[91]

The mitigation inquiry, like other factors discussed here, depends on the particular facts.   While the duty to mitigate extends to the acceptance of an unconditional offer of reinstatement, which would terminate accrual of the back pay obligation, [92] an employee does not fail to mitigate if she refuses to take a test designed to determine whether she might be able to perform a job nor if she declines a conditional offer of reinstatement.[93]

Mitigation, including looking for other jobs, also figures into the front pay assessment.[94]   However, courts have not demanded that

---

Discrimination in Employment Act case may include bonus and stock ownership rights).

[88]   Giles v. Gen. Elec. Co., 245 F.3d 474, 492-93 (5th Cir. 2001).   See Quint v. A.E. Staley Mfg. Co., 172 F.3d 1, 15-16 (1st Cir. 1999) (prevailing ADA plaintiff presumptively entitled to back pay, "provided it is made to appear that 'reasonable diligence [was exercised in the effort to secure] other suitable employment'") (quoting Ford Motor Co. v. EEOC, 458 U.S. 219, 231-32 (1982)).

[89]   Quint, 172 F.3d at 15-16.

[90]   Id. See also Greenway v. Buffalo Hilton Hotel, 143 F.3d 47, 54 (2d Cir. 1998); Weaver v. Casa Gallardo, Inc., 922 F.2d 1515, 1527 (11th Cir. 1991) (superseded by statute on other grounds) (Title VII race discrimination case); Sellers v. Delgado Coll., 902 F.2d 1189, 1193 (5th Cir. 1990) (Title VII gender discrimination case).

[91]   Giles, 245 F.3d at 492-93.

[92]   See Ford Motor Co., 458 U.S. at 230-31 (ADEA claim); Saladin v. Turner, 936 F.Supp. 1571, 1582 (N.D. Okla. 1996).

[93]   Hogan v. Bangor & Aroostook R.R.Co., 61 F.3d 1034, 1038 (1st Cir. 1995). See also Orzel v. City of Wauwatosa Fire Dep't, 697 F.2d 743 (7th Cir. 1983) (ADEA claim).

[94]   See Gotthardt v. Nat'l R.R. Passenger Corp., 191 F.3d 1148, 1157 (9th Cir. 1999) (ADEA case; front pay contemplates reasonable mitigation; "An

employees accept any job.[95] The job must be "comparable." There is, however, some confusion about how comparable it must be.

In a sex-discrimination case, the district court *instructed* the jury that "a position constitutes comparable employment if it would afford the plaintiff virtually identical promotional opportunities, compensation, job responsibilities, working conditions and status as the position from which she was discharged."[96] Nonetheless, the jury[97] rendered a verdict that could only be explained if it implicitly found that the plaintiff had failed to mitigate when she refused to take jobs with a 20 percent smaller salary.

The court of appeals held that the district court did not abuse its discretion in accepting the jury's recommendation. It found that the higher pay the plaintiff had received when working for the abusive employer was to compensate for the abusive environment; removing the abuse in effect meant lowering the pay as well. The market rate was thus a proper measure of plaintiff's position and she failed to mitigate when she would not accept work at that pay level.[98] There is, then, some flexibility in the use of the term "identical."

---

award of front pay does not contemplate that a plaintiff will sit idly by and be compensated for doing nothing."); Castle v. Sangamo Weston, Inc., 837 F.2d 1550, 1562 (11th Cir. 1988) (ADEA plaintiff has a duty to mitigate).

[95] Nor does a failure to mitigate affect the decision to reinstate. Dilley v. Supervalue, Inc., 296 F.3d 958, 967-68 (10th Cir. 2002) ("no logical link between a plaintiff's pursuit of alternative employment and whether he should be reinstated to the position from which he was wrongfully discharged").

[96] Hutchison v. Amateur Elec. Supply, 42 F.3d 1037, 1044 (7th Cir. 1994).

> "Title VII claimants are not obliged to go into another line of work, accept a demotion, or take a demeaning position," in order to mitigate their damages. Wheeler v. Snyder Buick, Inc., 794 F.2d 1228, 1235 (7th Cir. 1986) (citing Ford Motor Co. v. E.E.O.C., 458 U.S. 219, 231, 102 S.Ct. 3057, 3065, 73 L.Ed.2d 721 (1982)); see also Pierce, 65 F.3d at 575 (plaintiff who had been a senior analyst did not have to suffer the "great humiliation" of being a file room clerk in order to avoid a reduction in his award).

Ward v. Tipton County Sheriff Dep't, 937 F.Supp. 791, 797 (S.D. Ind. 1996). The court used the definition of "comparable" quoted above, but then found the plaintiff had failed to mitigate.

[97] The case was erroneously tried to a jury, but neither party objected. Hutchison, 42 F.3d at 1042 n.2.

[98] Id. at 1044.

Often a plaintiff will have been terminated, but also will have received benefits as a consequence of the termination, such as unemployment or increased pension benefits. Any front pay award must compensate the ex-employee plaintiff for losing his job, while avoiding a windfall for either the ex-employee or the employer.

Courts have analyzed these situations using a variant of the collateral source rule.[99] If the additional funds received by the ex-employee come from a source independent of the employer, such as unemployment benefits, courts will not deduct them from the back or front pay award,[100] because to do so would give the employer, assumedly a wrongdoer, an unfair windfall. On the other hand, a terminated employee may receive additional pension benefits because of her early (and wrongful) termination. While she may be entitled to front pay, permitting her to retain additional benefits as a result of the early termination would put her in a better position than if she had remained on the job. Accordingly, courts tend to deduct them from the front pay award.[101]

In the area of pension benefits, for example, some courts have used the following test:

> (1) whether the employee makes any contribution to funding of the disability payment; (2) whether the benefit plan arises as the result of a collective bargaining agreement; (3) whether the plan and payments thereunder cover both work-related and nonwork-related injuries; (4) whether payments from the plan are contingent upon length of service of the employee; and (5) whether the plan contains any specific language contemplating a set-off of

---

[99] Some courts use an abuse of discretion standard, Lussier v. Runyon, 50 F.3d 1103, 1109-10 (1st Cir. 1995) (whether to deduct collateral source payments within district court's discretion), while others consider it as part of a broader policy issue and thus treat it as a question for de novo review. Salitros v. Chrysler Corp., 306 F.3d 562, 573 (8th Cir. 2002).

[100] Moysis v. DTG Datanet, 278 F.3d 819, 828 (8th Cir. 2002) (workers compensation will not reduce back pay award) (citing Gaworski v. ITT Comm. Fin. Corp., 17 F.3d 1104, 1112 (8th Cir. 1994). But see Flowers v. Komatsu Mining Sys., Inc., 165 F.3d 554, 559 (7th Cir. 1999) (district court had discretion to deduct social security disability payments for periods plaintiff received back pay, despite collateral nature of payments).

[101] See Giles v. Gen. Elec. Co., 245 F.3d 474, 493-94 (5th Cir. 2001) (long term disability payments and disability pension used to reduce front pay award, because benefits designed to "compensate for [plaintiff's] inability to work in the future," just as front pay award is).

benefits received under the plan against a judgment received in a tort action.[102]

If the first four factors listed are affirmative and the fifth negative, it suggests that the employer should not benefit from the pension payout.[103]

B. *Compensatory Damages*

Compensatory damages include standard tort remedies, future monetary loss, pain and suffering, and the like. In 1991, Congress amended the Civil Rights Act to erase a number of decisions that had cut back on civil rights remedies and at the same time made equivalent compensatory and punitive damages available to those who suffered sex, religious and ethnic discrimination.[104] The statute provides compensatory damages if the defendant engages in "unlawful intentional discrimination (not an employment practice that is unlawful because of its disparate impact)."[105]

It extended the same remedies to violations of the ADA and the Rehabilitation Act.[106] However, it provides a safe harbor for employees who engage in good faith efforts to find a reasonable accommodation for the employee that will not impose undue hardship on the employer.[107]

---

[102] Phillips v. Western Co. of N. Am., 953 F.2d 923, 932 (5th Cir. 1992); see also Hamlin v. Charter Township of Flint, 165 F.3d 426, 435 (6th Cir. 1999) (following Phillips).

[103] See Salitros, 306 F.3d 562 at 573-74 (employer may not use sick pay, cause by illness employer caused, to reduce front pay award).

[104] H.R. Rep. No. 40(II), 102d Cong., 1st Sess. 1991, 1991 U.S.C.C.A.N. 549, 1991 WL 87020 (Leg. Hist.).

[105] 42 U.S.C. § 1981a(a)(1) (2000). In *Pollard v. E.I. DuPont de Nemours & Co.*, 532 U.S. 843, 852-54 (2001), the Supreme Court made it clear that compensatory damages are distinct from front pay. Most circuit courts had previously reached that conclusion. See Giles, 245 F.3d at 490 n.28, comparing Pals v. Schepel Buick & GMC Truck, Inc., 220 F.3d 495, 499-500 (7th Cir. 2000) (holding front pay exempt from cap); EEOC v. W & O, Inc., 213 F.3d 600, 618 & n.10 (11th Cir. 2000) (same); Gotthardt v. Nat'l R.R. Passenger Corp., 191 F.3d 1148, 1153-54 (9th Cir. 1999) (same); Martini v. Fed. Nat'l Mortgage Ass'n, 178 F.3d 1336, 1348-49 (D.C. Cir. 1999) (same); Medlock v. Ortho Biotech, Inc., 164 F.3d 545, 556 (10th Cir. 1999) (same); Kramer v. Logan County Sch. Dist., 157 F.3d 620, 626 (8th Cir. 1998) (same), with Pollard v. E.I. DuPont de Nemours & Co., 213 F.3d 933, 945 (6th Cir. 2000) (reasoning that front pay is compensatory in nature and therefore subject to the cap), rev'd 532 U.S. 843 (2001); Hudson v. Reno, 130 F.3d 1193, 1202-03 (6th Cir. 1997) (same).

[106] 42 U.S.C. § 1981a(a)(2).

[107] Id. § 1981a(a)(3).

At the same time, Congress placed limits on those damages. The sum of compensatory and punitive damages is limited as follows: [108]

> (A) for an employer with 15 to 100 employees in each of 20 or more calendar weeks in the current or preceding calendar year, $50,000;
>
> (B) for an employer with 101 to 200 employees in each of 20 or more calendar weeks in the current or preceding calendar year, $100,000;
>
> (C) for an employer with 201 to 500 employees in each of 20 or more calendar weeks in the current or preceding calendar year, $200,000; and
>
> (D) for an employer with more than 500 employees in each of 20 or more calendar weeks in the current or preceding calendar year, $300,000. [109]

The cap might be construed to cover compensatory and punitive damages separately, but courts have found that the correct reading is that the cap is an overall cap. [110]

ADA compensatory damages are subject to the same standards of proof as standard tort damages for emotional distress, pain and suffering, and loss of the enjoyment of life. The size of compensatory damages is, in the first instance, a question for the jury. "There is a strong presumption

---

[108] Id. § 1981a(a)(1).

[109] Id. § 1981a(b)(3). An individual may also seek state law remedies for the same behavior. If the state remedies are more generous, a court may award them. Gagliardo v. Connaught Labs., Inc., 311 F.3d 565, 570 (3d Cir. 2002).

> § 1981a does not prevent a claimant from recovering greater damages under a state law claim that is virtually identical to a capped federal claim. Passantino v. Johnson & Johnson, 212 F.3d 493, 510 (9th Cir. 2000) (discussing Title VII and the Washington Law Against Discrimination); Martini v. Fed. Nat'l Mortgage Ass'n, 178 F.3d 1336, 1349- 50 (D.C. Cir. 1999) (discussing Title VII and the District of Columbia Human Rights Act).

The Third Circuit relied on the statutory language: "Nothing in this chapter shall be construed to invalidate or limit the remedies, rights, and procedures of any Federal law or law of any State ... that provides greater or equal protection for the rights of individuals with disabilities than are afforded by this chapter." Id. See 42 U.S.C. § 12201(b) (2000).

[110] Hogan v. Bangor & Aroostook R.R.Co., 61 F.3d 1034, 1037 (1st Cir. 1995) (citing Commonwealth of Massachusetts v. Gately, 2 F.3d 1221, 1228 (1st Cir. 1993), cert. denied, 511 U.S. 1082 (1994)).

in favor of affirming a jury award of damages. The damage award may be overturned only upon a clear showing of excessiveness.... However, when [the] court is left with the perception that the verdict is clearly excessive, deference must be abandoned."[111]

C.   *Punitive Damages*

Congress added punitive damages to plaintiffs' arsenal of ADA Title I remedies in 1991.[112] Section 1981a adopts its own standard for imposing those damages, which is not necessarily congruent with common-law tests.[113] The Supreme Court first considered the test to establish an entitlement to punitive damages in *Kolstad*, supra, a sex discrimination case.   It held that the plaintiff must first prove an intentional act (sufficient to justify compensatory damages),[114] and must then prove that the employer had the requisite state of mind – "malice" or "reckless indifference to the federally protected rights of an aggrieved individual."[115]

---

[111] Giles v. Gen. Elec. Co., 245 F.3d 474, 488 (5th Cir. 2001) (quoting Eiland v. Westinghouse Elec. Corp., 58 F.3d 176, 183 (5th Cir. 1995) (believing a $300,000 verdict was excessive, the Fifth Circuit cut it in half)).   On the other hand, where an employer refused to permit an employee to return to work, viewing him as disabled, and thereby cut his $28,000 income in less than half, causing his wife to go to work, instead of caring for their small children, the First Circuit approved a $200,000 compensatory award. Hogan, 61 F.3d at 1037.

[112] In establishing the standard for punitive damages in the Civil Rights Act of 1991, Congress looked to *Smith v. Wade*, 461 U.S. 30 (1983).

> [T]he Report of the House Judiciary Committee states that the 'standard for punitive damages is taken directly from civil rights case law,' H.R. Rep. No. 102-40, pt. 2, p. 29 (1991), and proceeds to quote and cite with approval the very page in Smith that announced the punitive damages standard requiring 'evil motive or intent, or ... reckless or callous indifference to the federally protected rights of others,' 461 U.S., at 56, 103 S.Ct. 1625, quoted in H.R. Rep. No. 102-40, at 29. The Report of the House Education and Labor Committee echoed this sentiment. See H.R. Rep. No. 102-40, p. 74 (1991) (citing Smith with approval).

Kolstad v. Am. Dental Ass'n, 527 U.S. 526, 547 (1999) (Stevens, J., concurring and dissenting).

[113] Kolstad, 527 U.S. at 550 (Stevens, J., concurring and dissenting).

[114] Id. at 534.

[115] "Most often, however, eligibility for punitive awards is characterized in terms of a defendant's motive or intent. Indeed, '[t]he justification of exemplary damages lies in the evil intent of the defendant.' Accordingly,

"Malice" connotes an "evil motive or intent," which may include recklessness.[116] The state of mind for the "recklessness" prong of the test is "an employer must at least discriminate in the face of a perceived risk that its actions will violate federal law to be liable in punitive damages."[117]

Recklessness is distinct from malice toward the plaintiff. As a consequence, the *Kolstad* majority wrote that, where the employer either does not know about the federal law's requirements or believes its "discrimination is lawful," punitive damage liability will not lie.[118] One might argue that this interpretation puts a premium on remaining ignorant of the law and is superfluous to some degree in view of section 1981a(a)(3)'s reasonable accommodation safe harbor. However, the court apparently believed that the possibilities of lawful discrimination – permitted, for example, under the ADEA – militated in favor of permitting employers to show an absence of familiarity with governing standards.[119]

In *Kolstad*, the Supreme Court also addressed an employer's vicarious liability for an employee's acts. It rejected the Restatement (Second) of Torts/Restatement (Second) of Agency test for imposing punitive liability.[120] The Court was concerned that under the

---

'a positive element of conscious wrongdoing is always required.'" Id. at 538 (citations omitted).

[116] Id. at 536.

[117] Id. See Lovejoy-Wilson v. NOCO Motor Fuels, Inc., 242 F.Supp.2d 236, 245 (W.D.N.Y. 2003).

[118] Kolstad, 527 U.S. at 536-37.

[119] The imposition of punitive damages rests, in the first instance, with the jury. However, the court ultimately determines if the evidence is sufficient. This leads to a wide variability. For example, in Salitros, the jury had awarded punitive damages. The court of appeals wrote:

> [The] manager ... was quoted as saying he was going to teach Salitros a lesson, in circumstances that support the inference that the lesson to be learned was either not to file EEOC charges or not to protest work assignments that he thought exceeded his medical restrictions. [The manager] testified that he had received training on the Americans With Disabilities Act. A jury could conclude that [he] acted in reckless indifference to whether he was violating Salitros's federally protected rights.

Salitros v. Chrysler Corp., 306 F.3d 562, 570 (8th Cir. 2002); see also Dilley v. Supervalue, Inc., 296 F.3d 958, 963-64 (10th Cir. 2002) (court properly did not submit punitive damage issue to jury: evidence insufficient to show disregard of right).

[120] Kolstad, 527 U.S. at 542-43.

Restatement view, a principal may be liable for punitive damages for its agent's tortious acts if the agent acted in a managerial capacity and in the scope of her duties, even if the employer specifically forbid the acts.[121] "On this view, even an employer who makes every effort to comply with Title VII would be held liable for the discriminatory acts of agents acting in a 'managerial capacity.'"[122] This ran counter, in the Court's view, to the remedial goals of Title VII. It thus concluded, "[A]n employer may not be vicariously liable for the discriminatory employment decisions of managerial agents where these decisions are contrary to the employer's 'good-faith efforts to comply with Title VII.'"[123] Following *Kolstad*, courts have affirmed juries' imposition of punitive damages on employers based on their employees' knowledge in a range of situations.[124]

The courts have not come to rest on whether compensatory damages are a necessary prerequisite to an award of punitive damages. 42 U.S.C. § 1981a mentions no prerequisites, but that has not deterred courts. The Fourth Circuit requires compensatory damage – i.e., economic

---

> Punitive damages can properly be awarded against a master or other principal because of an act by an agent if, but only if: (a) the principal authorized the doing and the manner of the act, or (b) the agent was unfit and the principal was reckless in employing him, or (c) the agent was employed in a managerial capacity and was acting in the scope of employment, or (d) the principal or a managerial agent of the principal ratified or approved the act.

Restatement (Second) of Agency § 217 C (1958); see also Restatement (Second) of Torts § 909 (1979) (same).

[121] Kolstad, 527 U.S. at 543-44.

[122] Id. at 544.

[123] Id. at 545 (quoting Kolstad v. Am. Dental Ass'n, 139 F.3d 958, 974 (D.C. Cir. 1998) (en banc) (Tatel, J., dissenting)).

[124] See, e.g., Gagliardo v. Connaught Labs., Inc., 311 F.3d 565, 573 (3d Cir. 2002) ([1] employees showed reckless indifference to plaintiff's rights, because supervisor and human resources representative knew plaintiff had multiple sclerosis and latter, who also has MS, knew that requested accommodation was reasonable, but employer failed after various requests to provide accommodation; [2] defendant aware of rights because human resources representative, who was familiar with the ADA and responsible for ensuring defendant followed the ADA, was sufficiently high manager that her knowledge was imputed to defendant corporation); Salitros, 306 F.3d at 570 ("[The manager's] malice may be imputed to [the corporate defendant] because he was serving in a managerial capacity and acting in the scope of his employment."). Foster v. Time Warner Entm't Co., 250 F.3d 1189, 1196-97 (8th Cir. 2001) (quoting Kolstad, 527 U.S. at 543).

damage, or emotional distress damage – before it will permit punitive damages.[125] Its rule rests on the general necessity for compensatory damages in most common-law actions to justify punitive damages. The First and Eleventh Circuits consider an award of back pay, which they regard as compensatory, as sufficient. Some courts, such as the Third and Tenth Circuits, hold that a constitutional violation, even with only nominal damages, suffices.[126] Of course, an ADA violation is not a constitutional violation. Finally, some courts require no additional damage, basing their position on the unadorned words of the statute and the lack of any common-law consensus.[127]

D. *Prejudgment Interest*

Courts generally have recognized that prejudgment interest is presumptively available.[128] Nonetheless, because it is an element of an award that is at least partly equitable, its grant lies within the court's discretion.[129] The test used by some courts is whether the award makes the plaintiff whole. Thus, when the damage award is substantial in relation to the back pay award, a court may decline to order prejudgment interest.[130] That logic seems, however, to miss the point: if the plaintiff was entitled to back pay and compensatory damages, the back pay award should be augmented with interest or else the defendant has gained the time value of the wages it should have paid.

---

[125] People Helpers Found. v. Richmond, 12 F.3d 1321, 1327 (4th Cir. 1993).

[126] Goodwin v. Cir. Ct. of St. Louis County, 729 F.2d 541, 548 (8th Cir. 1984). In the Eighth Circuit, a constitutional violation automatically justifies at least nominal damages. Risdal v. Halford, 209 F.3d 1071, 1072 (8th Cir. 2000).

[127] Cush-Crawford v. Adchem Corp., 271 F.3d 352, 357-59 (2d Cir. 2001); Timm v. Progressive Steel Treating, Inc., 137 F.3d 1008, 1010 (7th Cir. 1998).

[128] McKnight v. Gen. Motors Corp., 973 F.2d 1366, 1372 (7th Cir. 1992); see also Hutchison v. Amateur Elec. Supply, Inc., 42 F.3d 1037, 1046 (7th Cir. 1994) ("Prejudgment interest is an element of complete compensation and a normal incident of relief under Title VII.").

[129] Criado v. IBM Corp., 145 F.3d 437, 446 (1st Cir. 1998) (citing Hogan v. Bangor & Aroostook R.R.Co., 61 F.3d 1034, 1038 (1st Cir. 1995)).

[130] Hogan, 61 F.3d at 1038 (denial of interest not an abuse of discretion, where damages almost three times back pay award).

Chapter 16 TITLE II – DISCRIMINATION BY PUBLIC ENTITES

§ 16.1 Introduction

Title II of the ADA attacks discrimination by "public entities."[1] Those include cities, counties, transportation districts and the like. It also include states, at least when the action is brought by the federal government. Title II addresses discrimination in public programs in subtitle A.[2] In subtitle B, it focuses on, in effect, bus and rail transportation systems.

Under the Supreme Court's recent interpretation of the ADA, individuals may not seek monetary damages against states and agencies of states under Title I,[3] but there remains an open question whether Congress validly abrogated the Eleventh Amendment in Title II.[4] The Department of Justice retains the power to enforce Title II[5] and, as of this writing, individuals still may seek injunctive and declaratory relief from the states.[6]

Title II's remedial provision reads simply, but in fact points in a set of confusing directions, because it proceeds from a base that is incongruent with its goals.[7] The remedial provisions were tailored to federal executive branch agencies and entities that receive federal funds, rather than state and local entities that do not receive federal funding. Confusion results, which the drafters might have avoided if they had been less wedded to following existing legislation and judicial decisions.[8]

---

[1] See discussion supra Chapter 10, § 10.2. It does not include the federal government, which is covered by the Rehabilitation Act of 1973.

[2] There is an open question whether Title II prohibits employment discrimination. Most courts have held that it does. See discussion supra Chapter 11, § 11.1.B.2.

[3] Bd. of Trs. of the Univ. of Ala. v. Garrett, 531 U.S. 356, 356 (2001).

[4] See discussion supra Chapter 10, § 10.2.

[5] 42 U.S.C. § 12134(a) (2000).

[6] See generally Chapter 10, § 10.2.

[7] Sande Buhai & Nina Golden, Adding Insult to Injury: Discriminatory Intent As a Prerequisite to Damages Under the ADA, 52 Rutgers L. Rev. 1121, 1128 (2000).

[8] On Title II's remedies, see Cheryl L. Anderson, Damages for Intentional Discrimination by Public Entities Under Title II of the Americans with Disabilities Act: A Rose by Any Other Name, but Are the Remedies the Same?, 9 BYU J. Pub. L. 235, 244 (1995); Buhai & Golden, supra note 7, at 1128-32; John J. Coleman, III & Marcel L. Debruge, A Practitioner's Introduction to ADA Title II, 45 Ala. L. Rev. 55, 92-96

The remedial language takes just one sentence:

> The remedies, procedures, and rights set forth in section 505 of the Rehabilitation Act of 1973 (29 U.S.C. 794a) shall be the remedies, procedures, and rights this title provides to any person alleging discrimination on the basis of disability in violation of section 202.

That would be fine if section 505 articulated remedies, but that section refers to "[t]he remedies, procedures, and rights set forth in section 717 of the Civil Rights Act of 1964 (42 U.S.C. 2000e-16), including the application of sections 706(f) through 706 (k), to any employee or applicant for employment aggrieved by the final disposition of such complaint ...."[9] With respect to non-employment disputes, it goes on, "[t]he remedies, procedures, and rights set forth in Title VI of the Civil Rights Act of 1964 (42 U.S.C. 2000d et seq.) shall be available to any person aggrieved by any act or failure to act by any recipient of Federal assistance or Federal provider of such assistance under section 794 of this title."[10] However, Title VI of the Civil Rights Act of 1964 does not spell out any remedies, so courts must imply them.[11]

Although the ADA was enacted pursuant to the Commerce Clause and section 5 of the Fourteenth Amendment, Title VI of the Civil Rights Act was enacted pursuant to the Constitution's Spending Clause.[12] The Supreme Court has, therefore, interpreted the remedies available under Title II to be those available pursuant to the Spending Clause.[13] Those remedies are such as would flow from a contract, expressed or implied, between the United States and the defendant. As we will see, this imposes limitations on the available relief; tort remedies, for example, are unavailable.

§ 16.2 Procedure

Title II adopts the remedial scheme of section 504 of the Rehabilitation Act, including the procedures of section 505.[14] As noted,

---

(1993); Mark C. Weber, Disability Discrimination by State and Local Government: The Relationship Between Section 504 of the Rehabilitation Act and Title II of the Americans with Disabilities Act, 36 Wm. & Mary L. Rev. 1089, 1104 (1995).

[9]   29 U.S.C. § 794a(a)(1) (2000).

[10]   Id. § 794a(a)(2). It also authorizes the recovery of attorneys' fees. Id. § 794a(b).

[11]   Cannon v. Univ. of Chi., 441 U.S. 677, 711-12 (1979).

[12]   U.S. Const. art. I, § 8, cl. 1.

[13]   Barnes v. Gorman, 536 U.S. 181, 184-89 (2002).

[14]   Those procedures apply to the entire subchapter, both parts A and B.

those, in turn, rest on Title VI of the Civil Rights Act. Individuals have two courses of action to attack alleged violations of Title II.[15]

First, they may pursue administrative remedies. As with Title I, the claimant must file within 180 days of the violation.[16] "An individual may file a complaint with any agency that he or she believes to be the appropriate agency designated under subpart G of this part, or with any agency that provides funding to the public entity that is the subject of the complaint, or with the Department of Justice for referral as provided in [28 C.F.R.] § 35.171(a)(2)."[17] Certain agencies have jurisdiction under section 504; agencies that do not have section 504 jurisdiction may be "designated agencies" – "for components of State and local governments that exercise responsibilities, regulate, or administer services, programs, or activities in [specified] functional areas."[18] The regulations specify how complaints are to be processed if filed with the agencies other than the Department of Justice.

The designated agency, which may be the Department of Justice, must investigate a complaint and attempt informal resolution.[19] If informal resolution fails, it issues findings of fact and conclusions of law, a description of the appropriate remedy and a notice to the complainant and the public entity.[20] If it finds non-compliance, it issues a letter of non-compliance, notifies the Assistant Attorney General in charge of the Civil Rights Division of the Department of Justice and attempts to negotiate to secure compliance.[21] If that fails it refers the matter to the Assistant Attorney General for litigation.

When the covered entity receives federal funding, the designated agency also may seek to revoke the federal funding under Section 504.[22]

---

[15] The Department of Justice regulations regarding Title II are found in 28 C.F.R. pt. 35.

[16] 28 C.F.R. § 35.170(b) (2003), unless the time is extended for good cause.

[17] Id. § 35.170.

[18] Id. § 35. 190(b). The designated agencies are the Departments of Agriculture, Education, Health and Human Services, Housing and Urban Development, Interior, Justice, Labor and Transportation. Id. Other departments' ADA responsibilities are spelled out in their own regulation. For example, the Department of Transportation's regulations are found at 49 C.F.R. pt. 27.

[19] 28 C.F.R. § 35.172.

[20] Id. § 35.172(a).

[21] Id. § 35.173(a).

[22] Id. § 42.108(a).

The regulations cabin that authority with a series of barriers that make attacks on funded programs quite difficult.[23]

Individuals' second option is a private suit. While individuals may elect to pursue administrative remedies, the courts have found uniformly that there is no need to exhaust administrative remedies in actions that are not against the federal government under the Rehabilitation Act.[24] In *Cannon v. University of Chicago*,[25] the Supreme Court found that those seeking relief under Title IX of the Civil Rights Act need not exhaust administrative remedies. Because the same enforcement procedures apply to Title IX of the Civil Rights Act, section 504 of the Rehabilitation Act, and Title II of the ADA, which all rest on Title VI of the Civil Rights

---

[23] The relevant regulation reads:

> No order suspending, terminating, or refusing to grant or continue Federal financial assistance shall become effective until: (1) The responsible Department official has advised the applicant or recipient of his failure to comply and has determined that compliance cannot be secured by voluntary means, (2) there has been an express finding on the record, after opportunity for hearing, of a failure by the applicant or recipient to comply with a requirement imposed by or pursuant to this subpart, (3) the action has been approved by the Attorney General pursuant to § 42.110, and (4) the expiration of 30 days after the Attorney General has filed with the committee of the House and the committee of the Senate having legislative jurisdiction over the program involved, a full written report of the circumstances and the grounds for such action.

Id. § 42.108(c).

[24] Tuck v. HCA Health Servs., 7 F.3d 465, 470-71 (6th Cir. 1993); cf. Smith v. Barton, 914 F.2d 1330, 1338 (9th Cir. 1990) (exhaustion not required under Rehabilitation Act). See 28 C.F.R. § 35.17(b). However, if the complainant must exhaust remedies under another statute, that exhaustion requirement trumps Title II's silence. See, e.g., Babicz v. Sch. Bd. of Broward County, 135 F.3d 1420, 1422 (11th Cir. 1998) (must exhaust Individuals with Disabilities Education Act remedies); Zulauf v. Ky. Educ. Television, 28 F.Supp.2d 1022, 1024 (E.D. Ky. 1998) (must exhaust remedies under Video Programming Accessibility Act). One must, of course, be careful: Employment claims against the federal government, rather than recipients of federal funds, arise under section 501 of the Rehabilitation Act, 29 U.S.C. § 794 (2000), which does require exhaustion. Spence v. Straw, 54 F.3d 196, 200-02 (3d Cir. 1995); Boyd v. U.S. Postal Serv., 752 F.2d 410, 412-13 (9th Cir. 1985).

[25] Cannon v. Univ. of Chi., 441 U.S. 677, 677 (1979).

Act, there is no exhaustion requirement.[26] That follows from the fact that the "administrative remedies, which result in suspension or termination of the federal assistance to the institutional recipient, do not afford individual complainants adequate relief."[27] If there were any doubt that exhaustion is not required under Title II of the ADA, Congress made it clear in the legislative history that it intended no such requirement.[28]

§ 16.3 Remedies

Both the federal government and private individuals may seek relief under Title II. They may not sue people in their individual capacity, since those targets are not defined "entities" under Title II. Nor may they seek relief for government actions that have a "disparate impact" on the subject group, as opposed to intentional discrimination; i.e., they have no private right of action for disparate impact discrimination.[29] The government may seek injunctive relief[30] and damages[31] in court and administratively may take actions such as cutting off funds for programs.[32]

The range, or perhaps more accurately, the available targets of remedies available to individuals under Title II remains problematic. Because the relief available under Title VI also is available under section 504 of the Rehabilitation Act, there are private rights of action under Title II.

---

[26] Camenisch v. Univ. of Tex., 616 F.2d 127 (5th Cir. 1980), vacated on other grounds, 451 U.S. 390, 135 (1981).

[27] Smith v. Barton, 914 F.2d 1330, 1338 (9th Cir. 1990); see also Greater L.A. Council on Deafness, Inc. v. Cmty. Television of S. Cal., 719 F.2d 1017, 1021 (9th Cir. 1983), cert. denied 467 U.S. 1252 (1984) (exhaustion not required under Rehabilitation Act); Pushkin v. Regents of Univ. of Colo., 658 F.2d 1372, 1380-82 (10th Cir. 1981) (same).

[28] H.R. Rep. No. 101-485, at 98 (1990), reprinted in 1990 U.S.C.A.A.N. 267, 381 ("As with § 504, there is also a private right of action ... which includes the full panoply of remedies. Again, consistent with section 504, it is not the Committee's intent that persons with disabilities need to exhaust Federal administrative remedies before exercising their private right of action.").

[29] Alexander v. Sandoval, 532 U.S. 275, 285-93 (2001).

[30] Barnes v. Gorman, 536 U.S. 181, 187 (2002).

[31] See, e.g., Martin v. Metro. Atlanta Rapid Transit Auth., 225 F.Supp.2d 1362, 1372 (N.D. Ga. 2002); People ex rel. Spitzer v. County of Del., 82 F.Supp.2d 12, 15-18 (N.D.N.Y. 2000).

[32] 42 U.S.C. §§ 2000e-5(f), 2000e-16 (2000). See 28 C.F.R. § 42.108 (2003) ("the responsible Department official may suspend or terminate, or refuse to grant or continue, Federal financial assistance, or use any other means authorized by law, to induce compliance with this subpart").

In 1972, in *Cannon v. University of Chicago*, the Supreme Court held that Title IX of the Civil Rights supports private rights of action.[33] As part of its reasoning, the Court recognized that Title IX's pertinent language is virtually identical to Title VI's.[34] A series of cases had found a private right of action under Title VI.[35] That background justified in part finding a private right of action under Title IX. The same reasoning applies to the Rehabilitation Act and from its early days, the Rehabilitation Act was held to establish a private right of action.[36] There is no question that the full range of remedies is available against all defendants except states. Given the resurgent Eleventh Amendment, it is not yet clear what view the Supreme Court will take of the range of those remedies as against states.

A. *Injunctive Relief*

In *Barnes v. Gorman*, the Supreme Court wrote that injunctive relief "is traditionally available in suits for breach of contract."[37] Because the remedies for Title VI are those for breaches of contract – the recipient's contract with the federal government – those remedies, even in the absence of a contract, are the remedies for Title II of the ADA. The United States may seek injunctive relief for violations of Title II.[38] Others may obtain injunctive relief, in general.[39] Of course, the usual standards for obtaining preliminary or permanent injunctive relief must be met.[40]

---

[33] Cannon v. Univ. of Chi., 441 U.S. 677, 689, 717 (1979). It followed the analytic scheme of *Cort v. Ash*, 422 U.S. 66, 80-85 (1975).

[34] Compare the language of Title VI ("No person in the United States shall, on the ground of race, color, or national origin, be excluded from participation in, be denied the benefits of, or be subjected to discrimination under any program or activity receiving Federal financial assistance."), 42 U.S.C. § 2000d, with that of Title IX ("No person in the United States shall, on the basis of sex, be excluded from participation in, be denied the benefits of, or be subjected to discrimination under any education program or activity receiving Federal financial assistance"), 20 U.S.C. § 1681 (2000).

[35] Cannon, 441 U.S. at 697-98 (citing Bossier Parish Sch. Bd. v. Lemon, 370 F.2d 847, 852 (5th Cir. 1967)).

[36] Pushkin v. Regents of Univ. of Colo., 658 F.2d 1372, 1377 (10th Cir. 1981) (citing numerous cases); see also Barnes v. Gorman, 536 U.S. 181, 181 (2002).

[37] Barnes, 536 U.S. at 187.

[38] 42 U.S.C. § 2000e-16(c); see United States v. City and County of Denver, 927 F.Supp. 1396 (D. Colo. 1996) (United States seeking injunctive relief).

[39] First Step, Inc. v. City of New London, 247 F.Supp.2d 135, 156-57 (D. Conn. 2003); Bertrand v. City of Mackinac Island, 662 N.W.2d 77, 78, 81-

The Supreme Court has not yet decided whether individuals may obtain equitable relief, such as injunctions, against states under Title II consistent with the Eleventh Amendment. That is, did Title II of the ADA

---

88 (Mich. Ct. App. 2003) (city required to permit resident use electric-assist tricycle, despite ordinance forbidding "motor vehicles").

[40] For a preliminary injunction, the plaintiff must show a "real or immediate threat of substantial or irreparable injury." Midgett v. Tri-County Metro. Transp. Dist., 254 F.3d 846, 850 (9th Cir. 2001) (citing Hodgers-Durgin v. De La Vina, 199 F.3d 1037, 1042 (9th Cir. 1999)); see also Jones v. City of Monroe, Mich., 341 F.3d 474, 476 (6th Cir. 2003) stating:

> When considering a motion for preliminary injunction, the district court should consider four factors: (1) whether the moving party has a strong likelihood of success on the merits; (2) whether the moving party will suffer irreparable injury without the injunction; (3) whether the issuance of the injunction would cause substantial harm to others; and (4) whether the public interest would be served by issuance of the injunction.

The court affirmed the refusal to issue a preliminary injunction where the plaintiff did not show the probability of success on her ADA Title II claim that defendant city's parking policies violated the ADA. Id. at 475. In *Martin v. Metropolitan Atlanta Rapid Transit Authority*, 225 F.Supp.2d 1362, 1372 (N.D. Ga. 2002), the court issued a preliminary injunction requiring the transit authority to comply with the ADA and requiring per 11th Circuit law:

> (1) a substantial likelihood that he will ultimately prevail on the merits; (2) that he will suffer irreparable injury unless the injunction issues; (3) that the threatened injury to the movant outweighs whatever damage the proposed injunction may cause the opposing party; and (4) that the injunction, if issued, would not be adverse to the public interest.

See People ex rel. Spitzer, 82 F.Supp.2d 12, 15-18 (N.D.N.Y. 2000) (irreparable harm most important element; shown by large number of people potentially denied right to vote by inaccessible polling places); Cupolo v. Bay Area Rapid Transit Dist., 5 F.Supp.2d 1078, 1082 (N.D. Cal. 1997) (quoting Rodeo Collection, Ltd. v. W. Seventh, 812 F.2d 1215, 1217 (9th Cir. 1987) (requiring per 9th Circuit law: "either: (1) a combination of probable success on the merits and the possibility of irreparable harm, or (2) that there exist serious questions regarding the merits and the balance of hardships tips sharply in its favor")). The governmental agency is granted substantial latitude in performing its functions. Rizzo v. Goode, 423 U.S. 362, 378-79 (1976).

validly abrogate the Eleventh Amendment? We consider the Eleventh Amendment issues in detail supra in Chapter 11.

Individuals may obtain prospective relief from state officials for continuing violations of federal law under the *Ex Parte Young*[41] doctrine. *Young* is an exception to Eleventh Amendment immunity, because the official is "stripped" of his mantle as a part of the state by virtue of his violation.

B. *Compensatory Damages*

Courts generally have found that plaintiffs may recover compensatory damages in Title VI cases.[42] In Rehabilitation Act § 504 cases, prevailing plaintiffs are entitled to the "full spectrum of legal and equitable remedies needed to redress their injuries."[43] Accordingly, ADA Title II plaintiffs may recover compensatory damages, including damages for emotional distress, pain and suffering, and economic losses.[44] Here, too, however, the Supreme Court has yet to consider whether individuals

---

[41] Ex Parte Young, 209 U.S. 123 (1908). See Carten v. Kent St. Univ., 282 F.3d 391, 395-97 (6th Cir. 2002). Under *Carten*, a request for reinstatement falls under the "continuing act" umbrella of *Carten*, because the termination is a continuing violation. Id.

[42] E.g., Guardians Ass'n v. Civil Serv. Comm'n, 463 U.S. 582, 602-03 (1983); Canutillo Indep. Sch. Dist. v. Leija, 101 F.3d 393, 397 (5th Cir. 1996), cert. denied, 520 U.S. 1265 (1997); Smith v. Univ. of Wash. Law Sch., 2 F.Supp.2d 1324, 1337 (W.D. Wash. 1998); Godby v. Montgomery County Bd. of Educ., 996 F.Supp. 1390, 1414 (M.D. Ala. 1998); Tafoya v. Bobroff, 865 F.Supp. 742, 749-50 (D.N.M. 1994), aff'd without op., 74 F.3d 1250 (10th Cir. 1996). See also Franklin v. Gwinnett County Pub. Sch., 503 U.S. 60, 70 (1992) (noting that "a clear majority" in Guardians Ass'n would allow damages in actions for intentional violations of Title VI).

[43] Matthews v. Jefferson, 29 F.Supp.2d 525, 535 (W.D. Ark. 1998) (quoting Gorman v. Bartch, 152 F.3d 907, 908 (8th Cir. 1998)).

[44] """Where legal rights have been invaded, and a federal statute provides for a general right to sue for such invasion, federal courts may use any available remedy to make good the wrong done.""" Niece v. Fitzner, 922 F.Supp. 1208, 1219 (E.D. Mich. 1996) (quoting Franklin, 503 U.S. at 66 (quoting Bell v. Hood, 327 U.S. 678, 684 (1946) (Title IX case))). Niece went on to quote Rodgers v. Magnet Cove Pub. Sch., 34 F.3d 642 (8th Cir. 1994) "[B]ecause Title IX was patterned after Title VI and Congress intended to create Title IX remedies comparable to those available under Title VI ..., the Court's holding on Title IX in Franklin applies equally to Title VI and Section 504 [of the Rehabilitation Act] cases." Niece, 922 F.Supp. at 1219 (citations omitted). A fortiori, those remedies are available to ADA plaintiffs.

may obtain the remedy against a state or whether the Eleventh Amendment bars it.[45]

What a plaintiff must show regarding the defendant's state of mind to recover compensatory damages has been disputed, but a consensus has developed. The courts distinguish between discrimination caused by the disparate impact of facially neutral actions[46] and discrimination caused by discriminatory intent. It is quite possible to argue that the Act's purpose, language and history do not make the intent to discriminate an element of a compensatory damage claim.[47] As a dissenting Ninth Circuit judge wrote, "Congress, the Supreme Court, and this circuit have recognized that discrimination against men and women with disabilities often results from thoughtlessness or a reluctance to employ the required resources to ensure accessibility, rather than from animus."[48]

The statute imposes duties on public entities to reasonably accommodate people with disabilities and where they do not, there is no statutory direction not to award all appropriate relief. The language does not mention an intent limitation. On the other hand, where Congress wished to limit relief, it did so, as in Title III, which does not provide monetary relief to private individuals. In addition, one of the statute's principal drafters, Senator Harkin, stated in the legislative record that compensatory damages were contemplated, without limiting their availability.[49] Finally, although the remedies are from Title VI of the

---

[45] See Carten, 282 F.3d at 394-95 (citing Popovich v. Cuyahoga County Ct. of Common Pleas, 276 F.3d 808 (6th Cir. 2002)).

[46] Guardians Ass'n, 463 U.S. at 598 (finding, in a suit based on the city police department's "last-hired, first-fired" policy, that discrimination "resulted from the disproportionate impact of the entry-level tests on racial minorities" but that "proof of discriminatory impact does not end the matter").

[47] See Ferguson v. City of Phoenix, 157 F.3d 668, 676 (9th Cir. 1998) (Tashima, J. dissenting).

[48] Id. at 679 (citing Alexander v. Choate, 469 U.S. 287, 295-298 (1985) (discussion of Congressional intent behind § 504)); see also Smith v. Barton, 914 F.2d 1330, 1339 (9th Cir. 1990).

[49]   [Under titles I & III of the ADA], the bill expressly limits relief to equitable remedies. However, title II of the act, covering public services, contains no such limitation. Title II of the bill makes available the rights and remedies also available under section 505 of the Rehabilitation Act, and damages remedies are available under that provision enforcing section 504 of the Rehabilitation Act and, therefore, also under title II of this bill.

135 Cong. Rec. S10742-60 (1989).

Civil Rights Act, which presupposes a contract, Title II of the ADA does not rest on a contract under the Constitution's Spending Clause, so rationales from contract-based analyses are inapposite.

The consensus of the courts facing the issue, however, rejects this reasoning. They hold that an individual seeking compensatory damages must show that the defendant intentionally discriminated, as opposed to engaging in a practice that had a discriminatory effect. Courts have relied on the relationship between Title II's remedies and those authorized by Title VI.

In the majority opinion in *Ferguson v. City of Phoenix*, the Ninth Circuit quoted the Supreme Court's opinion in *Gebser v. Lago Vista Independent School District*, decided under Title IX on the Civil Rights Act, which also uses Title VI's remedies:[50] "[I]n the absence of further direction from Congress ... we hold that a damages remedy will not lie under Title IX unless an official who at a minimum has authority to address the alleged discrimination and to institute corrective measures on the recipient's behalf has actual knowledge of discrimination in the recipient's programs and fails adequately to respond."[51] The Ninth Circuit held that such an intent was required for compensatory damages.

The Supreme Court probably has indirectly answered this question in *Barnes v. Gorman*, where the principal issue was whether punitive damages are available under Title II. Its analysis hangs on he contractual nature of Title II remedies.

> We have repeatedly characterized this statute and other Spending Clause legislation as "much in the nature of a contract: in return for federal funds, the [recipients] agree to comply with federally imposed conditions." [Citations omitted.] Just as a valid contract requires offer and acceptance of its terms, "[t]he legitimacy of Congress' power to legislate under the spending power ... rests on whether the [recipient] voluntarily and knowingly accepts the terms of the 'contract.' ... Accordingly, if Congress intends to impose a condition on the grant of federal moneys, it must do so unambiguously." [Citations omitted.] Although we have been careful not to imply that all contract-law rules apply to Spending Clause legislation, see, e.g., *Bennett v. Kentucky Dept. of Ed.*, 470 U.S. 656, 669, 105 S.Ct. 1544, 84

---

[50] Gebser v. Lago Vista Indep. Sch. Dist., 524 U.S. 274 (1998). It also relied heavily on *Guardians Association*, 463 U.S. at 584, a Title VI case, in which the Court used a "discriminatory animus" formulation. In addition, it noted two prior Rehabilitation Act cases in which courts of appeals had declined to award compensatory damages in the absence of discriminatory intent. Ferguson, 157 F.3d at 674 n.3.

[51] Ferguson, 157 F.2d at 674.

L.Ed.2d 590 (1985) (Title I), we have regularly applied the contract-law analogy in cases defining the scope of conduct for which funding recipients may be held liable for money damages. Thus, a recipient may be held liable to third-party beneficiaries for intentional conduct that violates the clear terms of the relevant statute, [citation omitted] but not for its failure to comply with vague language describing the objectives of the statute, [citation omitted] and, if the statute implies that only violations brought to the attention of an official with power to correct them are actionable, not for conduct unknown to any such official, see *Gebser*, supra, at 290, 118 S.Ct. 1989.[52]

In short, although the Supreme Court has not addressed the issue of the intent necessary for Title II compensatory damages, there is little doubt of the result, if it did.

The necessary level of intent for damages purpose has been characterized as "deliberate indifference."[53] The obvious case is when there is a "facial discrimination,"[54] but less may suffice. "Deliberate indifference requires both knowledge that a harm to a federally protected right is substantially likely, and a failure to act upon that likelihood."[55] The entity must know, for example, that an accommodation is required and must fail to make the accommodation in a way that bespeaks more than negligence, but has "an element of deliberateness,"[56] by, for example, failing to consider an individual's needs.[57]

C. *Punitive Damages*

In *Barnes v. Gorman*,[58] the Supreme Court held that punitive damages are not available under Title II. Building on the contractual nature of remedies to effectuate Title VI of the Civil Rights Act, the Court wrote:

---

[52] Barnes v. Gorman, 536 U.S. 181, 186-87 (2002).

[53] Duvall v. County of Kitsap, 260 F.3d 1124, 1139 (9th Cir. 2001).

[54] Lovell v. Chandler, 303 F.3d 1039, 1057 (9th Cir. 2002) (court affirmed summary judgment giving right to compensatory damages against Hawaii, because it (a) was chargeable with knowledge of the discrimination in violation of federally protected rights when it categorically excluded classes of people with disabilities from a state healthcare programs and (b) deliberately failed to protect their rights by denying them benefits.)

[55] Duvall, 260 F.3d at 1139 (citing City of Canton v. Harris, 489 U.S. 378, 389 (1989)).

[56] Id.

[57] Id. See also Lovell, 303 F.3d at 1056-58.

[58] Barnes v. Gorman, 536 U.S. 181 (2002).

Just as a valid contract requires offer and acceptance of its terms, "[t]he legitimacy of Congress' power to legislate under the spending power ... rests on whether the [recipient] voluntarily and knowingly accepts the terms of the 'contract.' ... Accordingly, if Congress intends to impose a condition on the grant of federal moneys, it must do so unambiguously."

...

A funding recipient is generally on notice that it is subject not only to those remedies explicitly provided in the relevant legislation, but also to those remedies traditionally available in suits for breach of contract.[59]

Because punitive damages are not "traditionally available" for breaches of contract, the Court held they are not available for violations of Title VI, and, by extension, for violations of Title II.

§ 16.4 A Note On ADA Title IV – Amendments To The Communications Act

Title IV of the ADA contains two sections, which are amendments to the Communications Act of 1934.[60] Section 401 of the ADA adds Section 225 to Title II of the Communications Act.[61] Section 225 provides in substance that each common carrier providing voice transmission shall provide "telecommunications relay services" (TRS) free of charge.[62]

TRS covers a number of modalities. It includes

- text to voice – the caller types on a text telephone (TTY) and a "communications assistant" (CA) reads the typing to the other party to the phone call;

- hearing carry over (HCO) – a person with a speech disability uses the TTY, the CA reads to the other party who speaks back directly to the speech impaired person;

- voice carry over (VCO) – a person who is hearing impaired, but who can speak, speaks directly to the other party who speaks back, but the speech is typed on a TTY by the CA;

- speech to speech relay – the CA is specially trained to understand speech with a variety of speech disorders; and

---

[59] Id. at 186-87 (quoting Pennhurst St. Sch. and Hosp. v. Halderman, 451 U.S. 1, 17 (1981)).

[60] 47 U.S.C. § 151 et seq. (2002).

[61] Id. § 225.

[62] Id. § 225(c).

- video relay services – a person who uses sign language can sign through a video device to the CA, who translates it into voice communication and translates the other party's voice communication into sign language.[63]

For interstate communications, the FCC regulates the carriers. States who wish to provide their own intrastate programs may be certified by the FCC.[64] Those states enforce their own regulations with respect to intrastate communications.[65] Intrastate communications in other states without a certificate are regulated by the FCC.[66]

Pursuant to Section 225(d), the FCC issued regulations for TRS.[67] The regulations deal with functional requirements for the TRS, minimum service standards, the requirement that the service be available "24/7"; the requirement that users pay no more than rates "paid for functionally equivalent voice communication services"; ensuring that carriers perform the services of the common carrier by not precluding calls or by limiting the length of calls and prohibiting carriers from revealing or altering any conversations.

The regulations establish a detailed complaint procedure.[68] As with cases under Title I, where states have a certified program, a consumer may file directly with the state or, if it files with the FCC, the complaint is referred to the state and the FCC only deals with it if the state fails to act within 180 days or such shorter time as the state's regulations may prescribe or the Commission finds that the state no longer has a valid certificate.[69] When the complaint goes to the Commission, there are informal and formal complaint procedures.[70]

The FCC's website provides information about each state with a certified program, including information about the complaints received by state authorities.[71] There have, however, been no cases that have decided

---

[63] See Consumer & Governmental Affairs Bureau, Federal Communications Comm'n, Telecommunications Relay Services – Consumer Facts, at http://www.fcc.gov/cgb/consumerfacts/trs.html (last modified Mar. 25, 2002). Note that the voice relay services are not required to be provided under the FCC regulations.

[64] 47 U.S.C. § 225(f).

[65] Id. § 225(c)(2).

[66] Id. § 225(c)(1).

[67] 47 C.F.R. §§ 64.601-64.605 (2002).

[68] Id. § 64.604(c)(6).

[69] Id. § 64.604(c)(6)(iii).

[70] Id. § 64.604(c)(6)(v).

[71] Consumer & Governmental Affairs Bureau, Federal Communications Comm'n, TRS by State and Territories, at http://www.fcc.gov/cgb/dro/trs_by_state.html (last modified Aug. 13, 2002).

issues under Section 225.[72] Presumably, the close regulation of telephone companies by the FCC and state utility regulators is sufficient to ensure that TRS is provided. However, like any utility service, there are likely to be complaints. We are aware of no studies that indicate that Section 225 has been ineffective.

Section 402 of the Act adds Section 611 to the Communications Act.[73] Section 611 provides that any public service announcement "produced or funded in whole or in part by any agency or instrumentality of the Federal Government shall include closed captioning of the verbal content of such announcement." Television licensees are not required to include closed captioning for announcements that fail to include it and are not liable for failing to broadcast those that do include it unless they do so intentionally.[74] There are no cases under Section 611 of which we are aware.

---

[72] In *GTE Arkansas, Inc. v. Arkansas Public Service Commission*, 961 S.W.2d 792 (Ark. Ct. App. 1998), GTE Arkansas, Inc. and various other local exchange carriers appealed from an order of the Arkansas Public Service Commission that had revoked a surcharge previously imposed on ratepayers to fund telecommunications relay service. The Court found, however, that the issue was moot.

[73] 47 U.S.C. § 611 (2000).

[74] Id.

Chapter 17 TITLE III – DISCRIMINATION IN PUBLIC ACCOMMODATIONS AND SERVICES OPERATED BY PRIVATE ENTITIES

§ 17.1 Introduction

Title III aims to provide "full and equal enjoyment" of "goods, services, facilities, privileges, advantages, or accommodations of any place of public accommodation" to people with disabilities.[1]

Title III does not look retrospectively. The remedies it gives to private parties are prospective and are based on section 204(a) of the Civil Rights Act of 1964.[2] Injunctive relief is available, including restraining orders. As Professor Colker has chronicled, the breadth of Title III's coverage was purchased at the cost of the strength of its remedies.[3] However, in addition to equitable remedies available to private parties, the Attorney General may seek monetary remedies and civil penalties in appropriate cases.

The ADA's remedial language for private parties asking for relief under Title III, section 308, reads:

(a) In General.

(1) Availability of remedies and procedures. The remedies and procedures set forth in section 204(a) of the Civil Rights Act of 1964 (42 U.S.C. 2000a-3(a)) are the remedies and procedures this title provides to any person who is being subjected to discrimination on the basis of disability in violation of this title or who has reasonable grounds for believing that such person is about to be subjected to discrimination in violation of section 303. Nothing in this section shall require a person with a disability to engage in a futile gesture if such person has actual notice that a person or organization covered by this title does not intend to comply with its provisions.

(2) Injunctive relief. In the case of violations of sections 302(b)(2)(A)(iv) and section 303(a), injunctive relief shall include an order to alter facilities to make such facilities readily accessible to and usable by individuals with disabilities to the extent required by this title. Where appropriate, injunctive relief shall also include requiring

---

[1] See supra Chapter 13.

[2] 42 U.S.C. § 2000a-3(a) (2000).

[3] Ruth Colker, ADA Title III: A Fragile Compromise, 21 Berkeley J. Emp. & Lab. L. 377, 382-85 (2000); see also Molly Hughes, Title III of the ADA: More Than an Employment Statute, S.C. Law. (Jan./Feb. 2001, at 18.

the provision of an auxiliary aid or service, modification of a policy, or provision of alternative methods, to the extent required by this title.[4]

The principal remedial issues under these sections is whether a claimant must hurdle a procedural barrier – notice – before bringing suit, and what constitutes appropriate remediation and standing.

§ 17.2 Procedure

There is a non-frivolous argument that requiring claimants to notify non-accommodating businesses would have been a useful addition to the Title III. One federal judge noted the apparent inefficiency in the statute:

> Requiring potential plaintiffs to notify offenders and provide an opportunity to remediate before filing suit is likely to solve access problems more efficiently than allowing all violators to be dragged into litigation regardless of their willingness to comply voluntarily with the ADA once informed if its infractions. The goals of the ADA do not include creating an incentive for attorneys to seek statutory fees by laying traps for those who are ignorant of the law. The Court believes that the purposes of the ADA are best served by reserving private enforcement actions for knowing violators who refuse to comply without an injunction.[5]

Championed by a well-known film actor/local politician, a movement developed to add a notice of violation and a 90-day waiting period to Title III of the ADA.[6] In this area, the factual environment may argue for and against an additional requirement to let businesses know that they may be inaccessible.

To begin with, the ADA's requirements are complex in some areas. The ADA's building accessibility standards are contained in the ADA

---

[4]   42 U.S.C. § 12188(a).

[5]   Snyder v. San Diego Flowers, 21 F.Supp.2d 1207, 1210-1211 (S.D. Cal. 1998) (notice required), superceded by Botosan v. Paul McNally Realty, 216 F.3d 827, 832 (9th Cir. 2000); see also Iverson v. Comsage, Inc., 132 F.Supp.2d 52, 55-56 (D. Mass. 2001) (suggesting why notice ought not to be required).

[6]   LawGuru.com Legal News, Congress Weighs 90-Day Delay for All Litigation Under ADA, at http://www.lawguru.com/newsletters/2000/06/35368.html (2000).

Accessibility Guidelines (ADAAG).[7] It would not be hard to envision owners of facilities not being familiar with all of ADAAG's details. Moreover, the burden on a potential plaintiff in giving notice of an architectural barrier is far less than that of litigation imposed on a defendant who is prepared to modify its facility. Because no action for damages lies under Title III, there is little redress for someone turned away from an establishment because of a disability. Congress' goal was not redress, but to change accessibility, for which notice before a suit might be most expeditious.

On the other hand, the ADA has been in effect for over 10 years (plus a nearly three-year grace period) and the standards are available, so it is difficult for owners of buildings and facilities to plead ignorance at this stage. Indeed, at least one court has held that a failure to follow ADAAG for new construction constitutes intentional discrimination.[8] Moreover, the ADA is not limited to physical access requirements and there is little purpose to notifying a business that its obviously exclusionary practices are illegal.

The drafters of the ADA may have believed that a business that had not made itself accessible years after the Act's passage and with ADAAG readily available were not likely voluntarily to change. Most important, they may have believed that people with disabilities should have access without recourse to notifying businesses, just as, for example, African-Americans have access without having to notifying businesses that the law requires it.

Early on, some courts found a notice requirement implied in the Act. [9] In order to resort to extrinsic interpretive aids, courts must find a statute ambiguous and those courts did so. Although it refers only to section 204(a) of the Civil Rights Act of 1964, those courts held that it could be read to indicate that Congress intended to import a notice requirement from section 204(c).[10]

---

[7] Access Board, ADA Accessibility Guidelines for Buildings and Facilities (ADAAG), at http://www.access-board.gov/adaag/html/ adaag.htm (Sept. 2002).

[8] Access Now, Inc. v S. Fla. Stadium Corp., 161 F.Supp.2d 1357, 1357, 1362 (S.D. Fla. 2001) (citing Ass'n for Disabled Ams., Inc. v. Concorde Gaming Corp., 158 F.Supp. 2d 1353, 1362 n.5 (S.D. Fla. 2001)).

[9] E.g., Burkhart v. Asean Shopping Ctr., Inc., 55 F.Supp.2d 1013 (D. Ariz. 1999), superseded by Botosan, 216 F.3d at 832; Snyder, 21 F.Supp.2d at 1210; Mayes v. Allison, 983 F.Supp.923, 925 (D. Nev. 1997); Daigle v. Friendly Ice Cream Corp., 957 F.Supp. 8, 10 (D.N.H. 1997); Howard v. Cherry Hills Cutters, Inc., 935 F.Supp. 1148, 1150 (D. Colo. 1996).

[10] See Adam A. Milani, Go Ahead. Make My 90 Days: Should Plaintiffs Be Required to Provide Notice to Defendants Before Filing Suit Under Title III of the Americans with Disabilities Act?, 2001 Wis. L. Rev. 107,

Even where courts found a notice "requirement" in the statute, two factors limit the effect of the requirement on people with disabilities and on property owners. First, even some courts that apply section 204(c) hold it is only a notice, not an exhaustion, requirement.[11] A plaintiff must simply wait 30 days. Second, those courts required only minimal notice and, at that, only substantial compliance.[12]

Despite early decisions requiring notice, the cases now have made it reasonably clear that notice is not required under Title III.[13] The statutory argument against notice is straightforward: the statute refers

---

118-125 (2001). Those courts noted that section 204(c) does not allow a party seeking relief, in a state "which has a State or local law prohibiting such act or practice and establishing or authorizing a State or local authority to grant or seek relief from such practice or to institute criminal proceedings with respect thereto," 42 U.S.C. § 2000a-3(c), to proceed without notifying the local authority by registered mail or in person and waiting 30 days. They read this as a limitation on section 204(a). Daigle, 957 F.Supp. at 10. They then, in some cases, looked to the second sentence of § 308 of the ADA, "[N]othing in this section shall require a person with a disability to engage in a futile gesture if such person has actual notice that a person or organization covered by this subchapter does not intend to comply with its provisions." See Milani, supra, at 116. They found that no further action is necessary if the facility already has actual notice. Thus, for example, if earlier potential patrons had informed a facility that it was in breach and it had done nothing, a suit could proceed. At this point, courts viewed it legitimate to review the legislative history. Again, it was possible to construe this source to find that Congress intended to incorporate all the remedial sections of Title II, including section 204(c). Burkhart, 55 F.Supp.2d at 1016.

[11] Id. at 1017.

[12] Daigle, 957 F.Supp. at 10-11 (unregistered letter to state attorney general asking for assistance, plus response from attorney general, obviated need for registered letter).

[13] Botosan, 216 F.3d at 831-32. Botosan also collects earlier cases rejecting a notice requirement: Guzman v. Denny's Inc., 40 F.Supp.2d 930, 934 (S.D. Ohio 1999); Moyer v. Showboat Casino Hotel, Atlantic City, 56 F.Supp.2d 498, 501 (D.N.J. 1999); Lewis v. Aetna Life Ins. Co., 993 F.Supp. 382, 387 (E.D. Va. 1998); Bercovitch v. Baldwin Sch., 964 F.Supp. 597, 605 (D.P.R. 1997), rev'd on other grounds, 133 F.3d 141 (1st Cir. 1998); Doukas v. Metro. Life Ins., No. Civ. 4-478-SD, 1997 WL 833134, at *3 (D.N.H. Oct. 21, 1997); Coalition of Montanans Concerned with Disabilities, Inc. v. Gallatin Airport Auth., 957 F.Supp. 1166, 1169 (D. Mont. 1997); Soignier v. Am. Bd. of Plastic Surgery, No. 95C2736, 1996 WL 6553, *1 (N.D. Ill. Jan. 8, 1996), aff'd, 92 F.3d 547 (7th Cir. 1996); Grubbs v. Med. Facilities of Am., Inc., Civ. A. No. 94-0009-D, 1994 WL 791708, at *3 (W.D. Va. Sept. 23, 1994).

only to section 204(a) of the Civil Rights Act of 1964, which says nothing about notice. To read a notification condition into the Act, one must import the procedures of section 204(c) of the Civil Rights Act of 1964, á là Title I. Because Congress did not do so, and did expressly include section 204(a), it can be concluded that it did not intend those procedures. As of this writing, no appellate courts have found a notice requirement in Title III.

§ 17.3 Remedies

A. *Injunctive Relief*

1. Consequences of lack of damages

As noted above, an essential feature of this remedy is the exclusion of damages for private plaintiffs.[14] This is not a matter that has been seriously disputed. Section 308 of the ADA refers to section 204(a) of the Civil Rights Act of 1964. Early on, the Supreme Court found – based on the unambiguous language quoted above – that private parties could not recover damages.[15] Courts deciding the issue under the ADA have followed suit.[16] Indeed, the District of Columbia Circuit rejected Department of Transportation regulations that would have imposed money damages, to be paid to passengers of bus companies whose trips were disrupted because the companies did not use accessible buses, since the ADA's remedies, which do not include damages, are exclusive.[17]

---

[14] Plaintiffs may seek damages for the same acts under applicable state statutes. E.g., Dudley v. Hannaford Bros. Co., 190 F.Supp.2d 69, 76-77 (D. Me. 2002) (plaintiff could recover penalty under Maine Human Rights Act).

[15] Newman v. Piggie Park Enters., Inc., 390 U.S. 400, 402 (1968) (per curiam). See also Pickern v. Holiday Quality Foods Inc., 293 F.3d 1133, 1136 (9th Cir. 2002).

[16] E.g., A.R. v. Kogan, 964 F.Supp. 269, 271 (N.D. Ill. 1997); cf. Blake v. Southcoast Health Sys., Inc., 145 F.Supp.2d 126, 127 (D. Mass. 2001). The *Blake* court held that the parents of the decedent lacked standing to sue for injunctive relief and damages were not available despite the grievous nature of the case:

> Behind the arid record of every legal case are genuine human beings with hopes, fears, aspirations, and an almost prayerful desire that sound laws will be wisely administered. Occasionally, though, there comes before the Court a situation evidencing such profound and shocking institutional incompetence leading to such unspeakable agony that the very stones of the courthouse would seem to cry out for relief.

[17] Am. Bus Ass'n v. Slater, 231 F.3d 1, 4-6 (D.C. Cir. 2000).

The unavailability of a damage remedy may be to diminish the overall effectiveness of Title III. Professor Colker has surveyed the appellate decisions and verdicts in Title III cases.[18] As of 2000, she found far fewer Title III appellate decisions (25) than Title I decisions (475).[19] Only 16% of ADA verdicts were in Title III cases.[20] She suggests that the relatively small number of Title III cases is due to the absence of a damage remedy incentive. In addition, cases must go to judges, who may be less plaintiff-oriented than juries.[21] The evidence, however, is not completely convincing, because there are far more employees than business establishments, so one might anticipate more suits, in general. Moreover, loss of or failure to obtain a job may be more significant, and thus more likely to lead to litigation, than the inability to use a business.

One longtime participant in the disability wars has, despite Title III's infirmities, expressed hope:

> Despite the flaws inherent in the ADA, the current situation is not totally bleak. There is some room for optimism. Notwithstanding its drawbacks, the ADA has helped in many respects to integrate people with disabilities into mainstream society. From a personal perspective, I can see significant changes.
>
> Prior to the ADA's enactment, for example, no hotels or motels had TDDs or closed captioned television sets for the use of their customers. Although I am frustrated by the fact that, ten years after the ADA Title III requirement that all hotels and motels have that equipment available, many (maybe most) hotels and motels have still not complied with the law, I am well aware that during that period more and more hotels and motels have acquired both TDDs and closed captioned TVs. This is progress.
>
> Similarly, since enactment of the ADA more and more entities have acquired TDDs for their own use, thus enabling me to communicate with those entities directly on

---

[18] Colker, supra note 3, at 399-406. She looked at settlements, as well, but was limited to those in which the Department of Justice brought the suit. Id. at 403-05.

[19] Id. at 399-400.

[20] Id. at 401. Of course, Title III cases will not go to a jury unless there is an associated state law claim for damages, since Title III's remedies are equitable.

[21] Id. at 402-03. She notes that, ironically, equitable relief to be decided by judges was the favored remedy for racial discrimination under the Civil Rights Act, because civil rights advocates feared judges less than prejudiced juries in southern states. In ADA cases, in contrast, juries appear to be more sympathetic to plaintiffs than judges.

the telephone. While I am frustrated by the fact that all entities required by the ADA to acquire TDDs and implement TDD lines have not yet done so, and that some entities that have acquired TDDs and installed TDD lines do not answer their TDD numbers (making TDDs virtually useless), the fact remains that progress has been made. I can now directly call many entities on TDD that I could not call ten years ago. Moreover, relay services, not generally available ten years ago, are now available nationwide. This is progress.

In addition, some public accommodations and state and local government entities have voluntarily complied with the ADA and have willingly made their programs and activities accessible to me — for example, the university theater that provided me with an oral interpreter so I could attend and understand a play. While I am frustrated that not all public accommodations and state and local governments have complied with the law, again the fact is that progress has been made. I, for one, am grateful for that progress.[22]

2. Standing

A plaintiff seeking relief under Title III must have not only the traditional level of standing — injury-in-fact, but must also show that the harm is likely to occur to him again.

> "[T]he plaintiff must have suffered an 'injury in fact' — an invasion of a legally protected interest which is (a) concrete and particularized; and (b) 'actual or imminent', not 'conjectural' or 'hypothetical.'" ... Second, there must be a causal connection between the injury and the conduct complained of. ... Finally, a plaintiff must show that it is likely that the injury will be redressed by a favorable decision.[23]

---

[22] Bonnie Poitras Tucker, The ADA'S Revolving Door: Inherent Flaws in the Civil Rights Paradigm, 62 Ohio St. L.J. 335, 382-83 (2001). One way to achieve access goals voluntarily is for organizations to require vendors to be accessible. E.g., Memorandum from the Task Force on Physicists with Disabilities, Am. Physical Soc'y (APS), to Judy Franz, Executive Officer (APS) (Apr. 21, 2001), at http://www.aps.org/exec/taskforce/disability.html (recommending that hotels chosen for conferences meet standards of accessibility).

[23] Deck v. Am. Haw. Cruises, Inc., 121 F.Supp.2d 1292, 1296-97 (D. Haw. 2000) (quoting and citing Lujan v. Defenders of Wildlife, 504 U.S. 555, 560 (1992)). Of course, if a plaintiff has never visited an accommodation, she lacks standing. Steger v. Franco, Inc., 228 F.3d 889, 894 (8th Cir. 2000)

Where a plaintiff seeks prospective relief, the causality and redressability prongs have been interpreted to demand the prospect of repeated harm.[24] Thus, where a plaintiff sued a cruise line after using it for one voyage, but could not show that she planned a trip on one of its ships in the future, she lacked standing.[25] On the other hand, the issue whether a plaintiff will return to an accommodation often is a question of fact, so that summary judgment for the defendant is inappropriate where the plaintiff can assert an intention to return. For example, a court found that a plaintiff had standing where he had previously gone to a stadium, continued to reside in the area, and stated that he would visit the stadium in the future.[26]

(denying standing for three plaintiffs who never visited facility before initiation of suit); Resnick v. Magical Cruise Co., Ltd., 148 F.Supp.2d 1298, 1301-02 (M.D. Fla. 2001) (no standing for person who never attempted to take cruise and only learned from defendant's website that its ships might not be accessible).

[24] Thus, although a plaintiff need not repeatedly suffer discrimination in order to assert her rights under Title III, ADA plaintiffs who seek injunctive relief must demonstrate that they themselves face a real and immediate threat of future harm; there must be sufficient immediacy, reality and causality between defendant's conduct and plaintiffs' allegations of future injury to warrant injunctive relief.

Deck, 121 F.Supp.2d at 1297 (citing O'Shea v. Littleton, 414 U.S. 488, 495-96 (1974)). The Eleventh Circuit has held that a plaintiff must allege "a real and immediate – as opposed to a merely conjectural or hypothetical – threat of future injury." Wooden v. Bd. of Regents of Univ. Sys. of Ga., 247 F.3d 1262, 1284 (11th Cir. 2001). See also Pickern v. Holiday Quality Foods, Inc., 293 F.3d 1133, 1138 (9th Cir. 2002) ("plaintiff who is threatened with harm in the future because of existing or imminently threatened non-compliance with the ADA suffers 'imminent injury'"); Shotz v. Cates, 256 F.3d 1077, 1081 (11th Cir. 2001); Malowney v. Fed. Collection Deposit Group, 193 F.3d 1342, 1348 (11th Cir. 1999).

[25] Deck, 121 F.Supp.2d at 1298-99. The court also cited a number of like cases. See also Moreno v. G & M Oil Co., 88 F.Supp.2d 1116, 1116 (C.D. Cal. 2000) (disabled plaintiff could not show actual injury with respect to defendant's other gas stations, because plaintiff "[did] not claim he wants to visit the other stations, or will ever do so").

[26] Access Now, Inc. v S. Fla. Stadium Corp., 161 F.Supp.2d 1357 (S.D. Fla. 2001); accord Pickern, 293 F.3d at 1138 (standing to sue store where plaintiff had visited "store in the past and states that he has actual knowledge of the barriers to access at that store. [Plaintiff] also states that he prefers to shop at Holiday markets and that he would shop at the Paradise market if it were accessible.").

Standing to seek redress for one type of inaccessibility does not equate to standing for other types. One court found that a person who used a wheelchair had standing to attack all barriers that affected the use of a wheelchair, whether or not previously encountered.[27] A second court held that a wheelchair user who was suing a stadium only could obtain an injunction with respect to those aspects of the stadium with which he "encountered difficulty."[28]

The distinction seems to be that the plaintiff in *Parr* learned about the ADAAG violations he had not personally encountered through an expert's evaluation of them, but the plaintiff in *Access Now* learned of those he had not seen personally via a non-expert. This seems to be a thin distinction. Note that the statute reads: "Nothing in this section shall require a person with a disability to engage in a futile gesture if such person has actual notice that a person or organization covered by this title does not intend to comply with its provisions." The statute does not by its terms require knowledge of specific violations.

---

[27] Plaintiff has standing to allege ADA violations in which he did not encounter, as long as Plaintiff is 'among the injured.' The legal interest at stake is Plaintiff's right to patronize L & L free from discrimination. The discrimination occurred as soon as Plaintiff encountered an architectural barrier. Plaintiff should not be required to encounter every barrier seriatim within L & L to obtain effective relief.

Parr v. L & L Drive-Inn Rest., 96 F.Supp.2d 1065, 1081 (D. Haw. 2000) (citation omitted).

[28] Access Now, Inc., 161 F.Supp.2d at 1363-66. The court distinguished *Parr*, 96 F.Supp.2d at 1081, on the ground that the plaintiff in *Parr* "had experienced certain barriers personally, and had 'actual notice' of their recurrence throughout the facility; as such, would not be required to confront each of those incidents of discrimination in order to demonstrate his entitlement to standing." Access Now, Inc., 161 F.Supp.2d at 1365. *Parr* did not say that, however. It stated,

> [t]o satisfy standing requirements to file suit, "'[a]ctual notice" of an intent not to comply with the ADA is sufficient.... Once Plaintiff either encountered discrimination or learned of the alleged violations through expert findings or personal observation, he had 'actual notice' that Defendant did not intend to comply with the ADA. Because Plaintiff is not required to engage in a 'futile gesture,' Plaintiff should be allowed to sue for the violations he did not encounter. See 42 U.S.C. § 12188(a)(1).

Parr, 96 F.Supp.2d at 1081.

Nor does standing to sue for one type of disability give standing to sue for others. A person with various kinds of psychological impairments does not have standing to seek relief for people who use wheelchairs or have vision or hearing impairments.[29] A party who uses a wheelchair may not seek relief for those with vision impairments.[30] In theory, this restriction may not be limiting, because the Attorney General can enforce the statute.[31] However, private parties still must convince the Attorney General to act.

3.   Examples of injunctive relief

Given the range of behavior prohibited by Title III, the range of injunctive relief is broad, limited principally by: (1) the necessity for eligibility criteria; (2) the avoidance of "fundamental alterations" in a program; and (3) if the remedy entails modifying an existing structure, the modification must be "readily achievable."[32]

In deciding whether a requested modification is reasonable or fundamentally alters the "goods, services, facilities, privileges, advantages, or accommodations," the "need of a disabled person [must] be evaluated on an individual basis."[33] Presumably, therefore, an accommodation proper for one person might not be necessary for another, although as a practical matter, if it is determined that a particular modification does not constitute a fundamental alteration, it would seem difficult to deny the benefit of that finding to others with a range of similar impairments. In *PGA Tour, Inc. v. Martin*,[34] for example, the PGA Tour had to modify its rules to permit Casey Martin to use a golf cart in tournaments. Others with similar impairments will certainly be able to

---

[29] Vandermolen v. City of Roosevelt Park, 1997 WL 853505, at *1-*2 (W.D. Mich. Oct. 28, 1997) (plaintiff who suffered from "depression, post-traumatic stress disorder, agoraphobia, claustrophobia, panic attacks, extreme sensitivity to sunlight, obesity, hypertension, hyperventilation, dizziness and a problem of the vocal cords" could not sue to make City "hall accessible to wheelchair-disabled, deaf and blind persons, [because] he himself is neither wheelchair-disabled, deaf or blind").

[30] Parr, 96 F.Supp.2d at 1082 ("Plaintiff seeks relief for barriers that are not related to his personal disability of non-mobility. For example, Plaintiff seeks ADA compliance for Braille sign violations which relate to sight impaired individuals. Such barriers do not specifically constitute discrimination against Plaintiff, yet are prohibited by the ADA nonetheless.").

[31] Id. at 1083.

[32] 42 U.S.C. § 12182(b) (2000). We address these substantive defenses in Chapter 13, §§ 13.6.E, 13.7.D and 13.8.

[33] PGA Tour, Inc. v. Martin, 532 U.S. 661, 690 (2001).

[34] Id. at 679-680.

take advantage of the change, absent a showing that the alteration is not "necessary" for them.

The range of injunctions requested has been broad:

- A sports arena was required to modify its seating to accommodate wheelchair users and was ordered not to "infill" seats for wheelchair patrons, until all seats for ambulatory patrons were sold. "If an ambulatory patron could still purchase a ticket for a conventional seat, then wheelchair users must be able to purchase tickets for comparable wheelchair spaces."[35] The court also ordered changes in the arena's sales of season tickets.[36]

- A court issued a preliminary injunction requiring a preschool to have its personnel undergo inhalation therapy training to assist an asthmatic child.[37]

- An airport making extensive alterations to its terminal was permanently enjoined to conform those alterations to ADAAG, by using an elevator, rather than a platform lift, to carry people with disabilities to the airport's restaurant.[38]

- A restaurant had to modify its entrance and parking spaces to conform to ADAAG.[39]

- The National Board of Medical Examiners was required to give a medical student with a reading disability additional

---

[35] Indep. Living Res. v. Or. Arena Corp., 1 F.Supp.2d 1159, 1165, 1170-71 (D. Or. 1998).

[36] Id.; see Ball v. AMC Entm't, Inc., 246 F.Supp.2d 17, 25-26 (D. D.C. 2003) (requiring installation of rear-window captioning system in 101 theatres would not fundamentally alter the nature of the service the theatres provide; factual question as to burden). But see Cornilles v. Regal Cinemas, Inc., 2002 WL 31469787, at *1 (D. Or. Mar. 19, 2002), approving a magistrate's recommendation (2002 WL 31440885, *6-*7 (D. Or. Jan. 3, 2002)) that a theatre chain is not required to install a rear-window captioning system in all theatres due to the unduly burdensome cost of $9,000 to $14,000 per theatre).

[37] Alvarez v. Fountainhead, Inc., 55 F.Supp.2d 1048, 1055-56 (N.D. Cal. 1999).

[38] Coalition of Montanans Concerned with Disabilities, Inc. v. Gallatin Airport Auth., 957 F.Supp. 1156, 1171 (D. Mont. 1997).

[39] Parr v. L & L Drive-Inn Rest., 96 F.Supp.2d 1065, 1087-88 (D. Haw. 2000).

time to take Step I of the Medical Licensing Examination.[40]

B. Enforcement By The Attorney General – Compensatory Damages And Civil Penalties

The statute gives the Attorney General broad powers to enforce Title III. The Attorney General has substantial investigative powers. [41] Moreover, unlike private parties, the Attorney General has authority to obtain compensatory damages in addition to the equitable relief available when individuals sue on their own behalf.[42] The Attorney General may – "to vindicate the public interest" – also seek civil penalties, which may not exceed $50,000 for a first violation or $100,000 for any subsequent violation.[43]

Despite this authority, there are relatively few reported cases in which the Attorney General has sought relief.[44] However, the absence of reported cases does not tell the whole story. Much of the Justice Department's activity is directed to obtaining consent decrees, which often affect a broad group of people.[45] These include such things as providing interpreters for hearing-impaired jurors, permitting students with hearing impairments to use assistive devices to take the certified public accountant examinations, improving the accessibility of university

---

[40] Rush v. Nat'l Bd. of Med.l Exam's, 268 F.Supp.2d 673, 679 (N.D. Tex. 2003).

[41] 42 U.S.C. § 12188(b)(1) (2000).

[42] Id. § 12188(b)(2). However, "[f]or purposes of subsection (b)(2)(B), the term monetary damages and such other relief does not include punitive damages." Id. § 12188(b)(4).

[43] Id. § 12188(b)(2)(C).

[44] A Westlaw® search performed in January 2003 located five reported cases in which the United States was a plaintiff or intervenor. See, e.g., United States v. AMC Entm't, Inc., 232 F.Supp.2d 1092, 1110-13 (C.D. Cal. 2002) (movie theatre patrons who used wheelchairs must be provided seating with "viewing angles comparable to those provided to members of general public" rule that would be given nationwide application).

[45] E.g., DeVinney v. Me. Med. Ctr., 1998 WL 271495 (D. Me. May 18, 1998). See generally U.S. Dep't of Justice, Enforcing the ADA: Looking Back on a Decade of Progress, at http://www.usdoj.gov/crt/ada/pubs/10thrpt.htm (July 2000) [hereinafter Enforcing the ADA]. The Disability Rights Section of the Civil Rights Division of the Department of Justice issues quarterly Status Reports on "Enforcing the ADA." For a recent report, see U.S. Dep't of Justice, Enforcing the ADA: A Status Report from the Department of Justice, http://www.usdoj.gov/crt/ada/statrpt.htm (Jan.-Mar. 2003).

campuses, and a brokerage's using larger print on its monthly statements.[46]

Both monetary damages and civil penalties are within the court's discretion[47] and the statute instructs the court to take the defendant's good faith into account in assessing penalties.[48] While damages can be substantial when awarded by a jury,[49] as indicated by the Justice Department's Enforcement Highlights, supra, which cover the first ten years of the ADA, in most cases the negotiated damage amounts are relatively modest.[50] The principal function of the Justice Department is to

---

[46] See Enforcing the ADA, supra note 45.

[47] United States v. York Obstetrics & Gynecology, 2001 WL 80082, at *1 n.3 (D. Me. Jan. 30, 2001).

[48] In a civil action under paragraph (1)(B), the court, when considering what amount of civil penalty, if any, is appropriate, shall give consideration to any good faith effort or attempt to comply with this Act by the entity. In evaluating good faith, the court shall consider, among other factors it deems relevant, whether the entity could have reasonably anticipated the need for an appropriate type of auxiliary aid needed to accommodate the unique needs of a particular individual with a disability.

42 U.S.C. § 12188(b)(5) (2000).

[49] See York Obstetrics & Gynecology, 2001 WL 80082, at *1-*2 (jury awarded $60,000 to deaf husband for whom his wife's obstetrician refused to provide sign-language interpreter on four to six occasions); Enforcing the ADA, supra note 45 (jury awarded $30,000 awarded to a blind person denied the right to sit on a jury).

[50] For example: $28,000 against a national bar review course operator which had "failed to provide appropriate auxiliary aids to students with vision and hearing impairments"; $7,500 against Duke University for failing to provide a campus accessible to a wheelchair-using student; an agreement by a CPA course to "pay $20,000 in damages to be distributed to deaf and hearing impaired students, and establish a $25,000 scholarship fund for accounting students at California State University who have hearing impairments";

the American Association of State Social Work Boards and Assessment Systems, Inc., agreed to ... pay $3,000 to a [blind] complainant who was not allowed to use his own reader for the social work license examination. Instead, he was allegedly required to use a college student who had been hired to work at the registration table and had never read for a person with a vision impairment. During the exam, the reader allegedly stumbled over technical terms and made mistakes in marking and recording the answers;

obtain broad relief, so the damages often appear calibrated to compensate the individual plaintiffs for their trouble in the litigation.

The penalties the Justice Department obtains serve two functions – to punish past behavior and to ensure that a defendant adheres to a settlement agreement. As noted, the court has discretion whether to award penalties. In *United States v. York Obstetrics & Gynecology*, supra, the court found that the compensatory award to the individual plaintiff was sufficient to deter future violative behavior and declined to impose a penalty.[51] Post-trial statements by the defendant to the press, in which he indicated he "still does not accept the fact that [his] duties under the ADA extend to all individuals who can reasonably be expected to use its services in any way," gave the court pause.[52] Even though the defendant had not shown good faith,[53] the government failed to present evidence of the amount of its requested penalty. It linked the penalty to its costs in prosecuting the case, but the ADA does not permit the government to recover its fees and costs,[54] so the court found it had not made a proper showing.

In *DeVinney v. Maine Medical Center*, supra, the court approved a consent decree that imposed an initial $25,000 penalty on the defendant – less than the statutory $50,000 for an initial penalty, because of the defendant's good faith. It also approved potential future penalties to be set by the court, in view of the defendant's good faith, for non-compliance, but levied a $3,000 penalty on the defendant each time it failed to provide a sign-language interpreter to a deaf person in accordance with the decree.

---

a 30-store discount department store chain agreed to pay $15,000 for not having ADA-compliant stores; a brokerage firm paid $1,500 for not having monthly statements legible to clients with vision impairments. However, in one case, the Department of Justice got a $550,000 damage award against a major real estate company that had refused to lease space to an advocacy group for people with disabilities. Enforcing the ADA, supra note 45.

[51] See York Obstetrics & Gynecology, 2001 WL 80082, at *2.

[52] Id.

[53] Id. at *3.

[54] 42 U.S.C. § 12205 (2000). The Justice Department's regulation provides:

> In any action or administrative proceeding commenced pursuant to the Act or this part, the court or agency, in its discretion, may allow the prevailing party, other than the United States, a reasonable attorney's fee, including litigation expenses, and costs, and the United States shall be liable to the foregoing the same as a private individual.

28 C.F.R. § 36.505 (2002).

All penalties were taken to be subsequent penalties under 42 U.S.C. § 12188(b)(2)(C)(ii).[55]

---

[55] DeVinney v. Me. Med. Ctr., 1998 WL 271495, at *16 (D. Me. May 18, 1998).

Chapter 18 STATUTES OF LIMITATIONS

Once an ADA claim has accrued – given rise to a claim for relief – the statute of limitations begins to run: if the complainant does not file within the statutory period, the claim is barred, unless it was tolled or the defendant is estopped from relying on it. The ADA presents an additional complication, because it does not have its own statute of limitations. Courts must thus determine which statute applies. Courts look to analogous state statutes and, while there is a near consensus, there is not unanimity on the appropriate sort of statute to use.

§ 18.1 Title I

As discussed above in section 15.2.B, Title I requires exhaustion of administrative remedies. Those remedies are exhausted when the claimant receives notice that the EEOC has issued a right to sue letter.[1] Title VII's 90-day limitation period to file suit then takes over. At that point, the cause of action has accrued and the complainant has 90 days to file a lawsuit.[2]

§ 18.2 Titles II And III

There is no exhaustion requirement under either Title II or Title III of the ADA. Therefore, one must look elsewhere to determine the limitations period. In *Wilson v. Garcia*,[3] the Supreme Court considered the limitations period for 42 U.S.C. § 1983 and noted, "when Congress has not established a time limitation for a federal cause of action, the settled

---

[1]   In *Ebbert v. DaimlerChrysler Corp.*, 319 F.3d 103, 114 (3d Cir. 2003), the Third Circuit held that oral notice may suffice, if it is as complete as written notice, i.e., states that the claimant has 90 days to file a suit. In *Ball v. Abbot Advertising, Inc.*, 864 F.2d 419, 421 (6th Cir. 1988), the court held that oral notice to the claimants attorney sufficed, without saying anything about the completeness of the notice. The *Ebbert* court speculated that the *Ball* court might have assumed the attorney was or should have been aware of the limitations period. Ebbert, 319 F.3d at 116 n.16. Actual receipt of a letter is not always required; constructive receipt will suffice in many jurisdictions. Zillyette v. Capital One Fin. Corp., 179 F.3d 1337, 1340-41 (11th Cir. 1999) (giving a survey of cases in different jurisdictions accepting various forms of constructive receipt as causing the start of the 90-day period). But see Hornsby v. United States Postal Serv., 787 F.2d 87, 91, 91 nn.4-7 (3d Cir. 1986) (postal form notifying the plaintiff that a letter addressed to him could be picked up at the Post Office but not identifying the sender, did not, by itself, constitute notice of an EEOC final action even if other circumstances short of actual receipt of the written notice would have sufficed).

[2]   42 U.S.C. § 2000e-5(f)(1) (2000); Taylor, 296 F.3d at 379. See infra Chapter 23, § 23.B.

[3]   Wilson v. Garcia, 471 U.S. 261, 266-67 (1985).

practice has been to adopt a local time limitation as federal law if it is not inconsistent with federal law or policy to do so."

Following *Burnett v. Grattan*,[4] the Court set forth the three-part test: (1) look to laws of the United States "so far as such laws are suitable"; (2) lacking a "suitable federal rule," the courts look to the common law of the forum state, "as modified and changed by the Constitution and statutes" of that state[5]; and (3) the Court applies the forum state's law if it is not inconsistent with the United States Constitution and laws. Federal law still is used to characterize the cause of action for the purpose of finding the appropriate state limitations period; state law only is used for determining the limitations period and the "closely related questions of tolling and application."[6]

Focusing on the need for uniformity in characterization of the federal statutes, the need for certainty and minimizing litigation costs, the Court declined to follow an approach that would adopt a different statute of limitations for each type of Section 1983 claim – of which there could be many.[7] Based upon the history of Section 1983, the Court concluded that state law limitations periods for personal injury actions best fit the purposes of that section.[8] It rejected the notion that state catch-all statutes for statutory claims was an appropriate approach, in part because Section 1983 did not itself define a wrong, but provided a remedy for certain kinds of wrongs.[9]

Two years after *Wilson* was decided, the Supreme Court found that actions under Title VII of the Civil Rights Act of 1964 and 42 U.S.C. § 1981 also were subject to state limitations statutes for personal injury actions.[10] The Court rejected the argument that since Section 1981 deals with the right to make contracts, it was primarily an economic statute and therefore subject to state law statutes of limitations related to property rights. "The provision asserts, in effect, that competence and capacity to contract shall not depend upon race. It is thus a part of a federal law barring racial discrimination, which, as the Court of Appeals said, is a fundamental injury to the individual rights of a person."[11]

Following the lead of *Wilson* and *Goodman* most courts that have considered the state statutes of limitations applicable to Titles II and III of the ADA have found that local personal injury statutes of limitations

---

4   Burnett v. Grattan, 468 U.S. 42, 47-48 (1984) (citing 42 U.S.C. § 1988).

5   Id.

6   Wilson, 471 U.S. at 269.

7   Id. at 469-76.

8   Id. at 276-280.

9   Id. at 278-79.

10   Goodman v. Lukens Steel Co., 482 U.S. 656, 661-64 (1987).

11   Id. at 661.

apply to both titles.[12] For example, in deciding a claim under Title III, the Seventh Circuit "agree[d] with the parties that this claim is best characterized as one for personal injury."[13]

Two principal issues often remain after a statute of limitations is selected: (1) what events constitute the accrual of a cause of action for limitations purposes, and (2) do tolling doctrines apply to mitigate the effects of a statute?

A.   *Accrual*

As noted, federal courts are directed by *Wilson* to look to state law on this issue.[14] Despite that injunction, most courts that consider the

---

[12]   Gaona v. Town & County Credit, 324 F.3d 1050, 1054-56 (8th Cir. 2003) Minnesota personal injury statute of limitations applies to claim under Title III of the ADA for lending institution's failure to provide interpreters to deaf borrowers; relying on prior Eighth Circuit decisions applying personal injury limitations period to Rehabilitation Act claims, the Court wrote, "because the ADA and the Rehabilitation Act enforce the same substantive rights, we conclude that the six-year limitations period ... applies to the Gaonas' ADA claim as well."); Everett v. Cobb County Sch. Dist., 138 F.3d 1407, 1409-10 (11th Cir. 1998) (applying Georgia personal injury statute of limitations claim under Title II of the ADA); Holmes v. Texas A&M Univ., 145 F.3d 681 (5th Cir. 1988) (Texas statute of limitations for personal injury claim applied to claim for employment discrimination under Title II of ADA).   One federal circuit refused to follow this trend, which in truth was not a trend in 1983 when it decided the issue.   In *Wolsky v. Medical College of Hampton Roads*, 1 F.3d 222 (4th Cir. 1993), the court held that Virginia's Rights of Persons with Disabilities Act, which "was modeled after and is almost identical to the Rehabilitation Act," and which had its own one-year statute of limitations was the analogous statute.   The remedies of Section 504 are, of course, the same remedies available under Title II of the ADA.   See also Kramer v. Regents of the Univ. of Cal., 81 F.Supp.2d 972 (N.D. Cal. 1999).   But see Gatto v. County of Somona, 120 Cal.Rptr.2d 550, 557 (Cal. Ct. App. 2002). The court in *Kramer* had assumed that California's three-year statute for actions on liabilities created by statute would apply, following two other federal court decisions. Kramer, 81 F.2d at 977.   However, the *Gatto* court concluded that the one-year statute of limitations for personal injury actually applied to relevant provisions of the California Civil Rights statute, demonstrating that courts must be quite careful in selecting state statutes of limitation.

[13]   Soignier v. Am. Bd. of Plastic Surgery, 92 F.3d 547, 551 (7th Cir. 1996).

[14]   The Supreme Court has directed that federal "[c]ourts thus should not unravel state limitations rules unless their full application would defeat

accrual of causes of action do not draw explicitly from state court jurisprudence. Rather, the rule appears to be that when a complainant knows that he has been discriminated against, such that all the elements of a cause of action exist, the statute of limitations begins to run.

For example in *Soignier,* the plaintiff, a plastic surgeon, alleged that the American Board of Plastic Surgeons had refused to accommodate his attention deficit disorder, auditory processing disability and dyslexia in the oral part of the Board's certification examination.[15] That occurred in 1992. Over the next three years, the plaintiff pursued various internal appeals with the Board, which eventually denied them. He sued in 1995 and the district court dismissed, finding that Illinois's two-year personal injury statute of limitations applied and that the claim arose when the Board refused to make the accommodation.[16] The Seventh Circuit affirmed and found, in 1992, the plaintiff knew that the Board had conducted a test without giving him an allegedly required accommodation, that he was disabled and otherwise qualified to take the examination.[17] Since all the elements of a claim were present, the statute began to run in November 1992 and was barred two years later. The fact that the plaintiff attempted to resolve the matter with the Board did not affect that conclusion.[18]

On the other hand, there are cases where the ADA violation can be seen as a series of discrete harms. Even though some of those harms may occur outside the limitation period, the ones that do occur within the limitation period are actionable. For example, in *Pickern,* supra, the plaintiff, who used a wheelchair, alleged that a grocery store did not provide proper accommodations so that he could use it.[19] He visited the

---

the goals of the federal statute at issue." Hardin v. Strav, 490 U.S. 536, 539 (1989).

[15] Soignier, 92 F.3d at 449-50.

[16] Id. at 551.

[17] Id. at 552.

[18] See also Holmes v. Texas A&M Univ., 145 F.3d 681, 684 (5th Cir. 1988) (professor allegedly terminated in violation of Title II of ADA had cause of action accrue when he was notified that termination would occur, not when termination actually took effect: "cause of action under a federal statute begins to run from the moment the plaintiff becomes aware that he has suffered an injury or has sufficient information to know that he has been injured.") (citing Helton v. Clements, 832 F.2d. 332, 334-35 (5th Cir. 1987), and Burfield v. Brown, Moore & Flint, 51 F.3d 583-589 (5th Cir. 1995)). The "unequivocal notice of facts giving rise to [a] claim or when a reasonable person would know of the facts" starts the statute running. Id.

[19] Pickern v. Holiday Quality Foods Inc., 293 F.3d 1133, 1136 (9th Cir. 2002).

store once prior to 1998, and once thereafter prior to filing his complaint in March 1999.

The district court granted summary judgment to the defendant on the ground that the complaint was time-barred, but the Ninth Circuit reversed. The court found that a plaintiff suffers an injury once he "has actually become aware of discriminatory conditions existing at a public accommodation and is thereby deterred from visiting or patronizing that accommodation."[20] The court when on, "so long as the discriminatory conditions continue, and so long as a plaintiff is aware of them and remains deterred, the injury under the ADA continues."[21]

There seems to be something of a tension between the notion of continuing violation in *Pickern* and the continuing violation doctrine the Supreme Court rejected in *Morgan*.[22] However, in *Morgan* the issue was whether the plaintiff could recover for a discriminatory act outside the 300-day period, whereas in *Pickern*, the issue was whether the plaintiff could enjoin an existing failure to make a public accommodation accessible. Certainly, if another person in a wheelchair had found the store inaccessible, that person could have filed a claim seeking the same injunctive relief. It would appear to make little sense to forbid a plaintiff who had noticed the violative conditions more than one year before he filed his complaint from bringing an action for prospective relief.

B.   *Equitable Tolling And Equitable Estoppel*

Under certain circumstances the running of a statute of limitations is tolled pending the occurrence of some event. This doctrine often is referred to as equitable tolling. It should not be confused – although it often is – with equitable estoppel, a doctrine which stops the running of the statute of limitations because of acts of the defendant, although some courts run the doctrines together, as we will discuss.

It is somewhat futile to attempt to categorize equitable tolling doctrines. The federal courts are required to adopt state law variants and the state laws run the gamut from no equitable tolling[23] to California's doctrine:

> [T]olling is appropriate where the record shows "(1) timely notice to the defendant in filing the first claim; (2) lack of

---

[20]   Id. at 1136-37.

[21]   Id. at 1137. Thus, the plaintiff's cause of action for injunctive relief – the only relief available under Title III – was not time-barred under the applicable one-year limitation statute.

[22]   Nat'l R.R. Passenger Corp. v. Morgan, 536 U.S. 101 (2002).

[23]   Estrada v. Trager, 2002 WL 31053819, at *6 (E.D. Pa. Sept. 12, 2002) ("equitable tolling ... is not a doctrine that is available under Pennsylvania law"; court also refused to apply federal equitable tolling principals).

prejudice to defendant in gathering evidence to defend against the second claim; and, (3) good faith and reasonable conduct by the plaintiff in filing the second claim."[24]

In *Daviton*, the plaintiffs were a hospital patient and her daughter, both hearing impaired, who alleged that the defendant hospital had denied them a qualified interpreter for emergency health care services, in violation of the Rehabilitation Act.[25] The violative act occurred on August 8, 1996. On February 7, 1997, the plaintiffs filed a complaint with the Federal Office of Civil Rights (OCR), which, on September 18, 1997 found that the defendant had violated Section 504.[26] On March 17, 1998, the plaintiffs filed their complaint in the Federal District Court. That court dismissed the claim on statute of limitations ground.

The Ninth Circuit reviewed the matter en banc to deal with an apparent conflict between two of its earlier decisions.[27] It held that the one year California statute of limitations applied.[28] It went on to hold, however, that the district court had improperly refused to apply the equitable tolling doctrine. That court, which had relied upon *Fobbs*, had required that the remedies sought in the two proceedings – the complaint in the OCR and the district court action – be the same. The court held that it was sufficient that the wrongs alleged in both the actions be the same, such that the defendant would be on notice of the facts alleged against it, so that it could prepare a defense.[29] In particular, the court found that California's version of the equitable tolling doctrine did not apply the threshold identity of claims requirement.[30] The court thus found that the notice in the OCR complaint was sufficient to permit the hospital to gather evidence against it and that the other elements of equitable estoppel were satisfied.[31]

But other states apply different versions of the equitable tolling doctrine. For example, in *Soignier*, the Seventh Circuit stated, "equitable

---

[24] Daviton v. Columbia/HCA Health Care Corp., 241 F.3d 1131, 1137-38 (9th Cir. 2001) (en banc) (quoting Collier v. City of Pasadena, 191 Cal.Rptr. 681 (Cal. Ct. App. 1983)). Collier, in turn, relied upon Addison v. State of California, 578 P.2d. 941 (Cal. 1978).

[25] Daviton, 241 F.3d at 1134.

[26] Id.

[27] Id. at 1133 (comparing Cervantes v. City of San Diego, 5 F.3d 1273 (9th Cir. 1993) and Fobbs v. Holy Cross Health Sys. Corp., 29 F.3d 1439 (9th Cir. 1994)).

[28] Id. at 1135-36.

[29] Id. at 1141.

[30] Id. at 1140.

[31] Id. at 1141-42.

tolling applies when the plaintiff, despite the exercise of due diligence and through no fault of his own, cannot determine information essential to bringing a complaint."[32] This is, of course, quite a different formulation of the doctrine from the California formulation set forth in *Daviton*. The point is that anyone seeking to rely upon the equitable tolling doctrine should look carefully at the law of the relevant jurisdiction.

Finally, equitable estoppel may provide yet another mitigant for a defendant that missed the statutory deadline.[33] Quoting again the *Soignier* case, "equitable estoppel requires that 'the defendant takes active steps to prevent the plaintiff from suing in time, ... such as by hiding evidence or promising not to plead the statute of limitations.'"[34] In *Soignier*, the Seventh Circuit found that the fact that the defendant had delayed hearing an internal appeal did not constitute misleading promises not to plead the statute of limitations and thus rejected the equitable estoppel claim.

---

[32] Soignier v. Am. Bd. of Plastic Surgery, 92 F.3d 547, 553 (7th Cir. 1996).

[33] Some courts conflate the two doctrines. See Estrada v. Trager, 2002 W.L. 31053819, at *6 (E.D. Pa. Sept. 10, 2002). *Estrada*, an unreported ADA Title III and Rehabilitation Act case, quotes *Lake v. Arnold*, 232 F.3d 360, 37 n.9 (3d Cir. 2000), for the proposition that, "equitable tolling is appropriate in three general scenarios: (1) where a defendant actively misleads a plaintiff with respect to her cause of action; (2) where the plaintiff has been prevented from asserting her claim as a result of other extraordinary circumstances; or (3) where the plaintiff asserts her claim in a timely manner but has done so in the wrong forum." Thus, the Third Circuit apparently runs together the doctrines of equitable tolling and equitable estoppel.

[34] Soignier, 92 F.3d at 554 (citing Thelen v. Marc's Big Boy Corp., 64 F.3d 264, 267 (7th Cir. 1995) (citing Cada v. Baxter Healthcare Corp., 920 F.2d 446, 450-51 (7th Cir. 1990))).

Chapter 19 ATTORNEYS' FEES

In any action or administrative proceeding commenced pursuant to the Americans with Disabilities Act, the court or agency, in its discretion, may allow the prevailing party, other than the United States, a reasonable attorneys fee, including litigation expenses, and costs, and the United States shall be liable for the foregoing the same as a private individual.[1]

The last battle in an ADA case is often waged over the parties' attorneys' fees requests.[2] Fees go to the prevailing party – other than the government. The disputes over attorneys' fees typically take two forms: (1) is the person seeking fees the prevailing party; (2) are the fees requested reasonable? On the first issue, the law presently seems to confer prevailing party status on someone who obtains a judgment and on someone who obtains a judicially enforceable agreement – a consent decree or a court-supervised settlement agreement. On the second issue, the courts have devised a multipart test to assess reasonableness.

§ 19.1 Prevailing Party

The Supreme Court has held:

The touchstone of the prevailing party inquiry must be the material alteration of the legal relationship of the parties in a manner which Congress sought to promote in the fee statute. Where such a change has occurred, the degree of the plaintiff's overall success goes to the reasonableness of the award under *Hensley* [*v. Eckerhart*, 461 U.S. 424 (1983)] not to the availability of a fee award *vel non*.[3]

Obviously, one who obtains a judgment is a prevailing party.[4] A difficult question had arisen when the plaintiff does not actually obtain a

---

[1]   42 U.S.C. § 12205 (2000). Note that section 107 of the ADA, 42 U.S.C. § 12117, which sets Title I's remedies, incorporates the remedies of Title VII of the Civil Rights Act of 1964. The latter permits attorneys' fees in cases section 505 might not. See infra note 33 and accompanying text. However, courts have applied the ADA-specific statute, rather than Title VII.

[2]   The prevailing party is also entitle to costs under Federal Rule of Civil Procedure 54(d)(1). See Miles v. State, 320 F.3d 986, 988-89 (9th Cir. 2003).

[3]   Tex. St. Teachers Ass'n v. Garland Indep. Sch. Dist., 489 U.S. 782, 792 (1989).

[4]   Buckhannon Bd. & Care Home, Inc. v. W.Va. Dep't of Health & Human Res., 532 U.S. 598, 603 (2001).

judgment, but the defendant changes its practices in response to the litigation – the "catalyst" theory.

In *Buckhannon Board & Care Home, Inc. v. West Virginia Dept. of Health & Human Resources*,[5] the Supreme Court rejected, in a five to four decision, the catalyst theory. In that case, the plaintiff sued West Virginia to force it to stop imposing a requirement that assisted living facilities comply with a state law that required people in the facilities to be capable of "self-preservation" – essentially that they be able to move themselves from situations involving imminent danger, such as fire.[6] West Virginia agreed to stay enforcement of the statute and the legislature then enacted two bills eliminating the requirement.[7] West Virginia then successfully moved to dismiss the lawsuit as moot. The plaintiffs requested attorneys' fees on the theory that they were the prevailing parties because their lawsuit had "brought about a voluntary change in the defendant's conduct."[8] Because the Fourth Circuit had previously rejected the catalyst theory,[9] the District Court denied the motion.

On certiorari, the Supreme Court began its analysis with Black's Law Dictionary, which defined prevailing party as a party "in whose favor a judgment is rendered, regardless of the amount of damages awarded."[10] The Court also noted that its precedents had authorized fee shifting on the basis of a consent decree.[11] "These decisions, taken together, establish that enforceable judgments on the merits and court-ordered consent decrees create the 'material alternation of the legal relationship of the parties' necessary to permit an award of attorneys' fees."[12]

The Court believed that the catalyst theory fell outside its prior cases because there was "no judicially sanctioned change in the legal relationship of the parties."[13] Reviewing the "American rule" against fee shifting, the Court rejected an argument based upon what it termed "at best ambiguous" legislative history, which stated, "[P]arties may be

---

[5]   Id. at 598.

[6]   Id. at 600.

[7]   Id.

[8]   Id.

[9]   S-1 and S-2 v. St. Bd. of Educ. of N.C., 21 F.3d 49, 41 (4th Cir. 1994) (en banc).

[10]   Buckhannon, 532 U.S. at 604.

[11]   Id.

[12]   Id. (citing Tex. St. Teachers Ass'n, 489 U.S. at 792-93).

[13]   Id. at 605.

considered to have prevailed when they vindicate rights through a consent judgment or without formally obtaining relief."[14]

The Court also rejected, as entirely speculative, the plaintiffs' arguments that doing away with the catalyst theory would prevent people from bringing possibly meritorious lawsuits. It pointed out that the possibility of incurring catalyst-based attorneys' fees might deter defendants from altering their conduct – which also seems speculative.[15]

Finally, the Court noted that this issue only arises when money damages are not at stake and that courts retain their power to declare conduct illegal "unless it is 'absolutely clear that the alleged wrongful behavior could not reasonably be expected to recur."[16] In view of that possibility, defendants have an incentive to enter into settlement agreements that reimburse plaintiffs their attorneys' fees.[17]

The Supreme Court's rejection of the catalyst theory did not go unnoticed in Congress. In November 2002, Senators Feingold, Kennedy and Jeffords introduced S.3161, which would have expressly provided that the definition of "prevailing party" includes:

> in addition to a party who substantially prevails through a judicial or administrative judgment or order, or an enforceable written agreement, a party whose pursuit of a non-frivolous claim or defense was a catalyst for a voluntary or unilateral change in position by the opposing party that provides any significant part of the relief sought.

A series of cases in the Ninth Circuit have explored the limits of *Buckhannon* when the parties enter into a settlement agreement. In *Barrios v. California Interscholastic Federation*,[18] the plaintiff had entered into a settlement agreement with the defendant providing for the payment of $10,000 to the plaintiff and providing that the plaintiff, a wheelchair-using baseball coach, would be allowed to coach on the field, contrary to

---

[14] Id. at 607-608 (quoting S. Rep. No. 94-1011, at 5 (1976), 1976 U.S.C.C.A.N. 5908, 5912).

[15] Buckhannon, 532 U.S. at 607-08.

[16] Id. at 609 (quoting Friends of the Earth, Inc. v. Laidlaw Env't Servs. (TOC), Inc., 528 U.S. 167, 189 (2000)).

[17] Four Justices dissented in an opinion written by Justice Ginsberg. The dissent pointed out that prior to 1994, every federal circuit court had approved the catalyst theory (with the exception of the Federal Circuit, which had not considered it), that in 1994 the Fourth Circuit, in a six to five en banc decision, rejected the theory, but that following that decision, nine courts of appeal had reaffirmed their earlier approach. Id. at 626-627. The dissent went on to argue that the catalyst approach was proper.

[18] Barrios v. Cal. Interscholastic Fed'n, 277 F.3d 1128 (9th Cir. 2002).

the prior decisions of the defendant.[19] Although the Court initially had entered the settlement agreement as an order of the court, it later granted the defendant's motion to set aside its order. Accordingly, only an agreement existed between the plaintiff and the defendant. Nonetheless, the Ninth Circuit concluded that the plaintiff was a prevailing party for purposes of recovering attorneys' fees.

Under prior Ninth Circuit law,

> [A] plaintiff 'prevails' when he or she enters into a legally enforceable settlement agreement against the defendant: "[A] plaintiff 'prevails' when actual relief on the merits of his claim materially alters the legal relationship between the parties by modifying the defendant's behavior in a way that directly benefits the plaintiff." The Court explained that "a material alteration of the legal relationship occurs [when] the plaintiff becomes entitled to enforce a judgment, consent decree, or settlement against the defendant."[20]

Thus, the issue was whether there was a material change in the relationship between the parties that is enforceable by a court. The Ninth Circuit concluded that *Buckhannon* did not alter that standard, because the plaintiff in *Barrios* did not claim merely to be a catalyst, but had obtained a legally enforceable settlement.[21]

More recently, the Ninth Circuit may have implicitly limited *Barrios*. In *Richard S. v. Department of Developmental Services*,[22] the court had awarded preliminary injunctive relief in favor of the individual plaintiffs and permanent injunctive relief on a motion brought by an advocacy group as an intervener. The parties entered into a settlement agreement in open court, agreeing that its terms would be binding and enforceable as if reduced to writing.[23]

On the plaintiffs' motion for attorneys' fees, the court originally awarded fees based in part on a catalyst theory, but held that the plaintiffs were not entitled to a fee due to their preliminary injunction, which only preserved the status quo.[24] Subsequently, the Supreme Court decided *Buckhannon* and the district court reversed its prior award of attorneys' fees. In so doing, the court relied upon a footnote in *Buckhannon*, which states, "Private settlements do not entail the judicial

---

[19]   Id. at 1133.

[20]   Id. at 1134 (citing Fischer v. SJB-P.D. Inc., 214 F.3d 1115, 1118 (9th Cir. 2000) (quoting Farrar v. Hobby, 506 U.S. 103, 111-12 (1992)).

[21]   Id. at 1134 n.5.

[22]   Richard S. v. Dep't of Developmental Serv., 317 F.3d 1080 (9th Cir. 2003).

[23]   Id. at 1088.

[24]   Id.

approval and oversight involved in consent decrees."[25] The Ninth Circuit distinguished this footnote, which is itself arguably *dicta*, on the ground that the magistrate judge presiding over the settlement negotiations had issued a minute order stating that the parties had entered into a binding and enforceable settlement agreement.[26]

One might ask whether this holding cuts back on prior holdings, which did not require that the settlement agreement be entered on the record. There are several arguments why that might not be the case, assuming that the settlement agreement does result in a change in the relationship between or among the parties. First, to the extent that a settlement agreement provides that parties will change their behavior, it would appear to be enforceable by a judicial proceeding. Second, it would appear to put form over substance to require that the settlement be entered on the record. Nonetheless, the Supreme Court may indeed follow what appears to be *dicta* in *Buckhannon's* footnote 7, so it would appear best for plaintiffs who intend to seek attorneys' fees to embody any settlement agreement in a consent decree or at least a judicially enforceable order.

The *Richard S.* court also found that a preliminary injunction could constitute a basis for finding that a plaintiff was a prevailing party.[27] However, other circuits have rejected that conclusion, finding that prevailing party status may not be based upon a decision that is not on the merits of a claim.[28] In short, the limits of the Supreme Court's

---

[25] Buckhannon Bd. & Care Home, Inc. v. W.Va. Dep't of Health & Human Res., 532 U.S. 598, 604 n.7 (2001).

[26] Richard S., 317 F.3d at 1088. See also Am. Disability Ass'n v. Chmielarz, 289 F.3d 1315, 1319-20 (11th Cir. 2002) stating that:

> Thus, it is clear that, even absent the entry of a formal consent decree, if the district court either incorporates the terms of a settlement into its final order of dismissal or expressly retains jurisdiction to enforce a settlement, it may thereafter enforce the terms of the parties' agreement. Its authority to do so clearly establishes a "judicially sanctioned change in the legal relationship of the parties," as required by Buckhannon, because the plaintiff thereafter may return to court to have the settlement enforced.

Id. at 1320.

[27] Richard S., 317 F.3d at 1088-89 (citing Watson v. County of Riverside, 300 F.3d 1092, 1093 (9th Cir. 2002) and Williams v. Alioto, 625 F.2d 845, 847-48 (1980)).

[28] Christopher P. v. Marcus, 915 F.2d 794, 805 (2d Cir. 1990); Smith v. Thomas, 687 F.2d 1113, 1115 (5th Cir. 1982). Of course, neither of these cases involves the ADA.

rejection of the catalyst theory have yet to fully be explored. Of course, plaintiffs often may be entitled to attorneys' fees under the appropriate state law if their award rests on state law claims.[29]

In *Buckhannon*, the Court decided that a prevailing party is "[a] party in whose favor a judgment is rendered, regardless of the amount of damages awarded." [30] Of course, if parties recover injunctive relief, that alone suffices for attorneys' fees.[31] Nor is prevailing party status determined by the degree of success achieved, assuming there is some degree of success.[32] On the other hand, in a "mixed-motive" case, the plaintiff may show, for example, that the defendant violated the ADA in firing her, but the defendant shows it would have taken the same action in the absence of the discrimination, so the plaintiff takes only a declaratory judgment. In those cases, the plaintiff is not entitled to attorneys' fees, because she is not a prevailing party under section 12205.[33]

Under the statute, not only the plaintiff, but the defendant as well, can recover attorneys' fees. However, the courts uniformly have held that the standard for awarding attorneys' fees to defendants is higher than that for awarding them to plaintiffs. As the Seventh Circuit put it, "an award of fees to an employer is appropriate only when the suit is brought in bad faith or when it is frivolous, unreasonable, or without

---

[29] The Ninth Circuit recently certified such a question to the California Supreme Court. Tipton-Whittingham v. City of L.A., 2003 WL 141281, at *1 (9th Cir. Jan. 21, 2003) (certifying question whether California Fair Employment & Housing Act, Business & Professions Code § 12965(b) and California Code of Civil Procedure § 1021.5 permit award of attorneys' fees on catalyst basis).

[30] Buckhannon, 532 U.S. at 603 (quoting Black's Law Dictionary 1145 (7th ed. 1999)).

[31] Fischer v. SJB-P.D. Inc., 214 F.3d 1115, 1118 (9th Cir. 2000).

[32] Richard S. v. Dep't of Developmental Serv., 317 F.3d 1080, 1087 (9th Cir. 2003). Rather, the degree of success may determine the amount of attorneys' fees. Id. at 1087 n.3. However, that formula may change when the plaintiff obtains only nominal damages.

[33] Pedigo v. P.A.M. Transp., Inc., 98 F.3d 396, 398 (8th Cir. 1996) ("Pedigo II"); see also Dehne v. Med. Shoppe Int'l, Inc., 2003 WL 21107302, at *3 (E.D. Mo. Mar. 31, 2003). Section 107 of the Civil Rights Act of 1991, 42 U.S.C. § 2000e-5(g)(2)(B)(i), which should apply to ADA Title I cases, allows attorneys' fees even when only declaratory relief is awarded. Pedigo v. P.A.M. Transp., Inc., 60 F.3d 1300, 1301 (8th Cir. 1995). However, in *Pedigo II*, a later case involving the same parties, the Eighth Circuit looked to ADA section 505 and found the plaintiff had not prevailed for attorneys' fees purposes. The ADA-specific statute trumped the more general Title VII provision.

foundation."[34] This asymmetry is a result of Congress' recognition that attorneys' fees under the ADA should be "interpreted in a manner consistent with the Civil Rights Attorneys' Fees Act [42 U.S.C. § 1988], including that statute's definition of prevailing party, as construed by the Supreme Court."[35] The court is not required to award attorneys' fees to a prevailing defendant even if the action is frivolous.[36]

Generally, subjective bad faith is not required to show frivolousness, rather it is sufficient that the action objectively arguably lacks a basis in law or fact.[37] In *Schutts v. Bently Nevada Corp.*,[38] the plaintiff was fired by the defendant after the plaintiff was arrested for and eventually convicted of hitting a person with a gun and holding the gun to the person's head, threatening to "blow his brains out." Holding that the law in the Ninth Circuit and elsewhere clearly gave an employer the right to fire an employee for improper acts even if those acts arose out of an alleged disability – here depression – the Court found that the facts and "controlling federal judicial authority extent prior to the initiation of this action, should have made plain to Plaintiff and his lawyer the futility – and impropriety – of filing the complaint and of opposing Defendant's meritorious summary judgment motion."[39] On those facts, the court awarded the defendant attorneys' fees under 42 U.S.C. § 12205 – and, showing its displeasure, under Federal Rule of Civil Procedure 11.

§ 19.2 Reasonableness Of Fees

The calculation of reasonable attorneys' fees in ADA cases is the same as that in other civil rights cases. The first element is to compute a "lodestar": the number of hours reasonably expended on the litigation

---

[34] Adkins v. Briggs & Stratton Corp., 159 F.3d 306, 307 (7th Cir. 1998) (citing Christiansburg Garment Co. v. EEOC, 434 U.S. 412, 421-22 (1978) (Civil Rights Act, Title VII employment discrimination case)); see also Bercovitch v. Baldwin Sch., Inc., 191 F.3d 8, 10 (1st Cir. 1999) (citing Hughes v. Rowe, 449 U.S. 5, 14 (1980) (per curiam) (noting that the Supreme Court has applied the same rule under 42 U.S.C. § 1983).

[35] H.R.Doc. No. 101-485 (III), at 73 (1990), 1990 U.S.C.C.A.N. 445, 496 (citing Christiansburg and Hughes).

[36] Adkins, 159 F.3d at 307; see Greenier v. Pace, Local No. 1188, 245 F.Supp.2d 247, 249, 250 (D. Me. 2003) ("[T]he frivolity showing required of a prevailing party applies with 'special force' in pro se actions. *Hughes v. Rowe*, 449 U.S. 5, 14-16 ... (applying the *Christiansburg* standard to pro se plaintiffs under the fee-shifting provision 42 U.S.C. § 1988)" and refusing to award fees to defendant, "[i]n light of Plaintiff's limited ability to grasp the legal significance of his actions as well as the sanctions already imposed in this matter").

[37] Neitzke v. Williams, 490 U.S. 319, 325 (1989).

[38] Schutts v. Bently Nev. Corp., 996 F.Supp. 1549 (D. Nev. 1997).

[39] Id. at 1557.

multiplied by the reasonable hourly rate of the individuals working on the matter.[40]

The court may, of course, determine either that the number of hours spent was inappropriate[41] or that the rates are too high.[42] For example, the district court in one case found that attorneys seeking fees had not properly established the reasons for having two attorneys at depositions.[43] The courts understand that the staffing needs of a case depend upon the complexity of the case.[44] The allowable rate is the current market rate at the time the petition is made, rather than the rates throughout the period litigation.[45] Note that both pre-filing services, such as drafting pleadings, and settlement efforts may be compensable.[46]

Obviously, the district court has substantial discretion in assessing the appropriateness of fees. Counsel who anticipate seeking such fees, should carefully prepare their bills from the outset. Interestingly, often these cases involve litigation on behalf of clients to whom no bills are sent, but that should not lead to laxity in preparing statements. It is not uncommon for courts to refuse to award fees where statements are not sufficiently detailed.[47] Moreover, counsel should

---

[40] E.g., Staton v. Boeing Co., 327 F.3d 938, 964 (9th Cir. 2003); Lanni v. New Jersey, 259 F.3d 146, 148 (3d Cir. 2001); Giles v. Gen. Elec. Co., 245 F.3d 474, 490-91 (5th Cir. 2001). "A 'strong presumption' exists that the lodestar figure represents a 'reasonable fee,' and therefore, it should only be enhanced or reduced in 'rare and exceptional cases.'" Fischer v. SJB-P.D. Inc., 214 F.3d 1115, 1119 n.4 (9th Cir. 2000) (quoting Pa Valley Citizens' Council for Clean Air, 478 U.S. 546, 565 (1986) (internal quotations omitted)). But see No Barriers, Inc., v. Brinker Chili's Tex., Inc., 262 F.3d 496, 500-01 (5th Cir. 2001) (court not required to use lodestar in simple case when court familiar with work done).

[41] For example, in *Lanni*, the Third Circuit affirmed the district court's denial of fees for a second partner at a trial, where the first partner was experienced in employment law. Lanni, 259 F.3d at 151.

[42] E.g., Giles, 245 F.3d at 490-91.

[43] Greenway v. Buffalo Hilton Hotel, 951 F.Supp. 1039, 1069 (W.D.N.Y. 1997).

[44] Roland v. Cellucci, 106 F.Supp.2d 128, 135-36 (D. Mass. 2000) (case involving a large class of individuals with disabilities and a number of novel time-consuming claims entitled to greater staffing); see also N.Y. St. Ass'n. for Retarded Children, Inc. v. Carey, 711 F.2d 1136, 1146 (2d Cir. 1983).

[45] Lanni, 259 F.3d at 149-50.

[46] Brinn v. Tidewater Transp. Dist. Comm'n, 105 F.Supp.2d 500, 505 (E.D. Va. 2000); Roland, 106 F.Supp.2d at 137-39.

[47] E.g., No Barriers, Inc. v. Brinker Chili's Tex., Inc., 262 F.3d 496, 500 (5th Cir. 2001).

carefully consider the staffing of cases in these matters, as it would do in any matter where the client was scrutinizing bills.

A number of courts have approved a list of 12 factors that may be used to assess attorneys' fees:

(1) The time and labor required;
(2) The novelty and difficulty of the questions;
(3) The skill requisite to perform a legal service properly;
(4) The preclusion of employment by the attorney due to acceptance of the case;
(5) The customary fees;
(6) Whether the fee is fixed or contingent;
(7) The time limitations imposed by the client or the circumstances;
(8) The amount involved and the results obtained;
(9) The experience, reputation, and ability of the attorney;
(10) The "undesirability" of the case;
(11) The nature and length of the professional relationship with the client; and
(12) Awards in similar cases.[48]

One of the principle factors involved in assessing fees is the measure of success. For example, where a party prevails only on a fraction of its claims, the court may reduce the award to reflect services on the losing claims.[49] On the other hand, where counsel achieves a particularly good result, for example, prevailing in a complex case, the court has discretion to award more than the lodestar.[50]

An interesting situation arises where the defendant obtains only nominal damages. The Supreme Court has written, "When a plaintiff recovers only nominal damages because of his failure to prove an essential element of his claim for monetary relief, the only reasonable fee is usually no fee at all."[51] That is, the size of the award determines, not whether a party prevails, but the size of the appropriate fee. For example, in *Red*

---

[48] Hamlin v. Charter Township of Flint, 165 F.3d 426, 437 (6th Cir. 1999) (citing Hensley v. Eckerhart, 461 U.S. 424, 430 n.3 (1983)); Johnson v. Ga. Highway Express, Inc., 488 F.2d 714, 717-19 (5th Cir. 1974).

[49] Lanni, 259 F.3d at 151 (approving reduction to account for lack of success on several claims and citing Hensley). Note that fees can be awarded for work on appeals in other cases, where the appeal helped preserve the client's rights. Armstrong v. Davis, 318 F.3d 965, 970-73 (9th Cir. 2003).

[50] Daggitt v. United Food & Comm. Workers Int'l Union, Local 304A, 245 F.3d 981, 989-90 (8th Cir. 2001).

[51] Farrar v. Hobby, 506 U.S. 103, 115 (1992) (citation omitted).

Cloud-Owen v. Albany Steel, Inc.,[52] the jury awarded the plaintiff $1. The district court cited *Carroll v. Blinken*[53] that "*Pino* [*v. Locasio*,[54]] stands for the proposition that in determining the reasonableness of a fee award ..., the quantity and quality of relief obtained is a critical factor. Where the damage award is nominal or modest, the injunctive relief has no systemic effect of importance, and no substantial public interest is served, a substantial fee award cannot be justified."[55] The court declined to award the plaintiff attorneys' fees. On the other hand, it also declined to award the defendant attorneys' fees, holding that "where evidence is introduced that, if credited, would suffice to support a judgment, fees are unjustified"[56] and there was such evidence, so it was inappropriate to award fees to the defendant.[57]

*   *   *

§ 19.3 A Note On The Taxability Of Attorneys' Fee Awards

Tax law is beyond the general scope of this treatise, but is touched upon infra in Part 10. However, taxes permeate everything, so it is important to bear them in mind when settling litigation.

Compensatory damages in ADA litigation generally will be taxable. To the extent a settlement is for back pay or front pay, it would not be excludable from income under section 104 of the Internal Revenue Code.[58] To the extent the settlement or award is for emotional distress and other forms of compensatory damages, unless it flows directly from personal injury or illness, it is not excludable, because it does not constitute personal injury under section 104(a)(2).[59] Finally, all punitive damages are taxable.[60]

---

[52] Red Cloud-Owen v. Albany Steel, Inc., 958 F.Supp. 94 (N.D.N.Y. 1997).

[53] Carroll v. Blinken, 105 F.3d 79, 81 (2d Cir. 1997); see also Flowers v. S. Reg'l Physicians Servs., Inc., 286 F.3d 798, 801-02 (5th Cir. 2002) (nominal award supports nominal $ 1 attorney's fee).

[54] Pino v. Locasio, 101 F.3d 235, 237 (2d Cir. 1996).

[55] Red Cloud-Owen, 958 F.Supp. at 96.

[56] Am. Fed'n of St., County & Mun. Employees v. County of Nassau, 96 F.3d 644, 652 (2d Cir. 1996).

[57] Red Cloud-Owen, 958 F.Supp. at 98.

[58] Comm'r of Internal Revenue v. Schleier, 515 U.S. 323, 328-32 (1995) (finding damages under ADEA to be taxable, since ADEA allows only lost pay and liquidated damages).

[59] Banaitis v. Comm'r of Internal Revenue, 2003 WL 22016822, at *6 (9th Cir. Aug. 27, 2003).

[60] O'Gilvie v. United States, 519 U.S. 79, 84-89 (1996).

The treatment of attorneys' fees is problematic.[61] The nature of a settlement for tax purposes depends upon the "nature and basis of the action settled, and amounts received in compromise of a claim must be considered as having the same nature as the right compromised."[62] Thus, in employment discrimination cases, where virtually all of the settlement will be taxable, courts that view the attorneys' fees portion of the settlement as income to the plaintiff, view the attorneys' fees as income as well.[63]

The taxability may, however, depend on the way state law treats such fees. Where state law treats them as property of the plaintiff, they are taxable.[64] Some courts have held that, where state law gives the attorney a lien or other right to a portion of the settlement, the fees are not income to the plaintiff, and thus not taxable.[65] However, many courts refuse to defer to state-law characterizations of the property interest in the part of the settlement or judgment that represents the fee.[66] In one

---

[61] To see just how problematic, see Jalali v. Root, 109 Cal.App.4th 1768, 1773 (2003) (client who received settlement in racial discrimination and sexual harassment case sued attorney for giving bad tax advice in relation to settlement).

[62] Alexander v. Internal Revenue Serv., 72 F.3d 938, 942 (1st Cir. 1995).

[63] It may, of course, be possible to allocate attorneys' fees to parts of a settlement that are not taxable, if such exist. In that event, the proponent of the fee allocation must prove that allocation. Although such evidence as attorneys' timesheets will be permitted, courts need not allocate pro rata based on the amounts of the settlement. Id. at 940.

[64] E.g., Sinyard v. Comm'r, 268 F.3d 756, 758-59 (9th Cir. 2001) (California law; ADEA claim); Benci-Woodward v. Comm'r, 219 F.3d 941, 943-44 (9th Cir. 2000) (California law; attorneys' fees portion of punitive damage award); Coady v. Comm'r, 213 F.3d 1187, 1190-91) (9th Cir. 2000) (Alaska law; wrongful termination).

[65] The first such case was *Cotnam v. Commissioner*, 263 F.2d 119, 125-26 (5th Cir. 1959) (Alabama law). See also Banaitis v. Comm'r of Internal Revenue, 2003 WL 22016822, at *6-*8 (9th Cir. Aug. 27, 2003) (California law); Foster v. United States, 249 F.3d 1275, 1279-80 (11th Cir. 2001) (extending Cotnam's holding to entire Eleventh Circuit); Srivastava v. Comm'r, 220 F.3d 353, 364-65 (5th Cir. 2000) (Texas law); Davis v. Comm'r, 210 F.3d 1346, 1347-48 (11th Cir. 2000) (Alabama law); Estate of Clarks v. United States, 202 F.3d 854, 856-58 (6th Cir. 2000) (Michigan law).

[66] Young v. Comm'r, 240 F.3d 369, 377-79 (4th Cir. 2001) (property dispute between former spouses; rejecting theory that state law controls and finding North Carolina law differs from Alabama law relied on in Cotnam); Kenseth v. Comm'r, 259 F.3d 881, 884-85 (7th Cir. 2001) (ADEA case; rejecting theory that contingent nature of fee rendered it not income); Campbell v. Comm'r, 274 F.3d 1312, 1313-14 (10th Cir. 2001)

case in which the state's law gave the taxpayer's attorney a lien on the recovery it still did not suffice to permit the plaintiff to net the attorneys' fees.[67]

If taxpayers have to take the attorneys' fees part of the award into their gross income, some might argue that they should be able to treat the inevitable "payment" to the attorney as a trade or business expense.[68] However, courts have rejected this approach. The attorneys' fees must be treated as a "miscellaneous itemized deduction" under Section 63 of the Internal Revenue Code.[69] This means that the deduction is taken "below the line," and is subject to a two percent minimum. Moreover, miscellaneous itemized deductions are subject to the alternative minimum tax – which may be even more problematic for many taxpayers.[70] In that computation, miscellaneous itemized deductions are not allowed.[71]

Thus, a person settling an ADA case and receiving substantial attorneys' fees indeed may wind up paying taxes on those fees. Some commentators have argued that, as a policy matter, that result undermines the statutes that provide attorneys' fees and promote the concept of a "private attorney general," by taking away a substantial part of the benefit.[72] The courts, however, are split, and the ones imposing the taxes point out that there is no injustice in treating a civil rights plaintiff differently financially than other similarly situated individuals.[73]

(Title VII case; rejecting theory that state law controls and finding, if it did, Missouri law does not give a lien, as do Alabama and Michigan statutes); O'Brien v. Comm'r, 319 F.2d 532 (3d Cir.1963), aff'g, 38 Tax Ct. 707, 711 (1962) (wrongful discharge case; refusing to apply Pennsylvania law).

[67] Baylin v. United States, 43 F.3d 1451, 1454 (Fed.Cir.1995).

[68] See 26 U.S.C. § 162(a) (2000).

[69] See Alexander v. Internal Revenue Serv., 72 F.3d 938, 944-46 (1st Cir. 1995).

[70] 26 U.S.C. §§ 55-57.

[71] Id. § 56(b)(1)(A)(i); Alexander, 72 F.3d at 946-74; Benci-Woodward v. Comm'r, 219 F.3d 941, 944 (9th Cir. 2000); Kenseth v. Comm'r, 114 T.C. 399 (2000), aff'd, 259 F.3d 881 (7th Cir. 2001). Thus, the taxpayer would get no benefit from the deduction.

[72] See Lara Sager & Stephen Cohen, How the Income Tax Undermines Civil Rights Law, 73 S. Cal. L. Rev. 1075, 1101 (2000).

[73] Alexander, 72 F.3d at 946.

Chapter 20 ALTERNATIVE DISPUTE RESOLUTION

§ 20.1 Mediation Of Disability Rights Disputes

The ADA encourages alternative dispute resolution as a way to resolve ADA claims. Section 513 of the Act[1] reads as follows:

> Where appropriate and to the extent authorized by law, the use of alternative means of dispute resolution, including settlement negotiations, conciliation, facilitation, mediation, fact-finding, mini-trials, and arbitration, is encouraged to resolve disputes under this Act.

Mediation is a voluntary procedure in which the parties to a dispute meet with a third party, typically an individual trained in assisting people to resolve their disputes. The third party has no power to impose a resolution on the individuals. However, at the conclusion of the mediation, the parties may enter into a settlement agreement that is binding. In carrying out their obligations under the Act, the EEOC and the Department of Justice have established mediation programs. The EEOC's program deals with employment disputes under Title I,[2] while the Justice Department's program addresses disputes under Titles II and III.[3]

The EEOC's mediation program applies, not just to the ADA, but also to Title VII of the Civil Rights Act of 1964, the Age Discrimination In Employment Act, and the Equal Pay Act.[4] The EEOC offers mediation to parties when a charge is filed. During the time the dispute is in mediation, the charge is not processed by the EEOC. If the EEOC has decided that the charge is without merit, it is not eligible for mediation. The EEOC maintains a staff of personnel, attorneys and non-attorneys, who have received training in mediation. Alternatively, the parties to the dispute may request a mediator outside the EEOC's structure. The process is confidential and is without charge to the parties. In 2000, the EEOC spent approximately $13 million on its mediation program.[5]

The Department of Justice's mediation program is limited to claims under Titles II and III of the ADA. The DOJ established its

---

[1]   42 U.S.C. § 12212 (2000).

[2]   See generally Equal Emp. Opportunity Comm'n, Mediation, http://www.eeoc.gov/mediate/index.html (last visited Aug. 15, 2003).

[3]   See generally U.S. Dep't of Justice, ADA Mediation Program, http://www.usdoj.gov/crt/ada/mediate.htm (last visited Aug. 15, 2003).

[4]   In addition to the language in specific statutes, the EEOC's program rests on the Administrative Dispute Resolution Act, 5 U.S.C. §§ 571-84 (2000).

[5]   Equal Emp. Opportunity Comm'n, History of EEOC Mediation Program, http://www.eeoc.gov/mediate/history.html (last visited Aug. 15, 2003).

program in 1994. Unlike the EEOC, the DOJ has completely outsourced its program to the Key Bridge Foundation.[6] According to its webpage, as of September 2002, the Key Bridge Foundation had handled nearly a thousand ADA complaints, resolving the majority successfully. Like the EEOC's program, the Justice Department's program is free and confidential.

As demonstrated in the examples of cases listed on the Department of Justice's ADA Mediation site,[7] where parties to the dispute are willing to compromise, and in particular where the potential defendant has at least some recognition that its actions have not fully conformed to statutory requirements, mediation can be a useful tool in resolving disputes.[8] It is less likely to be successful where there is a substantial amount of money at stake or one of the parties has an entrenched position. In addition, the quality of the mediator and the mediator's perceived independence obviously impacts on the process.

§ 20.2 Arbitration Of Disability Rights Disputes

Unlike mediation, arbitration results in a holding that binds the parties. Agreeing to arbitrate means giving up the right to a trial, and in particular a jury trial. In theory, the benefit of the agreement for potential (or actual) claimants is the speed of the process compared to a judicial resolution. The advantages for potential (or actual) defendants lie in the relative inexpensiveness and the avoidance of a jury. Arbitration awards may or may not be appealable, depending on the arbitration agreement, but where they are, the appellate review is generally quite limited.[9] Parties must agree to arbitrate their disputes, although they can do so in advance, before the dispute has arisen, or after it has arisen. Often the "agreement" is a clause in a more comprehensive document, such as an employment contract.

The core issue in any dispute over the applicability of an arbitration provision is whether a party to it effectively has waived her right to a jury trial, which would otherwise be available in any action for

---

[6] See Key Bridge Found., Center for Mediation, http://www.keybridge.org (last visited Aug. 15, 2003).

[7] See ADA Mediation Program, supra note 3.

[8] In 2001, the EEOC published a study that showed a 60% resolution rate. E. Patrick McDermott, et al., Equal Emp. Opportunity Comm'n, The EEOC Mediation Program: Mediators' Perspective on the Parties, Processes, and Outcomes, http://www.eeoc.gov/mediate/mcdfinal.html#IV (2001).

[9] Gilmer v. Interstate/Johnson Lane Corp., 500 U.S. 20, 32 n.4 (1991) (noting that judicial review of arbitration awards "'is sufficient to ensure that arbitrators comply with the requirements of the statute' at issue") (citation omitted).

damages. The arbitration of ADA disputes and, more generally, the arbitration of disputes under civil rights statutes, is, unlike the mediation of such disputes, a matter of some contention. Many parties, of course, elect to submit to binding arbitration, but problems arise where one party – an employer or a service provider – attempts to impose arbitration on the other party via the employment or service contract. Plaintiffs often object to mandatory arbitration clauses because of the perceived bias of arbitrators in favor of defendants, who are the repeat-users of their services.

Situations in which arbitration is part of a more comprehensive agreement pose a number of questions:

- Is arbitration even permissible for civil rights disputes?

- If it is permissible, does the particular arbitration clause cover the dispute?

- If the clause covers the dispute, is the arbitration procedure "effective"; i.e., is it fair?[10]

A. *Arbitrability Of ADA Disputes*

The backdrop of questions of arbitrability is the Federal Arbitration Act.[11] "Relying upon the federal policy favoring arbitration embodied in the Federal Arbitration Act (FAA), 9 U.S.C. § 1 et seq., [the Supreme Court] said that 'statutory claims may be the subject of an arbitration agreement, enforceable pursuant to the FAA.'"[12] The Supreme Court, however, has created its own level of confusion in this area.

In *Alexander v. Gardner-Denver Co.*[13] (*Gardner-Denver*), the Court held that an employee "does not forfeit his right to a judicial forum for claimed discriminatory discharge in violation of Title VII of the Civil Rights Act of 1964 ... if 'he first pursues his grievance through final

---

[10] Many states have their own analogues to the ADA and other civil rights statutes. Those states may, of course, authorize or reject arbitration of disputes under their civil rights statutes independently of what the federal government does under its statutes. See Armandariz v. Found. Psychcare Servs., Inc., 24 Cal.4th 83 (Cal. 2000).

[11] 9 U.S.C. § 1 et seq. (2000).

[12] Gilmer, 500 U.S. at 26. Similarly, arbitration agreements have been enforceable under the Sherman Act, the Racketeer Influenced and Corrupt Organizations Act (RICO), the Securities Exchange Act of 1934, and the Securities Act of 1933. Id. (citing e.g. Shearson/Am. Express, Inc. v. McMahon, 482 U.S. 220 (1987) (holding Securities Exchange Act and RICO claims arbitrable); Mitsubishi Motors Corp. v. Soler Chrysler-Plymouth, Inc., 473 U.S. 614 (1985) (arbitration in an antitrust action in part under the Sherman Act).

[13] Alexander v. Gardner-Denver Co., 415 U.S. 36 (1974).

arbitration under the non-discrimination clause of the collective bargaining agreement.'"[14] The notion is that the rights under the employee's collective bargaining agreement are separate from the employee's statutory rights under Title VII and "there can be no prospective waiver of an employee's rights under Title VII.[15]

On the other hand, in *Gilmer v. Interstate/Johnson Lane Corp.* the Supreme Court held that a claim under the Age Discrimination in Employment Act[16] (ADEA) could be the subject of a compulsory arbitration agreement in the standard U-4 Form used by the securities industry.[17] In *Mitsubishi Motors Corp.*, the Court had held that if the "parties' agreement to arbitrate reached the statutory issues," the court had to decide "whether legal constraints external to the parties' agreement foreclosed the arbitration of those claims."[18] The court could look to the text, the legislative history and the policy of the statute. The plaintiff in *Gilmer* argued that the FAA did not permit arbitration of a civil rights claim. The Court rejected that argument. It held that the party opposing arbitration has the burden of showing the words of the agreement are foreclosed.[19] It found that neither the language of the ADEA, which does not mention arbitration, nor its history precluded arbitration.[20] Nor was

---

[14] Wright v. Universal Mar. Serv. Corp., 525 U.S. 70, 75-76 (1998) (quoting Gardner-Denver, 415 U.S. at 49).

[15] Gardner-Denver, 415 U.S. at 51. Both before and after *Wright*, Courts have taken the position that statutory rights could not be waived in collective bargaining agreements. See, e.g., Rogers v. N.Y. Univ., 220 F.3d 73, 75 (2d Cir. 2000) (following Gardner-Denver, in finding that CBA could not waive the right to judicial forum for federal statutory claims); Pryner v. Tractor Supply Co., 109 F.3rd, 354, 363 (7th Cir. 1997); Wilmington v. J.I. Case Co., 793 F.2d 909, 918 (8th Cir. 1986) (§ 1981 claims independent of claims covered by CBA); Fowler v. Colfax Envelope Corp., 2002 WL 1676568, at *2-*3 (N.D. Ill. July 23, 2002) (CBA could not waive an ADEA claim); Scheiner v. N.Y. City Health & Hosp., 152 F.Supp.2d 487, 498-99 (S.D.N.Y. 2001) (CBA could not waive federal judicial forum for 42 U.S.C. § 1983 claim). But see Austin v. Owens-Brockway Glass Container, Inc., 78 F.3d 875, 880-82 (4th Cir. 1996) (employees can be compelled to submit ADA and Title VII claims to binding arbitration pursuant to collective bargaining agreement).

[16] 29 U.S.C. § 621, et seq. (2000).

[17] Gilmer, 500 U.S. at 26.

[18] Mitsubishi Motors Corp. v. Soler Chrysler-Plymouth, Inc., 473 U.S. 614, 628 (1985).

[19] Gilmer, 500 U.S. at 26.

[20] Id. at 27-30.

there any "inherent conflict" between arbitration and the statutory goals, since an arbitral panel was competent to provide all legal remedies.[21]

With some understatement, the Court has recognized that, "there is obviously some tension between these two lines of cases."[22] Although in *Wright*, various parties and amici suggested ways of resolving the two lines of cases, the Court found it did not need to do so in view of the contractual language in the case before it.[23] Nonetheless, circuit courts must plow on.

The courts of appeal that have considered whether ADA claims may be subject to a compulsory arbitration regime, have found that they can, at least where there is an individualized agreement.[24] They follow

---

[21] Id. at 32.

[22] Wright v. Universal Mar. Serv. Corp., 525 U.S. 70, 76 (1998).

[23] Certain parties advocated permitting individually executed (the U-4 is not individually negotiated) agreements prospectively to waive the right to a judicial proceeding, but not permitting collective bargaining agreements or, presumably, other collectively negotiated agreements to do so. On the other side, certain amici argued that the attitude toward arbitration had evolved to such an extent that all agreements could validly require compulsory arbitration.

[24] See Bercovitch v. Baldwin Sch., Inc., 133 F.3d 141, 148-51 (1st Cir. 1998) (ADA does not preclude waiver of the judicial forum in parents' agreement with private school); Miller v. Pub. Storage Mgmt., Inc., 121 F.2d 215, 218 (5th Cir. 1997) ("Congress did not intend to exclude the ADA from the scope of the FAA"); cf. Gibson v. Neighborhood Health Clinics, Inc., 121 F.3d 1126, 1130 (7th Cir. 1997) ("the parties agree that an employee and employer may contractually agree to submit federal claims, including Title VII and ADA to arbitration," citing Gilmer, 500 U.S. at 35). In addition, most Courts that have considered the issue have found that Title VII and ADEA claims are also arbitrable. E.g., Gilmer, 500 U.S. at 35 (ADEA Claim); Borg-Warner Protective Servs. Corp. v. EEOC, 245 F.3d 831, 834-36 (D.C. Cir. 2001) (dictum: Title VII dispute subject to arbitration); Desiderio v. Nat'l Ass'n of Sec. Dealers, Inc., 191 F.3d 198, 206 (2d Cir. 1999) (Title VII dispute subject to arbitration); Koveleskie v. SBC Capital Markets, Inc., 167 F.3d 361, 365 (7th Cir. 1999) (same); Rosenberg v. Merrill Lynch, Pierce, Fenner & Smith, Inc., 163 F.3d 1, 21 (1st Cir. 1998) (holding that "there was no congressional intent to preclude pre-dispute arbitration agreements manifested in the [Civil Rights Act of 1991]" but finding enforcement of the agreement inappropriate on facts of the case); Seus v. John Nuveen & Co., 146 F.3d 175, 182 (3d Cir. 1998) (Title VII dispute subject to arbitration) "), abrogated on other grounds by Blair v. Scott Specialty Gases, 283 F.3d 595, 599-602 (3d Cir. 2002); Cole v. Burns Int'l Security Servs., 105 F.3d 1465, 1482 (D.C. Cir. 1997) (same); Patterson v. Tenet Healthcare, Inc., 113 F.3d 832, 837 (8th Cir. 1997) (Title VII claims arbitrable under the FAA); Austin v. Owens-Brockway

Gilmer, but go farther, since, unlike the ADEA, the ADA expressly encourages arbitration in section 513.[25]

Section 118 of the Civil Rights Act of 1991 included language identical to section 513.[26] The statute was enacted after *Gilmer*. Courts have reasoned that Congress had *Gilmer* in mind when enacting section 118 and used that as an additional reason to find Title VII disputes arbitrable.[27]

For several years, the Ninth Circuit bucked the trend. In 1998, in *Duffield v. Robertson Stephans & Co.*,[28] the Ninth Circuit construed section 118 to preclude arbitration of Title VII claims in individually executed employment agreements. The court first found that the statutory language – "where appropriate and to the extent authorized by law" – was ambiguous; it therefore looked to the legislative history.[29]

The court began by noting that the two primary goals of the Civil Rights Act of 1991 were to "'restore ... civil rights laws' by 'overruling' a series of 1989 Supreme Court decisions that Congress believed narrowed

---

Glass Container, Inc., 78 F.3d 875, 881-82 (4th Cir. 1996) (Title VII claims arbitrable under a collective bargaining agreement); Metz v. Merrill Lynch, Pierce, Fenner & Smith, Inc., 39 F.3d 1482, 1487 (10th Cir. 1994) (Title VII claims arbitrable); Bender v. A.G. Edwards & Sons, Inc., 971 F.2d 698, 699 (11th Cir. 1992) (per curiam) (Title VII claims are subject to securities industry compulsory arbitration); Alford v. Dean Witter Reynolds, Inc. 939 F.2d 229, 230 (5th Cir. 1991) (same); cf. Willis v. Dean Witter Reynolds, Inc., 948 F.2d 305, 307 (6th Cir. 1991) (under Gilmer, an arbitration agreement in securities registration is enforceable with respect to Title VII claims, but noting that it is not an employment contract).

[25] 42 U.S.C. § 12212 (2000) ("Where appropriate and to the extent authorized by law, the use of alternative means of dispute resolution, including ... arbitration, is encouraged to resolve disputes arising under this chapter."); see Bercovich v. Baldwin Sch., Inc., 133 F.3d 141, 150 (1st Cir. 1998):

> If this language were not interpreted to permit prospective waiver of a judicial forum, it would be superfluous. Litigants are always permitted to resolve their disputes extrajudicially, with or without statutory language authorizing such action. This language adds nothing if it does not mean that litigants can anticipatorily waive a judicial forum for ADA claims.

[26] Pub.L. No. 102-166, § 118, 105 Stat. 1071 (codified at Notes to 42 U.S.C. § 1981).

[27] See cases supra note 24.

[28] Duffield v. Robertson Stephans & Co., 144 F.3d 1182 (9th Cir. 1998).

[29] Id. at 1193.

Title VII and (to) 'strengthen' Title VII by making it easier to bring and prove lawsuits."[30] The Ninth Circuit also noted that section 118 of the 1991 Civil Rights Act "track[ed] almost verbatim" section 513 of the ADA, whose legislative history "indicat[ed] that Congress intended to codify in the ADA the protections of the Court's holding in *Gardner-Denver*."[31] In particular, it cited the ADA's legislative history, which states that, "it is the intent of the conferees that the use of these alternative dispute resolution procedures is completely voluntary."[32]

At the point the ADA and the 1991 Civil Rights Act provisions were adopted, the Supreme Court had decided *Gardner-Denver*, which precluded provisions in collective bargaining agreements that required arbitrations of Title VII claims. It had not decided *Gilmer*, which permitted such clauses in individually negotiated claims. In view of *Gardner-Denver*, the Ninth Circuit believed that Congress understood that waiver of judicial fora in arbitration agreements was not "authorized by law."[33] Building on that, the court wrote, "it seems far more plausible that Congress meant to encourage *voluntary* agreements to arbitrate — agreements such as those that employers and employees enter into after a dispute has arisen because *both* parties consider arbitration to be a more satisfactory or expeditious method of resolving a disagreement."[34] The court then engaged in a detailed examination of the legislative history and determined that the U-4 agreement was unenforceable and that Congress intended only to permit arbitration agreements that are entered into voluntarily after a dispute has arisen.[35]

The *Duffield* analysis would apply to ADA claims. *Duffield*, however, has been overruled by the Ninth Circuit en banc.[36] In *Luce, Forward*, the EEOC brought a case on behalf of a person conditionally hired as a legal secretary at a law firm, who refused to execute an employment agreement that would have had the effect of waiving his right to sue for violations of federal anti-employment discrimination law. The *Luce, Forward* panel began by noting that section 118 of the Civil Rights Act of 1991 was passed against a backdrop of *Gilmer*.[37] Writing that the

---

[30] Id. at 1191.

[31] Duffield, 144 F.3d at 1192 n.10.

[32] H.R. Conf. Rep. No. 101-596, at 89 (1990), reprinted in 1990 U.S.C.C.A.N. 565, 598.

[33] Duffield, 144 F.3d at 1199.

[34] Id. at 1193.

[35] Id. at 1193-1200.

[36] EEOC v. Luce, Forward, Hamilton & Scripps, 2003 WL 22251382 (9th Cir. Sept. 30, 2003)) (en banc) ("Luce, Forward"). Three judges dissented. Id. at *9.

[37] EEOC v. Luce, Forward, Hamilton, & Scripps, 303 F.3d 994, 999 (9th Cir. 2002).

"Supreme Court's language and reasoning decimated *Duffield's* conclusion that Congress intended to preclude compulsory arbitration of Title VII claims,"[38] the *Luce, Forward* panel announced the death of *Duffield.*[39] Interestingly, the argument based on *Gilmer* does not apply to the ADA, which was enacted before the Supreme Court's *Gilmer* decision, but the court did not address that point.

The Ninth Circuit granted a petition for en banc review, thus vacating *Luce, Forward I* and leaving *Duffield* intact.[40] It then affirmed the panel's decision and overruled *Duffield.*[41] It found that the purpose of the Act was to encourage arbitration, that the language not only did not preclude pre-employment arbitration agreements, but promoted them and that the legislative history, while suggesting that Congress intended to retain a judicial forum, could be ignored, since the statutory language was unambiguous.[42]

In sum, most civil rights claims, including ADA claims, may be arbitrated. Still, despite the breadth of courts' language, courts have not fully addressed the arbitrability of ADA claims. In the first place, as noted, the ADA preceded *Gilmer*. In the second place, the ADA's legislative history indicates an intent to retain existing remedies. The House Judiciary Committee Report, incorporated into the House Conference Report stated:

> The Committee wishes to emphasize, however, that the use of alternative dispute resolution mechanisms is intended to supplement, not supplant, the remedies provided by this Act. Thus, for example, the Committee believes that any agreement to submit disputed issues to arbitration, whether in the context of a collective bargaining agreement or in an employment contract, does not preclude the affected person from seeking relief under the enforcement provisions of this Act. This view is consistent with the Supreme Court's interpretation of title VII of the Civil Rights Act of 1964, whose remedial provisions are incorporated by reference in title I. The Committee believes that the approach articulated by the Supreme Court in Alexander v. Gardner-Denver Co. applies equally to the ADA and does not intend that the inclusion of Section 513 [the ADA arbitration section] be used to preclude rights and

---

[38] Id. at 1002-03.

[39] Id. at 1003-04. One judge dissented. Id. at 1008 (Pregerson, J. dissenting).

[40] EEOC v. Luce, Forward, Hamilton & Scripps, 319 F.3d 1091 (9th Cir. 2003) (en banc).

[41] Luce, Forward, 2003 WL 22251382, at *9.

[42] Id. at *6-*9.

remedies that would otherwise be available to persons with disabilities.[43]

Bercovitch held that this language does not overcome the presumption in favor of arbitration and is designed to prevent arbitration when the complainant is not aware of the clause.[44]

B.   *Scope Of The Arbitration Clause*

The trend in the cases appears to accept arbitration agreements as appropriate, at least where they are between an individual and an employer or a service provider. Still, there must, in fact, be an agreement to arbitrate the specific dispute.

In *Wright v. Universal Maritime Service Corp.*,[45] the Supreme Court considered an arbitration provision in a collective bargaining agreement, which provided "matters under dispute" shall be submitted to a grievance proceeding and, if that fails, to arbitration. Recognizing, as noted above, the tension between *Gilmer* and *Gardner-Denver*, and leaving open the question of whether the latter survived in its full force, the Court found that the arbitration agreement did not cover an ADA dispute.

It began by noting the presumption of arbitrability under the Labor Management Relations Act, 29 U.S.C. Section 185.[46] "That presumption, however, does not extend beyond the reach of the principal rationale that justifies it, that arbitrators are in a better position than courts *to interpret the terms of a CBA [collective bargaining agreement].*"[47] The Court went on: "This rationale finds support in the very text of the LMRA, which announces '[f]inal adjustments by a method agreed upon by the parties is declared to be the desirable method for settlement of grievance disputes arising *over the application or interpretation* of an existing collective bargaining agreement.'"[48] The Court noted that the dispute before it involved the interpretation of a Federal statute, not the CBA, which "is distinct from any right conferred by the collective-bargaining agreement."[49] Although the contract stated that it was not intended to be violative of any state or Federal law, it did not specifically

---

[43]   H.R. Rep. No. 101-485 (III) (1990), reprinted in 1990 U.S.C.C.A.N. 445, 499 (footnote omitted); see also H.R. Rep. No. 101-596 (1990), reprinted in 1990 U.S.C.C.A.N. 445, 598.

[44]   Bercovitch v. Baldwin Sch., Inc., 133 F.3d 141, 150 (1st Cir. 1998)

[45]   Wright v. Universal Mar. Serv. Corp., 525 U.S. 70 (1998).

[46]   See generally United Steelworkers of Am. v. Enter. Wheel & Car Corp., 363 U.S. 593 (1960); United Steelworkers of Am. v. Am. Mfg. Co., 363 U.S. 564 (1960); United Steelworkers of Am. v. Warrior & Gulf Nav. Co., 363 U.S. 574, 582 (1960).

[47]   Wright, 525 U.S. at 78.

[48]   Id. (quoting 29 U.S.C. 173(d) (emphasis added)).

[49]   Id.

incorporate the ADA, so the Court refused to presume that the arbitrator's authority extended to interpretations of the ADA.[50] The Court held that "any CBA requirement to arbitrate [a statutory claim] must be 'explicitly stated.' More succinctly, the waiver must be clear and unmistakable."[51]

The Court focused on the particular context of the agreement. This was not a contract in which the individual had waived his own rights, but was a collective bargaining agreement that purported to waive union members' statutory claims. Unlike the CBAs in *Austin*[52] and *Gardner-Denver*,[53] this agreement contained no explicit anti-discrimination provisions of its own.[54] Finally, the Court rejected an attempt to use section 513 of the ADA to find that the agreement was an enforceable arbitration provision. It noted, "[A]bsent a clear waiver, it is not 'appropriate' within the meaning of this provision of the ADA, to find an agreement to arbitrate."[55]

Notably, *Wright* did not hold that no arbitration provision in a CBA purporting to cover the ADA is enforceable. Presumably, employers will attempt to write agreements that explicitly incorporate the ADA. In that event, there may be no need for a presumption that the agreement reaches to the ADA.[56]

Individuals can prosecute their own claims or can have the EEOC or Justice Department prosecute their claims for them. In the latter case, if there is an arbitration agreement between the claimant and the respondent, that agreement does not bind the EEOC or the Justice Department, as the case may be.

In *EEOC v. Waffle House, Inc.*,[57] the Supreme Court held that the EEOC, which was not a party to the arbitration agreement between the employee and the employer, was not bound by that arbitration agreement. Accordingly, the EEOC could seek relief, including victim specific relief, such as back pay, reinstatement or damages, in an ADA enforcement action against the employer.[58] According to the Court, when the agency

---

50   Id.

51   Id. (quoting Metro. Edison Co. v. NLRB, 460 U.S. 693, 708 (1983)).

52   Austin v. Owens-Brockway Glass Container, Inc., 78 F.3d 875 (4th Cir. 1996).

53   Alexander v. Gardner-Denver Co., 415 U.S. 36 (1974).

54   Wright, 525 U.S. at 81.

55   Id. at 82 n.2

56   Courts have interpreted Wright to be limited to collective bargaining agreements. See, e.g., Williams v. Imhoff, 203 F.3d 758, 763-64 (10th Cir. 2000) (U-4 Form properly provided for arbitrability); Kindred v. Second Judicial Dist. Ct., 996 P.2d 903, 908 n.4 (Nev. 2000) (same).

57   EEOC v. Waffle House, Inc., 534 U.S. 279 (2002).

58   Id. at 294-98.

seeks victim-specific relief, it may be vindicating the public interest and, therefore, should not be limited in the type of relief it may seek.

C. *Enforceability Of The Arbitration Agreement: Procedural And Substantive Unconscionability*

Although most courts have found that there is no statutory impediment to employers requiring employees to arbitrate ADA disputes, rather than take those disputes to court, courts still may police the fairness of the arbitration proceedings themselves.[59] Arbitration agreements are interpreted pursuant to the FAA, but are to be treated on an "equal footing with other contracts,"[60] so generally applicable state law governs the formation of the agreement.[61] While states differ, many follow the themes discussed here. If an agreement is "unfair" or unconscionable in ways that we will discuss, courts may refuse to enforce it, in whole or in part.

---

[59] Virtually all ADA-based arbitration disputes arise in the employment context.

[60] Waffle House, Inc., 534 U.S. at 293.

[61] First Options of Chicago, Inc. v. Kaplan, 514 U.S. 938, 943-44 (1995); Morrison v. Circuit City Stores, Inc., 317 F.3d 646, 666 (6th Cir. 2003). "Thus, generally applicable contract defenses, such as fraud, duress, or unconscionability, may be applied to invalidate arbitration agreements without contravening the FAA." Doctor's Assocs., Inc. v. Casarotto, 517 U.S. 681, 687 (1996), quoted in Posadas v. Pool Depot, Inc., 2003 WL 21480587, at *1 (La. App. June 27, 2003) (arbitration agreement unenforceable because print too small and relative positions of buyer and seller made enforcement unreasonable). State courts have, in a number of cases, established criteria for the propriety of arbitration agreements. Relying on Cole v. Burns Int'l Security Servs., 105 F.3d 1465 (D.C. Cir. 1997), the California Supreme Court adopted a five part test for the

> minimum requirements for the lawful arbitration of [civil] rights [disputes] pursuant to a mandatory employment arbitration agreement. Such an arbitration agreement is lawful if it "(1) provides for neutral arbitrators, (2) provides for more than minimal discoveries, (3) requires a written award, (4) provides for all of the types of relief that would otherwise be available in court, and (5) does not require employees to pay either unreasonable costs or any arbitrator's fees or expenses as a condition to the arbitration forum."

Armendariz v. Found. Psychcare Servs., Inc., 6 P.3d 669, 682 (Cal. 2000) (quoting Cole, 105 F.3d at 1482).

1.   Unconscionability

There are two aspects of fairness: procedural and substantive unconscionability, both of which must be present to justify refusing to enforce an arbitration clause. However, they need not always be present to the same degree. The California Supreme Court has established a sliding scale – the more substantively unconscionable a contract is, the less significant the procedural unconscionability may be.[62]

The explanations of procedural unconscionability vary. Some courts look to whether particular facts pertaining to a specific employee establish that there was no meeting of the minds.[63] Others look to the adhesive nature of the contract – the ability of the stronger party to impose it on the weaker.[64] The distinction can be dispositive. Since, in most employment settings, the employer has significant bargaining power, many employment contracts will prove adhesive and unconscionable under that test. Thus, in *Little v. Auto Steigler, Inc.*, the California Supreme Court found an arbitration agreement adhesive without any discussion of the employee's ability to bargain. On the other hand, in *Morrison v. Circuit City Stores, Inc.*, the Sixth Circuit, relying on Ohio law, in which the meeting of the minds was determinative,[65] found that an arbitration agreement between Circuit City, a major retailing chain, and an employee was not procedurally unconscionable, where the employee was a graduate of the Air Force Academy with a masters degree in administration, the language was plain and the plaintiff had three days to withdraw her consent.[66]

---

[62]   Armendariz, 6 P.3d at 690.

[63]   E.g., Morrison, 317 F.2d at 666 (citing Jeffrey Mining Prods., L.P. v. Left Fork Mining Co., 758 N.E.2d 1173, 1181 (Ohio Ct. App. 2001) (Ohio law)).

[64]   Little v. Auto Steigler, Inc., 29 Cal.4th 1064, 1071 (Cal. 2003).

[65]   Quoting the Ohio Appellate Court, Morrison indicated that: "'[t]he crucial question is whether "each party to the contract, considering his obvious education or lack of it, [had] a reasonable opportunity to understand the terms of the contract, or were the important terms hidden in a maze of fine print ...?"'" Morrison, 317 F.3d at 666 (quoting Ohio Univ. Bd. of Trs. v. Smith, 724 N.E.2d 1155, 1161 (Ohio Ct. App. 1999) (quoting Williams v. Walker-Thomas Furniture Co., 350 F.2d 445, 449 (D.C. Cir. 1965), and Lake Ridge Acad. v. Carney, 613 N.E.2d 183, 189 (1993))).

[66]   Morrison, 317 F.3d at 667-68. But see Szetela v. Discover Bank, 97 Cal.App.4th 1094, 1100 (2002) (Cal. Ct. App. 2002) (cited in Ingle v. Circuit City Stores, Inc., 328 F.3d 1165, 1172 (9th Cir. 2003) (time to consider agreement irrelevant to unconscionability determination) (holding that the availability of other options does not bear on whether a contract is procedurally unconscionable)).

The substantive unconscionability inquiry asks whether the agreement asymmetrically burdens the employee.[67] For example, the agreement may require the employee, but not the employer, to arbitrate,[68] or may limit the employee's, but not the employer's appeal rights.[69] Interestingly, the Ninth Circuit held in *Ingle v. Circuit City Stores, Inc.*, that, because only employees are likely to sue, arbitration clauses in employment agreements "raise a rebuttable presumption of substantive unconscionability."[70] Arbitration agreements may not force employees to abandon substantive rights.[71] Courts look carefully at whether the challenged provision will deter people from seeking their rights.[72]

Ingle presents a smorgasbord of ways an agreement may be substantively unconscionable:[73]

- The claims of employees had to be arbitrated, while any claims of the employer could be brought in court.

- A one-year limitations period deprived California Fair Employment and Housing Act plaintiffs of the benefits of the continuing violation doctrine.

- The prohibition on class actions was "'harsh and unfair' to those who could benefit from proceeding as a class and offensive to the policies underlying class actions, such as promoting 'judicial economy and streamlin[ing] the litigation process in appropriate cases.'"[74]

- The filing fee of $75 had to be paid to the employer. This was not the "type" of fee a person would pay in a judicial proceeding and might deter the claimant from bringing a claim.

---

[67] Morrison, 317 F.3d at 666; Little, 29 Cal.4th at 1071 (California law); Maxwell v. Fid. Fin. Servs., Inc., 907 P.2d 51 (Ariz. 1995) (Arizona law).

[68] Armendariz, 24 Cal.4th at 119.

[69] Little, 29 Cal.4th at 1072.

[70] Ingle v. Circuit City Stores, Inc., 328 F.3d 1165, 1174 (9th Cir. 2003).

[71] "[A] party does not forgo the substantive rights afforded by [a] statute [when she agrees to arbitrate a statutory claim but] only submits to their resolution in an arbitral, rather than a judicial, forum." Gilmer v. Interstate/Johnson Lane Corp., 500 U.S. 20, 26 (1991).

[72] Id. (filing fee that was not the type one would have to pay in federal court unconscionable).

[73] Ingle, 328 F.3d at 1173-79.

[74] Id. at 1175-76 (quoting Szetela v. Discover Bank, 97 Cal.App.4th 1094, 1101-02 (Cal. Ct. App. 2002)).

- The claimant had to pay half the costs of the arbitration and could be ordered to pay the employer's costs, as well.[75]

- The provision limited the available damage remedies more narrowly than federal law. Again, by itself, this made the provision substantively unconscionable.

- The employer, but not the employees, could terminate the agreement upon 30 days' notice.

In *Hooters of America, Inc. v. Phillips*,[76] the deficiency was not in the arbitration agreement, but in the procedure established pursuant to the agreement. In that case, the Fourth Circuit found that the agreement could not compel arbitration of the Title VII dispute where the panel was biased: Both the employer and the employee could pick members of a three arbitrator panel. The two members so chosen would choose a third member; however, the third member had to be chosen from a list supplied by the employer. "Under the rules, Hooters is free to devise lists of partial arbitrators who have existing relationships, financial or familial, with Hooters and its management."[77] The rules were so egregiously one-sided that a senior vice president of the American Arbitration Association testified that the AAA would refuse to arbitrate under the rules.[78] Thus, although there was an agreement to arbitrate, the employer breached the agreement by its required procedures and the employee was permitted to rescind.

Finally, an arbitration clause may be unenforceable, because there really is no agreement. In *Penn v. Ryan's Family Steakhouses, Inc.*,[79] the Court considered a somewhat unique scenario: Before beginning employment with Ryan's, the plaintiff was required to sign an agreement

---

[75] The court wrote:

> By itself, the fact that an employee could be held liable for Circuit City's share of the arbitration costs should she fail to vindicate employment-related claims renders this provision substantively unconscionable. Combined with the fact that Circuit City's fee-splitting scheme would sanction charging even a successful litigant for her share of arbitration costs, this scheme blatantly offends basic principles of fairness.

Id. at 1178. *Morrison* reaches a similar result regarding costs, but not on unconscionability grounds. Morrison v. Circuit City Stores, Inc., 317 F.3d 646, 668-70 (6th Cir. 2003).

[76] Hooters of America, Inc. v. Phillips, 173 F.2d 933 (4th Cir. 1999).

[77] Id. at 939.

[78] Id.

[79] Penn v. Ryan's Family Steakhouses, Inc., 269 F.3d 753 (7th Cir. 2001).

with a third party, Employment Dispute Services, Inc. (EDS), pursuant to which EDS provided an arbitration forum "for all employment related disputes between Ryan's and its employees.[80] However, the court found that the agreement was not enforceable because the obligations, if any, imposed upon EDS were "unascertainable, illusory."[81] While the obligations of Penn were quite clear, "nothing in the contract provides any details about the nature of the forum that EDS will provide or sets standards with which EDS must comply; EDS could fulfill its promise by providing Penn and Ryan's with a coin toss."[82] Nor was there any other contract that established the mutuality of obligation. Finally, the fact that a third party, such as Ryan's, might owe Penn a duty, did not suffice to create an enforceable contract with EDS.[83]

2. Severability

Where a particular provision in an arbitration agreement is substantively unconscionable, courts face the question of whether to sever the offensive provision, while letting the remainder of the agreement continue in operation, or refusing to enforce the entire agreement. In *Armendariz v. Foundation Psychcare Services, Inc.*, the California Supreme Court identified two reasons for maintaining the contract intact: (1) "to prevent parties from gaining undeserved benefit or suffering undeserved detriment as a result of voiding the entire contract – particularly when there has been full or partial performance of the contract";[84] (2) "to conserve a contractual relationship if to do so would not be condoning an illegal scheme. ... The overarching inquiry is whether "'the interests of justice ... would be furthered'" by severance."[85]

The *Armendariz* court observed that multiple unlawful provisions could "indicate a systematic effort to impose arbitration on an employee not simply as an alternative to litigation, but as an inferior forum that works to the employer's advantage."[86] In addition, the presence of a number of unlawful terms made it difficult to disentangle them from the possibly legal remainder of the contract.[87]

The Sixth Circuit and Ninth Circuit decisions in *Morrison*[88] and *Ingle*[89] provide an interesting point-counterpoint on this issue. Decided

---

[80] Id. at 755.

[81] Id. at 759.

[82] Id.

[83] Id. at 760.

[84] Armendariz v. Found. Psychcare Servs., Inc., 6 P.3d 669, 696 (Cal. 2000).

[85] Id. (citations omitted).

[86] Id.

[87] Id.

[88] Morrison v. Circuit City Stores, Inc., 317 F.3d 646 (6th Cir. 2003).

within two months of each other in 2003, both considered arbitration provisions in Circuit City's employment contract. The *Morrison* court found that two provisions of the contract – those dealing with cost-splitting and with limitations on statutory remedies – were unenforceable. It then looked to Ohio law to decide whether those provisions were severable. That law, in turn, looked to the intentions of the parties as to whether the contract was severable or not.[90] Although the contract contained a severability clause, the court found its application to the invalid clauses unclear. Thus, it could not define the parties' intent. Applying the presumption under the Federal Arbitration Act of resolving any doubts as to arbitrability in favor of arbitration articulated in *Moses H. Cone Memorial Hospital v. Mercury Construction Corp.*,[91] it declined to find the entire agreement unenforceable and severed the offending provisions.

In contrast to *Morrison*, the Ninth Circuit in *Ingle* found the entire agreement unenforceable. It had, of course, found a number of provisions in addition to those addressed by the *Morrison* court to be unconscionable. It had also addressed a previous version of the Circuit City agreement in an earlier decision, *Circuit City Stores v. Adams*[92] and was perhaps concerned about Circuit City's intransigence. Quoting *Armendariz*, because California law applied, it said the "issue was whether the 'central purpose of the contract was tainted with illegality' or whether 'the illegality is collateral to [its] main purpose'"[93] Although it too cited *Moses H. Cone Memorial Hospital* as to the presumption in favor of arbitrability, it found an "insidious pattern" to "stack the deck" in favor of the employer.[94] To excise the offending clauses would have required the court to redraft the contract, which it declined to do.[95]

---

89   Ingle v. Circuit City Stores, Inc., 328 F.3d 1165 (9th Cir. 2003).

90   Morrison, 317 F.3d. at 674-75 (citing Toledo Police Patrolmen's Ass'n. v. City of Toledo, 641 N.E.2d 779, 803 (Ohio 1994), appeal denied, 639 N.E.2d 795 (1994)).

91   Moses H. Cone Mem'l Hosp. v. Mercury Constr. Corp., 460 U.S.1, 24-25 (1983).

92   Circuit City Stores v. Adams, 279 F.3d 889 (9th Cir. 2002)

93   Ingle, 328 F.3d at 1180 (quoting Armendariz, 24 Cal.4th at 124).

94   Id.

95   Id.

Part 7

State Antidiscrimination Law
Analysis

Chapter 21 STATE ANTIDISCRIMINATION LAW

§ 21.1 Overview

When Congress passed the ADA, it was not drawing on a blank federal canvas; there already was a significant body of state antidiscrimination law. As discussed in Part 1 of this treatise, before the ADA, ten federal statutes prohibited discrimination, at least in part, on the basis of disability.[1] These statutes, like the Rehabilitation Act of 1973 (prohibiting discrimination in publicly funded state programs and services) and the Architectural Barriers Act (requiring accessibility for new federal buildings) covered narrow issue areas. As such, in the pre-ADA period, the states' civil rights model was the dominant form of antidiscrimination protection for people with disabilities.

The pre-ADA spectrum of state laws ran the gamut. Different states had laws covering nondiscrimination in employment, public accommodations, and state services. Many states covered one, but not the rest, of these areas. The passage of the ADA changed more than the federal landscape, as many states subsequently passed new or amended antidiscrimination laws modeled, at least in part, after the ADA.

This treatise has shown the many ways that federal courts, and in particular the Supreme Court, have interpreted the ADA. It is equally important to consider the different ways that states have reacted to these changes. Some state courts have fallen into step with the federal courts,

---

[1] See John T. Noonan, Narrowing the Nation's Power: The Supreme Court Sides with the States 114 (2002).

and interpreted their state laws to be consistent with the ADA. In other instances, state legislatures have amended their state laws to provide more protection for people with disabilities than the ADA, particularly as interpreted by the federal courts.

The ebb and flow between and among the federal and state laws is, of course, reflective of changing views about the role of the federal and state government in the lives of citizens.[2] With the recent narrowing by the Supreme Court of federal civil rights laws, and the ADA in particular, states' laws take on renewed importance for the protection of people with disabilities from discrimination.

A complete treatment of the different states' laws is beyond the scope of this treatise. This section highlights the disability discrimination laws of several representative states, with an eye toward how these civil rights laws interact and intersect with the ADA.

§ 21.2 Pre-ADA State Landscape

A. *Employment Law*

Many pre-ADA state laws dealing with disability civil rights focused on discrimination in employment. One study conducted a survey of pre-ADA state employment antidiscrimination law[3] and found that a majority of states (29) in the pre-ADA period had some form of disability antidiscrimination prohibitions. However, these state laws imposed no "reasonable accommodations" requirements on private employers.[4]

One such example is Georgia's law, passed in 1981, which provides in part that:

---

[2]   For an interesting treatment of this subject, see id.

[3]   See Christine Jolls & J.J. Prescott, The Effects of "Reasonable Accommodations" Requirements and Firing Costs on the Employment of Individuals with Disabilities (forthcoming 2003) (on file with authors). The thesis of this article is that the reasonable accommodations requirement of the ADA, rather than the ADA's imposition of firing costs, played the central role in recent empirical findings that the passage of the ADA reduced, rather than increased employment opportunities for people with disabilities. This article is discussed in more detail infra in Part 9 of this treatise. See also generally Samuel Bagenstos, Rational Discrimination, Accommodation, and the Politics of (Disability) Civil Rights, 89 Va. L. Rev. 825 (2003) (reviewing studies examining state disability laws).

[4]   Jolls & Prescott, supra note 3, at tbl. 1. These states are Alaska, California, Connecticut, Florida, Georgia, Hawaii, Illinois, Indiana, Kansas, Kentucky, Maine, Maryland, Michigan, Missouri, Montana, Nebraska, Nevada, New Hampshire, New Jersey, New York, North Dakota, Ohio, Oklahoma, South Carolina, South Dakota, Tennessee, Texas, Utah, and West Virginia.

No employer shall fail or refuse to hire nor shall any employer discharge or discriminate against any individual with disabilities with respect to wages, rates of pay, hours, or other terms or conditions of employment because of such person's disability unless such disability restricts that individual's ability to engage in the particular job or occupation for which he or she is eligible....[5]

The same study found that less than one-third of states (18) had pre-ADA disability antidiscrimination laws that contained reasonable accommodation requirements (or laws interpreted by their respective state courts in this fashion).[6]

An example of this type of law is Idaho's antidiscrimination law, passed in 1988, which provides in part that:

It shall be a prohibited act to discriminate against a person because of, or on a basis of ... disability ... provided that the prohibition against discrimination because of disability shall not apply if the particular disability, even with a reasonable accommodation by the employer, prevents the performance of the work required by the employer in that job.[7]

Finally, three states had no laws prohibiting disability discrimination by private employers before the ADA.[8]

Of the states that did have statutes prohibiting disability discrimination by private employers, most did not apply to people with cognitive disabilities (i.e., mental illness and mental retardation). Some of these statutes were amended before the passage of the ADA, to include people with mental disabilities.[9]

Some states had laws regulating disability discrimination by state employers. Mississippi, for example, a state that did not have a law

---

[5] Ga. Code Ann., § 34-6A-4 (1998).

[6] See Jolls & Prescott, supra note 3, at tbl. 2. These states are Arizona, Colorado, Delaware, Idaho, Iowa, Louisiana, Massachusetts, Minnesota, New Mexico, North Carolina, Oregon, Pennsylvania, Rhode Island, Vermont, Virginia, Washington, Wisconsin, and Wyoming.

[7] Idaho Code § 67-5909 (2003).

[8] See Jolls & Prescott, supra note 3, at tbl. 3. These states are Alabama, Arkansas, and Mississippi.

[9] Id. at tbl. A1. States that broadened their statutes to include protection for people with mental disabilities were Alaska (in 1987), California (in 1975), Connecticut (in 1978 and 1979), Montana (in 1975), New Jersey (1986 and 1987), New Mexico (in 1987), and Rhode Island (in 1981).

regulating disability discrimination by private employers, did have laws prohibiting disability discrimination by state employers.[10]

Mississippi's statute, passed in 1978, proscribes the refusal of employment by a state employer or employer funded by state funds "by reason of his being blind, visually handicapped, deaf, or otherwise physically handicapped, unless such disability shall materially affect the performance of the work required by the job."[11]

In contrast to the ADA, however, Mississippi's law did not have a reasonable accommodation requirement and did not apply to people with mental disabilities. Nor did the law extend to other state programs, services, or activities.

B. *Access And Public Accommodations Law*

Before the ADA, there also was a significant body of state statutory law prohibiting discrimination on the basis of disability in publicly owned buildings and in privately owned public accommodations. In the tradition of the Architectural Barriers Act (discussed in treatise Part 1), most of these statutes focused on removing barriers to ensure access to physical structures for people with disabilities.[12] But these statutes differed as to their coverage, application, and enforceability.

One study found that by 1977, twenty-nine states had statutes that applied only to state and locally funded buildings and facilities.[13] These statutes often were unclear, however, as to whether privately owned but publicly leased buildings were covered.[14] Twenty states had statutes that expressly applied to privately owned places of business, accommodation, or employment, in addition to publicly funded buildings and facilities.[15]

---

[10] See Herbert E. Gerson & J. Gregory Addison, Handicapped Discrimination Law and the Americans with Disabilities Act, 11 Miss. C. L. Rev. 233, 237 (1991).

[11] Miss. Code Ann. § 43-6-15 (2000).

[12] See Don F. Nicolai & William J. Ricci, Access to Buildings for the Disabled, 50 Temple L.Q. 1067, 1069 (1977).

[13] Id. at 1069 n.19. These states were Alaska, Arkansas, Colorado, Delaware, Indiana, Kansas, Louisiana, Maine, Maryland, Minnesota, Mississippi, Missouri, Montana, Nevada, New Hampshire, New Mexico, New York, North Dakota, Ohio, Oklahoma, South Dakota, Texas, Utah, Vermont, Virginia, and Wyoming.

[14] Id. at 1070 n.20.

[15] Id. at 1070 n.21. These states were Arizona, California, Connecticut, Idaho, Illinois, Iowa, Kentucky, Massachusetts, Michigan, Nebraska, New Jersey, Oregon, Pennsylvania, Rhode Island, South Carolina, Tennessee, Washington, West Virginia, and Wisconsin.

As a general matter, these state statutes were modest in their scope as compared with the ADA. As of 1977, only three states had statutes requiring the renovation of existing buildings to make them accessible to persons with disabilities.[16] Fifteen states did not specifically require accessibility when alteration, renovation, or remodeling of existing facilities was done.[17] Only three states covered public or private transportation services in their accessibility statutes.[18] And, only South Carolina allowed for recovery of damages in private suits for violations of barriers statutes.[19]

Some states attempted to give tax or other incentives for private individuals to make buildings accessible. In 1976, Florida passed a law providing that an owner of a building, which is open to the public and has been renovated to be accessible to persons with disabilities, could not be assessed a corresponding increase for property tax valuation (cf. treatise Part 10, discussion of tax policies and laws).[20] Similarly, in 1975, Oregon passed a law allowing the cost of renovating an existing building to eliminate barriers to be deductible from state income tax and corporate excise tax.[21]

Another example of an early public accommodations statute was observed when Mississippi passed a law in 1978 that provided: "[b]lind persons, visually impaired persons, deaf persons and other physically disabled persons shall have the same right as the able-bodied to the full and free use of the streets, highways, sidewalks, walkways, public buildings, public facilities, and other public places."[22] This statute also guaranteed this same class of people with disabilities full and equal access to public accommodations.[23]

There are, however, no reported cases pursuant to those Mississippi statutes. Perhaps it is testament to the effectiveness of these state statutes, or lack thereof, that when passing the ADA thirteen years later, Congress found widespread discrimination in places of public accommodations.

Some states that had broad public accommodations antidiscrimination statutes did not extend the coverage of these statutes to people with disabilities. For example, the Idaho antidiscrimination

---

[16] Id. at 1071 n.26.

[17] Id. at n.28.

[18] Nicolai & Ricci, supra note 12, at 1073 n.35.

[19] Id. at 1078.

[20] Id. at 1072 n.30; see Fla. Stat. Ann § 193.623 (2003).

[21] Nicolai & Ricci, supra note 12, at 1072 n.31 (citing Or. Rev. Stat. §§ 316.066, 316.067(h) (1975)).

[22] Miss. Code Ann. § 43-6-3 (2000).

[23] Id. § 43-6-5.

statute discussed above provided that no person may discriminate against an individual in the full and equal enjoyment of a place of public accommodation on the basis of race, color, religion, sex, or national origin.[24] The Idaho statute expressly did not extend this protection to people with disabilities.[25]

One study has confirmed that states have not offered as much protection from state discrimination on the basis of disability as does Title II of the ADA. In 2002, researchers compared the existing body of state disability law relating to discrimination in government programs, services, and activities with Title II of the ADA.[26] These researchers were interested in whether states had a level of protection regarding state discrimination that was comparable to that presented in Title II.

The study defined "Title II-like" protections as those statutes that: (a) prohibited discrimination in access to facilities; (b) prohibited discrimination in access to services; (c) provided a private right of action to enforce these protections, including compensatory damages; and (d) provided for the availability of attorneys' fees.[27] Thus defined, the study found that only twenty-four of fifty-one states provided clear statutory language with protections comparable to ADA Title II.[28]

§ 21.3 Post-ADA State Laws

After conducting nineteen hearings from 1988 to 1990, and reviewing the report of the Task Force on the Rights and Empowerment of Americans with Disabilities, Congress concluded that stronger federal legislation was needed.[29] The passage of the ADA marked a shift toward a comprehensive federal model of protection for a wide range of people with disabilities.

States have responded in different ways to the ADA and to U.S. Supreme Court interpretations of the law's protections.

A.   *Examples Of States That Have Expanded On Federal Protections*

1.   California

California represents a significant example of a state with a history, even pre-ADA, of strong legal protections for people with

---

[24]   Idaho Code § 67-5909(5) (2003).

[25]   Id.

[26]   See Ruth Colker & Adam Milani, Garrett, Disability Policy, and Federalism: A Symposium on Board of Trustees of the University of Alabama v. Garrett, 53 Ala. L. Rev. 1075 (2002).

[27]   Id. at 1082-83.

[28]   Id. at 1083.

[29]   See Noonan, supra note 1, at 114.

disabilities. California has reacted to the Supreme Court's interpretation of the ADA by providing state protections that are broader than federal law.

The California disability antidiscrimination statute, the Fair Employment and Housing Act ("FEHA"), is comprehensive in scope. FEHA prohibits discrimination in public and private employment, and contains a reasonable accommodation requirement.[30]

Another California statute, the Unruh Civil Rights Act, guarantees people with disabilities full and equal accommodations in all business establishments.[31] In addition to disability, the California statutes prohibit discrimination on the basis of sex, race, religion, and national origin. California has an extensive body of caselaw pursuant to passage of these statutes.

Moreover, after the U.S. Supreme Court's narrowing interpretation of the ADA's definition of "disability" in *Sutton v. United Air Lines, Inc.*,[32] *Albertson's Inc. v. Kirkingburg*,[33] and *Murphy v. United Parcel Service, Inc.*,[34] California responded by distinguishing its state law protections from the federal limits.

In 2000, California amended FEHA with the Prudence Kay Poppink Act.[35] The preface to these amendments states that the Legislature finds that:

> the law of this state in the areas of disabilities provides protections independent from those in the federal Americans with Disabilities Act .... Although the federal act provides a floor of protection, this state's law has always, even prior to passage of the federal act, afforded additional protections.[36]

---

[30] See generally Cal. Gov't Code §§ 12900-12996 (2003).

[31] See Cal. Civ. Code § 51 (2003) ("business establishment" has been interpreted very broadly to include even government bodies); see Gibson v. County of Riverside, 181 F.Supp.2d 1057 (C.D. Cal. 2002); see also Cal. Civ. Code § 54 ("Equal Rights to Public Facilities) and § 55 ("Right to Full Access to Public Facilities"); see Cal. Gov't Code § 11135 (prohibiting discrimination by state agencies and recipients of state funding).

[32] Sutton v. United Air Lines, Inc., 527 U.S. 471 (1999).

[33] Albertson's Inc. v. Kirkingburg, 527 U.S. 555 (1999).

[34] Murphy v. United Parcel Serv., Inc., 527 U.S. 516 (1999).

[35] Legal Aid Soc'y Emp. L. Ctr., The Prudence Kay Poppink Act, at www.las-elc.org/poppink.doc (last visited Oct. 11, 2003).

[36] Cal. Gov't Code § 12926.1(a) (2003).

The 2000 FEHA amendments provide greater protection than the ADA in several ways.[37] First, FEHA's definition of physical and mental disability require a "limitation" on a major life activity, as opposed to the "substantial limitation" required by the ADA.[38] The FEHA amendments make clear that "this distinction is intended to result in broader coverage...."[39]

In *Colmenares v. Braemar Country Club, Inc.*,[40] the California Supreme Court highlighted this distinction when it held that a plaintiff attempting to prove a physical disability under FEHA[41] must demonstrate: "(1) a physiological disease or condition affecting a body system; and (2) the disease or condition limited (as opposed to substantially limited, as required under federal ADA law) the plaintiff's ability to participate in major life activities."[42] The court also held that the limitation (as opposed to substantial limitation) element of the FEHA Amendments was retroactive, and applied to Mr. Colmenares back in 1997.[43]

Second, in *Sutton*, the Supreme Court interpreted the ADA to provide that a disability only exists where an impairment substantially limits a major life activity *considering* mitigating measures.[44] The FEHA amendments reject that view, providing that "under the law of this state, whether a condition limits a major life activity shall be determined without respect to any mitigating measures... ."[45]

Third, under *Sutton*, a plaintiff must show that she is "presently – not potentially or hypothetically – substantially limited in order to demonstrate a disability."[46] However, in *Goldman v. Standard Insurance*

---

[37] For an excellent comparison of FEHA, as amended, with the ADA, see Legal Aid Soc'y Emp. L. Ctr., Disability Discrimination in the Workplace – State Versus Federal Law Protections, at www.employmentlawcenter.org/adafehachart.pdf (last visited Sept. 12, 2003).

[38] Compare Cal. Gov't Code § 12926(c) with 42 U.S.C. § 12102(2)(A) (2000) and 29 C.F.R. Pt. 1630(j) (2003).

[39] Cal. Gov't Code § 12926(c).

[40] Colmenares v. Braemar Country Club, Inc., 130 Cal.Rptr.2d 662 (Cal. 2003).

[41] Cal. Gov't Code § 12900 et seq.

[42] See also Nat'l Council on Disability Policy Brief Series: Righting the ADA No. 9, *Chevron v. Echazabal*: The ADA's "Direct Threat to Self" Defense, www.ncd.gov/newsroom/publications/directthreat.html (2003).

[43] See Colmenares, 130 Cal.Rptr.2d at 670.

[44] Sutton v. United Air Lines, 527 U.S. 471, 483 (1992).

[45] Cal. Gov't Code § 12926.1 (2003).

[46] Sutton, 527 U.S. at 482.

Company,[47] the Ninth Circuit held that the *Sutton* mitigation interpretation did not apply to California's Unruh Act. Therefore, a California plaintiff suing under state discrimination law does not need to show that her employer regarded her as having a present limitation in a major life activity.[48]

Fourth, the FEHA amendments provide that "working" is a major life activity, and that a person who is limited in working need not be limited in a class or broad range of jobs.[49] In contrast, the ADA's EEOC regulations and federal court interpretations are more restrictive as to working being a major life activity, providing that a plaintiff must be unable to perform a broad range of jobs.[50]

This is a significant difference from ADA caselaw, especially for "regarded as" disabled cases.[51] Under federal law, it is difficult for plaintiffs to prove that their employers have viewed them as unable to work in a broad range of jobs.[52] Under California law, a plaintiff need only show that her employer viewed her as unable to work in her particular job. In theory, this approach avoids outcomes as in the Court's *Toyota Motor Manufacturing, Kentucky, Inc. v. Williams* decision, in which the plaintiff was required to show she was limited in common daily life activities and not just in her specific job tasks.[53]

The California expansions on the definition of disability do not just apply to California's employment discrimination statutes.[54] The FEHA

---

[47]   Goldman v. Standard Ins. Co., 2003 WL 22025139 (9th Cir. Aug. 29, 2003).

[48]   Id.

[49]   Cal. Gov't Code § 12926.1. This is consistent with a different section of the statute, which provides that "major life activities shall be broadly construed and shall include physical, mental, and social activities and working." Id. §§ 12926(i)(1)(C), (k)(1)(B)(iii).

[50]   See 29 C.F.R. § 1630.2(j)(3)(1) (2003) stating:

> Substantially limited in the major life activity of working means significantly restricted in the ability to perform either a class of jobs or a broad range of jobs in various classes as compared to the average person having comparable training, skills, and abilities. The inability to perform a single, particular job does not constitute a substantial limitation in the major life activity of working.

The Supreme Court has confirmed this view. See Sutton, 527 U.S. at 491.

[51]   See Legal Aid Soc'y Emp. L. Ctr., supra note 37.

[52]   Id.

[53]   Toyota Motor Mfg., Ky., Inc. v. Williams, 534 U.S. 184, 199 (2002).

[54]   See Cal. Civ. Code § 51(e)(1) (2003).

amendments apply to California's other disability discrimination statutes on public accommodations and state programs and services.[55]

Another significant difference between California and federal law is in the remedies for public accommodation discrimination. The California Unruh Civil Rights Act provides for up to treble damages for such discrimination.[56] Alternatively, it provides for statutory damages of $4,000.[57]

2.   New York

New York offers broad statutory protection for people with disabilities.[58] This includes protection from discrimination in employment and in the use and enjoyment of places of public accommodations.[59] Although New York's employment discrimination laws were passed in 1974, they did not include a reasonable accommodation requirement until 1998.[60]

Like California, New York's statutory disability protections are part of a broader statutory scheme prohibiting discrimination on the basis of race, sex, sexual orientation, and so on. Also like California, there are numerous New York cases brought pursuant to these statutes.

Even before the Supreme Court's 1999 *Sutton* Trilogy cases narrowing the definition of disability under the ADA, New York's laws had been interpreted to provide a broader definition of "disability" than the ADA. The New York Human Rights Law defines disability as "a physical, mental, or medical impairment resulting from anatomical, physiological, genetic or neurological conditions which prevents the exercise of a normal bodily function *or* is demonstrable by medically accepted clinical or laboratory diagnostic techniques ...."[61]

There are several state and federal cases holding that the second part of this definition means that individuals who are not "disabled" for the purposes of the ADA have a covered disability under New York's

---

[55]   See id. § 51; see also id. § 54 ("Equal Rights to Public Facilities") and § 55 ("Right to Full Access to Public Facilities").

[56]   Id. § 52.

[57]   Id. Notably, § 54.3 only provides $1,000 in statutory damages for the same conduct.

[58]   See N.Y. Human Rights Law (codified at N.Y. Exec. Law § 290-310 (2002)).

[59]   See N.Y. Exec. Law § 292(21).

[60]   See id.; see also Kwarren v. Am. Airlines, 303 A.D.2d 722, 757 N.Y.S.2d 105 (2 Dept. 2003).

[61]   N.Y. Exec. Law § 292(21).

Human Rights Law.[62] In *Reeves v. Johnson Controls World Services, Inc.*, for example, an individual diagnosed with "panic disorder with agoraphobia" sued his employer for firing him in violation of the ADA and New York's Human Rights Law.[63]

Reeves argued that he was substantially limited in the major life activity of "everyday mobility."[64] The Second Circuit declined to classify "everyday mobility" as a major life activity for purposes of the ADA, and therefore held that plaintiff did not have an ADA-covered disability.[65]

However, the Second Circuit held that the result was different under New York law, which treats a "medically diagnosable impairment as necessarily a disability."[66] Plaintiff therefore had a disability for purposes of the New York Human Rights Law.[67]

To date, there are no New York cases scaling back this expanded definition of disability in light of the U.S. Supreme Court's *Sutton* line of cases.

---

[62] See Fagan v. United Int'l Ins. Co., 128 F.Supp.2d 182, 186 (S.D.N.Y. 2001) ("The standard under New York State and City Human rights laws for proving a disability is broader than that of the ADA") (citations omitted); see also Roberts v. N.Y. St. Dep't of Correctional Servs., 63 F.Supp.2d 272, 290-91 (W.D.N.Y. 1999) (holding that individual with alcoholism was not disabled within the meaning of the ADA, but was disabled under New York's law); St. Div. of Human Rights v. Xerox Corp., 65 N.Y.2d 213, 218 (1985) ("In New York, the term 'disability' is more broadly defined [than typical disability statutes].").

[63] Reeves v. Johnson Controls World Servs., Inc., 140 F.3d 144, 153 (2d Cir. 1998).

[64] Id. at 147.

[65] Id. at 154.

[66] Id. at 155.

[67] Like New York's, the Connecticut definition of physical disability under its employment disability discrimination law has been held to be broader than the ADA. The Connecticut Fair Employment Practices Act (CFEPA), Conn. Gen. Stat. § 46a-51 et. seq., defines physical disability as "refer[ring] to any individual who has any chronic physical handicap, infirmity, or impairment." Conn. Gen. Stat. § 46a-51(15). In *Beason v. United Techs. Corp.*, 337 F.3d 271, the Second Circuit held that unlike the ADA, CFEPA does not require that a disabled individual be limited in a major life activity. Id. at 277. Therefore, even though an individual might not be covered by the ADA, she could be covered under CFEPA. Id. at 279. In a different case, the First Circuit held that an individual with a temporary condition can be disabled within the meaning of CFEPA. See Caruso v. Siemens Business Sys., Inc., 2003 WL 174791 (2d Cir. Jan. 23, 2003) (unpublished opinion).

3.   North Carolina

North Carolina has an extensive statutory scheme protecting people with disabilities from discrimination. In 1973, North Carolina enacted laws stating that it was the policy of the state to "encourage and enable handicapped persons to participate fully in the social and economic life of the State and to engage in remunerative employment."[68]

The North Carolina statute contained provisions, seemingly modest by today's standards, ensuring "handicapped persons" the same right as the "able-bodied" to the full and free use of the streets, highways, sidewalks, and other publicly and privately owned buildings which served the public,[69] and guaranteeing non-discrimination in housing.[70]

In 1985, North Carolina passed the "Persons With Disabilities Protection Act,"[71] which extended protection to employment (with a reasonable accommodation requirement),[72] public accommodations,[73] public services,[74] and public transportation.[75]

However, the North Carolina legislature took a different approach to the concept of the "undue hardship" defense than did the framers of the ADA. Whereas the ADA does not contain a precise mathematical formula as a guide to determine undue hardship,[76] the North Carolina statute offers guidance. The statute provides that any change that costs less than 5% of an employee's salary or annualized salary is presumed to not be an undue hardship.[77]

North Carolina has taken one significant step in responding to the Supreme Court's recent federalism rulings (see treatise Part 4 discussion). In *Board of Trustees of the University of Alabama v. Garrett*, the Supreme Court held that Congress had overstepped its authority pursuant to Section 5 of the Fourteenth Amendment in abrogating the states' sovereign immunity.[78] After this ruling, state employees could no longer sue their employers under Title I of the ADA for monetary damages.

---

[68]   N.C. Gen. Stat. § 168-A (2002).

[69]   Id. § 168-2.

[70]   Id. § 168-9.

[71]   Persons with Disabilities Protection Act (codified at N.C. Gen. Stat. § 168A-1-A-12).

[72]   Id. § 168A-4, 5.

[73]   Id. § 168A-6.

[74]   Id. § 168A-7.

[75]   Id. § 168A-8.

[76]   See 42 U.S.C. § 12111(10)(a)-(b) (2000).

[77]   N.C. Gen. Stat. § 168A-3(10)(a)(7).

[78]   Bd. of Trs. of the Univ. of Ala. v. Garrett, 531 U.S. 356 (2001).

Yet, despite Congress's failure to validly abrogate states' sovereign immunity for ADA Title I cases, states are able to waive this immunity voluntarily and consent to suit in federal court.[79] In 2001, North Carolina passed the "State Employee Federal Remedy Restoration Act," which waived its sovereign immunity for the purpose of allowing state employees to maintain lawsuits for monetary damages under the ADA.[80]

4.   Illinois

Like North Carolina, the legislature of the state of Illinois has reacted to the Supreme Court's decision in *Garrett*. On August 5, 2003, the legislature approved Illinois Public Act 93-414.[81] This law amended the Illinois State Sovereign Immunity Act to allow state employees, former employees, or prospective employees who are aggrieved by any conduct, action, or inaction of the State in violation of the ADA, to bring a lawsuit in state or federal court.[82]

To date, only North Carolina, Illinois and Minnesota[83] have expressly waived their sovereign immunity to allow ADA claims to be brought against them in federal court. Time will tell if other states follow their lead.

B.   *Examples Of States That Have Not Expanded On Federal Protections*

The states discussed above have provided greater protections than those offered by the ADA, either as written or as interpreted. In contrast, however, there are states that, when interpreting their own laws, have conformed to the federal courts' interpretation of the ADA.

1.   Texas

Like California and New York, Texas has a broad disability antidiscrimination statutory framework. Texas has a law specifically prohibiting discrimination in public facilities.[84] Its general provisions

---

[79] See Coll. Sav. Bank v. Fla. Prepaid Postsecondary Educ. Expense Bd., 527 U.S. 666, 670 (1999).

[80] See N.C. Gen. Stat. § 143-300.35.

[81] See "Civil Immunities – State Lawsuit Immunity – Exceptions To State Immunity," Ill. Pub. Act 93-414, http://www.iltla.com/Legislative%20Information/PA_93_0414.pdf (Aug. 26, 2003). This law becomes effective on January 1, 2004.

[82] Id. at § 1.5(d). This Act also waives Illinois's sovereign immunity under the Age Discrimination in Employment Act, the Fair Labor Standards Act, the Family and Medical Leave Act, and Title VII of the Civil Rights Act of 1964. Id. at § 1.5(a), (b), (c), (e).

[83] See Minn. Stat. § 1.05 (2002) (waiving Minnesota's sovereign immunity under the ADEA, Fair Labor Standards Act, FMLA, and ADA).

[84] See Tex. Hum. Res. Code Ann. § 121.001 (2003).

relating to antidiscrimination in private employment provide protection for people with disabilities.[85]

In contrast to California and New York, however, Texas has not passed amendments to its state disability antidiscrimination laws in light of recent Supreme Court cases; rather, its courts consistently have interpreted Texas state laws in ways similar to those in which federal courts have interpreted the ADA.

For example, in *Garcia v. Allen*, a terminated employee claimed that his employer fired him in violation of the Texas Commission on Human Rights Act.[86] The plaintiff was without a kneecap in his left knee. His employer knew of this condition when he was hired as an analyzer technician. After a subsequent surgery, the plaintiff's doctor prohibited him from climbing, squatting, kneeling, and crawling. His employer then terminated him.[87]

The plaintiff argued that he had a physical disability within the meaning of the Texas Commission on Human Rights Act, because he could not perform the major life activities of climbing, squatting, kneeling, and crawling. The Texas Court of Appeals, following the Supreme Court's decision in *Sutton*, held that these were not the same type of "major life activities" as caring for one's self, performing manual tasks, walking, seeing, hearing, speaking, breathing, learning, and working.[88]

The Texas court further held that even if plaintiff had argued an inability to perform the major life activity of "working," he still would not be disabled within the meaning of the Texas Commission on Human Rights Act. Again, following *Sutton*, the court reasoned that the plaintiff's impairments did not prohibit a large enough class of jobs to qualify as a covered disability.[89] Other Texas cases have followed this reasoning.[90]

---

[85] See Tex. Lab. Code Ann. §§ 21.051, 21.105 (2003) ("Texas Commission on Human Rights Act"). This statute has been interpreted to contain a reasonable accommodation requirement. See Columbia Plaza Med. Ctr. v. Szurek, 101 S.W.3d 161, 168 (Tx. Ct. App. 2003).

[86] Garcia v. Allen, 28 S.W.3d 587 (Tx. Ct. App. 2000).

[87] Id. at 590.

[88] Id. at 599.

[89] Id. at 599-600.

[90] See Kiser v. Original Inc., 32 S.W.3d 449 (Tex. Ct. of App. 2000) (plaintiff with epilepsy did not have substantial limitation in the major life activity of work); see also Union Carbide Corp. v. Mayfield, 66 S.W.3d 354 (Tx. Ct. of App. 2001) (plaintiff with severe flat-footedness did not have covered disability).

2.   Michigan

Michigan had an early and broad legislative scheme dealing with discrimination against people with disabilities. In 1976, Michigan passed the Handicappers' Civil Rights Act (MHCRA).[91]   This Law was later renamed the Persons with Disabilities Civil Rights Act (PWDCRA).[92]

As early as 1976, PWDCRA provided for nondiscrimination in employment, housing, public accommodations, public services, and educational facilities.[93]   In 1980, the law was amended to include a reasonable accommodation requirement in these areas.[94] The outer limit of the reasonable accommodation requirement is "undue hardship."[95]

PWDCRA's definition of "disability" parallels that of the ADA.[96] Like Texas, Michigan courts have interpreted this definition in the same way that the federal courts have interpreted the ADA's definition.

---

[91]   Mich. Comp. Laws § 37.1101-1607 (2003).

[92]   Hindelang v. Bay Med. Ctr., No. 97-003856-CL, slip op. at n.1 (Bay Cir. Ct. Aug. 11, 2000), at http://www.michbar.org/opinions/appeals/2000/081100/7865.html.

[93]   Mich. Comp. Laws § 37.1102(1).

[94]   Id. § 37.1102(2).

[95]   Id.

[96]   See id. § 37.1103(d) stating:

> "[D]isability" means 1 or more of the following: (i) a determinable physical or mental characteristic of an individual, which may result from disease, injury, congenital condition of birth, or functional disorder, if the characteristic: (A) For purposes of article 2 [employment], substantially limits one or more of the major life activities of that individual and is unrelated to the individual's ability to perform the duties of a particular job or position or substantially limits 1 or more of the major life activities of that individual and is unrelated to the individual's qualifications for employment or promotion.   (B) For purposes of article 3 [public accommodations], is unrelated to the individual's ability to utilize and benefit from a place of public accommodation or public service. (C) For purposes of article 4 (education), is unrelated to the individual's ability to utilize and benefit from educational opportunities, programs, and facilities at an educational institution.   (D) For purposes of article 5 (housing), substantially limits 1 or more of that individual's major life activities and is unrelated to the individual's ability to acquire, rent, or maintain property.   (ii) A history of a determinable physical or mental characteristic described

In the 1998 case *Chmielewski v. Xermac, Inc.*, an employee who had undergone a liver transplant and then was dependent on anti-rejection medication brought claim under the PWDCRA (at the time, called the MHCRA) after having been fired by his employer.[97] The plaintiff claimed that his employer had terminated him to avoid continued health insurance premium increases caused by the liver transplant and his consequent need to take costly anti-rejection medicine for the rest of his life.[98]

The Supreme Court of Michigan considered whether, for the purposes of deciding if he fell within the statutory definition of "disabled," the plaintiff should be considered with or without his medicine (it was undisputed that without these injections, he would die).[99] The court declined to go down the "slippery slope" of considering people in their unmedicated states, reasoning that it might "lead to the inclusion of many commonplace and relatively benign and easily remedied conditions into the act's definition of handicapped."[100]

One year later, in the *Sutton* case, the Supreme Court came to essentially the same conclusion under the ADA.[101] Subsequently, the Sixth Circuit (applying Michigan law) and the Michigan Court of Appeals have confirmed this interpretation of the PWDCRA.[102]

---

in subparagraph (i), (iii) Being regarded as having a determinable physical or mental characteristic described in subparagraph (i).

See also Curry v. Cyprian Ctr., 2001 WL 1006181, at *340 (6th Cir. Aug. 21, 2001) (claims of disability discrimination under PWDCRA essentially track those under ADA).

[97] Chmielewski v. Xermac, Inc., 580 N.W.2d 817 (Mich. Ct. App. 1998).

[98] Id. at 819.

[99] Id. at 820.

[100] Id. at 824.

[101] See Sutton v. United Air Lines, Inc., 527 U.S. 471, 488 (1999) (holding that disability is to be determined with reference to corrective measures).

[102] See Hein v. All Am. Plywood Co., 232 F.3d 482, 487 (6th Cir. 2000); see also Chiles v. Machine Shop, Inc., 606 N.W.2d 398, 410-11 (Mich. Ct. App. 2000) (citations omitted) stating:

As the Supreme Court emphasized in its recent cases ... too often the courts have simply accepted impairments as disabilities without strictly determining whether a plaintiff was disabled according to the language of the statutes; as a result, too many individuals have been designated "disabled" who were outside the contemplation of the legislative bodies that drafted these statutes.

§ 21.4 Looking Ahead – The States' Model Revisited

In light of the U.S. Supreme Court's narrowing of Congress's power to impose federal civil rights requirements on states – and the ADA in particular – it is worth reconsidering the states' model. As a doctrinal matter, the "new federalism" is based on the idea that states are the proper parties to regulate disability discrimination in state programs, services, activities, and employment. This model is premised on the idea that subjecting states to unwanted lawsuits for damages in federal courts impermissibly violates their dignity and sovereignty.[103]

As a whole, the states have not historically offered, nor do they currently provide, the broad and comprehensive protections afforded by the ADA against disability discrimination. With the exceptions of North Carolina, Minnesota, and Illinois, as discussed above, no state has voluntarily abrogated its sovereign immunity to consent to suits by state employees alleging disability discrimination in their employment.

The near wholesale lack of states willing to waive their immunity to suit in federal court could become more significant if the Supreme Court holds in *Tennessee v. Lane* that Congress did not validly abrogate states' sovereign immunity when it passed Title II of the ADA.[104] As the states' statutory schemes are less comprehensive and contain fewer protections than Title II,[105] the limiting of Title II may affect more than a shift from federal to state protection; it will create less civil rights protection overall and whatever legal protections do exist will vary from state to state.

Patricia Garrett, the losing plaintiff in *Board of Trustees of the University of Alabama v. Garrett*, serves as an apt example of how the above view has already become the trend in the area of state employment.[106] As described earlier in this treatise, Ms. Garrett, a registered nurse working for the hospital at the University of Alabama, alleged that after she underwent treatment for breast cancer, she was pressured to leave her job and ultimately forced to take a lower paying

---

Similarly, in the District of Columbia, courts have applied the Sutton analysis to preclude plaintiffs who are not substantially limited in their medicated states from being disabled under the DC Human Rights Act. See Grant v. May Dept. Stores, Co., 786 A.2d 580 (D.C. 2001); see also Strass v. Kaiser Found. Health Plan of Mid-Atlantic, 744 A.2d 1000 (D.C. 2000).

[103] See generally Noonan, supra note 1. See discussion supra Part 4, § 10.2 (regarding Tennessee v. Lane).

[104] See discussion supra Part 4, § 14.2 (regarding Tennessee v. Lane).

[105] See generally Colker & Milani, supra note 26.

[106] Bd. of Trs. of the Univ. of Ala. v. Garrett, 531 U.S. 356 (2001).

position.[107] Her doctor warned her that this workplace discrimination was harmful to her health.[108]

Since the *Garrett* case, those like Garrett, living in states like Alabama, effectively have had no ADA remedies; Alabama has not waived its sovereign immunity to suits against it under ADA Title I, nor does it have an ADA comparable state statute regulating employment discrimination based on disability when carried out by a state employer.[109]

Time will tell if more states voluntarily waive their sovereign immunity to suits under the ADA,[110] or pass stronger laws prohibiting disability discrimination in state programs, services, and activities. Until then, however, the shift from a federal to a state model continues to narrow civil rights protections for people with disabilities.

---

[107] See Brief for Respondents at *1-*5, Garrett, 531 U.S. 356 (2001), 2000 WL 1593420 (Aug. 11, 2000).

[108] Id.

[109] As a post-script, it is noteworthy that as things stand right now, Garrett will be entitled to receive damages under a different federal statute. On remand from the Supreme Court, the Eleventh Circuit held that Garrett could recover damages against Alabama pursuant to the Rehabilitation Act, because Alabama waived its sovereign immunity under the Rehabilitation Act by accepting federal funds. See Garrett v. Bd. of Trs. Of Univ. of Alabama at Birmingham, 2003 WL 22097772 (11th Cir. Sept. 11, 2003).

[110] It is also unclear if the present circuit split relating to whether states waive their immunity under the Rehabilitation Act by accepting federal funds, discussed infra in Part 4, will resolve itself in favor of expanded coverage.

Part 8

International Disability Rights Law
Analysis

Chapter 22 INTERNATIONAL LAW

§ 22.1 Overview

Our focus thus far has been on the ADA and related laws as an expression of United States attitudes toward the civil rights of people with disabilities. While the ADA developed solely in that context, the impact of the statute, or more accurately the movement of which it forms a part, has fallen outside the territorial boundaries of the United States. As the United States has developed its approach to those rights, other countries – generally referred to in this Part as "states" – have dealt in their own ways with identical social issues. Indeed, some, especially in Europe, have been dealing with those issues since before "disability rights" became a recognized branch of law.

As might be expected, states have pursued distinct policies predicated on their own political and social systems. Many, like France,[1] follow a medical or welfare model, which emphasizes preventing disabilities and providing special, albeit circumscribed, benefits to people with disabilities. Others follow a model like that in the United States, which depends crucially on removing barriers to the exercise of the same rights others enjoy. Even here, approaches vary. The United States and the United Kingdom[2] have extensive disability rights laws, but they are essentially standalone pieces of legislation. In Canada[3] and the developing law of the European Union,[4] disability rights are placed in the matrix of anti-discrimination legislation, including race and gender.

These divergent approaches flow from a conceptual distinction. Following World War II, disability rights have developed in parallel with and sometimes nurtured by broader concepts of human rights. In contrast, much of United States legislation is rooted in more limited post-Civil War notions of racial injustice, which established tiers of protection.

While operationally theories of equality and barrier removal motivate the ADA as they do other states' laws, in many cases, those others now ground their disability legal regimes explicitly in the language of human rights than does the United States in the ADA. That human rights foundation has caused states to interpret statutes that read like the ADA more capaciously than the United States now interprets the ADA. Ironically, as a consequence, in recent years, nations and international groups have enacted laws based upon the ADA, just as the United States courts have been trimming the ADA's reach, often based on notions of states' rights. Especially, in view of developments in Eleventh Amendment jurisprudence,[5] one might ask whether one approach or another is more useful.

Not only does examining other states expose theoretical issues about how disability rights are situated in the broader framework of rights, it also raises questions about models of disability rights. The

---

[1]   See infra Section 23.4.

[2]   Disability Discrimination Act, 1995, c. 50 (Eng.), http://www.hmso. gov.uk/acts/acts1995/1995050.htm (last visited Sept. 17, 2003). For a comparison of United Kingdom and United States disability discrimination statutes, see Suzanne Bruyère, A Comparison of the Implementation of the Employment Provisions of the Americans with Disabilities Act of 1990 (ADA) in the United States and the Disability Discrimination Act 1995 (DDA) in the United Kingdom (Cornell University Program on Employment and Disability School of Industrial and Labor Relations 1999).

[3]   See infra Section 23.3.A.

[4]   See infra Section 24.2.B.

[5]   See supra Section 10.2.

demarcation between rights models (including the ADA) and welfare models (such as France's) also may have practical consequences. The statistics in employment, for example, raise the question whether the rights model leads to better outcomes.

Increasingly, people with disabilities are being considered among those groups that merit international legal protection. Regional international organizations, such as the European Union and the Organization of American States, have adopted legal instruments pertaining to the rights of individuals with disabilities. In addition, advocacy organizations and individual states have initiated a process that could lead to a United Nations treaty requiring signatories to follow specified practices designed to assist people with disabilities. In regional and broader settings, the theories that motivate the ADA have played a role, but have not always displaced other approaches to disability rights.

This Part examines the laws of other states and developments at the international level, in part for what they instruct about other states' views of disability rights law and in part to chart where the ADA has had an impact. After a brief description of the international human rights regime, the following chapters will examine a range of systems adopted by several countries and international organizations.

As in much of the rest of this treatise, the law is changing as we write. That is exemplified by the final section on the on-going drafting of a United Nations convention on rights of people with disabilities. Throughout, we ask whether one methodology is superior in practice and whether the theory behind the statutes matters. In the end, one should judge the models by their effectiveness.

§ 22.2 International Human Rights Law

One can view the development of disability rights law in the United States and elsewhere as a more general expression of human rights law. Since the end of World War II, nations have signed a range of documents that aim to improve the international protection of human rights.[6]

---

[6] There is a vast literature on international human rights. See, e.g., International Human Rights: Problems of Law, Policy and Practice (Richard B. Lillich & Hurst Hannum eds., 3d ed. 1995); International Protection of Human Rights (Louis B. Sohn & Thomas Buergenthal eds., 1973); The International Dimensions of Human Rights (Karel Vasak & Philip Alston eds., 1982); Mark Janis, et al., European Human Rights Law: Text and Materials (1995); David Weissbrodt et al., International Human Rights: Law, Policy, and Process (3d ed. 2001). The Internet also holds untold riches in seeking information about international human rights law. See also Am. Soc'y of Int'l Law, ASIL Guide to Electronic Resources for International Law, http://www.asil.org/resource/

"Human rights" encompass civil and political rights, such as the rights to free speech and assembly, the right to vote, and due process rights in civil and criminal proceedings. They include economic and social rights, such as the right of workers to organize. They include the right to be free from torture and heightened protection for at-risk groups, such as women and children. Those at-risk groups now include people with disabilities.

A.   *The International Legal System*

Classically, one thought of international law as law regulating the relations among states.[7] That did not mean, however, that international law had no impact upon individuals or juridical entities within states. For example, in the first half of the 19th Century, when nations began to abolish slavery and the slave trade, they entered into treaties which permitted them to stop ships of other parties to the treaties on the high seas if the ships were engaged in the slave trade.[8] If no treaty permitted the arrest of the slave ship, states could not do so on the high seas.[9] Likewise, international humanitarian law – the law of war – has bound nations to standards of treatment of combatants and, later, noncombatants in situations of armed conflict since the Lieber codes of the mid-19th Century.[10]

International law takes two forms: customary international law (or custom) and treaties (or conventional international law).[11] "Custom in

---

humrts1.htm (last modified Oct. 3, 2003); University of Minn. Human Rights Ctr., University of Minnesota Human Rights Library, http://www1.umn.edu/humanrts/ (last visited Sept. 16, 2002). International human rights is distinct from "International Humanitarian Law," which deals with the treatment of individuals in situations of armed conflict, commonly known as the law of war.

[7]   See J.L. Brierly, The Law of Nations: An Introduction to the International Law of Peace 1 (Humphrey Waldock ed., 6th ed. 1963) defining International Law "as the body of rules and principals of action which are binding upon civilized states in their relations with one another."

[8]   The Amedie, 1 Acton's Rep. 240 (Vice-Adm. Ct. of Tortola 1810) (Claimant of property – slaves – seized on the high seas could have no right to them where the jurisdiction of the municipal law of the vessel gave no such right.) But see The Diana, 1 Dodson's Rep. 95 (Vice-Adm. Ct. of Sierra Leone 1813) (Cargo of Swedish vessel restored where Sweden had not entered into treaty with Great Britain).

[9]   See Le Louis, 2 Dodson 210 (British High Ct. of Adm. 1817).

[10]   The Lieber Code of 1863, http://www.civilwarhome.com/liebercode.htm (last visited Sept. 16, 2003).

[11]   Article 38 of the Statute of the International Court of Justice lists four sources of international law:

its legal sense means more than mere habit or usage; it is a usage felt by those who follow it to be an obligatory one."[12] This latter element of the obligatory nature of practice often is referred to as *opinio juris sive necessitas* or *opinio juris*.[13] Given its nature, there are substantial disputes – into which this treatise will not go – regarding the amount of practice necessary to constitute a custom[14] and how one determines whether states have a belief in the obligatory nature of the practice.[15]

Treaties are a source of international law in a different sense than custom. Rather than expressing the general sense of nations that a certain practice is binding, they establish consensual rules of conduct

---

"(a.) international conventions, whether general or particular, establishing rules expressly recognized by the contesting States; (b.) international custom, as evidence of a general practice accepted as law; (c.) the general principals of law recognized by civilized nations; (d.) subject to the provisions of Article 59, judicial decisions and the teachings of the most highly qualified publicists of the various nations, as subsidiary means for the determination of rules of law."

Article 59 provides that decisions of the International Court of Justice have no binding force except between the parties to a dispute. Statute of the International Court of Justice, June 26, 1945, 59 Stat. 1031, T.S. No. 993, 1945 WL 26967 (U.S. Treaty), http://www.icj-cij.org/icjwww/ibasicdocuments/Basetext/istatute.htm.

[12] J.L. Brierly, supra note 7, at 59; see also Restatement (Third) of the Foreign Relations Law of the United States § 102(2) (1986). On competing perceptions of custom compare Michael Akehurst, Custom as a Source of International Law, 47 Brit. Y.B. Int'l L. 1 (1974-1975) with Anthony D'Amato, The Concept of Custom in International Law (1971). See also Michael Akehurst & Anthony D'Amato, Note and Comment, Correspondence and Reply, 80 Am. J. Int'l L. 147 (1986), http://anthonydamato.law.northwestern.edu/Adobefiles/CR1-86-ake.pdf (last visited Sept. 24, 2003). On the formation of custom, see Comm. on the Formation of Customary (General) Int'l Law, Int'l Law Ass'n, Final Report: Statement of Principles Applicable to the Formation of General Customary International Law, Report of the 2000 Conference, http://www.ila-hq.org/pdf/CustomaryLaw.pdf (last visited Aug. 9, 2003).

[13] Michael Akehurst, supra note 12, at 31.

[14] E.g., Richard Baxter, Treaties and Custom, 129 Recueil de Cours pt.1, at 25, 67, 73 (1970).

[15] See Anthony D'Amato, supra note 12, at 81. On the way customary rules develop, using the Internet as a model, see Charles D. Siegal, Rule Formation in Non-Hierarchal Systems, 16 Temp. Envtl. L. & Tech. J. 173 (1998).

between and among states that are parties to the instrument. Even when states have ratified treaties, the domestic effect, for example, whether the treaty creates an obligation that may be enforced in domestic courts, depends on the law of particular states.

In the human rights area, treaties tend to be multilateral conventions, negotiated in the framework of the United Nations or of a regional organization, which a large number of the 191 plus states in the world are parties.[16] While some judicial opinions treat multilateral treaties as declarative of or evidence of customary international law,[17] that approach is problematic for those who have not formally exceeded to the instrument in question.

The development of human rights norms in the post-World War II era has almost completely followed the treaty path. Most obviously, many of the norms of international human rights law are at best only arguably practices of states as a whole. For example, many states have acceded to the Convention Against Torture and Other Cruel, Inhuman or Degrading Treatment or Punishment,[18] but one can hardly say that states do not as a general practice engage in behavior that a reasonable person would call torture.[19] In addition, many of the obligations undertaken pursuant to human rights treaties are relatively detailed and are not likely to arise via the accretion of custom.

With respect to rules of international disability rights, both of those reasons apply.[20] In the first place, it is virtually certain that no customary rules requiring particular treatment of people with disabilities presently exist.[21] In the second, the detail needed to describe how to

---

[16] Typically, a treaty is negotiated and "opened for signature." At that point, states may sign the treaty, but it typically has no binding effect on them until it has been ratified pursuant to their internal laws and a sufficient number of states have become parties to it so that it has entered into force.

[17] Filartiga v. Pena-Irala, 630 F.2d 876, 881 (2d Cir. 1980).

[18] Convention Against Torture and Other Cruel, Inhuman or Degrading Treatment or Punishment, Dec. 10 1984, 23 I.L.M. 1027 (1984), as modified, 24 I.L.M. 535 (1985), http://www.hrweb.org/legal/cat.html (last visited Sept. 24, 2003).

[19] E.g., Peter Maass, If a Terror Suspect Won't Talk, Should He Be Made To?, N. Y. Times, Mar. 9, 2003, at § 4, at 4.

[20] For an excellent recent overview of international law standards as applied to mental disabilities, see Eric Rosenthal and Clarence J. Sundram, International Human Rights in Mental Health Legislation, 21 N.Y.L. Sch. J. Int'l & Comp. L. 469 (2002).

[21] See Charles D. Siegal, International Disability Rights Law: Norm or Not?, International Civil Liberties Report 2001 (Am. Civil Liberties Union

respond to the needs of people with disabilities cannot easily accumulate in a common-law fashion.

B. *Human Rights Treaties*

The United Nations began developing a series of human rights instruments with the Universal Declaration on Human Rights in 1948.[22] Although the Universal Declaration, at least in the view of the United States, is not a legally binding document, it set the stage for later human rights treaties.

Over the course of the next eighteen years, United Nations members negotiated the two principal human rights documents that have the force of law, the International Covenant on Civil and Political Rights,[23] and the International Covenant on Economic, Social and Cultural Rights.[24] Together, these instruments establish a series of rights that apply to all people, "without distinction of any kind, such as race, colour, sex, language, religion, political or other opinion, national or social origin, property, birth or other status" – but not disability.[25] They require those who have acceded to the conventions – "States Parties" – to take action to ensure the rights established by the documents.[26]

They also establish monitoring mechanisms. The ICCPR establishes a Human Rights Committee to which States Parties are to provide "reports on the measures they have adopted which give effect to the rights recognized herein and on the progress made in the enjoyment of those rights."[27] States Parties to the ICESCR commit to provide reports to the United Nation's Economic and Social Council on the "measures which they have adopted and the progress made in achieving the observance of the rights recognized" in the ICESCR.[28]

2001) http://archive.aclu.org/library/iclr/2001/iclr2001_4.pdf (last visited Sept. 16, 2003).

[22] G.A. Res. 217A (III), at 71, U.N. Doc. A/180 (1948).

[23] G.A. Res. 2200A, 21 U.N. GAOR, Supp. No. 16, at 52, U.N. Doc. A/6316 (1966), http://www.unhchr.ch/html/menu3/b/a_ccpr.htm [hereinafter ICCPR].

[24] G.A. Res. 2200A, 21 U.N. GAOR, Supp. No. 16, at 49, U.N. Doc. A/6316 (1966), http://www.unhchr.ch/html/menu3/b/a_cescr.htm [hereinafter ICESCR].

[25] ICCPR, art. 2(1); ICESCR, art.2(2).

[26] ICESCR, art. 2(1).

[27] ICCPR, art. 40(1).

[28] ICESCR, art. 16.

The two overarching agreements have been followed by a legion of specific ones.[29] The various oversight mechanisms make clear what is implicit in human rights treaties – the obligations must be enforced locally to have a significant impact on the lives of people. However, this structure of agreements, until quite recently, ignored disability as a protected class.

The Universal Declaration mentions disability in Article 25:

> Everyone has the right to a standard of living adequate for the health and well-being of himself and of his family, including food, clothing, housing, and medical care and necessary social services, and the right to security in the event of unemployment, sickness, disability, widowhood, old age, or other lack of livelihood in circumstances beyond his control.

But disability is not recognized as a protected classification, like race, religion, or gender. The Declaration says nothing about employment, training or even treatment. Certainly, it says nothing about access. The ICESCR, where one might expect a reference, is silent, as is the ICCPR.[30] As two experts have commented, "Despite being one of the largest minority groups in the world, encompassing 600 million persons (of which two out of three live in developing countries), disabled people had been rather ignored during the first three decades of the United Nations' existence."[31]

---

[29] E.g., International Convention on the Elimination of All Forms of Racial Discrimination, G.A. Res. 2106 (1965); Convention on the Elimination of All Forms of Discrimination Against Women, G.A. Res. 34/180 (1979); The Convention on the Rights of a Child, G.A. Res. 44/25 (1989). A review of the links on the website of the Office of the High Commissioner for Human Rights, http://193.194.138.190/html/intlinst.htm (last visited Sept. 16, 2003), shows the many other human rights treaties, conventions, and protocols to treaties and conventions.

[30] See generally Charles D. Siegal, Fifty Years of Disability Law: The Relevance of the Universal Declaration, 5 ILSA J. Int'l & Comp. L. 267 (1999).

[31] Theresia Degener & Gerard Quinn, A Survey of International, Comparative and Regional Disability Law Reform, paper delivered at an international disability law and policy symposium, sponsored by the U.S. Social Security Administration and organized by the Disability Right Education and Defense Fund, pt. 1.B.1 (Oct. 22-26, 2000), http://www.sre.gob.mx/discapacidad/papertdegener1.htm.

Chapter 23 OTHER STATES' APPROACHES TO DISABILITY RIGHTS

While other states' domestic approaches to disability issues are not part of international law, it is worth at least a look at how various states address those issues to put domestic United States law into perspective. As states increasingly recognize the effects of disability discrimination and observe other states' efforts to ameliorate those effects, they have developed a range of approaches toward people with disabilities.

On the one hand, the philosophy of the state might be to situate disability discrimination with other civil or human rights issues, to grant equality to people with disabilities. On the other hand, the issues can be dealt with as part of the welfare program of the state, requiring public and private employers to set aside a fixed percentage of positions for people with disabilities, supporting their income and providing protected work environments for those who cannot work in the private sector. In addition, the legal matrix of the programs vary. The rights can be constitutional or statutory. If people are given rights, they also can be given causes of action to enforce them or there can be administrative enforcement bodies. Or, the state can enforce quotas through criminal penalties.[1]

We describe the legal regimes of other states with some diffidence. We have given several hundred pages to the ADA, but will give only small fractions of that to other states, which have equally venerable and complex systems. We have tried to ensure that our examples are not caricatures.

§ 23.1 Statistics On People With Disabilities

It is difficult to estimate the total number of people with disabilities throughout the world. The count depends on definitional issues, such as the meaning of disability.[2] Cultural differences come into play in the definitional process.[3] Moreover, many states lack an ability to

---

[1]   In Appendix 6, we present a list of states and references to their constitutional and statutory provisions relating to disability rights. The accompanying commentary is drawn from the Department of State's annual human rights reports. U.S. Dep't of St., Country Reports on Human Rights Practices, http://www.state.gov/g/drl/rls/hrrpt/2002/ (Mar. 31, 2003).

[2]   Ann Elwan, Poverty and Disability – A Survey of the Literature 3 (Soc. Protection Unit, World Bank Dec. 1999), http://wbln0018.worldbank. org/HDNet/HDdocs.nsf/2d5135ecbf351de6852566a90069b8b6/c112683be39 8a4c38525684e007787d9/$FILE/9932.pdf (last visited Sept. 17, 2003). See also supra Part 2.

[3]   See id. at 9-10 (gender distinctions in some states may affect estimates of people with disabilities).

survey their populations[4] and sampling techniques may vary. As discussed in section 27.1 below, even in the United States, the 43 million estimate of the number of people with disabilities used in the ADA is subject to interpretation. But, with all those caveats, the estimates remain substantial.

In 1981, the World Health Organization stated that the percentage could not be estimated more accurately than 10%.[5] A later UN study of 55 states found a range of 0.2% to 20.9%.[6] Another UN agency has conservatively estimated that about five percent of the people in developing countries are moderately to severely disabled.[7] It is likely that the measured rates in developing countries are higher than in developed countries – 10% to 25% of children under 15 are disabled in developing states vs. 4% in Austria to 11% in Canada.[8]

As in the United States, throughout the world, disability has a significant impact on social and economic indicators. The poverty in many developing states not only exacerbates the trends seen even in developed countries, but also makes addressing the conditions more difficult.

People with disabilities receive less education than others.

- Hong Kong: In 1981, 4% of the general population of 15-24 year olds had received no formal schooling versus 25% of those with disabilities;

- Canada: A 1983-84 survey showed that about 6% of the total population aged 15-24 had attended only eight years of schooling or less, while the proportion in the disabled group was 17%; and,

---

[4] Id. at iii-iv.

[5] World Health Org., Disability Prevention and Rehabilitation, Technical Report Series No. 668 (1981), cited in report by Leandro Despouy, Human Rights and Disabled Persons, Human Rights Series No. 6 (1988).

[6] U.N., Dep't of Int'l Econ. & Soc. Affairs, Statistical Office, Disability Statistics Compendium, Statistics on Special Population Groups, Series Y, No. 4, tbl. 6 (1990) [hereinafter UN Compendium].

[7] Hidden Sisters: Women and Girls with Disabilities in the Asian and Pacific Region, U.N. Econ. and Soc. Comm'n for Asia and the Pacific, UN Doc. ST/ESCAP/1548 (1995), http://www.unescap.org/decade/wwd1.htm [hereinafter Hidden Sisters] (citing Einer Helander, Prejudice and Dignity: An Introduction To Community-Based Rehabilitation (U.N. Dev. Programme Report 1992)).

[8] Elwan, supra note 2, at 6.

- Bahrain: In the 1981 census, 27% of all persons aged ten and over were illiterate, but in the same age group of the disabled population, the proportion was 77%.[9]

Likewise, people with disabilities participate in the economy far less than people without disabilities.

- Australia: A 1981 survey showed the proportion of disabled people not in the labor force was around 60%, twice as high as the proportion for the total population (30%).[10] In 1993, 46.5% of the disabled population participated in the labor force, compared with 73.6% for the general population.[11]

- Canada: In a 1983/84 survey, 41% of the disabled population aged 15-64 was employed, compared to 65% of the total population in the same age range.[12] In 1991, 44% of disabled people were not in the labor force, compared to 19% of non-disabled people.[13]

- United Kingdom: In 1981, 16% of the registered disabled people were unemployed – twice as many as in the workforce as a whole.[14]

- A 1984 study of the United States and several European countries found that, in terms of labor market participation, persons with disabilities were less likely to work, and when they did work, it was more likely to be part-time.[15]

---

[9] UN Compendium, supra note 6, at tbl. 6.

[10] Id. at tbl. 7.

[11] Disability and Self-Directed Employment: Business Development Models 173 (Alfred H. Neufeldt & Alison L. Albright, eds. 1998) citing Australian Bureau of Statistics (1993) (figures given for illustration of orders of magnitude only; without further review, the 1981 and 1993 figures should not be compared).

[12] UN Compendium, supra note 6, at tbl. 7. Again only a few tables present comparables for the total population.

[13] Neufeldt & Albright , supra note 11, at 186 (citing the Health Activity Limitation Survey in Canada (figures for illustration only; the 1983/4 and 1991 figures may not be comparable)).

[14] Caroline Glendinning & Sally Baldwin, The Costs of Disability, in Money Matters, Income, Wealth and Financial Welfare 63-80 (Robert Walker & Gillian Parker, eds. 1988) (citing Peter Townsend, Employment and Disability, in Disability in Britain: A Manifesto of Rights (Alan Walker & Peter Townsend, eds. 1981)).

[15] Neufeldt & Albright, supra note 11, at 8-9 (citing Robert H. Haveman et al., Public Policy Toward Disabled Workers: Cross-National Analyses of Economic Impacts (1984)); R. L. Metts & T. Oleson, Assisting Disabled

- The Swedish International Development Authority reports that only 16% of the disabled population in Mauritius is engaged in economic activities compared to 53% of the total population; and that in Botswana, the figures are 34% and 51%, respectively.[16]

The consequences are ineluctable – lower income levels among people with disabilities even in states with generous social welfare systems, lower assets, including home ownership, and higher poverty levels.[17]

Lack of access to resources diminishes the ability of people with disabilities to protect themselves. In Japan, between 1946 and 1992, over 16,000 women with disabilities were sterilized without their consent.[18] Likewise, people with disabilities are unable to fight against inhumane conditions in mental institutions.[19]

Historically, disability was overlooked as a civil or human rights issue. Part of the problem no doubt lay in the economic conditions of many states. Ameliorating disability discrimination via modification of the physical environment uses more resources than requiring employers to treat the genders equally. Part of the problem also sprang from a misunderstanding of the nature of disability that leads to a diminished appreciation for the abilities of people with disabilities. Indeed, that may have flowed from the medical model of disability, which still permeates the thinking in many states.

Over the past few decades, states have moved, first tentatively and now more aggressively, to attack the conditions illustrated by those statistics. A number have either added to their constitutions or enacted domestic legislation dealing with disability rights. They have begun to consider international agreements that establish rights.

Entrepreneurs in Kenya: Implications for Developed Countries, in Partners for Independence: Models that Work 313-22, Proceedings Before the N. Am. Reg'l Conference of Rehab. Int'l (1993).

[16] Swedish Int'l Dev. Auth., Poverty and Disability: A Position Paper 2 (Apr. 1995).

[17] Elwan, supra note 2, at 14-15.

[18] Bureau of Democracy, Human Rights, & Lab., U.S. Dep't of St., Country Reports on Human Rights Practices for 1999 (Feb. 25, 2000), http://www.usis.usemb.se/human/human1999/toc.html (last visited Sept. 17, 2003). There is also substantial literature demonstrating that when disability is coupled with being a woman, the discriminatory effects are multiplied. Hidden Sisters, supra note 7, at 11.

[19] See, e.g., the reports of Mental Disability Rights Int'l, at http://www.mdri.org/publications/index.htm (last visited Sept. 17, 2003) (reporting on conditions in Mexico, Kosovo, Hungary, Uruguay and Russia).

§ 23.2 Welfare/Medical Model Versus Rights Model

We discussed in Part 1 the models that governed societies' understanding of disabilities. Often, the models are only implicit; no one thinks she is imposing a particular concept on a set of facts until someone else looks at the same facts and suggests an alternate way to understand them. Only then does one realize that the implicit model may not only define what the "problem" is, but also determine the set of acceptable solutions.

In the classic example, if the problem is defined as "certain people are unable to climb stairs," one set a solutions may be appropriate. On the other hand, defining the problem as, "most buildings are constructed in a way that prevents a substantial number of people from entering them," suggests another solution set. Many countries developed programs to deal with disabilities using the former model, but are now reorienting their thinking and switching to the latter.

The long silence of the international community on disability issues is in part explained by the paradigm applied to disabilities. The controlling model that sees disability as primarily a medical problem attempts to relieve the symptoms of the medical condition. Once those are dealt with — to the extent medically possible — the only question is whether the state should provide support to the individual. Assuming that the state feels a need to do so, the remaining question is the level of support. The welfare state systems of post-World War II Europe accommodated well to that approach. Their disability laws, to the extent they existed, treated people with disabilities according to that model.

As early as the end of World War I, in view of the huge increase of people who suffered disabling injuries in combat, a number of European states had adopted programs to assist people with disabilities.[20] Most often those took the form of quotas for the number of disabled employees entities had to hire.[21] In some states, compliance was voluntary; in others, governments tried to impose systems of penalties for non-compliance.[22] In some, for example, France, the government undertakes part of the cost.[23] Whatever the particular means, states adopting quota systems understood the centrality of giving people access to jobs.

---

[20] Eric Besner, Employment Legislation for Disabled Individuals: What Can France Learn from the Americans with Disabilities Act? 16 Comp. Lab. L.J. 399, 401-02 (1995); Lisa Waddington, Reassessing the Employment of People with Disabilities in Europe: From Quotas to Anti-Discrimination Laws, 18 Comp. Lab. L.J. 62, 63-64 (1996).

[21] The quota approach to jobs endures in much of Western Europe. Lisa Waddington, supra note 20, at 64.

[22] Id. at 64-69.

[23] See infra Section 23.4.

However, the effectiveness of quotas appears to be limited.[24] Moreover, simply imposing quotas avoids recognizing the particular attributes of disability discrimination. Perhaps worst, the quotas stigmatize, by implying that workers with disabilities could not compete for equivalent jobs absent the mandate.

If one sees the issues through a "rights" lens, the questions and the set of potential answers morph.[25] People have equal rights to certain facets of societies. Equal rights must, of course, be given content. As Degener and Quinn point out, this can mean "(1) formal or juridical equality, (2) equality of results, and (3) equal opportunity or structural equality."[26] Formal equality requires that the law treat all people equally and, for example, does nothing to assist people who have the same formal "right" to vote, but who cannot see the ballot. Arguably, it is an illusory benefit.

Assuring the equality of results might be appropriate in the voting case, but generally pursuing it raises distributive justice issues in other cases. For example, it might be both expensive for employers and disturbing to people without disabilities to guarantee people with disabilities that they will have jobs for which they are not otherwise qualified. In addition, equalizing results may present problems from the perspective of a person with a disability:

> Segregated education for disabled students, for example, might be deemed legitimate if special schools for disabled students provide the same educational opportunities and degrees as regular schools. To put it bluntly, if we accept equality of results as the sole way of understanding equality, the mainstreaming of disabled students into regular schools could be viewed as an illegitimate goal.[27]

More typically, in the United States certainly, laws try to assure equality of opportunity. The ADA addresses this by requiring "reasonable" accommodations in its employment provisions and similar

---

[24] Lisa Waddington, supra note 20, at 69.

[25] See Theresia Degener & Gerard Quinn, A Survey of International, Comparative and Regional Disability Law Reform, paper delivered at an international disability law and policy symposium, pt. 1.A. (Oct. 22-26, 2000), http://www.sre.gob.mx/discapacidad/papertdegener1.htm. See also Aart Hendriks, The Significance of Equality and Non-Discrimination for the Protection of the Rights and Dignity of Disabled Persons, in Human Rights and Disabled Persons: Essays and Relevant Human Rights Instruments 40-62 (Theresia Degener & Yolan Koster-Dreese, eds. 1995); Gerard Quinn, The Human Rights of People with Disabilities Under EU Law, in The EU and Human Rights 281, 290 (Philip Alston, ed. 1999).

[26] Degener & Quinn, supra note 25, at pt. 1.A.2.

[27] Id.

limiting devices in its other commands.[28] That accords with the dominant free market economic gestalt: people with disabilities are given the right to compete in a setting where their disabilities must be ignored if they are not relevant to the job or the societal benefit.

But, in other states, even reasonable requirements for accommodations and other benefits may be problematic. In the first place, there is a question of who pays. In the employment context, in the United States, burdening private employers (especially in view of some tax incentives) does not place an insurmountable barrier in the way of equal opportunity. In other states, with substantially fewer economic resources, it is not clear that choice will work. In many states, moreover, it will not be feasible to have the government pay.

In the second place, any regime based on a reasonableness standard will generate disputes, which necessitates a functioning judicial or administrative dispute resolution structure. These kinds of institutions do not exist in all states and where they do, a complex ADA-like statute will impose additional burdens.

Despite those impediments, for the past decade, the trend in disability legislation has been to adopt a rights paradigm.[29] New legislation in Canada, South Africa and elsewhere – 40 new enactments since 1990 – and constitutional provisions in a number of countries rest on the rights paradigm, and many flatteringly mimic the ADA's words. The trend is not universal, however, and we have no evidence of whether such laws and other provisions as do exist are being enforced.

§ 23.3 States Following A Rights Model

A. *Developed States: Canada*

A number of states have begun to recognize disability rights, both constitutionally and legislatively. Certain states create wholly new apparatuses for disability rights, as the United States did. The United Kingdom is one.[30] Others place disability rights among their general

---

[28] The term "adjustments" replaces "accommodations" in the UK's Disability Discrimination Act. Disability Discrimination Act, 1995, c. 50 (Eng.) § 6 [hereinafter DDA], http://www.hmso.gov.uk/acts/acts1995/1995050.htm (last visited Sept. 17, 2003).

[29] See, e.g., Rodrigo Jimenez, The Americans with Disabilities Act and Its Impact on International and Latin American Law, 52 Ala. L. Rev. 419, 420-22 (2000) (discussing Latin American statutes adopting the rights-based model and, in particular, Costa Rican cases).

[30] The DDA forbids discrimination in employment (Part II), "goods, facilities and services" and "premises" (Part III), education (Part IV) and "public transport" (Part V). Employers have an obligation to make "reasonable adjustments." "(1) Where – (a) any arrangements made by or on behalf of an employer, or (b) any physical feature of premises occupied

equality protections, although they must have some specific legislation to deal with the differences between disability and other protected statuses, such as race and gender. One might ask whether situating disability rights among other human rights laws does not conduce to a broader conception of disability rights.

The provisions in other states' laws face the same problems the drafters of the ADA faced, but sometimes address them differently. We will consider the Canadian approach, although we might just as well have considered, for example, New Zealand.[31]

---

by the employer, place the disabled person concerned at a substantial disadvantage in comparison with persons who are not disabled, it is the duty of the employer to take such steps as it is reasonable, in all the circumstances of the case, for him to have to take in order to prevent the arrangements or feature having that effect." Id. § 6(1). Sections 5(3) and 5(4) of the DDA provide:

> (3) Subject to subsection (5), for the purposes of subsection (1) treatment is justified if, but only if, the reason for it is both material to the circumstances of the particular case and substantial. [¶] (4) For the purposes of subsection (2), failure to comply with a section 6 duty is justified if, but only if, the reason for the failure is both material to the circumstances of the particular case and substantial.

For a critique of the English courts' treatment of the justification defense, see Jackie Davies, A Cuckoo in the Nest? A 'Range of Reasonable Responses', Justification and the Disability Discrimination Act 1995, 32 Indus. L.J. 164 (2003).

[31] Human Rights Act, 1993 (N.Z.) [hereinafter HRA] http://www.legislation.govt.nz/browse_vw.asp?content-set=pal_statutes (last visited on Sept. 17, 2003). The HRA prohibits discrimination generally and then in specific areas, such as employment, education, provision of goods and services, and provision of "land, housing and other accommodations." Id. §§ 21, 22, 42, 44, 53 & 57. It then creates certain circumscribed exceptions, among them exceptions related to disability. See § 21(h) (prohibiting discrimination on the basis of disability); § 29(a) (exception to § 22 requirement of non-discrimination in employment where "[t]he position is such that the person could perform the duties of the position satisfactorily only with the aid of special services or facilities and it is not reasonable to expect the employer to provide those services or facilities"); § 43(2) (excepting from public access requirement of § 42 cases in which, "by reason of the disability of that person, special services or special facilities to enable any such person to gain access to or use any place or vehicle when it would not be reasonable to require the provision of such special services or facilities"); § 43(3) (excepting from public access requirement of § 42 cases in which "the disability of a person is such that

At the federal level, Canada has situated its disability discrimination legislation squarely within its apparatus for dealing with all forms of discrimination. It substantially amended its Constitution in 1982, including its Charter of Rights and Freedoms. Article 15 of the Charter expressly prohibits discrimination on the basis of mental or physical disability:

> (1) Every individual is equal before and under the law and has the right to the equal protection and equal benefit of the law without discrimination and, in particular, without discrimination based on race, national or ethnic origin, colour, religion, sex, age or mental or physical disability.

> (2) Subsection (1) does not preclude any law, program or activity that has as its object the amelioration of conditions of disadvantaged individuals or groups including those that are disadvantaged because of race, national or ethnic origin, colour, religion, sex, age or mental or physical disability.[32]

1.   Definitions of disability

Canada has sets of human rights laws and commissions at the federal and provincial levels. The 1985 Canadian Human Rights Act prohibits discrimination on the basis of "race, national or ethnic origin, colour, religion, age, sex, sexual orientation, marital status, family status, disability and conviction for which a pardon has been granted."[33] This statute applies to the Canadian federal government and businesses regulated by the federal government, such as banks, and reaches employment, as well as government, services.[34] In addition, the Employment Equity Act, passed in 1995, specifically extends protection for people with disabilities and other classes to private employment. The Employment Equity Act defines persons with disabilities as:

---

there would be a risk of harm to that person or to others, including the risk of infecting others with an illness, if that person were to have access to or use of any place or vehicle and it is not reasonable to take that risk"); § 60 (dealing with exceptions to non-discrimination requirements for educational institutions).

[32] Constitution Act (1982), art. 15, http://www.solon.org/Constitutions/ Canada/English/ca_1982.html (last visited Sept. 30, 2003) (enacted as part of Schedule B to Canada Act 1982 (UK), 1982, c. 11). Note that Canada finesses anti-affirmative action attacks on the Constitution by specifically allowing affirmative action as a matter of constitutional law.

[33] Canadian Human Rights Act, R.S.C., c. H-6, § 3 (1985) (Can.).

[34] Employment Equity Act, S.C., c. 44, § 4 (1995) (Can.) 42-43-44 Eliz. II, 1994-95, http://laws.justice.gc.ca/en/E-5.401/48801.html. Section 4 addresses private and public sector employers.

persons who have a long-term or recurring physical, mental, sensory, psychiatric or learning impairment and who

(a) consider themselves to be disadvantaged in employment by reason of that impairment, or

(b) believe that an employer or potential employer is likely to consider them to be disadvantaged in employment by reason of that impairment,

and includes persons whose functional limitations owing to their impairment have been accommodated in their current job or workplace ....[35]

Note that the disabling characteristic is viewed from the perspective of the person with the disability.

Although deploying many ideas from the ADA, the Canadian statute differs in material ways. For example, it deals expressly with the mitigation issue by including those who have been accommodated, rather than defining away the disability, as the United States Supreme Court did in *Sutton*.[36] The Canadian Supreme Court recognized this distinction between the ADA and the Canadian statute in *Granovsky v. Minister of Employment and Immigration*.[37]

In addition to the federal statute, each province and territory has its own disability rights legislation as part of the provincial human rights act or code.[38] As one might expect, their approaches differ slightly. For example, New Brunswick defines "mental disability" as"

(a) any condition of mental retardation or impairment,

(b) any learning disability, or dysfunction in one or more of the mental processes involved in the comprehension or use of symbols or spoken language, or

(c) any mental disorder

---

[35] Id. § 3.

[36] See discussion supra Section 3.2.B.2.

[37] Granovsky v. Minister of Employment and Immigration [2000] 1 S.C.R. 703, ¶ 36.

[38] E.g., R.S.N.B. 1973, c. H-11, s. 3 (New Brunswick). These statutes are all available on WestLaw®. For another listing, see generally Learning Disabilities Ass'n of Canada, LD and the Law, at http://www.ldac-taac.ca/ld-law/canadian/HRClist.htm (last visited Aug. 26, 2003). The Supreme Court of Canada may render decisions on provincial statutes. E.g., Québec (Commission des droits de la personne & des droits de la jeunesse) v. Montréal (Ville), [2000] 1 S.C.R. 665, 185 D.L.R. (4th) 385, 2000 CarswellQue 650 (2000) ("*Québec v. Montreal*").

and physical disability as

> any degree of disability, infirmity, malformation or
> disfigurement of a physical nature caused by bodily injury,
> illness or birth defect and, without limiting the generality of
> the foregoing, includes any disability resulting from any
> degree of paralysis or from diabetes mellitus, epilepsy,
> amputation, lack of physical co-ordination, blindness or
> visual impediment, deafness or hearing impediment,
> muteness or speech impediment, or physical reliance on a
> guide dog or on a wheelchair, cane, crutch or other remedial
> device or appliance.[39]

Nova Scotia, on the other hand, defines both together and expands
the definition explicitly to cover learning disabilities:

> (l) "physical disability or mental disability" means an actual
> or perceived
>
> (i) loss or abnormality of psychological, physiological or
> anatomical structure or function,
>
> (ii) restriction or lack of ability to perform an activity,
>
> (iii) physical disability, infirmity, malformation or
> disfigurement, including, but not limited to, epilepsy and
> any degree of paralysis, amputation, lack of physical
> coordination, deafness, hardness of hearing or hearing
> impediment, blindness or visual impediment, speech
> impairment or impediment or reliance on a hearing-ear dog,
> a guide dog, a wheelchair or a remedial appliance or device,
>
> (iv) learning disability or a dysfunction in one or more of the
> processes involved in understanding or using symbols or
> spoken language,
>
> (v) condition of being mentally handicapped or impaired,
>
> (vi) mental disorder, or
>
> (vii) previous dependency on drugs or alcohol.[40]

As in the Canadian federal context, provincial legislation may strike out
beyond the ADA. In both sets of definitions, for example, analogous to the
federal statute, reliance on a remedial device is an indicium of disability,
not a way to find there is no disability.

2. Interpretive rules

Drawing on the inclusion of disability rights with other human
rights, Canadian courts have broadened the reach of disability rights

---

[39] R.S.N.B. 1973, c. H-11, s. 2.
[40] R.S.N.S. 1989, c. 214, s. 3.

statutes. *Québec v. Montreal* dealt with three individuals who had "physical anomalies" but no "functional limitations" with respect to particular jobs. Two, however, were fired from their jobs and one was not hired. The issue was the definition of "handicap" under section 10 of the Québec Charter of Human Rights and Freedoms:

> Every person has a right to full and equal recognition and exercise of his human rights and freedoms, without distinction, exclusion or preference based on race, colour, sex, pregnancy, sexual orientation, civil status, age except as provided by law, religion, political convictions, language, ethnic or national origin, social condition, a handicap or the use of any means to palliate a handicap.[41]

Focusing on the inquiry in a human rights lens, the Canadian Supreme Court wrote:

> [G]iven its fundamental and quasi-constitutional status, human rights legislation prevails over other legislation.... The Court has also held that because of its quasi-constitutional status, the [Québec] *Charter* must be interpreted in light of both its context and objectives ....

> More generally, in *Driedger on the Construction of Statutes* (3rd ed. 1994), at pp. 383-84, Professor R. Sullivan summarized as follows the rules of interpretation that apply to human rights legislation:

> (1) Human rights legislation is given a liberal and purposive interpretation. Protected rights receive a broad interpretation, while exceptions and defenses are narrowly construed.

> (2) In responding to general terms and concepts, the approach is organic and flexible. The key provisions of the legislation are adapted not only to changing social conditions but also to evolving conceptions of human rights.

> ...

> This Court has repeatedly stressed that it is inappropriate to rely solely on a strictly grammatical analysis, particularly with respect to the interpretation of legislation which is constitutional or quasi-constitutional in nature....

> The preamble suggests that the [Quebec] Charter's objective is to protect the dignity and equality rights of all

---

41 Quebec Charter of Human Rights and Freedoms R.S.Q., c. C-12, s. 10 (2003), http://www.cdpdj.qc.ca/en/commun/docs/charter.pdf (last modified June 24, 2000).

human beings and, by logical extension, to eliminate discrimination....

Distinctions based on personal characteristics attributed to an individual solely on the basis of association with a group will rarely escape the charge of discrimination, while those based on an individual's merits and capacities will rarely be so classed.[42]

---

[42] Québec v. Montreal, supra note 38, at ¶¶ 27-35. The court also cited a 1984 report of the Canadian government:

> In the following passage from the Report of the Commission on Equality in Employment (1984) (also called the "Abella Report"), at p. 2, the Commission eloquently explained that:

> Equality in employment means that no one is denied opportunities for reasons that have nothing to do with inherent ability. It means equal access free from arbitrary obstructions. Discrimination means that an arbitrary barrier stands between a person's ability and his or her opportunity to demonstrate it. If the access is genuinely available in a way that permits everyone who so wishes the opportunity to fully develop his or her potential, we have achieved a kind of equality. It is equality defined as equal freedom from discrimination.

> *Discrimination* in this context *means practices or attitudes that have, whether by design or impact, the effect of limiting an individual's or group's right to the opportunities generally available because of attributed rather than actual characteristics. What is impeding the full development of the potential is not the individual's capacity but an external barrier that artificially inhibits growth.*

Id. at ¶ 37 (emphasis added). See also Ins. Corp. of B.C. v. Heerspink, [1982] 2 S.C.R. 145, 157-58, 1982 CarswellBC 224, [1983] 1 W.W.R. 137, stating that:

> When the subject matter of a law is said to be the comprehensive statement of the "human rights" of the people living in that jurisdiction, then there is no doubt in my mind that the people of that jurisdiction have through their legislature clearly indicated that they consider that law, and the values it endeavours to buttress and protect, are, save their constitutional laws, more important than all others.

Accordingly, after an extended analysis, and recognizing the subjective nature of the notion of handicap, the Court held that "handicap" does not require a functional limitation.[43]

One might contrast the Canadian and United States interpretive schemes. Early on, applying tiered levels of scrutiny, the United States Supreme Court held that disability is not a "suspect class," entitled to the same degree of protection as race, or even as gender.[44] The more comprehensive approach of Canadian statutes places disabilities with other protected criteria and provides broader protection.

The Canadian courts' references to human rights concepts may tend to result in a slightly less restrictive interpretation of Canadian legislation than the United States Supreme Court precedent.[45] On the other hand, the court has stressed the individualized nature of the notion of disability. In a case where parents of a disabled child wished her to be mainstreamed in school, but the school authorities decided she was being segregated in that environment, the court wrote:

---

[43] Québec v. Montreal, supra note 38, at ¶ 71. That is, one can be "handicapped" without being limited in the ability to perform tasks. The court also wrote:

> The Preamble to the [Quebec] Charter suggests that its objective is to protect the dignity and equality rights of all human beings, and to eliminate discrimination. The objectives of the Charter will not be achieved unless it is recognized that discriminatory acts may be based on perception and myths and stereotypes, and not just actual functional limitations. The exclusion of persons with handicaps that do not lead to functional limitations would undermine the very essence of discrimination.

2000 CarswellQue at 3.

[44] Eldridge v. British Columbia, [1997] 151 D.L.R. (4th) 577, 3 S.C.R. 624 (hospital funded by province required by Constitution to provide sign language interpreter to hearing impaired patient); City of Cleburne v. Cleburne Living Ctr., 473 U.S. 432, 442-47 (1985).

[45] Gibbs v. Battlefords & Dist. Co-operative Ltd. [1997] 1 W.W.R. 1, 140 D.L.R. (4th) 1 (1996) (differential disability insurance benefits given in collective bargaining agreement to person with mental disability in relation to people with physical disabilities violated Saskatchewan Human Rights Act); Berg v. Univ. of B.C. Sch. of Family and Nutritional Scis., [1993] 102 D.L.R. (4th) 665, 2 S.C.R. 353, ("service customarily available to the public" interpreted expansively so that services provided to students without disabilities must be provided to plaintiff with mental disability).

It follows that disability, as a prohibited ground, differs from other enumerated grounds such as race or sex because there is no individual variation with respect to these grounds. However, with respect to disability, this ground means vastly different things depending upon the individual and the context. This produces, among other things, the "difference dilemma" referred to by the Interveners whereby segregation can be both protective of equality and violative of equality depending upon the person and the state of disability.

In some cases, special education is a necessary adaptation of the mainstream world which enables some disabled pupils access to the learning environment they need in order to have an equal opportunity in education. While integration should be recognized as the norm of general application because of the benefits it generally provides, a presumption in favour of integrated schooling would work to the disadvantage of pupils who require special education in order to achieve equality. Schools focused on the needs of the blind or deaf, and special education for students with learning disabilities indicate the positive aspects of segregated education placement. Integration can be either a benefit or a burden depending on whether the individual can profit from the advantages that integration provides.[46]

The court held that mainstreaming was not in the child's best interests.

3. Accommodations

Canadian law also must face the issue of how to accommodate individuals with disabilities. It employs a variant of the reasonable accommodation approach. Section 15(1) of the Human Rights Act defines "exceptions" to human rights requirements. The first is:

(a) any refusal, exclusion, expulsion, suspension, limitation, specification or preference in relation to any employment is established by an employer to be based on a *bona fide* occupational requirement; ...

(g) in the circumstances described in section 5 or 6, an individual is denied any goods, services, facilities or accommodation or access thereto or occupancy of any commercial premises or residential accommodation or is a victim of any adverse differentiation and there is *bona fide* justification for that denial or differentiation.

The Human Rights Act goes on to say:

---

[46] Eaton v. Brant (County) Bd. of Educ., [1997] 1 S.C.R. 241, 142 D.L.R. (4th) 385, at ¶ 69.

For any practice mentioned in paragraph (1)(a) to be considered to be based on a *bona fide* occupational requirement and for any practice mentioned in paragraph (1)(g) to be considered to have a *bona fide* justification, it must be established that accommodation of the needs of an individual or a class of individuals affected would impose undue hardship on the person who would have to accommodate those needs, considering health, safety and cost.[47]

Canadian courts have developed a test for appropriate accommodations in the sex discrimination area. In *British Columbia (Public Service Employee Relations Commission) v. BCGSEU*,[48] a gender discrimination case brought under a British Columbia statute worded the same way as section 15 of the Human Rights Act, the Canadian Supreme Court rejected its prior distinction between direct discrimination and adverse effect discrimination.[49] It held that to constitute a bona fide occupational requirement ("BFOR"):

An employer may justify the impugned standard by establishing on the balance of probabilities:

(1) that the employer adopted the standard for a purpose rationally connected to the performance of the job;

(2) that the employer adopted the particular standard in an honest and good faith belief that it was necessary to the fulfillment of that legitimate work-related purpose; and

---

[47] Canadian Human Rights Act, R.S., c. H-6,, § 15(2) (1985) (Can.), http://laws.justice.gc.ca/en/H-6/.

[48] British Columbia (Public Service Employee Relations Commission) v. BCGSEU [1999] 3 S.C.R. 3 Can.▓ ▓ (*"Meiorin"*), http://www.lexum.umontreal.ca/csc-scc/en/pub/1999/vol3/html/1999scr3_0003.html.

[49] The court noted that section 15 of the Human Rights Act does not support such a distinction, stating that

[w]hile it is well established that it is open to a s. 15(1) claimant to establish discrimination by demonstrating a discriminatory legislative purpose, proof of legislative intent is not required in order to found a s. 15(1) claim: .... What is required is that the claimant establish that either the purpose or the effect of the legislation infringes s. 15(1), such that the onus may be satisfied by showing only a discriminatory effect.

Id. at ¶ 47 (citation omitted).

(3) that the standard is reasonably necessary to the accomplishment of that legitimate work-related purpose. To show that the standard is reasonably necessary, it must be demonstrated that it is impossible to accommodate individual employees sharing the characteristics of the claimant without imposing undue hardship upon the employer.[50]

The court then applied the *Meiorin* standard in a disability rights case.[51] In *Grismer*, the Superintendent of Motor Vehicles denied the complainant a drivers' license because of his impaired peripheral vision. As the court wrote: "The issue is whether the member designated by the British Columbia Council of Human Rights ... erred in holding that a blanket refusal [to grant a license] in Mr. Grismer's case, without the possibility of individual assessment, constituted discrimination contrary to the British Columbia Human Rights Act, S.B.C. 1984, c. 22 (now the Human Rights Code, R.S.B.C. 1996, c. 210)."[52]

The court held that, under the *Meiorin* test, the member had not erred. It noted: "All too often, persons with disabilities are assumed to be unable to accomplish certain tasks based on the experience of able-bodied individuals. The thrust of human rights legislation is to eliminate such assumptions and break down the barriers that stand in the way of equality for all."[53] The blanket prohibition met the first two prongs of the *Meiorin* test, but the Superintendent failed to show that it was reasonably necessary to the goal of public safety. He could not demonstrate that people with Grismer's condition should not be permitted to drive at all.[54] Nor could he demonstrate that performing individualized assessments was unduly burdensome.[55] Because there were tests that could be used to

---

[50] Id. at ¶ 54.

[51] British Columbia (Superintendent of Motor Vehicles) v. British Columbia (Council of Human Rights), [1999] 181 D.L.R. (4th) 385, S.C.R. 868 ("Grismer"), http://www.lexum.umontreal.ca/csc-scc/en/pub/1999/vol3/html/1999scr3_0868.html (last visited Sept. 6, 2003). Notably, English courts have not adopted rules relating to race or gender discrimination in the disability context. See Clark v. TDG Ltd t/a Novacold, [1999] 2 All E.R. 977 (Eng. C.A.).

[52] Grismer at ¶ 1.

[53] Id. at ¶ 2.

[54] Id. at ¶¶ 34-37.

[55] Id. at ¶¶ 38-42 ("While in some circumstances excessive cost may justify a refusal to accommodate those with disabilities, one must be wary of putting too low a value on accommodating the disabled. It is all too easy to cite increased cost as a reason for refusing to accord the disabled equal treatment.").

determine whether Grismer could drive safely, the government had to perform an individual assessment.[56]

Whether, under the ADA or state analogues, the result in a *Grismer*-like case would have been different is unclear. However, the reliance on a standard with its origin in gender discrimination law in a disability discrimination case may separate Canadian thinking about disability rights from the paradigm used by United States courts.[57]

B.   *Developing States: South Africa*

Determining the legal situation of disability rights in developing states is complicated by the lack of transparency. South Africa presents a good example. The Constitution of 1996, widely hailed as a model, expressly outlaws discrimination based upon disability:[58]

> 9. (1) Everyone is equal before the law and has the right to equal protection and benefit of the law.
>
> (2) Equality includes the full and equal enjoyment of all rights and freedoms. To promote the achievement of equality, legislative and other measures designed to protect or advance persons, or categories of persons, disadvantaged by unfair discrimination may be taken.
>
> (3) The state may not unfairly discriminate directly or indirectly against anyone on one or more grounds, including race, gender, sex, pregnancy, marital status, ethnic or social origin, colour, sexual orientation, age, disability, religion, conscience, belief, culture, language and birth.
>
> (4) No person may unfairly discriminate directly or indirectly against anyone on one or more grounds in terms

---

[56]   See also Justice Inst. of B.C. v. British Columbia (Attorney Gen.), [1999] B.C.J. No. 1571; 17 Admin. L.R. (3d) 267 (B.C. Supreme Ct.) ((a) police trainee had a learning disability that could be accommodated by allowing him to take examinations in an alternate way (such as having more time to write the exam). (b) trainee's needs must be accommodated in a manner that respected his dignity but did not cause undue hardship to the Academy)); Canada (Attorney Gen.) v. Green (T.D.) [2000] F.C.J. No. 778; [2000] 4 F.C. 629 (Fed. Ct. Can.) (public agency had to accommodate dyslexic employee who needed to learn French for promotion by giving her more time on test and additional mandatory language training).

[57]   Of course, as discussed in Part 6, many remedies in the ADA expressly rest on the Civil Rights Act's remedies.

[58]   Constitution of the Republic of South Africa Act 108 of 1996 § 9, http://www.concourt.gov.za/constitution/index.html (last visited Sept. 25, 2003).

of subsection (3). National legislation must be enacted to prevent or prohibit unfair discrimination.

(5) Discrimination on one or more of the grounds listed in subsection (3) is unfair unless it is established that the discrimination is fair.

South Africa has also enacted an Employment Equity Act,[59] which provides:

(1) No person may unfairly discriminate, directly or indirectly, against an employee, in any employment policy or practice, on one or more grounds, including race, gender, sex, pregnancy, marital status, family responsibility, ethnic or social origin, colour, sexual orientation, age, disability, religion, HIV status, conscience, belief, political opinion, culture, language and birth.

(2) It is not unfair discrimination to –

1. take affirmative action measures consistent with the purpose of this Act; or

2. distinguish, exclude or prefer any person on the basis of an inherent requirement of a job.

Affirmative action measures include: "making reasonable accommodation for people from designated groups in order to ensure that they enjoy equal opportunities and are equitably represented in the workforce of a designated employer."[60] In addition, the act limits medical and psychometric testing.[61]

---

[59] Employment Equity Act 55 of 1998 § 6, http://www.labour.gov.za/docs/legislation/eea/act98-055.html (last visited Sept. 25, 2003); see also S. Afr. Dep't of Lab., Employment Equity, http://www.labour.gov.za/docs/legislation/eea/ (last visited Sept. 25, 2003).

[60] Employment Equity Act 55 of 1998 § 15(2)(c).

[61] Sections 7 and 8 of the act read:

7. Medical testing. – (1) Medical testing of an employee is prohibited, unless –

a. legislation permits or requires the testing; or

b. it is justifiable in the light of medical facts, employment conditions, social policy, the fair distribution of employee benefits or the inherent requirements of a job.

(2) Testing of an employee to determine that employee's HIV status is prohibited unless such testing is determined justifiable by the Labour Court in terms of section 50 (4) of this Act.

Complaints under the Employment Equity Act may be brought to a governmental labour inspector, the Commission for Employment Equity established under the act, or the Director-General of the Department of Labour.[62] The employer may object to any proposed compliance order. If the Director-General issues an order, an aggrieved employer may appeal to the Labour Court.[63]

The act is implemented by a Code of Good Practice, which came into effect in August 2002 and sets forth detailed rules for dealing with employees with disabilities.[64] The Code represents South Africa's attempt to address many of the issues that have bedeviled ADA interpretation. For example:

- It defines a long-term impairment, as one that "has lasted or is likely to persist for at least twelve months. A short-term or temporary illness or injury is not an impairment which gives rise to a disability."[65]

- With respect to "substantially-limiting," it states: "Some impairments are so easily controlled, corrected or lessened, that they have no limiting effects. For example, a person who wears spectacles or contact lenses does not have a disability unless even with spectacles or contact lenses the person's vision is substantially impaired."[66]

- On public policy grounds, it excludes, among other things "compulsive gambling, tendency to steal or light fires; [and] disorders that affect a person's mental or physical state if they are caused by current use of illegal drugs or alcohol,

---

8. Psychometric testing. – Psychometric testing and other similar assessments of an employee are prohibited unless the test or assessment being used –

a. has been scientifically shown to be valid and reliable;

b. can be applied fairly to employees; and

c. is not biased against any employee or group.

62   Id. § 34.

63   Id. § 40.

64   Ministry of Lab., Code of Good Practice on Key Aspects of Disability in the Workplace (draft document Apr. 19, 2001), http://www.labour.gov.za/docs/legislation/eea/codegoodpractise.htm (published for public comment).

65   Id. § 5.1.1(i).

66   Id. § 5.1.3(ii).

unless the affected person is participating in a recognised programme of treatment."[67]

- It requires reasonable accommodations, but provides: "The employer need not accommodate a qualified applicant or an employee with a disability if this would impose an unjustifiable hardship on the business of the employer."

- "Unjustifiable hardship is action that requires significant or considerable difficulty or expense and that would substantially harm the viability of the enterprise. This involves considering the effectiveness of the accommodation and the extent to which it would seriously disrupt the operation of the business."

- "An accommodation that imposes an unjustifiable hardship for one employer at a specific time may not be so for another or for the same employer at a different time."[68]

- Its requirements for testing and interviewing are very much like the ADA's.[69]

Awareness of disability issues appears high in South Africa. But it is difficult to gauge the effect of the legislation. According the United States Department of State's 2002 Human Rights Report on South Africa, in practice discrimination against people with disabilities continues to exist.[70] It also wrote, "The law mandates access to buildings for persons with disabilities; however, such regulations rarely were enforced, and public awareness of them remained minimal."[71]

Statistically, in 2001, only 0.2% of the public sector workforce was disabled, although people with disabilities constituted 5.9% of the population. But the statistics must be judged against South Africa's other problems. A disability rights activist in South Africa's Parliament was quoted in 2001:

> The Employment Equity Act is having an effect. It is slow and there have been problems, but its demands are gradually being realized. ...
>
> But, bit by bit, some of the fruits of the disabled's struggle for their place in the sun are ripening. There is still

---

[67] Id. § 5.1.3(iv).

[68] Id. §§ 6.11-6.13.

[69] Id. §§ 7-8.

[70] U.S. Dep't of St., Country Reports on Human Rights Practices: South Africa (Mar. 31, 2003), http://www.state.gov/g/drl/rls/hrrpt/2002/18227.htm (last visited April 5, 2003).

[71] Id.

stereotyping. Blind people are mostly employed as switchboard operators, but the equity plans presently being submitted to the Department of Labour are going to show that real progress has been made.[72]

As seen in Appendix 6, many developing states have adopted disability rights legislation. The question is whether those new laws will have any actual effect, given the other imperative needs of those states.

§ 23.4 States Following A Welfare/Medical Model: France

Another approach to disability rights is to provide special treatment and programs for people with disabilities, rather than to attempt to situate them in mainstream settings by providing them equalizing assistance. The system either mandates quotas[73] – an epithet in the United States – or gives people with disabilities a priority.[74]

---

[72] Peta Thornycroft, Beating the Drum, Johannesburg Globe & Mail, July 27, 2001 (quoting Hendrietta Bogopane), reprinted in Peta Thornycroft, Disabled Take Struggle to Parliament, The Braille Monitor, Dec. 2001, at http://www.nfb.org/BM/BM01/BM0112/bm011208.htm (last visited Sept. 6, 2003).

[73] For example, Germany, Japan or Greece. See Katharina C. Heyer, The ADA on the Road: Disability Rights in Germany, 27 Law & Soc. Inquiry 723, 728-31 (2002) (describing German quota system); Katharina Heyer, From Special Needs to Equal Rights: Japanese Disability Law, 1 Asian-Pac. L. & Pol'y J. 7 (2000) (describing Japanese quota system); Org. for Econ. Co-Operation and Dev., Labour Market and Social Policy, Occasional Papers, Employment Policies for People with Disabilities, Occasional Papers No. 8, OCDE/GD(92)7 at ¶ 123 (1992) (describing Greek quota system); Koula Labropoulou & Eva Soumeli, Euro. Indus. Relations Observatory, Workers with Disabilities: Law, Bargaining and the Social Partners, http://www.eiro.eurofound.eu.int/2001/02/Study/TN0102201S.html (2001).

[74] For example, Denmark: "Legislation introduced in 1960 provides for preferential access to certain jobs in the public sector (such as switchboard operators). In practice, however, the law is barely used, and applied to only 76 persons in 1991." Disability, Employment and the Law in Europe ~ Part Two, Eur. Indus. Rel. Rev. 252 (Jan. 1995), reprinted in Global Applied Disability Research & Info. Network on Employment & Training, Disability, Employment and the Law In Europe ~ Part Two, at http://www.gladnet.org/index.cfm?fuseaction=research.SearchResultsDispl ay&FileToReturn=337.htm (last visited August 13, 2003) (citing Neil Lunt & Patricia Thornton, Research Series No. 16, Employment Policies for Disabled People – a Review of Legislation and Services in 15 Countries (1993)).

Perhaps the best example of the attitudinal difference is this quote from the French Senate's website describing various states' approaches to placing people with disabilities in jobs: "La loi de 1990 [the ADA] ne crée aucune obligation d'emploi des handicapés." ("The law of 1990 does not establish any duty to employ handicapped people.")[75] The French would not leave it to private employers to apply non-discriminatory criteria, but would rely on the government to mandate employment.

That approach keeps alive the focus on disabilities as factors that set people apart, in place of a focus on the environment as excluding people who are differently-abled. It also entails substantial and often complex state intervention. However, given the mixed evidence on the success of the rights model, in theory application of aspects of the welfare model could be beneficial.[76] On the other hand, even states that follow this model are adopting some aspects of the rights model.[77]

France exemplifies the welfare model.[78] It does not – or at least until recently did not – consider disability a human rights issue.[79] Its

---

[75] Sénat, L'Insertion des Handicapes dans L'Entreprise: Les États-Unis, at http://www.senat.fr/lc/lc116/lc1167.html#toc31 (last visited Aug. 28, 2003).

[76] See Mark C. Weber, Reciprocal Lessons of the ADA and European Disability Law, 93 Am. Soc'y Int'l L. Proc. 338, 339-41 (1999); Mark C. Weber, Beyond the Americans with Disabilities Act: A National Employment Policy for People with Disabilities, 46 Buff. L. Rev. 123, 166-74 (1998). While these articles argue in favor of such welfare programs as job set-asides, they present no data on the benefits of those programs.

[77] E.g., see the Decree "Relatif à l'Accessibilité aux Personnes Handicapées des Locaux d'Habitation, des Établissements et Installations Recevant du Public, Modifiant et Complétant le Code de la Construction et de l'Habitation et la Code de l'Urbanisme." Décret No.° 94-86, Jan. 26, 1994, Journal Official [J.O.] Jan. 28, 1994, 1585, http://www.legifrance. gouv.fr/WAspad/Visu?cid=101466&indice=2&table=JORF&ligneDeb=1 (last visited Sept. 30, 2003). This decree changes building codes to require that all buildings must make known to people with disabilities that they can enter, move about, exit and avail themselves of all the benefits the establishment offers to the public. Id.

[78] The French government maintains a website that provides access to its laws: http://www.legifrance.gouv.fr/ (last visited Sept. 30, 2003).

[79] In 1987, in debates about the need for a United Nations convention, the French delegate stated, "the issue of the disabled was one of national solidarity ... was not a human rights issue warranting the drafting of further legal instruments." U.N. Doc. A/C.3/42/SR.18, 4 (1987), quoted in Osamu Nagase, Difference, Equality and Disabled People: Disability Rights and Disability Culture, http://www.arsvi.com/0w/no01/1995.htm (last visited Sept. 4, 2004).

disability laws date to the post-World War I period, when it had to deal with large numbers of disabled veterans.[80] Over the next 65 years, the law was expanded from veterans, military widows and orphans to all those designated as disabled by the Commission technique d'orientation et de reclassement professionnel ("COTOREP"), a French government commission.[81] The original 1924 law applied to any enterprise employing more than 10 workers and required such employers to have 10% of their workforce be disabled veterans.[82] In 1955, the law was extended to people who had suffered workplace injuries, but the quota was only 3%.

A law of November 23, 1957 required private employers to hire people with disabilities on a priority basis.[83] Département level committees classified workers into various categories and skill levels.[84]

> The 1957 act laid the foundations for compulsory employment, a quota system for the private and public sectors, and reserved employment for particular categories of workers in certain occupational activities. There were no penalties for non-compliance. Employers were expected to conform to a laid-down procedure for notifying to the employment offices vacancies in reserved jobs or where the quota had not been obtained. If the employment office could not produce a candidate within eight days (later 15 days), the employer was free to engage any worker. In calculating whether the quota had been met, a weighting was attached to workers classified in different categories by the committee for vocational guidance.[85]

The 1957 law also permitted people who could not work in normal environments to work in sheltered workshops ("ateliers protégés"), "centres d'aide par le travail" ("CATs"), or home-work distribution centers ("centres de distribution de travail à domicile").[86] However, it failed to

---

[80] Eric A. Besner, Employment Legislation For Disabled Individuals: What Can France Learn From The Americans With Disabilities Act? 16 Comp. Lab. L.J. 399, 401 (1995).

[81] Id. at 401-02.

[82] Patricia Thornton & Neil Lunt, Employment Policies for Disabled People in Eighteen Countries: A Review 90-91 (1997).

[83] Law No. 57-1223, Nov. 23, 1957, J.O., Nov. 24, 1957, p. 10,858, 1957 D.L. 346 (codified at Code du Travail, art. L. 323-9 et seq.).

[84] Thornton and Lunt, supra note 82, at 91.

[85] Id.

[86] Id.

meet expectations of employing people in ordinary jobs, largely due to its "ponderous and complex" structure.[87]

In 1975, France enacted a law establishing a broad charter of rights for people with disabilities, young and old, including education, training and social integration.[88] It was intended comprehensively to deal with disability issues. But, in the employment area it generally built on existing – dysfunctional – laws.

The 1975 law does not define disability. COTOREP, an agency composed of multi-disciplinary teams, replaces the prior vocational guidance committees and determines the degree of one's disability.[89] Guided by a person's degree of disability, the employment section of COTOREP classifies the person into specific categories of jobs. COTOREP "orientates the individual to mainstream employment, to a sheltered employment or to a vocational training program."[90] The law guaranteed a minimum wage based upon the wages of people in open and in sheltered employment.

Still, as with earlier laws, the 1975 law lacked any effective mechanism for moving people into the labor force. It exempted employers who entered a contract with a CAT or a sheltered workshop. By the mid-1980s, it was evident that the law was not working:[91]

- The percentage of people with disabilities in the population was about 5%, but only about 0.6% of private sector employees and 1% of public sector employees ("according to the most optimistic statistics") were "handicapés."

- Fifty-five percent of workers recognized by COTOREP as disabled were unemployed and their periods of unemployment averaged twice as long as non-disabled workers in 1985.

---

[87] See Marie-Louise Cros-Courtial, Les Obligations Patronales à l'Égard des Handicaps Après la Loi du 10 Juillet 1987 [Protective Obligations Toward Handicapped People Following the Law of July 10, 1987], Droit Social 598 (Juillet-Août 1988).

[88] Law No. 75-534 of July 1, 1975, J.O., No. 150, July 1, 1975, p. 6596, 975 D.S.L. 207 (codified at Code du Travail, art. L. 323-9 et seq.). See Cros-Courtial, supra note 87, at 598.

[89] Serge Ebersold, Comparative Analysis and Assessment of the Policy Implications of Alternative Legal Definitions of Disability on Policies for People with Disabilities[:] Progress Report About the French System 13-18 (Brunel Univ. June 2001), http://www.brunel.ac.uk/depts/govn/research/France.doc. (on file with authors).

[90] Id. at 16-17.

[91] Cros-Courtial, supra note 87, at 598.

- Although the number of people with disabilities employed in regular business had increased from 20,000 in 1965 to 75,000 in 1987, the number of people in "protected" work had increased from 3,000 to 69,000.

France most recently confronted disabilities issues broadly in the law of July 10, 1987, which, like its predecessors, is codified in the Code du Travail (Labor Code).[92] It imposes an enforceable obligation on public sector employers and on private sector employers with 20 or more employees to meet a fixed quota, which increased from 3% in 1988 to 6% in 1991, with employees hired weighted according to their disability. It also encouraged employers and employees' organizations to adopt joint plans to assist workers with disabilities to integrate in the workforce. Moreover, if an employee is referred by COTOREP, the employer cannot refuse to hire her. However, the employer can pay a smaller wage, the difference being made up by the state.

Although the 1987 law retains a number of features of earlier legislation,[93] it does depart from them. First, it imposes a duty on employers before particular potential employees are identified. Second, it focuses, not primarily on those injured in war, to whom the country owes a debt, but "handicapped workers." Thus, more than earlier legislation, it stresses the obligation to improve the conditions of all people with disabilities. In 1990, France added a statute that increased the penalties for refusing to hire people with disabilities.[94]

The 1987 law, however, resulted from a political compromise. One of its authors noted that "it is neither possible nor desirable to impose [the direct hiring of persons with disabilities] on a business which does not want to employ its quota of disabled workers or even an amount under

---

[92] Law No. 87-517, July 10, 1987, J.O., No. 160, July 12, 1987, p. 7822, 1987 D.S.L. 282 (codified at Code du Travail, art. L. 323-1 et seq.).

[93] They include:

> obligations to war-disabled workers; the recognition of disability by a commission, the weighting of categories of disability; compulsory employment with a percentage of workforce quota; scope to meet part of the quota obligation by contracting with sheltered workshops; [and] the right to a minimum working wage in open and sheltered employment.

Thornton and Lunt, supra note 82, at 91.

[94] Law No. 90-602, July 12, 1990, J.O., No. 162, July 12, 1990, p. 8272, 1990 D.S.L. 321 (vol. 2) (codified in part at Code du Travail, art. L. 122-45).

quota."[95]   A French commentator, Marie-Louise Cros-Courtial, has said that the way the law takes "economic realisme" into account results in a law that seems like a retreat.[96]

This attitude no doubt underlies provisions that blunt the law's effect.   In the first place, the beneficiaries of the act include not those recognized by COTOREP as "handicaps," but eight other categories, including those who suffered at least 10% permanent incapacity due to workplace injuries, holders of social security pensions, and war widows and orphans under 21.[97]   An employer can meet his quota by hiring the "socially handicapped," not losing any perceived efficiency and not employing people with disabilities.

In addition to the implicit loophole, the law contains three alternatives to regular employment, each of which meets the quota requirements.[98]

1.   Employers may meet up to half their quota by establishing protected workshops, home work distribution centers or CATs.[99]

2.   Employers can enter into "enterprise accords," approved by Departmental Commission of Handicapped Workers, War-Mutilated, and the Equivalent (CDTHMGA), in which they agree to implement one or more of a hiring program, a training program, technological adaptive measures or a program for maintaining people with disabilities in times of cutbacks.[100]   This provision applies only to people with disabilities recognized by COTOREP.   However, it has no enforcement mechanism and requires only a plan, not action.

3.   Employers may make an annual contribution for each person they would have employed to a fund overseen by the Association de gestion du fonds de développement pour l'insertion professionnelle des handicapeés (AGEFIPH), an

---

[95]   Philippe Auvergnon, L'Obligation d'Emploi des Handicapes [The Obligation to Employ Persons with Disabilities], Droit Social 596, 602 (Juillet-Août 1991) (quoting D. Jacquart , Rapport du Projet de Loi au Nom de la Commission des Affaires Culturelles, Familiales et Sociales de l'Assemblée Nationale [Report of the Legal Project in the Name of the Commission of Cultural, Domestic, and Social Affairs of the National Assembly] 30 (1987)).

[96]   Cros-Courtial, supra note 87, at 603.

[97]   Code du Travail, art. L. 323-3.

[98]   Id. art. L. 323-4.

[99]   Id. art. L. 323-8.

[100]   Id. art. L. 323-8-1.

organization of people with disabilities, employers and others created by the Code du Travail.[101]

The availability of those avoidance devices, inter alia, lead Cros-Courtial to predict that the 1987 law would not open many doors to employment for people with disabilities and that the hopes pinned on it could lead to disillusion.[102] Statistics from the early years of the law seem to validate those concerns. The percentage of people with disabilities employed stayed almost constant at 3% from 1988 to 1994; even accounting for the severity of the disability, it rose to only 4.11%.[103] "In 1994, 36 per cent of establishments met or exceeded the six per cent target; 27 per cent employed at least one disabled worker; and 37 per cent employed none. These proportions are almost identical to those in 1991."[104]

During the same period, contracts with sheltered workshops rose from 6,900 to 18,100, but still only represented 0.1% of the private sector workforce.[105] Moreover, "In 1990, 32 per cent of firms with contracts had no disabled employees, rising to 36 per cent in 1991; in 1994 the proportion was also 36 per cent."[106] The number of contributions to AGEFIPH rose from 317 million francs in 1988 to 1,593 million francs in 1984.[107] Employers thus opted to pay a bounty rather than hire people with disabilities.

More recent data also indicate that the law has not had a dramatic effect. In 1998, AGEFIPH estimated that 92,000 people with disabilities were employed in the "mainstream area."[108] In 1996, 13,446 people with disabilities were employed in shelters and 83,666 in CATs.[109] Thus, the ratio between "mainstream" and sheltered had not changed materially in

---

[101] Id. art. L. 323-8-2.

[102] Cros-Courtial, supra note 87, at 609.

[103] Thornton and Lunt, supra note 82, at 100 (citing Ministry of Labour, Employment and Training, 1993; Ministry of Labour and Social Affairs, 1996). This figure remained constant to 1998. See Euro. Indus. Relations Observatory On-Line, http://www.eiro.eurofound.eu.int/2001/02/word/fr0010194s.doc (last visited Sept. 29, 2003) ("EIRO").

[104] Id.

[105] Id.

[106] Id.

[107] Id. (citing Association de gestion du fonds pour l'insertion professionnelle des personnes handicapées (AGEFIPH) [Disabled Persons' Occupational Integration Fund] , Rapport d'Activité (1995)).

[108] Serge Ebersold, supra note 89, at 17 n.11 (citing AGEFIPH, Les Personnes Handicapées et l'Emploi, Données Chiffrées Disponibles en Mai 1999, Paris, la Documentation Française, 2001).

[109] Serge Ebersold, supra note 89, at 18.

the 8 to 10 years after the 1987 law became effective. Data compiled by the European Industrial Relations Observatory indicate that people with disabilities are unemployed twice as long as others and their unemployment rate has increased twice as fast as non-disabled employees.[110]

While the statistics on employment of people with disabilities in France indicate that the 1987 law, including its amendments, have not reversed the trend of gross under-employment, they do not present a picture so different from the United States statistics in Part 9, so that one cannot say from an outcome point of view that one system is obviously superior. That suggests that some combination of the welfare model and the rights model may be superior to either.

Like many other states, France has recently enacted legislation in areas other than employment.[111] For example, French law provides:

1. Children with disabilities are first to be taught in mainstream classes.[112]

2. Transportation for "gravely disabled" students must be provided.[113]

3. Buildings must be made accessible. Law Number 91-663 of July 13, 1991, recognized that the 1975 law had not been fully complied with. The 1991 law extended accessibility requirements to multifamily apartments. Notably, it also provided that advocacy groups could bring cases if accessibility standards were not complied with.

In summary, France has explored a number of possibilities to bring people with disabilities into the mainstream. As in all countries, there remain questions of the success of the approaches.

* * *

There is a wide range of national models.[114] While many commentators express a preference for a rights-based approach to

---

[110] EIRO, supra note 103.

[111] See Personnes Handicapées, Note d'Orientation de la Loi Relative à l'égalité des chances des personnes handicapées (Apr. 24, 2003), http://www.handicap.gouv.fr/point_presse/doss_pr/pdf/note.pdf (last visited Aug. 9, 2003) (describing various laws for people with disabilities); Personnes Handicapées, Ressources, at http://www.handicap.gouv.fr/dossiers/ressources/index.htm (last modified Apr. 2003) (resources for people with disabilities).

[112] Code d'Éducation, art. L. 351-1.

[113] Id. at art. L. 213-11.

disability law,[115] there exists little empirical evidence that people with disabilities have more favorable outcomes in those regimes than in others.

---

[114] See infra Appendix 6; see also Disability Rights Educ. and Defense Fund, Country Laws Index, http://www.dredf.org/symposium/lawindex.html (last visited April 26, 2003) (texts of disability laws of many nations); Euro. Indus. Relations Observatory On-Line, http://www.eiro.eurofound.eu.int/2001/02/study/ (last visited Aug. 31, 2003) (providing access to numerous European Union states' and other international disability laws).

[115] Degener & Quinn, supra note 25, at pt. 1.

Chapter 24 REGIONAL ORGANIZATIONS

Between the level of individual states and the United Nations, regional groups of states can establish policies keyed to the abilities of states in the region to respond. In the 1990s, regional initiatives accelerated until they touched every continent, except perhaps Antarctica.

As we shall discuss, the Organization of American States ("OAS") and the European Union ("EU") have adopted specific instruments aimed at eliminating disability discrimination. In 1992, Asian and Pacific countries declared the Asian and Pacific Decade of Disabled Persons to run from 1993 to 2002.[1] And, in 1999, the African Union, formerly known as the Organization of African Unity, proclaimed 2000 to 2009 the African Decade of Disabled Persons.[2]

The documents that have emerged from these efforts tend to reflect the degree of legal integration of the groupings. The OAS members have agreed to what could be described as general non-discrimination goals, keyed in large part to pre-existing human rights instruments. The EU, which has the authority to issue regulations binding on its members, has promulgated a directive, requiring action by its member states not later than 2006.[3] In each case, the international agreement rests with the broader human rights framework.

§ 24.1 Organization Of American States

The Organization of American States was the first regional body to adopt a treaty on disability rights.[4] Beginning in 1993, in a series of resolutions,[5] the OAS addressed the issues of disability.

---

[1] UN Doc. A/CONF 157/P C/61/Add.1. See generally U.N. Econ. & Soc. Comm'n for Asia and the Pacific (UNECAP), Asia & Pacific Decade of Disabled Persons 1993-2002, at http://www.unescap.org/decade/ (last modified May 8, 2000) (last visited April 27, 2003).

[2] Org. of Afr. Unity and Afr. Rehab Inst., Declaration of the African Decade of the Disabled Persons (1999-2009), Decision CM/De.535 (LXXII) Rev. 1 (July 2000), http://www.disability.dk/images/docpics/1047369246_OAU-ARI_DECLARATION_OF_THE_AFRICAN_DECADE.doc (last visited April 27, 2003).

[3] Council Directive 2000/78/EC of 27 (Nov. 27, 2000). 303 Official J. Eur. Communities 16 (Nov. 2000), http://europa.eu.int/comm/employment_social/news/2001/jul/dir200078_en.html (last visited Sept. 6, 3003).

[4] Inter-American Convention on the Elimination of All Forms of Discrimination Against Persons with Disabilities, June 7, 1999, AG/ RES. 1608, 29th Sess., O.E.A. Doc. OEA/Ser. P AG/doc.3826/ 99 (June 7, 1999), http://www.oas.org/juridico/english/ga-res99/eres1608.htm (last visited Sept. 6, 2003) [hereinafter Inter-American Convention].

In 1996, the OAS passed the Panama Commitment to Persons with Disabilities in the American Hemisphere, which "instruct[ed] the Permanent Council, through the appropriate Working Group, to prepare a draft Inter-American Convention on the Elimination of All Forms of Discrimination by Reason of Disability, taking into account other existing instruments."[6] The OAS considered drafts of a convention in 1997 and 1998 and adopted the Inter-American Convention on the Elimination of All Forms of Discrimination Against Persons with Disabilities on June 7, 1999.[7] Following the requisite six ratifications, the Convention entered into force on September 1, 2001.[8]

The OAS Charter[9] and the American Convention on Human Rights[10] mandate the Inter-American Commission on Human Rights to review complaints by private individuals against states parties for violations of human rights norms. Those norms include the rights in the Convention. However, at this point, there has been no litigation under it.

The Convention describes disability in a way that will be familiar to United States lawyers:

---

[5]   Declaration of Caracas of the Pan Am. Health Org.: Situation of Persons with Disabilities in the American Hemisphere, AG/RES. 1356 (June 9, 1995), http://www.oas.org/EN/PINFO/RES/RESGA95/ agd1356.htm (last visited Sept. 6, 2003).

[6]   Panama Commitment to Persons with Disabilities in the American Hemisphere, AG/res. 1369 (June 5, 1996) http://www.oas.org/juridico/ english/ga-res96/res-1369.htm (last visited April 27, 2003).

[7]   E.g., Draft Inter-American Convention on the Elimination of All Forms of Discrimination Against Persons with Disabilities, AG/RES. 1564 (June 2, 1998), http://www.oas.org/juridico/english/ga-Res98/Eres1564.htm (last visited Sept. 6, 2003).

[8]   See Technical Secretariat for Legal Cooperation Mechanisms, Org. of Am. States, General Information of the Treaty: A-65 (Inter-American Convention on the Elimination of All Forms of Discrimination Against Persons with Disabilities June 7, 1999), http://www.oas.org/juridico/ english/sigs/a-65.html (last visited Aug. 31, 2003). The United States is not a signatory.

[9]   Charter of the Organization of American States, April 30, 1948, 2 U.S.T. 2394, T.I.A.S. No. 2361, http://www.oas.org/juridico/english/ charter.html (last visited Sept. 6, 2003) [hereinafter OAS Charter]. The OAS Charter was signed at Bogota on April 30, 1948, and entered into force December 13, 1951.

[10]   American Convention on Human Rights, Nov. 22, 1969, O.A.S. Treaty Series No. 36, 1144 U.N.T.S. 123, http://www1.umn.edu/humanrts/ oasinstr/zoas3con.htm [hereinafter OAS Human Rights Convention] (entered into force July 18, 1978) (last visited June 12, 2003).

1. Disability

The term "disability" means a physical, mental, or sensory impairment, whether permanent or temporary, that limits the capacity to perform one or more essential activities of daily life, and which can be caused or aggravated by the economic and social environment.

2. Discrimination against persons with disabilities

a. The term "discrimination against persons with disabilities" means any distinction, exclusion, or restriction based on a disability, record of disability, condition resulting from a previous disability, or perception of disability, whether present or past, which has the effect or objective of impairing or nullifying the recognition, enjoyment, or exercise by a person with a disability of his or her human rights and fundamental freedoms.

b. A distinction or preference adopted by a state party to promote the social integration or personal development of persons with disabilities does not constitute discrimination provided that the distinction or preference does not in itself limit the right of persons with disabilities to equality and that individuals with disabilities are not forced to accept such distinction or preference. If, under a state's internal law, a person can be declared legally incompetent, when necessary and appropriate for his or her well-being, such declaration does not constitute discrimination.[11]

Subsection 2.b appears to pave the way for some affirmative action.

The Convention characterizes discrimination as interference with "human rights and fundamental freedoms." Those rights and freedoms are defined elsewhere, in particular the OAS Charter and the American Convention on Human Rights. The former outlines a number of social rights. For example, "All human beings, without distinction as to race, sex, nationality, creed, or social condition, have a right to material well-being and to their spiritual development, under circumstances of liberty, dignity, equality of opportunity, and economic security."[12] Again, it provides a right to education.[13]

The American Convention on Human Rights establishes a rather comprehensive list of civil and political rights – including the right to life, to humane treatment, to a fair trial, to privacy, freedom of assembly and

---

[11] Inter-American Convention, supra note 4, at art. I, §§ 1, 2.

[12] OAS Charter, supra note 9, at art. 45(a).

[13] Id. at art. 49.

association.[14] It adverts to the economic, social and cultural rights "implicit in the economic, social, educational, scientific, and cultural standards set forth in the Charter of the Organization of American States as amended by the Protocol of Buenos Aires,"[15] but those rights are not spelled out.

The Inter-American Convention does not itself detail the obligations of states. Rather, it sets out general duties in Articles III.

> 1. To adopt the legislative, social, educational, labor-related, or any other measures needed to eliminate discrimination against persons with disabilities and to promote their full integration into society, including, but not limited to:
>
> a. Measures to eliminate discrimination gradually and to promote integration by government authorities and/or private entities in providing or making available goods, services, facilities, programs, and activities such as employment, transportation, communications, housing, recreation, education, sports, law enforcement and administration of justice, and political and administrative activities;
>
> b. Measures to ensure that new buildings, vehicles, and facilities constructed or manufactured within their respective territories facilitate transportation, communications, and access by persons with disabilities;
>
> c. Measures to eliminate, to the extent possible, architectural, transportation, and communication obstacles to facilitate access and use by persons with disabilities; and
>
> d. Measures to ensure that persons responsible for applying this Convention and domestic law in this area are trained to do so.
>
> 2. To work on a priority basis in the following areas:
>
> a. Prevention of all forms of preventable disabilities;
>
> b. Early detection and intervention, treatment, rehabilitation, education, job training, and the provision of comprehensive services to ensure the optimal level of independence and quality of life for persons with disabilities; and
>
> c. Increasing of public awareness through educational campaigns aimed at eliminating prejudices, stereotypes,

---

[14] OAS Human Rights Convention, supra note 10, at arts. 3-25.

[15] Id. at art. 26.

and other attitudes that jeopardize the right of persons to live as equals, thus promoting respect for and coexistence with persons with disabilities;[16]

Consistent with the spectrum of legal and economic situations in the signatory countries, the Inter-American Convention provides a framework, rather than a detailed plan. Although it does have both physical and programmatic accessibility as goals, it commits its signatories only to "eliminate discrimination gradually." Putting that undefined exhortation aside, one might ask what its consequences are if it only directs states not to prevent people from realizing other fundamental rights, for which remedies presumably already exist. Perhaps the answer is that, assuming states adhere to the other human rights norms in the OAS Charter and Human Rights Convention, they are permitted to depart from those rules when there is a "rational basis" – in United States constitutional parlance – for doing so, but the Convention assures that disability will not be a rational basis.

A pre-Convention case, where one might now expect relief to be sought under the Convention, illustrates the situation. In *Damião Ximenes Lopes*,[17] the sister of a man with a psychiatric condition petitioned that a "rest home," to which her brother had been admitted for treatment, mistreated him so badly that he died. She filed her petition in 1999, before the Convention entered into force, and sought relief against Brazil, a state party to the Convention, for "alleged violations of Articles 4, 5, 11, and 25 of the American Convention on Human Rights ..., on the

---

[16] Inter-American Convention, supra note 4, at art. III, §§ 1-2. Article IV reads:

> 1. To achieve the objectives of this Convention, the states parties undertake to:
>
> Cooperate with one another in helping to prevent and eliminate discrimination against persons with disabilities;
>
> 2. Collaborate effectively in:
>
> a. Scientific and technological research related to the prevention of disabilities and to the treatment, rehabilitation, and integration into society of persons with disabilities; and
>
> b. The development of means and resources designed to facilitate or promote the independence, self-sufficiency, and total integration into society of persons with disabilities, under conditions of equality ....

[17] Damião Ximenes Lopes v. Brazil, Inter-Am. C.H.R.(Oct. 9, 2002) Case 12.237, Report No. 38/02, at http://www.cidh.org/annualrep/2002eng/Brazil.12237.htm. (last visited April 27, 2003).

right to life, the right to humane treatment, the right to privacy, and the right to judicial protection." In October 2002, the Commission declared the case admissible. One would think that she now also has a claim based on the Convention.

§ 24.2 Council Of Europe And European Union

To understand the treatment of disability rights by what is now known as the European Union, it is useful to understand a bit of the development of post-World War II institutions in Europe.[18] In respect of human rights, in particular, the situation is complicated because Europe has proceeded on two institutional tracks, which only recently have begun to coalesce.[19]

A.   *Council Of Europe*

The Council of Europe was established in 1949 in large part to promote human rights.[20] In 1950, the Council of Europe adopted the European Convention on Human Rights ("ECHR").[21] The ECHR and its five protocols[22] recognize a panoply of civil rights (right to life (Article 2), right not to be subjected to torture (Article 3), right to be free from slavery and compulsory labor (Article 4), right to fair trials in criminal proceedings (Article 6), freedom of "thought, conscience and religion" (Article 9(1)), freedom of expression (Article 10)).

The ECHR creates two enforcement bodies.[23] One is the European Commission of Human Rights ("Commission");[24] the other is the European

---

[18]   There is a mass of literature on this subject, which we will not attempt to cover. See, e.g., John McCormick, Understanding the European Union (2d ed. 2002); Neill Nugent, The Government and Politics of the European Union (5th ed. 2003); see also Euro. Union, Teaching Resources: Teaching the EU, at http://www.eurunion.org/infores/teaching/resource.htm (last visited Aug. 31, 2003) (providing a selected bibliography).

[19]   For a listing of current statutes in EU states, see Eur. Indus. Relations Observatory, supra note 73.

[20]   Statute of the Council of Europe, May 5, 1949, E.T.S. 1, U.N.T.S. 1168, http://conventions.coe.int/treaty/en/Treaties/Html/001.htm.

[21]   European Convention for the Protection of Human Rights and Fundamental Freedoms, Nov. 4, 1950, 213 U.N.T.S. 221, http://www.echr.coe.int/Convention/webConvenENG.pdf (entering into force on September 3, 1953) [hereinafter ECHR].

[22]   See Protocols to the Convention for the Protection of Human Rights and Fundamental Freedoms: No.1, Mar. 20, 1952, E.T.S. 9 (Paris); No. 2, May 6, 1963, E.T.S. 44 (Strasbourg); No. 3, May 6, 1963, E.T.S. 45 (Strasbourg); No. 5, Jan. 20, 1966 (Strasbourg); No. 8, Mar. 19, 1985, E.T.S. 118 (Vienna).

[23]   ECHR, supra note 21, at art. 19.

Court of Human Rights.[25] "High Contracting Parties – those states who are parties to the ECHR – may bring alleged breaches to the Commission. Individuals may bring petitions to the Commission, "provided that the High Contracting Party against which the complaint has been lodged has declared that it recognizes the competence of the Commission to receive" such petitions.[26]

The cases we discuss arose prior to 1998. Until 1998, the enforcement mechanism was as follows. After all domestic remedies had been exhausted, the Commission could investigate the matter and try to effectuate a "friendly settlement" of a dispute. Failing that, it could issue a report to the Committee of Ministers of the Council of Europe, which would decide whether there had been a violation of the ECHR. The Committee of Ministers could then prescribe a period for compliance and if compliance was not achieved would "decide ... what effect shall be given to its original decision and shall publish the Report [of the Commission]."[27] That decision was binding upon the High Contracting Parties. However, if the matter was referred to the Court within three months of the time the Commission issued its Report, the Commission would not act.

A matter could be brought to the Court by the Commission, the High Contracting Parties "whose national is alleged to be a victim," the High Contracting Party "which referred the case to the Commission," and the High Contracting Party "against which the complaint has been lodged."[28] The Court could issue a decision, which the parties undertook to abide and which was supervised by the Committee of Ministers.[29]

The ECHR does not mention disability. However, some applicants brought what amount to disability cases under other provisions of the ECHR. In two cases, students in the UK sought relief under Article 2 of Protocol No. 1, which provides that "no person shall be denied the right to education." In one case,[30] the court found that a local education authority's decision not to provide free transportation to a more distant school for a student with special learning needs did not violate the ECHR, since the child's parents did not contend that the closer school was inadequate, but simply that they philosophically preferred the farther school.

---

[24] Id. at art. 20 to 37.

[25] Id. at art. 38 to 56.

[26] Id. at art. 25.

[27] Id. at art. 32(3).

[28] Id. at art. 48.

[29] ECHR, supra note 21, at arts. 53-54.

[30] Cohen v. United Kingdom, No. 25959-94, 21 Eur. H.R. Rep. CD104 (Feb. 28, 1996) (decision on admissibility).

In a second case,[31] the Commission found that the local educational authority's decision not to conduct additional psychological testing on a dyslexic child and its failure to remove the child from a school (the child had already been removed from three other schools), which the mother believed was inadequate for his educational purposes, did not violate Article 2 of Protocol 1. The Commission "recognize[d] that there must be a wide measure of discretion left to the appropriate authorities as to how to make the best use possible of the resources available to them in the interest of disabled children generally," and also pointed out that, "it is not the Commission's task to assess the standard of teaching provided by schools." Accordingly, it decided that there was not a denial to the right to education and declared the Application inadmissible. Arguably, this decision is somewhat formalistic.

On the other hand, there have been situations in which the Court responded to disability-related claims made under provisions of the ECHR. In *X&Y v. Netherlands,*[32] a "mentally handicapped" woman claimed that by failing to provide an appropriate criminal penalty against a man who had raped her, the Netherlands deprived her of her rights under Article 8, which protects "the right to respect for his private and family life." Netherlands criminal law was at the time incapable of providing a penalty to someone of the complaining party's age (16) where she could not testify that physical force had been used or that promises had been made.[33] The Court found that this failure on the part of the Netherlands violated Article 8 and imposed a monetary penalty on the Netherlands.

The case of *Botta v. Italy*[34] presented a different and broader question. In that case, the plaintiff, a person with a disability, alleged that certain private beaches had failed to build ramps and accessible lavatory facilities, as required by Italian law.[35] After exhausting his remedies under Italian law, he filed a petition with the Commission.

> He complained (a) that he had been subjected to inhuman and degrading treatment (Article 3 of the Convention);

---

[31] S.P. v. United Kingdom, No. 28915/95, 23 Eur. H.R. Rep. CD139 (Jan. 17, 1997) (decision on admissibility).

[32] X&Y v. Netherlands, No. 16/1983/72/110, 8 Eur. H.R. Rep. 235, 1986 WL 407898 (Eur. Ct. H.R. Mar. 28, 1985).

[33] The Court noted that at the hearings, counsel for the Netherlands "informed the Court that the Ministry of Justice had *prepared* a Bill modifying the provisions of the Criminal Code that related to sexual offenses. Under the Bill, it would be an offense to make sexual advances to a mentally handicapped person." Id. at *238 (emphasis added).

[34] Botta v. Italy, No. 153/1996/772/973, 26 Eur. H.R. Rep. 241, 1998 WL 1043389 (Eur. Ct. H.R. Feb. 24, 1998).

[35] Id. at *242-43.

(b) of restrictions on his right to liberty and security of person (Article 5); (c) of discrimination affecting the enjoyment of his rights on account of his physical disability (Article 14); (d) that he had not had an effective remedy before a national authority (Article 13); and (e) of an infringement of his right to a fair hearing within a reasonable time by an independent and impartial tribunal (Article 6 § 1).[36]

The Commission found that the application was admissible as to the first three claims, taking them in conjunction with Article 8 of the Convention, which protects "private and family life." Having declared the Application admissible, the Commission then found that there was no violation.[37]

The applicant and Italy brought the matter to the Court, which affirmed, holding that there was no violation. The Court held that "private life" "includes a person's physical and psychological integrity," and "is primarily intended to ensure the development, without outside interference, of the personality of each individual in his relations with other human beings ...."[38] The Court held that this sometimes requires action by the state. Nonetheless, the Court found that:

> [T]he right asserted by Mr. Botta, namely the right to gain access to the beach and the sea at a place distant from his normal place of residence during his holidays, concerns interpersonal relations of such broad and indeterminate scope that there can be no conceivable direct link between the measures the State was urged to take in order to make good the omissions of the private bathing establishments and the applicant's private life.[39]

Interestingly, by the time of *Botta*, the Council of Europe had taken a number of further steps to recognize disability rights. As early as 1961, the Council had recognized the issue of disability, but was fixed in a welfare mode. The European Social Charter[40] provides in its general part, "Disabled persons have the right to vocational training, rehabilitation and resettlement, whatever the origin and nature of their disability."[41] Article 15 articulates what that requires in more detail:

---

[36] Id. at 246.

[37] Id. at 246-47.

[38] Id. at 257.

[39] Id. at 258.

[40] European Social Charter, Oct. 18, 1961, E.T.S. 035, http://conventions.coe.int/Treaty/en/Treaties/Html/035.htm (entering into force on Feb. 26, 1965).

[41] Id. at pt. I, art. 15.

Article 15 – The right of physically or mentally disabled persons to vocational training, rehabilitation and social resettlement

With a view to ensuring the effective exercise of the right of the physically or mentally disabled to vocational training, rehabilitation and resettlement, the Contracting Parties undertake:

1. to take adequate measures for the provision of training facilities, including, where necessary, specialised institutions, public or private;

2. to take adequate measures for the placing of disabled persons in employment, such as specialised placing services, facilities for sheltered employment and measures to encourage employers to admit disabled persons to employment.

In 1992, the Committee of Ministers issued Recommendation No. r(92)6 "on a coherent policy for people with disabilities."[42] The general principals upon which the resolution rests are set forth in Section 1:

A coherent and global policy in favour of people with disabilities or who are in danger of acquiring them should aim at:

– preventing or eliminating disablement, preventing its deterioration and alleviating its consequences;

– guaranteeing full and active participation in community life;

– helping them to lead independent lives, according to their own wishes.

It is an ongoing and dynamic process of mutual adaptation, involving on the one hand people with disabilities living according to their own wishes, choice and abilities, which must be developed as far as possible, and on the other hand, society which must demonstrate its support by taking specific and appropriate steps to ensure equality of opportunity.[43]

Then, in 1996, the Council adopted a revised European Social Charter that fundamentally changed the theory of the prior article 15

---

[42] Recommendation No. r(92)6 of the Comm. of Ministers, http://cm.coe.int/stat/E/Public/1992/92r6.htm (adopted Apr. 9, 1992 at the 474th meeting of the Ministers' Deputies) (last visited May 17, 2003).
[43] Id.

from one of rehabilitation and segregation to one of "independence, social integration and participation in the life of the community."[44]

> Article 15 – The right of persons with disabilities to independence, social integration and participation in the life of the community
>
> With a view to ensuring to persons with disabilities, irrespective of age and the nature and origin of their disabilities, the effective exercise of the right to independence, social integration and participation in the life of the community, the Parties undertake, in particular:
>
> to take the necessary measures to provide persons with disabilities with guidance, education and vocational training in the framework of general schemes wherever possible or, where this is not possible, through specialised bodies, public or private;
>
> to promote their access to employment through all measures tending to encourage employers to hire and keep in employment persons with disabilities in the ordinary working environment and to adjust the working conditions to the needs of the disabled or, where this is not possible by reason of the disability, by arranging for or creating sheltered employment according to the level of disability. In certain cases, such measures may require recourse to specialised placement and support services;
>
> to promote their full social integration and participation in the life of the community in particular through measures, including technical aids, aiming to overcome barriers to communication and mobility and enabling access to transport, housing, cultural activities and leisure.[45]

This and other resolutions,[46] evince an awareness on the part of

---

[44] European Social Charter, May 3 1996, E.T.S. 163, http://conventions.coe.int/Treaty/en/Treaties/html/163.htm (last visited May 17, 2003).

[45] Id. at art. 15.

[46] The Council of Europe Parliamentary Assembly Recommendation 1185 (1992) states that: "[s]ociety has a duty to adapt its standards to the specific needs of disabled people in order to ensure that they can lead independent lives." See Parliamentary Assembly Recommendation 1185 (1992), http://assembly.coe.int/Main.asp?link=http%3A%2F%2Fassembly. coe.int%2FDocuments%2FAdoptedText%2Fta92%2FEREC1185.htm (last visited Sept. 12, 2003). The Council of Europe's web site, http://www.coe.int/DefaultEN.asp (last modified Oct. 17, 2003), provides a very useful portal to the documents of the Council's organs.

the Council of Europe that additional legislation is necessary to realize rights of people with disabilities. However, these recommendations in the European Social Charter have limited legal impact. The recommendations are just that. The Social Charter provides that a signatory must "consider itself bound by at least six of the following nine articles of Part II of this Charter: Articles 1, 5, 6, 7, 12, 13, 16, 19 and 20."[47] Therefore, the disability provision is not binding.

In 1998, the Council significantly overhauled procedures under the ECHR. It abolished the Commission and instituted a process by which all matters go to the Court. The Court now sits in committees of 3, chambers of 7 and a grand chamber of 17, which hears only exceptional cases.[48] The Committee may unanimously declare applications inadmissible or strike out from the list of cases individual applications "where such a decision can be taken without further examination."[49] That decision is final.

If there is no final decision by a Committee, a chamber of seven decides on the admissibility and the merits of the applications, both when brought by states and by individuals. Again, the decision of the Chamber is final unless it relinquishes jurisdiction to the Grand Chamber, in cases that raise "a serious question affecting the interpretation of the Convention or the protocols thereto" or where there is a possibility of inconsistency with their prior judgment.[50] The decision of the Grand Chamber is final.

It is not clear if recent developments in the Charter and Resolutions have impacted the decisions of the Court under the new regime. In one unreported case, *Zehnalová v. Czech Republic*,[51] the plaintiff alleged that the Czech Republic had failed to enforce its own laws on accessibility of public buildings. The plaintiff structured his claim much like the plaintiff in *Botta*. The Court, according to a comment discussing the case, wrote: "Article 8 was not necessarily applicable whenever the first applicant's everyday life was affected, but only in the exceptional circumstances where the lack of access to public buildings would hinder her rights to personal development and to establish and maintain relations with the outside world and others."[52] It thus found the application inadmissible.

---

47 European Social Charter, supra note 44, at pt. III, art. A(1)(b).

48 See ECHR, supra note 21, at art. 27.

49 Id. at art. 28.

50 Id. at art. 29.

51 Zehnalová and Zehnal v. Czech Republic, No. 38621/97, unreported (Eur. Ct. H.R. May 14, 2002), cited in Case Comment, Employment and Discrimination: Failure to Ensure Public Buildings Are Accessible to the Disabled, Eur. Hum. Rts. L. Rev. 673, 673 (2002).

52 Id.

It seems relatively clear from *Botta* and *Zehnálova* that the European court does not consider the ECHR to reach as far as to require contracting parties to enforce their own laws on accessibility of buildings. In both *Botta* and *Zehnálova*, the Court limited the reach of Article 8. In the absence of more targeted treaty language, the Court seems willing to give local officials a good deal of discretion in enforcing their own disability rights statutes.

However, where actions by authorities impacted an individual because of that person's disabilities, in a way that deprived the individual of rights guaranteed by the ECHR, there has been redress. In *Price v. United Kingdom*[53] the applicant suffered from phocomelia, as a result of Thalidomide, as well as kidney problems. She was held in contempt of court in a civil proceeding and sentenced to seven days in prison. A court officer refused to allow her to take her wheelchair's battery charger with her. Because she could not be sent to prison on the first night of her incarceration, she spent the night in a cell in a local jail, where she alleged she had to sleep in her chair because the bed was too hard and would have caused pain in her legs and where the toilet was inaccessible to her. The cell was so cold she had to be wrapped in two blankets.[54]

On the second day, the applicant was transferred to a prison, where she was put in a special medical facility. She alleged that during the second evening, she was placed on a toilet by a female prison officer and then had to wait for over three hours until she agreed to allow a male nursing officer to clean her and help her off the toilet.[55] She also alleged that a female nursing officer undressed her in the presence of two male prison nursing officers.[56] The government denied these allegations.[57]

After she was released from prison, the applicant claimed that she suffered health problems for ten weeks as a result of her treatment, but did not provide any direct medical evidence in support of that claim.[58] After exhausting her remedies in the United Kingdom, she petitioned the Court, alleging a breach of the requirement in Article 3 of the Convention that, "No one shall be subjected to torture or to inhuman or degrading treatment or punishment."

The evidentiary record was sparse and disputed; however there were doctors and nurses' notes that indicated "concern over the problems that were likely to be encountered during [applicant's] detention,

---

[53] Price v. United Kingdom, No. 33394/96, 34 Eur. H.R. Rep. 53, 2001 WL 825435 (ECHR) (Eur. Ct. H.R. July 10, 2001).

[54] Id. at ¶ 9, 2001 WL 825435, at *1288.

[55] Id. at ¶ 15, 2001 WL 825435, at *1290.

[56] Id.

[57] Id.

[58] Id. at ¶ 18, 2001 WL 825435, at *1291.

including reaching the bed and toilet, hygiene and fluid intake, and mobility if the battery of her wheelchair ran down."[59] In fact, the prison governor authorized his staff to try to find a place in an outside hospital for her, but they could not do so because she had no specific medical condition.[60] The Court found a violation of Article 3:

> There is no evidence in this case of any positive intention to humiliate or debase the applicant. However, the Court considers that to detain a severely disabled person in conditions where she is dangerously cold, risks developing sores because her bed is too hard or unreachable, and is unable to go to the toilet or keep clean without the greatest of difficulty, constitutes degrading treatment contrary to Article 3. It therefore finds a violation of this provision in the present case.[61]

Significantly, the Court did not find it was necessary that there be an intention to humiliate the applicant. The condition sufficed. Although the applicant requested £50,000 as damages, the Court awarded £4,500 for non-pecuniary damage and £4,000 (less 5,300 francs previously paid as legal aid by the Council of Europe) plus post-judgment interest.

Three judges concurred in two separate opinions. In one, the judges wrote that the "primary responsibility" for the violation rested not with the police, "but with the judicial authorities who committed the applicant to an immediate term of imprisonment for contempt of court," without "at the very least ensuring in advance that there existed both adequate facilities for detaining her and conditions of detention in which her special needs could be met."[62]

The other concurring opinion, by Judge Greve, cited an earlier case, *Thlimmenos v. Greece*:[63] "The right not to be discriminated against in the enjoyment of the rights guaranteed under the Convention is also violated when States without an objective and reasonable justification fail to treat differently persons whose situations are significantly different." That judge wrote that ameliorating and compensating for the person's disabilities "form part of the disabled person's bodily integrity."[64] The judge felt that that bodily integrity had been violated. He wrote:

> The applicant's disabilities are not hidden or easily overlooked. It requires no special qualification, only a

---

59 Price, ¶ 29, 2001 WL 825435, at *1294.

60 Id.

61 Id. at ¶ 30, 2001 WL 825435, at *1294.

62 Id. at *1295-96 (Bratza, J., concurring).

63 Thlimmenos v. Greece, No. 34369/97, 31 Eur. H.R. Rep. 15 (Eur. Ct. H.R. Apr. 6, 2000).

64 Price, 2001 WL 825435, at *1296 (Greve, J., concurring).

minimum of ordinary human empathy, to appreciate her situation and to understand that to avoid unnecessary hardship – that is, hardship not implicit in the imprisonment of an able-bodied person – she has to be treated differently from other people because her situation is significantly different.[65]

It is unclear how far Judge Greve intended to take his analysis. It could well impose duties on states to differentiate among people that transcend obligations presently contemplated by most anti-discrimination legislation.[66]

B. *European Union*

Unlike the Council of Europe, the principal focus of the entity presently known as the European Union ("EU") was not human rights. Rather, the EU has grown out of post-World War II attempts to unify Europe economically and then politically.

The EU and European Community ("EC") formally came into being in July 1992 at Maastricht, Netherlands with the signings of the Treaty on European Union[67] and the Treaty Establishing the European Community.[68] The EU Treaty amended the three constituent treaties of the European Economic Community ("EEC"), the Treaty Establishing the European Economic Community;[69] the Treaty Establishing the European

---

[65] Id. at *1297 (Greve, J., concurring).

[66] The year 2003 was the European year of people with disabilities. See Eur. Year of People with Disabilities, Official Website (2003), http://www.eypd2003.org/eypd/index.jsp (last visited Sept. 12, 2003). On May 8, 2003, the second European conference of Ministers responsible for integration policies for people with disabilities adopted the Malaga Ministerial Declaration on People with Disabilities. That Declaration sets forth the elements of a European action plan to be implemented over the next decade. See Malaga Ministerial Declaration on People with Disabilities: "Progressing Towards Full Participation As Citizens" (May 8, 2003), http://eurociu.implantecoclear.org/declamalaga_en.htm.

[67] Treaty on European Union, July 29, 1992, O.J. (C 191) 1 (1992), http://europa.eu.int/en/record/mt/top.html [hereinafter EU Treaty].

[68] Treaty Establishing the European Community, July 31, 1992 O.J. (C 224) [hereinafter EC Treaty] ("O.J." is the Official Journal of the European Communities.) The consolidated version of the treaty, Dec. 24, 2002 O.J. C325, can be accessed via Eur-Lex, at http://europa.eu.int/eur-lex/en/search/search_treaties.html.

[69] Treaty Establishing the European Economic Community, Mar. 25, 1957, 298 U.N.T.S. 3, 4 Eur. Y.B. 412 [hereinafter EEC Treaty or Treaty of Rome].

Atomic Energy Community,[70] and the Treaty Establishing the European Coal And Steel Community.[71] The institutions that presently govern the EU are the Parliament (elected by the people of the EU), the Council (composed of the governments), the Commission (the executive body), the Court of Justice and the Court of Auditors.[72]

The impetus toward human rights has, over the past ten years, percolated into the structure of the EU.[73] Human rights advocates have promoted the incorporation of human rights into EU documents, such as the EC Treaty and the subsequent Treaty of Amsterdam.[74] Moreover, the EU has become increasingly active in the employment area and in other areas it traditionally avoided. Its philosophy is rights-based, consistent with developments in the Council of Europe and is motivated in part by the ADA.

Article F(2) of the EU Treaty (now Article 6 of the Amsterdam Treaty) provides as follows:

> The Union shall respect fundamental rights, as guaranteed by the European Convention for the Protection of Human Rights and Fundamental Freedoms[75] signed in Rome on 4 November 1950 and as they result from the constitutional traditions common to the Member States, as general principles of Community law.

---

[70] Treaty Establishing the European Atomic Energy Community, Mar. 25, 1957, 298 U.N.T.S. 259, 5 Eur. Y.B. 454 http://europa.eu.int/abc/obj/treaties/en/entoc38.htm [Euratom Treaty].

[71] Treaty Establishing the European Coal and Steel Community, Apr. 18, 1951, 261 U.N.T.S. 140 http://europa.eu.int/abc/obj/treaties/en/entoc29.htm [hereinafter ECSC Treaty or Treaty of Paris].

[72] See generally Europa, Institutions of the European Union, http://europa.eu.int/inst-en.htm (last visited Sept. 6, 2003). The present structure of the EU is set forth in the Treaty of Amsterdam Amending the Treaty on European Union, the Treaties Establishing the European Communities and Related Acts, signed November 10, 1997, O.J. C 340 173 (1997), art. 7 and Part 5 ("Treaty of Amsterdam"). The Treaty of Nice Amending the Treaty on European Union, the Treaties Establishing the European Communities and Certain Related Acts, signed February 14, 2000, O.J. C 80 1 (2001) ("Treaty of Nice"), amended the earlier treaties.

[73] A useful web site for European developments is the Euro. Indus. Relations Observatory Online, at http://www.eiro.eurofound.ie (last visited Sept. 24, 2003).

[74] Gerard Quinn, Human Rights of People with Disabilities Under EU Law, in The EU and Human Rights, 281, 298-305 (Philip Alston, ed., 1999).

[75] See ECHR, supra note 21.

The EC Treaty also provides:

Community policy in this area shall contribute to the general objective of developing and consolidating democracy and the rule of law, and to that of respecting human rights and fundamental freedoms.[76]

Without prejudice to the other provisions of this Treaty the Council, acting in accordance with the procedure referred to in Article 189c, shall adopt the measures necessary to further the objectives referred to in Article 130u. Such measures may take the form of multiannual programmes.[77]

Despite those principles, the EU's competence in the area of human rights was limited. In 1994, a number of member states asked for an advisory opinion from the European Court of Justice as to whether the EU, like its constituent States, could accede to the ECHR. In Opinion 2/94, the court answered that it could not.[78] The court found that the EU lacked power under then Article 235 of the EC Treaty[79] to accede to the ECHR, because that was not within one of the powers defined by the EU Treaty.

Although the European Court of Justice previously had found that human rights were part of general principals of European Union law, the fact that specific provisions of that law did not apply to the EU limited its scope in certain areas, in particular disability rights. For example, in *Jacqueline Lisa Grant v. Southwest Trains Ltd,*[80] the European Court of Justice held that the general anti-discrimination provisions in the ECHR did not inure to the benefit of people with disabilities.[81]

---

[76] EC Treaty, supra note 68, at art. 130u (as amended at art. 177).

[77] Id. at art. 130w (as amended at art. 179).

[78] Accession by the Community to the European Convention for the Protection of Human Rights and Fundamental Freedoms, Opinion 2/94, [1996] ECR I-1759 (Eur. Ct. Justice 1996). See Judith Hippler Bello et al., European Union – Accession of the Community to the European Convention on Human Rights – Competence of the Community Under Article 235 of the Treaty Establishing European Community – Need to Amend the Treaty, 90 Am. J. Int'l L. 664, 666 (1996) ("The parallel existence of these two systems [the EU and the ECHR] portends a double standard of human rights protection in Europe"); Koen Lenaerts, Respect for Fundamental Rights as a Constitutional Principal of the European Union, 6 Colum. J. Eur. L. 1, 1-2 (2000) (noting impetus decision gave to strengthening human rights protections in Treaty of Amsterdam).

[79] Article 235 is now article 308.

[80] Grant v. Southwest Trains Ltd., No. C-249/96, [1998] Eur. Ct. Rep. I-621 (Feb. 17, 1998).

[81] See Quinn, supra note 74, at 299.

In 1997, the Amsterdam Treaty significantly amended the EU Treaty. It added a chapter on employment and in that context the EU first explicitly recognized the rights of people with disabilities. Article 13 reads:

> Without prejudice to the other provisions of this Treaty and within the limits of the powers conferred by it upon the Community, the Council, acting unanimously on a proposal from the Commission and after consulting the European Parliament, may take appropriate action to combat discrimination based on sex, racial or ethnic origin, religion or belief, disability, age or sexual orientation.[82]

---

[82] In 1989, the eleven members of the EC (the UK did not sign, although it did in 1999, after the Blair government came to power) adopted the Community Charter of Fundamental Social Rights for Workers, which states that:

> All disabled persons, whatever the origin and nature of their disablement, must be entitled to additional concrete measures aimed at improving their social and professional integration. These measures must concern, in particular, according to the capacities of the beneficiaries, vocational training, ergonomics, accessibility, mobility, means of transport and housing.

Community Charter of Fundamental Social Rights for Workers ("Social Charter"), Dec. 9, 1989, ¶ 26, quoted in Comm. on Citizens' Freedoms and Rights, Justice and Home Affairs, Eur. Parliament, § 3 "European Union Law," at http://www.europarl.eu.int/comparl/libe/elsj/charter/art26/default_en.htm (last visited Sept. 7, 2003) [hereinafter Comm. on Citizens' Freedoms and Rights]. On December 7, 2000, at Nice, the presidents of the EU Council, Parliament and Commission "proclaimed" the Charter of Fundamental Rights of the European Union, O.J. C 364 1 (2000), http://www.europarl.eu.int/charter/pdf/text_en.pdf, which incorporates ideas from the Social Charter. The Charter is not legally binding, yet, although courts have referred to it. Article 26 states:

> The Union recognises and respects the right of persons with disabilities to benefit from measures designed to ensure their independence, social and occupational integration and participation in the life of the community.

The European Parliament's Committee on Citizens' Freedoms and Rights, Justice and Home Affairs commentary on article 26 states:

> In accordance with the principle of non-discrimination, the rights of persons with disabilities are recognised by the United Nations and the Council of Europe in the context of their work (resolutions or recommendations) in the social

The EU has, since the mid-90's, focused on disability issues in a number of ways.[83] However, with the adoption of Article 13 of the EC treaty, the EU began systematically to address problems of discrimination, including disability discrimination.[84] In the 1999 Communication, the Commission proposed a three-pronged action plan to address disability. The first was a directive designed to "combat discrimination in the labour market on all grounds referred to in Article 13," except for sex which is covered in pre-existing Community legislation.[85] The second is a directive designed to address racial and ethnic origin discrimination outside the labour market.[86]

Finally, the Commission proposed a program of action to support individual states' efforts to combat discrimination.[87] Following the 1999

---

and employment fields. The revised European Social Charter of 1996 is the only binding text which expressly protects the rights of persons with disability, beyond access to work, but it has been ratified by only six member states of the European Union.

The Treaty of Amsterdam has made the fight against all forms of discrimination one of the principles of the European Community (article 13 EC). In the context of social policy, the Community has put in place measures and action plans intended to improve the professional integration of persons with disabilities, in accordance with the European Charter on the Fundamental Social Rights of Workers proclaimed in 1989.

Comm. on Citizens' Freedoms and Rights, supra at § 1 "Overview." See Quinn, supra note 74, at 303.

[83] See Communication from the Commission to the Council, the European Parliament, the Economic and Social Committee and the Committee of the Regions on Certain Community Measures to Combat Discrimination COM/99/0564 final, Annex II at 15 (Nov. 25, 1999), available at http://europa.eu.int/cgi-bin/eur-lex/udl.pl?REQUEST=Seek-Deliver&COLLECTION=com&SERVICE=eurlex&LANGUAGE=en&DOC ID=599PC0564&FORMAT=pdf (last visited Sept. 13, 2003) [hereinafter Community Measures]. The EU maintains a "portal to European Union law" at http://europa.eu.int/eur-lex/en/index.html (last visited Sept. 13, 2003).

[84] See Community Measures, supra note 83, at 1.

[85] Id. at 8.

[86] Id.

[87] Id. By 1999, virtually all states then members of the EU had constitutional or legislative provisions that dealt with discrimination. See id. at 3 nn.3-6 and Annexes V and VI. However, the scope of those

Communication, the Council issued two documents at the end of 2000 that addressed disability issues; Council Directive 2000/78/EC, "establishing a general framework for equal treatment in employment and occupation,"[88] and Council Decision of 27 November 2000 "establishing a Community action programme to combat discrimination (2001 to 2006)."[89]

The Framework Directive provides, among many other things, in its preambular paragraphs:

> (8) The Employment Guidelines for 2000 agreed by the European Council at Helsinki on 10 and 11 December 1999 stress the need to foster a labour market favourable to social integration by formulating a coherent set of policies aimed at combating discrimination against groups such as persons with disability. They also emphasise the need to pay particular attention to supporting older workers, in order to increase their participation in the labour force.
>
> ...
>
> (11) Discrimination based on religion or belief, disability, age or sexual orientation may undermine the achievement of the objectives of the EC Treaty, in particular the attainment of a high level of employment and social protection, raising the standard of living and the quality of life, economic and social cohesion and solidarity, and the free movement of persons.
>
> (12) To this end, any direct or indirect discrimination based on religion or belief, disability, age or sexual orientation as regards the areas covered by this Directive should be prohibited throughout the Community.

The Framework Directive requires EU members to adopt a number of kinds of measures to address discrimination generally. It defines both "direct" and "indirect" discrimination. Direct discrimination occurs "where one person is treated less favorably than another is, has been or would be treated in a comparable situation," on any of the protected grounds.[90] Indirect discrimination occurs "where an apparently neutral provision, criterion or practice" would disadvantage a person with particular criteria compared with other persons unless:

---

provisions varied, some being general, and some being limited to employment, and not all provisions provided a means of redress.

88 O.J. L 303 16 (2000) [hereinafter Framework Directive].

89 O.J. L 303 23 (2000) [hereinafter Community Action Programme].

90 Framework Directive, art. 2, ¶ 2(a).

(i) that provision, criterion or practice is objectively justified by a legitimate aim and the means of achieving that aim are appropriate and necessary, or

(ii) as regards persons with a particular disability, the employer or any person or organisation to whom this Directive applies, is obliged, under national legislation, to take appropriate measures in line with the principles contained in Article 5 in order to eliminate disadvantages entailed by such provision, criterion or practice.[91]

Article 5 is the reasonable accommodation provision and reads:

In order to guarantee compliance with the principle of equal treatment in relation to persons with disabilities, reasonable accommodation shall be provided. This means that employers shall take appropriate measures, where needed in a particular case, to enable a person with a disability to have access to, participate in, or advance in employment, or to undergo training, unless such measures would impose a disproportionate burden on the employer. This burden shall not be disproportionate when it is sufficiently remedied by measures existing within the framework of the disability policy of the Member State concerned.

Article 5 is subject to Article 4, which provides that different treatment based upon a protected characteristic "shall not constitute discrimination where, by reason of the nature of the particular occupational activities concerned or of the context in which they are carried out, such a characteristic constitutes a genuine and determining occupational requirement, provided that the objective is legitimate and the requirement is proportionate."[92]

The Framework Directive also attempts to deal with a number of other issues that have arisen in U.S. antidiscrimination statutes. Article 7, for example, provides that the "principle of equal treatment" shall not preclude a member state from putting specific measure into place to compensate for disadvantages linked to the protective characteristics.[93] Article 9 provides not only that there shall be "judicial and/or administrative procedures" to enforce the obligations under the Framework Directive but that organizations that have a "legitimate interest in ensuring that the provisions of [the Framework Directive] are

---

[91] Id., art. 2, ¶ 2(b)(i), (ii).

[92] Id., art. 4.

[93] Id., art. 7.

complied with" may participate in support of a complainant in the enforcement proceedings.[94]

Article 10 deals with the burden of proof issue, shifting the burden to the respondent once the complainant has raised a presumption of "direct or indirect discrimination," and not preventing member states from using burdens of proof that are even more favorable.[95] The Directive also provides that Member States "shall lay down the rules on sanctions applicable to infringements of the national provisions adopted pursuant to this Directive," which sanctions may include compensation to the victim.[96]

The Framework Directive is to be implemented no later than December 2, 2003, although states may request an additional three years, to December 2, 2006, for compliance. The Community Action Programme is designed to assist Member States in implementing the Framework Directive. It will conduct analyses of "factors related to discrimination" and evaluate anti-discrimination legislation and practice, promote transnational cooperation and promote awareness raising.[97]

The Framework Directive has not been without controversy. Where states had existing disability rights legislation, there was concern as to the Directive's impact. Prior to its adoption, a select committee of the House of Lords issued a report that raised procedural and substantive issues on many aspects of the Directive.[98] The committee questioned whether the Directive provided greater disability discrimination protection than the United Kingdom's Disability Discrimination Act.[99] It was concerned that the Directive, which forbids indirect discrimination, unless justified by a legitimate aim or the subject of reasonable accommodation under national legislation, was "uncertain" as the interrelationship between the Article 2 obligations and the Article 5 obligation to provide reasonable accommodations.[100]

---

[94] Id., art. 9, ¶¶ 1-2.

[95] Id., art. 10, ¶¶ 1-2.

[96] Framework Directive, art. 17.

[97] Community Action Programme, art. 3.

[98] Select Comm. on the EE, Fourth Report (19 Dec. 2000), http://www.publications.parliament.uk/pa/ld200001/ldselect/ldeucom/13/13 02.htm [hereinafter HL Report] (last visited Sept. 22, 2003).

[99] Id. at ¶ 8.

[100] HL Report, supra note 98, at ¶ 41. Discussing conceptions of disability, the Fourth Report states that:

> Article 5 creates a free-standing obligation to provide reasonable accommodation, which all Member States are bound to implement. In the light of this it is not clear whether, and in what circumstances, the prohibition on indirect discrimination against the disabled in Article

In Norway, which is not an EU member, but has agreed to follow its directives, certain minority parties in parliament objected that the burden of proof provisions would unduly burden employers, causing them to "focus more on formal education and qualifications, and less on other more intangible qualities that make a person qualified for a specific job."[101] This, of course, is precisely the kind of discretion anti-discrimination legislation seeks to combat.

There also is a countervailing concern that the Article 2(5)'s limitation on the definition of discrimination to protect "rights and freedoms of others"[102] might be read too broadly.[103] Whittle points to an Irish case that interpreted the Irish constitution's property rights guarantee to prohibit more than "nominal" costs in making accommodations.[104] Ironically, Whittle warns that "confusion" about the duty to accommodate has arisen in the ADA cases and "[i]t is of great importance, therefore, that such confusion does not take place within the European Union and that the recent difficulties associated with the ADA do not also occur as regards the Framework Directive and its provisions on disability (either in its implementation by the Member States or interpretation by the courts)."[105]

2(2)(b) will apply. Moreover, it is unclear to what extent Article 2(2)(b)(i) and (ii) themselves are intended to be complementary or mutually exclusive. We are uncertain whether an employee or employer would be able to turn to (i) where there has been a failure, either on the part of a Member State or an employer, to meet the requirements of Article 5.

[101] Euro. Indus. Relations Observatory On-line, Norway: Legal Framework on Discrimination Strengthened, http://www.eiro.eurofound.ie/2001/08/feature/NO0108138F.html (last visited May 26, 2003).

[102] The Framework Directive "shall be without prejudice to measures laid down by national law which, in a democratic society, are necessary for public security, for the maintenance of public order and the prevention of criminal offences, for the protection of health and for the protection of the rights and freedoms of others." Framework Directive, art. 2, ¶ 5.

[103] Richard Whittle, The Framework Directive for Equal Treatment in Employment and Occupation: An Analysis from a Disability Rights Perspective (June 2, 2002) (paper presented at the European Disability Forum seminar on current and future disability rights at European level, Brussels, 8 - 9 Feb. 2002), http://www.edf-feph.org/Papers/pospaper/01-08/EDF01-8-Empl_Dir_analysis.pdf (last visited Sept. 22, 2003).

[104] Id. at 15, n.44 (citing Re Employment Equality Bill, 1996, [1997] 2 I.R. 321 at 355).

[105] Id. at 10.

Despite the – somewhat muted – controversy over specifics, it appears that EU states are moving to implement the Framework Directive. The United Kingdom has issued draft regulations, which are scheduled to go into effect in 2004.[106] Likewise, Norway, a non-member which has agreed to follow EU directives, enacted disability rights legislation in 2001, but has expressed its intent to implement the Framework Directive by December 2, 2003.[107]

Although EU Member States and those states, like Norway, which have agreed to follow EU directives, likely are to enact legislation implementing the Framework Directive, there is little reason to expect any less diversity in their interpretations of the Directive then is found in United States' courts interpretations of the ADA. One assumes that many of those cases will percolate up to the European Court of Justice, which will provide some coherence to this body of law. Moreover, the Framework Directive applies only in the employment area; it remains to be seen whether the EU will attempt to use its authority under Article 13 to promote broader anti-discrimination legislation.

Eventually, the effect of any anti-discrimination legislation dealing with employment issues will be measured by the change in employment among the protected groups. At the present time, European employment statistics for people with disabilities show, like their United States analogues, underemployment and under education, despite rather generalized awareness of and, at least as expressed to pollsters, sensitivity to disability issues.

For example, 97% of Europeans responding to a poll believed that "something should be done to integrate people with disabilities more into society" and 93% of the respondents believed that "more money should be spent on removing physical barriers which complicate the lives of physically disabled people."[108] About 50% of respondents thought that the national government should be responsible for effecting improvements to

---

[106] The draft regulations are accessible at Dep't of Trade & Indus., Equality and Diversity – The Way Ahead, at http://www.dti.gov.uk/er/equality/wayahead.htm (last modified Aug. 6, 2003).

[107] Euro. Indus. Relations Observatory On-line, Norway: Committee Makes Recommendations on Implementation of EU Equal Treatment Directive, http://www.eiro.eurofound.ie/2003/01/InBrief/NO0301102N.html (last visited Sept. 22, 2003).

[108] Euro. Opinion Research Group for the Educ. & Culture Directorite–General, Euro. Comm'n, Attitudes of Europeans to Disability: Eurobarometer 54.2 p. 62 (May 2001), http://Europa.EU.int/comm/employment_social/publications/2002/cev502001_en.pdf (last visited on Sept. 22, 2003).

integrate people with disabilities; only about 24% believed that employers and companies should be responsible.[109]

But even with a generally accepting attitude, the employment situation for people with disabilities in Europe evinces the same sorts of disparities seen in the United States. In August 2001, EIM Business and Policy Research prepared a study on the employment situation of people with disabilities in the European Union.[110] The EIM report found that about 14% of working age people in Europe – or about 26 million people – self reported a disability.[111] About 40% of those reporting themselves as disabled were 55 years of age or older.[112] The study, based upon 1966 data, indicated that approximately 40% of people with disabilities in the EU were employed and another approximately 5% were unemployed, but active in the labor market, while the corresponding figures for people without disabilities were approximately 65% and approximately 7%.[113] Interestingly, this study found less disparity among wages once people became employed.[114]

Other studies indicate that the actual percentage of people in the work force with disabilities is quite low – 1.9% in Finland; 3% in France in the public sector; 2% in the Netherlands and 3.9% in Germany.[115] In the end, only additional study will determine whether the various directives will increase the number of people with disabilities who are in fact employed.[116]

---

[109] Id. at 56.

[110] EIM Business & Pol'y Research, The Employment Situation of People with Disabilities in the European Union (Aug. 2001), http://europa.eu.int/ comm/employment_social/news/2001/dec/2666complete_en.pdf (last visited Sept. 22, 2003).

[111] Id. at 38.

[112] Id.

[113] Id. at 39.

[114] Id. at 49.

[115] Eur. Indus. Relations Observatory, supra note 73.

[116] The EU is also expanding its activities beyond the employment realm. In December 2000, the Commission issued a communication, Towards A Barrier Free Europe For People With Disabilities, COM (2000) 284 (Dec. 5, 2000), http://europa.eu.int/comm/employment_social/equ_opp/com284f/ com_284f_en.pdf (last visited Sept. 22, 2003), which addressed the reduction of access barriers for people with disabilities, including improving mobility, formational issues, assistive technology and consumer issues. Finally, we note that 2003 has been designated by the European Union as the European Year of People with Disabilities. See http://www.eypd2003.org/eypd/index.jsp (last visited Sept. 22, 2003).

Chapter 25 UNITED NATIONS

The United Nations,[1] founded in 1945 with 51 member states, presently has 191 member states.[2] The trajectory of disability issues on the UN's radar screen reprises the development of those issues in individual states – beginning with complete ignorance, moving to advisory, rather than legally binding, measures in selected areas, such as mental health and employment, and, as this is written, possibly to a broad legally-binding document, a treaty.

The history of disability rights at the UN displays all the crosscurrents that have made the passage of domestic legislation difficult, from philosophical uncertainty about overall approaches to the disparate economic abilities among states beset with many competing needs.[3] We will not attempt to cover it in detail, but will sketch its outlines.

§ 25.1 United Nations Initiatives Prior To 2001[4]

Internationally, disability issues hardly reached the agenda until the 1970s and, even then, the efforts were tentative. The seminal human rights text, the 1948 UN General Assembly Universal Declaration of Human Rights,[5] mentions disability once, to say that people have a right

---

[1] See generally U.N. website, http://www.un.org (last modified Apr. 23, 2003).

[2] U.N., Growth in United Nations Memberships, 1945-2003, http://www.un.org/Overview/growth.htm (last modified April 23, 2003).

[3] See generally Theresia Degener & Gerard Quinn, The Current Use and Future Potential of United Nations Human Rights Instruments in the Context of Disability (2002).

[4] In international human rights matters, much of the impetus for legal change comes from non-governmental organizations – NGOs. Among the principal ones in this area are Disabled People International (http://www.dpi.org (last visited Sept. 23, 2003)), Inclusion International (http://www.inclusion-international.org/ (last visited Sept. 23, 2003)), Rehabilitation International (http://www.rehab-international.org (last visited Sept. 23, 2003)), World Blind Union (http://umc.once.es/home.cfm (last visited Sept. 23, 2003)), World Federation of the Deaf (http://www.wfdnews.org (last visited Sept. 23, 2003)), Landmine Survivors Network (http://www.landminesurvivors.org (last visited Sept. 23, 2003)), the Inter-American Institute on Disability (http://www.iidisability.org/eng/index.htm (last visited Sept. 23, 2003)) and the Disability Rights Education and Defense Fund (http://www.dredf.org/ (last visited Sept. 23, 2003)).

[5] Adopted by the General Assembly at its 3d session, New York, 10 Dec. 1948, GA Res. 217A (III), U.N. Doc A/810 at 71 (1948) ("Universal Declaration").

to an adequate standard of living, even if they are disabled.[6] One of the first overt efforts of the international community was the 1971 Declaration of the Rights of Mentally Retarded Persons.[7] Although broadly phrased, it was a substantial jump. Article 3 reads:

> The mentally retarded person has a right to economic security and to a decent standard of living. He has a right to perform productive work or to engage in any other meaningful occupation to the fullest possible extent of his capabilities.

It emphasized integration, promising employment to the fullest extent of "his" capabilities. However, the 1971 Declaration was hortatory; it established no legal obligations.

The 1975 Declaration on the Rights of Disabled Persons[8] was the first detailed attempt at the UN to articulate rights of people with disabilities generally. It represents a major doctrinal step beyond the 1971 Declaration. Article 5 posits an entitlement "to the measures designed to enable them [people with disabilities] to become as self-reliant as possible." Articles 6 and 7 read:

> 6. Disabled persons have the right to medical, psychological and functional treatment, including prosthetic and orthetic appliances, to medical and social rehabilitation, education, vocational training and rehabilitation, aid, counselling, placement services and other services *which will enable them to develop their capabilities and skills to the maximum and will hasten the process of their social integration or reintegration.*
>
> 7. Disabled persons have the right to economic and social security and to a decent level of living. They have the right,

---

[6] Article 25 states that:

> [e]veryone has the right to a standard of living adequate for the health and well-being of himself and of his family, including food, clothing, housing and medical care and necessary social services, and the right to security in the event of unemployment, sickness, disability, widowhood, old age or other lack of livelihood in circumstances beyond his control.

[7] Adopted by the General Assembly at its 26th session, 2027th plenary meeting, New York, 20 Dec. 1971, G.A. Res. 2856 (XXVI), 26 U.N. GAOR Supp. (No. 29) at 93, U.N. Doc. A/8429 (1971).

[8] Adopted by the General Assembly at its 30th session, 2433rd plenary meeting, New York, 9 Dec. 1975, G.A. Res. 3447 (XXX), 30 U.N. GAOR Supp. (No. 34) at 88, U.N. Doc. A/10034 (1975).

according to their capabilities, to secure and retain employment or to engage in a useful, productive and remunerative occupation and to join trade unions.[9]

In a sense, the 1975 Declaration added "disability" as a protected class. Still, note the silence on exactly how the entitlement will be realized. The 1975 Declaration provides no guidance. Nor does it establish any legally binding duties. Thus, as of the mid-1970s, the UN had not addressed disability rights in a juridical framework. In context, however, that is not startling: the United States had just enacted the Rehabilitation Act two years earlier; Canada would wait seven years to add disability to its Charter of Rights and Freedoms; the United States would wait 15 years to pass the ADA (although many of the United States would by then have disability legislation).

During the 1980s, the UN and various of its subsidiary bodies began to view disability issues in a range of contexts. Those appear to have promoted a consensus on the significance of disability issues, although they left open the modalities for dealing with them.[10]

- 1980 – The World Health Organization published the International Classification of Impairments, Disabilities and Handicaps.[11]

- 1981 – UN International Year of Disabled Persons.[12] The UN set out to define the rights of people with disabilities, increase public awareness, and encourage the formation of advocacy organizations.

- 1983 – World Programme of Action Concerning Disabled Persons.[13] The UN incorporated the lessons from the International Year of Disabled Persons into the World Programme of Action. Beyond prevention and rehabilitation, it stressed "equalization of opportunities."[14] It linked national

---

[9] Id. arts. 6-7 (emphasis added).

[10] Many relevant documents are available at the U.N. Persons with Disabilities website, at http://www.un.org/esa/socdev/enable/index.html (last modified Oct. 15, 2003). Those with access to U.N. documents can use U.N., Persons with Disabilities, at http://www.un.org/partners/civil_society/docs/d-disabl.htm#featured (last modified July 5, 2003).

[11] World Health Org., International Classification of Impairments, Disabilities and Handicaps (ICIDH) (1980).

[12] Adopted by the General Assembly at its 31st session, New York, 16 Dec. 1976, GA Res. 123 (XXXI) (1976).

[13] Adopted by the General Assembly at its 37th session GA Res. 37/52, UN Doc. A/RES/37/52, GAOR, 37th session, Supplement No. 51 (1982).

[14] General Assembly Resolution 37152 states that:

legislation, as part of member states' human rights efforts, to ensuring equal opportunities. This linkage expressed the growing view that the task of the disability rights agenda was to develop ways to put people with disabilities on an equal footing, rather than find them isolated but protected social niches.

- 1983 – International Labor Organisation (ILO) Convention No. 159, Vocational Rehabilitation and Employment (Disabled Persons) Convention.[15] Here, the signatories agreed to provide equal vocational rehabilitation opportunities to people with and without disabilities. The convention evinces the duality in disability rights: strict equality may be ineffective. "The said policy shall be based on the principle of equal opportunity between disabled workers and workers generally. Equality of opportunity and treatment for disabled men and women workers shall be respected. Special positive measures aimed at effective equality of opportunity and treatment between disabled workers and other workers shall not be regarded as discriminating against other workers."[16]

- 1983-1992 – UN Decade of Disabled Persons.[17] The UN proclaimed a decade of disabled persons, which began a significant effort directed to a range of

---

'Equalization of opportunities' is a central theme of the WPA and its guiding philosophy for the achievement of full participation of persons with disabilities in all aspects of social and economic life. An important principle underlying this theme is that issues concerning persons with disabilities should not be treated in isolation, but within the context of normal community services.

UN Doc. A/37/351/Add.1 and Corr.1, annex, § VIII, recomm. 1 (IV), cited in U.N. and Persons with Disabilities, World Programme of Action Concerning Disabled Persons, at http://www.un.org/esa/socdev/enable/diswpa00.htm (last modified June 11, 2003).

[15] The Convention entered into force June 20, 1983. Int'l Labour Office, C159 Vocational Rehabilitation and Employment (Disabled Persons) Convention, 1983, http://www.logos-net.net/ilo/150_base/en/instr/c_159.htm (last visited Sept. 23, 2003).

[16] Id. art. 4.

[17] Adopted at the 90th plenary meeting, 3 Dec. 1982, GA Res. 37/53, UN Doc. A/RES/37/53 (1982).

projects to implement the World Programme of Action. However, to quote Bengt Lindqvist, the UN's Special Rapporteur on disabilities,

During the first years of the Decade a lot of attention was given to disability matters in many countries. A few years later, however, this interest seemed to fade away. This was noted at the mid-term evaluation of the Decade, at an expert meeting in 1987. In the report from the meeting a number of measures were suggested to strengthen the leadership role of the United Nations in implementing the new disability policy. The final response to this request was the elaboration and adoption of the UN Standard Rules on the Equalization of Opportunities for Persons with Disabilities.[18]

- 1984 – The UN Sub-Commission on Prevention of Discrimination and Protection of Minorities[19] appointed a Special Rapporteur, Leandro Despouy, to conduct a comprehensive study on the relationship between human rights and disability.[20]

- 1987 – UN rejected a proposed Convention on the Elimination of All Forms of Discrimination Against Disabled Persons.[21]

- 1989 – Convention on the Rights of the Child.[22] This for the first time, albeit in a limited context, tries to put into law programs necessary to achieve equality. Art. 23(1) reads:

States Parties recognize that a mentally or physically disabled child should enjoy a full and decent life, in

---

[18] See Soc. Dev. Div., U.N., Asian & Pacific Decade of Disabled Persons 1993-2002, at http://www.unescap.org/decade/benqtrpt.htm#background (last modified May 8, 2000) (providing a copy of the U.N. Standard Rules).

[19] Sub-Commission on Prevention of Discrimination and Protection of Minorities resolution 1984/20.

[20] See Leandro Despouy, Human Rights and Disabled Persons, Human Rights Study Series No. 6 (1988), at http://www.un.org/esa/socdev/enable/dispaperdes0.htm (last visited Sept. 23, 2003).

[21] See generally Theresia Degener, Disabled Persons and Human Rights: The Legal Framework, in Human Rights and Disabled Persons 12 (Theresia Degener & Yolan Koster-Dreese, eds. 1995).

[22] G.A. Res. 44/25, annex, 44 U.N. GAOR Supp. (No. 49) at 167, U.N. Doc. A/44/49 (1989), entered into force 2 September 1990, http://www.unicef.org/crc/fulltext.htm (last visited Sept. 23, 2003).

conditions which ensure dignity, promote self-reliance and facilitate the child's active participation in the community.

Article 23(4) requires that assistance provided to children with disabilities:

shall be designed to ensure that the disabled child has effective access to and receives education, training, health care services, rehabilitation services, preparation for employment and recreation opportunities in a manner conducive to the child's achieving the fullest possible social integration and individual development, including his or her cultural and spiritual development.

The problem is that the Convention does not commit the parties to provide any assistance.

- 1989 – Tallinn Guidelines for Action on Human Resources Development in the Field of Disability.[23] These urged governments to adopt certain measures to promote the full participation of people with disabilities in society. Among other things, Article 11 recommended that information be provided in formats, such as Braille, that gave people with disabilities access to it, and Article 12 recommended that governments "adopt, enforce and fund" access standards for buildings and transportation.

- 1991 – General Assembly adopted the Principles for the Protection of Persons with Mental Illness and for the Improvement of Mental Health Care.[24] These principles are a broad set of rights for people with mental illnesses or disabilities, including, *inter alia*, rights to treatment, civil and political rights, the right to live in the community and the right to confidentiality. Like the other resolutions, this is non-binding, but the General Assembly here recognized a panoply of civil rights, which, if they attain the status of customary international law, would bind states.

---

[23] Adopted by the General Assembly in its 78th plenary meeting, 8 Dec. 1989, G.A. Res. 44/70, UN Doc. A/RES/44/70 (1989).

[24] Adopted by the General Assembly at the 75th plenary meeting, 46th session, 17 Dec. 1991, G.A. Res. 46/119 and Annex: Principles for the Protection of Persons with Mental Illness and for the Improvement of Mental Health Care U.N. Doc. A/RES/46/119 (1989).

With the foregoing as prologue, in 1994, the United Nations adopted the Standard Rules on the Equalization of Opportunities for Persons with Disabilities.[25] To date, the 22 Standard Rules represent the UN's most complete statement of the rights of people with disabilities. Their stated purpose is to "ensure that girls, boys, women and men with disabilities, as members of their societies, may exercise the same rights and obligations as others."

While explicitly recognizing that they are not "compulsory, they can become international customary rules when they are applied by a great number of States with the intention of respecting a rule in international law." The Rules touch address the "preconditions," such as consciousness raising and rehabilitation services, the "target areas" in which equality must be established (accessibility, both to the physical environment and information, education, employment, income maintenance and social security, family life and personal integrity, culture, recreation and sports, and religion), and a range of "implementation measures," such as legislation, "policy and planning," "work coordination" and "technical and economic cooperation."

One of the more interesting things the Rules do is create a monitoring mechanism, much as other UN human rights treaties have monitors. The monitoring, under the direction of a Special Rapporteur, who was appointed in March 1994,[26] was designed to "assist each State in assessing its level of implementation of the Rules and in "measuring its progress" under them.[27] As part of that effort, the Special Rapporteur surveys states, UN organizations and NGOs. To date, the Special Rapporteur's original three-year mandate has been extended twice and he has produced three reports on whether states follow the individual rules.[28]

---

[25] Adopted by the General Assembly at the 85th plenary meeting, 48th session, 20 Dec. 1993, GA Res. 48/96, annex, UN Doc. A/RES/48/96 (1993), at http://www.un.org/esa/socdev/enable/dissre00.htm (last modified June 11, 2003).

[26] See Soc. Dev. Div., supra note 18.

[27] Id. ¶8.

[28] See Monitoring the Implementation of the Standard Rules on the Equalization of Opportunities for Persons with Disabilities, UN Doc. E/CN.5/2002/4 (2002) (Report on Third Mandate of the Special Rapporteur); Monitoring the Implementation of the Standard Rules on the Equalization of Opportunities for Persons with Disabilities, UN Doc. E/CN.5/2000/3 (2000) (Report on Second Mandate of the Special Rapporteur); Monitoring the Implementation of the Standard Rules on the Equalization of Opportunities for Persons with Disabilities, UN Doc. A/52/56 (1997) (Report on First Mandate of the Special Rapporteur) ("1997 Special Rapporteur's Report"). See U.N. Documents and Reports, at http://www.un.org/esa/socdev/enable/disparl.htm (last modified Oct. 15, 2003). In addition, the World Health Organization (WHO) has conducted

In the Special Rapporteur's Third Report, he proposed a Supplement to the Standard Rules to focus on specific problems of the most disadvantaged people with disabilities.[29]

Also, in 1994 the UN Committee on Economic, Social and Cultural Rights in 1994 issued general comment No. 5[30] to the International

---

a survey of three of the Rules that relate to health issues. World Health Organization, The UN Standard Rules on the Equalization of Opportunities for Persons with Disabilities: Government Responses to the Implementation of the Rules on Medical Care, Rehabilitation, Support Services and Personnel Training: Summary, vol. I (WHO/ DAR/01.1) (1999) and Main Report, vol. II (WHO/DAR/01.2) (1999). WHO also broke its work into various regional reports: (1) Regional Report AFRO (WHO/DAR/01.3) (1999); (2) Regional Report AMRO (WHO/DAR/01.4) (1999); (3) Regional Report EMRO (WHO/DAR/01.5) (1999); (4) Regional Report EURO (WHO/DAR/01.6) (1999); (5) Regional Report SEARO (WHO/DAR/01.7) (1999); (6) Regional Report WPRO (WHO/DAR/01.8) (1999). Id.; see also Dimitris Michailakis, Government Action on Disability Policy: A Global Survey (1997), available at http://www. independentliving.org/standardrules/UN_Answers/UN.pdf (last visited Sept. 23, 2003), which assembles the data from the first surveys.

[29] U.N., Report of the Special Rapporteur of the Commission for Social Development on Monitoring the Implementation of the Standard Rules on the Equalization of Opportunities for Persons with Disabilities on His Third Mandate, 2000-2002, available at http://www.un.org/esa/socdev/ enable/disecn520024e2.htm (2003).

[30] The Official Records of the Economic and Social Council, 1995, Supplement No. 3 (E/1995/22), annex IV, state the:

> Covenant [on Economic, Social and Cultural Rights] does not refer explicitly to persons with disabilities. Nevertheless, the Universal Declaration of Human Rights recognizes that all human beings are born free and equal in dignity and rights and, since the Covenant's provisions apply fully to all members of society, persons with disabilities are clearly entitled to the full range of rights recognized in the Covenant. In addition, insofar as special treatment is necessary, States parties are required to take appropriate measures, to the maximum extent of their available resources, to enable such persons to seek to overcome any disadvantages, in terms of the enjoyment of the rights specified in the Covenant, flowing from their disability. Moreover, the requirement contained in article 2 (2) of the Covenant that the rights "enunciated ... will be exercised without discrimination of any kind" based on certain specified grounds "or other status" clearly applies to discrimination on the grounds of disability.

Covenant of Economic, Social and Cultural Rights. The comment effectively incorporates people with disabilities as a category protected by the ICESCR.[31]

After nearly 20 years of increasing activity in the area of disability rights, as of 2003, the United Nations' most articulated instrument was the Standard Rules, which implement the World Programme of Action. The Special Rapporteurs' reports indicate that individual States are adopting policies that provide various rights to people with disabilities. Some States say that they have changed their policies in response to the Standard Rules.[32] The Special Rapporteur wrote in his 2002 report, "[I]t is evident that the Standard Rules play a major role assisting in policy development and serving as a tool for advocacy."[33]

Nonetheless, none of the United Nations' instruments is legally binding, save for the Convention on the Rights of the Child, which binds only its signatories (virtually every nation in the world save the United States and Somalia). The instruments do not constitute customary international law at this stage, since there does not appear to be any indication that states that have adopted, for example, the principles of the Standard Rules have done so out of a sense of legal obligation, rather than a sense that they represent sound policy.

For example, the European Commission issued a resolution on December 20, 1996, entitled "A New European Community Disability Strategy."[34] The resolution states that, "[w]hile the Standard Rules are not compulsory in the strict legal sense, they imply a strong moral and political commitment on behalf of States to take action. They also invite States to cooperate in the development of policies for the equalization of opportunities for people with disabilities."[35] The Committee viewed the resolution as "endorsement" of the Standard Rules.[36]

Id. at ¶ 5.

[31] Id.

[32] 1997 Final Report of the Special Rapporteur, http://www.un.org/esa/socdev/enable/dismsre6.htm#B ("Most Governments indicated either that they had already acted in the spirit of the Rules or that they were drafting new policies in accordance with them;" "Many countries had translated the Rules into their native language;" some countries have adopted or were adopting legislation using the principles of the Rules. Four countries reported that they were creating new institutions to implement the Rules.) (last visited Sept. 23, 2003).

[33] See Report of the Special Rapporteur, supra note 29.

[34] See Euro. Parliament, http://europa.eu.int/comm/employment_social/soc-prot/disable/com406/index_en.htm (last visited Sept. 23, 2003).

[35] Id. ¶ 28.

[36] Id. ¶ 27.

As will be discussed in the next section, throughout much of the 1980s and 1990s, some organizations called for an international treaty on disability rights law. However, it is at least arguable that if the Standard Rules, augmented by the phalanx of the United Nations' instruments, including Comment 5 to the ICESCR, have resulted in domestic policy changes and legislation, then a treaty is unlikely to add anything. International law is, as noted at the outset, in large part consensual. If states are willing to modify their internal legislation to incorporate disability rights, there may be no need for an additional international convention.

States that have not found it in their interest to follow the Standard Rules and other instruments may be unlikely to sign onto a convention that requires them to do what the Standard Rules require. Additional research may help to determine whether the Standard Rules have been adopted broadly, and whether their precepts have filtered into customary international law.

On the other hand, the utility of a binding international instrument might be broadened enforcement opportunities. The enforcement mechanisms available under individual states' legislation may vary in their scope and whether they provide sufficient and useful remedies. If an international convention has an enforcement body, such as the Inter American Convention does, the treaty could provide a backup mechanism for people with grievances against their states. However, litigating those matters first to the point of exhaustion of local remedies and then through an international tribunal, perhaps thousands of miles from the home of the complainant with a disability – often a person of minimal means – is unlikely to provide the sort of remedy most people require when faced, for example, with an illegal stairway that prevents them from accepting a job.

§ 25.2 Convention On The Rights Of Persons With Disabilities

The next step in the evolution of United Nations' consideration of disability issues appears to be the drafting of an international convention on the rights of people with disabilities. As discussed above, the United Nations has developed a substantial infrastructure for enforcing human rights in general. There is a United Nations' High Commissioner on Human Rights and there are monitoring bodies for the other major human rights treaties, but disability rights initiatives have developed largely outside the context of "mainstream" human rights.

Indeed, most of the work on disability rights has not been under the aegis of the United Nations' Human Rights Commission or the Office of the High Commissioner on Human Rights, but under the Commission for Social Development.[37] The 1994 Comment 5 to the ICESCR was an attempt to bring disability rights within the larger tent, but some argue that does not suffice.[38]

The notion of a convention was raised as early as the mid 1980's.[39] NGOs promoted the idea. In 1998, the United Nations convened the Consultative Expert Group and Meeting on International Norms and Standards Relating to Disability, which discussed a new international convention.[40] The report of the Expert Group Meeting recognized the arguments for and against a convention, including the possibility that by establishing a separate convention, disability issues would become marginalized from mainstream human rights issues. Nonetheless, momentum toward a convention continued.

The Government of Mexico adopted such a convention as a major policy initiative at the United Nations. Through its efforts, the Program of Action adopted by the World Conference against Racism, Racial Discrimination, Xenophobia and Related Intolerance included a paragraph inviting the "United Nations General Assembly to consider elaborating an integral and comprehensive international convention to protect and promote the rights and dignity of disabled people."[41]

Largely as a result of these efforts, at the end of 2001, the General Assembly passed a resolution creating an Ad Hoc Committee to consider proposals for a Convention "based on the holistic approach in the work done in the fields of social development, human rights and non-discrimination."[42] It also called for states to hold regional conferences on such a proposal.

---

[37] The EU has adopted a resolution setting forth its "full support" for a convention. Communication COM/2003/16 (24/01/03), Towards a United Nations Legally Binding Instrument to Promote and Protect the Rights and Dignity of Persons with Disabilities.

[38] For a brief discussion, see Report of the Special Rapporteur, supra note 29.

[39] See supra text accompanying note 21.

[40] See U.N. Enable, at http://www.un.org/esa/socdev/enable/disberk0.htm (last visited Sept. 24, 2003).

[41] World Conference Against Racism, Racial Discrimination, Xenophobia and Related Intolerance, Durban, South Africa, 31 August – 8 September 2001, UN Doc. A/CONF. 189/12, Chapter 1, ¶ 180.

[42] Adopted by the General Assembly 18 December 2001 GA Res. 56/168, UN Doc. A/RES/56/168 (2001), available at http://www.un.org/esa/socdev/enable/disA56168e1.htm (last visited Sept. 24, 2003).

In 2002, the Ad Hoc Committee met in New York.[43] The Report also called for Regional Meetings; the American regional meeting took place in Quito in April 2003 and other regional meetings were scheduled for Johannesburg in early May 2003, Beirut in late May 2003 and Bangkok in June 2003.[44] The second session of the Ad Hoc Committee took place mid June 2003 at the United Nations Headquarters in New York.[45] There will be a third session in 2004.[46]

A number of drafts have been proposed for a Convention.[47] Rather than considering the different variations, we will look at the proposal from the Government of Mexico. (For convenience, the 2002 Proposal is appended hereto as Appendix 7.)[48]

The Draft Text Elements begin with a series of preambular clauses that refer to the history leading up to the convention and the broad purposes of the convention. We will not deal with the preambular language here.

The substance of the draft begins by setting forth the Convention's broad objects.[49] Where it refers to rights of people with disabilities, it

---

[43] See U.N. Enable, Meeting of the Ad Hoc Committee 29 July-9 August 2002 United Nations, New York, at http://www.un.org/esa/socdev/ enable/rights/adhocmeet.htm (last modified June 12, 2003).

[44] Links to those meetings can be found at U.N. Enable, at http://www. un.org/esa/socdev/enable/ (last modified Oct. 15, 2003).

[45] See Report of the Ad Hoc Committee on a Comprehensive and Integral International Convention on Protection and Promotion of the Rights and Dignity of Persons with Disabilities, U.N. Doc. A/58/118, 3 July 2003, http://www.un.org/esa/socdev/enable/rights/a_58_118_e.htm (last visited Sept. 24, 2003).

[46] Id.

[47] See Secretaria de Relaciones Exteriores, Contributed Papers, at http://www.sre.gob.mx/discapacidad/papers.htm (last modified July 3, 2002). For discussion of the opinions of various states on the broad thrust of the Convention, views submitted by Governments, intergovernmental organizations and United Nations bodies concerning a comprehensive and integral international convention on the protection and promotion of the rights and dignity of persons with disabilities, see U.N. Enable, at http://www.un.org/esa/socdev/enable/rights/a_ac265_2003_4e.htm#4 (last modified June 14, 2003).

[48] Ministry of Foreign Affairs, Presidential Office for the Promotion and Soc. Integration of Persons with Disabilities, Elements for a Future United Nations Comprehensive and Integral Convention to Promote and Protect the Rights and Dignity of Persons with Disabilities, http://www.sre.gob.mx/discapacidad/elementsproposal.htm (last modified July 15, 2002) [hereinafter Draft Text Elements].

[49] Id. art. 1.

would be read to include all rights, such as civil, political and economic rights. That goal is evident in the specific clauses of the document. But beyond protecting rights, it has a promotional aspect -- to "[p]romote the autonomy and independent lives of persons with disabilities and achieve their full participation in economic, social, cultural, civil, and political life under conditions of equality."[50] The Draft Text Elements thus face up to the argument that society must inject resources to promote the opportunities of people with disabilities.

The draft then moves, in Article 2, to definitions. The Draft Text Elements define only disability and discrimination.[51] The disability definition arguably suffers from the defects in the ADA's definition and indeed more so. For example, it refers to limitations on "the capacity to perform one or more essential activities of daily life,"[52] without defining what those activities are or whether the ability to perform them with or without assistive devices, such as eyeglasses or hearing aids, takes them out of the scope of disabilities. In this regard, it is less expansive than, for example, the Canadian federal and provincial legislation discussed earlier.[53]

The definitions define "discrimination" in terms of the way a person is treated because of a disability, record of a disability or perception of a disability (all like the ADA) and whether that treatment impairs the exercise of human rights or fundamental freedoms.[54] Clearly, this leaves a huge scope to the definition of "human rights and fundamental freedoms." Note that the preambular language in subparagraph (c) refers to the United Nations Human Rights Covenants, so that arguably any interference with any of the rights elaborated in those instruments would constitute discrimination.

However, one might ask whether that addresses, for example, accessibility limitations that prevent a person from being employed at a particular job, as opposed to simply being employed. One might argue that the breadth of the Convention sacrifices some of the utility of the more precisely aimed rule, such as that set out in the ADA.

In Article 3, states parties agree to adopt "legislative, judicial, administrative, and any other kind of measures aimed at achieving the

---

[50] Id. art. 1(c).

[51] A later draft expanded the definitions. See Text of Elements for a United Nations Comprehensive and Integral International Convention to Promote and Protect the Rights and Dignity of Persons with Disabilities, http://www.sre.gob.mx/discapacidad/elements.htm (May 16, 2002) (last visited Sept. 28, 2003).

[52] Draft Text Elements, supra note 48, at art. 2(a).

[53] See supra Section 23,3.1.

[54] Draft Text Elements, supra note 48, at art. 2(b).

objectives of this Convention." Not only do they agree to incorporate the principal of equality and non-discrimination in their legislation, but they also agree to establish appropriate sanctions and to ensure that the rights "contained in this Convention and other related international instruments have the legal protection of the competent national courts."[55] Interestingly, via that route, states might be required to establish legal protection for rights contained in the ICCPR or the ICESCR. States also, under Article 3, have affirmative duties to enact laws to "establish ... the necessary positive actions to promote the autonomy and independent lives of persons with disabilities" and to achieve their full integration into various aspects of society.[56]

Article 4 emphasizes that positive aspect of the obligations by requiring states to "promote ... positive or compensatory measures." The Convention thus makes it clear that states have duties beyond assuring access or removal of barriers. Indeed, it requires its members to "adopt specific measures to protect persons with disabilities who are in special situations of vulnerability."[57]

Articles 6, 7 and 8 address access, including the kind of access guaranteed by the ADA to public services and facilities and public transportation,[58] but also in Article 7 and 8, access to information and to the right to communicate. Article 6 does not address access to private structures, other than perhaps housing. Article 7 obligates states to "promote access to different forms of alternative communication," which might include one supposes TTYs, Braille or sign languages.

Like many of the other operative provisions of the text, the access requirements are general, leaving to individual states parties the decisions how best to realize the treaty's obligations and practice. We have seen that in the United States detailed regulations accompany the ADA, which is itself more detailed than any of the proposed conventions. Both the Standard Rules and the World Action Program provide guidance to the Convention, but given the detailed nature of, for example, access requirements, it will be interesting to observe how states implement it and how citizens of those states attempt to enforce it.

Article 10(1)(a) requires states to commit to provide legal counsel and interpretation or translation services for free to all persons with disabilities. In the first place, if the United States signed this Convention, one could imagine a significant Eleventh Amendment problem, since most judicial proceedings occur in state courts. Second, it would provide people with disabilities, even disabilities that have no real bearing on their ability to appear in court, with free legal counsel, including free counsel in

---

[55]   Id. art. 3(2)(c).

[56]   Id. art. 3(2)(d).

[57]   Id. art. 4(2).

[58]   Id. art. 6.

civil proceedings. Article 10(1)(b) inhibits discrimination during legal proceedings or during "the serving of a prison sentence." That would seem to address the issues that arose in *Price v. United Kingdom*.[59]

Article 11 attempts to integrate people with disabilities into the political life of the country. Subparagraph (a) addresses voting rights, a subject that has bedeviled the United States.[60] It also aims to provide people with information sufficiently affirmative to allow their participation in governmental decision-making.[61] In subparagraph (d) it guarantees people with disabilities the right of freedom of association, which would not seem to go beyond their rights under the First Amendment of the United States Constitution.

But in subpart (e), where it requires states to "promote the participation of persons with disabilities and their organizations in the design of government policies related to disability," it clearly could raise problems. Does that mean, for example, that the United States Executive Branch must take account of the goals of people with disabilities in designing legislation? Does it mean that they must be at least involved in the decision-making process? Would there, for example, be a cause of action if a disability rights organization were not permitted to be present during consideration of new legislation? The answer to all these questions is probably no, but they raise drafting questions for the convention.

Articles 12 and 13 deal with rights to education and medical/rehabilitation services. Although Article 12 has a number of provisions requiring states to take action to ensure educational opportunities for persons with disabilities, it arguably expresses no preference as to whether they should be trained in mainstream or separate facilities, although it allows them to be retained in separate facilities if they so desire.[62]

Arguably, when, in Article 12(2), it requires states to "provide the resources needed to allow their inclusion in the formal education system," it means the mainstream education system. Here, some wording changes would be useful to clarify the convention's goal. Article 12 requires states to spend money for services and training features. There could be a question whether this international obligation takes precedence over other educational needs, especially in times when funds are scarce. The convention does not address that issue.

---

[59] Price v. United Kingdom, No. 33394/96, 34 Eur. H.R. Rep. 53, 2001 WL 825435 (ECHR) (Eur. Ct. H.R. July 10, 2001), discussed supra Section 24.2.A.

[60] See generally Michael Waterstone, Constitutional and Statutory Voting Rights for People with Disabilities, 14 Stan. L. & Pol'y Rev. 353 (2003). See also supra Part 4.

[61] Draft Text Elements, art. 11(b).

[62] Id. art. 12(3).

Article 13 deals with a wide variety of issues relating to medical care. As with other articles, it stresses providing people with disabilities with information such that they can make intelligent choices – here a choice of treatments.[63] Article 13(c), which guarantees people with disabilities "quality medical attention within the state health care systems," includes breastfeeding mothers among people with disabilities. More important, perhaps, it assumes that there are "state health care systems," which is not the case in the United States, except in a limited sense.

Article 14 deals comprehensively with employment issues. Uncontroversially, it guarantees equal pay for equal work and, like the ADA, requires "the adoption of positive measures that allows persons with disabilities access to and continuance in employment." However, it appears to go farther than the ADA, since among other things it has no minimum size requirement for an employer and does not limit "positive measures" to those that are "reasonable."[64] It also raises issues about the interaction between collective bargaining agreements and protection of people with disabilities.

In subpart (a), it requires states parties to "[g]uarantee that individual and collective labor agreements and regulations protect persons with disabilities in regard with [sic] employment, job promotion, and working conditions ...." Does this mean that protection of people with disabilities trumps union seniority agreements? One could see that unions in all parts of the world might have problems with this provision, just as employers might have problems with the unlimited requirements of other provisions of this section.

Article 16 illustrates the scope of drafters' concerns about integrating people with disabilities into society as well as the failure of the instrument to distinguish between public and private activities. That article deals with "access to and the enjoyment of ... Recreational, cultural, and sports activities through adaptations which facilitate them the use of related facilities and services." [sic] What does this mean with respect to the *Martin*[65] types of issues? In its requirement that people with disabilities be integrated into "routine sports activities and national as well as international competitions" it gives no guidance on how states are to deal with athletes with disabilities. Nor does it distinguish public recreational, cultural and sports activities with private versions of the same activities.

---

63 Id. art. 13(b).

64 Id. art. 14 (d). There is no such requirement in the EU's Framework Directive, either, which requires some states, such as the UK, to modify existing legislation.

65 PGA Tour v. Martin, 532 U.S. 661 (2001). See supra Part 5.

Assuming that one accepts the goals of the convention, it obviously presents drafting problems. It is best seen as an instrument that will commit its members to take broadly defined actions in various arenas, but not one that spells those actions out in detail. A legal issue that then arises is how one aggrieved by a perceived violation of the convention can state a claim for relief. Certainly, in the most gross situations, if the state engaged in compulsory sterilization or provided no access to public buildings or refused to permit blind people to have facilities to vote in secrecy, one could make arguments about violations.

The more difficult questions pit legitimate concerns against other legitimate concerns, for example, seniority rights of non-disabled labor union members versus job accommodation rights of people with disabilities. Those sorts of issues show the limitations on international human rights agreements. What is weighed against them, however, is the ability of such agreements to effect moral conceptions and thereby impel states to take action, even if each state takes different actions and not all achieve similar ends.

Part 9

Disability And Employment, Welfare, And Health Care Policy

Analysis

Chapter 26 INTRODUCTION

§ 26.1 Overview

Important issues are emerging about the ADA's reach and applicability to American social and economic policy. The issues are compelling in light of the dramatic changes that have occurred in the last twenty-five years in employment, welfare, and health care policy. Contemporary employment and welfare policies, for example, are focused on increasing the labor force participation of qualified persons with disabilities and reducing their dependence on government entitlement programs.

Federal laws such as the Workforce Investment Act of 1998 (WIA), the Ticket to Work and Work Incentives Improvement Act of 1999 (TWWIIA), along with the ADA, illustrate public support for enhancing employment opportunities for working age adults with disabilities and preventing discrimination in the workplace and society. Despite these policy initiatives and the emerging ADA case law, there is little analysis of their interrelationship. This Part examines the applicability of the ADA to three areas of evolving policy: employment, welfare, and health care.

Chapter 27 DISABILITY AND EMPLOYMENT POLICY

While the U.S. Supreme Court and legal commentators have grappled over the reach of the ADA, there has been a parallel debate in the social sciences on how to assess the real-world impact of the ADA's Title I employment provisions. The central question is how to measure the law's impact on the employment prospects and economic independence of individuals with disabilities.[1]

Much of the research attempting to determine the effects of Title I is not conclusive. Studies finding that the employment levels of individuals with work disabilities declined in the early 1990s conclude that Title I is the likely cause.[2] Other studies find increased employment levels since the enactment of the ADA; however, these samples may not be representative of the population covered by the law.[3] Nevertheless, these later studies show that individuals with severe functional limitations that do not prevent them from working markedly improved their relative employment levels in the early 1990s.[4]

A primary difference in the findings on employment outcomes hinges on how researchers define and measure disability.[5] Of course, how researchers identify the group of individuals with disabilities is fundamental to whether their findings are informative as to the impact of the ADA.[6]

---

[1] Peter Blanck et al., Calibrating the Impact of the ADA's Employment Provisions, 14 Stan. L. & Pol'y Rev. 267, 267-68 (2003) [hereinafter Blanck, Calibrating the Impact].

[2] Richard V. Burkhauser et al., A User's Guide to Current Statistics on the Employment of People with Disabilities, in The Decline in Employment of People with Disabilities: A Policy Puzzle (David C. Stapleton & Richard V. Burkhauser eds., forthcoming 2003) [hereinafter Policy Puzzle]; David C. Stapleton et al., Have Changes in Job Requirements Reduced the Number of Workers with Disabilities?, in Policy Puzzle, supra.

[3] Stephen H. Kaye, Improved Employment Opportunities for People with Disabilities (Nat'l Inst. of Disability and Rehab. Res. 2003); Douglas Kruse & Lisa Schur, Employment of People with Disabilities Following the ADA, 42 Indus. Relations 31, 50-51 (2003) (paper presented at the Industrial Relations Research Association Conference in New Orleans in January 2001, and the Employment & Disability Policy Institute, sponsored by Cornell University in Washington, D.C. in October 2001).

[4] See supra note 3.

[5] Blanck, Calibrating the Impact, supra note 1, at 268.

[6] See Susan Schwochau & Peter Blanck, The Economics of the Americans with Disabilities Act, Part III: Does the ADA Disable the Disabled?, 21 Berkeley J. Emp. & Lab. L. 271, 299 (2000).

As discussed in prior Parts of this treatise, there are many reasons why individuals with disabilities are less likely to be employed, and, when employed, receive lower wages than nondisabled workers. Employment rates are suppressed by an inability to invest in training and education, workplace barriers that curtail productivity such as lack of workplace accommodations, and the inability to receive adequate health insurance.[7]

This chapter examines the applicability of disability rights principles to the Workforce Investment Act of 1998 (WIA)[8] and then to the Ticket to Work and Work Incentives Improvement Act of 1999 (TWWIIA).[9] WIA was enacted to assist individuals with disabilities to obtain employment through the provision of job-related supports, work incentives, and access to health care benefits.[10] To support this goal, WIA establishes "one stop" employment and job training centers.[11]

In a complementary manner, TWWIIA, through its "Ticket to Work" program, allows eligible recipients of disability insurance (SSDI) and supplemental income (SSI) to receive a "ticket" to obtain services from Employment Networks (ENs). ENs are public or private entities that provide services such as workplace accommodations, peer mentoring, job training, and transportation assistance to Ticket participants seeking employment. TWWIIA and WIA, working together, are meant to eliminate disincentives that have limited the employment options for disabled persons.[12]

§ 27.1 Disability Prevalence And The Case Of Employment

With the evolution of disability civil rights law and policy, critical questions are emerging about the composition, quality, and

---

[7] Id. at 284-85.

[8] Workforce Investment Act of 1998, Pub. L. No. 105-220, 112 Stat. 936 (codified as amended in scattered sections of 29 U.S.C.); 29 U.S.C. §§ 2801-2945 (2000).

[9] Ticket to Work and Work Incentives Improvement Act of 1999, Pub. L. No. 106-170, 113 Stat. 1860 (codified as amended in scattered sections of 42 U.S.C.).

[10] Peter Blanck & Helen A. Schartz, Towards Researching a National Employment Policy for Persons with Disabilities, 2001 Switzer Monograph (22nd Mary E. Switzer Memorial Seminar: Emerging Workforce Issues: WIA, Ticket to Work and Partnerships), http://www.mswitzer.org/sem00/papers/blanck.html (2000).

[11] Blanck, Calibrating the Impact, supra note 1, at 289.

[12] Id. For instance, these laws allow for deferral of medical reviews for those who return to work, and expedited reinstatement of benefits for those who cannot continue to be employed.

competitiveness of the American work force of the 21st century, including millions of workers with disabilities. These questions include:

- What types of work skills will be needed for American employers to remain competitive in the U.S. and abroad?

- Will our increasingly diversified and aging work force include millions of persons with disabilities?

- What will be the characteristics and qualifications of the work force of persons with disabilities?

- What types of job training, technology, and accommodations will be available to that work force? and,

- How will the changes that have occurred in the last quarter of the 20th century in disability antidiscrimination law, and welfare and health care policy affect that work force?

Part 1 of the treatise described how disability laws and policies have undergone a dramatic shift from a model of charity and compensation, to medical oversight, and then to civil rights. Contemporary employment policies and laws, for instance, are focused on increasing the labor force participation of persons with disabilities and reducing their dependence on government programs.

Federal laws such as the WIA,[13] the TWWIIA,[14] and the ADA, illustrate public support for enhancing employment opportunities for, and health care available to, working age adults with disabilities and preventing discrimination in the workplace.

Despite these and other public and private initiatives, there is little definitive evidence that American disability policies and laws have resulted in substantial increases in the numbers of persons with disabilities participating fully in American society. Even in periods of high employment, millions of persons with disabilities remain unemployed or underemployed. Persons with disabilities are less likely to have full-time employment, and, even when employed, earn less income than their nondisabled peers.[15]

---

[13] Pub. L. No. 105-220, 112 Stat. 936 (codified as amended in scattered sections of 29 U.S.C.); 29 U.S.C. §§ 2801-2945 (2000).

[14] Pub. L. No. 106-170, 113 Stat. 1860 (codified as amended in scattered sections of 42 U.S.C.).

[15] For reviews, see Peter Blanck et al., Is it Time to Declare the ADA a Failed Law?, in Policy Puzzle, supra note 2, at 335-72; Richard Burkhauser et al., A User's Guide to Current Statistics on the Employment of People with Disabilities, in Policy Puzzle, supra note 2.

A.   *Demographics Of Disability*

Despite the new approach toward a national disability policy of inclusion, millions of individuals with disabilities who are capable of working remain unemployed or underemployed. The 2000 National Organization on Disability/Harris Survey of Americans with Disabilities reports that 32% of disabled individuals are employed, compared to 81% of individuals without disabilities.[16]

The 1998 Current Population Survey (CPS) found that approximately 27% of individuals with disabilities were employed, compared to 78% of their nondisabled peers.[17] About 64% of individuals with disabilities who were employed held full-time jobs, compared to 82% of employees without disabilities.

Those employees with disabilities with full-time, year round employment had average annual earnings of $29,513, over $8,000 less than the $37,961 average earnings of nondisabled counterparts. In short, even in prosperous economic times, individuals with disabilities are less likely to be employed, and, if they are employed, are more likely to be working part-time and earning far less than their peers.

Moreover, in the future, individuals with disabilities may be even less prepared for competitive employment. Individuals with disabilities, on average, attain less formal education than individuals without disabilities. According to the CPS, nearly 31% of those with work-related disabilities had not completed high school, compared to about 18% of individuals without disabilities.[18]

Although almost one quarter (24%) of individuals without disabilities had more than 16 years of education, less than 11% of individuals with disabilities attained that level of education.[19] Considering that the Bureau of Labor Statistics predicts continued employment growth into 2008, with the fastest growing occupations being in information technology, limited education will place individuals with disabilities at a significant disadvantage in the labor force.[20]

---

[16]   Nat'l Org. on Disability, Executive Summary: The 2000 N.O.D./Harris Survey of Americans with Disabilities, at http://www.nod.org/content. cfm?id=1076 (July 10, 2002).

[17]   U.S. Bureau of Lab. Statistics & U.S. Bureau of the Census, Disability Data from March Current Population Survey, http://www.bls.census. gov/cps/cpsmain.htm (last visited Oct. 12, 2003) [hereinafter CPS].

[18]   Id.

[19]   Id.

[20]   See Kate D. Seelman, Employment of Individuals with Disabilities – Opportunities and Challenges – The Best of Times/the Worst of Times

Not all of the available information paints a dismal picture for individuals with disabilities. Researchers report increases in employment since passage of the ADA among people aged 21-64 with severe functional limitations. Others find that since 1990 employment rates declined among those reporting "work disabilities," but improved among those reporting severe functional limitations without a work disability.[21]

B.   *Research Into The Impact Of The ADA On Employment*

We began this treatise in Part 1 describing the tension between the ADA's employment-expanding goal and economic theory, which has caused a range of researchers to examine the impact of the ADA on employment of people with disabilities. Historically, of course, people with disabilities have been employed at substantially lower rates than people without disabilities,[22] although the rates tended to fluctuate with overall economic conditions.[23] While the ADA was designed to improve the employment of people with disabilities, as early as 1996 commentators were asserting that the employment situation of people with disabilities actually had deteriorated in relation to other groups.[24]

(2000) (paper presented at Employment and Disability Pol'y Summer Institute, Cornell Univ., Ithaca, N.Y.).

[21] For a review of these studies, see Blanck, Calibrating the Impact, supra note 1; Schwochau & Blanck, supra note 6.

[22] See, e.g., Edward H. Yelin & Patricia P. Katz, Labor Force Trends of Persons With and Without Disabilities, 117 Monthly Lab. Rev. 36, 38-41 (Oct. 1994). The employment rate for people with disabilities between 1970 and 1992, for all ages and both genders, fluctuated between 42 and 49 percent as opposed to rates between 75 and 95 percent for men without disabilities of all ages and 45 to 78 percent for women of all ages without disabilities. Id. at 39-41. The data are from the CPS. The data also indicate that employment for males of all ages generally "trended" down for older (55 to 64 years old) males, while holding reasonably steady for younger males, but it rose dramatically for younger women, while holding steady for older women. For people with disabilities, the employment rates for men generally declined over the relevant period and declined more than the rates for men without disabilities when those rates were declining. On the other hand, the increase in employment among younger women generally also was reflected in an increase in employment among women with disabilities. Id. at 38.

[23] See Richard V. Burkhouser, Post-ADA: Are People With Disabilities Expected to Work? 549 Annals Am. Acad. Pol. & Soc. Sci. 71, 78 (1997).

[24] See Walter Y. Oi, Employment and Benefits for People with Diverse Disabilities, in Disability, Work and Cash Benefits Disability, Work and Cash Benefits, 103 (Jerry L. Mashaw et al., eds. 1996) (suggesting that percentage of disabled individuals with jobs had fallen from 33% in 1986

The period following the enactment of the ADA has been one of rapid changes in the economic structure of the United States. Manufacturing sector jobs have declined in favor of service industry jobs; job mobility has increased; and the economy has seen an upsurge and, at the end of decade, a substantial retrenchment. In the face of those large-scale changes in the economy, a number of authors have attempted to determine the impact of the ADA on employment of people with disabilities.[25]

Researchers have developed various theoretical models to predict the effects of the ADA and statistical approaches to test their predictions. We describe two of the models to illustrate their approaches. In doing so, we do not plumb their mathematical details, which are sophisticated, and the interested reader should examine the original articles. We do point out issues with respect to their methodology.

Acemoglu and Angrist model what they perceive as the three principal impacts of the ADA on employment.[26] First, they include the firing costs generated by (disabled and nondisabled) employees who sue for wrongful termination in violation of the ADA, including attorneys' fees and the potential for damages.

---

to 31% in 1996). Other, less academic, writers concur. See e.g., Lisa J. Stansky, Opening Doors, A.B.A. J. 66 (Mar. 1996).

[25] See generally, Daron Acemoglu & Joshua D. Angrist, Nat'l Bur. of Econ. Research, Consequences of Employment Protection? The Case of the Americans with Disabilities Act, 109 J. Pol. Econ. 915 (2001) (Working Paper No. 6670 (1998)), http://www.nber.org/papers/w6670.pdf; Thomas DeLeire, The Wage and Employment Effects of the Americans with Disabilities Act, 35 J. Hum. Res. 693, 694 (2000) (curiously, DeLeire begins his analysis in 1990, before Title I was effective); Christine Jolls, Accommodation Mandates, 53 Stan. L. Rev. 223, 228-29 (2000); see also John J. Donohue III, Understanding the Reasons for an Impact of Legislatively Mandated Benefits for Selected Workers, 53 Stan. L. Rev. 897, 898-99 (2001) (commenting on Jolls).

[26] See Acemoglu & Angrist, supra note 25, at 921. Their factual assumptions are arguable. For example, in attempting to estimate the cost of the ADA, they state that employees file 40,000 "discrimination" cases each year and win "almost 60%" of the time. Id. at 920. However, they lump all discrimination cases together – gender, age, race and disability. Id. Moreover, statistics on disability cases show that employees or applicants, in fact, lose their cases over 94% of the time. ABA Comm'n on Mental and Physical Disability Law, 2002 Employment Decisions Under the ADA Title I–Survey Update, http://www.abanet.org/disability/title_survey.pdf (2002). The hostility of the federal courts to ADA cases has led many plaintiffs to bring cases in state courts under state law, where that law is more hospitable.

Second, they include the costs of reasonable accommodations for workers with disabilities.

Third, they include the costs to the employer of potential (disabled and nondisabled) applicants suing for failure to hire in violation of the ADA, which includes the potential for damages as well as attorneys' fees, even if the applicant loses.

Because hiring additional people, including people with disabilities, will diminish potential litigation over failing to hire, "hiring costs" effectively act as subsidies.[27] They treat hiring and firing costs as taxes on the firms, rather than transfers to the applicants/employees. Using a production function that takes into account the (assumed) differing efficiencies of workers with disabilities and workers without disabilities, they write a function that expresses the profits of firms that employ workers with and without disabilities, incorporating terms for each of the three factors they consider most important.[28]

Assuming that firms immediately adjust to steady employment levels, as well as a number of other simplifying conditions, Acemoglu and Angrist derive a pair of partial differential equations for the wages and employment levels of disabled and nondisabled employees.[29] They derive the wage rates for disabled employees,[30] from which they calculate the employment levels for workers with and without disabilities.[31]

Acemoglu and Angrist make a number of predictions from their model:

- Because hiring people with disabilities effectively creates a subsidy versus not hiring them, depending on the cost of hiring and firing nondisabled employees, the ADA can increase employment and wages for people with disabilities.

- However, they suggest that "the ADA appears to have increased" the firing costs for disabled employees substantially over the hiring costs, so that, added to the new

---

[27] Acemoglu & Angrist, supra note 25, at 922.

[28] Id.

[29] Id.

[30] They assume that the "market clears" for workers without disabilities; i.e., that the wages of workers without disabilities multiplied by the supply function for those workers equals the number of firms in the market at equilibrium times the number of applicants for each job from those workers without disabilities. Id. at 923. They also assume that the number of firms is determined by the maximized profits' being equal to the entry costs or that there is no entry. Id.

[31] Id.

costs of accommodation, the ADA is more likely to reduce employment and wages.

- The ADA's equal pay requirement may increase wages for people with disabilities, thus creating involuntary unemployment and preventing wages from falling to account for firing costs and accommodation costs, further leading to a decline in employment among people with disabilities.

- Because the hiring costs effectively reduce profits, some firms may close, causing disabled and nondisabled employment and wages to fall.

- The ADA might affect employment for those without disabilities, who may sue, claiming to have disabilities.[32]

They conclude:

The theoretical discussion shows that the net effect of the ADA depends on which provisions are most important. Accommodation and firing costs are likely to reduce employment, whereas hiring costs have the opposite effect. If the equal-pay provision is not binding, equilibrium will be on the labor supply curves of disabled and nondisabled workers, and employment declines will be accompanied by declines in wages. More generally, however, the equal-pay provision creates "involuntary unemployment" off the supply curve.[33]

Because, presumably, it would be virtually impossible to assemble actual data to test their equilibrium conditions, Acemoglu and Angrist propose a "reduced" equation to attempt to fit the data to their model.[34] They applied their theory to a sample of data drawn from the March 1988-1997 CPS of the Census Bureau.

Workers with disabilities were identified in the March CPS Income Supplemental by the question "Do you have a health problem or disability which prevents you from working or which limits the kind and amount of work you can do?" Acemoglu and Angrist evaluate the ADA's

---

[32] Acemoglu & Angrist, supra note 25, at 924.

[33] Id.

[34] Id. at 924-25. Note that they do not attempt to estimate the variables or parameters in their equilibrium model. Rather, they attempt to measure the changes due to the ADA using nondisabled individuals as a control group. See Christine Jolls & J. J. Prescott, The Effects of "Reasonable Accommodations" Requirements and Firing Costs on the Employment of Individuals with Disabilities 10 and tbl. 5 (on file with authors).

impact by looking at the number of weeks worked and the average weekly earnings.

Taking the effects of the ADA to start in 1993, because it was effective for most businesses in mid-1992, they find drops in the number of weeks worked by disabled men in the 21-39 age group in 1993 and 1995. They find similar results for women in the same age group, but the decline began in 1992. They likewise find a drop in the employment of men in the 48-50 year age group, but do not find one for women in that group. They find little effect on the relative wages of workers with and without disabilities.[35]

Acemoglu and Angrist attempt to account for a number factors that might bias their results.[36] First, they deal with composition bias — the possibility that, after the ADA became law, being viewed as a person with a disability became more socially acceptable, so more people identified themselves as disabled.[37] They control for this by using a matched sample of people who reported they were disabled in 1993 and 1994 and people who reported they were disabled in neither year. They find that this limitation has little effect on the results for men between 40 and 58 and for women between 21 and 39.[38] The results for men age 21 to 39 declined, but they discount that because disability rates for men in that age were lower at the end of the sample.[39]

Second, they attempt to control for changes in the Supplemental Security Income ("SSI") and Disability Insurance ("DI") programs in the early 1990s, both of which increased payments at that time. They find that those changes did not explain the magnitude of the hours lost.[40]

Finally, they attempt to determine whether their results varied by state, because, in view of the fact that labor forces in states have different compositions, awareness of the ADA might vary, and states have different employment laws of their own. They find that there was a negative effect in 1993-1994 for weeks worked in states with a large number of ADA charges versus other states.[41]

Because the non-ADA factors do not explain the data, Acemoglu and Angrist conclude that the ADA had negative impacts on the employment of people with disabilities under age 39. They explain the

---

[35] Acemoglu & Angrist, supra note 25, at 929-32, 948-49.

[36] Id. at 935.

[37] Id.

[38] Id.

[39] Id.

[40] Id. at 935-39.

[41] Acemoglu & Angrist, supra note 25, at 944-48. Acemoglu and Angrist attempted to determine impact of the ADA on hirings and separations and the impact of firm size on the results. Id. at 940-44.

absence of effects on older women workers by the effects of the Age Discrimination in Employment Act (ADEA), which protects workers over age 40, and Title VII of the Civil Rights Act of 1964, which protects women.

Because wages, in the data, did not decline for workers with disabilities, they attribute part of the fall in employment to wage stability; i.e., employers dealt with increased costs by hiring fewer people. They find, however, that the ADA did not result in lower separation rates. Their data indicate accommodation costs are greater than the costs of wrongful termination lawsuits and thus are likely to be at least as important a factor for employers as the fear of litigation. If that is so, employers would be more likely to terminate than to accommodate.[42]

Significantly, they find no effect of the ADA on the employment of people without disabilities. That finding would allay concerns that the ADA could result in an overall decrease in employment.

Instead of focusing specifically on the ADA, another commentator, Jolls, has developed a model of the impact of "accommodation mandates" – legislatively mandated benefits that apply to a defined subset of employees.[43] The ADA is such a mandate, as is the Family and Medical Leave Act.[44] Jolls first notes, like Acemoglu and Angrist, that one must consider two labor markets, the demand for and supply of workers to whom an accommodation is due ("disadvantaged workers") and workers to whom an accommodation is not due ("nondisadvantaged workers").[45] One then must determine the impact of the statutory mandate on the supply of and demand for each group.[46]

Jolls emphasizes the effect of the binding or non-binding nature of the mandate – what the law requires and how readily it is enforced.[47] She finds that, contrary to Summers' general theory of mandates, under certain circumstances, the disadvantaged group may benefit from accommodations.

Briefly to summarize Jolls' conclusions:

---

[42] Id. at 950.

[43] Jolls, supra note 25, at 231. Her work generalizes that of Lawrence Summers on mandates that affect all workers. See generally, Lawrence H. Summers, Some Simple Economics of Mandated Benefits, 79 Am. Econ. Rev. 177 (1989).

[44] 29 U.S.C. § 2612(a)(1) (2000).

[45] Jolls, supra note 25, at 241.

[46] Id.

[47] Id. at 241, 263-72 (discussion of conditions under which restrictions are binding). Compare id. at 243-63 (which does not factor in litigation costs) with Acemoglu & Angrist, supra note 25, at 950 (which does factor in litigation costs).

(1) If wage and employment mandates are binding:

- If the value to the employee of an accommodation exceeds its cost to the employer, the disadvantaged worker's wage will fall less than the value of the accommodation (whose cost is spread among all workers) and the employment level of the disadvantaged workers will rise, since, in effect, the supply of disadvantaged workers will increase faster than the demand for them falls.[48]

- If the value to the employee of an accommodation exceeds its cost to the employer, then it is not certain that disadvantaged groups will benefit. However, if the proportion of disadvantaged employees is small enough and the cost of accommodation is small enough, disadvantaged workers will benefit because the effect of the accommodation on the total marginal revenue will be small.[49]

(2) If restrictions on wage differentials are binding, but restrictions on employment differentials are not:

- The wages of the disadvantaged group either stay the same or rise, but the number of disadvantaged employees will fall.[50]

(3) If restrictions on wage differentials are not binding:

- It does not matter if employment restrictions are binding, since employers can adjust wages to compensate for any inefficiencies associated with hiring people with disabilities.

- The wage rates of the disadvantaged group always will fall, but their employment rates will depend on whether the value of the accommodation exceeds its cost.

---

[48] Jolls, supra note 25, at 247-48.
[49] Id. at 249.
[50] Id. at 255.

Jolls applies her theory to the ADA. She notes that wage differential restrictions likely are to be binding. But, because of the difficulty of determining who is disabled and whether that person can perform essential job functions, employment differential restrictions are likely not to be binding. Under her analysis, wage levels will remain the same, but employment levels will drop.[51] That is consistent with Acemoglu and Angrist's conclusions.

In a subsequent article, to separate the effects of accommodation from those of traditional antidiscrimination laws, Jolls and Prescott examine the impact of the ADA on three groups of states: (1) states that, prior to the ADA, had no disability discrimination law; (2) states that, prior to the ADA, had only a "traditional" disability discrimination law – one that simply prevented discrimination on the basis of disability ("protection without accommodation" states); and (3) states that had an ADA-like statute – one that prohibited discrimination and also required reasonable accommodations ("accommodation" states).

Their theory is that if the changes in employment – if any – are most pronounced in states where there was no prior kind of disability discrimination regime, and least in those states where there was an ADA-like regime, one could more easily infer a causal link between the accommodation requirement of the ADA and the changes.[52]

Jolls and Prescott's results support the findings of Acemoglu and Angrist, but also contain the same limitations (e.g., limitations of the applicability of their samples to ADA qualified individuals). They find people with disabilities in "protection without accommodation" states worked 1.515 fewer weeks following the effective date of the ADA as opposed to those in accommodation states. Given that the total number of weeks worked by the former disabled group was 15.985 and in the latter disabled group was 17.247, the drop was significant – approximately 10%.[53] There was a much smaller and statistically insignificant relative drop in accommodation states.[54] That is, they argue, attributable to the imposition of reasonable accommodation requirements.

They find a slightly smaller, but statistically insignificant, drop when comparing the states with no preexisting antidiscrimination requirement to the protection without accommodation states.[55] They conclude that the accommodation and the traditional antidiscrimination

---

[51] Id. at 275. This does not result when the accommodations are one-time events, such as building a ramp. Id. at 276.

[52] Jolls & Prescott, supra note 34, at 3.

[53] Id. at 11.

[54] Id. at 11 & tbl. 5.

[55] Id. at 12 & tbl. 5.

provisions of the ADA negatively affected employment, but the accommodation requirement was more significant.[56]

Thus, some studies suggest that the accommodation provisions and, to a lesser extent, the other antidiscrimination sections of the ADA, have a *negative* impact on the employment of people with disabilities. However, a number of other commentators, including Blanck, one of the authors of this treatise, have suggested those studies fail to demonstrate a causal relationship between the ADA and the employment effects they report.[57] As one author writes, "By confounding employment outcomes with labor supply decisions, these previous studies have not provided a complete, or even fair, assessment of the labor market provisions of the ADA."[58]

Thus, there are a number of substantial limitations to the prior studies:[59]

- Is the definition that is used in the background data appropriate? In particular, the ADA addresses employment of "qualified" people with disabilities. The Census Bureau question, on the other hand, asks whether people "have a health problem or disability which prevents [them] from working or which limits the kind and amount of work [they] can do." It may, therefore, select out precisely the people at whom the ADA was directed.[60]

---

[56] See also id. at tbl. 6, which shows the effect of the reasonable accommodation requirement in total leads to a drop of 2.009 weeks of work (with a 0.789 standard deviation) while the effect of a traditional antidiscrimination requirement is a drop of 0.936 weeks of work (with a standard deviation of 1.176). Jolls and Prescott also studied a number of effects that might potentially affect their results. Those do not affect their major conclusions.

[57] E.g., Kathleen Beegle & Wendy A. Stock, The Labor Market Effects of Disability Discrimination Laws, 38 J. Hum. Res. 806, 807 (2003); Schwochau & Blanck, supra note 6, at 273; Kruse & Schur, supra note 3, at 60-61; Julie L. Hotchkiss, A Closer Look at the Employment Impact of the Americans with Disabilities Act 15, http://www.people.virginia.edu/~sns5r/microwkshp/EmpADA_3_02.pdf (Mar. 2002).

[58] Hotchkiss, supra note 57, at 1.

[59] Indeed, the authors of those studies recognize their limits. E.g., Jolls, supra note 25, at 278 (noting that the available employment data are not congruent with the ADA's definition of disabled).

[60] As a policy matter, however, one could argue that the ADA is addressed more broadly to people with disabilities, so the research should not be limited to qualified people with disabilities. See Blanck, Calibrating the Impact, supra note 1, at 276-78.

- Do the studies properly account for the general downward trends in employment among people with disabilities?

- Do the studies properly account for the increase in transfer payments to people with disabilities during the same period that the ADA became effective?

- Do the studies even answer the question "what is the probability of entering the labor force and being employed?," rather than the question "what is the probability of being employed?"[61]

In beginning to address such questions, Kruse and Schur investigated various definitions of disability. The many people who can and do work, and who have an impairment of some sort, are the proper subject for an analysis to address the impact of the ADA's employment provisions. Others included in, for example, Acemoglu and Angrist's and DeLeire's analyses, are not the target of Title I and are not properly considered in employment studies. Kruse and Schur find that if the definition of the disability is drawn closely from the ADA, meaning that the population studied is restricted to those who are not work limited but are functionally limited, following the ADA there was an actual *increase* in employment among the population studied.[62]

Kruse and Schur also emphasize the change in composition of those reporting disabilities. During the period studied, more people reported functional and daily activity limitations, while fewer reported being able to work.[63] Partly, this may be due to increased SSDI payments during the relevant period and partly, ironically, to changing perceptions that stigmatized disabilities less. The employment decline in the data used by others may result from those changes. Indeed, if more people with disabilities have jobs, fewer may view themselves – and report themselves – as disabled. While Acemoglu and Angrist tested for that compositional effect, Kruse and Schur argue that their employment and disability populations cover different times and measure a decrease in employment among those with newly acquired impairments, but miss the increase among those with older impairments.[64]

Beegle and Stock analyze employment data to account for state antidiscrimination laws and preexisting trends in labor market outcomes for people with and without disabilities.[65] In addition, they perform an analysis that takes into account states' supplementation (or lack thereof)

---

[61] Hotchkiss, supra note 57, at 9.

[62] See Kruse & Schur, supra note 3, at 50-51; see also Blanck, Calibrating the Impact, supra note 1, at 276-78.

[63] Kruse & Schur, supra note 3, at 53.

[64] Id. at 37.

[65] Beegle & Stock, supra note 57, at 7.

of federal SSI in determining whether states have reasonable accommodation requirements.[66]

Of course, there are potential problematic elements in this analysis, as Beegle and Stock note. For example, there is a substantial variation among individual states' laws, for which it is not practical to control. It is not clear whether an analysis like Jolls and Prescott's, which separates different state laws, would alter the Beegle and Stock findings.

Second, there is a timing problem: They use three time periods, pre-1970, pre-1980 and pre-1990. A state that adopted a law in 1981 may look much like a state that adopted one in 1980, but it is considered with states in the next decade. Finally, they are mindful of the possibility that the definition of disability is exogenous — that individuals self-define themselves and that definition may depend on the legal environment at a given time. They consider that to be a small effect.[67]

Beegle and Stock find that disabled workers in states with disability discrimination laws have approximately 12 percentage points lower labor force participation rates than in states with no such laws. However, when they control for differential trends among the disabled and nondisabled, the difference shrinks to about 1%. This finding is similar for employment rates.[68]

Moreover, when they control for temporal trends, they find that the differential time trend of employment of people with disabilities, rather than the applicable statutory regime, drives the difference. They find that, at least with respect to state legislation, "reasonable accommodation appears not to have been a driving force in the legislation's possible effects for the disabled."[69] Unlike Acemoglu and Angrist, they find a small negative effect on the earnings of people with disabilities.

Finally, a recent study by Hotchkiss reaches results similar to Kruse and Schur's. She finds that "the reduction in the labor force participation rate among the disabled is *not* the result of the disabled leaving the labor force, but, rather, a reclassification of non-disabled labor force non-participants as disabled. This phenomenon likely occurred as a result of more stringent welfare requirements and more generous federal disability benefits."[70] Where people already were in the labor force, the employment of people with disabilities relative to those without disabilities did not change after the implementation of the ADA.[71]

---

[66] Id. at 15.

[67] Id. at 17.

[68] Id. at 23-24.

[69] Id. at 24-25.

[70] Hotchkiss, supra note 57, at 21.

[71] Id.

Hotchkiss analyzes the Social Security Administration's Survey of Income and Program Participation ("SIPP") data, which permits one to disaggregate the data by type of disability.

She finds a positive employment impact of the ADA on people with mental disorders and "other" disabilities, but workers with musculoskeletal and internal system disabilities did not experience different employment probability growth than people without those disabilities.[72] Hotchkiss concludes that the fact that all states had passed anti-disability discrimination legislation prior to 1990, when the ADA was passed, may explain why the ADA has had little employment impact.[73] However, Hotchkiss' conclusions continue to show a negative impact on people not already participating in the labor market. Certainly, one of the goals of the ADA was to bring people into the labor market.

To summarize, a decade after the employment provisions of the ADA became effective, it appears that certain groups of persons with different disabilities are benefiting more than others from the law's antidiscrimination and accommodation mandates. The studies that find a negative relationship between the ADA and employment of people with disabilities may focus on a broader definition of disabilities than the ADA covers. These researchers thus may be asking a question that is largely irrelevant to an analysis of the ADA's impact.

Still, there is evidence that the ADA has not moved the anticipated large numbers of people with disabilities from the non-participant category to the worker category. Given that the ADA came into being during a time of tremendous, albeit fleeting, economic prosperity, it will be interesting to see how the antidiscrimination and accommodation mandates fare in the less bullish post-2000 period.

§ 27.2 Workforce Investment Act (WIA)

A. Overview

The Workforce Investment Act of 1998 (WIA) establishes state and local Workforce Investment Boards responsible for developing a "one-stop" delivery system of accessible, innovative, and comprehensive employment services.[74] They partner with local vocational rehabilitation agencies,

---

[72] Id.

[73] Id. at 21-22. Prior to 1990, in Alabama, Arkansas and Mississippi, the legislation was limited to public employers. Id. at tbl. 5.

[74] Blanck & Schartz, supra note 10; Michael Morris, Building Relationships at a Community Level: Lessons Learned from Work Incentive Grantees (WIGs) 2, available at http://disability.law.uiowa.edu/lhpdc/projects/doltech.html (Rehab. Res. and Training Ctr. on Workforce Investment and Emp. Pol'y for Persons with Disabilities, Mar. 2002).

businesses, and job training and education programs to assist local communities in increasing employment.[75]

Furthermore, the one-stop system provides assistance in job search activities, career planning, job skill assessments and training, and childcare resources.[76] One-stops also provide resources for job and entrepreneurial training, transportation and housing assistance, and access to affordable health coverage.[77]

B.   *Applicability Of The ADA To WIA*

WIA is designed to help individuals with disabilities achieve employment, economic independence, and inclusion into society.[78] It is the federal funding vehicle for states to provide rehabilitation services and employment opportunities to people with disabilities.[79]

The programs and services supported by WIA are covered by the antidiscrimination provisions of the ADA and Section 504 of the Rehabilitation Act of 1973.[80] The antidiscrimination provisions apply to state and local agencies supported with WIA funds, state and local workforce boards, one-stop operators, and employment providers.[81]

---

[75] See e.g., Cal. Workforce Inv. Bd., Our Partners: Local, State & Federal, at http://www.calwia.org/partners/index.tpl (last visited July 27, 2003); Cal. Workforce Inv. Bd., What is Workforce Development, at http://www.calwia.org/workforce_development/index.tpl (last visited July 27, 2003) (describing the local Board's role in helping companies find skilled workers, overseeing job training activities, increasing workers' employment and earnings potential, increasing workers' educational and occupational skills, and reducing welfare dependence).

[76] See generally Iowa Workforce Dev., at http://www.iowaworkforce.org (last visited July 18, 2003); Texas Workforce Comm'n, at http://www.twc.state.tx.us/twc.html (last visited July 18, 2003).

[77] Morris, supra note 74.

[78] 29 U.S.C. § 701(b)(1) (2000).

[79] Letter from Lex Frieden, Chairperson, NCD to Congressman John A. Boehner, Chair, Education and the Workforce Committee (Mar. 18, 2003), at http://www.jfanow.org/cgi/getli.pl?1694 (last visited July 11, 2003).

[80] David Hoff, The Workforce Investment Act: Opportunities and Issues for the Disability Community (Nat'l Ctr. On Workforce and Disability, Dec. 1, 2000), at http://www.onestops.info/print.php?article_id=119.

[81] Robert Silverstein, Provisions in the Workforce Investment Act Relating to Nondiscrimination on the Basis of Disability and the Development by the Governor of a Written Methods of Administration, 2(3) Policy Brief, http://www.communityinclusion.org/publications/text/pb4text.html (Ctr. for the Study and Advancement of Disability Pol'y, Mar. 2000).

"Disability" is defined under WIA consistently with the regulations implementing the ADA.[82] Employees of private service providers are protected by Title I. State and local activities are covered under Title II. Title III's public accommodation provisions apply to private service providers receiving WIA funds from workforce boards.

A qualified person with a disability is entitled to effective benefits and services provided under WIA. One-stops and service providers must administer their programs in the most integrated setting possible[83] and not impose criteria that screen out individuals with disabilities.[84] They must provide reasonable accommodations to qualified applicants, participants, and employees with disabilities, unless doing so causes undue hardship. They also must make reasonable modifications to policies and practices to avoid discrimination.[85]

Secretary of Labor Elaine L. Chao, on the eve of the thirteenth anniversary of the ADA, announced the dissemination of the "WIA Section 188 Checklist" to all one-stop centers, workforce agencies, WIA grantees, and Job Corps directors and contractors.[86] The checklist provides policy and procedure guidance "to ensure nondiscrimination and equal opportunities for persons with disabilities."[87] Examples of the antidiscrimination protections applicable to persons with disabilities in the employment provider context are provided in the following chapter on the applicability of the ADA to TWWIIA.

§ 27.3 Ticket To Work And Work Incentives Improvement Act (TWWIIA)

A. Overview

TWWIIA provides benefits to eligible individuals with disabilities who want to and are capable of working.[88] One benefit allows working individuals with disabilities the option of maintaining Medicaid health insurance coverage. This promotes the ability of participants to return to work without the loss of essential health care benefits. Another benefit is

---

[82] 29 C.F.R. § 37.4 (2003).

[83] Id. § 37.7(d).

[84] Id. § 37.7(i).

[85] Id. § 37.8(a)-(b).

[86] Press Release, Dep't of Labor, U.S. Department of Labor Issues WIA Compliance Assistance Checklist to Help People with Disabilities, at http://www.dol.gov/opa/media/press/odep/ODEP2003400.htm (July 25, 2003). The checklist is available at http://www.dol.gov/oasam/programs/crc/section188.htm (last visited July 31, 2003).

[87] Id.

[88] 20 C.F.R § 411.125(B) (2003).

providing "tickets" for persons with disabilities to choose, rather than be assigned to, service providers for employment training.

Historically, one of the barriers to work for persons with disabilities has been the inability to obtain health care coverage.[89] Disability-based payments often diminish incentives to work, particularly when the attempt to work itself reduces eligibility for such benefits.[90] Cash benefits, for instance under the SSI and SSDI programs, primarily have been available to individuals who could not engage in "substantial gainful activity."[91]

Among working Americans with disabilities, almost one-fifth have no health insurance coverage, largely because their incomes (though low by most standards) exceed Medicaid eligibility levels and their employers do not offer coverage.[92] TWWIIA was passed to address these issues.[93]

TWWIIA allows states to permit qualified individuals with disabilities and incomes above the poverty level the option of purchasing Medicaid health insurance or of maintaining their coverage throughout their employment. TWWIIA also covers people returning to work from SSDI (e.g., after being injured on the job) who may risk the loss of health insurance coverage.[94]

TWWIIA's Ticket to Work and Self-Sufficiency Program provides recipients of disability insurance with a "ticket" to purchase employment training services from qualified Employment Networks (ENs).[95] The goal is to encourage individuals with disabilities to seek employment

---

[89] Schartz et al., Employment of Persons with Disabilities in Information Technology Jobs: Literature for "IT Works", 20 Behav. Sci & L. 637, 640 (2002).

[90] Pacer Ctr., Work Incentives for Persons with Disabilities, http://www.pacer.org/text/employ/workinc.htm (last visited July 31, 2003).

[91] Peter Blanck et al., Applicability of the ADA to "Ticket to Work" Employment Networks, 20 Behav. Sci. & L. 621, 625-27 (2002).

[92] Jack McNeil, U.S. Census Bureau, Current Population Reports, Americans with Disabilities: Household Economic Studies, 1997, pp. 70-73 (2001).

[93] Robert F. Rich et al., Critical Legal and Policy Issues for People with Disabilities, 6 DePaul J. Health Care L. 1, 21 (2002).

[94] Allen Jensen & Robert Silverstein, Improvements to the SSDI and SSI Work Incentives and Expanded Availability of Health Care Services to Workers with Disabilities under the Ticket to Work and Work Incentives Improvement Act of 1999, 2(1) Pol'y Brief, at http://www.community inclusion.org/publications/text/pb2text.html (Rehab. Research and Training Ctr., Feb. 2000).

[95] See 20 C.F.R. § 411.300 (2003) (defining the EN's purpose).

rehabilitation services that aid in attaining employment[96] and to reduce dependence on governmental benefit programs.[97] Ticket program services include the provision of case management, workplace accommodations, peer mentoring, job training, and transportation assistance.

ENs receive payment from SSA when they succeed in placing the participant in employment. Public and private organizations may apply to be ENs,[98] as may family and friends who meet the EN qualifications.[99] To date, more than one-third of the states have implemented TWWIIA and others have passed legislation creating similar programs.[100]

B. Applicability Of The ADA To TWWIIA's Employment Networks (ENs)

Individuals with disabilities covered by TWWIIA are considered qualified individuals with disabilities under the ADA.[101] The applicability of the ADA to ENs depends on the classification of the EN. ENs include individuals, cooperatives, and public and private rehabilitation providers.

Although Title I protects employees of an EN, the relationship between an EN and its Ticket participants is governed by Title II provisions for public entities or Title III provisions for private entities as places of public accommodation. A state agency serving as an EN is a public entity governed by Title II. A private community rehabilitation provider is a public accommodation covered under Title III.[102] Public and private ENs receiving federal grants or contracts also are subject to the antidiscrimination provisions of Section 504 of the Rehabilitation Act of 1973.[103]

A Ticket participant is a person with a disability for purposes of SSI or SSDI and likely covered under the ADA as an individual with a

---

[96] The Ticket to Work and Self-Sufficiency Program, 66 Fed. Reg. 67,370, 67,370 (Dec. 28, 2001).

[97] Id.

[98] Id. at 67,433.

[99] Id. at 67,397.

[100] Donna Folkemer et al., Medicaid Buy-In Programs: Case Studies of Early Implementer States, at http://aspe.hhs.gov/daltcp/reports/EIcasest.htm (U.S. Dep't Health & Hum. Servs., May 2002).

[101] 42 U.S.C. § 12131(2) (2000).

[102] Id. § 12181(7)(k).

[103] Nondiscrimination on the Basis of Disability by Public Accommodations and in Commercial Facilities, 56 Fed. Reg. 35544, 35552 (July 26, 1991).

disability.[104] Title II requires that ENs not exclude a qualified individual with disabilities from their services and programs.[105] As such, these ENs must be physically and programmatically accessible.[106]

State or local government ENs, covered under Title II, must ensure that their programs, when viewed in their entirety, are accessible.[107] Title III requires that privately-run ENs provide access to all persons with disabilities, not just those who are "qualified" for a particular program or service.[108] An individual, family member, or friend of a Ticket participant who owns, leases, or operates a place of public accommodation as an EN is subject to Title III. Privately-run ENs must remove barriers in existing buildings or provide services through alternative methods when "readily achievable."[109]

As ADA Title II or III entities, ENs must ensure effective communication with and physical and programmatic access to facilities and services for Ticket applicants, participants, their families, and the public.[110] ENs may not adopt program eligibility criteria that screen out people with certain disabilities (or individuals who have an association with people with disabilities) from programs or services, unless such criteria are necessary to program operation.[111] Public and private ENs must reasonably modify their policies, practices, and procedures when necessary to allow people with disabilities to participate, unless doing so would fundamentally alter the program.[112]

A program participant may assign her Ticket to a public or private EN willing and able to provide services.[113] The program encourages a range of service choices in which the participant and the EN choose their

---

[104] 42 U.S.C. § 12102(2). Being "disabled" under SSA regulations does not necessarily mean an individual is disabled under the ADA. Cleveland v. Pol'y Mgmt. Sys. Corp. 526 U.S. 795, 807 (1999).

[105] 42 U.S.C. § 12132.

[106] 20 C.F.R. § 411.315(a)(2) (2003).

[107] 28 C.F.R. §§ 35.149-150 (2002).

[108] 42 U.S.C. § 12182(a) (stating that "*No* individual shall be discriminated against on the basis of disability.") (emphasis added); see also Wendy E. Parmet, Title III – Public Accommodations, in Implementing the Americans with Disabilities Act 123 (Lawrence Gostin & Henry Beyer, eds., 1993).

[109] 42 U.S.C. § 12181(9); 28 C.F.R. § 36.304 (2003).

[110] Id. § 12182(b)(2)(A)(iv); Peter Blanck & Leonard A. Sandler, ADA Title III and the Internet: Technology and Civil Rights, 24 Mental & Physical Disability L. Rep. 855, 855-59 (2000).

[111] 42 U.S.C. § 12182(b)(2)(A)(i).

[112] 28 C.F.R. §§ 35.130(b)(7), 36.202.

[113] 20 C.F.R. § 411.140 (2003).

working partners.[114] Likewise, a participant is able to choose her EN and deposit the Ticket to receive services from that EN or the state VR agency, and may choose to re-assign the Ticket to another EN.[115]

Program and service choice is a central theme in the new disability policy framework:

> The Ticket to Work program provides for a voluntary relationship between the beneficiary and the EN. While an EN may not discriminate in the provision of services based on a beneficiary's age, gender, race, color, creed, or national origin, *an EN may select the beneficiaries to whom it will offer services based on factors such as its assessment of the needs of the beneficiary and its ability to help the individual.*[116]

There are sound reasons why ENs may specialize in service to particular groups of individuals.[117] Specialization can provide for greater efficiency and effectiveness in the delivery of services.

Where an EN is not qualified to serve a particular individual, the ADA's undue burden provision does not require the EN to serve that Ticket holder. When accommodation is possible and reasonable, public or private ENs may not charge an individual to cover their costs.[118]

However, questions remain about TWWIIA implementation. What is an EN's responsibility under the ADA to serve individuals with multiple disabilities? In the case of a Ticket participant who is deaf and blind, does an EN specializing in serving deaf Ticket holders violate the ADA's nondiscrimination provisions by not providing materials in Braille, effectively excluding the blind and deaf individual from services?

Addressing such issues under the ADA, an EN's core obligation to Ticket holders is nondiscrimination in the provision of program access and services. An EN's decision not to provide service to a Ticket holder with multiple or secondary disabilities must be substantiated by evidence that such secondary disabilities require a service modification that would either fundamentally alter the program or pose an undue burden. Regardless, an EN must ensure physical access to potential program

---

[114] Id. §§ 411.145, 411.150.

[115] 20 C.F.R. § 411.150 (placing limitations on Ticket reassignment).

[116] The Ticket to Work and Self-Sufficiency Program, 66 Fed. Reg. 67,370, 67,400 (Dec. 28, 2001) (emphasis added).

[117] Id. at 67,399.

[118] 28 C.F.R. §§ 36.301(c), 35.130(f) (2003).

participants and their families, for instance, by using alternative means of meeting with clients or their representatives.[119]

Another prominent question related to Ticket implementation is whether the ADA prevents ENs from choosing to provide services only to the pool of least disabled and "creamed" participants. Disability advocates' concerns about program implementation reflect the emergence of two separate and perhaps unequal markets for EN services, one served by private specialized ENs and another by state VR providers.[120]

The economic incentives in the Ticket Program encourage ENs to serve participants who need the fewest and least costly services (e.g. workplace accommodations and job training), and those who are able to return to work for an extended period of time.[121] Subsequently, disability advocates are concerned that state VR agencies will bear a greater burden of serving individuals with more involved disabilities and costly service needs.[122]

By the year 2002, approximately 85 to 95 percent of program participants had assigned their tickets to state VR agencies.[123] The trends suggest that most program participants either have not used their Tickets or have remained in the state VR system instead of assigning their ticket to an EN of their choice.[124] Education that explains the Ticket Program is vital for beneficiaries and service providers as well as for other stakeholders on the local, state, and federal levels.[125] Moreover, Ticket participants must be knowledgeable about their rights and responsibilities under the program.

Information on the Ticket Program is crucial to assess questions such as: Who is being served and rejected? What is the nature of program

---

[119] Ticket to Work and Work Incentives Advisory Panel, Testimony 35-37 (May 3, 2002) (statement of Peter Blanck, Dir. of the Law, Health Pol'y, & Disability Ctr., Univ. of Iowa College of Law) (transcript on file with authors).

[120] Id. at 26 (statement of Andrew Imparato, President and CEO, Am. Ass'n of People with Disabilities).

[121] Id. at 38.

[122] Id. at 20-21 (statement of Ray Cebula, Senior Staff Attorney, Disability Law Ctr.).

[123] Id. at 72 (statement of Sallie Rhodes, Dir. of External Relations, Council of St. Administrators of Vocational Rehab.); id. at 227 (statement of Ken McGill, Dir. of the Office of Employment Support Programs, Soc. Security Admin.).

[124] Ticket to Work and Work Incentives Advisory Panel, Soc. Security Admin., Annual Report to the President and Congress: Year Two (SSA Pub. No. 63-011) 17 (Aug. 2002).

[125] Id. at 11.

access and accommodation for beneficiaries with multiple disabilities (and their families or representatives)? Will the ADA's antidiscrimination provisions and TWWIIA's reform of work incentives affect employers' and co-workers' attitudes about Ticket holders as job applicants and workers with disabilities? And, will the ADA and TWWIIA impact the attitudes of disabled individuals themselves with regard to their employment goals?

Chapter 28 DISABILITY AND WELFARE POLICY

§ 28.1 Temporary Assistance For Needy Families (TANF) Programs

A. *Overview*

In 1996, the Personal Responsibility and Work Opportunity Reconciliation Act (PRWOR) created the Temporary Assistance for Needy Families (TANF) program. TANF replaced the Aid to Families with Dependent Children program as a shift away from long-term welfare services and toward the requirement of employment for welfare recipients.[1]

Among other goals, the TANF program strives to promote job preparation and employment to help reduce dependency on government welfare.[2] TANF's work requirements aim to encourage eligible recipients to seek employment and self-sufficiency. Recipients must begin working when the state determines they are ready for employment, or after twenty-four cumulative months of assistance.[3] Families receiving TANF benefits must participate in work activities for at least twenty hours per week, with two-parent families required to work at least thirty-five hours per week. A state has the option to exempt single parents with a child under one year of age from these requirements.[4]

With a focus on reducing the number of welfare recipients, monetary benefits end after a total of sixty months, regardless of whether an individual has found gainful employment.[5] TANF agencies may reduce or terminate benefits if a recipient refuses to work.[6] There are exceptions to the work term limit for personal hardship and situations involving family violence.[7]

TANF places requirements on the state administering agencies. The agency is responsible for developing an individual responsibility plan (IRP) for participants by assessing job skills, prior work experience, and prospects for employability.[8] The IRP is intended to help the individual

---

[1] Lindsay Mara Schoen, Note, Working Welfare Recipients: A Comparison of the Family Support Act and the Personal Responsibility and Work Opportunity Reconciliation Act, 24 Fordham Urb. L.J. 635, 635 (1997).

[2] 45 C.F.R. § 260.20(b) (2001).

[3] Schoen, supra note 1, at 646.

[4] Id. at 647-48.

[5] Id. at 648-49 (citations omitted).

[6] 42 U.S.C. § 607(e)(1) (2000).

[7] Schoen, supra note 1, at 648-49 (citations omitted).

[8] Id.

achieve employment and to increase job responsibility over time.[9] States are subject to declines in federal assistance if they do not satisfy minimum participation rates,[10] comply with work term time limits,[11] or sanction recipients who refuse to work.[12]

In 2001, TANF services were provided to more than two million families comprising some five million individuals. Over four million of the recipients were children.[13] Families typically end TANF services when they locate employment.[14] However, many families that have left the TANF program continue to rely on governmental programs such as Medicaid, Food Stamps, and the Earned Income Tax Credit.[15]

The TANF program is not directed specifically towards individuals with disabilities. Yet, a substantially higher proportion of TANF recipients reported having physical or mental impairments than did adults in the non-TANF population.[16] Many TANF families include a child with a disability[17] or a member with an undiagnosed disability.[18] Psychiatric disabilities and learning disabilities also are prevalent in the TANF population.[19]

---

[9] 42 U.S.C. § 608(b)(2)(A)(3) (emphasis added).

[10] 45 C.F.R. § 262.1(a)(4).

[11] Id. § 262.1(a)(9).

[12] Id. § 262.1(a)(14).

[13] Office of Family Assistance, U.S. Dep't of Health and Hum. Servs., Temporary Assistance for Needy Families Program: Fifth Annual Report to Congress X184-230, http://www.acf.dhhs.gov/programs/ofa/annual report5/ (Feb. 3, 2003).

[14] Id. at X84.

[15] Welfare Reform: Hearing Before the Subcomm. on Hum. Res., Comm. of Ways and Means, 107th Cong. (2001) (statement of Christine Devere, Analyst in Soc. Legislation, Library of Cong.), http://waysandmeans. house.gov/legacy/humres/107cong/3-15-01/107-5final.htm (last visited July 30, 2003).

[16] Nat'l Council on Disability, TANF and Disability – Importance of Supports for Families with Disabilities in Welfare Reform, http://www.ncd.gov/newsroom/publications/familysupports.html (Mar. 14, 2003) [hereinafter TANF Disability Position Paper].

[17] Id.

[18] Cary LaCheen, Using Title II of the Americans with Disabilities Act on Behalf of Clients in TANF Programs, 8 Geo. J. Poverty L. & Pol'y 1, 88 (2001) (citations omitted).

[19] Id.

B.   *Applicability Of The ADA To TANF*

Programs and activities supported by TANF funds are subject to federal antidiscrimination laws such as the ADA, the Age Discrimination in Employment Act, Section 504 of the Rehabilitation Act of 1973, and Title VI of the Civil Rights Act of 1964.[20] However, an individual with a physical or mental limitation receiving TANF benefits does not qualify automatically as an "individual with a disability" under the ADA.[21]

Many TANF recipients have undiagnosed disabilities, and their histories of disability do not establish a record of a substantially limiting impairment.[22] As TANF agencies develop and maintain recipient profiles and track their progress, information about participants' records of disabilities may develop.[23]

Subject to restrictions, state TANF programs may establish exceptions to the mandatory work requirements.[24] To date, state programs have not ordinarily applied the ADA's definition of disability when defining exceptions.[25] For instance, California's TANF program (CalWORKS) exempts from work requirements individuals with a doctor's verification that the disability likely will last at least thirty days, and that it significantly impairs the ability to be employed or participate in welfare-to-work activities.[26] New York's program exempts individuals who are "disabled or incapacitated" based on a determination by the welfare agency or a private doctor referred by the agency.[27] New York also exempts those who are ill or injured when unable to engage in work for up to three months.[28]

Professor LaCheen suggests several issues related to the applicability of ADA law to state TANF programs. For instance, if a claim of discrimination arises from lack of access to the application process, individuals with disabilities who are covered by the ADA need not qualify for TANF benefits to raise such a challenge.[29] However, where a job-

---

[20] 45 C.F.R. § 260.35 (2001).

[21] LaCheen, supra note 18, at 89-90.

[22] Id. at 89.

[23] Id.

[24] Id. at 90.

[25] Terri S. Thompson et al., The Urb. Inst. and the U.S Dep't of Health & Hum. Servs., State Welfare-to-Work Policies for People with Disabilities: Changes Since Welfare Reform; Executive Summary), at http://aspe.hhs.gov/daltcp/reports/wel2wkes.htm (Oct. 1998).

[26] Cal. Welf. & Inst. Code § 11320.3(b)(3)(A) (2003).

[27] N.Y. Comp. Codes R. & Regs. tit.12 § 1300.2(b)(4) (2002).

[28] Id. § 1300.2(b)(1).

[29] LaCheen, supra note 18, at 94.

training program requires participants to have a certain diploma to participate, and the applicant with a disability does not have such a diploma, the ineligibility requirement for program participation may properly preclude an ADA challenge.[30] Lastly, some states may argue that individuals who have not been compliant with TANF work requirements are not qualified individuals for purposes of an ADA challenge.[31]

One unresolved issue is whether TANF program work requirements will have an unfair impact on persons with disabilities.[32] To date, no study has assessed whether TANF recipients with disabilities face more significant barriers to employment than nondisabled recipients.[33] To strengthen protections for persons with disabilities in TANF programs, one advocacy group has recommended that states give assurances that participants with disabilities are screened with appropriate diagnostic tools, and that work activities include rehabilitation activities (e.g., as supported by TWWIIA) to help the individual attain work.

In addition, states might train their staffs who serve TANF recipients on issues related to disabilities to, for instance, aid in access to Medicaid or other health coverage when recipients move from welfare to work. In the end, compliance may require regular reviews to ensure that TANF programs comply with the ADA and Section 504 requirements.[34]

---

[30] Id. at 95.

[31] Id.

[32] Id. at 109.

[33] TANF Disability Position Paper, supra note 16.

[34] Id.

Chapter 29 DISABILITY AND HEALTH CARE POLICY

§ 29.1 The ADA And Genetic Discrimination

A. *Overview*

The Human Genome Project (HGP) is a federally funded research effort that seeks to map and sequence every human gene.[1] This chapter describes the dialogue on the interplay between the HGP and the employment provisions of ADA Title I.

The HGP has engendered a revolution in the diagnosis of human genetic conditions. Scores of new genetic tests have been identified with the potential for discovering the causes of inheritable diseases.[2] The rapid advances in genetic testing, therapy, and technology, however, have increased the possibility of stigmatization and discrimination against qualified individuals with current and possible future genetic disorders in the employment context and in other areas of daily life. [3]

At present, no federal statutes are specifically designed to protect against genetic discrimination in employment-related settings,[4] though legislation has been proposed.[5] Researchers, courts, and policy makers

---

[1]   Peter Blanck & Mollie W. Marti, Genetic Discrimination and the Americans with Disabilities Act: Legal, Health and Policy Implications, 14 Behav. Sci. & L. 411, 411-32 (1996).

[2]   Wendy McGoodwin, Genie Out of the Bottle; Genetic Testing and the Discrimination It's Creating, Wash. Post, May 5, 1996, at C03, 1996 WL 3077898.

[3]   Peter Blanck, Reflections on the Law and Ethics of the Human Genome Project, in Genes and Human Self-Knowledge 185 (Robert F. Weir eds., 1994).

[4]   Anita Silvers & Michael Ashley Stein, An Equality Paradigm for Preventing Genetic Discrimination, 55 Vand. L. Rev. 1341, 1376-79 (2003) (noting pending federal legislation in the Genetic Nondiscrimination in Health Insurance and Employment Act, H.R. 602, 107th Cong. (2001)).

[5]   Genetic Information Nondiscrimination Act, S. 1053, 108th Cong. (2003). On October 14, 2003, the Senate passed a version of the Genetic Information Nondiscrimination Act in a 95 to 0 vote. The Senate bill would:

> [b]an[ ] the use and disclosure of genetic information for health insurance coverage decisions. ... [p]rohibit[ ] health insurers from collecting genetic information before enrollment in any plan. ... "[p]rohibit[ ] the use of genetic information in employment decisions, such as hiring, firing, job assignments and promotions. ... [p]revent[ ] employers from acquiring or disclosing genetic information. ... [e]stablish[ ] a single federal standard to

are beginning to explore how the ADA and its judicial and legislative progeny safeguard against genetic discrimination in the employment relationship in particular, and in the provision of insurance and health care benefits in general.[6]

At the same time, insurance companies, private employers, governments, and educational institutions each have a legitimate interest in promoting genetic screening to help identify and appropriately treat individuals with genetic disorders.[7] Identifying health risks or heightened susceptibility to injury from workplace exposures due to an individual's genetic composition is an application central to the advancing knowledge of the HGP.[8]

In situations where employers, insurers or others use medically-related information from genetic testing to deny equal employment opportunities, exclude qualified individuals from work or work-related benefits, or limit health care coverage to qualified individuals, the antidiscrimination provisions of ADA Title I are implicated. Adverse employment-related decisions are harmful when they are premature, rendered on the basis of false assumptions or attitudes, and not based on current research regarding the nature and predictability of genetic tests.

B.   *Asymptomatic Genetic Traits Under The ADA*

ADA Title I prohibits covered entities from discriminating against a qualified person with a disability in employment.[9] As discussed in Part 2 of this treatise, a person with a disability covered by the law has a physical or mental condition that substantially limits major life activities, has a record of, or is regarded as having such a physical or mental

---

protect genetic information, replacing existing state laws. ... and [p]rovide[ ] that the Office of Civil Rights in the Department of Health and Human Services will enforce privacy provisions of the law. Civil and criminal penalties may be applied when violations are established.

John A. MacDonald, Genetic Testing Safeguards Pass Senate, Head to House, Hartford Courant, Oct. 15, 2003, at A7.

[6]   See Larry Gostin, Genetic Discrimination: The Use of Genetically Based Diagnostic and Prognostic Tests by Employers and Insurers, 17 Am. J.L. & Med. 109, 120-42 (1991); see also Marvin R. Natowicz et al., Genetic Discrimination and the Law, 50 Am. J. Hum. Genetics 465, 471 (1992).

[7]   Paul R. Billings et al., Discrimination as a Consequence of Genetic Testing, 50 Am. J. Hum. Genetics 476, 480-81 (1992).

[8]   Marne E. Brom, Note, Insurers and Genetic Testing: Shopping for the Perfect Pair of Genes, 40 Drake L. Rev. 121, 138 (1991).

[9]   42 U.S.C. § 12112(a) (2000).

condition.[10] What is less certain, however, is under what circumstances the ADA restricts discrimination when a genetic condition is asymptomatic.[11]

In Part 3 of this treatise, we have described how Title I limits disability-related pre-employment inquiries and medical examinations, except those examinations conducted after a conditional job offer has been made.[12] If the medical examination reveals that the applicant has the gene for Huntington's disease, for example, does Title I protect the applicant when the employer withdraws the offer because of his asymptomatic genetic trait?[13]

Although the reasoning underlying *Bragdon v. Abbott*[14] may support the application of the ADA to individuals with asymptomatic genetic disorders and genetic predispositions,[15] this decision also may limit the ADA's reach.[16] The Court relied on two findings in holding that HIV is a disability under the ADA even when the infection has not yet progressed to the symptomatic phase.

First, HIV infection is a physiological disorder *from the moment of the infection*, thereby satisfying the definition of a physical impairment during every stage of the disease.[17] Second, HIV infection places a substantial limitation on a woman's major life activity of reproduction.[18] Some commentators suggest that the extension of *Bragdon* to asymptomatic genetic conditions is limited to similar circumstances.[19] Whether an asymptomatic genetic condition constitutes a substantial limitation of a major life activity depends largely on the ability of medical

---

[10] Id. § 12102(2). ADA Title I also prohibits discrimination on the basis of an association with a person with a disability. Id. § 12112(b)(4).

[11] Marisa Anne Pagnattaro, Genetic Discrimination and the Workplace: Employee's Right to Privacy v. Employer's Need to Know, 39 Am. Bus. L. J. 139, 160 (2001).

[12] 42 U.S.C. § 12112(d)(3).

[13] Pagnattaro, supra note 11, at 160-61.

[14] Bragdon v. Abbott, 524 U.S. 624 (1998).

[15] Paul Steven Miller, Is there a Pink Slip in My Genes? Genetic Discrimination in the Workplace, 3 J. Health Care L. & Pol'y 225, 242 (2000).

[16] Pagnattaro, supra note 11, at 164.

[17] Bragdon, 524 U.S. at 628 (emphasis added).

[18] Id. at 639-40.

[19] Pagnattaro, supra note 11, at 164-65.

science to accurately identify the genetic defect and predict with some certainty its effects.[20]

Under *Bragdon*, to be covered as an actual disability, the defect must have some current physiological effect and that effect must limit a major life activity. The *Bragdon* Court did not rely on the possible future effects of HIV in rendering its decision.

The EEOC has issued guidance extending protections to qualified federal employees who experience employment discrimination on the basis of their genetic profiles.[21] The EEOC guidance refers to a hypothetical scenario about a qualified job applicant whose genetic profile reveals an increased susceptibility to colon cancer, but where no actual link to the development of the disease is present.[22] After making the qualified applicant a conditional offer of employment, the employer learns from genetic testing about the applicant's increased susceptibility. The employer withdraws the job offer because of generalized concerns about the applicant's future productivity, insurance costs, and absences from work. The EEOC suggests that the applicant would be covered by the third prong of the definition of "disability," because the employer is regarding and treating the asymptomatic applicant as having an impairment that substantially limits the major life activity of work.

If an employer can demonstrate that hiring or accommodating the applicant's disability would create an undue hardship, discriminatory action is not prohibited.[23] In addition, persons with genetic disabilities may be determined to be unqualified for a job if they pose a direct safety or health threat to themselves or others in the workplace.[24] But patronizing assumptions, generalized fears, and speculative risks of incurring a genetic condition or disease are not sufficient to constitute a

---

[20] Deborah Gridley, Genetic Testing under the ADA: A Case for Protection from Employment Discrimination, 89 Geo. L. J. 973, 988-89 (2001).

[21] EEOC Policy Guidance on Executive Order 13145: To Prohibit Discrimination in Federal Employment Based on Genetic Information, http://www.eeoc.gov/docs/guidance-genetic.html (July 26, 2000) [hereinafter EEOC Policy Guidance]; see also Silvers & Stein, supra note 4, at 1349, 1360 (discussing EEOC approach).

[22] EEOC Policy Guidance, supra note 21.

[23] Gridley, supra note 20, at 993-94.

[24] Chevron U.S.A. Inc. v. Echazabal, 536 U.S. 73, 76-85 (2002) (finding that an EEOC determination, permitting an employer to refuse hiring an individual whose own health would be endangered in the performance of the job, did not exceed EEOC authority under ADA). See supra treatise Part 3.

"direct threat" defense to a Title I claim.[25] Those lawfully excluded from employment because of a direct threat of harm often involve individuals with potential sudden onset conditions, not those who may become disabled at some point in the future.[26]

As a result of the Supreme Court's analysis in *Chevron v. Echazabal*,[27] it is not clear for purposes of ADA analysis whether an employer may refuse to hire a qualified individual, even though asymptomatic, if occupational exposure to certain substances is likely to increase the employee's known genetic susceptibility to disease, even with the provision of reasonable accommodations.[28] However, few instances of genetic conditions that require differential treatment in the workplace have been documented or studied systematically.[29]

The EEOC specifies that blood tests to detect genetic markers or diseases are medical examinations for purposes of the ADA.[30] It further specifies that discrimination by covered entities may include actions

---

[25] See 29 C.F.R. § 1630.2(r) (2003) ("The determination that an individual poses a 'direct threat' [is] based on an individualized assessment of the individual's present ability to safely perform the essential functions of the job. This assessment [is] based on a reasonable medical judgment that relies on the most current medical knowledge and/or on the best available objective evidence."); Pope L. Moseley et al., Hospital Privileges and the Americans with Disabilities Act, 21 Spine 2288, 2291 (1996).

[26] Mark A. Rothstein, Genetic Discrimination in Employment and the Americans with Disabilities Act, 29 Hous. L. Rev. 23, 73 (1992).

[27] Chevron U.S.A. v. Echazabal, 536 U.S. 73 (2002). See detailed discussion supra treatise Part 3.

[28] See Muller v. Costello, 1996 WL 191977, at *5, *8 (N.D.N.Y. Apr. 16, 1996) (holding that corrections officer with asthma, triggered by exposure to secondhand smoke on the job, may proceed with his claims alleging ADA violations); see also Occupational Safety and Health Admin., U.S. Dep't of Labor, Guidelines for Preventing Workplace Violence for Health Care and Social Service Workers OSHA 3148-2003 (Revised) 5 http://www.osha.gov/Publications/osha3148.pdf (2003) (stating management commitment should include organizational concern for employee emotional and physical safety and health).

[29] Natowicz et al., supra note 6, at 467.

[30] See EEOC Enforcement Guidance: Disability-Related Inquiries and Medical Examinations of Employees Under the Americans with Disabilities Act (ADA), http://www.eeoc.gov/docs/guidance-inquiries.html (July 27, 2000).

against qualified individuals on the basis of actual or perceived genetic conditions or impairments.[31]

Employees may be subjected legitimately to urine and blood tests to screen for alcohol or substance use.[32] However, in one case settled with the EEOC, the Burlington Northern and Santa Fe Railway Company (BNSF) required that certain employees who had filed claims of work-related carpal tunnel syndrome injuries against the company submit blood samples for genetic screening.[33] BNSF required the genetic tests without the employees' knowledge or consent. As a result of a mediated settlement, BNSF agreed to pay $2.2 million to thirty-six employees who were ordered to submit to the testing.[34]

In addition to direct testing, employers often obtain the results of genetic testing conducted in other contexts and may potentially use that information to restrict the employment opportunities of qualified applicants and employees.[35] Federal legislation affecting confidentiality issues arising from the use of genetic information in the workplace has been proposed.[36] Twenty-eight states have enacted laws that limit the ability of employers to collect, use, and disclose genetic information.[37] For example, Colorado, Florida and Georgia have given individuals property

---

[31] Id. See also Miller, supra note 15, at 238-39 (stating that the ADA protects the individual with a manifested genetically-related illness that substantially limits a major life activity, and the individual with "a prior record of a genetically-related disability").

[32] See Patricia A. Montgomery, Workplace Drug Testing: Are There Limits?, 32(2) Tenn. Bar J. 20, 21 (1996) (discussing employers that use random employee drug testing and Tennessee law which denies employment compensation to employees that leave their jobs to avoid testing).

[33] Press Release, Equal Employment Opportunity Comm'n, EEOC and BNSF Settle Genetic Testing Case Under Americans with Disabilities Act, http://www.eeoc.gov/press/5-8-02.html (May 8, 2002).

[34] Cf. E.E.O.C. v. Woodbridge Corp, 263 F.3d 812 (8th Cir. 2001) (holding that company did not violate the ADA when excluding applicants from employment on a manufacturing line, based on test results that indicate they may be susceptible to injuries from repetitive motion; plaintiffs held not to be covered as persons with disabilities under the ADA).

[35] Rothstein, supra note 26, at 62-68. This information may be obtained through releases by employees, health insurance claims, or voluntary medical examinations and wellness programs. Id.

[36] See Genetic Information Nondiscrimination Act, supra note 1. See also George P. Smith II, Accessing Genetic Information or Safeguarding Genetic Privacy, 9 J.L. & Health 121, 130 (1994-1995).

[37] Sonia M. Suter, The Allure and Peril of Genetics Exceptionalism: Do We Need Special Genetics Legislation?, 79 Wash. U. L.Q. 669, 692 (2001).

rights over their DNA.[38] In addition, individuals may find privacy protection in the state common-law duty of confidentiality, which limits physicians' disclosure of their patients' medical records to employers.[39]

No courts have addressed the issue of whether genetic predisposition to disease is an actual or "regarded as" disability under the ADA. However, according to the EEOC, employment discrimination under § 501 of the Rehabilitation Act may include unequal treatment on the basis of a genetic condition or disability in any terms, conditions and privileges of employment.[40] An employer receiving federal funds cannot use actual or perceived medical histories as a pretext for refusing to hire, firing, or taking other adverse action against a qualified applicant or employee.[41]

Although an employer cannot use the results of genetic screening conducted as part of a post-offer medical examination to withdraw an offer of employment to a qualified applicant, the results may be used to modify health care coverage provided through the employer's self-funded benefits plan.

The ADA does not prohibit insurance companies from underwriting and classifying medical health risks, if the classifications are consistent with state law practices.[42] Third party insurers or employers self-funding their insurance plans may classify employees with regard to health insurance coverage on the basis of their medical and health histories.[43] Limitations on health insurance coverage or exclusions of certain genetic conditions from coverage are permitted under the ADA when not a "subterfuge" for disability-based discrimination.[44] For example, a self-funded employer may offer a health insurance policy to all employees that does not cover experimental treatment for Huntington's disease. However, under the ADA, a self-insured employer with an employee whose child develops cystic fibrosis may not withdraw dependent coverage for that particular employee on the basis of that disability.

---

[38] See Fla. Stat. Ann. § 760.40 (2)(a) (2003); Colo. Rev. Stat. Ann. § 10-3-1104.7(1)(a) (2002); Ga. Code Ann. § 33-54-1(1) (2002).

[39] Lawrence O. Gostin, Health Information Privacy, 80 Cornell L. Rev. 451, 508 (1995).

[40] EEOC Policy Guidance, supra note 21.

[41] Id.

[42] 29 C.F.R. § 1630.16(f) (2003).

[43] Because the ADA's legislative history only addresses health insurance, it is uncertain whether employees may be denied life and disability insurance provided by employers. S. Rep. No. 101-116 at 29 (1989); Natowicz et al., supra note 6, at 471.

[44] Id.

States have enacted legislative protections against health insurance denial based solely on genetic status.[45] State laws, however, often do not provide protection for those who obtain their health insurance coverage through employer-based plans, because the Federal Employee Retirement Income Security Act (ERISA) exempts self-funded plans from state oversight.[46]

C.   *Future Issues*

The possibility of discrimination in employment, insurance, or other areas may have a chilling effect on the use of genetic testing. Individuals may avoid genetic testing because of fear of discrimination. This avoidance may lead individuals with genetic predispositions to miss preventive opportunities and, thus, increase the likelihood that they will actually contract the disease. If we fail to adequately address discrimination, the development of genetic research may, ironically, increase our susceptibility to genetic disease.

Myths and stereotypes in society contribute to the potential for genetic discrimination by employers, insurers, and the general public.[47] This is true even though genetic testing does not establish that all individuals with a genetic predisposition for a condition or disease will inevitably contract that disease.

Misconceptions about the usefulness of genetic testing may lead to increased discrimination against people with genetic impairments and their relatives. In the employment realm, genetic discrimination based on misinformation may preclude qualified people from being hired, hold people hostage to their current employment because of a reluctance to seek a new job without new health insurance, or serve as a basis for firing.

As discussed above in the employment context, in the insurance arena, discrimination may result in the denial of coverage, inequitable premiums, or unwarranted exclusions for particular genetic conditions. Given the advances in the development of genetic tests, the economic incentives for insurance companies and employers to use them, and the presence of certain abnormal genes in all individuals, increasing numbers

---

[45]   See Silvers & Stein, supra note 4, at 1343-44 (noting about half of the jurisdictions prohibit workplace discrimination on the grounds of genetic information, and a handful of jurisdictions have established individuals' property rights to their personal DNA information).

[46]   29 U.S.C. § 1144(a) (2000).

[47]   Paul Steven Miller, Genetic Alliance, Genetic Discrimination in the Workplace, at http://www.geneticalliance.org/geneticissues/eeoc.html (Mar. 12, 2001).

of qualified individuals may be in jeopardy of encountering genetic discrimination.[48]

Genetic discrimination involving health and life insurance may include discrimination against asymptomatic individuals or their relatives once a genetic diagnosis has been established, or the failure of group insurance plans to provide equitable coverage for qualified individuals with a genetic diagnosis or their relatives.[49] Research suggests that people who are currently healthy and asymptomatic are being denied health insurance and employment opportunities based solely on predictions that they may become "unhealthy" in the future.[50] Many healthy, asymptomatic individuals are treated as if they were presently disabled or chronically ill.

There are flaws in equating the presence of a particular genotype with the existence of a severe illness and the lack of effective treatment. First, many genetic conditions are variable in expressivity; that is, not all individuals with the genotype develop clinical manifestations of the disease.[51] With the growth in therapies for genetic conditions, it is likely that additional therapies may be available by the time an asymptomatic person actually contracts a predicted genetic disease.

Second, when decisions regarding insurance and employment are based solely on a diagnostic label, the severity or range of the individual's condition is disregarded. The course and severity of many diseases vary among individuals, and the presence of a gene cannot foretell how disabling a genetic condition or disease may be to a specific person.[52] Nevertheless, the worst possible scenario often is used as the standard for policy decisions regarding persons with genetic conditions or impairments.[53]

Third, few genetic conditions are caused by a single gene.[54] Many common health conditions, such as coronary disease and cancer, have been shown to have many causes. Focusing on the role of genetics also

---

[48] Joseph S. Alper et al., Genetic Discrimination and Screening for Hemochromatosis, 15 J.Pub. Health Pol'y 345, 354 (1994); Lisa N. Geller et al., Individual, Family, and Societal Dimensions of Genetic Discrimination: A Case Study Analysis, 2 Sci. & Engineering 71, 72 (1996); see also Tom Harkin, The Americans with Disabilities Act: Four years later – Commentary on Blanck, 79 Iowa L. Rev. 935, 936 (1994).

[49] Geller et al, supra note 48, at 75.

[50] Billings et al., supra note 7, at 481; Geller, et al., supra note 48, at 82.

[51] Alper et al., supra note 48, at 353.

[52] Billings et al., supra note 7, at 479-80.

[53] Id.

[54] Abigail Trafford, Ethics and Genetics, Wash. Post, April 16, 1996, at Z06, 1996 WL 3074614.

minimizes the attention given to other social conditions, such as poverty, or environmental conditions, such as pollution, that have been shown to be related to poor health and higher mortality rates.[55] An attitudinal bias or overemphasis on genetic conditions may divert researchers and resources from addressing the underlying economic and social mediating factors.[56]

Fourth, errors in testing and interpretation occur.[57] Because of a high rate of false positive test results, the medical records of individuals who do not have a particular genetic condition sometimes suggest treatment for the disease.[58] False positive tests can have a dramatic impact on an individual's life.[59] Psychometric studies from statisticians, actuaries, psychologists, and others are needed on the predictive validity of each genetic test.

In addition, the chance of developing a genetic condition or disease is perceived differently than a similar probability of contracting an illness not produced primarily by genetic factors.[60] People commonly commit base-rate judgment errors when attempting to predict the outcome of events on the basis of fallible data.[61] The phenomenon of base-rate error has been demonstrated empirically in studies about the prediction of disease onset.[62]

In a study of state insurance commissioners, findings showed that respondents ignored base rate information about the prevalence and onset of genetic conditions.[63] Regardless of actual risk, the commissioners treated applicants who were at genetic risk for developing breast cancer or coronary artery disease less harshly than those with other genetic

---

[55] McGoodwin, supra note 2.

[56] Id.; see infra text accompanying notes 60-62 (discussing base-rate fallacy).

[57] Alper et al., supra note 48, at 352-53.

[58] Id. at 353.

[59] Montgomery, supra note 32, at 24. The National Breast Cancer Coalition "opposes open marketing of a test for the so-called breast cancer gene, BRCA1. . . . [T]he test's generally ambiguous results may trigger unnecessary panic in many women." Rick Weiss, Tests' Availability Tangles Ethical and Genetic Codes, Wash. Post, May 26, 1996, at A01, 1996 WL 3081637.

[60] Billings et al., supra note 7, at 480.

[61] Amos Tversky & Daniel Kahneman, Judgment Under Uncertainty: Heuristics and Biases, 185 Science 1124, 1124 (1974).

[62] Ward Casscells et al., Interpretation by Physicians of Clinical Laboratory Results, 299 New Eng. J. Med. 999-1000 (1978).

[63] Jean E. McEwen et al., A Survey of State Insurance Commissioners Concerning Genetic Testing and Life Insurance, 51 Am. J. Hum. Gen. 785 (1992).

conditions, such as Huntington's disease or cystic fibrosis.[64]   The respondents reported that they were as willing to permit the denial of insurance to an adult with spina bifida as to an adult with cystic fibrosis, even though a young adult with spina bifida has a significantly higher life expectancy.[65]

Another stereotype is that the onset of a genetic condition or disability indicates the end of one's productive work life. One study that examined the extent to which workers, through their own actions or their employer's accommodations, adjust to their health limitations and continue working, found that only about one-quarter of those who become impaired while employed exited the labor force on a permanent basis.[66] Over half of the individuals studied remained with their employers, and the remaining individuals continued to work for different employers.[67] Moreover, significantly more employees who remained with their employers after the onset of their impairment reported receiving accommodations from their employers, compared with those who changed employers.[68]

The use of genetic tests by employers and insurers raises additional issues concerning informed consent, privacy, and confidentiality in research, diagnosis, and therapy.[69] Issues involving confidentiality are prominent as medical records are loaded into computer databases that are accessible to a large number of individuals and companies.[70] Commentators have proposed the use of anonymous genetic counseling and testing.[71]

Congress appears poised to address at least some of these issues. The proposed Genetic Information Nondiscrimination Act (Senate Bill

---

[64]   Id. at 791. It is not in violation of the ADA for insurers and organizations administering health plans to charge higher premiums for certain conditions, to exclude certain conditions, to exclude dependents, or to limit coverage of certain conditions, as a matter of "underwriting risks, classifying risks, or administering such risks," as long as such actions do not violate state law. 42 U.S.C. § 12201(c) (2000).

[65]   McEwen, et al., supra note 63, at 791.

[66]   Mary C. Daly & John Bound, Worker Adaptation and Employer Accommodation Following the Onset of a Health Impairment, NBER Working Paper No. 5169, at 31 tbl. 1, http://www.nber.org/papers/w5169.pdf (July 1995).

[67]   Id.

[68]   Id. at 37 tbl. 5.

[69]   Cf. Trafford, supra note 54.

[70]   Natowicz, supra note 6, at 473.

[71]   Maxwell J. Mehlman et al., The Need for Anonymous Genetic Counseling and Testing, 58 Am. J. Hum. Gen. 393, 393-397 (1996).

1053) would provide protection from intentional discrimination in employment based on genetic testing.[72] Employers covered by the law would include employment agencies, labor organizations, and training programs.[73] The bill's enforcement provisions include compensatory and punitive damages.[74] The Act permits certain uses of genetic information where doing so is shown to be job-related and consistent with business necessity.[75]

---

[72] Genetic Information Nondiscrimination Act, S. 1053, 108th Cong. § 202(b) (2003). See supra note 1.

[73] Id. §§ 203(b), 204(b), 205(b).

[74] Id. § 208(a).

[75] Id. § 202(d)(1). See 42 U.S.C. § 12113(a) (2000).

Part 10

Applications Of The ADA To Technology Policy And Tax Policy

Analysis

Chapter 30 INTRODUCTION

§ 30.1 Overview

The rise of the disability civil rights movement, bolstered by passage of antidiscrimination laws described in Part 1 of this treatise, has coincided with a wave of technological advances that enhance the inclusion and equal participation in society of persons with disabilities.[1] Most emblematic of the wave of technological advances is the development and use of the Internet. Equal access to the Internet by persons with disabilities now is a prominent topic of discussion in disability law and policy.

The drafters of the ADA could not contemplate the significance of the Internet and the World Wide Web (WWW).[2] Nonetheless, as we discuss, issues of Internet accessibility for persons with disabilities are implicated by the public accommodations language of Title III and by state and the local governmental activities covered by Title II. In addition, public entities are subject to Sections 504 and 508 of the Rehabilitation Act of 1973.[3] Section 508, for example, requires government agencies to purchase accessible technology.

Parallel to the Internet, since passage of the ADA, computers and assistive technologies have come to play a central role in the lives of workers with disabilities covered by Title I.[4] The importance of technology in the workplace has broad implications for the employment of people with disabilities.[5] Thus, computer technologies compensate for the physical limitations inherent in some disabilities – those without finger dexterity use voice-recognition software to run a computer, and those with speech impairments use special software to "speak" through the computer.[6]

Computer skills provide occupational options where disability is of little or no relevance. For instance, most wheelchair users operate computers in the same way as those who do not use wheelchairs, yet a lack of computer skills can drastically restrict occupational options for

---

[1] David Klein et al., Electronic Doors to Education: Study of High School Website Accessibility in Iowa, 21 Behav. Sci. & L. 27, 42 (2003).

[2] Id. at 29.

[3] 29 U.S.C. §§ 794, 794d (2000).

[4] Peter Blanck et al., Calibrating the Impact of the ADA's Employment Provisions, 14 Stan. L. & Pol'y Rev. 267, 284 (2003).

[5] See generally Heather Ritchie & Peter Blanck, The Promise of the Internet for Disability: A Study of On-line Services and Web Site Accessibility at Centers for Independent Living, 21 Behav. Sci. & L. 5 (2003); Kevin Schartz et al., Employment of Persons with Disabilities in Information Technology Jobs: Literature Review for "IT Works," 20 Behav. Sci. & L. 637 (2002).

[6] Nonetheless, in *Thornton v. McClatchy Newspapers, Inc.*, 292 F.3d 1045, 1046 (9th Cir. 2002), the Ninth Circuit rejected a newspaper employee's ADA claim that her inability to use a computer and engage in continuous keyboarding constituted a substantial limitation on a major life activity, distinguishing substantial limitation from "diminished" ability.

people with disabilities. Professors Krueger and Kruse find that among people with spinal cord injuries (SCIs), those using computers prior to their SCI had more rapid returns to work.[7] Furthermore, nonusers of computers with SCI faced severe earnings penalties when attempting to return to work after injury.[8]

Despite the positive effects of computer use and the Internet on the employment and earnings of people with disabilities, research shows that people with disabilities generally are less likely to be computer users. A 2002 study by the National Telecommunications and Information Administration indicated that 74.9% and 61.7% of persons with severe vision impairments use computers and the Internet, respectively, compared to 83.4% and 75.1% of persons without disabilities.[9] Additionally, among full-time workers, almost half of those without disabilities use computers at work, compared to one-third of those with disabilities.[10]

Many employees with disabilities who do not use computers at work regularly use them elsewhere, or say they could do so without difficulty.[11] Moreover, computer and Internet use appears to be increasing significantly among persons with disabilities. Studies indicate that between 2000 and 2002, Internet use among persons with disabilities increased from 10% to as high as 57%, depending upon the type of disability.[12] These statistics indicate the potential for increased

---

[7] Alan Krueger & Douglas Kruse, Labor Market Effects of Spinal Cord Injuries in the Dawn of the Computer Age (Working Paper No. 5302) 3 (Nat'l Bureau of Econ. Research), http://www.nber.org/papers/w5302.pdf (1995).

[8] Id.

[9] Nat'l Telecomms. and Info. Admin., A Nation Online: How Americans Are Expanding Their Use of the Internet 67, tbl. 7-3, http://www.ntia.doc.gov/ntiahome/dn/anationonline2.pdf (Feb. 2002) (reflecting computer use at home) [hereinafter NTIA Study].

[10] Lisa Schur & Douglas Kruse, Non-standard Work Arrangements and Disability Income 21 (Report to the Disability Research Inst.), http://www.als.uiuc.edu/dri/pubs/schur_kruse_final.pdf (2002).

[11] Krueger & Kruse, supra note 7, at 30-31.

[12] H. Stephen Kaye, Computer and Internet Use Among People with Disabilities, Disability Statistics Report No. 13, at 5 (U.S. Dep't of Educ., Nat'l Inst. on Disability and Rehab. Research), http://dsc.ucsf.edu/UCSF/pdf/REPORT13.pdf (2000); NTIA Study, supra note 9, at 67 tbl. 7-2. See generally H. Stephen Kaye, The Status of People with Disabilities in the United States (Disability Rights Advocates), http://www.dralegal.org/publications/dw/disability-watch.pdf (1997) (discussing these and related statistics from national Current Population Survey conducted in

employment of people with disabilities given the importance of computer skills in the workplace.[13]

This Part addresses issues related to the applicability of the ADA and other disability antidiscrimination laws to Internet and technological accessibility in workplaces, homes and schools.

In addition, the Part examines the applicability of federal and state tax policies to the procurement and use of AT in the workplace, homes and elsewhere. Tax policy has been a tool for enhancing the employment of persons with disabilities, for instance, through federal provisions such as the "disabled access credit" and the small business tax deduction for expenses incurred making workplaces accessible. As such, the tax laws provide opportunities for persons with disabilities to attain and retain employment, and thereby accumulate assets.

December 1998 and March 1999 by Census Bureau for Bureau of Labor Statistics).

[13]   Krueger & Kruse, supra note 7, at 34.

Chapter 31 DISABILITY POLICY AND PRIVATE INTERNET SITES

§ 31.1 Internet Accessibility

The issue of Internet accessibility has received national attention. In 1999, the National Federation of the Blind (NFB) filed a class action lawsuit against America Online, Inc. (AOL).[1] NFB alleged that AOL's Internet browser and services were not accessible to blind users and did not comply with the accessibility requirements of ADA Title III.[2] The plaintiffs claimed that AOL's online service sign-up form, welcome screens, and chat rooms were not accessible because screen readers could not read text hidden within graphic displays.[3]

In 2000, the AOL lawsuit and the applicability of the ADA to private internet sites were the subject of congressional hearings.[4] Testimony was presented by persons with disabilities, technology specialists, industry executives, and legal analysts. Later in 2000, the parties to the AOL litigation announced they had reached a settlement. AOL agreed to make its Internet browsing software compatible with screen reader assistive technology, which makes AOL software accessible to blind users. It also agreed to make the existing and future content of

---

[1] Nat'l Fed'n of the Blind v. Am. Online, Inc., No. 99CV12303EFH (D. Mass. filed Nov. 4, 1999). See also Peter Blanck & Leonard A. Sandler, ADA Title III and the Internet: Technology and Civil Rights, 24 Men. & Phys. Dis. L. Rptr. 855-59 (2000) (with thanks to Professor Sandler for the co-development of many of the ideas in this Chapter).

[2] Cynthia D. Waddell, The National Federation of the Blind Sues AOL, 27 Hum. Rights 22, 22-24 (2000).

[3] "Screen readers" use an artificial voice to read aloud text appearing on the computer monitor. People who are blind or deaf-blind use "refreshable Braille" computer displays that move pins to form Braille letters, which a user can then read. Screen readers and Braille displays cannot be used with non-accessible web-based formats (e.g., with certain graphic images with descriptive text). People with significant impairments affecting their manual dexterity (e.g., cerebral palsy or quadriplegia) who cannot use a computer mouse benefit from accessible formats that allow the user to use other commands (e.g., arrows or tabs) for Internet navigation.

[4] Applicability of the Americans with Disabilities Act (ADA) to Private Internet Sites: Hearing Before the Subcomm. on the Constitution of the House Judiciary Comm., 106th Cong. (2000), at http://commdocs.house. gov/committees/judiciary/hju65010.000/hju65010_0f.htm   [hereinafter Private Internet Site Hearing].

AOL services accessible to blind users, and to publish an Accessibility Policy and post it on its website.[5]

NFB and other groups and individuals, working sometimes in concert with government enforcement agencies, continue to examine the accessibility of Internet service providers and websites.[6] Former President Clinton proposed an initiative to "bridge the digital divide" by broadening access to the Internet and promoting online applications that help Americans use computer technologies to their fullest potential.[7]

President Bush has set out a comprehensive "New Freedom Initiative" to ensure that Americans with disabilities participate fully in the life of their communities, with emphasis on access to communications technologies such as the Internet.[8] The following chapters examine the particular application of Title III's accessibility requirements to private and public Internet websites and services.

§ 31.2 Title III Caselaw And The "Place" Requirement

One of the ADA's major goals is to remove architectural and communication barriers. Congress was careful in drafting the ADA's accessibility provisions to balance the needs of people with disabilities and the legitimate concerns of entities covered by the law, such as businesses, non-profit organizations, and state and local governments.

As discussed supra in Part 5 of this treatise, Title III prohibits discrimination against persons with disabilities in the equal enjoyment of places of public accommodation.[9] A public accommodation generally is a private entity in one of twelve categories that offers goods and services to the public.[10]

Federal circuit courts are split on the issue whether Title III covers only physical "places."[11] The Third Circuit, in *Ford v. Schering-*

---

[5] Nat'l Fed'n of the Blind/America Online Accessibility Agreement, at http://www.nfb.org/Tech/accessibility.htm (July 26, 2000).

[6] Judy Heim, Locking Out the Disabled, PC World, Sept. 1, 2000, at 181, 2000 WL 9395458.

[7] Mary Hillebrand, Clinton Launches Initiative to Bridge Digital Divide, E-Commerce Times, Dec. 10, 1999, at http://www.ecommercetimes.com/perl/story/1956.html.

[8] Remarks Announcing the New Freedom Initiative, 37 Weekly Comp. Pres. Doc. 5 (Feb. 1, 2001); George W. Bush, Presidential Address: New Freedom Initiative, http://www.whitehouse.gov/news/freedominitiative/freedominitiative.html (last visited Oct. 13, 2003).

[9] 42 U.S.C. § 12182(a) (2000).

[10] Id. § 12181(7).

[11] See supra Section 18.1(E).

Plough Corp.[12] and the Sixth Circuit in *Parker v. Metropolitan Insurance Co.*[13] have held that public accommodations are limited to physical places.

The First, Second and Seventh circuits have held otherwise.[14] The First Circuit, in *Carparts Distribution Center, Inc. v. Automotive Wholesaler's Association of New England, Inc.*,[15] found that the "services" of a health insurance provider may be covered under Title III. The court reasoned that the term "place of public accommodation" is not limited to actual physical structures.

Thus, by including travel services among the list of Title III public accommodations, the First Circuit concluded that service establishments, including providers of services that do not require a person to enter an actual physical structure, should be covered by Title III. The court based this conclusion on the fact that travel agencies conduct business by telephone and email and do not require customers to enter an office.

As the First Circuit stated in *Carparts*:

> [O]ne can easily imagine the existence of other service establishments conducting business by mail and phone without providing facilities to their customers to enter in order to utilize their services. It would be irrational to conclude that persons who enter an office to purchase services are protected by the ADA, but persons who purchase the same services over the telephone or by mail are not.[16]

Following the logic of the First Circuit, web-based activities of public accommodations that also have a physical presence (e.g., certain travel agents, insurance companies, online catalogues, and retail stores) likely are subject to Title III provisions. There would be a violation if services offered online were not accessible to people with disabilities. For the same reason, exclusively web-based service industries (e.g., e-commerce retail companies) likely would be considered Title III covered entities and their Internet services would have to be accessible.

---

[12] Ford v. Schering-Plough Corp., 145 F.3d 601, 612-13 (3d Cir. 1998).

[13] Parker v. Metro. Life Ins. Co., 121 F.3d 1006, 1008 (6th Cir. 1997).

[14] Pallozzi v. Allstate Life Ins. Co., 198 F.3d 28, 32 (2d Cir. 1999) (ADA guarantees "more than mere physical access"); Doe v. Mutual of Omaha Ins. Co., 179 F.3d 557, 559 (7th Cir. 1999); Carparts Distribution Ctr., Inc. v. Automotive Wholesaler's Ass'n of New England, Inc., 37 F.3d 12 (1st Cir. 1994).

[15] Carparts, 37 F.3d at 18-19.

[16] Id.

In *Pallozzi v. Allstate Life Insurance Co.*,[17] the Second Circuit held that Title III's requirement that persons with disabilities have equal access to the goods and services of a public accommodation suggests that the ADA guarantees them "more than mere physical access." Likewise, in *Doe v. Mutual of Omaha Insurance Co.*, the Seventh Circuit concluded that the plain meaning of ADA Title III mandates that the owner or operator of a public website "cannot exclude disabled persons from entering the facility and, once in, from using the facility in the same way that the nondisabled do."[18] The Eleventh Circuit would require at least a nexus with a physical place, although the discrimination need not occur at the place.[19]

Rendon v. Valleycrest Prods., Ltd. addressed the reach of Title III where individuals with manual dexterity impairments sued the producers of the television game show "Who Wants To Be A Millionaire." Plaintiffs alleged that use of an automated telephone selection process violated the ADA because it excluded individuals with disabilities from participating.

The Eleventh Circuit in *Rendon* held the telephone selection process to be a "discriminatory screening mechanism."[20] The court concluded that "[t]here is nothing in the [ADA] to suggest that discrimination via an imposition of screening or eligibility requirements must occur on site."[21] Moreover, the Eleventh Circuit noted that plaintiffs stated a viable claim under Title III because they demonstrated "a nexus between the challenged service and the premises of the public accommodation."[22]

In 2002, a Florida court, in *Access Now, Inc. v. Southwest Airlines*, examined the applicability of the ADA to a private Internet site. Access Now, a non-profit advocacy organization for persons with disabilities and an individual who is blind sued defendant Southwest Airlines. Plaintiffs contended that Southwest's Internet website (southwest.com, a virtual ticket counter) was not accessible in violation of ADA Title III. The court concluded that southwest.com was not a "place of public accommodation" covered by Title III, and therefore granted Southwest's motion to dismiss the case.[23]

In reaching its decision, the court stated that southwest.com was not a literal "place of public accommodation" as defined by the language of

---

[17] Pallozzi, 198 F.3d at 32.

[18] Doe, 179 F.3d at 559 (citation omitted).

[19] Rendon v. Valleycrest Prods., Ltd., 294 F.3d 1279 (11th Cir. 2002).

[20] Id. at 1286.

[21] Id. at 1283-84.

[22] Id. at 1284 n.8.

[23] Access Now, Inc. v. Southwest Airlines, Co., 227 F.Supp.2d 1312, 1318, 1322 (S.D. Fla. 2002).

Title III.[24] The court concluded that the site did not bar plaintiffs' access to, or have a nexus with, a physical space operated by Southwest Airlines, such as an airline ticket counter.[25]

In *Noah v. AOL Time Warner, Inc.*,[26] the court addressed whether an Internet chatroom is a public accommodation under Title II of the Civil Rights Act. The court held that "'places of public accommodation' are limited to actual, physical places and structures, and thus cannot include chat rooms, which are not actual physical facilities but instead virtual forums for communication."[27]

The courts have not yet addressed situations in which an entity that clearly is a place of public accommodation also offers its services via a website. Thus, for example, a department store, which has a physical store, as well as an Internet site, is more likely to be covered by Title III than AOL Time Warner, which has no physical place open to the public or an airline, like Southwest, which is not covered by Title III.

§ 31.3 Title III And The Internet: Emerging Issues

A. *Effective Communication*

The issue in *Access Now, Inc. v. Southwest Airlines* was whether plaintiffs were excluded in violation of Title III from the services offered by the airline. Discrimination under Title III would include the failure of a place of public accommodation to provide appropriate auxiliary aids or services (e.g., sign-language interpreters, assistive listening devices, Braille, or audiocassettes for individuals with sensory impairments) to ensure effective communication with customers with disabilities.[28] As mentioned, such accommodation is mandated unless it would fundamentally alter the nature of the services provided or result in an undue burden to the public accommodation.[29]

In a policy letter concerning website accessibility, the U.S. Department of Justice (DOJ) concludes that, pursuant to Titles II and III, state and local governments and the business sector must provide "effective communication" whenever they convey information, through the Internet or otherwise, regarding their programs, goods, or services.

---

[24] Id. at 1318.

[25] Id. at 1321. The *Access Now* court distinguished *Rendon v. Valleycrest Productions, Ltd.* from its holding. Id. at 1320. Notably, airlines are not places of public accommodation, so the "nexus" approach could not be relied upon.

[26] Noah v. AOL Time Warner, Inc., 261 F.Supp.2d 532, 540-45 (E.D. Va. 2003).

[27] Id. at 541.

[28] 28 C.F.R. § 36.303 (2003).

[29] 42 U.S.C. § 12182(b)(2)(A)(ii) (2000).

Referring to persons with vision disabilities who use screen readers,[30] DOJ suggests that providing an electronic text, rather than solely a graphical format, helps to ensure accessibility.[31]

The U.S. Department of Education, Office of Civil Rights (OCR), also defines the term effective communication in the context of Title II as the transfer of information with three basic components: timeliness of delivery; accuracy of the translation; and provision in a manner and medium appropriate to the significance of the message and the abilities of the individual with the disability.[32] Although not yet applied to Title III, this interpretation provides a framework for evaluating Internet activities as well.

From a technological standpoint, accessible web design often is a more effective and efficient way of ensuring access than other auxiliary aids. Accessible web design reduces or eliminates the need for translation into Braille, thereby avoiding the introduction of inaccuracies. In addition, it enables the "timeliness of delivery" requirement to be satisfied in cost-effective and technologically efficient ways that do not require entities to engage in case-by-case accommodations for individuals needing accessibility.[33] Accessible web design further allows communication to take place in a manner and medium appropriate for all individuals without case-by-case judgments of the significance of the message and the abilities of the individual.

Still, courts have been hesitant to require website modifications that might "jeopardize the overall viability" or solvency of public accommodations.[34] However, this threat appears exaggerated because

---

[30] See supra note 4 for description of screen readers.

[31] Letter from Deval Patrick, Assistant Attorney General, Civil Rights Division, U.S. Dep't Justice, to Tom Harkin, U.S. Senate (Sept. 9, 1996), (reprinted in 10 Nat'l Disability L. Rep. ¶ 240 (1996)); see also Cynthia D. Waddell, The Growing Digital Divide in Access for People with Disabilities: Overcoming Barriers to Participation, Remarks at Understanding the Digital Economy Conference, Washington, D.C., http://www.icdri.org/CynthiaW/the_digital_divide.htm (May 25-26, 1999).

[32] U.S. Dep't of Educ., Office of Civil Rights, Letter of Resolution, Docket No. 09-97-2002 (Apr. 7, 1997) (noting that entities covered under ADA Title II and III must meet the "effective communication" requirement).

[33] But see Private Internet Site Hearing, supra note 4, at 114 (statement of Walter Olson, Fellow at the Manhattan Institute) (discussing "the ADA's application [to the Internet] as a serious threat to the freedom, spontaneity and continued growth of the Web").

[34] Emery v. Caravan of Dreams, 879 F. Supp. 640, 643 (N.D. Tex. 1995) (citing N.M. Ass'n For Retarded Citizens v. New Mexico, 678 F.2d 847 (10th Cir. 1982)); see also Roberts v. KinderCare Learning Ctrs., 896 F.

Title III requires a public accommodation to make only "reasonable modifications in policies, practices, or procedures,"[35] and the effective communication requirement does not require a public accommodation to undertake an undue burden.[36]

As an alternative to providing accessibility through the Internet, Title III entities may offer their services in other effective formats. A public accommodation may choose to make its services available through a telephone help-line or offer print catalogues in Braille format. The help-line – which Title III would require to be staffed in a fashion equal to the services provided to nondisabled customers via their website (e.g., presumably 24 hours a day) – would be costly relative to website access. Likewise, producing an updated print catalogue in Braille is costly relative to placing the information online in a format accessible to screen readers and refreshable Braille.

B.   *First Amendment Issues*

It is likely that the application of Title III to private Internet sites and services does not violate the First Amendment,[37] which guarantees private parties the right to engage in expressive activities without governmental interference. Title III does not require a covered entity to change the subject matter or content of websites and services, but only to address the manner by which information is presented.[38]

Title III does not restrict editorial discretion over material transmitted or displayed on websites, nor does it require a site to display or otherwise engage in any speech "that is not their own."[39] Lastly, Title

---

Supp. 921, 926 (D. Minn. 1995); Easley by Easley v. Snider, 36 F.3d 297, 304 (3d Cir. 1994).

[35]   42 U.S.C. § 12182(b)(2)(A)(ii) (2000).

[36]   28 C.F.R. §36.104 (2003).

[37]   See Private Internet Site Hearing, supra note 4, at 120-33 (statement of Charles J. Cooper, Counsel for Cooper & Kirk, PLLC). But see id. at 92 (statement of Elizabeth K. Dorminey, Counsel for Wimberly, Lawson, Steckel, Nelson & Schneider, PC) (arguing that if websites were required to be in a text-based form, the freedom of expression of those who wished to present non-text information would be abridged).

[38]   See Paul Taylor, The Americans with Disabilities Act and the Internet, 7 B.U. J. Sci. & Tech. L. 26, 45 (2001) (stating that requiring websites to mirror content in an accessible form is not "forced speech").

[39]   See Private Internet Sites Hearing, supra note 4, at 121 (statement of Charles J. Cooper).

III does not target speech or any group of speakers, but applies equally to all entities covered by the law.[40]

Given Title III's undue hardship defense, accessibility is unlikely to impose conditions that stifle speech.[41] Rather, information technology has the potential to transform the limitations of print media by enabling the message to be communicated in multiple modes effectively and in ways that separate style from content.[42]

C. *Section 508 Of The Rehabilitation Act*

The implementation of Section 508 of the Rehabilitation Act[43] was designed to spur innovation throughout the e-commerce industry. Enacted as part of the Workforce Investment Act of 1998 (WIA) discussed supra in Part 9 of this treatise,[44] Section 508 requires that electronic and information technology (EIT), such as federal websites, telecommunications, software, and information kiosks, be usable by persons with disabilities.

Federal agencies may not purchase, maintain, or use EIT that is not accessible to persons with disabilities, unless accessibility poses an undue burden. The Electronic and Information Technology Accessibility Standards, finalized on December 21, 2000, detail the requirements for federal entities.[45] Section 508 does not require private companies that market technologies to the federal government to modify the EIT products used by company employees, or to make their Internet sites accessible to people with disabilities.[46]

---

[40] Id. at 122 (concluding that the fact that the cost of compliance will divert an organization's funds away from its speech activities or toward accessibility requirements does not implicate the First Amendment).

[41] Id. (indicating that the heightened scrutiny test under the First Amendment is not applicable where Title III applicability does not constitute a direct regulation of speech content).

[42] Waddell, supra note 2. "For example, screen reader technology permits persons with visual impairments or reading difficulties to 'read' accessibly coded websites via converting the website contents into Braille or synthesized speech." Id.

[43] 29 U.S.C. § 701(b)(1) (2000).

[44] Workforce Investment Act of 1998, Pub. L. 105-220, 112 Stat. 936 (1998); see supra Part 9, Chapter 27 for a discussion of WIA.

[45] Architectural and Transp. Barriers Compliance Bd., Electronic and Information Technology Accessibility Standards, http://www.access-board.gov/sec508/508standards.htm (last visited July 23, 2003).

[46] Dep't of Justice, Information Technology and People With Disabilities: The Current State of Federal Accessibility, Executive Summary & Recommendations (Report from Attorney Gen. Janet Reno to President Bill Clinton, Apr. 2000), http://www.usdoj.gov/crt/508/report/exec.htm.

Other shifts in law and policy benefit technology innovation and induce market activity for accessible Internet sites, goods, and services.[47] Section 508 and the ADA function in a complementary and technology stimulating manner by motivating covered entities to be accessible and accommodate individuals with disabilities.[48] Economically and socially beneficial implementation of anti-discrimination laws is furthered by communicating information in accessible formats to persons with disabilities.[49]

Review of economic activity in the assistive technology market illustrates that laws like the ADA and Section 508 foster technological innovation and economic activity in the Internet-based service industry in ways unanticipated at the time that these laws were passed.[50] This "push-pull" of disability policy is fostering research initiatives of individual and corporate inventors. The regulatory "push," introduced by the ADA and furthered by Section 508, expanded the market for accessible technology to include a range of consumer groups, including persons with disabilities; the elderly; employers; and public, municipal, and governmental entities.

Financial incentives and investment (the "pull") provide research and development opportunities to Internet inventors and e-commerce companies.[51] One such strategy involves enhancing the e-commerce

---

[47] Heidi M. Berven & Peter Blanck, Economics of the Americans with Disabilities Act: Part II–Patents, Innovations and Assistive Technology, 12 Notre Dame J.L. Ethics & Pub. Pol'y 9, 18-19 (1998).

[48] Heidi M. Berven & Peter Blanck, Assistive Technology Patenting Trends and the Americans with Disabilities Act, 17 Behav. Sci. & L. 47, 49 (1999); cf. Susan Schwochau & Peter Blanck, The Economics of the Americans with Disabilities Act: Part III–Does the ADA Disable the Disabled?, 21 Berkeley J. Emp. & Lab. L. 271, 286 (2000) (discussing the economic theory that "a firm chooses the most profitable and efficient means of production, given the state of technology, demand for the product, and relative cost of capital and labor").

[49] Web Accessibility Initiative, Economic Factors for Consideration in a Business Case for Web Accessibility, at http://www.w3.org/WAI/EO/Drafts/bcase/econ.html (last visited Aug. 1, 2003); Web Accessibility Initiative, Presenting the Case for Web Accessibility: Social Factors, at http://www.w3.org/WAI/EO/Drafts/bcase/soc.html (last visited Aug. 1, 2003).

[50] See Berven & Blanck, supra notes 47-48 (discussing this line of research).

[51] See Leonard A. Sandler & Peter Blanck, Corporate Culture, Disability, and Competitive Strategy: A Case Study of a Large Technology Company, 22 Behav. Sci. & L. (forthcoming 2004) (examining the relation among corporate culture, technological innovation, and disability).

industry by increasing support for programs that encourage small business research, innovation, and entrepreneurship.[52] These and related programs are important in light of studies showing that web accessibility solutions are inexpensive and reflect effective web design strategies.[53]

Competition within the e-commerce market for consumers with and without disabilities continues to foster technological innovation and development. According to a 1992 survey, of the 2.5 million persons who had an unmet need for assistive technology, about half (1.2 million) were of working age (25-64).[54]

§ 31.4 Summary

The applicability of ADA Title III to private Internet sites and services requires analysis of technologies, e-commerce, and accessibility (e.g., through endeavors such as The World Wide Web Consortium, Web Accessibility Initiative).[55]

Study is needed about persons with disabilities in terms of their capabilities and value to employers and the American economy. Evaluation and implementation of accessible Internet technologies and universal design concepts is needed as applied to persons with and without disabilities, including initiatives in e-commerce, employment, health care, and education.[56]

---

[52] See Peter Blanck et al., The Emerging Workforce of Entrepreneurs with Disabilities: Preliminary Study of Entrepreneurship in Iowa, 85 Iowa L. Rev. 1583, 1648 (2000) (discussing the importance of technology to entrepreneurs with disabilities).

[53] See Private Internet Site Hearing, supra note 4, at 48-50 (statement of Judy Brewer, Dir. of Web Accessibility Initiative of the World Wide Web Consortium) (discussing technological aspects of accessible web design). In addition, a tax credit is available to small businesses to offset expenses in complying with the ADA and for website accessibility improvements. Id. at 109 n.18 (statement of Peter D. Blanck, Prof. of Law, Univ. of Iowa College of Law), and discussed infra Chapter 33.

[54] Mitchell P. LaPlante et al., Assistive Technology Devices and Home Accessibility Features: Prevalence, Payment, Need, and Trends, No. 217 (Ctr. for Disease Control and Nat'l Ctr. for Health Statistics) 4, http://www.cdc.gov/nchs/data/ad/ad217.pdf (Sept. 16, 1992).

[55] See Private Internet Site Hearing, supra note 4, at 48-50 (statement of Judy Brewer (discussing the W3C, Web Accessibility Initiative, and guidelines describing common approaches to Web accessibility).

[56] See id. at 69, 73 (statement of Dennis C. Hayes, Chairman of the U.S. Internet Indus. Ass'n) (discussing the Internet "as an evolving media," and stating that "the answer to the problem of accessibility is not regulation, but rather education and participation").

It also is essential to analyze the relation among Internet technologies and services and federal and state disability policies (e.g., WIA and TWWIIA discussed supra Part 9 of this treatise).[57] Examination of the application of the ADA to Internet services and sites is needed, not only for people with disabilities, but for all underrepresented individuals in society – the poor and isolated, and the vulnerable.

---

[57] Peter Blanck, Researching the Work Environment: Disability, Employment Policy, and the ADA (Working Paper), at http://www.itaa.org/workforce/studies/taks.htm (2000) (examining under-represented groups in the IT workforce, including persons with disabilities); Steven Mendelsohn, Nat'l Council on Disability, When the Americans with Disabilities Act Goes Online: Application of the ADA to the Internet and the Worldwide Web, http://www.ncd.gov/newsroom/publications/adainternet.html (July 10, 2008).

Chapter 32 DISABILITY POLICY AND PUBLIC INTERNET SITES

§ 32.1 Access To Data

The Internet has transformed the nature of access to information. Library card catalog systems have lost practical use, in large part due to the difficulty of maintaining them as compared to the efficiency of technology to constantly update and search the vast electronic catalogs. However, even when a public library uses accessible software to search these databases, persons with disabilities often encounter barriers posed by inaccessible website design.[1]

Estimates suggest that one-fifth of Americans have disabilities[2] and one in twelve school-age children has a disability.[3] Students with disabilities are three times less likely to use the Internet to perform routine tasks than their nondisabled peers.[4]

Similarly, persons with disabilities (ages 15 and over) are nearly four times less likely to use the Internet than their nondisabled peers.[5] The inequality of Internet access disproportionately impedes individuals with disabilities at school, work, and home.[6]

Sparse case law has addressed the accessibility of public Internet programs and services provided via the Internet. However, the U.S.

---

[1] Cynthia D. Waddell, Applying the ADA to the Internet: A Web Accessibility Standard, at http://www.icdri.org/CynthiaW/applying_the_ada_to_the_internet.htm (June 17, 1998).

[2] Nat'l Council on Disability, Access to Multimedia Technology by People with Sensory Disabilities, http://www.ncd.gov/newsroom/publications/sensory.html (Mar. 13, 1998).

[3] D'Vera Cohn, U.S. Counts One in 12 Children As Disabled, Wash. Post, July 5, 2002, at B01, 2002 WL 23851525.

[4] John M. Slatin, Inst. for Tech. and Learning, The Imagination Gap: Making Web-Based Instructional Resources Accessible to Students and Colleagues with Disabilities, Currents in Electronic Literacy: Computers, Writing, Research, and Learning in the Lab, 6, at http://currents.cwrl.utexas.edu/spring02/slatin.html (Spring 2002).

[5] H. Stephen Kaye, Computer and Internet Use Among People with Disabilities, Disability Statistics Report No. 13, at 5 tbl. A (U.S. Dep't of Educ., Nat'l Inst. on Disability and Rehab. Research), http://dsc.ucsf.edu/UCSF/pdf/REPORT13.pdf (2000); see id. at 7 fig. 3 (indicating that among adults age 18-64, 74.3% of those without a disability use the Internet and 37.2% of those with a disability use the Internet).

[6] David Klein et al., Electronic Doors to Education: Study of High School Website Accessibility in Iowa, 21 Behav. Sci. & L. 27, 28 (2003).

Departments of Education and Justice consider the ADA and Rehabilitation Act applicable to these issues.

§ 32.2 Applications Of The ADA

ADA Title II prohibits discrimination against persons with disabilities by public entities, including state and local governmental programs and services.[7] As mentioned, the U.S. Department of Education and the Department of Justice consider Titles II and III to apply to the Internet.[8] This position arises from the ADA mandate that public entities employ methods of effective communication with the population of individuals with disabilities.[9] Unlike Title III, Title II does not include a "place" requirement to limit its application to Internet sites.

The federal court for the Northern District of Georgia, in *Martin v. Metropolitan Atlanta Rapid Transit Authority (MARTA)*, found that a transit authority's website providing scheduling information for bus and other transit services must be accessible under Title II of the ADA.[10] In the *MARTA* case, the court granted plaintiffs' motion for a preliminary injunction because of MARTA's failure to provide access to its website for people who are blind.

The district court noted that MARTA conceded that its web page was not formatted so that it could be read by persons who are blind, who use screen reader computer software. The court concluded that "until these deficiencies are corrected, MARTA is violating the ADA mandate of 'making adequate communications capacity available, through accessible formats and technology, to enable users to obtain information and schedule service' as required by the Department of Transportation Regulations implementing Title II of the ADA."[11]

Public entities, for instance, also must purchase computer software and hardware that remove accessibility barriers for persons with disabilities. A public entity may not claim an undue cost burden to

---

[7]   42 U.S.C. §§ 12131-12132 (2000).

[8]   Dep't of Justice, ADA Accessibility Requirements Apply to Internet Web Pages, 10 NDLR ¶ 240 (Sept. 9, 1996); Letter to Dr. James Rosser, President of Cal. St. Univ. at L.A., from Adriana Cardenas, Team Leader, Office for Civil Rights, U.S. Dept. of Educ. (April 7, 1997), http://www.rit.edu/~easi/law/csula.htm. Alternately see Letter to Senator Tom Harkin, Iowa, from Deval L. Patrick, Assistant Attorney Gen., Civil Rights Div. (Sept. 9, 1996), http://www.usdoj.gov/crt/foia/tal712.txt. This letter is the basis for the Department of Justice's Policy "ADA Accessibility Requirements Apply to Internet Web Pages."

[9]   28 C.F.R. § 35.160(a) (2003).

[10]   Martin v. Metro. Atlanta Rapid Trans. Auth., 225 F.Supp.2d 1362, 1377 (N.D. Ga. 2002).

[11]   Id. at 1377.

replace or update inaccessible technology, due to its own shortsightedness.[12]

State governments are moving toward making their resources and services available online as a means of reducing costs and increasing citizen participation. The Information Technology Technical Assistance and Training Center (ITTATC) completed its initial survey addressing how states are promoting the accessibility of electronic and information technology.[13] The ITTATC study indicated that most state accessibility improvements focus on website accessibility, in comparison to application development, hardware and software procurement, and public access to hardware.[14]

Website accessibility standards vary widely by state but tend to be drawn from Section 508 standards and the World Wide Web Consortium (W3C) Web Content Accessibility Guidelines (WCAG). Other states have developed their own standards.[15] Nevertheless, to the extent that public websites remain inaccessible to persons with disabilities, concurrent reductions in traditional communications due to cost or other reasons may impede the availability of programs and services.[16]

§ 32.3 Applications Of Section 504 Of The Rehabilitation Act

In addition to the ADA, Section 504 of the Rehabilitation Act prohibits disability discrimination by state and private entities receiving

---

[12] Letter to Dr. James Rosser, supra note 8; see also Delano-Pyle v. Victoria County, 302 F.3d 567, 575 (5th Cir. 2002) (stating that "a plain reading of the ADA evidences that Congress intended to impose an affirmative duty on public entities to create policies or procedures to prevent discrimination based on disability").

[13] Info. Tech. Technical Assistance and Training Ctr., National Assessment of State E&IT Accessibility Initiatives, at http://www.ittatc. org/laws/report_3.cfm (Apr. 2003). The complete results of the survey are available at Info. Tech. Technical Assistance and Training Ctr., Overview of State Accessibility Laws, Policies, Standards and Other Resources Available On-line [hereinafter ITTATC Overview], at http://www.ittatc. org/laws/stateLawAtGlance.cfm (last visited Aug. 6, 2003).

[14] ITTATC Overview, supra note 13.

[15] Id.

[16] Nat'l Council on Disability, When the Americans with Disabilities Act Goes Online: Application of the ADA to the Internet and the Worldwide Web, http://www.ncd.gov/newsroom/publications/adainternet.html (2003) [hereinafter ADA Goes Online].

federal funding. The failure to provide programs and services in accessible formats violates Section 504.[17]

In public schools, for instance, students with disabilities are entitled to services that are equal to and as effective as those provided for other students.[18] When Internet access is required for successful completion of homework assignments or a program only is available via the Web (e.g., a distance-learning course), inaccessible technologies that prevent access by students with disabilities violate Section 504.[19]

Additionally, students with disabilities increasingly use their own personal assistive technology devices in the classroom (e.g., electronic screen readers).[20] Public schools need to keep pace in a manner accessible to these new technologies.[21]

§ 32.4 Applications Of Section 508 Of The Rehabilitation Act

As discussed above, the WIA amendments included in Section 508 of the Rehabilitation Act[22] mandate accessible Internet use for federal government employees whose work requires access to electronic and information technology. Section 508 requires federal government websites, telecommunications, software, and information kiosks to be accessible to and usable by persons with disabilities.[23] Federal agencies may not purchase, maintain, or use electronic information technology that is not accessible, unless doing so would pose an undue burden.[24]

The Architectural and Transportation Barriers Compliance Board (Access Board discussed supra in Part 5 of this treatise) is charged with developing the rules to implement Section 508. The Access Board published its final regulations, the Electronic and Information Technology Accessibility Standards (EITAS), in December 2000.[25]

The EITAS provides accessibility standards for federal agencies in areas related to hardware and software products, technical criteria and

---

[17] Klein et al., supra note 6, at 29.

[18] 34 C.F.R. §§ 104.4(b)(ii) (2003); id. § 104.4(b)(iii)-(iv).

[19] Klein et al., supra note 6, at 29.

[20] Id.

[21] Id. at 30.

[22] Workforce Investment Act of 1998, Pub. L. 105-220, 112 Stat. 936 (1998); 29 U.S.C. § 701(b)(1) (2000).

[23] 36 C.F.R. § 1194 (2003).

[24] Id. § 1194.2.

[25] Architectural and Transp. Barriers Compliance Bd., Electronic and Information Technology Accessibility Standards, http://www.access-board.gov/sec508/508standards.htm (last visited July 29, 2003).

performance-based requirements, web-based information and applications, telecommunications, video and multi-media, and compatibility with the adaptive equipment used by persons with disabilities for information and communication access.[26]

Although the Section 508 standards do not apply specifically to the states' use and procurement of technology,[27] most states are implementing policies, and in some cases enacting statutes, imposing accessibility standards. These laws frequently parallel Section 508 with regard to state governmental services, purchase of IT products, website design, and hardware.[28] In addition, the U.S. Department of Education has interpreted Section 508 to apply to states that receive federal funds under the Assistive Technology for Individuals with Disabilities Act of 1998, with guidance forthcoming.[29]

§ 32.5 Other Policy Issues

As discussed, there is a strong practical and policy-oriented tie between the goals of the ADA and the development of accessible Internet sites and services. As the policy and attitudinal shifts fostered by the ADA expand the market for goods and services that improve accessibility, employers and entities affecting commerce are vying for positive economic opportunities associated with the law's implementation.[30]

---

[26] Id. The EITAS are encoded at 36 C.F.R. § 1194. To keep pace with technological advances, the Access Board is required to periodically update the EITAS. 29 U.S.C. § 794d(a)(2)(B). The EITAS currently reflect revisions as of July 1, 2002. 36 C.F.R. § 1194.1.

[27] Klein et al., supra note 6, at 30.

[28] See ITTATC Overview, supra note 13.

[29] Assistive Technology for Individuals with Disabilities Act of 1998, Pub. L. No. 105-394, 112 Stat. 3627 (codified in scattered sections of Titles 15 and 29 U.S.C.); Constance S. Hawke & Anne L. Jannarone, Emerging Issues of Web Accessibility: Implications for Higher Education, 160 Educ. L. Rep. 715, 719 (2002).

[30] Applicability of the Americans with Disabilities Act (ADA) to Private Internet Sites: Hearing Before the Subcomm. on the Constitution of the House Judiciary Comm., 106th Cong. (2000), at http://commdocs.house.gov/committees/judiciary/hju65010.000/hju65010_0f.htm [hereinafter Private Internet Site Hearing] (statement of Charles J. Cooper, Counsel for Cooper & Kirk, PLLC). Mr. Cooper, quoting the Supreme Court, describes the Internet as:

> comparable . . . to both a vast library including millions of readily available and indexed publications and a sprawling mall offering goods and services. From the publishers' point of view, it constitutes a vast platform from which to

Universal design and accessibility, for instance, are fundamental components of e-business and e-government plans. Goods, services, and information are thereby posted and promoted to the widest possible customer base.

E-commerce involves Internet links to commercial, governmental, and public and private partners, whose websites may be accessible to persons with sensory, physical, mobility, cognitive, mental, and other impairments. By creating a universal platform – not "separate but equal" sites – e-businesses are cultivating brand and consumer loyalty while reducing the costs of services and websites.

Although accessibility may make technological and business sense, the marketplace has been slow in prompting innovation on its own. Elaborate site "art" (e.g., banners and sales lures) has been developed at the expense of accessibility.[31] In addition, e-businesses and website developers often lack the skills or incentives to make their sites usable by persons with disabilities.

Despite these problems, the government has helped provide the catalyst for change. For instance, the National Federation of the Blind and the Connecticut Attorney General's office reached an agreement with HDVest, Intuit, H & R Block, and Gilman and Ciocia to provide accessible on-line tax filing services.[32] The Internal Revenue Service had listed these companies on its site as partners for e-filing, but users with screen readers could not file returns on those sites. Here, the accessibility laws helped promote innovative solutions.

---

address and hear from a world-wide audience of millions of readers, viewers, researchers, and buyers.

Reno v. Am. Civil Liberties Union, 521 U.S. 844, 853 (1997).

[31] Leonard A. Sandler & Peter Blanck, Corporate Culture, Disability, and Competitive Strategy: A Case Study of a Large Technology Company, 22 Behav. Sci. & L. (forthcoming 2004) (examining the relation among corporate culture, technological innovation, and disability).

[32] Press Release, Conn. Attorney General's Office, National Federation of Blind Applaud On-Line Tax Filing Services for Agreeing to Make Sites Blind-Accessible (Apr. 17, 2000), http://lists.w3.org/Archives/Public/w3c-wai-ig/2000AprJun/0194.html.

Chapter 33 DISABILITY AND TAX POLICY

§ 33.1 Overview: Tax Policy And Persons With Disabilities[1]

American tax policy exists to spur asset accumulation, economic independence and social empowerment.[2] For many who advocate for inclusion of Americans with disabilities in the economic mainstream, the subject of tax policy and asset accumulation is unfamiliar.[3]

The field of tax policy and asset development for low-income Americans has emerged in recent years, with the tenet that owning assets is a core value of citizenship.[4] In 1998, Congress passed the Assets for Independence Act (AFIA)[5] that allowed for matched savings accounts for

---

[1] Many of the ideas and sections in this chapter are derived from Peter Blanck, Michael Morris, Johnette Hartnet and Steven Mendelson, Grant Proposal to The National Institute on Disability and Rehabilitation Research–Tax Policy and Asset Accumulation Strategies (July, 2003) available at http://disability.law.uiowa.edu/lhpdc/projects/assetdevtaxpol. html (grant funded by NIDRR, Nov. 1, 2003) [hereinafter Grant Proposal] (with listing of other grant contributor partners, and particular thanks to Johnette Hartnet and Michael Morris).

[2] See id. (citing Beyond Child Poverty: The Social Exclusion of Children (A. Kahn & S. Kamerman eds., 2002); Ray Boshara, Building Assets: A Report on the Asset-Development and IDA Field (Corp. for Enter. Dev. 2001); Steve Mendelsohn, Federal Income Tax Law: A Tool for Increasing Employment Opportunities for Americans with Disabilities, Report to the Presidential Task Force on Employment of Adults with Disabilities (2002); Isabel Sawhill & Strobe Talbott, One Percent for the Kids: New Policies, Brighter Futures for America's Children (2003); Michael Sherraden, From Research to Policy: Lessons from Individual Development Accounts (2001); Mark Schreiner, What Do Individual Development Accounts Cost? The First Three Years at CAPTC (Research Report for the Ctr. for Soc. Dev.), http://www.microfinance.com/English/Papers/IDA_Costs_98_01.pdf (Feb. 1, 2001); Gregory M. Stanton, Unblocking Obstacles to Capital Markets for Community Development Lenders (White Paper), http://www.bos.frb. org/commdev/conf/orient/stanton2.pdf (Jan. 2003) (references discussed throughout this chapter)).

[3] Mendelsohn, supra note 2.

[4] Grant Proposal, supra note 1, at 7.

[5] Assets for Independence Act of 1998, Pub. L. No. 105-285, § 416, 112 Stat 2579 (1998). The Assets for Independence Demonstration Program (IDA Program) was established by the Assets for Independence Act (AFI Act), under Title IV of the Community Opportunities, Accountability, and Training and Educational Services Act of 1998 (codified as amended at 42 U.S.C. §§ 604 et seq. See Office of Cmty. Servs., Admin. of Children &

the poor to enhance their economic and social growth.[6] The goals of AFIA include creating asset accumulation opportunities for households eligible for Temporary Assistance for Needy Families (for the discussion of the TANF Program, see supra treatise Part 9) and other eligible individuals and working families.[7]

The development of asset-based policy is important because traditionally, for low income persons with disabilities on government benefits programs that are means-tested, owning assets has meant disqualification from their benefits.[8] Studies show that individuals with disabilities participating in government benefits programs (e.g., TANF and SSI programs discussed supra in treatise Part 9) that are means- or asset-tested have low saving rates.[9]

Promoting economic and social independence is at the heart of disability civil rights laws like the Individuals with Disabilities Education Act (IDEA), the Rehabilitation Act of 1973, and the ADA. However, to date, national disability policies in employment, housing, health care, and technology have focused on the limits of asset accumulation, not on its potentials.

§ 33.2 Tax Policy, Asset Accumulation And Disability Policy

Fundamental to asset accumulation strategies for people with disabilities is the idea that social and economic independence equates with

---

Families, U.S. Dep't of Health & Human Servs., AFIA Legal Requirements & Regulations, at http://www.acf.hhs.gov/programs/ocs/demo/ida/ocs_present.html (last modified Sept. 10, 2001). Individual Development Accounts (IDAs) are matched savings accounts designed to help low-income and low-wealth families accumulate assets for high-return investments in education or job training, homeownerships, and microenterprise. Corp. for Enter. Dev., 2002 Federal IDA Briefing Book 8, http://www.cbpp.org/10-29-02wel.pdf. Low-income individuals save regularly, typically over a three-year period, and have their savings matched by public or private funders. Financial institutions, foundations, churches, private donors, and state and local governments fund the matches to the personal saving of IDA holders (usually at a rate ranging from $1 to $4 for each dollar saved). Accountholders typically receive financial education and counseling.

[6] Grant Proposal, supra note 1, at 18.

[7] For a description of AFIA, see 66 Fed. Reg. 12688-12721 (Feb. 27, 2001).

[8] Peter R. Orszag, Asset Tests and Low Saving Rates Among Lower-Income Families Ctr. on Budget & Pol'y Priorities 16, http://www.cbpp.org/4-13-01wel.pdf (Apr. 13, 2001).

[9] Id.

civil rights. Conversely, sustained poverty leads to social dependence. A crucial correlate is that economic advancement in and of itself does not equate with the alleviation of disability.

In fact, quite the opposite: economic advancement helps eliminate discrimination on the basis of disability (or any other characteristic) that is based on social dependency. Thus, tax policy and "asset accumulation, and the effects of economic independence, lead to recognition of difference, not continued discrimination, and to social recognition and equal participation in society as contributing citizens."[10]

As described in Part 1 of the treatise, because disability historically has been viewed as a "problem to fix," people in the business of building private wealth, as well as many disability policymakers, have not examined the potential of persons with disabilities to accumulate assets. Yet, nearly one in five Americans, or 19 percent of the U.S. population, are classified as having a disability, and one in ten Americans have a severe disability.[11]

Of the 50 million Americans with disabilities, 18.6 million are employed, and 31.1 (63%) are unemployed, as compared to a 6.4 percent unemployment rate of people without disabilities.[12] "Homeownership for people with significant disabilities is under 10 percent. Over 50 percent of 7 million people receiving Supplemental Security Insurance (SSI) are unbanked, having no checking or savings accounts."[13] In addition, many persons participating in income maintenance programs such as SSI and TANF who do have access to asset producing strategies have low participation rates.

Traditionally, economic advancement programs targeting people with disabilities have included subsidized services. These services have included payments or tax credits for goods and services (AT (assistive technology), subsidized housing, and specialized employment training) and income maintenance (notably, through SSDI and SSI).[14]

Yet, when it comes to employment, housing, technology access, education, health care and other key elements of modern life, the availability of these economic strategies to most Americans is structured by tax policy. For example, it is not possible to assess our nation's health insurance system without recognizing the favored tax status afforded those who obtain the fringe benefits of employment.

---

[10] Grant Proposal, supra note 1, at 8.

[11] U.S. Census Bureau, Facts for Features: Anniversary of Americans with Disabilities Act (July 26) CB03-FF.10, at http://www.census.gov/Press-Release/www/2003/cb03ff-10.html (July 14, 2003).

[12] Id.

[13] Grant Proposal, supra note 1, at 9.

[14] Id.

Similarly, the proliferation of home ownership among Americans would not have occurred without the tax deductibility of home mortgage interest and tax features that subsidize the residential real estate market. Even the existence of low-income subsidized housing would be markedly different without provisions such as the low-income housing credit.

Although tax policy has been a tool for enhancing the employment of persons with disabilities – as discussed in this chapter infra, through provisions such as the disabled access or small business accommodation credit – decisions about tax policy "have been made without particular consideration of people with disabilities."[15] As a result, tax policies have not had the same positive effects on the lives of people with disabilities.

There is a need, therefore, for analysis of the laws promoting asset accumulation through the tax system and the laws limiting the accumulation of assets (such as through means-testing) by people with disabilities. One example of the failure of tax-based asset accumulation policies to benefit persons with disabilities is illustrated in the area of home ownership.

Although homeownership levels for the population as a whole exceed 70 percent, those for persons with disabilities hover in the single digits. Research also shows that "34 percent of persons with disabilities live in households with total incomes of $15,000 or less, compared to only 12 percent of those without disabilities," and explains why many persons with disabilities are less likely to take advantage of tax incentives.[16]

For similar reasons, to the degree that the tax laws encourage home ownership or other forms of asset accumulation, they tend to work effectively for people with continuous employment and rising incomes. Yet, these are not necessarily the work history patterns encountered by many people with disabilities.

Studies of the use of technology find that only 25 percent of people with disabilities own computers compared to 66 percent of U.S. adults without disabilities.[17] At the same time, expenses incurred by workers with disabilities – for AT, for specialized training or other work-related costs – often are considerably higher than for the average worker without a disability.

Despite their current shortcomings, the tax laws potentially provide opportunities for persons with disabilities to accumulate assets and use capital to their benefit. These strategies help persons with

---

[15]   Id. at 10.

[16]   Id. at 11.

[17]   White House, Executive Summary: Fulfilling America's Promise to Americans with Disabilities, at www.whitehouse.gove/news/ freedominitiative/freedominitiatve.html (2001).

disabilities "reach beyond the traditional 'income maintenance' mindset that has framed ... disability policy for more than seventy years."[18]

§ 33.3 Tax Policies And The ADA: Applications To Technology And Other Areas

The ADA places a burden on private businesses to eliminate some of the societal barriers traditionally excluding people with disabilities. To offset some of that burden, the federal government has provided tax incentives for compliance with the law. When businesses make use of the tax advantages of ADA compliance, the benefits and burdens of compliance are shared between the business and the federal government.

However, studies indicate that the tax incentives are not fulfilling their potential. According to the National Council on Disability (NCD), "[a] [General Accounting Office] study completed in late 2002 concludes that the three major Internal Revenue Code provisions aimed at enhancing employment of persons with disabilities *cannot be demonstrated to have had significant effect*."[19]

There are several federal tax provisions set out in the Internal Revenue Code available to business to foster ADA implementation and compliance.[20] There is a "disabled access credit" available for small businesses,[21] a tax deduction available to any business when improving accessibility for customers and employees with disabilities, and a tax credit available to any employer for a percentage of the first and second year wages of a new employee with a disability.

In addition, there are state tax code provisions applicable to small businesses to foster the hiring and retention of employees with disabilities.

---

[18] Grant Proposal, supra note 1, at 17.

[19] Nat'l Council on Disability, National Disability Policy: A Progress Report December 2001-December 2002 p. 101, http://www.ncd.gov/newsroom/publications/pdf/progressreport_final.pdf (July 26, 2003) (emphasis added) (citation omitted).

[20] For a review, see Office of the Attorney Gen., Tax Incentives Packet on the Americans with Disabilities Act, http://www.usdoj.gov/crt/ada/taxpack.htm (July 26, 2001) (noting that the tax credit is established under Section 44 of the Internal Revenue Code (1990) to help small businesses cover ADA-related expenditures). See Internal Revenue Code, 26 U.S.C. §§ 44, 51, 190 (2000).

[21] See Tax Incentive Packet, supra note 20 (including the Internal Revenue Service (IRS) form and instructions for claiming the disabled access credit).

A. *Disabled Access Credit*

Title 26 of the IRS Code, Section 44, provides a small business disabled tax credit for architectural adaptations (but not new construction), equipment acquisitions such as AT (assistive technology), and services such as sign language interpreters. Small businesses, including service firms such as law firms and physician practice groups, may be eligible for the credit, for instance to defray the cost of accommodations for interpreters for client meetings.[22]

The tax credit is subtracted from tax liability after the calculation of taxes owed. Businesses with revenues of $1,000,000 or less or with fewer than 31 full-time workers, may use the credit. The tax credit may equal up to 50% of the eligible access expenditures in a year, to a maximum expenditure of $10,250. There is no credit for the first $250 of expenditures; therefore, the maximum tax credit is $5,000.

B. *Tax Deduction For Removal Of Architectural And Transportation Barriers*

A tax deduction can be used for architectural or transportation adaptations under Title 26, Section 190 of the IRS Code. The tax deduction is subtracted from total income before taxes, to establish the taxable income rate.

Presently, the tax deduction is a maximum of $15,000 per year. Businesses of any size (including active owners of an apartment building) may use the deduction for the removal of architectural and transportation barriers. Small businesses may use the Section 190 tax deduction and the Section 44 disabled tax credit in combination.

The Justice Department provides the example that a small business that spends $20,000 to widen bathroom doors and install a ramp as access adaptations may take a maximum tax credit of $5000 (based on $10,250 of expenditures) and a deduction of $15,000.

C. *Work Opportunity Credit*

The Work Opportunity Credit provides businesses an incentive to hire individuals with disabilities and others with historically high unemployment rates.[23] A business can claim the credit for 40 percent of

---

[22] See, e.g., Beth Gallie & Deirdre M. Smith, Representing Deaf Clients: What Every Lawyer Should Know, 15 Me. B.J. 128, 130 n.18 (Apr. 2000).

[23] The Job Creation and Worker Assistance Act of 2002, Pub. L. No. 107-134, 115 Stat. 2427 (codified in scattered sections of 26 U.S.C.) extended the Work Opportunity Tax Credit from January 1, 2002 to December 31, 2003. Quicken.com, The Job Creation and Worker Assistance Act of 2002, at http://www.quicken.com/cms/viewers/article/taxes/57021 (last visited Oct. 15, 2003). For one example of a review of the program, see Okla. Emp. Sec. Comm'n, Work Opportunity Tax Credit: What You Need to

the first $6,000 of first-year wages (or $2,400) of a new employee who has a disability.[24]

To qualify for this credit, the worker must have been employed for at least 400 hours. For employees working fewer than 400 hours, but at least 120 hours, a 25 percent credit toward the first $6,000 in wages (or $1,500) credit is available.

D.   *Welfare-To-Work Tax Credit*

The Welfare-to-Work Tax Credit provides employers an incentive to hire and retain persons with disabilities who have been long-term welfare recipients (e.g., see treatise Part 9 for discussion of TANF Program recipients) or who have been referred on completion of a state vocational rehabilitation program.

To qualify, new hires must be employed 400 or more hours. Employers may receive a 35 percent credit toward the first $10,000 of qualified wages for the first year and 50 percent of the second year earnings (for a total potential credit of $8,500 over the two years).[25]

Employers may not claim for the same employee both the Work Opportunity Credit (described above) and the Welfare-to-Work Tax Credit during the same employment period. However, there is no limit on the number of employees an employer may claim for either tax credit.[26]

E.   *State Tax Policy Illustrations*

Many states are developing tax policies as a tool to enhance the economic and social independence of persons with disabilities. The state policies typically mirror the federal tax credit and deduction initiatives designed to enhance accessibility and the procurement of assistive technology.

Know to Save Up to $2,400 Per Employee on Federal Taxes, at http://www.oesc.state.ok.us/ES/default.htm?http://www.oesc.state.ok.us/ES/WOTC.htm (last modified Sept. 4, 2003).

[24]   For eligible summer youth employees, 40 percent of the first $3,000 can be claimed (or a $1,200 credit). U.S. Chamber of Commerce, Business Tax Credits & Deductions for Employment of Persons with Disabilities 2 (Jan. 2000).

[25]   For one example of a review of the program, see Ill. Dep't of Emp. Sec. Tax Credits, at http://www.ides.state.il.us/employer/uitax/credits.htm (last visited Oct. 15, 2003).

[26]   There are various forms that must be completed by the employer to receive the tax credits, e.g., IRS FORM 8850, "Work Opportunity Credit Pre-Screening Notice and Certification Request," and Department of Labor ETA FORM 9061, "Individual Characteristics Form" FORM 9062, "Conditional Certification Form." See id.

The Rehabilitation Engineering and Assistive Technology Society of North America (RESNA) has undertaken a "Technical Assistance Project" to increase access to AT for persons with disabilities.[27] The project provides information about the procurement and funding of AT in regard to available tax credits and tax revenue initiatives in all states funded under the Assistive Technology Act of 1998.[28] Other illustrative state tax policy initiatives related to AT and general accessibility are highlighted below.[29]

1.   Iowa assistive device tax credit

Small businesses in Iowa can receive a tax credit by buying or renting accessible equipment and making the workplace accessible. To qualify for the Iowa tax credit, Iowa businesses must employ fewer than 15 full time employees or have $3 million dollars or less in gross annual receipts. The credit is for one-half of the first $5,000 for qualifying expenses, with an annual cap of $2,500.[30]

2.   Kansas individual developmental accounts

In 2001, Kansas passed legislation allowing for "Assistive Technology Individual Development Accounts (IDAs)." Eligible individuals (who earn 200 percent of poverty or less) may use earned income toward home ownership, education and training, the procurement of AT, and small business endeavors.

---

[27] See Rehab. Eng'g & Assistive Tech. Soc'y of N. Am., Technical Assistance Project, at http://128.104.192.129/taproject/ (last modified July 9, 2003).

[28] See Assistive Technology Act of 1998, Pub. L. No. 105-394, 112 Stat. 3627 (codified in scattered sections of 29 U.S.C.). For a review of state initiatives, see Technical Assistance Project, Rehab. Eng'g & Assistive Tech. Soc'y of N. Am., Policy Information Pipeline Funding, Tax Credits and Tax Revenue Initiatives of the Assistive Technology Act Projects, at http://128.104.192.129/taproject/policy/funding/taxcredit.html (last modified Jan. 12, 2003). For an excellent series of articles on AT access and financing, see 14 J. Disability Pol'y Stud. 66-125 (2003) (discussing federal and state policies).

[29] In addition, some states provide for a sales tax exemption and tax credit for AT. See id.

[30] For information on the Iowa tax credit, see Clarinda Econ. Dev., Financial Assistance: Assistive Device Tax Credit, at http://www.developiowa.net/assistive_device_tax_credit.htm (last visited Oct. 15, 2003), and Iowa Program for Assistive Tech., 15(1) Infotech Newsletter (Fall 2001), at http://www.uiowa.edu/infotech/News15-1.htm. See also Iowa Code §§ 422.11E, 422.33 (2003); Iowa Admin. Code §§ 261-66 (2001), 701-42.14 (2002).

3.   California Revenue and Tax Code: general accessibility

California Revenue and Tax Code Section 24383 provides a deduction of up to $15,000 for the cost of repair or remodeling of a building, facility, or vehicle to make it more accessible to people with disabilities.

§ 33.4 Illustrative Caselaw: Tax Policy And Disability

In *Hubbard and Hubbard v. Commissioner of Internal Revenue*,[31] the IRS had determined a $5,814 deficiency in Hubbard's Federal income tax for 1997.[32] The issue before the U.S. Tax Court was whether the cost of equipment purchased by Hubbard for use in his optometric practice qualified under Section 44 for the Disabled Access Tax Credit.

During the years in question, Hubbard ran the only optometric practice located in a three-county area of Nevada, with other practices 120 miles away. To aid in the diagnosis of his patients with disabilities, Hubbard purchased for $4,495 a height-adjustable instrument stand that made his tools accessible to patients who use wheelchairs. Using the accessible instrument stand, he was able to conduct his examinations on all of his patients in a more accessible manner.

In 1997, Hubbard claimed on his Federal income tax return a Section 44 Disabled Access Credit of $5,000 for the cost of purchasing the accessible instrument stand. In a notice of deficiency, the IRS disallowed his claimed tax credit because the diagnostic equipment also was used to treat nondisabled patients. Hubbard appealed the decision to the Tax Court.

The court reviewed the case in the context of ADA Title III, noting that professional offices of health care providers, such as Hubbard's optometric practice, are covered places of public accommodation.[33] As such, to comply with Title III's prohibition of discrimination, Hubbard was required to make reasonable modifications to provide services to individuals with disabilities.

As discussed above, Section 44(a) allows certain small businesses a Federal income tax credit equal to 50 percent of eligible access expenditures exceeding $250 and up to $10,250 (with a maximum credit of $ 5,000) to enable businesses to comply with ADA.[34]

---

[31] Hubbard and Hubbard v. Comm'r of Internal Revenue, T.C. Memo 2003-245, 2003 WL 21940724 (T.C. 2003).

[32] Id. In 1997, petitioner's practice had gross receipts of $586,649. Id.

[33] Id. (citing 42 U.S.C. § 12181(7)(F) (2000)).

[34] "Eligible small businesses" are businesses with gross receipts less than $1 million or with less than 30 employees which elect to be treated as

The tax court concluded that Hubbard's entitlement to the Disabled Access Tax Credit was not improper simply because the equipment in question also was used to treat nondisabled patients.

The court noted that there is no exclusive use or benefit test requirement in § 44(a): "a wheelchair ramp into a restaurant for disabled access will be used by nondisabled customers of the restaurant, and nothing in section 44 or the regulations would deprive the restaurant owner of the disabled access tax credit with regard thereto."[35]

Because there also was evidence that it was reasonable and necessary for Hubbard to purchase the equipment to treat patients with disabilities to comply with ADA's prohibition of discrimination, his cost for the equipment was held to be eligible for the Section 44 Disabled Access Tax Credit.

In contrast to the outcome in *Hubbard*, in *Fan v. Commissioner*,[36] a Disabled Access Tax Credit claimed by a dentist relating to the cost of an intra-oral camera system was disallowed.

In *Fan*, the credit was disallowed because, prior to purchasing the camera system, the dentist was in compliance with ADA, for instance, through the use of handwritten notes to communicate with patients with hearing impairments. The Tax Court noted that the equipment in question had general usefulness in treating all of the dentist's patients.[37]

---

such by filing a Form 8826 with the IRS. See 26 U.S.C. § 44(b) (2000). "Eligible access expenditures" are "amounts paid or incurred" by eligible small businesses in complying with ADA, including: (1) Expenditures to "remov[e] architectural, communication, physical, or transportation barriers ... prevent[ing] a business from being accessible to, or usable by, individuals with disabilities;" and (2) expenditures "to acquire or modify equipment" for use by or to benefit individuals with disabilities. See id. §§ 44(c)(2)(A), 44(c)(2)(D). Also, to qualify as eligible access expenditures the expenditures must be reasonable and necessary. Id. § 44(c)(3).

[35] Hubbard and Hubbard, 2003 WL 21940724 (citing 28 C.F.R. § 36.304(b)(1) (2003)).

[36] Fan v. Comm'r, 117 T.C. 32, 34-35, 37 (T.C. 2001).

[37] Cf. Internal Revenue Serv., Misuse of Disabled Access Credits – Law and Arguments, Digital Daily, at http://www.irs.gov/businesses/small/article/0,,id=106480,00.html (last visited Aug. 15, 2003).

APPENDICES

I. FEDERAL AND STATE STATUTES

APPENDIX 1

AMERICANS WITH DISABILITIES ACT OF 1990
CODIFIED AS 42 U.S.C. § 12101 *et seq.*

TABLE OF CONTENTS

§ 12101. Findings and purpose

A Findings

The Congress finds that--

(1) some 43,000,000 Americans have one or more physical or mental disabilities, and this number is increasing as the population as a whole is growing older;

(2) historically, society has tended to isolate and segregate individuals with disabilities, and, despite some improvements, such forms of discrimination against individuals with disabilities continue to be a serious and pervasive social problem;

(3) discrimination against individuals with disabilities persists in such critical areas as employment, housing, public accommodations, education, transportation, communication, recreation, institutionalization, health services, voting, and access to public services;

(4) unlike individuals who have experienced discrimination on the basis of race, color, sex, national origin, religion, or age, individuals who have experienced discrimination on the basis of disability have often had no legal recourse to redress such discrimination;

(5) individuals with disabilities continually encounter various forms of discrimination, including outright intentional exclusion, the discriminatory effects of architectural, transportation, and communication barriers, overprotective rules and policies, failure to make modifications to existing facilities and practices, exclusionary qualification standards and criteria, segregation, and relegation to lesser services, programs, activities, benefits, jobs, or other opportunities;

(6) census data, national polls, and other studies have documented that people with disabilities, as a group, occupy an inferior status in our society, and are severely disadvantaged socially, vocationally, economically, and educationally;

(7) individuals with disabilities are a discrete and insular minority who have been faced with restrictions and limitations, subjected to a history of purposeful unequal treatment, and relegated to a position of political powerlessness in our society, based on characteristics that are beyond the control of such individuals and resulting from stereotypic assumptions not truly indicative of the individual ability of such individuals to participate in, and contribute to, society;

(8) the Nation's proper goals regarding individuals with disabilities are to

assure equality of opportunity, full participation, independent living, and economic self-sufficiency for such individuals; and

(9) the continuing existence of unfair and unnecessary discrimination and prejudice denies people with disabilities the opportunity to compete on an equal basis and to pursue those opportunities for which our free society is justifiably famous, and costs the United States billions of dollars in unnecessary expenses resulting from dependency and nonproductivity.

B Purpose

It is the purpose of this chapter--

(1) to provide a clear and comprehensive national mandate for the elimination of discrimination against individuals with disabilities;

(2) to provide clear, strong, consistent, enforceable standards addressing discrimination against individuals with disabilities;

(3) to ensure that the Federal Government plays a central role in enforcing the standards established in this chapter on behalf of individuals with disabilities; and

(4) to invoke the sweep of congressional authority, including the power to enforce the fourteenth amendment and to regulate commerce, in order to address the major areas of discrimination faced day-to-day by people with disabilities.

§ 12102. Definitions

As used in this chapter:

(1) Auxiliary aids and services

The term "auxiliary aids and services" includes--

(A) qualified interpreters or other effective methods of making aurally delivered materials available to individuals with hearing impairments;

(B) qualified readers, taped texts, or other effective methods of making visually delivered materials available to individuals with visual impairments;

(C) acquisition or modification of equipment or devices; and

(D) other similar services and actions.

(2) Disability

The term "disability" means, with respect to an individual--

(A) a physical or mental impairment that substantially limits one or more of the major life activities of such individual;

(B) a record of such an impairment; or

(C) being regarded as having such an impairment.

(3) State

The term "State" means each of the several States, the District of Columbia, the Commonwealth of Puerto Rico, Guam, American Samoa, the Virgin Islands, the Trust Territory of the Pacific Islands, and the Commonwealth of the Northern Mariana Islands.

SUBCHAPTER I – EMPLOYMENT

§ 12111. Definitions

As used in this subchapter:

(1) Commission

The term "Commission" means the Equal Employment Opportunity Commission established by section 2000e-4 of this title.

(2) Covered entity

The term "covered entity" means an employer, employment agency, labor organization, or joint labor-management committee.

(3) Direct threat

The term "direct threat" means a significant risk to the health or safety of others that cannot be eliminated by reasonable accommodation.

(4) Employee

The term "employee" means an individual employed by an employer. With respect to employment in a foreign country, such term includes an individual who is a citizen of the United States.

(5) Employer

(A) In general

The term "employer" means a person engaged in an industry affecting commerce who has 15 or more employees for each working day in each of 20 or more calendar weeks in the current or preceding calendar year, and any agent of such person, except that, for two years following the effective date of this subchapter, an employer means a person engaged in an industry affecting commerce who has 25 or more employees for each working day in each of 20 or more calendar weeks in the current or preceding year, and any agent of such person.

(B) Exceptions

The term "employer" does not include--

(i) the United States, a corporation wholly owned by the government of the United States, or an Indian tribe; or

(ii) a bona fide private membership club (other than a labor organization) that is exempt from taxation under section 501(c) of Title 26.

(6) Illegal use of drugs

(A) In general

The term "illegal use of drugs" means the use of drugs, the possession or distribution of which is unlawful under the Controlled Substances Act [21 U.S.C.A. § 801 et seq.]. Such term does not include the use of a drug taken under supervision by a licensed health care professional, or other uses authorized by the Controlled Substances Act or other provisions of Federal law.

(B) Drugs

The term "drug" means a controlled substance, as defined in schedules I through V of section 202 of the Controlled Substances Act [21 U.S.C.A. § 812].

(7) Person, etc.

The terms "person", "labor organization", "employment agency", "commerce", and "industry affecting commerce", shall have the same meaning given such terms in section 2000e of this title.

(8) Qualified individual with a disability

The term "qualified individual with a disability" means an individual with a disability who, with or without reasonable accommodation, can perform the essential functions of the employment position that such individual holds or desires. For the purposes of this subchapter, consideration shall be given to the employer's judgment as to what functions of a job are essential, and if an employer has prepared a written description before advertising or interviewing applicants for the job, this description shall be considered evidence of the essential functions of the job.

(9) Reasonable accommodation

The term "reasonable accommodation" may include--

(A) making existing facilities used by employees readily accessible to and usable by individuals with disabilities; and

(B) job restructuring, part-time or modified work schedules, reassignment to a vacant position, acquisition or modification of equipment or devices, appropriate adjustment or modifications of examinations, training materials or policies, the provision of qualified readers or interpreters, and other similar accommodations for individuals with disabilities.

(10) Undue hardship

(A) In general

The term "undue hardship" means an action requiring significant difficulty or expense, when considered in light of the factors set forth in subparagraph (B).

(B) Factors to be considered

In determining whether an accommodation would impose an undue hardship on a covered entity, factors to be considered include--

(i) the nature and cost of the accommodation needed under this chapter;

(ii) the overall financial resources of the facility or facilities involved in the provision of the reasonable accommodation; the number of persons employed at such facility; the effect on expenses and resources, or the impact otherwise of such accommodation upon the operation of the facility;

(iii) the overall financial resources of the covered entity; the overall size of the business of a covered entity with respect to the number of its employees; the number, type, and location of its facilities; and

(iv) the type of operation or operations of the covered entity, including the composition, structure, and functions of the workforce of such entity; the geographic separateness, administrative, or fiscal relationship of the facility or facilities in question to the covered entity.

§ 12112. Discrimination

(a) General rule

No covered entity shall discriminate against a qualified individual with a disability because of the disability of such individual in regard to job application procedures, the hiring, advancement, or discharge of employees, employee compensation, job training, and other terms, conditions, and privileges of employment.

(b) Construction

As used in subsection (a) of this section, the term "discriminate" includes--

(1) limiting, segregating, or classifying a job applicant or employee in a way that adversely affects the opportunities or status of such applicant or employee because of the disability of such applicant or employee;

(2) participating in a contractual or other arrangement or relationship that has the effect of subjecting a covered entity's qualified applicant or employee with a disability to the discrimination prohibited by this subchapter (such relationship includes a relationship with an employment or referral agency, labor union, an organization providing fringe benefits to an employee of the covered entity, or an organization providing training and apprenticeship programs);

(3) utilizing standards, criteria, or methods of administration--

(A) that have the effect of discrimination on the basis of disability; or

(B) that perpetuate the discrimination of others who are subject to common administrative control;

(4) excluding or otherwise denying equal jobs or benefits to a qualified individual because of the known disability of an individual with whom the qualified individual is known to have a relationship or association;

(5)(A) not making reasonable accommodations to the known physical or mental limitations of an otherwise qualified individual with a disability who is an applicant or employee, unless such covered entity can demonstrate that the accommodation would impose an undue hardship on the operation of the business of such covered entity; or

(B) denying employment opportunities to a job applicant or employee who is an otherwise qualified individual with a disability, if such denial is based on the need of such covered entity to make reasonable accommodation to the physical or mental impairments of the employee or applicant;

(6) using qualification standards, employment tests or other selection criteria that screen out or tend to screen out an individual with a disability or a class of individuals with disabilities unless the standard, test or other selection criteria, as used by the covered entity, is shown to be job-related for the position in question and is consistent with business necessity; and

(7) failing to select and administer tests concerning employment in the most effective manner to ensure that, when such test is administered to a job applicant or employee who has a disability that impairs sensory, manual, or speaking skills, such test results accurately reflect the skills, aptitude, or whatever other factor of such applicant or employee that such test purports to measure, rather than reflecting the impaired sensory, manual, or speaking skills of such employee or applicant (except where such skills are the factors that the test purports to measure).

(c) Covered entities in foreign countries

(1) In general

It shall not be unlawful under this section for a covered entity to take any action that constitutes discrimination under this section with respect to an employee in a workplace in a foreign country if compliance with this section would cause such covered entity to violate the law of the foreign country in which such workplace is located.

(2) Control of corporation

(A) Presumption

If an employer controls a corporation whose place of incorporation is a foreign country, any practice that constitutes discrimination under this section and is engaged in by such corporation shall be presumed to be engaged in by such employer.

(B) Exception

This section shall not apply with respect to the foreign operations of an employer that is a foreign person not controlled by an American employer.

(C) Determination

For purposes of this paragraph, the determination of whether an employer controls a corporation shall be based on--

(i) the interrelation of operations;

(ii) the common management;

(iii) the centralized control of labor relations; and

(iv) the common ownership or financial control, of the employer and the corporation.

(d) Medical examinations and inquiries

(1) In general

The prohibition against discrimination as referred to in subsection (a) of this section shall include medical examinations and inquiries.

(2) Preemployment

(A) Prohibited examination or inquiry

Except as provided in paragraph (3), a covered entity shall not conduct a medical examination or make inquiries of a job applicant as to whether such applicant is an individual with a disability or as to the nature or severity of such disability.

(B) Acceptable inquiry

A covered entity may make preemployment inquiries into the ability of an applicant to perform job-related functions.

(3) Employment entrance examination

A covered entity may require a medical examination after an offer of employment has been made to a job applicant and prior to the commencement of the employment duties of such applicant, and may condition an offer of employment on the results of such examination, if--

(A) all entering employees are subjected to such an examination regardless of disability;

(B) information obtained regarding the medical condition or history of the applicant is collected and maintained on separate forms and in separate medical files and is treated as a confidential medical record, except that--

(i) supervisors and managers may be informed regarding necessary restrictions on the work or duties of the employee and necessary accommodations;

(ii) first aid and safety personnel may be informed, when appropriate, if the disability might require emergency treatment; and

(iii) government officials investigating compliance with this chapter shall be provided relevant information on request; and

(C) the results of such examination are used only in accordance with this subchapter.

(4) Examination and inquiry

(A) Prohibited examinations and inquiries

A covered entity shall not require a medical examination and shall not make inquiries of an employee as to whether such employee is an individual with a disability or as to the nature or severity of the disability, unless such examination or inquiry is shown to be job-related and consistent with business necessity.

(B) Acceptable examinations and inquiries

A covered entity may conduct voluntary medical examinations, including voluntary medical histories, which are part of an employee health program available to employees at that work site. A covered entity may make inquiries into the ability of an employee to perform job-related functions.

(C) Requirement

Information obtained under subparagraph (B) regarding the medical condition or history of any employee are subject to the requirements of subparagraphs (B) and (C) of paragraph (3).

§ 12113. Defenses

(a) In general

It may be a defense to a charge of discrimination under this chapter that an alleged application of qualification standards, tests, or selection criteria that screen out or tend to screen out or otherwise deny a job or benefit to an individual with a disability has been shown to be job-related and consistent with business necessity, and such performance cannot be accomplished by reasonable accommodation, as required under this subchapter.

(b) Qualification standards

The term "qualification standards" may include a requirement that an individual shall not pose a direct threat to the health or safety of other individuals in the workplace.

(c) Religious entities

(1) In general

This subchapter shall not prohibit a religious corporation, association, educational institution, or society from giving preference in employment to individuals of a particular religion to perform work connected with the carrying on by such corporation, association, educational institution, or society of its activities.

(2) Religious tenets requirement

Under this subchapter, a religious organization may require that all applicants and employees conform to the religious tenets of such organization.

(d) List of infectious and communicable diseases

(1) In general

The Secretary of Health and Human Services, not later than 6 months after July 26, 1990, shall--

(A) review all infectious and communicable diseases which may be transmitted through handling the food supply;

(B) publish a list of infectious and communicable diseases which are transmitted through handling the food supply;

(C) publish the methods by which such diseases are transmitted; and

(D) widely disseminate such information regarding the list of diseases and their modes of transmissability [FN1] to the general public.

Such list shall be updated annually.

(2) Applications

In any case in which an individual has an infectious or communicable disease that is transmitted to others through the handling of food, that is included on the list developed by the Secretary of Health and Human Services under paragraph (1), and which cannot be eliminated by reasonable accommodation, a covered entity may refuse to assign or continue to assign such individual to a job involving food handling.

(3) Construction

Nothing in this chapter shall be construed to preempt, modify, or amend any State, county, or local law, ordinance, or regulation applicable to food handling which is designed to protect the public health from individuals who pose a significant risk to the health or safety of others, which cannot be eliminated by reasonable accommodation, pursuant to the list of infectious or communicable diseases and the modes of transmissability [FN1] published by the Secretary of Health and Human Services.

§ 12114. Illegal use of drugs and alcohol

(a) Qualified individual with a disability

For purposes of this subchapter, the term "qualified individual with a disability" shall not include any employee or applicant who is currently engaging in the illegal use of drugs, when the covered entity acts on the basis of such use.

(b) Rules of construction

Nothing in subsection (a) of this section shall be construed to exclude as a qualified individual with a disability an individual who--

(1) has successfully completed a supervised drug rehabilitation program and is no longer engaging in the illegal use of drugs, or has otherwise been rehabilitated successfully and is no longer engaging in such use;

(2) is participating in a supervised rehabilitation program and is no longer engaging in such use; or

(3) is erroneously regarded as engaging in such use, but is not engaging in such use;

except that it shall not be a violation of this chapter for a covered entity to adopt or administer reasonable policies or procedures, including but not limited to drug testing, designed to ensure that an individual described in paragraph (1) or (2) is no longer engaging in the illegal use of drugs.

(c) Authority of covered entity

A covered entity--

(1) may prohibit the illegal use of drugs and the use of alcohol at the workplace by all employees;

(2) may require that employees shall not be under the influence of alcohol or be engaging in the illegal use of drugs at the workplace;

(3) may require that employees behave in conformance with the requirements established under the Drug-Free Workplace Act of 1988 (41 U.S.C. 701 et seq.);

(4) may hold an employee who engages in the illegal use of drugs or who is an alcoholic to the same qualification standards for employment or job performance and behavior that such entity holds other employees, even if any unsatisfactory performance or behavior is related to the drug use or alcoholism of such employee; and

(5) may, with respect to Federal regulations regarding alcohol and the illegal use of drugs, require that--

(A) employees comply with the standards established in such regulations of the Department of Defense, if the employees of the covered entity are employed in an industry subject to such regulations, including complying with regulations (if any) that apply to employment in sensitive positions in such an industry, in the case of employees of the covered entity who are employed in such positions (as defined in the regulations of the Department of Defense);

(B) employees comply with the standards established in such regulations of the Nuclear Regulatory Commission, if the employees of the covered entity are employed in an industry subject to such regulations, including complying with regulations (if any) that apply to employment in sensitive positions in such an industry, in the case of employees of the covered entity who are employed in such positions (as defined in the regulations of the Nuclear Regulatory Commission); and

(C) employees comply with the standards established in such regulations of the Department of Transportation, if the employees of the covered entity are employed in a transportation industry subject to such regulations, including complying with such regulations (if any) that apply to employment in sensitive positions in such an industry, in the case of employees of the covered entity who are employed in such positions (as defined in the regulations of the Department of Transportation).

(d) Drug testing

(1) In general

For purposes of this subchapter, a test to determine the illegal use of drugs shall not be considered a medical examination.

(2) Construction

Nothing in this subchapter shall be construed to encourage, prohibit, or authorize the conducting of drug testing for the illegal use of drugs by job applicants or employees or making employment decisions based on such test results.

(e) Transportation employees

Nothing in this subchapter shall be construed to encourage, prohibit, restrict, or authorize the otherwise lawful exercise by entities subject to the jurisdiction of the Department of Transportation of authority to--

(1) test employees of such entities in, and applicants for, positions involving safety-sensitive duties for the illegal use of drugs and for on-duty impairment by alcohol; and

(2) remove such persons who test positive for illegal use of drugs and on-duty impairment by alcohol pursuant to paragraph (1) from safety-sensitive duties in implementing subsection (c) of this section.

§ 12115. Posting notices

Every employer, employment agency, labor organization, or joint labor-management committee covered under this subchapter shall post notices in an accessible format to applicants, employees, and members describing the applicable provisions of this chapter, in the manner prescribed by section 2000e-10 of this title.

§ 12116. Regulations

Not later than 1 year after July 26, 1990, the Commission shall issue regulations in an accessible format to carry out this subchapter in accordance with subchapter II of chapter 5 of Title 5.

§ 12117. Enforcement

(a) Powers, remedies, and procedures

The powers, remedies, and procedures set forth in sections 2000e-4, 2000e-5, 2000e-6, 2000e-8, and 2000e-9 of this title shall be the powers, remedies, and procedures this subchapter provides to the Commission, to the Attorney General, or to any person alleging discrimination on the basis of disability in violation of any provision of this chapter, or regulations promulgated under section 12116 of this title, concerning employment.

(b) Coordination

The agencies with enforcement authority for actions which allege employment discrimination under this subchapter and under the Rehabilitation Act of 1973 [29 U.S.C.A. § 701 et seq.] shall develop procedures to ensure that administrative complaints filed under this subchapter and under the Rehabilitation Act of 1973 are dealt with in a manner that avoids duplication of effort and prevents imposition of inconsistent or conflicting standards for the same requirements under this subchapter and the Rehabilitation Act of 1973. The Commission, the Attorney General, and the Office of Federal Contract Compliance Programs shall establish such coordinating mechanisms (similar to provisions contained in the joint regulations promulgated by the Commission and the Attorney General at part 42 of title 28 and part 1691 of title 29, Code of Federal Regulations, and the Memorandum of Understanding between the Commission and the Office of Federal Contract Compliance Programs dated January 16, 1981 (46 Fed.Reg. 7435, January 23, 1981)) in regulations implementing this subchapter and Rehabilitation Act of 1973 not later than 18 months after July 26, 1990.

SUBCHAPTER II - PUBLIC SERVICES

§ 12131. Definitions

As used in this subchapter:

(1) Public entity

The term "public entity" means--

(A) any State or local government;

(B) any department, agency, special purpose district, or other instrumentality of a State or States or local government; and

(C) the National Railroad Passenger Corporation, and any commuter authority (as defined in section 502(8) of Title 45).

(2) Qualified individual with a disability

The term "qualified individual with a disability" means an individual with a disability who, with or without reasonable modifications to rules, policies, or practices, the removal of architectural, communication, or transportation barriers, or the provision of auxiliary aids and services, meets the essential eligibility requirements for the receipt of services or the participation in programs or activities provided by a public entity.

§ 12132. Discrimination

Subject to the provisions of this subchapter, no qualified individual with a disability shall, by reason of such disability, be excluded from participation in or be denied the benefits of the services, programs, or activities of a public entity, or be subjected to discrimination by any such entity.

§ 12133. Enforcement

The remedies, procedures, and rights set forth in section 794a of Title 29 shall be the remedies, procedures, and rights this subchapter provides to any person alleging discrimination on the basis of disability in violation of section 12132 of this title.

§ 12134. Regulations

(a) In general

Not later than 1 year after July 26, 1990, the Attorney General shall promulgate regulations in an accessible format that implement this part. Such regulations shall not include any matter within the scope of the authority of the Secretary of Transportation under section 12143, 12149, or 12164 of this title.

(b) Relationship to other regulations

Except for "program accessibility, existing facilities", and "communications", regulations under subsection (a) of this section shall be consistent with this chapter and with the coordination regulations under part 41 of title 28, Code of Federal Regulations (as promulgated by the Department of Health, Education, and Welfare on January 13, 1978), applicable to recipients of Federal financial assistance under section 794 of Title 29. With respect to "program accessibility, existing facilities", and "communications", such regulations shall be consistent with regulations and analysis as in part 39 of title 28 of the Code of Federal Regulations, applicable to federally conducted activities under such section 794 of Title 29.

(c) Standards

Regulations under subsection (a) of this section shall include standards applicable to facilities and vehicles covered by this part, other than facilities, stations, rail passenger cars, and vehicles covered by part B of this subchapter. Such standards shall be consistent with the minimum guidelines and requirements issued by the Architectural and Transportation Barriers Compliance Board in accordance with section 12204(a) of this title.

§ 12141. Definitions

As used in this subpart:

(1) Demand responsive system

The term "demand responsive system" means any system of providing designated public transportation which is not a fixed route system.

(2) Designated public transportation

The term "designated public transportation" means transportation (other than public school transportation) by bus, rail, or any other conveyance (other than transportation by aircraft or intercity or commuter rail transportation (as defined in section 12161 of this title)) that provides the general public with general or special service (including charter service) on a regular and continuing basis.

(3) Fixed route system

The term "fixed route system" means a system of providing designated public transportation on which a vehicle is operated along a prescribed route according to a fixed schedule.

(4) Operates

The term "operates", as used with respect to a fixed route system or demand responsive system, includes operation of such system by a person under a contractual or other arrangement or relationship with a public entity.

(5) Public school transportation

The term "public school transportation" means transportation by schoolbus vehicles of schoolchildren, personnel, and equipment to and from a public elementary or secondary school and school-related activities.

(6) Secretary

The term "Secretary" means the Secretary of Transportation.

§ 12142. Public entities operating fixed route systems

(a) Purchase and lease of new vehicles

It shall be considered discrimination for purposes of section 12132 of this title and section 794 of Title 29 for a public entity which operates a fixed route system to purchase or lease a new bus, a new rapid rail vehicle, a new light rail vehicle, or any other new vehicle to be used on such system, if the solicitation for such purchase or lease is made after the 30th day following July 26, 1990, and if such bus, rail vehicle, or other vehicle is not readily accessible to and usable by individuals with disabilities, including individuals who use wheelchairs.

(b) Purchase and lease of used vehicles

Subject to subsection (c)(1) of this section, it shall be considered discrimination for purposes of section 12132 of this title and section 794 of Title 29 for a public entity which operates a fixed route system to purchase or lease, after the 30th day following July 26, 1990, a used vehicle for use on such system unless such entity makes demonstrated good faith efforts to purchase or lease a used vehicle for use on such system that is readily accessible to and usable by individuals with disabilities, including individuals who use wheelchairs.

(c) Remanufactured vehicles

(1) General rule

Except as provided in paragraph (2), it shall be considered discrimination for purposes of section 12132 of this title and section 794 of Title 29 for a public entity which operates a fixed route system--

(A) to remanufacture a vehicle for use on such system so as to extend its usable life for 5 years or more, which remanufacture begins (or for which the solicitation is made) after the 30th day following July 26, 1990; or

(B) to purchase or lease for use on such system a remanufactured vehicle which has been remanufactured so as to extend its usable life for 5 years or more, which purchase or lease occurs after such 30th day and during the period in which the usable life is extended;

unless, after remanufacture, the vehicle is, to the maximum extent feasible, readily accessible to and usable by individuals with disabilities, including individuals who use wheelchairs.

(2) Exception for historic vehicles

(A) General rule

If a public entity operates a fixed route system any segment of which is included on the National Register of Historic Places and if making a vehicle of historic character to be used solely on such segment readily accessible to and usable by individuals with disabilities would significantly alter the historic character of such vehicle, the public entity only has to make (or to purchase or lease a remanufactured vehicle with) those modifications which are necessary to meet the requirements of paragraph (1) and which do not significantly alter the historic character of such vehicle.

(B) Vehicles of historic character defined by regulations

For purposes of this paragraph and section 12148(b) of this title, a vehicle of historic character shall be defined by the regulations issued by the Secretary to carry out this subsection.

§ 12143. Paratransit as a complement to fixed route service

(a) General rule

It shall be considered discrimination for purposes of section 12132 of this title and section 794 of Title 29 for a public entity which operates a fixed route system (other than a system which provides solely commuter bus service) to fail to provide with respect to the operations of its fixed route system, in accordance with this section, paratransit and other special transportation services to individuals with disabilities, including individuals who use wheelchairs, that are sufficient to provide to such individuals a level of service (1) which is comparable to the level of designated public transportation services provided to individuals without disabilities using such system; or (2) in the case of response time, which is comparable, to the extent practicable, to the level of designated public transportation services provided to individuals without disabilities using such system.

(b) Issuance of regulations

Not later than 1 year after July 26, 1990, the Secretary shall issue final regulations to carry out this section.

(c) Required contents of regulations

(1) Eligible recipients of service

The regulations issued under this section shall require each public entity which operates a fixed route system to provide the paratransit and other special transportation services required under this section--

(A)(i) to any individual with a disability who is unable, as a result of a physical or mental impairment (including a vision impairment) and without the assistance of another individual (except an operator of a wheelchair lift or other boarding assistance device), to board, ride, or disembark from any vehicle on the system which is readily accessible to and usable by individuals with disabilities;

(ii) to any individual with a disability who needs the assistance of a wheelchair lift or other boarding assistance device (and is able with such assistance) to board, ride, and disembark from any vehicle which is readily accessible to and usable by individuals with disabilities if the individual wants to travel on a route on the system during the hours of operation of the system at a time (or within a reasonable period of such time) when such a vehicle is not being used to provide designated public transportation on the route; and

(iii) to any individual with a disability who has a specific impairment-related condition which prevents such individual from traveling to a boarding location or from a disembarking location on such system;

(B) to one other individual accompanying the individual with the disability; and

(C) to other individuals, in addition to the one individual described in subparagraph (B), accompanying the individual with a disability provided that space for these additional individuals is available on the paratransit vehicle carrying the individual with a disability and that the transportation of such additional individuals will not result in a denial of service to individuals with disabilities.

For purposes of clauses (i) and (ii) of subparagraph (A), boarding or disembarking from a vehicle does not include travel to the boarding location or from the disembarking location.

(2) Service area

The regulations issued under this section shall require the provision of paratransit and special transportation services required under this section in the service area of each public entity which operates a fixed route system, other than any portion of the service area in which the public entity solely provides commuter bus service.

(3) Service criteria

Subject to paragraphs (1) and (2), the regulations issued under this section shall establish minimum service criteria for determining the level of services to be required under this section.

(4) Undue financial burden limitation

The regulations issued under this section shall provide that, if the public entity is able to demonstrate to the satisfaction of the Secretary that the provision of paratransit and other special transportation services otherwise required under this section would impose an undue financial burden on the public entity, the public entity, notwithstanding any other provision of this section (other than paragraph (5)), shall only be required to provide such services to the extent that providing such services would not impose such a burden.

(5) Additional services

The regulations issued under this section shall establish circumstances under which the Secretary may require a public entity to provide, notwithstanding paragraph (4), paratransit and other special transportation services under this section beyond the level of paratransit and other special transportation services which would otherwise be required under paragraph (4).

(6) Public participation

The regulations issued under this section shall require that each public entity which operates a fixed route system hold a public hearing, provide an opportunity for public comment, and consult with individuals with disabilities in preparing its plan under paragraph (7).

(7) Plans

The regulations issued under this section shall require that each public entity which operates a fixed route system--

(A) within 18 months after July 26, 1990, submit to the Secretary, and commence implementation of, a plan for providing paratransit and other special transportation services which meets the requirements of this section; and

(B) on an annual basis thereafter, submit to the Secretary, and commence implementation of, a plan for providing such services.

(8) Provision of services by others

The regulations issued under this section shall--

(A) require that a public entity submitting a plan to the Secretary under this section identify in the plan any person or other public entity which is providing a paratransit or other special transportation service for individuals with disabilities in the service area to which the plan applies; and

(B) provide that the public entity submitting the plan does not have to provide under the plan such service for individuals with disabilities.

(9) Other provisions

The regulations issued under this section shall include such other provisions and requirements as the Secretary determines are necessary to carry out the objectives of this section.

(d) Review of plan

(1) General rule

The Secretary shall review a plan submitted under this section for the purpose of determining whether or not such plan meets the requirements of this section, including the regulations issued under this section.

(2) Disapproval

If the Secretary determines that a plan reviewed under this subsection fails to meet the requirements of this section, the Secretary shall disapprove the plan and notify the public entity which submitted the plan of such disapproval and the reasons therefor.

(3) Modification of disapproved plan

Not later than 90 days after the date of disapproval of a plan under this subsection, the public entity which submitted the plan shall modify the plan to meet the requirements of this section and shall submit to the Secretary, and commence implementation of, such modified plan.

(e) "Discrimination" defined

As used in subsection (a) of this section, the term "discrimination" includes--

(1) a failure of a public entity to which the regulations issued under this section apply to submit, or commence implementation of, a plan in accordance with subsections (c)(6) and (c)(7) of this section;

(2) a failure of such entity to submit, or commence implementation of, a

modified plan in accordance with subsection (d)(3) of this section;

(3) submission to the Secretary of a modified plan under subsection (d)(3) of this section which does not meet the requirements of this section; or

(4) a failure of such entity to provide paratransit or other special transportation services in accordance with the plan or modified plan the public entity submitted to the Secretary under this section.

(f) Statutory construction

Nothing in this section shall be construed as preventing a public entity--

(1) from providing paratransit or other special transportation services at a level which is greater than the level of such services which are required by this section,

(2) from providing paratransit or other special transportation services in addition to those paratransit and special transportation services required by this section, or

(3) from providing such services to individuals in addition to those individuals to whom such services are required to be provided by this section.

§ 12144. Public entity operating a demand responsive system

If a public entity operates a demand responsive system, it shall be considered discrimination, for purposes of section 12132 of this title and section 794 of Title 29, for such entity to purchase or lease a new vehicle for use on such system, for which a solicitation is made after the 30th day following July 26, 1990, that is not readily accessible to and usable by individuals with disabilities, including individuals who use wheelchairs, unless such system, when viewed in its entirety, provides a level of service to such individuals equivalent to the level of service such system provides to individuals without disabilities.

§ 12145. Temporary relief where lifts are unavailable

(a) Granting

With respect to the purchase of new buses, a public entity may apply for, and the Secretary may temporarily relieve such public entity from the obligation under section 12142(a) or 12144 of this title to purchase new buses that are readily accessible to and usable by individuals with disabilities if such public entity demonstrates to the satisfaction of the Secretary--

(1) that the initial solicitation for new buses made by the public entity specified that all new buses were to be lift-equipped and were to be otherwise accessible to and usable by individuals with disabilities;

(2) the unavailability from any qualified manufacturer of hydraulic, electromechanical, or other lifts for such new buses;

(3) that the public entity seeking temporary relief has made good faith efforts to locate a qualified manufacturer to supply the lifts to the manufacturer of such buses in sufficient time to comply with such solicitation; and

(4) that any further delay in purchasing new buses necessary to obtain such lifts would significantly impair transportation services in the community served by the public entity.

(b) Duration and notice to Congress

Any relief granted under subsection (a) of this section shall be limited in duration by a specified date, and the appropriate committees of Congress shall be notified of any such relief granted.

(c) Fraudulent application

If, at any time, the Secretary has reasonable cause to believe that any relief granted under subsection (a) of this section was fraudulently applied for, the Secretary shall--

(1) cancel such relief if such relief is still in effect; and

(2) take such other action as the Secretary considers appropriate.

§ 12146. New facilities

For purposes of section 12132 of this title and section 794 of Title 29, it shall be considered discrimination for a public entity to construct a new facility to be used in the provision of designated public transportation services unless such facility is readily accessible to and usable by individuals with disabilities, including individuals who use wheelchairs.

§ 12147. Alterations of existing facilities

(a) General rule

With respect to alterations of an existing facility or part thereof used in the provision of designated public transportation services that affect or could affect the usability of the facility or part thereof, it shall be considered discrimination, for purposes of section 12132 of this title and section 794 of Title 29, for a public entity to fail to make such alterations (or to ensure that the alterations are made) in such a manner that, to the maximum extent feasible, the altered portions of the facility are readily accessible to and usable by individuals with disabilities, including individuals who use wheelchairs, upon the completion of such alterations. Where the public entity is undertaking an alteration that affects or could affect usability of or access to an area of the facility containing a primary function, the entity shall also make the alterations in such a manner that, to the maximum extent feasible, the path of travel to the altered area and the bathrooms, telephones, and drinking fountains serving the altered area, are readily accessible to and usable by individuals with disabilities, including individuals who use wheelchairs, upon completion of such alterations, where such alterations to the path of travel or the bathrooms, telephones, and drinking fountains serving the altered area are not disproportionate to the overall alterations in terms of cost and scope (as determined under criteria established by the Attorney General).

(b) Special rule for stations

(1) General rule

For purposes of section 12132 of this title and section 794 of Title 29, it shall be considered discrimination for a public entity that provides designated public transportation to fail, in accordance with the provisions of this subsection, to make key stations (as determined under criteria established by the Secretary by regulation) in rapid rail and light rail systems readily accessible to and usable by individuals with disabilities, including individuals who use wheelchairs.

(2) Rapid rail and light rail key stations

(A) Accessibility

Except as otherwise provided in this paragraph, all key stations (as determined under criteria established by the Secretary by regulation) in rapid rail and light rail systems shall be made readily accessible to and usable by individuals with disabilities, including individuals who use wheelchairs, as soon as practicable but in no event later than the last day of the 3-year period beginning on July 26, 1990.

(B) Extension for extraordinarily expensive structural changes

The Secretary may extend the 3-year period under subparagraph (A) up to a 30- year period for key stations in a rapid rail or light rail system which stations need extraordinarily expensive structural changes to, or replacement of, existing facilities; except that by the last day of the 20th year following July 26, 1990, at least 2/3 of such key stations must be readily accessible to and usable by individuals with disabilities.

(3) Plans and milestones

The Secretary shall require the appropriate public entity to develop and submit to the Secretary a plan for compliance with this subsection--

(A) that reflects consultation with individuals with disabilities affected by such plan and the results of a public hearing and public comments on such plan, and

(B) that establishes milestones for achievement of the requirements of this subsection.

§ 12148. Public transportation programs and activities in existing facilities and one car per train rule

(a) Public transportation programs and activities in existing facilities

(1) In general

With respect to existing facilities used in the provision of designated public transportation services, it shall be considered discrimination, for purposes of section 12132 of this title and section 794 of Title 29, for a public entity to fail to operate a designated public transportation program or activity conducted in such facilities so that, when viewed in the entirety, the program or activity is readily accessible to and usable by individuals with disabilities.

(2) Exception

Paragraph (1) shall not require a public entity to make structural changes to existing facilities in order to make such facilities accessible to individuals who use wheelchairs, unless and to the extent required by section 12147(a) of this title (relating to alterations) or section 12147(b) of this title (relating to key stations).

(3) Utilization

Paragraph (1) shall not require a public entity to which paragraph (2) applies, to provide to individuals who use wheelchairs services made available to the general public at such facilities when such individuals could not utilize or benefit from such services provided at such facilities.

(b) One car per train rule

(1) General rule

Subject to paragraph (2), with respect to 2 or more vehicles operated as a train by a light or rapid rail system, for purposes of section 12132 of this title and section 794 of Title 29, it shall be considered discrimination for a public entity to fail to have at least 1 vehicle per train that is accessible to individuals with disabilities, including individuals who use wheelchairs, as soon as practicable but in no event later than the last day of the 5-year period beginning on the effective date of this section.

(2) Historic trains

In order to comply with paragraph (1) with respect to the remanufacture of a vehicle of historic character which is to be used on a segment of a light or rapid rail system which is included on the National Register of Historic Places, if making such vehicle readily accessible to and usable by individuals with disabilities would significantly alter the historic character of such vehicle, the public entity which operates such system only has to make (or to purchase or lease a remanufactured vehicle with) those modifications which are necessary to meet the requirements of section 12142(c)(1) of this title and which do not significantly alter the historic character of such vehicle.

§ 12149. Regulations

(a) In general

Not later than 1 year after July 26, 1990, the Secretary of Transportation shall issue regulations, in an accessible format, necessary for carrying out this subpart (other than section 12143 of this title).

(b) Standards

The regulations issued under this section and section 12143 of this title shall include standards applicable to facilities and vehicles covered by this part. The standards shall be consistent with the minimum guidelines and requirements issued by the Architectural and Transportation Barriers Compliance Board in accordance with section 12204 of this title.

§ 12150. Interim accessibility requirements

If final regulations have not been issued pursuant to section 12149 of this title, for new construction or alterations for which a valid and appropriate State or local building permit is obtained prior to the issuance of final regulations under such section, and for which the construction or alteration authorized by such permit begins within one year of the receipt of such permit and is completed under the terms of such permit, compliance with the Uniform Federal Accessibility Standards in effect at the time the building permit is issued shall suffice to satisfy the requirement that facilities be readily accessible to and usable by persons with disabilities as required under sections 12146 and 12147 of this title, except that, if such final regulations have not been issued one year after the Architectural and Transportation Barriers Compliance Board has issued the supplemental minimum guidelines required under section 12204(a) of this title, compliance with such supplemental minimum guidelines shall be necessary to satisfy the requirement that facilities be readily accessible to and usable by persons with disabilities prior to issuance of the final regulations.

§ 12161. Definitions

As used in this subpart:

(1) Commuter authority

The term "commuter authority" has the meaning given such term in section 502(8) of Title 45.

(2) Commuter rail transportation

The term "commuter rail transportation" has the meaning given the term "commuter rail passenger transportation" in section 502(9) of Title 45.

(3) Intercity rail transportation

The term "intercity rail transportation" means transportation provided by the National Railroad Passenger Corporation.

(4) Rail passenger car

The term "rail passenger car" means, with respect to intercity rail transportation, single-level and bi-level coach cars, single-level and bi-level dining cars, single-level and bi-level sleeping cars, single-level and bi-level lounge cars, and food service cars.

(5) Responsible person

The term "responsible person" means--

(A) in the case of a station more than 50 percent of which is owned by a public entity, such public entity;

(B) in the case of a station more than 50 percent of which is owned by a private party, the persons providing intercity or commuter rail transportation to such station, as allocated on an equitable basis by regulation by the Secretary of Transportation; and

(C) in a case where no party owns more than 50 percent of a station, the persons providing intercity or commuter rail transportation to such station and the owners of the station, other than private party owners, as allocated on an equitable basis by regulation by the Secretary of Transportation.

(6) Station

The term "station" means the portion of a property located appurtenant to a right-of-way on which intercity or commuter rail transportation is operated, where such portion is used by the general public and is related to the provision of such transportation, including passenger platforms, designated waiting areas, ticketing areas, restrooms, and, where a public entity providing rail transportation owns the property, concession areas, to the extent that such public entity exercises control over the selection, design, construction, or alteration of the property, but such term does not include flag stops.

§ 12162. Intercity and commuter rail actions considered discriminatory

(a) Intercity rail transportation

(1) One car per train rule

It shall be considered discrimination for purposes of section 12132 of this title and section 794 of Title 29 for a person who provides intercity rail transportation to fail to have at least one passenger car per train that is readily accessible to and usable by individuals with disabilities, including individuals who use wheelchairs, in accordance with regulations issued under section 12164 of this title, as soon as practicable, but in no event later than 5 years after July 26, 1990.

(2) New intercity cars

(A) General rule

Except as otherwise provided in this subsection with respect to individuals who use wheelchairs, it shall be considered discrimination for purposes of section 12132 of this title and section 794 of Title 29 for a person to purchase or lease any new rail passenger cars for use in intercity rail transportation, and for which a solicitation is made later than 30 days after July 26, 1990, unless all such rail cars are readily accessible to and usable by individuals with disabilities, including individuals who use wheelchairs, as prescribed by the Secretary of Transportation in regulations issued under section 12164 of this title.

(B) Special rule for single-level passenger coaches for individuals who use wheelchairs

Single-level passenger coaches shall be required to--

(i) be able to be entered by an individual who uses a wheelchair;

(ii) have space to park and secure a wheelchair;

(iii) have a seat to which a passenger in a wheelchair can transfer, and a space to fold and store such passenger's wheelchair; and

(iv) have a restroom usable by an individual who uses a wheelchair, only to the extent provided in paragraph (3).

(C) Special rule for single-level dining cars for individuals who use wheelchairs

Single-level dining cars shall not be required to--

(i) be able to be entered from the station platform by an individual who uses a wheelchair; or

(ii) have a restroom usable by an individual who uses a wheelchair if no restroom is provided in such car for any passenger.

(D) Special rule for bi-level dining cars for individuals who use wheelchairs

Bi-level dining cars shall not be required to--

(i) be able to be entered by an individual who uses a wheelchair;

(ii) have space to park and secure a wheelchair;

(iii) have a seat to which a passenger in a wheelchair can transfer, or a space to fold and store such passenger's wheelchair; or

(iv) have a restroom usable by an individual who uses a wheelchair.

(3) Accessibility of single-level coaches

(A) General rule

It shall be considered discrimination for purposes of section 12132 of this title and section 794 of Title 29 for a person who provides intercity rail transportation to fail to have on each train which includes one or more single- level rail passenger coaches--

(i) a number of spaces--

(I) to park and secure wheelchairs (to accommodate individuals who wish to remain in their wheelchairs) equal to not less than one-half of the number of single-level rail passenger coaches in such train; and

(II) to fold and store wheelchairs (to accommodate individuals who wish to transfer to coach seats) equal to not less than one-half of the number of single-level rail passenger coaches in such train,

as soon as practicable, but in no event later than 5 years after July 26, 1990; and

(ii) a number of spaces--

(I) to park and secure wheelchairs (to accommodate individuals who wish to remain in their wheelchairs) equal to not less than the total number of single- level rail passenger coaches in such train; and

(II) to fold and store wheelchairs (to accommodate individuals who wish to transfer to coach seats) equal to not less than the total number of single-level rail passenger coaches in such train,

as soon as practicable, but in no event later than 10 years after July 26, 1990.

(B) Location

Spaces required by subparagraph (A) shall be located in single-level rail passenger coaches or food service cars.

(C) Limitation

Of the number of spaces required on a train by subparagraph (A), not more than two spaces to park and secure wheelchairs nor more than two spaces to fold and store wheelchairs shall be located in any one coach or food service car.

(D) Other accessibility features

Single-level rail passenger coaches and food service cars on which the spaces required by subparagraph (A) are located shall have a restroom usable by an individual who uses a wheelchair and shall be able to be entered from the station platform by an individual who uses a wheelchair.

(4) Food service

(A) Single-level dining cars

On any train in which a single-level dining car is used to provide food service--

(i) if such single-level dining car was purchased after July 26, 1990, table service in such car shall be provided to a passenger who uses a wheelchair if--

(I) the car adjacent to the end of the dining car through which a wheelchair may enter is itself accessible to a wheelchair;

(II) such passenger can exit to the platform from the car such passenger occupies, move down the platform, and enter the adjacent accessible car described in subclause (I) without the necessity of the train being moved within the station; and

(III) space to park and secure a wheelchair is available in the dining car at the time such passenger wishes to eat (if such passenger wishes to remain in a wheelchair), or space to store and fold a wheelchair is available in the dining car at the time such passenger wishes to eat (if such passenger wishes to transfer to a dining car seat); and

(ii) appropriate auxiliary aids and services, including a hard surface on which to eat, shall be provided to ensure that other equivalent food service is available to individuals with disabilities, including individuals who use wheelchairs, and to passengers traveling with such individuals.

Unless not practicable, a person providing intercity rail transportation shall place an accessible car adjacent to the end of a dining car described in clause (i) through which an individual who uses a wheelchair may enter.

(B) Bi-level dining cars

On any train in which a bi-level dining car is used to provide food service--

(i) if such train includes a bi-level lounge car purchased after July 26, 1990, table service in such lounge car shall be provided to individuals who use wheelchairs and to other passengers; and

(ii) appropriate auxiliary aids and services, including a hard surface on which to eat, shall be provided to ensure that other equivalent food service is available to individuals with disabilities, including individuals who use wheelchairs, and to passengers traveling with such individuals.

(b) Commuter rail transportation

(1) One car per train rule

It shall be considered discrimination for purposes of section 12132 of this title and section 794 of Title 29 for a person who provides commuter rail transportation to fail to have at least one passenger car per train that is readily accessible to and usable by individuals with disabilities, including individuals who use wheelchairs, in accordance with regulations issued under section 12164 of this title, as soon as practicable, but in no event later than 5 years after July 26, 1990.

(2) New commuter rail cars

(A) General rule

It shall be considered discrimination for purposes of section 12132 of this title and section 794 of Title 29 for a person to purchase or lease any new rail passenger cars for use in commuter rail transportation, and for which a solicitation is made later than 30 days after July 26, 1990, unless all such rail cars are readily accessible to and usable by individuals with disabilities, including individuals who use wheelchairs, as prescribed by the Secretary of Transportation in regulations issued under section 12164 of this title.

(B) Accessibility

For purposes of section 12132 of this title and section 794 of Title 29, a requirement that a rail passenger car used in commuter rail transportation be accessible to or readily accessible to and usable by individuals with disabilities, including individuals who use wheelchairs, shall not be construed to require--

(i) a restroom usable by an individual who uses a wheelchair if no restroom is provided in such car for any passenger;

(ii) space to fold and store a wheelchair; or

(iii) a seat to which a passenger who uses a wheelchair can transfer.

(c) Used rail cars

It shall be considered discrimination for purposes of section 12132 of this title and section 794 of Title 29, for a person to purchase or lease a used rail passenger car for use in intercity or commuter rail transportation, unless such person makes demonstrated good faith efforts to purchase or lease a used rail car that is readily accessible to and usable by individuals with disabilities, including individuals who use wheelchairs, as prescribed by the Secretary of Transportation in regulations issued under section 12164 of this title.

(d) Remanufactured rail cars

(1) Remanufacturing

It shall be considered discrimination for purposes of section 12132 of this title and section 794 of Title 29 for a person to remanufacture a rail passenger car for use in intercity or commuter rail transportation so as to extend its usable life for 10 years or more, unless the rail car, to the maximum extent feasible, is made readily accessible to and usable by individuals with disabilities, including individuals who use wheelchairs, as prescribed by the Secretary of Transportation in regulations issued under section 12164 of this title.

(2) Purchase or lease

It shall be considered discrimination for purposes of section 12132 of this title and section 794 of Title 29 for a person to purchase or lease a remanufactured rail passenger car for use in intercity or commuter rail transportation unless such car was remanufactured in accordance with paragraph (1).

(e) Stations

(1) New stations

It shall be considered discrimination for purposes of section 12132 of this title and section 794 of Title 29 for a person to build a new station for use in intercity or commuter rail transportation that is not readily accessible to and usable by individuals with disabilities, including individuals who use wheelchairs, as prescribed by the Secretary of Transportation in regulations issued under section 12164 of this title.

(2) Existing stations

(A) Failure to make readily accessible

(i) General rule

It shall be considered discrimination for purposes of section 12132 of this title and section 794 of Title 29 for a responsible person to fail to make existing stations in the intercity rail transportation system, and existing key stations in commuter rail transportation systems, readily accessible to and usable by individuals with disabilities, including individuals who use wheelchairs, as prescribed by the Secretary of Transportation in regulations issued under section 12164 of this title.

(ii) Period for compliance

(I) Intercity rail

All stations in the intercity rail transportation system shall be made readily accessible to and usable by individuals with disabilities, including individuals who use wheelchairs, as soon as practicable, but in no event later than 20 years after July 26, 1990.

(II) Commuter rail

Key stations in commuter rail transportation systems shall be made readily accessible to and usable by individuals with disabilities, including individuals who use wheelchairs, as soon as practicable but in no event later than 3 years after July 26, 1990, except that the time limit may be extended by the Secretary of Transportation up to 20 years after July 26, 1990, in a case where the raising of the entire passenger platform is the only means available of attaining accessibility or where other extraordinarily expensive structural changes are necessary to attain accessibility.

(iii) Designation of key stations

Each commuter authority shall designate the key stations in its commuter rail transportation system, in consultation with individuals with disabilities and organizations representing such individuals, taking into consideration such factors as high ridership and whether such station serves as a transfer or feeder station. Before the final designation of key stations under this clause, a commuter authority shall hold a public hearing.

(iv) Plans and milestones

The Secretary of Transportation shall require the appropriate person to develop a plan for carrying out this subparagraph that reflects consultation with individuals with disabilities affected by such plan and that establishes milestones for achievement of the requirements of this subparagraph.

(B) Requirement when making alterations

(i) General rule

It shall be considered discrimination, for purposes of section 12132 of this title and section 794 of Title 29, with respect to alterations of an existing station or part thereof in the intercity or commuter rail transportation systems that affect or could affect the usability of the station or part thereof, for the responsible person, owner, or person in control of the station to fail to make the alterations in such a manner that, to the maximum extent feasible, the altered portions of the station are readily accessible to and usable by individuals with disabilities, including individuals who use wheelchairs, upon completion of such alterations.

(ii) Alterations to a primary function area

It shall be considered discrimination, for purposes of section 12132 of this title and section 794 of Title 29, with respect to alterations that affect or could affect the usability of or access to an area of the station containing a primary function, for the responsible person, owner, or person in control of the station to fail to make the alterations in such a manner that, to the maximum extent feasible, the path of travel to the altered area, and the bathrooms, telephones, and drinking fountains serving the altered area, are readily accessible to and usable by individuals with disabilities, including individuals who use wheelchairs, upon completion of such alterations, where such alterations to the path of travel or the bathrooms, telephones, and drinking fountains serving the altered area are not disproportionate to the overall alterations in terms of cost and scope (as determined under criteria established by the Attorney General).

(C) Required cooperation

It shall be considered discrimination for purposes of section 12132 of this title and section 794 of Title 29 for an owner, or person in control, of a station governed by subparagraph (A) or (B) to fail to provide reasonable cooperation to a responsible person with respect to such station in that responsible person's efforts to comply with such subparagraph. An owner, or person in control, of a station shall be liable to a responsible person for any failure to provide reasonable cooperation as required by this subparagraph. Failure to receive reasonable cooperation required by this subparagraph shall not be a defense to a claim of discrimination under this chapter.

§ 12163. Conformance of accessibility standards

Accessibility standards included in regulations issued under this subpart shall be consistent with the minimum guidelines issued by the Architectural and Transportation Barriers Compliance Board under section 12204(a) of this title.

§ 12164. Regulations

Not later than 1 year after July 26, 1990, the Secretary of Transportation shall issue regulations, in an accessible format, necessary for carrying out this subpart.

§ 12165. Interim accessibility requirements

(a) Stations

If final regulations have not been issued pursuant to section 12164 of this title, for new construction or alterations for which a valid and appropriate State or local building permit is obtained prior to the issuance of final regulations under such section, and for which the construction or alteration authorized by such permit begins within one year of the receipt of such permit and is completed under the terms of such permit, compliance with the Uniform Federal Accessibility Standards in effect at the time the building permit is issued shall suffice to satisfy the requirement that stations be readily accessible to and usable by persons with disabilities as required under section 12162(e) of this title, except that, if such final regulations have not been issued one year after the Architectural and Transportation Barriers Compliance Board has issued the supplemental minimum guidelines required under section 12204(a) of this title, compliance with such supplemental minimum guidelines shall be necessary to satisfy the requirement that stations be readily accessible to and usable by persons with disabilities prior to issuance of the final regulations.

(b) Rail passenger cars

If final regulations have not been issued pursuant to section 12164 of this title, a person shall be considered to have complied with the requirements of section 12162(a) through (d) of this title that a rail passenger car be readily accessible to and usable by individuals with disabilities, if the design for such car complies with the laws and regulations (including the Minimum Guidelines and Requirements for Accessible Design and such supplemental minimum guidelines as are issued under section 12204(a) of this title) governing accessibility of such cars, to the extent that such laws and regulations are not inconsistent with this subpart and are in effect at the time such design is substantially completed.

SUBCHAPTER III - PUBLIC ACCOMMODATIONS AND SERVICES OPERATED BY PRIVATE ENTITIES

§ 12181. Definitions

As used in this subchapter:

(1) Commerce

The term "commerce" means travel, trade, traffic, commerce, transportation, or communication--

(A) among the several States;

(B) between any foreign country or any territory or possession and any State; or

(C) between points in the same State but through another State or foreign country.

(2) Commercial facilities

The term "commercial facilities" means facilities--

(A) that are intended for nonresidential use; and

(B) whose operations will affect commerce.

Such term shall not include railroad locomotives, railroad freight cars, railroad cabooses, railroad cars described in section 12162 or covered under this subchapter, railroad rights-of-way, or facilities that are covered or expressly exempted from coverage under the Fair Housing Act of 1968 (42 U.S.C. 3601 et seq.).

(3) Demand responsive system

The term "demand responsive system" means any system of providing transportation of individuals by a vehicle, other than a system which is a fixed route system.

(4) Fixed route system

The term "fixed route system" means a system of providing transportation of individuals (other than by aircraft) on which a vehicle is operated along a prescribed route according to a fixed schedule.

(5) Over-the-road bus

The term "over-the-road bus" means a bus characterized by an elevated passenger deck located over a baggage compartment.

(6) Private entity

The term "private entity" means any entity other than a public entity (as defined in section 12131(1) of this title).

(7) Public accommodation

The following private entities are considered public accommodations for purposes of this subchapter, if the operations of such entities affect commerce--

(A) an inn, hotel, motel, or other place of lodging, except for an establishment located within a building that contains not more than five rooms for rent or hire and that is actually occupied by the proprietor of such establishment as the residence of such proprietor;

(B) a restaurant, bar, or other establishment serving food or drink;

(C) a motion picture house, theater, concert hall, stadium, or other place of exhibition or entertainment;

(D) an auditorium, convention center, lecture hall, or other place of public gathering;

(E) a bakery, grocery store, clothing store, hardware store, shopping center, or other sales or rental establishment;

(F) a laundromat, dry-cleaner, bank, barber shop, beauty shop, travel service, shoe repair service, funeral parlor, gas station, office of an accountant or lawyer, pharmacy, insurance office, professional office of a health care provider, hospital, or other service establishment;

(G) a terminal, depot, or other station used for specified public transportation;

(H) a museum, library, gallery, or other place of public display or collection;

(I) a park, zoo, amusement park, or other place of recreation;

(J) a nursery, elementary, secondary, undergraduate, or postgraduate private school, or other place of education;

(K) a day care center, senior citizen center, homeless shelter, food bank, adoption agency, or other social service center establishment; and

(L) a gymnasium, health spa, bowling alley, golf course, or other place of exercise or recreation.

(8) Rail and railroad

The terms "rail" and "railroad" have the meaning given the term "railroad" in section 431(e) of Title 45.

(9) Readily achievable

The term "readily achievable" means easily accomplishable and able to be carried out without much difficulty or expense. In determining whether an action is readily achievable, factors to be considered include--

(A) the nature and cost of the action needed under this chapter;

(B) the overall financial resources of the facility or facilities involved in the action; the number of persons employed at such facility; the effect on expenses and resources, or the impact otherwise of such action upon the operation of the facility;

(C) the overall financial resources of the covered entity; the overall size of the business of a covered entity with respect to the number of its employees; the number, type, and location of its facilities; and

(D) the type of operation or operations of the covered entity, including the composition, structure, and functions of the workforce of such entity; the geographic separateness, administrative or fiscal relationship of the facility or facilities in question to the covered entity.

(10) Specified public transportation

The term "specified public transportation" means transportation by bus, rail, or any other conveyance (other than by aircraft) that provides the general public with general or special service (including charter service) on a regular and continuing basis.

(11) Vehicle

The term "vehicle" does not include a rail passenger car, railroad locomotive, railroad freight car, railroad caboose, or a railroad car described in section 12162 of this title or covered under this subchapter.

§ 12182. Prohibition of discrimination by public accommodations

(a) General rule

No individual shall be discriminated against on the basis of disability in the full and equal enjoyment of the goods, services, facilities, privileges, advantages, or accommodations of any place of public accommodation by any person who owns, leases (or leases to), or operates a place of public accommodation.

(b) Construction

(1) General prohibition

(A) Activities

(i) Denial of participation

It shall be discriminatory to subject an individual or class of individuals on the basis of a disability or disabilities of such individual or class, directly, or through contractual, licensing, or other arrangements, to a denial of the opportunity of the individual or class to participate in or benefit from the goods, services, facilities, privileges, advantages, or accommodations of an entity.

(ii) Participation in unequal benefit

It shall be discriminatory to afford an individual or class of individuals, on the basis of a disability or disabilities of such individual or class, directly, or through contractual, licensing, or other arrangements with the opportunity to participate in or benefit from a good, service, facility, privilege, advantage, or accommodation that is not equal to that afforded to other individuals.

(iii) Separate benefit

It shall be discriminatory to provide an individual or class of individuals, on the basis of a disability or disabilities of such individual or class, directly, or through contractual, licensing, or other arrangements with a good, service, facility, privilege, advantage, or accommodation that is different or separate from that provided to other individuals, unless such action is necessary to provide the individual or class of individuals with a good, service, facility, privilege, advantage, or accommodation, or other opportunity that is as effective as that provided to others.

(iv) Individual or class of individuals

For purposes of clauses (i) through (iii) of this subparagraph, the term "individual or class of individuals" refers to the clients or customers of the covered public accommodation that enters into the contractual, licensing or other arrangement.

(B) Integrated settings

Goods, services, facilities, privileges, advantages, and accommodations shall be afforded to an individual with a disability in the most integrated setting appropriate to the needs of the individual.

(C) Opportunity to participate

Notwithstanding the existence of separate or different programs or activities provided in accordance with this section, an individual with a disability shall not be denied the opportunity to participate in such programs or activities that are not separate or different.

(D) Administrative methods

An individual or entity shall not, directly or through contractual or other arrangements, utilize standards or criteria or methods of administration--

(i) that have the effect of discriminating on the basis of disability; or

(ii) that perpetuate the discrimination of others who are subject to common administrative control.

(E) Association

It shall be discriminatory to exclude or otherwise deny equal goods, services, facilities, privileges, advantages, accommodations, or other opportunities to an individual or entity because of the known disability of an individual with whom the individual or entity is known to have a relationship or association.

(2) Specific prohibitions

(A) Discrimination

For purposes of subsection (a) of this section, discrimination includes--

(i) the imposition or application of eligibility criteria that screen out or tend to screen out an individual with a disability or any class of individuals with disabilities from fully and equally enjoying any goods, services, facilities, privileges, advantages, or accommodations, unless such criteria can be shown to be necessary for the provision of the goods, services, facilities, privileges, advantages, or accommodations being offered;

(ii) a failure to make reasonable modifications in policies, practices, or procedures, when such modifications are necessary to afford such goods, services, facilities, privileges, advantages, or accommodations to individuals with disabilities, unless the entity can demonstrate that making such modifications would fundamentally alter the nature of such goods, services, facilities, privileges, advantages, or accommodations;

(iii) a failure to take such steps as may be necessary to ensure that no individual with a disability is excluded, denied services, segregated or otherwise treated differently than other individuals because of the absence of auxiliary aids and services, unless the entity can demonstrate that taking such steps would fundamentally alter the nature of the good, service, facility, privilege, advantage, or accommodation being offered or would result in an undue burden;

(iv) a failure to remove architectural barriers, and communication barriers that are structural in nature, in existing facilities, and transportation barriers in existing vehicles and rail passenger cars used by an establishment for transporting individuals (not including barriers that can only be removed through the retrofitting of vehicles or rail passenger cars by the installation of a hydraulic or other lift), where such removal is readily achievable; and

(v) where an entity can demonstrate that the removal of a barrier under clause (iv) is not readily achievable, a failure to make such goods, services, facilities, privileges, advantages, or accommodations available through alternative methods if such methods are readily achievable.

(B) Fixed route system

(i) Accessibility

It shall be considered discrimination for a private entity which operates a fixed route system and which is not subject to section 12184 of this title to purchase or lease a vehicle with a seating capacity in excess of 16 passengers (including the driver) for use on such system, for which a solicitation is made after the 30th day following the effective date of this subparagraph, that is not readily accessible to and usable by individuals with disabilities, including individuals who use wheelchairs.

(ii) Equivalent service

If a private entity which operates a fixed route system and which is not subject to section 12184 of this title purchases or leases a vehicle with a seating capacity of 16 passengers or less (including the driver) for use on such system after the effective date of this subparagraph that is not readily accessible to or usable by individuals with disabilities, it shall be considered discrimination for such entity to fail to operate such system so that, when viewed in its entirety, such system ensures a level of service to individuals with disabilities, including individuals who use wheelchairs, equivalent to the level of service provided to individuals without disabilities.

(C) Demand responsive system

For purposes of subsection (a) of this section, discrimination includes--

(i) a failure of a private entity which operates a demand responsive system and which is not subject to section 12184 of this title to operate such system so that, when viewed in its entirety, such system ensures a level of service to individuals with disabilities, including individuals who use wheelchairs, equivalent to the level of service provided to individuals without disabilities; and

(ii) the purchase or lease by such entity for use on such system of a vehicle with a seating capacity in excess of 16 passengers (including the driver), for which solicitations are made after the 30th day following the effective date of this subparagraph, that is not readily accessible to and usable by individuals with disabilities (including individuals who use wheelchairs) unless such entity can demonstrate that such system, when viewed in its entirety, provides a level of service to individuals with disabilities equivalent to that provided to individuals without disabilities.

(D) Over-the-road buses

(i) Limitation on applicability

Subparagraphs (B) and (C) do not apply to over-the-road buses.

(ii) Accessibility requirements

For purposes of subsection (a) of this section, discrimination includes (I) the purchase or lease of an over-the-road bus which does not comply with the regulations issued under section 12186(a)(2) of this title by a private entity which provides transportation of individuals and which is not primarily engaged in the business of transporting people, and (II) any other failure of such entity to comply with such regulations.

(3) Specific construction

Nothing in this subchapter shall require an entity to permit an individual to participate in or benefit from the goods, services, facilities, privileges, advantages and accommodations of such entity where such individual poses a direct threat to the health or safety of others. The term "direct threat" means a significant risk to the health or safety of others that not be eliminated by a modification of policies, practices, or procedures e provision of auxiliary aids or services.

§ 12183. New construction and alterations in public accommodations and commercial facilities

(a) Application of term

Except as provided in subsection (b) of this section, as applied to public accommodations and commercial facilities, discrimination for purposes of section 12182(a) of this title includes--

(1) a failure to design and construct facilities for first occupancy later than 30 months after July 26, 1990, that are readily accessible to and usable by individuals with disabilities, except where an entity can demonstrate that it is structurally impracticable to meet the requirements of such subsection in accordance with standards set forth or incorporated by reference in regulations issued under this subchapter; and

(2) with respect to a facility or part thereof that is altered by, on behalf of, or for the use of an establishment in a manner that affects or could affect the usability of the facility or part thereof, a failure to make alterations in such a manner that, to the maximum extent feasible, the altered portions of the facility are readily accessible to and usable by individuals with disabilities, including individuals who use wheelchairs. Where the entity is undertaking an alteration that affects or could affect usability of or access to an area of the facility containing a primary function, the entity shall also make the alterations in such a manner that, to the maximum extent feasible, the path of travel to the altered area and the bathrooms, telephones, and drinking fountains serving the altered area, are readily accessible to and usable by individuals with disabilities where such alterations to the path of travel or the bathrooms, telephones, and drinking fountains serving the altered area are not disproportionate to the overall alterations in terms of cost and scope (as determined under criteria established by the Attorney General).

(b) Elevator

Subsection (a) of this section shall not be construed to require the installation of an elevator for facilities that are less than three stories or have less than 3,000 square feet per story unless the building is a shopping center, a shopping mall, or the professional office of a health care provider or unless the Attorney General determines that a particular category of such facilities requires the installation of elevators based on the usage of such facilities.

§ 12184. Prohibition of discrimination in specified public transportation services provided by private entities

(a) General rule

No individual shall be discriminated against on the basis of disability in the full and equal enjoyment of specified public transportation services provided by a private entity that is primarily engaged in the business of transporting people and whose operations affect commerce.

(b) Construction

For purposes of subsection (a) of this section, discrimination includes--

(1) the imposition or application by a [FN1] entity described in subsection (a) of this section of eligibility criteria that screen out or tend to screen out an individual with a disability or any class of individuals with disabilities from fully enjoying the specified public transportation services provided by the entity, unless such criteria can be shown to be necessary for the provision of the services being offered;

(2) the failure of such entity to--

(A) make reasonable modifications consistent with those required under section 12182(b)(2)(A)(ii) of this title;

(B) provide auxiliary aids and services consistent with the requirements of section 12182(b)(2)(A)(iii) of this title; and

(C) remove barriers consistent with the requirements of section 12182(b)(2)(A) of this title and with the requirements of section 12183(a)(2) of this title;

(3) the purchase or lease by such entity of a new vehicle (other than an automobile, a van with a seating capacity of less than 8 passengers, including the driver, or an over-the-road bus) which is to be used to provide specified public transportation and for which a solicitation is made after the 30th day following the effective date of this section, that is not readily accessible to and usable by individuals with disabilities, including individuals who use wheelchairs; except that the new vehicle need not be readily accessible to and usable by such individuals if the new vehicle is to be used solely in a demand responsive system and if the entity can demonstrate that such system, when viewed in its entirety, provides a level of service to such individuals equivalent to the level of service provided to the general public;

(4)(A) the purchase or lease by such entity of an over-the-road bus which does not comply with the regulations issued under section 12186(a)(2) of ' title; and

ther failure of such entity to comply with such regulations; and

(5) the purchase or lease by such entity of a new van with a seating capacity of less than 8 passengers, including the driver, which is to be used to provide specified public transportation and for which a solicitation is made after the 30th day following the effective date of this section that is not readily accessible to or usable by individuals with disabilities, including individuals who use wheelchairs; except that the new van need not be readily accessible to and usable by such individuals if the entity can demonstrate that the system for which the van is being purchased or leased, when viewed in its entirety, provides a level of service to such individuals equivalent to the level of service provided to the general public;

(6) the purchase or lease by such entity of a new rail passenger car that is to be used to provide specified public transportation, and for which a solicitation is made later than 30 days after the effective date of this paragraph, that is not readily accessible to and usable by individuals with disabilities, including individuals who use wheelchairs; and

(7) the remanufacture by such entity of a rail passenger car that is to be used to provide specified public transportation so as to extend its usable life for 10 years or more, or the purchase or lease by such entity of such a rail car, unless the rail car, to the maximum extent feasible, is made readily accessible to and usable by individuals with disabilities, including individuals who use wheelchairs.

(c) Historical or antiquated cars

(1) Exception

To the extent that compliance with subsection (b)(2)(C) or (b)(7) of this section would significantly alter the historic or antiquated character of a historical or antiquated rail passenger car, or a rail station served exclusively by such cars, or would result in violation of any rule, regulation, standard, or order issued by the Secretary of Transportation under the Federal Railroad Safety Act of 1970 [45 U.S.C.A. § 431 et seq.], such compliance shall not be required.

(2) Definition

As used in this subsection, the term "historical or antiquated rail passenger car" means a rail passenger car--

(A) which is not less than 30 years old at the time of its use for transporting individuals;

(B) the manufacturer of which is no longer in the business of manufacturing rail passenger cars; and

(C) which--

(i) has a consequential association with events or persons significant to the past; or

(ii) embodies, or is being restored to embody, the distinctive characteristics of a type of rail passenger car used in the past, or to represent a time period which has passed.

§ 12185. Study

(a) Purposes

The Office of Technology Assessment shall undertake a study to determine--

(1) the access needs of individuals with disabilities to over-the-road buses and over-the-road bus service; and

(2) the most cost-effective methods for providing access to over-the-road buses and over-the-road bus service to individuals with disabilities, particularly individuals who use wheelchairs, through all forms of boarding options.

(b) Contents

The study shall include, at a minimum, an analysis of the following:

(1) The anticipated demand by individuals with disabilities for accessible over-the-road buses and over-the-road bus service.

(2) The degree to which such buses and service, including any service required under sections 12184(b)(4) and 12186(a)(2) of this title, are readily accessible to and usable by individuals with disabilities.

(3) The effectiveness of various methods of providing accessibility to such buses and service to individuals with disabilities.

(4) The cost of providing accessible over-the-road buses and bus service to individuals with disabilities, including consideration of recent technological and cost saving developments in equipment and devices.

(5) Possible design changes in over-the-road buses that could enhance accessibility, including the installation of accessible restrooms which do not result in a loss of seating capacity.

(6) The impact of accessibility requirements on the continuation of

over-the- road bus service, with particular consideration of the impact of such requirements on such service to rural communities.

(c) Advisory committee

In conducting the study required by subsection (a) of this section, the Office of Technology Assessment shall establish an advisory committee, which shall consist of--

(1) members selected from among private operators and manufacturers of over- the-road buses;

(2) members selected from among individuals with disabilities, particularly individuals who use wheelchairs, who are potential riders of such buses; and

(3) members selected for their technical expertise on issues included in the study, including manufacturers of boarding assistance equipment and devices.

The number of members selected under each of paragraphs (1) and (2) shall be equal, and the total number of members selected under paragraphs (1) and (2) shall exceed the number of members selected under paragraph (3).

(d) Deadline

The study required by subsection (a) of this section, along with recommendations by the Office of Technology Assessment, including any policy options for legislative action, shall be submitted to the President and Congress within 36 months after July 26, 1990. If the President determines that compliance with the regulations issued pursuant to section 12186(a)(2)(B) of this title on or before the applicable deadlines specified in section 12186(a)(2)(B) of this title will result in a significant reduction in intercity over-the-road bus service, the President shall extend each such deadline by 1 year.

(e) Review

In developing the study required by subsection (a) of this section, the Office of Technology Assessment shall provide a preliminary draft of such study to the Architectural and Transportation Barriers Compliance Board established under section 792 of Title 29. The Board shall have an opportunity to comment on such draft study, and any such comments by the Board made in writing within 120 days after the Board's receipt of the draft study shall be incorporated as part of the final study required to be submitted under subsection (d) of this section.

§ 12186. Regulations

(a) Transportation provisions

(1) General rule

Not later than 1 year after July 26, 1990, the Secretary of Transportation shall issue regulations in an accessible format to carry out sections [FN1] 12182(b)(2)(B) and (C) of this title and to carry out section 12184 of this title (other than subsection (b)(4)).

(2) Special rules for providing access to over-the-road buses

(A) Interim requirements

(i) Issuance

Not later than 1 year after July 26, 1990, the Secretary of Transportation shall issue regulations in an accessible format to carry out sections 12184(b)(4) and 12182(b)(2)(D)(ii) of this title that require each private entity which uses an over-the-road bus to provide transportation of individuals to provide accessibility to such bus; except that such regulations shall not require any structural changes in over-the-road buses in order to provide access to individuals who use wheelchairs during the effective period of such regulations and shall not require the purchase of boarding assistance devices to provide access to such individuals.

(ii) Effective period

The regulations issued pursuant to this subparagraph shall be effective until the effective date of the regulations issued under subparagraph (B).

(B) Final requirement

(i) Review of study and interim requirements

The Secretary shall review the study submitted under section 12185 of this title and the regulations issued pursuant to subparagraph (A).

(ii) Issuance

Not later than 1 year after the date of the submission of the study under section 12185 of this title, the Secretary shall issue in an accessible format new regulations to carry out sections 12184(b)(4) and 12182(b)(2)(D)(ii) of this title that require, taking into account the purposes of the study under section 12185 of this title and any recommendations resulting from such study, each private entity which uses an over-the-road bus to provide transportation to individuals to provide accessibility to such bus to individuals with disabilities, including individuals who use wheelchairs.

(iii) Effective period

Subject to section 12185(d) of this title, the regulations issued pursuant to this subparagraph shall take effect--

(I) with respect to small providers of transportation (as defined by the Secretary), 3 years after the date of issuance of final regulations under clause (ii); and

(II) with respect to other providers of transportation, 2 years after the date of issuance of such final regulations.

(C) Limitation on requiring installation of accessible restrooms

The regulations issued pursuant to this paragraph shall not require the installation of accessible restrooms in over-the-road buses if such installation would result in a loss of seating capacity.

(3) Standards

The regulations issued pursuant to this subsection shall include standards applicable to facilities and vehicles covered by sections 12182(b)(2) and 12184 of this title.

(b) Other provisions

Not later than 1 year after July 26, 1990, the Attorney General shall issue regulations in an accessible format to carry out the provisions of this subchapter not referred to in subsection (a) of this section that include standards applicable to facilities and vehicles covered under section 12182 of this title.

(c) Consistency with ATBCB guidelines

Standards included in regulations issued under subsections (a) and (b) of this section shall be consistent with the minimum guidelines and requirements issued by the Architectural and Transportation Barriers Compliance Board in accordance with section 12204 of this title.

(d) Interim accessibility standards

(1) Facilities

If final regulations have not been issued pursuant to this section, for new construction or alterations for which a valid and appropriate State or local building permit is obtained prior to the issuance of final regulations under this section, and for which the construction or alteration authorized by such permit begins within one year of the receipt of such permit and is completed under the terms of such permit, compliance with the Uniform Federal Accessibility Standards in effect at the time the building permit is issued shall suffice to satisfy the requirement that facilities be readily accessible to and usable by persons with disabilities as required under section 12183 of this title, except that, if such final regulations have not been issued one year after the Architectural and Transportation Barriers Compliance Board has issued the supplemental minimum guidelines required under section 12204(a) of this title, compliance with such supplemental minimum guidelines shall be necessary to satisfy the requirement that facilities be readily accessible to and usable by persons with disabilities prior to issuance of the final regulations.

(2) Vehicles and rail passenger cars

If final regulations have not been issued pursuant to this section, a private entity shall be considered to have complied with the requirements of this subchapter, if any, that a vehicle or rail passenger car be readily accessible to and usable by individuals with disabilities, if the design for such vehicle or car complies with the laws and regulations (including the Minimum Guidelines and Requirements for Accessible Design and such supplemental minimum guidelines as are issued under section 12204(a) of this title) governing accessibility of such vehicles or cars, to the extent that such laws and regulations are not inconsistent with this subchapter and are in effect at the time such design is substantially completed.

§ 12187. Exemptions for private clubs and religious organizations

The provisions of this subchapter shall not apply to private clubs or establishments exempted from coverage under title II of the Civil Rights Act of 1964 (42 U.S.C. 2000-a(e)) [42 U.S.C.A. § 2000a et seq.] or to religious organizations or entities controlled by religious organizations, including places of worship.

§ 12188. Enforcement

(a) In general

(1) Availability of remedies and procedures

The remedies and procedures set forth in section 2000a-3(a) of this title are the remedies and procedures this subchapter provides to any person who is being subjected to discrimination on the basis of disability in violation of this subchapter or who has reasonable grounds for believing that such person is about to be subjected to discrimination in violation of section 12183 of this title. Nothing in this section shall require a person with a disability to engage in a futile gesture if such person has actual notice that a person or organization covered by this subchapter does not intend to comply with its provisions.

(2) Injunctive relief

In the case of violations of sections 12182(b)(2)(A)(iv) and section [FN1] 12183(a) of this title, injunctive relief shall include an order to alter facilities to make such facilities readily accessible to and usable by individuals with disabilities to the extent required by this subchapter. Where appropriate, injunctive relief shall also include requiring the provision of an auxiliary aid or service, modification of a policy, or provision of alternative methods, to the extent required by this subchapter.

(b) Enforcement by Attorney General

(1) Denial of rights

(A) Duty to investigate

(i) In general

The Attorney General shall investigate alleged violations of this subchapter, and shall undertake periodic reviews of compliance of covered entities under this subchapter.

(ii) Attorney General certification

On the application of a State or local government, the Attorney General may, in consultation with the Architectural and Transportation Barriers Compliance Board, and after prior notice and a public hearing at which persons, including individuals with disabilities, are provided an opportunity to testify against such certification, certify that a State law or local building code or similar ordinance that establishes accessibility requirements meets or exceeds the minimum requirements of this chapter for the accessibility and usability of covered facilities under this subchapter. At any enforcement proceeding under this section, such certification by the Attorney General shall be rebuttable evidence that such State law or local ordinance does meet or exceed the minimum requirements of this chapter.

(B) Potential violation

If the Attorney General has reasonable cause to believe that--

(i) any person or group of persons is engaged in a pattern or practice of discrimination under this subchapter; or

(ii) any person or group of persons has been discriminated against under this subchapter and such discrimination raises an issue of general public importance,

the Attorney General may commence a civil action in any appropriate United States district court.

(2) Authority of court

In a civil action under paragraph (1)(B), the court--

(A) may grant any equitable relief that such court considers to be appropriate, including, to the extent required by this subchapter--

(i) granting temporary, preliminary, or permanent relief;

(ii) providing an auxiliary aid or service, modification of policy, practice, or procedure, or alternative method; and

(iii) making facilities readily accessible to and usable by individuals with disabilities;

(B) may award such other relief as the court considers to be appropriate, including monetary damages to persons aggrieved when requested by the Attorney General; and

(C) may, to vindicate the public interest, assess a civil penalty against the entity in an amount--

(i) not exceeding $50,000 for a first violation; and

(ii) not exceeding $100,000 for any subsequent violation.

(3) Single violation

For purposes of paragraph (2)(C), in determining whether a first or subsequent violation has occurred, a determination in a single action, by judgment or settlement, that the covered entity has engaged in more than one discriminatory act shall be counted as a single violation.

(4) Punitive damages

For purposes of subsection (b)(2)(B) of this section, the term "monetary damages" and "such other relief" does not include punitive damages.

(5) Judicial consideration

In a civil action under paragraph (1)(B), the court, when considering what amount of civil penalty, if any, is appropriate, shall give consideration to any good faith effort or attempt to comply with this chapter by the entity. In evaluating good faith, the court shall consider, among other factors it deems relevant, whether the entity could have reasonably anticipated the need for an appropriate type of auxiliary aid needed to accommodate the unique needs of a particular individual with a disability.

§ 12189. Examinations and courses

Any person that offers examinations or courses related to applications, licensing, certification, or credentialing for secondary or post-secondary education, professional, or trade purposes shall offer such examinations or courses in a place and manner accessible to persons with disabilities or offer alternative accessible arrangements for such individuals.

SUBCHAPTER IV - MISCELLANEOUS PROVISIONS

§ 12201. Construction

(a) In general

Except as otherwise provided in this chapter, nothing in this chapter shall be construed to apply a lesser standard than the standards applied under title V of the Rehabilitation Act of 1973 (29 U.S.C. 790 et seq.) or the regulations issued by Federal agencies pursuant to such title.

(b) Relationship to other laws

Nothing in this chapter shall be construed to invalidate or limit the remedies, rights, and procedures of any Federal law or law of any State or political subdivision of any State or jurisdiction that provides greater or equal protection for the rights of individuals with disabilities than are afforded by this chapter. Nothing in this chapter shall be construed to preclude the prohibition of, or the imposition of restrictions on, smoking in places of employment covered by subchapter I of this chapter, in transportation covered by subchapter II or III of this chapter, or in places of public accommodation covered by subchapter III of this chapter.

(c) Insurance

Subchapters I through III of this chapter and title IV of this Act shall not be construed to prohibit or restrict--

(1) an insurer, hospital or medical service company, health maintenance

organization, or any agent, or entity that administers benefit plans, or similar organizations from underwriting risks, classifying risks, or administering such risks that are based on or not inconsistent with State law; or

(2) a person or organization covered by this chapter from establishing, sponsoring, observing or administering the terms of a bona fide benefit plan that are based on underwriting risks, classifying risks, or administering such risks that are based on or not inconsistent with State law; or

(3) a person or organization covered by this chapter from establishing, sponsoring, observing or administering the terms of a bona fide benefit plan that is not subject to State laws that regulate insurance.

Paragraphs (1), (2), and (3) shall not be used as a subterfuge to evade the purposes of subchapter [FN1] I and III of this chapter.

(d) Accommodations and services

Nothing in this chapter shall be construed to require an individual with a disability to accept an accommodation, aid, service, opportunity, or benefit which such individual chooses not to accept.

§ 12202. State immunity

A State shall not be immune under the eleventh amendment to the Constitution of the United States from an action in [FN1] Federal or State court of competent jurisdiction for a violation of this chapter. In any action against a State for a violation of the requirements of this chapter, remedies (including remedies both at law and in equity) are available for such a violation to the same extent as such remedies are available for such a violation in an action against any public or private entity other than a State.

§ 12203. Prohibition against retaliation and coercion

(a) Retaliation

No person shall discriminate against any individual because such individual has opposed any act or practice made unlawful by this chapter or because such individual made a charge, testified, assisted, or participated in any manner in an investigation, proceeding, or hearing under this chapter.

(b) Interference, coercion, or intimidation

It shall be unlawful to coerce, intimidate, threaten, or interfere with any individual in the exercise or enjoyment of, or on account of his or her having exercised or enjoyed, or on account of his or her having aided or encouraged any other individual in the exercise or enjoyment of, any right granted or protected by this chapter.

(c) Remedies and procedures

The remedies and procedures available under sections 12117, 12133, and 12188 of this title shall be available to aggrieved persons for violations of subsections (a) and (b) of this section, with respect to subchapter I, subchapter II and subchapter III of this chapter, respectively.

§ 12204. Regulations by Architectural and Transportation Barriers Compliance Board

(a) Issuance of guidelines

Not later than 9 months after July 26, 1990, the Architectural and Transportation Barriers Compliance Board shall issue minimum guidelines that shall supplement the existing Minimum Guidelines and Requirements for Accessible Design for purposes of subchapters II and III of this chapter.

(b) Contents of guidelines

The supplemental guidelines issued under subsection (a) of this section shall establish additional requirements, consistent with this chapter, to ensure that buildings, facilities, rail passenger cars, and vehicles are accessible, in terms of architecture and design, transportation, and communication, to individuals with disabilities.

(c) Qualified historic properties

(1) In general

The supplemental guidelines issued under subsection (a) of this section shall include procedures and requirements for alterations that will threaten or destroy the historic significance of qualified historic buildings and facilities as defined in 4.1.7(1)(a) of the Uniform Federal Accessibility Standards.

(2) Sites eligible for listing in National Register

With respect to alterations of buildings or facilities that are eligible for listing in the National Register of Historic Places under the National Historic Preservation Act (16 U.S.C. 470 et seq.), the guidelines described in paragraph (1) shall, at a minimum, maintain the procedures and requirements established in 4.1.7(1) and (2) of the Uniform Federal Accessibility Standards.

(3) Other sites

With respect to alterations of buildings or facilities designated as historic under State or local law, the guidelines described in paragraph (1) shall establish procedures equivalent to those established by 4.1.7(1)(b) and (c) of the Uniform Federal Accessibility Standards, and shall require, at a minimum, compliance with the requirements established in 4.1.7(2) of such standards.

§ 12205. Attorney's fees

In any action or administrative proceeding commenced pursuant to this chapter, the court or agency, in its discretion, may allow the prevailing party, other than the United States, a reasonable attorney's fee, including litigation expenses, and costs, and the United States shall be liable for the foregoing the same as a private individual.

§ 12206. Technical assistance

(a) Plan for assistance

(1) In general

Not later than 180 days after July 26, 1990, the Attorney General, in consultation with the Chair of the Equal Employment Opportunity Commission, the Secretary of Transportation, the Chair of the Architectural and Transportation Barriers Compliance Board, and the Chairman of the Federal Communications Commission, shall develop a plan to assist entities covered under this chapter, and other Federal agencies, in understanding the responsibility of such entities and agencies under this chapter.

(2) Publication of plan

The Attorney General shall publish the plan referred to in paragraph (1) for public comment in accordance with subchapter II of chapter 5 of Title 5 (commonly known as the Administrative Procedure Act).

(b) Agency and public assistance

The Attorney General may obtain the assistance of other Federal agencies in carrying out subsection (a) of this section, including the National Council on Disability, the President's Committee on Employment of

People with Disabilities, the Small Business Administration, and the Department of Commerce.

(c) Implementation

(1) Rendering assistance

Each Federal agency that has responsibility under paragraph (2) for implementing this chapter may render technical assistance to individuals and institutions that have rights or duties under the respective subchapter or subchapters of this chapter for which such agency has responsibility.

(2) Implementation of subchapters

(A) Subchapter I

The Equal Employment Opportunity Commission and the Attorney General shall implement the plan for assistance developed under subsection (a) of this section, for subchapter I of this chapter.

(B) Subchapter II

(i) Part A

The Attorney General shall implement such plan for assistance for part A of subchapter II of this chapter.

(ii) Part B

The Secretary of Transportation shall implement such plan for assistance for part B of subchapter II of this chapter.

(C) Subchapter III

The Attorney General, in coordination with the Secretary of Transportation and the Chair of the Architectural Transportation Barriers Compliance Board, shall implement such plan for assistance for subchapter III of this chapter, except for section 12184 of this title, the plan for assistance for which shall be implemented by the Secretary of Transportation.

(D) Title IV

The Chairman of the Federal Communications Commission, in coordination with the Attorney General, shall implement such plan for assistance for title IV.

(3) Technical assistance manuals

Each Federal agency that has responsibility under paragraph (2) for implementing this chapter shall, as part of its implementation responsibilities, ensure the availability and provision of appropriate technical assistance manuals to individuals or entities with rights or duties under this chapter no later than six months after applicable final regulations are published under subchapters I, II, and III of this chapter and title IV.

(d) Grants and contracts

(1) In general

Each Federal agency that has responsibility under subsection (c)(2) of this section for implementing this chapter may make grants or award contracts to effectuate the purposes of this section, subject to the availability of appropriations. Such grants and contracts may be awarded to individuals, institutions not organized for profit and no part of the net earnings of which inures to the benefit of any private shareholder or individual (including educational institutions), and associations representing individuals who have rights or duties under this chapter. Contracts may be awarded to entities organized for profit, but such entities may not be the recipients or [FN1] grants described in this paragraph.

(2) Dissemination of information

Such grants and contracts, among other uses, may be designed to ensure wide dissemination of information about the rights and duties established by this chapter and to provide information and technical assistance about techniques for effective compliance with this chapter.

(e) Failure to receive assistance

An employer, public accommodation, or other entity covered under this chapter shall not be excused from compliance with the requirements of this chapter because of any failure to receive technical assistance under this section, including any failure in the development or dissemination of any technical assistance manual authorized by this section.

§ 12207. Federal wilderness areas

(a) Study

The National Council on Disability shall conduct a study and report on the effect that wilderness designations and wilderness land management practices have on the ability of individuals with disabilities to use and enjoy the National Wilderness Preservation System as established under the Wilderness Act (16 U.S.C. 1131 et seq.).

(b) Submission of report

Not later than 1 year after July 26, 1990, the National Council on Disability shall submit the report required under subsection (a) of this section to Congress.

(c) Specific wilderness access

(1) In general

Congress reaffirms that nothing in the Wilderness Act [16 U.S.C.A. § 1131 et seq.] is to be construed as prohibiting the use of a wheelchair in a wilderness area by an individual whose disability requires use of a wheelchair, and consistent with the Wilderness Act [16 U.S.C.A. § 1131 et seq.] no agency is required to provide any form of special treatment or accommodation, or to construct any facilities or modify any conditions of lands within a wilderness area in order to facilitate such use.

(2) "Wheelchair" defined

For purposes of paragraph (1), the term "wheelchair" means a device designed solely for use by a mobility-impaired person for locomotion, that is suitable for use in an indoor pedestrian area.

§ 12208. Transvestites

For the purposes of this chapter, the term "disabled" or "disability" shall not apply to an individual solely because that individual is a transvestite.

§ 12209. Instrumentalities of the Congress

The General Accounting Office, the Government Printing Office, and the Library of Congress shall be covered as follows:

(1) In general

The rights and protections under this chapter shall, subject to paragraph (2), apply with respect to the conduct of each instrumentality of the Congress.

(2) Establishment of remedies and procedures by instrumentalities

The chief official of each instrumentality of the Congress shall establish remedies and procedures to be utilized with respect to the rights and protections provided pursuant to paragraph (1).

(3) Report to Congress

The chief official of each instrumentality of the Congress shall, after establishing remedies and procedures for purposes of paragraph (2), submit to the Congress a report describing the remedies and procedures.

(4) Definition of instrumentality

For purposes of this section, the term "instrumentality of the Congress" means the following:, [FN1]   the General Accounting Office, the Government Printing Office, and the Library of Congress,. [FN2]

(5) Enforcement of employment rights

The remedies and procedures set forth in section 2000e-16 of this title shall be available to any employee of an instrumentality of the Congress who alleges a violation of the rights and protections under sections 12112 through 12114 of this title that are made applicable by this section, except that the authorities of the Equal Employment Opportunity Commission shall be exercised by the chief official of the instrumentality of the Congress.

(6) Enforcement of rights to public services and accommodations

The remedies and procedures set forth in section 2000e-16 of this title shall be available to any qualified person with a disability who is a visitor, guest, or patron of an instrumentality of Congress and who alleges a violation of the rights and protections under sections 12131 through 12150 or section 12182 or 12183 of this title that are made applicable by this section, except that the authorities of the Equal Employment Opportunity Commission shall be exercised by the chief official of the instrumentality of the Congress.

(7) Construction

Nothing in this section shall alter the enforcement procedures for individuals with disabilities provided in the General Accounting Office Personnel Act of 1980 and regulations promulgated pursuant to that Act.

§ 12210. Illegal use of drugs

(a) In general

For purposes of this chapter, the term "individual with a disability" does not include an individual who is currently engaging in the illegal use of drugs, when the covered entity acts on the basis of such use.

(b) Rules of construction

Nothing in subsection (a) of this section shall be construed to exclude as an individual with a disability an individual who--

(1) has successfully completed a supervised drug rehabilitation program and is no longer engaging in the illegal use of drugs, or has otherwise been rehabilitated successfully and is no longer engaging in such use;

(2) is participating in a supervised rehabilitation program and is no longer engaging in such use; or

(3) is erroneously regarded as engaging in such use, but is not engaging in such use;

except that it shall not be a violation of this chapter for a covered entity to adopt or administer reasonable policies or procedures, including but not limited to drug testing, designed to ensure that an individual described in paragraph (1) or (2) is no longer engaging in the illegal use of drugs; however, nothing in this section shall be construed to encourage, prohibit, restrict, or authorize the conducting of testing for the illegal use of drugs.

(c) Health and other services

Notwithstanding subsection (a) of this section and section 12211(b)(3) of this title, an individual shall not be denied health services, or services provided in connection with drug rehabilitation, on the basis of the current illegal use of drugs if the individual is otherwise entitled to such services.

(d) "Illegal use of drugs" defined

(1) In general

The term "illegal use of drugs" means the use of drugs, the possession or distribution of which is unlawful under the Controlled Substances Act [21 U.S.C.A. § 801 et seq.]. Such term does not include the use of a drug taken under supervision by a licensed health care professional, or other uses authorized by the Controlled Substances Act [21 U.S.C.A. § 801 et seq.] or other provisions of Federal law.

(2) Drugs

The term "drug" means a controlled substance, as defined in schedules I through V of section 202 of the Controlled Substances Act [21 U.S.C.A. § 812].

§ 12211. Definitions

(a) Homosexuality and bisexuality

For purposes of the definition of "disability" in section 12102(2) of this title, homosexuality and bisexuality are not impairments and as such are not disabilities under this chapter.

(b) Certain conditions

Under this chapter, the term "disability" shall not include--

(1) transvestism, transsexualism, pedophilia, exhibitionism, voyeurism, gender identity disorders not resulting from physical impairments, or other sexual behavior disorders;

(2) compulsive gambling, kleptomania, or pyromania; or

(3) psychoactive substance use disorders resulting from current illegal use of drugs.

§ 12212. Alternative means of dispute resolution

Where appropriate and to the extent authorized by law, the use of alternative means of dispute resolution, including settlement negotiations, conciliation, facilitation, mediation, factfinding, minitrials, and arbitration, is encouraged to resolve disputes arising under this chapter.

§ 12213. Severability

Should any provision in this chapter be found to be unconstitutional by a court of law, such provision shall be severed from the remainder of this chapter and such action shall not affect the enforceability of the remaining provisions of this chapter.

CIVIL RIGHTS ACT OF 1991,
AMENDING CIVIL RIGHTS ACT OF 1964 §§ 701, 702, 703, 704, 705, 706 and 717, and AMERICANS WITH DISABILITIES ACT OF 1990 §§ 101(4) and 102
Codified at 42 U.S.C. §§ 1981a, 2000e, 2000e-1, 2000e-2, 2000e-4, 2000e-5, 2000e-16, 12111(4) and 12112

SECTION 1. SHORT TITLE.

This Act may be cited as the "Civil Rights Act of 1991".

SEC. 2. FINDINGS.

The Congress finds that -

(1) additional remedies under Federal law are needed to deter unlawful harassment and intentional discrimination in the workplace;

(2) the decision of the Supreme Court in Wards Cove Packing Co. v. Antonio, 490 U.S. 642 (1989) has weakened the scope and effectiveness of Federal civil rights protections; and

(3) legislation is necessary to provide additional protections against unlawful discrimination in employment.

SEC. 3. PURPOSES.

The purposes of this Act are -

(1) to provide appropriate remedies for intentional discrimination and unlawful harassment in the workplace;

(2) to codify the concepts of "business necessity" and "job related" enunciated by the Supreme Court in Griggs v. Duke Power Co., 401 U.S. 424 (1971), and in the other Supreme Court decisions prior to Wards Cove Packing Co. v. Antonio, 490 U.S. 642 (1989):

(3) to confirm statutory authority and provide statutory guidelines for the adjudication of disparate impact suits under title VII of the Civil Rights Act of 1964 (42 U.S. C. 2000e et seq.); and

(4) to respond to recent decisions of the Supreme Court by

expanding the scope of relevant civil rights statutes in order to provide adequate protection to victims of discrimination.

TITLE I - FEDERAL CIVIL RIGHTS REMEDIES

SEC. 101. PROHIBITION AGAINST ALL RACIAL DISCRIMINATION IN THE MAKING AND ENFORCEMENT OF CONTRACTS.

Section 1977 of the Revised Statutes (42 U.S.C. 1981) is amended -

(1) by inserting "(a)" before "All persons within"; and

(2) by adding at the end the following new subsections;

(b) For purposes of this section, the term "make and enforce contracts" includes the making, performance, modification, and termination of contracts, and the enjoyment of all benefits, privileges, terms, and conditions of the contractual relationship.

(c) The rights protected by this section are protected against impairment by nongovernmental discrimination and impairment under color of State law.

SEC. 102. DAMAGES IN CASES OF INTENTIONAL DISCRIMINATION.

The Revised Statutes are amended by inserting after section 1977 (42 U.S.C. 1981) the following new section:

"SEC. 1977A. DAMAGES IN CASES OF INTENTIONAL DISCRIMINATION IN EMPLOYMENT.

[42 U.S.C. 1981a.]

Sec. 1981a. - Damages in cases of intentional discrimination in employment

(a) Right of recovery

(1) Civil rights

In an action brought by a complaining party under section 706 or 717 of the Civil Rights Act of 1964 (42 U.S.C. 2000e-5, 2000e-16) against a respondent who engaged in unlawful intentional discrimination (not an employment practice that is unlawful because of its disparate impact) prohibited under section 703, 704, or 717 of the Act (42 U.S.C. 2000e-2, 2000e-3, 2000e-16), and provided that the complaining party cannot recover under section 1981 of this title, the complaining party may recover compensatory and punitive damages as allowed in subsection (b) of this section, in addition to any relief authorized by section 706(g) of the Civil Rights Act of 1964, from the respondent.

(2) Disability

In an action brought by a complaining party under the powers, remedies, and procedures set forth in section 706 or 717 of the Civil Rights Act of 1964 (42 U.S.C. 2000e-5, 2000e-16) (as provided in section 107(a) of the Americans with Disabilities Act of 1990 (42 U.S.C. 12117(a)), and section 794a(a)(1) of title 29, respectively) against a respondent who engaged in unlawful intentional discrimination (not an employment practice that is unlawful because of its disparate impact) under section 791 of title 29 and the regulations implementing section 791 of title 29, or who violated the requirements of section 791 of title 29 or the regulations implementing section 791 of title 29 concerning the provision of a reasonable accommodation, or section 102 of the Americans with Disabilities Act of 1990 (42 U.S.C. 12112), or committed a violation of section 102(b)(5) of the Act, against an individual, the complaining party may recover compensatory and punitive damages as allowed in subsection (b) of this section, in addition to any relief authorized by section 706(g) of the Civil Rights Act of 1964, from the respondent.

(3) Reasonable accommodation and good faith effort

In cases where a discriminatory practice involves the provision of a reasonable accommodation pursuant to section 102(b)(5) of the Americans with Disabilities Act of 1990 (42 U.S.C. 12112(b)(5)) or regulations implementing section 791 of title 29, damages may not be awarded under this section where the covered entity demonstrates good faith efforts, in consultation with the person with the disability who has informed the covered entity that accommodation is needed, to identify and make a reasonable accommodation that would provide such individual with an equally effective opportunity and would not cause an undue hardship on the operation of the business.

(b) Compensatory and punitive damages

(1) Determination of punitive damages

A complaining party may recover punitive damages under this section against a respondent (other than a government, government agency or political subdivision) if the complaining party demonstrates that the respondent engaged in a discriminatory practice or discriminatory practices with malice or with reckless indifference to the federally protected rights of an aggrieved individual.

(2) Exclusions from compensatory damages

Compensatory damages awarded under this section shall not include backpay, interest on backpay, or any other type of relief authorized under section 706(g) of the Civil Rights Act of 1964 (42 U.S.C. 2000e-5(g)).

(3) Limitations

The sum of the amount of compensatory damages awarded under this section for future pecuniary losses, emotional pain, suffering, inconvenience, mental anguish, loss of enjoyment of life, and other nonpecuniary losses, and the amount of punitive damages awarded under this section, shall not exceed, for each complaining party -

(A) in the case of a respondent who has more than 14 and fewer than 101 employees in each of 20 or more calendar weeks in the current or preceding calendar year, $50,000;

(B) in the case of a respondent who has more than 100 and fewer than 201 employees in each of 20 or more calendar weeks in the current or preceding calendar year, $100,000; and

(C) in the case of a respondent who has more than 200 and fewer than 501 employees in each of 20 or more calendar weeks in the current or preceding calendar year, $200,000; and

(D) in the case of a respondent who has more than 500 employees in each of 20 or more calendar weeks in the current or preceding calendar year, $300,000.

(4) Construction

Nothing in this section shall be construed to limit the scope of, or the relief available under, section 1981 of this title.

(c) Jury trial

If a complaining party seeks compensatory or punitive damages under this section -

(1) any party may demand a trial by jury; and

(2) the court shall not inform the jury of the limitations described in subsection (b)(3) of this section.

(d) Definitions

As used in this section:

(1) Complaining party

The term "complaining party" means -

(A) in the case of a person seeking to bring an action under subsection (a)(1) of this section, the Equal Employment Opportunity Commission, the Attorney General, or a person who may bring an action or proceeding under title VII of the Civil Rights Act of 1964 (42 U.S.C. 2000e et seq.); or

(B) in the case of a person seeking to bring an action under subsection (a)(2) of this section, the Equal Employment Opportunity Commission, the Attorney General, a person who may bring an action or proceeding under section 794a(a)(1) of title 29, or a person who may bring an action or proceeding under title I of the Americans with Disabilities Act of 1990 (42 U.S.C. 12111 et seq.).

(2) Discriminatory practice

The term "discriminatory practice" means the discrimination described in paragraph (1), or the discrimination or the violation described in paragraph (2), of subsection (a) of this section

SEC. 103. ATTORNEY'S FEES.

The last sentence of section 722 of the Revised Statutes (42 U.S.C. 1988) is amended by inserting, "1977A" after "1977".

SEC. 104. DEFINITIONS.

Section 701 of the Civil Rights Act of 1964 (42 U.S.C. 2000e) is amended by adding at the end the following new subsections:

(1) The term "complaining party" means the Commission, the Attorney General, or a person who may bring an action or proceeding under this title.

(2) The term "demonstrates" means meets the burdens of production and persuasion.

(3) The term "respondent" means an employer, employment agency, labor organization, joint labor-management committee controlling apprenticeship or other training or retraining program, including an on-the-job training program, or Federal entity subject to section 717.

SEC. 105. BURDEN OF PROOF IN DISPARATE IMPACT CASES.

(a) Section 703 of the Civil Rights Act of 1964 (42 U.S.C. 2000e-2) is amended by adding at the end the following new subsection:

"(k)(1)(A) An unlawful employment practice based on disparate impact is established under this title only if -

"(i) a complaining party demonstrates that a respondent uses a particular employment practice that causes a disparate impact on the basis of race, color, religion, sex, or national origin and the respondent fails to demonstrate that the challenged practice is job related for the position in question and consistent with business necessity; or

"(ii) the complaining party makes the demonstration described in subparagraph (C) with respect to an alternative employment practice and the respondent refuses to adopt such alternative employment practice.

"(B)(i) With respect to demonstrating that a particular employment practice causes a disparate impact as described in subparagraph (A)(i), the complaining party shall demonstrate that each particular challenged employment practice causes a disparate impact, except that if the complaining party can demonstrate to the court that the elements of a respondent's decisionmaking process are not capable of separation for analysis, the decisionmaking process may be analyzed as one employment practice.

"(ii) If the respondent demonstrates that a specific employment practice does not cause the disparate impact, the respondent shall not be required to demonstrate that such practice is required by business necessity.

"(C) The demonstration referred to by subparagraph (A)(ii) shall be in accordance with the law as it existed on June 4, 1989, with respect to the concept of 'alternative employment practice'.

"(2) A demonstration that an employment practice is required by business necessity may not be used as a defense against a claim of intentional discrimination under this title.

"(3) Notwithstanding any other provision of this title, a rule barring the employment of an individual who currently and knowingly uses or possesses a controlled substance, as defined in schedules I and II of section 102(6) of the Controlled Substances Act (21 U.S.C. 802(6)), other than the use or possession of a drug taken under the supervision of a licensed health care professional, or any other use or possession authorized by the Controlled Substances Act or any other provision of

Federal law, shall be considered an unlawful employment practice under this title only if such rule is adopted or applied with an intent to discriminate because of race, color, religion, sex, or national origin."

(b) No statements other than the interpretative memorandum appearing at Vol. 137 Congressional Record S 15276 (daily ed. Oct. 25, 1991) shall be considered legislative history of, or relied upon in any way as legislative history in construing or applying, any provision of this Act that relates to Wards Cove - Business necessity/cumulation/alternative business practice.

SEC. 106. PROHIBITION AGAINST DISCRIMINATORY USE OF TEST SCORES.

Section 703 of the Civil Rights Act of 1964 (42 U.S.C. 2000e-2) (as amended by section 105) is further amended by adding at the end the following new subsection:

"(1) It shall be an unlawful employment practice for a respondent, in connection with the selection or referral of applicants or candidates for employment or promotion, to adjust the scores of, use different cutoff scores for, or otherwise alter the results of, employment related tests on the basis of race, color, religion, sex, or national origin."

SEC. 107. CLARIFYING PROHIBITION AGAINST IMPERMISSIBLE CONSIDERATION OF RACE, COLOR, RELIGION, SEX, OR NATIONAL ORIGIN IN EMPLOYMENT PRACTICES.

(a) In General. - Section 703 of the Civil Rights Act of 1964 (42 U.S.C. 2000e-2) (as amended by sections 105 and 106) is further amended by adding at the end the following new subsection:

"(m) Except as otherwise provided in this title, an unlawful employment practice is established when the complaining party demonstrates that race, color, religion, sex, or national origin was a motivating factor for any employment practice, even though other factors also motivated the practice."

(b) Enforcement Provisions. - Section 706(g) of such Act (42 U.S.C. 2000e-5(g)) is amended-

(1) by designating the first through third sentences as paragraph (1);

(2) by designating the fourth sentence as paragraph (2)(A) and indenting accordingly; and

(3) by adding at the end the following new subparagraph:

"(B) On a claim in which an individual proves a violation under section 703(m) and a respondent demonstrates that the respondent would have taken the same action in the absence of the impermissible motivating factor, the court -

"(i) may grant declaratory relief, injunctive relief (except as provided in clause (ii)), and attorney's fees and costs demonstrated to be directly attributable only to the pursuit of a claim under section 703(m); and

"(ii) shall not award damages or issue an order requiring any admission, reinstatement, hiring, promotion, or payment, described in subparagraph (A)."

SEC. 108. FACILITATING PROMPT AND ORDERLY RESOLUTION OF CHALLENGES TO EMPLOYMENT PRACTICES IMPLEMENTING LITIGATED OR CONSENT JUDGMENTS OR ORDERS.

Section 703 of the Civil Rights Act of 1964 (42 U.S.C. 2000e-2) (as amended by sections 105, 106, and 107 of this title) is further amended by adding at the end the following new subsection:

"(n)(1)(A) Notwithstanding any other provision of law, and except as provided in paragraph (2), an employment practice that implements and is within the scope of a litigated or consent judgment or order that resolves a claim of employment discrimination under the Constitution or Federal civil rights laws may not be challenged under the circumstances described in subparagraph (B).

"(B) A practice described in subparagraph (A) may not be challenged in a claim under the Constitution or Federal civil rights laws -

"(i) by a person who, prior to the entry of the judgment or order described in subparagraph (A), had -

"(I) actual notice of the proposed judgment or order sufficient to apprise such person that such judgment or order might adversely affect the interests and legal rights of such person and that an opportunity was available to present objections to such judgment or order by a future date certain; and

"(II) a reasonable opportunity to present objections to such judgment or order; or

"(ii) by a person whose interests were adequately represented by another person who had previously challenged the judgment or order on the same legal grounds and with a similar factual situation, unless there has been an intervening change in law or fact.

"(2) Nothing in this subsection shall be construed to -

"(A) alter the standards for intervention under rule 24 of the Federal Rules of Civil Procedure or apply to the rights of parties who have successfully intervened pursuant to such rule in the proceeding in which the parties intervened;

"(B) apply to the rights of parties to the action in which a litigated or consent judgment or order was entered, or of members of a class represented or sought to be represented in such action, or of members of a group on whose behalf relief was sought in such action by the Federal Government;

"(C) prevent challenges to a litigated or consent judgment or order on the ground that such judgment or order was obtained through collusion or fraud, or is transparently invalid or was entered by a court lacking subject matter jurisdiction; or

"(D) authorize or permit the denial to any person of the due process of law required by the Constitution.

"(3) Any action not precluded under this subsection that challenges an employment consent judgment or order described in paragraph (1) shall be brought in the court, and if possible before the judge, that entered such judgment or order. Nothing in this subsection shall preclude a transfer of such action pursuant to section 1404 of title 28, United States Code."

SEC. 109. PROTECTION OF EXTRATERRITORIAL EMPLOYMENT.

(a) Definition of Employee. - Section 701(f) of the Civil Rights Act of 1964 (42 U.S.C. 2000e(f)) and section 101(4) of the Americans with Disabilities Act of 1990 (42 U.S.C. 12111(4)) are each amended by adding at the end the following: "With respect to employment in a foreign country, such term includes an individual who is a citizen of the United States."

(b) Exemption. -

(1) Civil rights act of 1964. - Section 702 of the Civil Rights Act of 1964 (42 U.S.C. 2000e-1) is amended -

(A) by inserting "(a)" after "Sec. 702"; and

(B) by adding at the end the following:

"(b) It shall not be unlawful under section 703 or 704 for an employer (or a corporation controlled by an employer), labor organization, employment agency, or joint labor-management committee controlling apprenticeship or other training or retraining (including on-the-job training programs) to take any action otherwise prohibited by such section, with respect to an employee in a workplace in a foreign country if compliance with such section would cause such employer (or such corporation), such organization, such agency, or such committee to violate the law of the foreign country in which such workplace is located.

"(c)(1) If an employer controls a corporation whose place of incorporation is a foreign country, any practice prohibited by section 703 or 704 engaged in by such corporation shall be presumed to be engaged in by such employer.

"(2) Sections 703 and 704 shall not apply with respect to the foreign person not controlled by an American employer.

"(3) For purposes of this subsection, the determination of whether an employer controls a corporation shall be based on -

"(A) the interrelation of operations;

"(B) the common management;

"(C) the centralized control of labor relations; and

"(D) the common ownership or financial control, of the employer and the corporation."

(2) Americans with Disabilities Act of 1990. - Section 102 of the Americans with Disabilities Act of 1990 (42 U.S.C. 12112) is amended -

(A) by redesignating subsection (c) as subsection (d); and

(B) by inserting after subsection (b) the following new subsection:

"(c) Covered Entities in Foreign Countries. -

"(I) In general. - It shall not be unlawful under this section for a covered entity to take any action that constitutes discrimination under this section with respect to an employee in a workplace in a foreign country if compliance with this section would cause such covered entity to violate the law of the foreign country in which such workplace is located.

"(2) Control of corporation. -

"(A) Presumption. - If an employer controls a corporation whose place of incorporation is a foreign country, any practice that constitutes discrimination under this section and is engaged in by such corporation shall be presumed to be engaged in by such employer.

"(B) Exception. - This section shall not apply with respect to the foreign operations of an employer that is a foreign person not controlled by an American employer.

"(C) Determination. - For purposes of this paragraph, the determination of whether an employer controls a corporation shall be based on -

"(i) the interrelation of operations;

"(ii) the common management;

"(iii) the centralized control of labor relations; and

"(iv) the common ownership or financial control, of the employer and the corporation."

(c) Application of Amendments. - The amendments made by this section shall not apply with respect to conduct occurring before the date of the enactment of this Act.

SEC. 110. TECHNICAL ASSISTANCE TRAINING INSTITUTE.

(a) Technical Assistance. - Section 705 of the Civil Rights Act of 1964 (42 U.S.C. 2000e-4) is amended by adding at the end the following new subsection:

"(i)(1) The Commission shall establish a Technical Assistance Training Institute, through which the Commission shall provide technical assistance and training regarding the laws and regulations enforced by the Commission.

"(2) An employer or other entity covered under this title shall not be excused from compliance with the requirements of this title because of any failure to receive technical assistance under this subsection.

"(3) There are authorized to be appropriated to carry out this subsection such sums as may be necessary for fiscal year 1992."

(b) Effective Date. - The amendment made by this section shall take effect on the date of the enactment of this Act.

SEC. 111. EDUCATION AND OUTREACH.

Section 705(h) of the Civil Rights At of 1964 (42 U.S.C. 2000e-4(h) is amended -

(1) by inserting "(1)" after "(h)"; and

(2) by adding at the end the following new paragraph:

"(2) In exercising its powers under this title, the Commission shall carry out educational and outreach activities (including dissemination of information in languages other than English) targeted to -

"(A) individuals who historically have been victims of employment discrimination and have not been equitably served by the Commission; and

"(B) individuals on whose behalf the Commission has authority to enforce any other law prohibiting employment discrimination, concerning rights and obligations under this title or such law, as the case may be."

SEC. 112. EXPANSION OF RIGHT TO CHALLENGE DISCRIMINATORY SENIORITY SYSTEMS.

Section 706(e) of the Civil Rights Act of 1964 (42 U.S.C. 2000e-5(e)) is amended -

(1) by inserting "(1)" before "A charge under this section..."; and

(2) by adding at the end the following new paragraph:

"(2) For purposes of this section, an unlawful employment practice occurs, with respect to a seniority system that has been adopted for an intentionally discriminatory purpose in violation of this title (whether or not that discriminatory purpose is apparent on the face of the seniority provision), when the seniority system is adopted, when an individual becomes subject to the seniority system, or when a person aggrieved is injured by the application of the seniority system or provision of the system."

SEC. 113. AUTHORIZING AWARD OF EXPERT FEES.

(a) Revised Statutes. - Section 722 of the Revised Statutes is amended -

(1) by designating the first and second sentences as subsections (a) and (b), respectively, and indenting accordingly; and

(2) by adding at the end the following new subsection:

"(c) In awarding an attorney's fee under subsection (b) in any action or proceeding to enforce a provision of sections 1977 or 1977A of the Revised Statutes, the court, in its discretion, may include expert fees as part of the attorney's fee."

(b) Civil Rights Act of 1964. - Section 706(k) of the Civil Rights Act of 1964 (42 U.S.C. 2000e-5(k)) is amended by inserting "(including expert fees)" after "attorney's fee".

SEC. 114. PROVIDING FOR INTEREST AND EXTENDING THE STATUTE OF LIMITATIONS IN ACTIONS AGAINST THE FEDERAL GOVERNMENT.

Section 717 of the Civil Rights Act of 1964 (42 U.S.C. 2000e-16) is amended -

(1) in subsection (c), by striking 'thirty days' and inserting '90 days'; and

(2) in subsection (d), by inserting before the period "and the same interest to compensate for delay in payment shall be available as in cases involving nonpublic parties."

SEC. 115. NOTICE OF LIMITATIONS PERIOD UNDER THE AGE DISCRIMINATION IN EMPLOYMENT ACT OF 1967.

Section 7(e) of the Age Discrimination in Employment Act of 1967 (29 U.S.C. 626(e)) is amended -

(1) by striking paragraph (2);

(2) by striking the paragraph designation in paragraph (1);

(3) by striking "Sections 6 and" and inserting "Section"; and

(4) by adding at the end the following: "If a charge filed with the Commission under this Act is dismissed or the proceedings of the Commission are otherwise terminated by the Commission, the Commission shall notify the person aggrieved. A civil action may be brought under this section by a person defined in section 11(a) against the respondent named in the charge within 90 days after the date of the receipt of such notice."

SEC. 116. LAWFUL COURT-ORDERED REMEDIES, AFFIRMATIVE ACTION, AND CONCILIATION AGREEMENTS NOT AFFECTED.

Nothing in the amendments made by this title shall be construed to affect court-ordered remedies, affirmative action, or conciliation agreements, that are in accordance with the law.

SEC. 117. COVERAGE OF HOUSE OF REPRESENTATIVES AND THE AGENCIES OF THE LEGISLATIVE BRANCH.

(a) Coverage of the House of Representatives. -

(1) In general. - Notwithstanding any provision of title VII of the Civil Rights Act of 1964 (42 U.S.C. 2000e et seq.) or of other law, the purposes of such title shall, subject to paragraph (2), apply in their entirety to the House of Representatives.

(2) Employment in the house.-

(A) Application. - The rights and protections under title VII of the Civil Rights Act of 1964 (42 U.S.C. 2000e et seq.) shall, subject to subparagraph (B), apply with respect to any employee in an employment position in the House of Representatives and any employing authority of the House of Representatives.

(B) Administration. -

(i) In general. - In the administration of this paragraph, the remedies and procedures made applicable pursuant to the resolution described in clause (ii) shall apply exclusively.

(ii) Resolution. - The resolution referred to in clause (i) is the Fair Employment Practices Resolution (House Resolution 558 of the One Hundredth Congress, as agreed to October 4, 1988), as incorporated into the Rules of the House of Representatives of the One Hundred Second Congress as Rule LI, or any other provision that continues in effect the provisions of such resolution.

(C) Exercise of rulemaking power. - The provisions of subparagraph (B) are enacted by the House of Representatives as an exercise of the rulemaking power of the House of Representatives, with full recognition of the right of the House to change its rules, in the same manner, and to the same extent as in the case of any other rule of the House.

(b) Instrumentalities of Congress.-

(1) In general. - The rights and protections under this title and title VII of the Civil Rights Act of 1964 (42 U.S.C. 2000e et seq.) shall, subject to paragraph (2), apply with respect to the conduct of each instrumentality of the Congress.

(2) Establishment of remedies and procedures by instrumentalities. - The chief official of each instrumentality of the Congress shall establish remedies and procedures to be utilized with respect to the rights and protections provided pursuant to paragraph (1). Such remedies and procedures shall apply exclusively, except for the employees who are defined as Senate employees, in section 301(c)(1).

(3) Report to Congress. - The chief official of each instrumentality of the Congress shall, after establishing remedies and procedures for purposes of paragraph (2), submit to the Congress a report describing the remedies and procedures.

(4) Definition of instrumentalities. - For purposes of this section, instrumentalities of the Congress include the following: The Architect of the Capitol, the Congressional Budget Office, the General Accounting Office, the Government Printing Office, the Office of Technology Assessment, and the United States Botanic Garden.

(5) Construction. - Nothing in this section shall alter the enforcement procedures for individuals protected under section 717 of title VII for the Civil Rights Act of 1964 (42 U.S.C. 2000e-16).

SEC. 118. ALTERNATIVE MEANS OF DISPUTE RESOLUTION.

Where appropriate and to the extent authorized by law, the use of alternative means of dispute resolution, including settlement negotiations, conciliation, facilitation, mediation, fact finding, minitrials, and arbitration, is encouraged to resolve disputes arising under the Acts or provisions of Federal law amended by this title.

2. Equal Employment Opportunity Commission

42 U.S.C. § 2000e-5. Enforcement provisions

(a) Power of Commission to prevent unlawful employment practices

The Commission is empowered, as hereinafter provided, to prevent any person from engaging in any unlawful employment practice as set forth in section 2000e-2 or 2000e-3 of this title.

(b) Charges by persons aggrieved or member of Commission of

unlawful employment practices by employers, etc.; filing; allegations; notice to respondent; contents of notice; investigation by Commission; contents of charges; prohibition on disclosure of charges; determination of reasonable cause; conference, conciliation, and persuasion for elimination of unlawful practices; prohibition on disclosure of informal endeavors to end unlawful practices; use of evidence in subsequent proceedings; penalties for disclosure of information; time for determination of reasonable cause

Whenever a charge is filed by or on behalf of a person claiming to be aggrieved, or by a member of the Commission, alleging that an employer, employment agency, labor organization, or joint labor-management committee controlling apprenticeship or other training or retraining, including on-the-job training programs, has engaged in an unlawful employment practice, the Commission shall serve a notice of the charge (including the date, place and circumstances of the alleged unlawful employment practice) on such employer, employment agency, labor organization, or joint labor-management committee (hereinafter referred to as the "respondent") within ten days, and shall make an investigation thereof. Charges shall be in writing under oath or affirmation and shall contain such information and be in such form as the Commission requires. Charges shall not be made public by the Commission. If the Commission determines after such investigation that there is not reasonable cause to believe that the charge is true, it shall dismiss the charge and promptly notify the person claiming to be aggrieved and the respondent of its action. In determining whether reasonable cause exists, the Commission shall accord substantial weight to final findings and orders made by State or local authorities in proceedings commenced under State or local law pursuant to the requirements of subsections (c) and (d) of this section. If the Commission determines after such investigation that there is reasonable cause to believe that the charge is true, the Commission shall endeavor to eliminate any such alleged unlawful employment practice by informal methods of conference, conciliation, and persuasion. Nothing said or done during and as a part of such informal endeavors may be made public by the Commission, its officers or employees, or used as evidence in a subsequent proceeding without the written consent of the persons concerned. Any person who makes public information in violation of this subsection shall be fined not more than $1,000 or imprisoned for not more than one year, or both. The Commission shall make its determination on reasonable cause as promptly as possible and, so far as practicable, not later than one hundred and twenty days from the filing of the charge or, where applicable under subsection (c) or (d) of this section, from the date upon which the Commission is authorized to take action with respect to the charge.

(c) State or local enforcement proceedings; notification of State or local authority; time for filing charges with Commission; commencement of proceedings

In the case of an alleged unlawful employment practice occurring in a State, or political subdivision of a State, which has a State or local law prohibiting the unlawful employment practice alleged and establishing or authorizing a State or local authority to grant or seek relief from such practice or to institute criminal proceedings with respect thereto upon receiving notice thereof, no charge may be filed under subsection ([b]) of this section by the person aggrieved before the expiration of sixty days after proceedings have been commenced under the State or local law, unless such proceedings have been earlier terminated, provided that such sixty-day period shall be extended to one hundred and twenty days during the first year after the effective date of such State or local law. If any requirement for the commencement of such proceedings is imposed by a State or local authority other than a requirement of the filing of a written and signed statement of the facts upon which the proceeding is based, the proceeding shall be deemed to have been commenced for the purposes of this subsection at the time such statement is sent by registered mail to the appropriate State or local authority.

(d) State or local enforcement proceedings; notification of State or local authority; time for action on charges by Commission

In the case of any charge filed by a member of the Commission alleging an unlawful employment practice occurring in a State or political subdivision of a State which has a State or local law prohibiting the practice alleged and establishing or authorizing a State or local authority to grant or seek relief from such practice or to institute criminal proceedings with respect thereto upon receiving notice thereof, the Commission shall, before taking any action with respect to such charge, notify the appropriate State or local officials and, upon request, afford them a reasonable time, but not less than sixty days (provided that such sixty-day period shall be extended to one hundred and twenty days during the first year after the effective day of such State or local law), unless a shorter period is requested, to act under such State or local law to remedy the practice alleged.

(e) Time for filing charges; time for service of notice of charge on respondent; filing of charge by Commission with State or local agency; seniority system

(1) A charge under this section shall be filed within one hundred and eighty days after the alleged unlawful employment practice occurred and notice of the charge (including the date, place and circumstances of the alleged unlawful employment practice) shall be served upon the person against whom such charge is made within ten days thereafter,

except that in a case of an unlawful employment practice with respect to which the person aggrieved has initially instituted proceedings with a State or local agency with authority to grant or seek relief from such practice or to institute criminal proceedings with respect thereto upon receiving notice thereof, such charge shall be filed by or on behalf of the person aggrieved within three hundred days after the alleged unlawful employment practice occurred, or within thirty days after receiving notice that the State or local agency has terminated the proceedings under the State or local law, whichever is earlier, and a copy of such charge shall be filed by the Commission with the State or local agency.

(2) For purposes of this section, an unlawful employment practice occurs, with respect to a seniority system that has been adopted for an intentionally discriminatory purpose in violation of this subchapter (whether or not that discriminatory purpose is apparent on the face of the seniority provision), when the seniority system is adopted, when an individual becomes subject to the seniority system, or when a person aggrieved is injured by the application of the seniority system or provision of the system.

(f) Civil action by Commission, Attorney General, or person aggrieved; preconditions; procedure; appointment of attorney; payment of fees, costs, or security; intervention; stay of Federal proceedings; action for appropriate temporary or preliminary relief pending final disposition of charge; jurisdiction and venue of United States courts; designation of judge to hear and determine case; assignment of case for hearing; expedition of case; appointment of master

(1) If within thirty days after a charge is filed with the Commission or within thirty days after expiration of any period of reference under subsection (c) or (d) of this section, the Commission has been unable to secure from the respondent a conciliation agreement acceptable to the Commission, the Commission may bring a civil action against any respondent not a government, governmental agency, or political subdivision named in the charge. In the case of a respondent which is a government, governmental agency, or political subdivision, if the Commission has been unable to secure from the respondent a conciliation agreement acceptable to the Commission, the Commission shall take no further action and shall refer the case to the Attorney General who may bring a civil action against such respondent in the appropriate United States district court. The person or persons aggrieved shall have the right to intervene in a civil action brought by the Commission or the Attorney General in a case involving a government, governmental agency, or political subdivision. If a charge filed with the Commission pursuant to subsection (b) of this section is dismissed by the Commission, or if within one hundred and eighty days from the filing of such charge or the expiration of any period of reference under subsection

(c) or (d) of this section, whichever is later, the Commission has not filed a civil action under this section or the Attorney General has not filed a civil action in a case involving a government, governmental agency, or political subdivision, or the Commission has not entered into a conciliation agreement to which the person aggrieved is a party, the Commission, or the Attorney General in a case involving a government, governmental agency, or political subdivision, shall so notify the person aggrieved and within ninety days after the giving of such notice a civil action may be brought against the respondent named in the charge (A) by the person claiming to be aggrieved or (B) if such charge was filed by a member of the Commission, by any person whom the charge alleges was aggrieved by the alleged unlawful employment practice. Upon application by the complainant and in such circumstances as the court may deem just, the court may appoint an attorney for such complainant and may authorize the commencement of the action without the payment of fees, costs, or security. Upon timely application, the court may, in its discretion, permit the Commission, or the Attorney General in a case involving a government, governmental agency, or political subdivision, to intervene in such civil action upon certification that the case is of general public importance. Upon request, the court may, in its discretion, stay further proceedings for not more than sixty days pending the termination of State or local proceedings described in subsections (c) or (d) of this section or further efforts of the Commission to obtain voluntary compliance.

(2) Whenever a charge is filed with the Commission and the Commission concludes on the basis of a preliminary investigation that prompt judicial action is necessary to carry out the purposes of this Act, the Commission, or the Attorney General in a case involving a government, governmental agency, or political subdivision, may bring an action for appropriate temporary or preliminary relief pending final disposition of such charge. Any temporary restraining order or other order granting preliminary or temporary relief shall be issued in accordance with rule 65 of the Federal Rules of Civil Procedure. It shall be the duty of a court having jurisdiction over proceedings under this section to assign cases for hearing at the earliest practicable date and to cause such cases to be in every way expedited.

(3) Each United States district court and each United States court of a place subject to the jurisdiction of the United States shall have jurisdiction of actions brought under this subchapter. Such an action may be brought in any judicial district in the State in which the unlawful employment practice is alleged to have been committed, in the judicial district in which the employment records relevant to such practice are maintained and administered, or in the judicial district in which the aggrieved person would have worked but for the alleged unlawful employment practice, but if the respondent is not found within any such district, such an action may be brought within the judicial district in

which the respondent has his principal office. For purposes of sections 1404 and 1406 of Title 28, the judicial district in which the respondent has his principal office shall in all cases be considered a district in which the action might have been brought.

(4) It shall be the duty of the chief judge of the district (or in his absence, the acting chief judge) in which the case is pending immediately to designate a judge in such district to hear and determine the case. In the event that no judge in the district is available to hear and determine the case, the chief judge of the district, or the acting chief judge, as the case may be, shall certify this fact to the chief judge of the circuit (or in his absence, the acting chief judge) who shall then designate a district or circuit judge of the circuit to hear and determine the case.

(5) It shall be the duty of the judge designated pursuant to this subsection to assign the case for hearing at the earliest practicable date and to cause the case to be in every way expedited. If such judge has not scheduled the case for trial within one hundred and twenty days after issue has been joined, that judge may appoint a master pursuant to rule 53 of the Federal Rules of Civil Procedure.

(g) Injunctions; appropriate affirmative action; equitable relief; accrual of back pay; reduction of back pay; limitations on judicial orders

(1) If the court finds that the respondent has intentionally engaged in or is intentionally engaging in an unlawful employment practice charged in the complaint, the court may enjoin the respondent from engaging in such unlawful employment practice, and order such affirmative action as may be appropriate, which may include, but is not limited to, reinstatement or hiring of employees, with or without back pay (payable by the employer, employment agency, or labor organization, as the case may be, responsible for the unlawful employment practice), or any other equitable relief as the court deems appropriate. Back pay liability shall not accrue from a date more than two years prior to the filing of a charge with the Commission. Interim earnings or amounts earnable with reasonable diligence by the person or persons discriminated against shall operate to reduce the back pay otherwise allowable.

(2)(A) No order of the court shall require the admission or reinstatement of an individual as a member of a union, or the hiring, reinstatement, or promotion of an individual as an employee, or the payment to him of any back pay, if such individual was refused admission, suspended, or expelled, or was refused employment or advancement or was suspended or discharged for any reason other than discrimination on account of race, color, religion, sex, or national origin or in violation of section 2000e-3(a) of this title.

(B) On a claim in which an individual proves a violation under section 2000e- 2(m) of this title and a respondent demonstrates that the respondent would have taken the same action in the absence of the impermissible motivating factor, the court--

(i) may grant declaratory relief, injunctive relief (except as provided in clause (ii)), and attorney's fees and costs demonstrated to be directly attributable only to the pursuit of a claim under section 2000e- 2(m) of this title; and

(ii) shall not award damages or issue an order requiring any admission, reinstatement, hiring, promotion, or payment, described in subparagraph (A).

(h) Provisions of chapter 6 of Title 29 not applicable to civil actions for prevention of unlawful practices

The provisions of chapter 6 of Title 29 shall not apply with respect to civil actions brought under this section.

(i) Proceedings by Commission to compel compliance with judicial orders

In any case in which an employer, employment agency, or labor organization fails to comply with an order of a court issued in a civil action brought under this section, the Commission may commence proceedings to compel compliance with such order.

(j) Appeals

Any civil action brought under this section and any proceedings brought under subsection (i) of this section shall be subject to appeal as provided in sections 1291 and 1292, Title 28.

42 U.S.C. § 2000e-6. Civil Actions by the Attorney General

(a) Complaint

Whenever the Attorney General has reasonable cause to believe that any person or group of persons is engaged in a pattern or practice of resistance to the full enjoyment of any of the rights secured by this subchapter, and that the pattern or practice is of such a nature and is intended to deny the full exercise of the rights herein described, the Attorney General may bring a civil action in the appropriate district court of the United States by filing with it a complaint (1) signed by him (or in his absence the Acting Attorney General), (2) setting forth facts pertaining to such pattern or practice, and (3) requesting such relief, including an application for a permanent or temporary injunction, restraining order or other order against the person or persons responsible for such pattern or practice, as he deems necessary to insure the full enjoyment of the rights herein described.

(b) Jurisdiction; three-judge district court for cases of general public importance: hearing, determination, expedition of action, review by Supreme Court; single judge district court: hearing, determination, expedition of action

The district courts of the United States shall have and shall exercise jurisdiction of proceedings instituted pursuant to this section, and in any such proceeding the Attorney General may file with the clerk of such court a request that a court of three judges be convened to hear and determine the case. Such request by the Attorney General shall be accompanied by a certificate that, in his opinion, the case is of general public importance. A copy of the certificate and request for a three-judge court shall be immediately furnished by such clerk to the chief judge of the circuit (or in his absence, the presiding circuit judge of the circuit) in which the case is pending. Upon receipt of such request it shall be the duty of the chief judge of the circuit or the presiding circuit judge, as the case may be, to designate immediately three judges in such circuit, of whom at least one shall be a circuit judge and another of whom shall be a district judge of the court in which the proceeding was instituted, to hear and determine such case, and it shall be the duty of the judges so designated to assign the case for hearing at the earliest practicable date, to participate in the hearing and determination thereof, and to cause the case to be in every way expedited. An appeal from the final judgment of such court will lie to the Supreme Court.

In the event the Attorney General fails to file such a request in any such proceeding, it shall be the duty of the chief judge of the district (or in his absence, the acting chief judge) in which the case is pending immediately to designate a judge in such district to hear and determine the case. In the event that no judge in the district is available to hear and determine the case, the chief judge of the district, or the acting chief judge, as the case may be, shall certify this fact to the chief judge of the circuit (or in his absence, the acting chief judge) who shall then designate a district or circuit judge of the circuit to hear and determine the case.

It shall be the duty of the judge designated pursuant to this section to assign the case for hearing at the earliest practicable date and to cause the case to be in every way expedited.

(c) Transfer of functions, etc., to Commission; effective date; prerequisite to transfer; execution of functions by Commission

Effective two years after March 24, 1972, the functions of the Attorney General under this section shall be transferred to the Commission, together with such personnel, property, records, and unexpended balances of appropriations, allocations, and other funds employed, used, held, available, or to be made available in connection with such functions unless the President submits, and neither House of Congress vetoes, a reorganization plan pursuant to chapter 9 of title 5, inconsistent with the provisions of this subsection. The Commission shall carry out such functions in accordance with subsections (d) and (e) of this section.

(d) Transfer of functions, etc., not to affect suits commenced pursuant to this section prior to date of transfer

Upon the transfer of functions provided for in subsection (c) of this section, in all suits commenced pursuant to this section prior to the date of such transfer, proceedings shall continue without abatement, all court orders and decrees shall remain in effect, and the Commission shall be substituted as a party for the United States of America, the Attorney General, or the Acting Attorney General, as appropriate.

(e) Investigation and action by Commission pursuant to filing of charge of discrimination; procedure

Subsequent to March 24, 1972, the Commission shall have authority to investigate and act on a charge of a pattern or practice of discrimination, whether filed by or on behalf of a person claiming to be aggrieved or by a member of the Commission. All such actions shall be conducted in accordance with the procedures set forth in section 2000e-5 of this title.

42 U.S.C. § 2000e-8 and 2000e-9: These sections deal with evidentiary matters, discovery, and the conduct of hearings by the EEOC.

42 U.S.C. § 2000e-10. - Posting of notices; penalties

(a) Every employer, employment agency, and labor organization, as the case may be, shall post and keep posted in conspicuous places upon its premises where notices to employees, applicants for employment, and members are customarily posted a notice to be prepared or approved by the Commission setting forth excerpts from or, summaries of, the pertinent provisions of this subchapter and information pertinent to the filing of a complaint.

(b) A willful violation of this section shall be punishable by a fine of not more than $100 for each separate offense

42 U.S.C. § 2000e-16. Employment by Federal Government

(a) Discriminatory practices prohibited; employees or applicants for employment subject to coverage

All personnel actions affecting employees or applicants for employment (except with regard to aliens employed outside the limits of the United States) in military departments as defined in section 102 of Title 5, in executive agencies as defined in section 105 of Title 5 (including employees and applicants for employment who are paid from nonappropriated funds), in the United States Postal Service and the Postal Rate Commission, in those units of the Government of the District of Columbia having positions in the competitive service, and in those units of the judicial branch of the Federal Government having positions in the competitive service, in the Smithsonian Institution, and in the Government Printing Office, the General Accounting Office, and the Library of Congress shall be made free from any discrimination based on race, color, religion, sex, or national origin.

(b) Equal Employment Opportunity Commission; enforcement powers, issuance of rules, regulations, etc.; annual review and approval of national and regional equal employment opportunity plans; review and evaluation of equal employment opportunity programs and publication of progress reports; consultations with interested parties; compliance with rules, regulations, etc.; contents of national and regional equal employment opportunity plans; authority of Librarian of Congress

Except as otherwise provided in this subsection, the Equal Employment Opportunity Commission shall have authority to enforce the provisions of subsection (a) of this section through appropriate remedies, including reinstatement or hiring of employees with or without back pay, as will effectuate the policies of this section, and shall issue such rules, regulations, orders and instructions as it deems necessary and appropriate to carry out its responsibilities under this section. The Equal Employment Opportunity Commission shall--

(1) be responsible for the annual review and approval of a national and regional equal employment opportunity plan which each department and agency and each appropriate unit referred to in subsection (a) of this section shall submit in order to maintain an affirmative program of equal employment opportunity for all such employees and applicants for employment;

(2) be responsible for the review and evaluation of the operation of all agency equal employment opportunity programs, periodically obtaining and publishing (on at least a semiannual basis) progress reports from each such department, agency, or unit; and

(3) consult with and solicit the recommendations of interested individuals, groups, and organizations relating to equal employment opportunity.

The head of each such department, agency, or unit shall comply with such rules, regulations, orders, and instructions which shall include a provision that an employee or applicant for employment shall be notified of any final action taken on any complaint of discrimination filed by him thereunder. The plan submitted by each department, agency, and unit shall include, but not be limited to--

(1) provision for the establishment of training and education programs designed to provide a maximum opportunity for employees to advance so as to perform at their highest potential; and

(2) a description of the qualifications in terms of training and experience relating to equal employment opportunity for the principal and operating officials of each such department, agency, or unit responsible for carrying out the equal employment opportunity program and of the allocation of personnel and resources proposed by such department, agency, or unit to carry out its equal employment opportunity program.

With respect to employment in the Library of Congress, authorities granted in this subsection to the Equal Employment Opportunity Commission shall be exercised by the Librarian of Congress.

(c) Civil action by employee or applicant for employment for redress of grievances; time for bringing of action; head of department, agency, or unit as defendant

Within 90 days of receipt of notice of final action taken by a department, agency, or unit referred to in subsection (a) of this section, or by the Equal Employment Opportunity Commission upon an appeal from a decision or order of such department, agency, or unit on a complaint of discrimination based on race, color, religion, sex or national origin, brought pursuant to subsection (a) of this section, Executive Order 11478 or any succeeding Executive orders, or after one hundred and eighty days from the filing of the initial charge with the department, agency, or unit or with the Equal Employment Opportunity Commission on appeal from a decision or order of such department, agency, or unit until such time as final action may be taken by a department, agency, or unit, an employee or applicant for employment, if aggrieved by the final disposition of his complaint, or by the failure to take final action on his complaint, may file a civil action as provided in section 2000e-5 of this title, in which civil action the head of the department, agency, or unit, as appropriate, shall be the defendant.

(d) Section 2000e-5(f) through (k) of this title applicable to civil actions

The provisions of section 2000e-5(f) through (k) of this title, as applicable, shall govern civil actions brought hereunder, and the same interest to compensate for delay in payment shall be available as in cases involving nonpublic parties.

(e) Government agency or official not relieved of responsibility to assure nondiscrimination in employment or equal employment opportunity

Nothing contained in this Act shall relieve any Government agency or official of its or his primary responsibility to assure nondiscrimination in employment as required by the Constitution and statutes or of its or his responsibilities under Executive Order 11478 relating to equal employment opportunity in the Federal Government.

APPENDIX 3

REHABILITATION ACT OF 1973
§§ 501, 504, 505, 508, codified in
29 U.S.C. §§ 791, 794, 794a and 794d

§ 501, 29 U.S.C. § 791. Employment of individuals with disabilities

(a) Interagency Committee on Employees who are Individuals with Disabilities; establishment; membership; co-chairmen; availability of other Committee resources; purpose and functions

There is established within the Federal Government an Interagency Committee on Employees who are Individuals with Disabilities (hereinafter in this section referred to as the "Committee"), comprised of such members as the President may select, including the following (or their designees whose positions are Executive Level IV or higher): the Chairman of the Equal Employment Opportunity Commission (hereafter in this section referred to as the "Commission"), the Director of the Office of Personnel Management, the Secretary of Veterans Affairs, the Secretary of Labor, the Secretary of Education, and the Secretary of Health and Human Services. Either the Director of the Office of Personnel Management and the Chairman of the Commission shall serve as co-chairpersons of the Committee or the Director or Chairman shall serve as the sole chairperson of the Committee, as the Director and Chairman jointly determine, from time to time, to be appropriate. The resources of the President's Committees on Employment of People With Disabilities and on Mental Retardation shall be made fully available to the Committee. It shall be the purpose and function of the Committee (1) to provide a focus for Federal and other employment of individuals with disabilities, and to review, on a periodic basis, in cooperation with the Commission, the adequacy of hiring, placement, and advancement practices with respect to individuals with disabilities, by each department, agency, and instrumentality in the executive branch of Government and the Smithsonian Institution, and to insure that the special needs of such individuals are being met; and (2) to consult with the Commission to assist the Commission to carry out its responsibilities under subsections (b), (c), and (d) of this section. On the basis of such review and consultation, the Committee shall periodically make to the Commission such recommendations for legislative and administrative changes as it deems necessary or desirable. The Commission shall timely transmit to the appropriate committees of Congress any such recommendations.

(b) Federal agencies; affirmative action program plans

Each department, agency, and instrumentality (including the United States Postal Service and the Postal Rate Commission) in the executive branch and the Smithsonian Institution shall, within one hundred and eighty days after September 26, 1973, submit to the Commission and to the Committee an affirmative action program plan for the hiring, placement, and advancement of individuals with disabilities in such department, agency, instrumentality, or Institution. Such plan shall include a description of the extent to which and methods whereby the special needs of employees who are individuals with disabilities are being met. Such plan shall be updated annually, and shall be reviewed annually and approved by the Commission, if the Commission determines, after consultation with the Committee, that such plan provides sufficient assurances, procedures and commitments to provide adequate hiring, placement, and advancement opportunities for individuals with disabilities.

(c) State agencies; rehabilitated individuals, employment

The Commission, after consultation with the Committee, shall develop and recommend to the Secretary for referral to the appropriate State agencies, policies and procedures which will facilitate the hiring, placement, and advancement in employment of individuals who have received rehabilitation services under State vocational rehabilitation programs, veterans' programs, or any other program for individuals with disabilities, including the promotion of job opportunities for such individuals. The Secretary shall encourage such State agencies to adopt and implement such policies and procedures.

(d) Report to Congressional committees

The Commission, after consultation with the Committee, shall, on June 30, 1974, and at the end of each subsequent fiscal year, make a complete report to the appropriate committees of the Congress with respect to the practices of and achievements in hiring, placement, and advancement of individuals with disabilities by each department, agency, and instrumentality and the Smithsonian Institution and the effectiveness of the affirmative action programs required by subsection (b) of this section, together with recommendations as to legislation which have been submitted to the Commission under subsection (a) of this section, or other appropriate action to insure the adequacy of such practices. Such report shall also include an evaluation by the Committee of the effectiveness of the activities of the Commission under subsections (b) and (c) of this section.

(e) Federal work experience without pay; non-Federal status

An individual who, as a part of an individualized plan for employment under a State plan approved under this chapter, participates in a program of unpaid work experience in a Federal agency, shall not, by reason thereof, be considered to be a Federal employee or to be subject to the provisions of law relating to Federal employment, including those relating to hours of work, rates of compensation, leave, unemployment compensation, and Federal employee benefits.

(f) Federal agency cooperation; special consideration for positions on President's Committee on Employment of People With Disabilities

(1) The Secretary of Labor and the Secretary of Education are authorized and directed to cooperate with the President's Committee on Employment of People With Disabilities in carrying out its functions.

(2) In selecting personnel to fill all positions on the President's Committee on Employment of People With Disabilities, special consideration shall be given to qualified individuals with disabilities.

(g) Standards used in determining violation of section

The standards used to determine whether this section has been violated in a complaint alleging nonaffirmative action employment discrimination under this section shall be the standards applied under title I of the Americans with Disabilities Act of 1990 (42 U.S.C. 12111 et seq.) and the provisions of sections 501 through 504, and 510, of the Americans with Disabilities Act of 1990 (42 U.S.C. 12201-12204 and 12210), as such sections relate to employment.

§ 504, 29 U.S.C. § 794. Nondiscrimination under Federal grants and programs

(a) Promulgation of rules and regulations

No otherwise qualified individual with a disability in the United States, as defined in section 705(20) of this title, shall, solely by reason of her or his disability, be excluded from the participation in, be denied the benefits of, or be subjected to discrimination under any program or activity receiving Federal financial assistance or under any program or activity conducted by any Executive agency or by the United States Postal Service. The head of each such agency shall promulgate such regulations as may be necessary to carry out the amendments to this section made by the Rehabilitation, Comprehensive Services, and Developmental Disabilities Act of 1978. Copies of any proposed regulation shall be submitted to appropriate authorizing committees of the Congress, and such regulation may take effect no earlier than the thirtieth day after the date on which such regulation is so submitted to such committees.

(b) "Program or activity" defined

For the purposes of this section, the term "program or activity" means all of the operations of--

(1)(A) a department, agency, special purpose district, or other instrumentality of a State or of a local government; or

(B) the entity of such State or local government that distributes such assistance and each such department or agency (and each other State or local government entity) to which the assistance is extended, in the case of assistance to a State or local government;

(2)(A) a college, university, or other postsecondary institution, or a public system of higher education; or

(B) a local educational agency (as defined in section 7801 of Title 20), system of vocational education, or other school system;

(3)(A) an entire corporation, partnership, or other private organization, or an entire sole proprietorship--

(i) if assistance is extended to such corporation, partnership, private organization, or sole proprietorship as a whole; or

(ii) which is principally engaged in the business of providing education, health care, housing, social services, or parks and recreation; or

(B) the entire plant or other comparable, geographically separate facility to which Federal financial assistance is extended, in the case of any other corporation, partnership, private organization, or sole proprietorship; or

(4) any other entity which is established by two or more of the entities described in paragraph (1), (2), or (3);

any part of which is extended Federal financial assistance.

(c) Significant structural alterations by small providers

Small providers are not required by subsection (a) of this section to make significant structural alterations to their existing facilities for the purpose of assuring program accessibility, if alternative means of providing the services are available. The terms used in this subsection shall be construed with reference to the regulations existing on March 22, 1988.

(d) Standards used in determining violation of section

The standards used to determine whether this section has been violated in a complaint alleging employment discrimination under this section shall be the standards applied under title I of the Americans with Disabilities Act of 1990 (42 U.S.C. 12111 et seq.) and the provisions of sections 501 through 504, and 510, of the Americans with Disabilities Act of 1990 (42 U.S.C. 12201 to 12204 and 12210), as such sections relate to employment.

§ 505, 29 U.S.C. § 794a. Remedies and attorney fees

(a)(1) The remedies, procedures, and rights set forth in section 717 of the Civil Rights Act of 1964 (42 U.S.C. 2000e-16), including the application of sections 706(f) through 706(k) (42 U.S.C. 2000e-5(f) through (k)), shall be available, with respect to any complaint under section 791 of this title, to any employee or applicant for employment aggrieved by the final disposition of such complaint, or by the failure to take final action on such complaint. In fashioning an equitable or affirmative action remedy under such section, a court may take into account the reasonableness of the cost of any necessary work place accommodation, and the availability of alternatives therefor or other appropriate relief in order to achieve an equitable and appropriate remedy.

(2) The remedies, procedures, and rights set forth in title VI of the Civil Rights Act of 1964 [42 U.S.C.A. § 2000d et seq.] shall be available to any person aggrieved by any act or failure to act by any recipient of Federal assistance or Federal provider of such assistance under section 794 of this title.

(b) In any action or proceeding to enforce or charge a violation of a provision of this subchapter, the court, in its discretion, may allow the prevailing party, other than the United States, a reasonable attorney's fee as part of the costs.

§ 508, 29 U.S.C. § 794d. Electronic and information technology

(a) Requirements for Federal departments and agencies

    (1) Accessibility

    (A) Development, procurement, maintenance, or use of electronic and information technology

When developing, procuring, maintaining, or using electronic and information technology, each Federal department or agency, including the United States Postal Service, shall ensure, unless an undue burden would be imposed on the department or agency, that the electronic and information technology allows, regardless of the type of medium of the technology--

(i) individuals with disabilities who are Federal employees to have access to and use of information and data that is comparable to the access to and use of the information and data by Federal employees who are not individuals with disabilities; and

(ii) individuals with disabilities who are members of the public seeking information or services from a Federal department or agency to have access to and use of information and data that is comparable to the access to and use of the information and data by such members of the public who are not individuals with disabilities.

(B) Alternative means efforts

When development, procurement, maintenance, or use of electronic and information technology that meets the standards published by the Access Board under paragraph (2) would impose an undue burden, the Federal department or agency shall provide individuals with disabilities covered by paragraph (1) with the information and data involved by an alternative means of access that allows the individual to use the information and data.

(2) Electronic and information technology standards

(A) In general

Not later than 18 months after August 7, 1998, the Architectural and Transportation Barriers Compliance Board (referred to in this section as the "Access Board"), after consultation with the Secretary of Education, the Administrator of General Services, the Secretary of Commerce, the Chairman of the Federal Communications Commission, the Secretary of Defense, and the head of any other Federal department or agency that the Access Board determines to be appropriate, including consultation on relevant research findings, and after consultation with the electronic and information technology industry and appropriate public or nonprofit agencies or organizations, including organizations representing individuals with disabilities, shall issue and publish standards setting forth--

(i) for purposes of this section, a definition of electronic and information technology that is consistent with the definition of information technology specified in section 11101(6) of Title 40; and

(ii) the technical and functional performance criteria necessary to implement the requirements set forth in paragraph (1).

(B) Review and amendment

The Access Board shall periodically review and, as appropriate, amend the standards required under subparagraph (A) to reflect technological advances or changes in electronic and information technology.

(3) Incorporation of standards

Not later than 6 months after the Access Board publishes the standards required under paragraph (2), the Federal Acquisition Regulatory Council shall revise the Federal Acquisition Regulation and each Federal department or agency shall revise the Federal procurement policies and directives under the control of the department or agency to incorporate those standards. Not later than 6 months after the Access Board revises any standards required under paragraph (2), the Council shall revise the Federal Acquisition Regulation and each appropriate Federal department or agency shall revise the procurement policies and directives, as necessary, to incorporate the revisions.

(4) Acquisition planning

In the event that a Federal department or agency determines that compliance with the standards issued by the Access Board under paragraph (2) relating to procurement imposes an undue burden, the documentation by the department or agency supporting the procurement shall explain why compliance creates an undue burden.

(5) Exemption for national security systems

This section shall not apply to national security systems, as that term is defined in section 11103 of Title 40.

(6) Construction

(A) Equipment

In a case in which the Federal Government provides access to the public to information or data through electronic and information technology, nothing in this section shall be construed to require a Federal department or agency--

(i) to make equipment owned by the Federal Government available for access and use by individuals with disabilities covered by paragraph (1) at a location other than that where the electronic and information technology is provided to the public; or

(ii) to purchase equipment for access and use by individuals with disabilities covered by paragraph (1) at a location other than that where the electronic and information technology is provided to the public.

(B) Software and peripheral devices

Except as required to comply with standards issued by the Access Board under paragraph (2), nothing in paragraph (1) requires the installation of specific accessibility-related software or the attachment of a specific accessibility-related peripheral device at a workstation of a Federal employee who is not an individual with a disability.

(b) Technical assistance

The Administrator of General Services and the Access Board shall provide technical assistance to individuals and Federal departments and agencies concerning the requirements of this section.

(c) Agency evaluations

Not later than 6 months after August 7, 1998, the head of each Federal department or agency shall evaluate the extent to which the electronic and information technology of the department or agency is accessible to and usable by individuals with disabilities described in subsection (a)(1) of this section, compared to the access to and use of the technology by individuals described in such subsection who are not individuals with disabilities, and submit a report containing the evaluation to the Attorney General.

(d) Reports

(1) Interim report

Not later than 18 months after August 7, 1998, the Attorney General shall prepare and submit to the President a report containing information on and recommendations regarding the extent to which the electronic and information technology of the Federal Government is accessible to and usable by individuals with disabilities described in subsection (a)(1) of this section.

(2) Biennial reports

Not later than 3 years after August 7, 1998, and every 2 years thereafter, the Attorney General shall prepare and submit to the President and Congress a report containing information on and recommendations regarding the state of Federal department and agency compliance with the requirements of this section, including actions regarding individual complaints under subsection (f) of this section.

(e) Cooperation

Each head of a Federal department or agency (including the Access Board, the Equal Employment Opportunity Commission, and the General Services Administration) shall provide to the Attorney General such information as the Attorney General determines is necessary to conduct the evaluations under subsection (c) of this section and prepare the reports under subsection (d) of this section.

(f) Enforcement

(1) General

(A) Complaints

Effective 6 months after the date of publication by the Access Board of final standards described in subsection (a)(2) of this section, any individual with a disability may file a complaint alleging that a Federal department or agency fails to comply with subsection (a)(1) of this section in providing electronic and information technology.

(B) Application

This subsection shall apply only to electronic and information technology that is procured by a Federal department or agency not less than 6 months after the date of publication by the Access Board of final standards described in subsection (a)(2) of this section.

(2) Administrative complaints

Complaints filed under paragraph (1) shall be filed with the Federal department or agency alleged to be in noncompliance. The Federal department or agency receiving the complaint shall apply the complaint procedures established to implement section 794 of this title for resolving allegations of discrimination in a federally conducted program or activity.

(3) Civil actions

The remedies, procedures, and rights set forth in sections 794a(a)(2) and 794a(b) of this title shall be the remedies, procedures, and rights available to any individual with a disability filing a complaint under paragraph (1).

(g) Application to other Federal laws

This section shall not be construed to limit any right, remedy, or procedure otherwise available under any provision of Federal law (including sections 791 through 794a of this title) that provides greater or equal protection for the rights of individuals with disabilities than this section.

APPENDIX 4

FAIR HOUSING ACT
Codified in 42 U.S.C. § 3604, et seq.

SUBCHAPTER I--GENERALLY

§ 3604. Discrimination in the sale or rental of housing and other prohibited practices

As made applicable by section 3603 of this title and except as exempted by sections 3603(b) and 3607 of this title, it shall be unlawful--

(a) To refuse to sell or rent after the making of a bona fide offer, or to refuse to negotiate for the sale or rental of, or otherwise make unavailable or deny, a dwelling to any person because of race, color, religion, sex, familial status, or national origin.

(b) To discriminate against any person in the terms, conditions, or privileges of sale or rental of a dwelling, or in the provision of services or facilities in connection therewith, because of race, color, religion, sex, familial status, or national origin.

(c) To make, print, or publish, or cause to be made, printed, or published any notice, statement, or advertisement, with respect to the sale or rental of a dwelling that indicates any preference, limitation, or discrimination based on race, color, religion, sex, handicap, familial status, or national origin, or an intention to make any such preference, limitation, or discrimination.

(d) To represent to any person because of race, color, religion, sex, handicap, familial status, or national origin that any dwelling is not available for inspection, sale, or rental when such dwelling is in fact so available.

(e) For profit, to induce or attempt to induce any person to sell or rent any dwelling by representations regarding the entry or prospective entry into the neighborhood of a person or persons of a particular race, color, religion, sex, handicap, familial status, or national origin.

(f)(1) To discriminate in the sale or rental, or to otherwise make unavailable or deny, a dwelling to any buyer or renter because of a handicap of--

(A) that buyer or renter, [FN1]

(B) a person residing in or intending to reside in that dwelling after it is so sold, rented, or made available; or

(C) any person associated with that buyer or renter.

(2) To discriminate against any person in the terms, conditions, or privileges of sale or rental of a dwelling, or in the provision of services or facilities in connection with such dwelling, because of a handicap of--

(A) that person; or

(B) a person residing in or intending to reside in that dwelling after it is so sold, rented, or made available; or

(C) any person associated with that person.

(3) For purposes of this subsection, discrimination includes--

(A) a refusal to permit, at the expense of the handicapped person, reasonable modifications of existing premises occupied or to be occupied by such person if such modifications may be necessary to afford such person full enjoyment of the premises except that, in the case of a rental, the landlord may where it is reasonable to do so condition permission for a modification on the renter agreeing to restore the interior of the premises to the condition that existed before the modification, reasonable wear and tear excepted. [FN2]

(B) a refusal to make reasonable accommodations in rules, policies, practices, or services, when such accommodations may be necessary to afford such person equal opportunity to use and enjoy a dwelling; or

(C) in connection with the design and construction of covered multifamily dwellings for first occupancy after the date that is 30 months after September 13, 1988, a failure to design and construct those dwellings in such a manner that--

(i) the public use and common use portions of such dwellings are readily accessible to and usable by handicapped persons;

(ii) all the doors designed to allow passage into and within all premises within such dwellings are sufficiently wide to allow passage by handicapped persons in wheelchairs; and

(iii) all premises within such dwellings contain the following features of adaptive design:

(I) an accessible route into and through the dwelling;

(II) light switches, electrical outlets, thermostats, and other environmental controls in accessible locations;

(III) reinforcements in bathroom walls to allow later installation of grab bars; and

(IV) usable kitchens and bathrooms such that an individual in a wheelchair can maneuver about the space.

(4) Compliance with the appropriate requirements of the American National Standard for buildings and facilities providing accessibility and usability for physically handicapped people (commonly cited as "ANSI A117.1") suffices to satisfy the requirements of paragraph (3)(C)(iii).

(5)(A) If a State or unit of general local government has incorporated into its laws the requirements set forth in paragraph (3)(C), compliance with such laws shall be deemed to satisfy the requirements of that paragraph.

(B) A State or unit of general local government may review and approve newly constructed covered multifamily dwellings for the purpose of making determinations as to whether the design and construction requirements of paragraph (3)(C) are met.

(C) The Secretary shall encourage, but may not require, States and units of local government to include in their existing procedures for the review and approval of newly constructed covered multifamily dwellings, determinations as to whether the design and construction of such dwellings are consistent with paragraph (3)(C), and shall provide technical assistance to States and units of local government and other persons to implement the requirements of paragraph (3)(C).

(D) Nothing in this subchapter shall be construed to require the Secretary to review or approve the plans, designs or construction of all covered multifamily dwellings, to determine whether the design and construction of such dwellings are consistent with the requirements of paragraph 3(C).

(6)(A) Nothing in paragraph (5) shall be construed to affect the authority and responsibility of the Secretary or a State or local public agency certified pursuant to section 3610(f)(3) of this title to receive and process complaints or otherwise engage in enforcement activities under this subchapter.

(B) Determinations by a State or a unit of general local government under paragraphs (5)(A) and (B) shall not be conclusive in enforcement proceedings under this subchapter.

(7) As used in this subsection, the term "covered multifamily dwellings" means--

(A) buildings consisting of 4 or more units if such buildings have one or more elevators; and

(B) ground floor units in other buildings consisting of 4 or more units.

(8) Nothing in this subchapter shall be construed to invalidate or limit any law of a State or political subdivision of a State, or other jurisdiction in which this subchapter shall be effective, that requires dwellings to be designed and constructed in a manner that affords handicapped persons greater access than is required by this subchapter.

(9) Nothing in this subsection requires that a dwelling be made available to an individual whose tenancy would constitute a direct threat to the health or safety of other individuals or whose tenancy would result in substantial physical damage to the property of others.

APPENDIX 5

STATE OF CALIFORNIA
GOVERNMENT CODE
FAIR EMPLOYMENT AND HOUSING ACT (SELECTED EXCERPTS)
DIVISION 3. EXECUTIVE DEPARTMENT
PART 2.8. DEPARTMENT OF FAIR EMPLOYMENT AND HOUSING

§ 12921. Civil rights; employment and housing without discrimination

(a) The opportunity to seek, obtain and hold employment without discrimination because of race, religious creed, color, national origin, ancestry, physical disability, mental disability, medical condition, marital status, sex, age, or sexual orientation is hereby recognized as and declared to be a civil right.

(b) The opportunity to seek, obtain, and hold housing without discrimination because of race, color, religion, sex, sexual orientation, marital status, national origin, ancestry, familial status, disability, or any other basis prohibited by Section 51 of the Civil Code is hereby recognized as and declared to be a civil right.

§ 12926. Additional definitions

As used in this part in connection with unlawful practices, unless a different meaning clearly appears from the context:

(a) "Affirmative relief" or "prospective relief" includes the authority to order reinstatement of an employee, awards of backpay, reimbursement of out-of-pocket expenses, hiring, transfers, reassignments, grants of tenure, promotions, cease and desist orders, posting of notices, training of personnel, testing, expunging of records, reporting of records, and any other similar relief that is intended to correct unlawful practices under this part.

(b) "Age" refers to the chronological age of any individual who has reached his or her 40th birthday.

(c) "Employee" does not include any individual employed by his or her parents, spouse, or child, or any individual employed under a special license in a nonprofit sheltered workshop or rehabilitation facility.

(d) "Employer" includes any person regularly employing five or more persons, or any person acting as an agent of an employer, directly or indirectly, the state or any political or civil subdivision of the state, and cities, except as follows:

"Employer" does not include a religious association or corporation not organized for private profit.

(e) "Employment agency" includes any person undertaking for compensation to procure employees or opportunities to work.

(f) "Essential functions" means the fundamental job duties of the employment position the individual with a disability holds or desires. "Essential functions" does not include the marginal functions of the position.

(1) A job function may be considered essential for any of several reasons, including, but not limited to, any one or more of the following:

(A) The function may be essential because the reason the position exists is to perform that function.

(B) The function may be essential because of the limited number of employees available among whom the performance of that job function can be distributed.

(C) The function may be highly specialized, so that the incumbent in the position is hired for his or her expertise or ability to perform the particular function.

(2) Evidence of whether a particular function is essential includes, but is not limited to, the following:

(A) The employer's judgment as to which functions are essential.

(B) Written job descriptions prepared before advertising or interviewing applicants for the job.

(C) The amount of time spent on the job performing the function.

(D) The consequences of not requiring the incumbent to perform the function.

(E) The terms of a collective bargaining agreement.

(F) The work experiences of past incumbents in the job.

(G) The current work experience of incumbents in similar jobs.

(g) "Labor organization" includes any organization that exists and is constituted for the purpose, in whole or in part, of collective bargaining or of dealing with employers concerning grievances, terms or conditions of employment, or of other mutual aid or protection.

(h) "Medical condition" means either of the following:

(1) Any health impairment related to or associated with a diagnosis of cancer or a record or history of cancer.

(2) Genetic characteristics. For purposes of this section, "genetic characteristics" means either of the following:

(A) Any scientifically or medically identifiable gene or chromosome, or combination or alteration thereof, that is known to be a cause of a disease or disorder in a person or his or her offspring, or that is determined to be associated with a statistically increased risk of development of a disease or disorder, and that is presently not associated with any symptoms of any disease or disorder.

(B) Inherited characteristics that may derive from the individual or family member, that are known to be a cause of a disease or disorder in a person or his or her offspring, or that are determined to be associated with a statistically increased risk of development of a disease or disorder, and that are presently not associated with any symptoms of any disease or disorder.

(i) "Mental disability" includes, but is not limited to, all of the following:

(1) Having any mental or psychological disorder or condition, such as mental retardation, organic brain syndrome, emotional or mental illness, or specific learning disabilities, that limits a major life activity. For purposes of this section:

(A) "Limits" shall be determined without regard to mitigating measures, such as medications, assistive devices, or reasonable accommodations, unless the mitigating measure itself limits a major life activity.

(B) A mental or psychological disorder or condition limits a major life activity if it makes the achievement of the major life activity difficult.

(C) "Major life activities" shall be broadly construed and shall include physical, mental, and social activities and working.

(2) Any other mental or psychological disorder or condition not described in paragraph (1) that requires special education or related services.

(3) Having a record or history of a mental or psychological disorder or condition described in paragraph (1) or (2), which is known to the employer or other entity covered by this part.

(4) Being regarded or treated by the employer or other entity covered by this part as having, or having had, any mental condition that makes achievement of a major life activity difficult.

(5) Being regarded or treated by the employer or other entity covered by this part as having, or having had, a mental or psychological disorder or condition that has no present disabling effect, but that may become a mental disability as described in paragraph (1) or (2).

"Mental disability" does not include sexual behavior disorders, compulsive gambling, kleptomania, pyromania, or psychoactive substance use disorders resulting from the current unlawful use of controlled substances or other drugs.

(j) "On the bases enumerated in this part" means or refers to discrimination on the basis of one or more of the following: race, religious creed, color, national origin, ancestry, physical disability, mental disability, medical condition, marital status, sex, age, or sexual orientation.

(k) "Physical disability" includes, but is not limited to, all of the following:

(1) Having any physiological disease, disorder, condition, cosmetic disfigurement, or anatomical loss that does both of the following:

(A) Affects one or more of the following body systems: neurological, immunological, musculoskeletal, special sense organs, respiratory, including speech organs, cardiovascular, reproductive, digestive, genitourinary, hemic and lymphatic, skin, and endocrine.

(B) Limits a major life activity. For purposes of this section:

(i) "Limits" shall be determined without regard to mitigating measures such as medications, assistive devices, prosthetics, or reasonable accommodations, unless the mitigating measure itself limits a major life activity.

(ii) A physiological disease, disorder, condition, cosmetic disfigurement, or anatomical loss limits a major life activity if it makes the achievement of the major life activity difficult.

(iii) "Major life activities" shall be broadly construed and includes physical, mental, and social activities and working.

(2) Any other health impairment not described in paragraph (1) that requires special education or related services.

(3) Having a record or history of a disease, disorder, condition, cosmetic disfigurement, anatomical loss, or health impairment described in paragraph (1) or (2), which is known to the employer or other entity covered by this part.

(4) Being regarded or treated by the employer or other entity covered by this part as having, or having had, any physical condition that makes achievement of a major life activity difficult.

(5) Being regarded or treated by the employer or other entity covered by this part as having, or having had, a disease, disorder, condition, cosmetic disfigurement, anatomical loss, or health impairment that has no present disabling effect but may become a physical disability as described in paragraph (1) or (2).

(6) "Physical disability" does not include sexual behavior disorders, compulsive gambling, kleptomania, pyromania, or psychoactive substance use disorders resulting from the current unlawful use of controlled substances or other drugs.

(l) Notwithstanding subdivisions (i) and (k), if the definition of "disability" used in the Americans with Disabilities Act of 1990 (Public Law 101-336) would result in broader protection of the civil rights of individuals with a mental disability or physical disability, as defined in subdivision (i) or (k), or would include any medical condition not included within those definitions, then that broader protection or coverage shall be deemed incorporated by reference into, and shall prevail over conflicting provisions of, the definitions in subdivisions (i) and (k).

(m) "Race, religious creed, color, national origin, ancestry, physical disability, mental disability, medical condition, marital status, sex, age, or sexual orientation" includes a perception that the person has any of those characteristics or that the person is associated with a person who has, or is perceived to have, any of those characteristics.

(n) "Reasonable accommodation" may include either of the following:

(1) Making existing facilities used by employees readily accessible to, and usable by, individuals with disabilities.

(2) Job restructuring, part-time or modified work schedules, reassignment to a vacant position, acquisition or modification of equipment or devices, adjustment or modifications of examinations, training materials or

policies, the provision of qualified readers or interpreters, and other similar accommodations for individuals with disabilities.

(o) "Religious creed," "religion," "religious observance," "religious belief," and "creed" include all aspects of religious belief, observance, and practice.

(p) "Sex" includes, but is not limited to, pregnancy, childbirth, or medical conditions related to pregnancy or childbirth.

(q) "Sexual orientation" means heterosexuality, homosexuality, and bisexuality.

(r) "Supervisor" means any individual having the authority, in the interest of the employer, to hire, transfer, suspend, lay off, recall, promote, discharge, assign, reward, or discipline other employees, or the responsibility to direct them, or to adjust their grievances, or effectively to recommend that action, if, in connection with the foregoing, the exercise of that authority is not of a merely routine or clerical nature, but requires the use of independent judgment.

(s) "Undue hardship" means an action requiring significant difficulty or expense, when considered in light of the following factors: (1) the nature and cost of the accommodation needed, (2) the overall financial resources of the facilities involved in the provision of the reasonable accommodations, the number of persons employed at the facility, and the effect on expenses and resources or the impact otherwise of these accommodations upon the operation of the facility, (3) the overall financial resources of the covered entity, the overall size of the business of a covered entity with respect to the number of employees, and the number, type, and location of its facilities, (4) the type of operations, including the composition, structure, and functions of the workforce of the entity, and (5) the geographic separateness, administrative, or fiscal relationship of the facility or facilities.

§ 12927. Housing accommodations; definitions

As used in this part in connection with housing accommodations, unless a different meaning clearly appears from the context:

(a) "Affirmative actions" means any activity for the purpose of eliminating discrimination in housing accommodations because of race, color, religion, sex, marital status, national origin, ancestry, familial status, or disability.

(b) "Conciliation council" means a nonprofit organization, or a city or county human relations commission, which provides education, factfinding, and mediation or conciliation services in resolution of complaints of housing discrimination.

(c)(1) "Discrimination" includes refusal to sell, rent, or lease housing accommodations; includes refusal to negotiate for the sale, rental, or lease of housing accommodations; includes representation that a housing accommodation is not available for inspection, sale, or rental when that housing accommodation is in fact so available; includes any other denial or withholding of housing accommodations; includes provision of inferior terms, conditions, privileges, facilities, or services in connection with those housing accommodations; includes harassment in connection with those housing accommodations; includes the cancellation or termination of a sale or rental agreement; includes the provision of segregated or separated housing accommodations; includes the refusal to permit, at the expense of the disabled person, reasonable modifications of existing premises occupied or to be occupied by the disabled person, if the modifications may be necessary to afford the disabled person full enjoyment of the premises, except that, in the case of a rental, the landlord may, where it is reasonable to do so condition permission for a modification on the renter's agreeing to restore the interior of the premises to the condition that existed before the modification (other than for reasonable wear and tear), and includes refusal to make reasonable accommodations in rules, policies, practices, or services when these accommodations may be necessary to afford a disabled person equal opportunity to use and enjoy a dwelling.

(2) "Discrimination" does not include either of the following:

(A) Refusal to rent or lease a portion of an owner-occupied single-family house to a person as a roomer or boarder living within the household, provided that no more than one roomer or boarder is to live within the household, and the owner complies with subdivision (c) of Section 12955, which prohibits discriminatory notices, statements, and advertisements.

(B) Where the sharing of living areas in a single dwelling unit is involved, the use of words stating or tending to imply that the housing being advertised is available only to persons of one sex.

(d) "Housing accommodation" means any building, structure, or portion thereof that is occupied as, or intended for occupancy as, a residence by one or more families and any vacant land that is offered for sale or lease for the construction thereon of any building, structure, or portion thereof intended to be so occupied.

(e) "Owner" includes the lessee, sublessee, assignee, managing agent, real estate broker or salesperson, or any person having any legal or equitable right of ownership or possession or the right to rent or lease housing accommodations, and includes the state and any of its political subdivisions and any agency thereof.

(f) "Person" includes all individuals and entities that are described in Section 3602(d) of Title 42 of the United States Code, and in the definition of "owner" in subdivision (e) of this section, and all institutional third parties, including the Federal Home Loan Mortgage Corporation.

(g) "Aggrieved person" includes any person who claims to have been injured by a discriminatory housing practice or believes that the person will be injured by a discriminatory housing practice that is about to occur.

(h) "Real estate-related transactions" include any of the following:

(1) The making or purchasing of loans or providing other financial assistance that is for the purpose of purchasing, constructing, improving, repairing, or maintaining a dwelling, or that is secured by residential real estate.

(2) The selling, brokering, or appraising of residential real property.

(3) The use of territorial underwriting requirements, for the purpose of requiring a borrower in a specific geographic area to obtain earthquake insurance, required by an institutional third party on a loan secured by residential real property.

§ 12932. Legislative recognition; employment of disabled persons; conciliation assistance; confidentiality; disciplinary action

(a) The Legislature recognizes that the avoidance of discriminatory practices in the employment of disabled persons is most effectively achieved through the ongoing efforts of state agencies involved in the vocational rehabilitation and job placement of the disabled. The department may utilize the efforts and experience of the Department of Rehabilitation in the development of job opportunities for the disabled by requesting the Department of Rehabilitation to foster good will and to conciliate on employment policies with employers who, in the judgment of the department, have employment practices or policies that discriminate against disabled persons. Nothing contained in this paragraph shall be construed to transfer any of the functions, powers, or duties from the department to the Department of Rehabilitation.

(b) The activities of the department in providing conciliation assistance shall be conducted in confidence and without publicity, and the department shall hold confidential any information acquired in the regular performance of its duties upon the understanding that it would be so held.

(c) No employee of the department shall engage in the performance of investigative or prosecuting functions of any department or agency in any litigation arising out of a dispute in which he or she acted on behalf of the department. Any employee of the department, who makes public in any manner whatever any information in violation of this subdivision, is guilty of a misdemeanor and, if a member of the state civil service, shall be subject to disciplinary action under the State Civil Service Act (Part 2 (commencing with Section 18500) of Division 5 of Title 2).

(d) When contacted by the department, employers, labor organizations, or employment agencies shall be informed whether a particular discussion, or portion thereof, constitutes either of the following:

(1) Endeavors at conference, conciliation, and persuasion which may not be disclosed by the department or received in evidence in any formal hearing or court action.

(2) Investigative processes, which are not so protected.

§ 12940. Employers, labor organizations, employment agencies and other persons; unlawful employment practice; exceptions

It shall be an unlawful employment practice, unless based upon a bona fide occupational qualification, or, except where based upon applicable security regulations established by the United States or the State of California:

(a) For an employer, because of the race, religious creed, color, national origin, ancestry, physical disability, mental disability, medical condition, marital status, sex, age, or sexual orientation of any person, to refuse to hire or employ the person or to refuse to select the person for a training program leading to employment, or to bar or to discharge the person from employment or from a training program leading to employment, or to discriminate against the person in compensation or in terms, conditions, or privileges of employment.

(1) This part does not prohibit an employer from refusing to hire or discharging an employee with a physical or mental disability, or subject an employer to any legal liability resulting from the refusal to employ or the discharge of an employee with a physical or mental disability, where the employee, because of his or her physical or mental disability, is unable to perform his or her essential duties even with reasonable accommodations, or cannot perform those duties in a manner that would not endanger his or her health or safety or the health or safety of others even with reasonable accommodations.

(2) This part does not prohibit an employer from refusing to hire or discharging an employee who, because of the employee's medical

condition, is unable to perform his or her essential duties even with reasonable accommodations, or cannot perform those duties in a manner that would not endanger the employee's health or safety or the health or safety of others even with reasonable accommodations. Nothing in this part shall subject an employer to any legal liability resulting from the refusal to employ or the discharge of an employee who, because of the employee's medical condition, is unable to perform his or her essential duties, or cannot perform those duties in a manner that would not endanger the employee's health or safety or the health or safety of others even with reasonable accommodations.

(3) Nothing in this part relating to discrimination on account of marital status shall do either of the following:

(A) Affect the right of an employer to reasonably regulate, for reasons of supervision, safety, security, or morale, the working of spouses in the same department, division, or facility, consistent with the rules and regulations adopted by the commission.

(B) Prohibit bona fide health plans from providing additional or greater benefits to employees with dependents than to those employees without or with fewer dependents.

(4) Nothing in this part relating to discrimination on account of sex shall affect the right of an employer to use veteran status as a factor in employee selection or to give special consideration to Vietnam era veterans.

(5) Nothing in this part prohibits an employer from refusing to employ an individual because of his or her age if the law compels or provides for that refusal. Promotions within the existing staff, hiring or promotion on the basis of experience and training, rehiring on the basis of seniority and prior service with the employer, or hiring under an established recruiting program from high schools, colleges, universities, or trade schools do not, in and of themselves, constitute unlawful employment practices.

(b) For a labor organization, because of the race, religious creed, color, national origin, ancestry, physical disability, mental disability, medical condition, marital status, sex, age, or sexual orientation of any person, to exclude, expel or restrict from its membership the person, or to provide only second-class or segregated membership or to discriminate against any person because of the race, religious creed, color, national origin, ancestry, physical disability, mental disability, medical condition, marital status, sex, age, or sexual orientation of the person in the election of officers of the labor organization or in the selection of the labor organization's staff or to discriminate in any way against any of its members or against any employer or against any person employed by an employer.

(c) For any person to discriminate against any person in the selection or training of that person in any apprenticeship training program or any other training program leading to employment because of the race, religious creed, color, national origin, ancestry, physical disability, mental disability, medical condition, marital status, sex, age, or sexual orientation of the person discriminated against.

(d) For any employer or employment agency to print or circulate or cause to be printed or circulated any publication, or to make any non-job-related inquiry of an employee or applicant, either verbal or through use of an application form, that expresses, directly or indirectly, any limitation, specification, or discrimination as to race, religious creed, color, national origin, ancestry, physical disability, mental disability, medical condition, marital status, sex, age, or sexual orientation, or any intent to make any such limitation, specification or discrimination. Nothing in this part prohibits an employer or employment agency from inquiring into the age of an applicant, or from specifying age limitations, where the law compels or provides for that action.

(e)(1) Except as provided in paragraph (2) or (3), for any employer or employment agency to require any medical or psychological examination of an applicant, to make any medical or psychological inquiry of an applicant, to make any inquiry whether an applicant has a mental disability or physical disability or medical condition, or to make any inquiry regarding the nature or severity of a physical disability, mental disability, or medical condition.

(2) Notwithstanding paragraph (1), an employer or employment agency may inquire into the ability of an applicant to perform job-related functions and may respond to an applicant's request for reasonable accommodation.

(3) Notwithstanding paragraph (1), an employer or employment agency may require a medical or psychological examination or make a medical or psychological inquiry of a job applicant after an employment offer has been made but prior to the commencement of employment duties, provided that the examination or inquiry is job-related and consistent with business necessity and that all entering employees in the same job classification are subject to the same examination or inquiry.

(f)(1) Except as provided in paragraph (2), for any employer or employment agency to require any medical or psychological examination of an employee, to make any medical or psychological inquiry of an employee, to make any inquiry whether an employee has a mental disability, physical disability, or medical condition, or to make any inquiry regarding the nature or severity of a physical disability, mental disability, or medical condition.

(2) Notwithstanding paragraph (1), an employer or employment agency may require any examinations or inquiries that it can show to be job-related and consistent with business necessity. An employer or employment agency may conduct voluntary medical examinations, including voluntary medical histories, which are part of an employee health program available to employees at that worksite.

(g) For any employer, labor organization, or employment agency to harass, discharge, expel, or otherwise discriminate against any person because the person has made a report pursuant to Section 11161.8 of the Penal Code that prohibits retaliation against hospital employees who report suspected patient abuse by health facilities or community care facilities.

(h) For any employer, labor organization, employment agency, or person to discharge, expel, or otherwise discriminate against any person because the person has opposed any practices forbidden under this part or because the person has filed a complaint, testified, or assisted in any proceeding under this part.

(i) For any person to aid, abet, incite, compel, or coerce the doing of any of the acts forbidden under this part, or to attempt to do so.

(j)(1) For an employer, labor organization, employment agency, apprenticeship training program or any training program leading to employment, or any other person, because of race, religious creed, color, national origin, ancestry, physical disability, mental disability, medical condition, marital status, sex, age, or sexual orientation, to harass an employee, an applicant, or a person providing services pursuant to a contract. Harassment of an employee, an applicant, or a person providing services pursuant to a contract by an employee other than an agent or supervisor shall be unlawful if the entity, or its agents or supervisors, knows or should have known of this conduct and fails to take immediate and appropriate corrective action. An entity shall take all reasonable steps to prevent harassment from occurring. Loss of tangible job benefits shall not be necessary in order to establish harassment.

(2) The provisions of this subdivision are declaratory of existing law, except for the new duties imposed on employers with regard to harassment.

(3) An employee of an entity subject to this subdivision is personally liable for any harassment prohibited by this section that is perpetrated by the employee, regardless of whether the employer or covered entity knows or

should have known of the conduct and fails to take immediate and appropriate corrective action.

(4)(A) For purposes of this subdivision only, "employer" means any person regularly employing one or more persons or regularly receiving the services of one or more persons providing services pursuant to a contract, or any person acting as an agent of an employer, directly or indirectly, the state, or any political or civil subdivision of the state, and cities. The definition of "employer" in subdivision (d) of Section 12926 applies to all provisions of this section other than this subdivision.

(B) Notwithstanding subparagraph (A), for purposes of this subdivision, "employer" does not include a religious association or corporation not organized for private profit.

(C) For purposes of this subdivision, "harassment" because of sex includes sexual harassment, gender harassment, and harassment based on pregnancy, childbirth, or related medical conditions.

(5) For purposes of this subdivision, "a person providing services pursuant to a contract" means a person who meets all of the following criteria:

(A) The person has the right to control the performance of the contract for services and discretion as to the manner of performance.

(B) The person is customarily engaged in an independently established business.

(C) The person has control over the time and place the work is performed, supplies the tools and instruments used in the work, and performs work that requires a particular skill not ordinarily used in the course of the employer's work.

(k) For an employer, labor organization, employment agency, apprenticeship training program, or any training program leading to employment, to fail to take all reasonable steps necessary to prevent discrimination and harassment from occurring.

(l) For an employer or other entity covered by this part to refuse to hire or employ a person or to refuse to select a person for a training program leading to employment or to bar or to discharge a person from employment or from a training program leading to employment, or to discriminate against a person in compensation or in terms, conditions, or privileges of employment because of a conflict between the person's religious belief or observance and any employment requirement, unless the employer or other entity covered by this part demonstrates that it has explored any available reasonable alternative means of accommodating the religious belief or observance, including the possibilities of excusing the person from those duties that conflict with his or her religious belief or observance or permitting those duties to be performed at another time or by another person, but is unable to reasonably accommodate the religious belief or observance without undue hardship on the conduct of the business of the employer or other entity covered by this part. Religious belief or observance, as used in this section, includes, but is not limited to, observance of a Sabbath or other religious holy day or days, and reasonable time necessary for travel prior and subsequent to a religious observance.

(m) For an employer or other entity covered by this part to fail to make reasonable accommodation for the known physical or mental disability of an applicant or employee. Nothing in this subdivision or in paragraph (1) or (2) of subdivision (a) shall be construed to require an accommodation that is demonstrated by the employer or other covered entity to produce undue hardship to its operation.

(n) For an employer or other entity covered by this part to fail to engage in a timely, good faith, interactive process with the employee or applicant to determine effective reasonable accommodations, if any, in response to a request for reasonable accommodation by an employee or applicant with a known physical or mental disability or known medical condition.

(o) For an employer or other entity covered by this part, to subject, directly or indirectly, any employee, applicant, or other person to a test for the presence of a genetic characteristic.

§ 12943. School districts; unlawful employment practice based on pregnancy or temporary disability

It shall be an unlawful employment practice unless based upon a bona fide occupational qualification:

(a) For the governing board of any school district, because of the pregnancy of any female person, to refuse to hire or employ her, or to refuse to select her for a training program leading to employment, or to bar or to discharge her from employment or from a training program leading to employment, or to discriminate against her in compensation or in terms, conditions, or privileges of employment.

(b) For the governing board of any school district to terminate any employee who is temporarily disabled, pursuant to or on the basis of an employment policy under which insufficient or no leave is available, if the policy has a disparate impact on employees of one sex and is not justified by necessity of the public schools.

12944. Licensing boards; unlawful acts based on examinations and qualifications; determination of unlawfulness; inquiries; reasonable accommodations; records

(a) It shall be unlawful for a licensing board to require any examination or establish any other qualification for licensing that has an adverse impact on any class by virtue of its race, creed, color, national origin or ancestry, sex, age, medical condition, physical disability, mental disability, or sexual orientation, unless the practice can be demonstrated to be job related.

Where the commission, after hearing, determines that an examination is unlawful under this subdivision, the licensing board may continue to use and rely on the examination until such time as judicial review by the superior court of the determination is exhausted.

If an examination or other qualification for licensing is determined to be unlawful under this section, that determination shall not void, limit, repeal, or otherwise affect any right, privilege, status, or responsibility previously conferred upon any person by the examination or by a license issued in reliance on the examination or qualification.

(b) It shall be unlawful for a licensing board to fail or refuse to make reasonable accommodation to an individual's mental or physical disability or medical condition.

(c) It shall be unlawful for any licensing board, unless specifically acting in accordance with federal equal employment opportunity guidelines or regulations approved by the commission, to print or circulate or cause to be printed or circulated any publication, or to make any non-job-related inquiry, either verbal or through use of an application form, which expresses, directly or indirectly, any limitation, specification, or discrimination as to race, religious creed, color, national origin, ancestry, physical disability, mental disability, medical condition, sex, age, or sexual orientation or any intent to make any such limitation, specification, or discrimination. Nothing in this subdivision shall prohibit any licensing board from making, in connection with prospective licensure or certification, an inquiry as to, or a request for information regarding, the physical fitness of applicants if that inquiry or request for information is directly related and pertinent to the license or the licensed position the applicant is applying for. Nothing in this subdivision shall prohibit any licensing board, in connection with prospective examinations, licensure, or certification, from inviting individuals with physical or mental disabilities to request reasonable accommodations or from making inquiries related to reasonable accommodations.

(d) It is unlawful for a licensing board to discriminate against any person because the person has filed a complaint, testified, or assisted in any proceeding under this part.

(e) It is unlawful for any licensing board to fail to keep records of applications for licensing or certification for a period of two years following the date of receipt of the applications.

(f) As used in this section, "licensing board" means any state board, agency, or authority in the State and Consumer Services Agency that has the authority to grant licenses or certificates which are prerequisites to employment eligibility or professional status.

§ 12945. Pregnancy; childbirth or related medical condition; unlawful practice by employers; benefits and leaves of absence; transfer of position

It shall be an unlawful employment practice, unless based upon a bona fide occupational qualification:

(a) For any employer, because of the pregnancy, childbirth, or related medical condition of any female employee, to refuse to promote her, or to refuse to select her for a training program leading to promotion, provided she is able to complete the training program at least three months prior to the anticipated date of departure for her pregnancy leave, or to discharge her from employment or from a training program leading to promotion, or to discriminate against her in compensation or in terms, conditions, or privileges of employment.

(b) For any employer to refuse to allow a female employee affected by pregnancy, childbirth, or related medical conditions either:

(1) To receive the same benefits or privileges of employment granted by that employer to other persons not so affected who are similar in their ability or inability to work, including to take disability or sick leave or any other accrued leave that is made available by the employer to temporarily disabled employees. For purposes of this section, pregnancy, childbirth, and related medical conditions are treated as any other temporary disability. However, no employer shall be required to provide a female employee disability leave on account of normal pregnancy, childbirth, or related medical condition for a period exceeding six weeks. This section shall not be construed to require an employer to provide his or her employees with health insurance coverage for the medical costs of pregnancy, childbirth, or related medical conditions. The inclusion in any health insurance coverage of any provisions or coverage relating to medical costs of pregnancy, childbirth, or related medical conditions shall not be construed to require the inclusion of any other provisions or coverage, nor shall coverage of any related medical conditions be required by virtue of coverage of any medical costs of pregnancy, childbirth, or

other related medical conditions.

(2) To take a leave on account of pregnancy for a reasonable period of time not to exceed four months. The employee shall be entitled to utilize any accrued vacation leave during this period of time. Reasonable period of time means that period during which the female employee is disabled on account of pregnancy, childbirth, or related medical conditions. This paragraph shall not be construed to limit the provisions of paragraph (1) of subdivision (b).

An employer may require any employee who plans to take a leave pursuant to this subdivision to give the employer reasonable notice of the date the leave shall commence and the estimated duration of the leave.

(c)(1) For any employer, including both employers subject to and not subject to Title VII of the federal Civil Rights Act of 1964, to refuse to provide reasonable accommodation for an employee for conditions related to pregnancy, childbirth, or related medical conditions, if she so requests, with the advice of her health care provider.

(2) For any employer, including both employers subject to and not subject to Title VII of the federal Civil Rights Act of 1964, who has a policy, practice, or collective bargaining agreement requiring or authorizing the transfer of temporarily disabled employees to less strenuous or hazardous positions for the duration of the disability to refuse to transfer a pregnant female employee who so requests.

(3) For any employer, including both employers subject to and not subject to Title VII of the federal Civil Rights Act of 1964, to refuse to temporarily transfer a pregnant female employee to a less strenuous or hazardous position for the duration of her pregnancy if she so requests, with the advice of her physician, where that transfer can be reasonably accommodated. However, no employer shall be required by this section to create additional employment that the employer would not otherwise have created, nor shall the employer be required to discharge any employee, transfer any employee with more seniority, or promote any employee who is not qualified to perform the job.

(d) This section shall not be construed to affect any other provision of law relating to sex discrimination or pregnancy, or in any way to diminish the coverage of pregnancy, childbirth, or medical conditions related to pregnancy or childbirth under any other provisions of this part, including subdivision (a) of Section 12940.

(e) Except for subdivision (c) and paragraph (2) of subdivision (b), this section is inapplicable to any employer subject to Title VII of the federal Civil Rights Act of 1964.

§ 12945.2. Family care and medical leave; definitions; conditions; unlawful employment practices.

(a) Except as provided in subdivision (b), it shall be an unlawful employment practice for any employer, as defined in paragraph (2) of subdivision (c), to refuse to grant a request by any employee with more than 12 months of service with the employer, and who has at least 1,250 hours of service with the employer during the previous 12-month period, to take up to a total of 12 workweeks in any 12-month period for family care and medical leave. Family care and medical leave requested pursuant to this subdivision shall not be deemed to have been granted unless the employer provides the employee, upon granting the leave request, a guarantee of employment in the same or a comparable position upon the termination of the leave. The commission shall adopt a regulation specifying the elements of a reasonable request.

(b) Notwithstanding subdivision (a), it shall not be an unlawful employment practice for an employer to refuse to grant a request for family care and medical leave by an employee if the employer employs less than 50 employees within 75 miles of the worksite where that employee is employed.

(c) For purposes of this section:

(1) "Child" means a biological, adopted, or foster child, a stepchild, a legal ward, or a child of a person standing in loco parentis who is either of the following:

(A) Under 18 years of age.

(B) An adult dependent child.

(2) "Employer" means either of the following:

(A) Any person who directly employs 50 or more persons to perform services for a wage or salary.

(B) The state, and any political or civil subdivision of the state and cities.

(3) "Family care and medical leave" means any of the following:

(A) Leave for reason of the birth of a child of the employee, the placement of a child with an employee in connection with the adoption or foster care of the child by the employee, or the serious health condition of a child of the employee.

(B) Leave to care for a parent or a spouse who has a serious health condition.

(C) Leave because of an employee's own serious health condition that makes the employee unable to perform the functions of the position of that employee, except for leave taken for disability on account of pregnancy, childbirth, or related medical conditions.

(4) "Employment in the same or a comparable position" means employment in a position that has the same or similar duties and pay that can be performed at the same or similar geographic location as the position held prior to the leave.

(5) "FMLA" means the federal Family and Medical Leave Act of 1993 (P.L. 103-3).

(6) "Health care provider" means any of the following:

(A) An individual holding either a physician's and surgeon's certificate issued pursuant to Article 4 (commencing with Section 2080) of Chapter 5 of Division 2 of the Business and Professions Code, an osteopathic physician's and surgeon's certificate issued pursuant to Article 4.5 (commencing with Section 2099.5) of Chapter 5 of Division 2 of the Business and Professions Code, or an individual duly licensed as a physician, surgeon, or osteopathic physician or surgeon in another state or jurisdiction, who directly treats or supervises the treatment of the serious health condition.

(B) Any other person determined by the United States Secretary of Labor to be capable of providing health care services under the FMLA.

(7) "Parent" means a biological, foster, or adoptive parent, a stepparent, a legal guardian, or other person who stood in loco parentis to the employee when the employee was a child.

(8) "Serious health condition" means an illness, injury, impairment, or physical or mental condition that involves either of the following:

(A) Inpatient care in a hospital, hospice, or residential health care facility.

(B) Continuing treatment or continuing supervision by a health care provider.

(d) An employer shall not be required to pay an employee for any leave taken pursuant to subdivision (a), except as required by subdivision (e).

(e) An employee taking a leave permitted by subdivision (a) may elect, or an employer may require the employee, to substitute, for leave allowed under subdivision (a), any of the employee's accrued vacation leave or other accrued time off during this period or any other paid or unpaid time off negotiated with the employer. If an employee takes a leave because of the employee's own serious health condition, the employee may also elect, or the employer may also require the employee, to substitute accrued sick leave during the period of the leave. However, an employee shall not use sick leave during a period of leave in connection with the birth, adoption, or foster care of a child, or to care for a child, parent, or spouse with a serious health condition, unless mutually agreed to by the employer and the employee.

(f)(1) During any period that an eligible employee takes leave pursuant to subdivision (a) or takes leave that qualifies as leave taken under the FMLA, the employer shall maintain and pay for coverage under a "group health plan," as defined in Section 5000(b)(1) of the Internal Revenue Code of 1986, for the duration of the leave, not to exceed 12 workweeks in a 12-month period, commencing on the date leave taken under the FMLA commences, at the level and under the conditions coverage would have been provided if the employee had continued in employment continuously for the duration of the leave. Nothing in the preceding sentence shall preclude an employer from maintaining and paying for coverage under a "group health plan" beyond 12 workweeks. An employer may recover the premium that the employer paid as required by this subdivision for maintaining coverage for the employee under the group health plan if both of the following conditions occur:

(A) The employee fails to return from leave after the period of leave to which the employee is entitled has expired.

(B) The employee's failure to return from leave is for a reason other than the continuation, recurrence, or onset of a serious health condition that entitles the employee to leave under subdivision (a) or other circumstances beyond the control of the employee.

(2) Any employee taking leave pursuant to subdivision (a) shall continue to be entitled to participate in employee health plans for any period during which coverage is not provided by the employer under paragraph (1), employee benefit plans, including life, short-term, or long-term disability or accident insurance, pension and retirement plans, and supplemental unemployment benefit plans to the same extent and under the same conditions as apply to an unpaid leave taken for any purpose other than those described in subdivision (a). In the absence of these conditions an employee shall continue to be entitled to participate in these plans and, in the case of health and welfare employee benefit plans, including life, short-term, or long-term disability or accident insurance, or other similar plans, the employer may, at his or her discretion, require the employee to

pay premiums, at the group rate, during the period of leave not covered by any accrued vacation leave, or other accrued time off, or any other paid or unpaid time off negotiated with the employer, as a condition of continued coverage during the leave period. However, the nonpayment of premiums by an employee shall not constitute a break in service, for purposes of longevity, seniority under any collective bargaining agreement, or any employee benefit plan.

For purposes of pension and retirement plans, an employer shall not be required to make plan payments for an employee during the leave period, and the leave period shall not be required to be counted for purposes of time accrued under the plan. However, an employee covered by a pension plan may continue to make contributions in accordance with the terms of the plan during the period of the leave.

(g) During a family care and medical leave period, the employee shall retain employee status with the employer, and the leave shall not constitute a break in service, for purposes of longevity, seniority under any collective bargaining agreement, or any employee benefit plan. An employee returning from leave shall return with no less seniority than the employee had when the leave commenced, for purposes of layoff, recall, promotion, job assignment, and seniority-related benefits such as vacation.

(h) If the employee's need for a leave pursuant to this section is foreseeable, the employee shall provide the employer with reasonable advance notice of the need for the leave.

(i) If the employee's need for leave pursuant to this section is foreseeable due to a planned medical treatment or supervision, the employee shall make a reasonable effort to schedule the treatment or supervision to avoid disruption to the operations of the employer, subject to the approval of the health care provider of the individual requiring the treatment or supervision.

(j)(1) An employer may require that an employee's request for leave to care for a child, a spouse, or a parent who has a serious health condition be supported by a certification issued by the health care provider of the individual requiring care. That certification shall be sufficient if it includes all of the following:

(A) The date on which the serious health condition commenced.

(B) The probable duration of the condition.

(C) An estimate of the amount of time that the health care provider believes the employee needs to care for the individual requiring the care.

(D) A statement that the serious health condition warrants the participation of a family member to provide care during a period of the treatment or supervision of the individual requiring care.

(2) Upon expiration of the time estimated by the health care provider in subparagraph (C) of paragraph (1), the employer may require the employee to obtain recertification, in accordance with the procedure provided in paragraph (1), if additional leave is required.

(k)(1) An employer may require that an employee's request for leave because of the employee's own serious health condition be supported by a certification issued by his or her health care provider. That certification shall be sufficient if it includes all of the following:

(A) The date on which the serious health condition commenced.

(B) The probable duration of the condition.

(C) A statement that, due to the serious health condition, the employee is unable to perform the function of his or her position.

(2) The employer may require that the employee obtain subsequent recertification regarding the employee's serious health condition on a reasonable basis, in accordance with the procedure provided in paragraph (1), if additional leave is required.

(3)(A) In any case in which the employer has reason to doubt the validity of the certification provided pursuant to this section, the employer may require, at the employer's expense, that the employee obtain the opinion of a second health care provider, designated or approved by the employer, concerning any information certified under paragraph (1).

(B) The health care provider designated or approved under subparagraph (A) shall not be employed on a regular basis by the employer.

(C) In any case in which the second opinion described in subparagraph (A) differs from the opinion in the original certification, the employer may require, at the employer's expense, that the employee obtain the opinion of a third health care provider, designated or approved jointly by the employer and the employee, concerning the information certified under paragraph (1).

(D) The opinion of the third health care provider concerning the information certified under paragraph (1) shall be considered to be final and shall be binding on the employer and the employee.

(4) As a condition of an employee's return from leave taken because of the employee's own serious health condition, the employer may have a uniformly applied practice or policy that requires the employee to obtain certification from his or her health care provider that the employee is able to resume work. Nothing in this paragraph shall supersede a valid collective bargaining agreement that governs the return to work of that employee.

(*l*) It shall be an unlawful employment practice for an employer to refuse to hire, or to discharge, fine, suspend, expel, or discriminate against, any individual because of any of the following:

(1) An individual's exercise of the right to family care and medical leave provided by subdivision (a).

(2) An individual's giving information or testimony as to his or her own family care and medical leave, or another person's family care and medical leave, in any inquiry or proceeding related to rights guaranteed under this section.

(m) This section shall not be construed to require any changes in existing collective bargaining agreements during the life of the contract, or until January 1, 1993, whichever occurs first.

(n) The amendments made to this section by the act adding this subdivision shall not be construed to require any changes in existing collective bargaining agreements during the life of the contract, or until February 5, 1994, whichever occurs first.

(o) The provisions of this section shall be construed as separate and distinct from those of Section 12945.

(p) Leave provided for pursuant to this section may be taken in one or more periods. The 12-month period during which 12 workweeks of leave may be taken under this section shall run concurrently with the 12-month period under the FMLA, and shall commence the date leave taken under the FMLA commences.

(q) In any case in which both parents entitled to leave under subdivision (a) are employed by the same employer, the employer shall not be required to grant leave in connection with the birth, adoption, or foster care of a child that would allow the parents family care and medical leave totaling more than the amount specified in subdivision (a).

(r)(1) Notwithstanding subdivision (a), an employer may refuse to reinstate an employee returning from leave to the same or a comparable position if all of the following apply:

(A) The employee is a salaried employee who is among the highest paid 10 percent of the employer's employees who are employed within 75 miles of the worksite at which that employee is employed.

(B) The refusal is necessary to prevent substantial and grievous economic injury to the operations of the employer.

(C) The employer notifies the employee of the intent to refuse reinstatement at the time the employer determines the refusal is necessary under subparagraph (B).

(2) In any case in which the leave has already commenced, the employer shall give the employee a reasonable opportunity to return to work following the notice prescribed by subparagraph (C).

(s) Leave taken by an employee pursuant to this section shall run concurrently with leave taken pursuant to the FMLA, except for any leave taken under the FMLA for disability on account of pregnancy, childbirth, or related medical conditions. The aggregate amount of leave taken under this section or the FMLA, or both, except for leave taken for disability on account of pregnancy, childbirth, or related medical conditions, shall not exceed 12 workweeks in a 12-month period. An employee is entitled to take, in addition to the leave provided for under this section and the FMLA, the leave provided for in Section 12945, if the employee is otherwise qualified for that leave.

§ 12946. Retention of applications, records and files for two years; failure to retain as unlawful practice by employers, labor organization and employment agencies

It shall be an unlawful practice for employers, labor organizations, and employment agencies subject to the provisions of this part to fail to maintain and preserve any and all applications, personnel, membership, or employment referral records and files for a minimum period of two years after the records and files are initially created or received, or for employers to fail to retain personnel files of applicants or terminated employees for a minimum period of two years after the date of the employment action taken. For the purposes of this section, the State Personnel Board is exempt from the two-year retention requirement and shall instead, maintain the records and files for a period of one year. Upon notice that a verified complaint against it has been filed under this part, any such employer, labor organization, or employment agency shall maintain and preserve any and all records and files until the complaint is fully and finally disposed of and all appeals or related proceedings terminated. The commission shall adopt suitable rules, regulations, and standards to carry out the purposes of this section. Where necessary, the department, pursuant to its powers under Section 12974, may seek temporary or preliminary judicial relief to enforce this section.

§ 12955. Unlawful practices

<Text of section operative until Jan. 1, 2005.>

It shall be unlawful:

(a) For the owner of any housing accommodation to discriminate against or harass any person because of the race, color, religion, sex, sexual orientation, marital status, national origin, ancestry, familial status, source of income, or disability of that person.

(b) For the owner of any housing accommodation to make or to cause to be made any written or oral inquiry concerning the race, color, religion, sex, sexual orientation, marital status, national origin, ancestry, familial status, or disability of any person seeking to purchase, rent or lease any housing accommodation.

(c) For any person to make, print, or publish, or cause to be made, printed, or published any notice, statement, or advertisement, with respect to the sale or rental of a housing accommodation that indicates any preference, limitation, or discrimination based on race, color, religion, sex, sexual orientation, marital status, national origin, ancestry, familial status, source of income, or disability or an intention to make any such preference, limitation, or discrimination.

(d) For any person subject to the provisions of Section 51 of the Civil Code, as that section applies to housing accommodations, to discriminate against any person on the basis of sex, sexual orientation, color, race, religion, ancestry, national origin, familial status, marital status, disability, source of income, or on any other basis prohibited by that section.

(e) For any person, bank, mortgage company or other financial institution that provides financial assistance for the purchase, organization, or construction of any housing accommodation to discriminate against any person or group of persons because of the race, color, religion, sex, sexual orientation, marital status, national origin, ancestry, familial status, source of income, or disability in the terms, conditions, or privileges relating to the obtaining or use of that financial assistance.

(f) For any owner of housing accommodations to harass, evict, or otherwise discriminate against any person in the sale or rental of housing accommodations when the owner's dominant purpose is retaliation against a person who has opposed practices unlawful under this section, informed law enforcement agencies of practices believed unlawful under this section, has testified or assisted in any proceeding under this part, or has aided or encouraged a person to exercise or enjoy the rights secured by this part. Nothing herein is intended to cause or permit the delay of an unlawful detainer action.

(g) For any person to aid, abet, incite, compel, or coerce the doing of any of the acts or practices declared unlawful in this section, or to attempt to do so.

(h) For any person, for profit, to induce any person to sell or rent any dwelling by representations regarding the entry or prospective entry into the neighborhood of a person or persons of a particular race, color, religion, sex, sexual orientation, marital status, ancestry, disability, source of income, familial status, or national origin.

(i) For any person or other organization or entity whose business involves real estate-related transactions to discriminate against any person in making available a transaction, or in the terms and conditions of a transaction, because of race, color, religion, sex, sexual orientation, marital status, national origin, ancestry, source of income, familial status, or disability.

(j) To deny a person access to, or membership or participation in, a multiple listing service, real estate brokerage organization, or other service because of race, color, religion, sex, sexual orientation, marital status, ancestry, disability, familial status, source of income, or national origin.

(k) To otherwise make unavailable or deny a dwelling based on discrimination because of race, color, religion, sex, sexual orientation, familial status, source of income, disability, or national origin.

(l) To discriminate through public or private land use practices, decisions, and authorizations because of race, color, religion, sex, sexual orientation, familial status, marital status, disability, national origin, source of income, or ancestry. Discrimination includes, but is not limited to, restrictive covenants, zoning laws, denials of use permits, and other actions authorized under the Planning and Zoning Law (Title 7 (commencing with Section 65000)), that make housing opportunities unavailable.

Discrimination under this subdivision also includes the existence of a restrictive covenant, regardless of whether accompanied by a statement that the restrictive covenant is repealed or void. This paragraph shall become operative on January 1, 2001.

(m) As used in this section, "race, color, religion, sex, sexual orientation, marital status, national origin, ancestry, familial status, source of income, or disability" includes a perception that the person has any of those characteristics or that the person is associated with a person who has, or is perceived to have, any of those characteristics.

(n) To use a financial or income standard in the rental of housing that fails to account for the aggregate income of persons residing together or proposing to reside together on the same basis as the aggregate income of married persons residing together or proposing to reside together.

(o) In instances where there is a government rent subsidy, to use a financial or income standard in assessing eligibility for the rental of housing that is not based on the portion of the rent to be paid by the tenant.

(p)(1) For the purposes of this section, "source of income" means lawful, verifiable income paid directly to a tenant or paid to a representative of a tenant.

(2) For the purposes of this section, it shall not constitute discrimination based on source of income to make a written or oral inquiry concerning the level or source of income.

(q) This section shall remain in effect only until January 1, 2005, and as of that date is repealed, unless a later enacted statute, that is enacted before January 1, 2005, deletes or extends that date.

II.   INTERNATIONAL MATERIALS

APPENDIX 6

CONSTITUTIONAL PROVISIONS AND LEGISLATION PROTECTING THE RIGHTS OF PERSONS WITH DISABILITIES IN OTHER STATES

	AFRICA[1]
Angola	There is no legislation mandating accessibility for persons with disabilities in public or private facilities, and, in view of the degradation of the country's infrastructure and high unemployment rate, it was difficult for persons with disabilities to find employment or participate in the education system.
Benin	Although the Constitution provides that the State should care for persons with disabilities, the Government does not mandate accessibility for them. It operates a number of social centers for persons with disabilities to assist their social integration.
Botswana	The Government does not require accessibility for public buildings and public conveyances for persons with disabilities, and the NGO community only recently has begun to address the needs of persons with disabilities. The Government has a national policy that provides for integrating the needs of persons with disabilities into all aspects of government policymaking. The Government funded NGOs that provide rehabilitation services and supported small-scale work projects by workers with disabilities.
Burkina Faso	While there are modest government subsidies for workshops for persons with disabilities, there is no government mandate or legislation concerning accessibility for persons with disabilities. There also is no legislation to protect persons with disabilities from discrimination. Programs to aid persons with disabilities are limited, and their advocates report that such persons often face social and economical discrimination.

---

[1] The textual material is excerpted from the United States Department of State website. United States Department of State, Country Reports on Human Rights Practices, http://www.state.gov/g/drl/rls/hrrpt/2002/ (last visited on Aug. 26, 2003).

Burundi	The Government has not enacted legislation or otherwise mandated access to buildings or government services for persons with disabilities. Discrimination against persons with disabilities is a problem. There are few job opportunities for persons with physical disabilities in the country, where most jobs involve significant manual labor.
Cameroon	The law provides certain rights to persons with disabilities. These include access to public institutions, medical treatment, and education. The Government is obliged to bear part of the educational expenses of persons with disabilities, to employ them where possible, and to provide them with public assistance when necessary. However, the Government rarely respects these rights. The law does not mandate special access provisions to buildings and facilities for persons with disabilities. *Specific Legislation:* Protection of Disabled Persons Act No. 83/13, 21 July 1983.
Cape Verde	The Constitution prohibits discrimination based on race, sex, religion, disability, language, or social status. However, despite the Government's increasing efforts to enforce all relevant constitutional provisions, it still does not do so effectively, and not all elements of society, particularly women and children, enjoy full protection against discrimination. Although the Constitution mandates "special protection" for the aged and persons with disabilities, the Government does not require access to public buildings or services for persons with disabilities. *Specific Legislation:* Cape Verde Const. of 1992, art. 59, 67 & 72 (amended 1999), <http://confinder.richmond.edu/capeverde.htm> (last visited on August 13, 2003)
Central African Republic	There are no legislated or mandated accessibility provisions for persons with disabilities. There are several government and NGO-initiated programs designed to assist persons with disabilities, including handicraft training for the blind and the distribution of wheelchairs and carts by the Ministry of Social Services.
Chad	There is no official discrimination against persons with disabilities; however, the Government operated only a few therapy, education, or employment programs for persons with disabilities, and no laws mandate access to buildings for persons with disabilities. Several local NGOs provide skills training to the deaf and blind. *Specific Legislation:* Chad Const. of 1996, art. 40, <http://droit.francophonie.org/BJ/TexteHTM/TD0/TD0C0001A.htm> (last visited on August 26, 2003)
Comoros	There are no laws that mandate access to buildings for persons with disabilities.

Congo, Democratic Republic of the	The law does not mandate accessibility to buildings or government services for persons with disabilities. There are some special schools, many staffed with missionaries, that use private funds and limited public support to provide education and vocational training to students who are blind or have physical disabilities.
Congo, Republic of	The Fundamental Act prohibits discrimination based on physical condition; however, in practice this prohibition generally was not enforced, because the ministry charged with implementation faced severe financial constraints. There were no laws mandating access for persons with disabilities.
Cote d'Ivoire	The law requires the Government to educate and train persons with disabilities, to hire them or help them find jobs, to design houses and public facilities for wheelchair access, and to adapt machines, tools, and work spaces for access and use by persons with disabilities. The law covers persons with physical, mental, visual, auditory, and cerebral motor disabilities. The Government is working to put these regulations into effect; however, the law had not been implemented fully by year's end. Wheelchair accessible facilities for persons with disabilities are not common, and there are few training and job assistance programs for persons with disabilities.
Djibouti	The Government does not mandate accessibility to buildings or government services for persons with disabilities. Although persons with disabilities have access to education and public health facilities, there is no specific law that addresses the needs of persons with disabilities, and there are no laws or regulations that prevent job discrimination against persons with disabilities. Persons with disabilities have difficulty finding employment in an economy where at least 60 percent of the able-bodied adult male population is underemployed or jobless.
Equatorial Guinea	There is no constitutional or legal provision to protect persons with disabilities from discrimination in employment, education, or the provision of other state services; however, there is no evidence of discrimination against persons with disabilities in practice. The law does not mandate access for persons with disabilities to buildings.
Eritrea	The Constitution and the transitional civil code prohibit discrimination against persons with disabilities, and the Government enforces these provisions. The long war for independence and the conflict with Ethiopia left thousands of men and women with physical disabilities from injuries they received as guerrillas, soldiers, and civilian victims. The Government spends a large share of its resources to support and train these fighters, who are regarded as heroes, and does not discriminate against them in training, education, or employment. There are no laws mandating access for persons with disabilities to public thoroughfares or public or private buildings; however, many newly constructed buildings provide access for persons with disabilities. *Specific Legislation*: (a) Eri. Constitution of 1997, art. 14, <http://www.oefre.unibe.ch/law/icl/er00000_.html> (last visited on August 13, 2003) (b) Transitional Civil Code.

Ethiopia	The Constitution stipulates that the state shall provide rehabilitation and assistance to persons with physical and mental disabilities; however, the Government devoted few resources for these purposes. There are approximately six million persons with disabilities in the country. At year's end, the Government had not yet put into place mechanisms to enforce a law mandating equal rights for persons with disabilities. The Government does not mandate access to buildings or government services for persons with disabilities, and persons with minor disabilities sometimes complain of job discrimination. The conflict with Eritrea resulted in numerous soldiers losing limbs, many from landmine explosions. Wheelchairs are rare in the country. According to a 1998 NGO report, only 500 of the approximately 700,000 visually impaired persons in the country have access to employment opportunities. Although there are approximately 800,000 mentally ill persons estimated in the country, there is only 1 mental hospital and only 10 psychiatrists. In the past several years, the mental hospital trained 117 psychiatric nurses to work in 33 rural clinics; however, half of these nurses subsequently left their jobs. *Specific Legislation*: (a) Eth. Const. of 1994, art. 41, <http://www.oefre.unibe.ch/law/icl/et00000_.html> (last visited on August 13, 2003) (b) The Rights of Disabled Persons to Employment Proclamation, No. 101/1994, of 26 August 1994, <http://natlex.ilo.org/txt/E94ETH01.htm> (last visited on August 18, 2003)
Gabon	There are no laws that prohibit discrimination against persons with disabilities or that provide for access to buildings or services.
Gambia	The Constitution prohibits discrimination based on race, sex, religion, disability, language, or social status and the Government generally respected these prohibitions There are no statutes or regulations requiring accessibility for persons with disabilities. Persons with severe disabilities subsisted primarily through private charity. *Specific Legislation*: Gam. Const. (Second Republic of Gambia, 1996), § 31, <http://www.dredf.org/symposium/gambia.html> (last visited on August 13, 2003)

Ghana	The Constitution prohibits discrimination on the basis of race, sex, religion, disability, language, or social status. The Constitution specifically provides for the rights of persons with disabilities, including protection against exploitation and discrimination. The Constitution also states that "as far as practicable, every place to which the public has access shall have appropriate facilities for disabled persons." However, in practice this provision has yet to be implemented. *Specific Legislation*: (a) Ghana Const. of 1992, art. 29, <http://www.psr.keele.ac.uk/docs/ghanaconst.pdf> (last visited on August 13, 2003) (b) The Disabled Persons Act, 1993, <http://www.dredf.org/symposium/Ghana2.html> (last visited on August 18, 2003)
Guinea	The Constitution provides that all persons are equal before the law. There are no special constitutional provisions for persons with disabilities. The Government has not mandated accessibility for persons with disabilities, and few persons with disabilities work, although some develop opportunities in the informal sector.
Guinea-Bissau	There is no law mandating accessibility. The law does not prohibit specifically discrimination against persons with disabilities, and the Government does not ensure equal access to employment and education; however, there were no reports of overt societal discrimination. The Government has made some efforts to assist veterans with disabilities through pension programs, but these programs do not address adequately veterans' health, housing, and food needs; there are no reports of funds for special programs for persons with disabilities.
Kenya	Government policies do not discriminate against persons with disabilities in employment, education, or in the provision of other state services; however, persons with disabilities frequently are denied drivers' licenses. There are no mandated provisions of accessibility for persons with disabilities to public buildings or transportation. KTN broadcasts some news programs in sign language. A bill to address problems faced by persons with disabilities was pending before Parliament at year's end. The bill aims to outlaw discrimination against persons with disabilities and to assist them through provisions such as mandatory education for children with disabilities. *Specific Legislation*: Rights for disabled persons should be drafted into Constitution soon, <http://www.nationaudio.com/News/DailyNation/Adverts/constitution/constitution_full.pdf> (Draft Bill of the Constitution, 2002)
Lesotho	Discrimination against persons with physical disabilities in employment, education, or provision of other government services is unlawful; however, societal discrimination is common. The Government has not legislated or mandated accessibility to public buildings for persons with disabilities.

Liberia	As a result of the civil war, a large number of persons have permanent disabilities, in addition to those disabled by accident or illness. It is illegal to discriminate against persons with disabilities; however, in practice they do not enjoy equal access to public buildings or government services. No laws mandate accessibility to public buildings or services.
Madagascar	There is no systematic discrimination against persons with disabilities in employment, education, or in the provision of other state services. There is no law mandating access to buildings for persons with disabilities. In April the Government issued an implementing decree for a law, passed by the National Assembly in 1998, to define the rights of persons with disabilities. *Specific Legislation*: (a) Decree No. 2001-162 of February 21, 2001, application of the law No 97-044, Rights of Handicapped Persons, <http://natlex.ilo.org/txt/F98MDG01.htm> (last visited on August 26, 2003) (b) Labor Code No. 94-027 of September 29, 1994, Code of hygiene, safety and the environment of work.
Malawi	The Government has not mandated accessibility to buildings and services for persons with disabilities, but one of the national goals in the Constitution is to support persons with disabilities through greater access to public places, fair opportunities in employment, and full participation in all spheres of society. *Specific Legislation*: (a) Malawi Const. (Republic of Malawi Act, 1994), §§ 20, 30, 31. <http://www.sdnp.org.mw/constitut/chapter4.html> (last visited on August 14, 2003) (b) Handicapped Persons Act No. 48, 1971, Annual Volume of the Laws, Vol. I (1971), <http://www.dredf.org/symposium/malawi48.html> (last visited on August 18, 2003)
Mali	There is no specific legislation protecting the rights of persons with physical or mental disabilities or mandating accessibility. The Government does not discriminate against persons with physical disabilities in regard to employment, education, and other state services; however, the Government has not made provision for persons with disabilities in these areas. There is no societal discrimination against persons with disabilities; however, in view of the high unemployment rate, persons with physical disabilities often are unable to find work.

Mauritania	The law does not provide specifically for persons with disabilities, and the Government does not mandate preference in employment or education or public accessibility for persons with disabilities. However, it does provide some rehabilitation and other assistance for persons with disabilities. NGOs increasingly have become active in raising public awareness of issues affecting persons with disabilities. The school for the deaf and the blind in Nouakchott operated 6 classrooms and enrolled 35 students (20 girls and 15 boys) during the year; however, the school lacked trained staff. In 2000 the school obtained the services of a volunteer expert who provided professional training for the staff.
Mauritius	The law requires organizations that employ more than 10 persons to set aside at least 3 percent of their positions for persons with disabilities. There is no law mandating access to public buildings or facilities. *Specific Legislation*: The Training and Employment of Disabled Persons Act No. 9, 1996, § 18, Supplement To The Labour Laws Of Mauritius 1992 & Mauritius Laws 1996, <http://natlex.ilo.org/txt/E96MUS01.htm> (last visited on August 18, 2003)

Mozambique	The Constitution forbids discrimination based on race, sex, religion, or disability; however, in practice discrimination against women and persons with disabilities persists.
	The Constitution states that "disabled citizens shall enjoy fully the rights" that it provides for; however, the Government provided few resources to implement this provision. War veterans with disabilities are among the most politically organized citizens with disabilities. Approximately 1.9 percent of citizens have physical or mental disabilities.
	The Government only provides four schools nationwide for the hearing and vision impaired and for persons with physical and mental disabilities. There are few job opportunities for persons with disabilities in the formal sector, although the 1997 census reported that 55 percent of such persons worked or held a job.
	During the year, the Government provided scholarships for 615 children with disabilities in education facilities.
	The Government continued to rely on NGOs to assist persons with disabilities. The Association of Disabled Mozambicans (ADEMO) addresses social and economic needs of persons with disabilities. ADEMO's effectiveness during the year was hindered by internal conflicts. Smaller NGOs also have formed, including the Association of Handicapped Military and Paramilitary Mozambicans, the Association of Blind and Visually Impaired Mozambicans (ACDVM), the Association of Mozambican Disabled Soldiers (ADEMIMO), the Association of Deaf Mozambicans (ASUMO), the Association of Demobilized War Veterans (AMODEC), and the Association of Disabled Divorced Women (AMODD). In 2000 ADEMO held a conference to address the rights of persons with disabilities.
	The only provisions that the Government has enacted for accessibility to buildings and transportation for persons with disabilities were in the electoral law governing the country's first multiparty elections, which addressed the needs of voters with disabilities in the polling booths. Special access facilities are rare.
	Specific Legislation: Mozam. Const. of 1990, art. 68, 95, <http://oncampus.richmond.edu/~jjones//confinder/MOZ.htm> (last visited on August 14, 2003)

Namibia	While discrimination on the basis of disability is not addressed in the Constitution, the Labor Act prohibits discrimination against persons with disabilities in employment; however, enforcement in this area was weak. Although there was no legal discrimination against persons with disabilities, societal discrimination persists. The Government legally does not require special access to public buildings for persons with disabilities, and many ministries remain inaccessible to them. *Specific Legislation*: (a) Labor Act No. 6, 1992, § 107, <http://natlex.ilo.org/txt/E92NAM01.htm> (last visited on August 18, 2003) (b) National Vocational Training Act No. 18, 1994, <http://www.dredf.org/symposium/namb2.html> (last visited on August 18, 2003)
Niger	The Constitution mandates that the State provide for persons with disabilities; however, the Government has yet to implement regulations to mandate accessibility to buildings and education for those with special needs. Regulations do not mandate accessibility to public transport, of which there is little... *Specific Legislation*: Niger Const. of 1993, art. 20 (amended 1999).
Nigeria	While the Government called for private business to institute policies that ensured fair treatment for persons with disabilities, it did not enact during the year any laws requiring greater accessibility to buildings or public transportation, nor did it formulate any policy specifically ensuring the right of persons with disabilities to work. *Specific Legislation:* (a) Nig. Constitution of 1999, art. 16, <http://www.nigeria-law.org/ConstitutionOfTheFederalRepublicOfNigeria.htm> (last visited on August 14, 2003) (b) Nigerians with Disability Decree, 1993, <http://www.dredf.org/symposium/nig1.html> (last visited on August 18, 2003)
Rwanda	Although there are no laws restricting persons with disabilities from employment, education, or other state services, in practice few persons with disabilities have access to education or employment. There is no law mandating access to public facilities.
Sao Tome and Principe	The law does not mandate access to buildings, transportation, or services for persons with disabilities. There are no reports of discrimination against persons with disabilities.

Senegal	There are no laws that mandate accessibility for persons with disabilities, and in practice most persons with disabilities generally were unable to participate in many occupations due to physical barriers and a lack of equipment and training opportunities. In 2000 the Council of State (the country's highest administrative court) ruled on an antidiscrimination lawsuit filed in 1999 by the National Association of Disabled People (ANHMS) against the regional educational board in the eastern province of Tambacounda. The board had refused to hire a candidate with physical disabilities who had passed a recruitment test, on the grounds that persons with physical disabilities were not qualified for the job of teaching. The court overruled the board's decision on the grounds that a physical disability did not represent a valid legal ground for barring a person from teaching.
Seychelles	There is no legislation providing for access to public buildings, transportation, or state services.
Sierra Leone	Public facility access and discrimination against persons with disabilities are not considered public policy concerns. No laws mandate accessibility to buildings or provide for other assistance for persons with disabilities. Although a few private agencies and organizations attempted to train persons with disabilities in useful work, there was no government policy or program directed particularly at persons with disabilities. There does not appear to be outright discrimination against persons with disabilities in housing or education; however, given the high rate of general unemployment, work opportunities for persons with disabilities are few. Some of the many individuals who were maimed in the fighting, or had their limbs amputated by rebel forces, are receiving special assistance from various local and international humanitarian organizations. Such programs involve reconstructive surgery, prostheses, and vocational training to help them acquire new work skills. Although the Lome Accord also called for the creation of a special fund to implement a program for rehabilitation of war victims, the fund had not yet been established by year's end. Attention to amputees increased the access of other persons with disabilities to health care and treatment.
Somalia	In the absence of a functioning state, the needs of persons with disabilities are not addressed. There are several local NGOs in Somaliland that provide services for persons with disabilities.

South Africa	The Constitution prohibits discrimination on the grounds of race, religion, disability, ethnic or social origin, color, age, culture, language, sex, pregnancy, or marital status. The Promotion of Equality and Prevention of Unfair Discrimination Act, which entered into force on August 9, outlaws unfair discrimination against any person on the grounds of gender, race, and disability, and places a responsibility on the State and any person in the public domain to promote equality. The act addresses discrimination in a broad context in the workplace, health care, education, services, pensions, and other socio-economic areas
	The Constitution prohibits discrimination on the basis of disability. Society is increasingly open to the concept of persons with disabilities as a minority whose civil rights must be protected. The Government attempts to ensure that all government-funded projects take account of the needs of citizens with disabilities. However, in practice Government and private sector discrimination against persons with disabilities in employment still exists. The law mandates access to buildings for persons with disabilities, but such regulations rarely are enforced, and public awareness of them remains minimal. The law requires employers with more than 50 workers to create an affirmative action plan with provisions for achieving employment equity for persons with disabilities.
	Specific Legislation: (a) S. Afr. Const. (Bill of Rights, 1996), § 9, <http://www.oefre.unibe.ch/law/icl/sf00000_.html> (last visited on August 13, 2003) (b) §§ 6, 15, & 53 of Employment Equity Act No. 55 of 1998, BSRSA, Vol. 11, <http://www.dredf.org/symposium/safrbill60.html> (last visited on August 18, 2003) (c) § 6 of Skills Development Act No. 97 of 1998, BSRSA, Vol. 11, <http://www.logos-net.net/ilo/150_base/en/init/sa_8.htm> (last visited on August 18, 2003) (d) Income Tax Act No. 58 of 1962, in Silke On South African Income Tax (2001/ 2002), <http://www.polity.org.za/html/govdocs/legislation/misc/act58-1962.pdf> (last visited on August 18, 2003) (e) §§ 9 & 28 of The Promotion of Equality and Prevention of Unfair Discrimination Act No. 4 of 2000, BSRSA, Vol. 5A, <http://www.polity.org.za/html/govdocs/legislation/2000/act4.pdf> (last visited on August 18, 2003)

Sudan	The General Education Act stipulates equal opportunity in education for persons with disabilities. The Government does not discriminate against persons with disabilities but has not enacted any special legislation for them, such as mandating accessibility to public buildings and transportation. The General Education Act requires equal educational opportunities for persons with disabilities. *Specific Legislation*: (a) Sudan Const. (Draft Constitution of the Republic of the Sudan, 1998), art. 11, <http://www.sudani.co.za/Documents%20and%20Issues/Constitution.htm> (last visited on August 14, 2003) (b) General Education Act of 1992.
Swaziland	The Ministry of Home Affairs has called for equal treatment of persons with disabilities; however, there are no laws that protect the rights of those with disabilities or that mandate accessibility for persons with disabilities to buildings, transportation, or government services. There has been no progress on legislation that would give preferential treatment to persons with disabilities for building access and other needs; however, all new government buildings under construction include improvements for those with disabilities, including accessibility ramps.
Tanzania	The Government does not mandate access to public buildings, transportation, or government services for persons with disabilities. Although there is no official discrimination against persons with disabilities, in practice persons with physical disabilities effectively are restricted in their access to education, employment, and provision of other state services due to physical barriers. The Government provides only limited funding for special facilities and programs.
Togo	The Government does not mandate accessibility to public or private facilities for persons with disabilities. Although the Constitution nominally obliges the Government to aid persons with disabilities and shelter them from social injustice, the Government provides only limited assistance in practice. There is no overt state discrimination against persons with disabilities and some hold Government positions. However, persons with disabilities have no meaningful recourse against private sector or societal discrimination, and in practice there is discrimination against persons with disabilities.

Uganda	The Constitution provides that persons with disabilities have "a right to respect and human dignity" and requires that authorities take appropriate measures "to ensure that they realize their full mental and physical potential;" however, despite this provision, there was no statutory requirement for government services or facilities, such as accessibility of buildings for persons with disabilities. Widespread discrimination by society and employers limits job and educational opportunities for those with physical disabilities. The Children's Statute also requires children with disabilities to be treated and given necessary special facilities—a provision hampered in execution by inadequate funding. *Specific Legislation*: (a) Uganda Const. (Constitution of the Republic of Uganda, 1995), art. 21, 32, 35, <http://www.trybunal.gov.pl/constit/constitu/constit/uganda/uganda-e.htm> (last visited on August 14, 2003) (b) Local Government Act of 1997.
Zambia	Persons with disabilities faced significant societal discrimination in employment and education. The Government took steps to ameliorate their hardships, including establishing a national trust fund to provide loans to persons with disabilities to help them start businesses, but its efforts were limited by scarce resources. The Government did not legislate or otherwise mandate accessibility to public buildings and services for persons with disabilities. *Specific Legislation*: The Persons with Disabilities Act No. 33 of 1996, <http://natlex.ilo.org/txt/E96ZMB01.htm> (last visited on August 19, 2003)
Zimbabwe	President Mugabe appointed a disability activist to Parliament in 1995 to represent the needs of persons with disabilities. The law specifically prohibits discrimination against persons with disabilities in employment, admission to public places, or provision of services and is viewed by advocates of persons with disabilities as model legislation. However, in practice the lack of resources for training and education severely hampers the ability of persons with disabilities to compete for scarce jobs. The law stipulates that government buildings should be accessible to persons with disabilities; however, implementation of this policy has been slow. The Sexual Offenses Act, enacted in August, expanded the definition of sexual offenses to include an immoral or indecent act with a person with mental disabilities. *Specific Legislation*: (a) Disabled Persons Act of 1992, <http://natlex.ilo.org/txt/E92ZWE01.htm> (last visited on August 19, 2003) (b) Sexual Offenses Act of 2001.

	East Asia and the Pacific
Australia	Legislation prohibits discrimination against persons with disabilities in employment, education, or other state services. The Disability Discrimination Commissioner promotes compliance with federal laws that prohibit discrimination against persons with disabilities. The Commissioner also promotes implementation and enforcement of state laws that require equal access and otherwise protect the rights of persons with disabilities. The law makes it illegal to discriminate against a person on the grounds of disability in employment, education, provision of goods, services, and facilities, access to premises, and other areas. The law also provides for investigation of discrimination complaints by the HREOC, authorizes fines against violators, and awards damages to victims of discrimination. *Specific Legislation*: Disability Discrimination Act No. 135, 1992, <http://www.dredf.org/symposium/Ausdda.html> (last visited on August 19, 2003)
Brunei	The law does not mandate accessibility or other assistance for persons with disabilities. The Government is attempting to provide educational services for children with disabilities, although these efforts are not yet adequate. Teachers still must be trained to deal with children with disabilities, and some such children have no educational opportunities. A special facility with trained educators is needed to accommodate the children with disabilities who cannot be assimilated into normal classrooms, and the Ministry of Education continues to study the problem.
Burma	In principle official assistance to persons with disabilities includes two-thirds of pay for up to 1 year of a temporary disability and a tax-free stipend for permanent disability; however, in practice assistance is extremely limited. There is no law mandating accessibility to buildings, public transportation, or government facilities. While there are several small-scale organizations to assist persons with disabilities, most must rely on their families to provide for their welfare. Military veterans with disabilities receive available benefits on a priority basis. Because of landmine detonations, there are a large number of amputees.

Cambodia	The Government does not require that buildings or government services be accessible to persons with disabilities. According to the Government, approximately 1 in 250 citizens is missing at least one limb. This statistic reflects the continuing effects of landmine detonations. *Specific Legislation:* Cambodia Const. of 1993, art. 74 (amended 1999), <http://www.oefre.unibe.ch/law/icl/cb00000_.html> (last visited on August 14, 2003)
China (Includes Hong Kong and Macau)	There are laws designed to protect women, children, persons with disabilities, and minorities. However, in practice, societal discrimination based on ethnicity, gender, and disability persists. The Government has adopted legislation that protects the rights of the country's persons with disabilities. According to the official press, all local governments have drafted specific measures to implement the law. The press publicizes both the plight of persons with disabilities and the Government's efforts to assist them. The Government, at times in conjunction with NGOs such as the Lions Club International, sponsors a wide range of preventive and rehabilitative programs, including efforts to reduce congenital birth defects, treat cataracts, and treat hearing disorders. The goal of many of these programs is to allow persons with disabilities to be integrated into the rest of society. *Specific Legislation*: (a) P.R.C. Const. of 1982, art. 45, <http://www.oefre.unibe.ch/law/icl/ch00000_.html> (last visited on August 12, 2003) (b) Law of the People's Republic of China on the Protection of Disabled Persons, (1990), <http://natlex.ilo.org/txt/E90CHN01.htm> (last visited on August 12, 2003) (c) Labour Law of the People's Republic of China, 1994, §§ 14 & 73, China Laws for Foreign Business: Business Regulation, <http://www.chinalaborwatch.org/laws/laws.htm> (last visited on August 19, 2003) (d) Hong Kong Special Administrative Region: Disability Discrimination (Investigation and Conciliation) (Amendment) Rules 1997 (L.N. 630 of 1997), Hong Kong SAR Gazette, Legal Supplement No. 2, 1997-12-24, Vol. 1, No. 26, p. B1549) (e) Sex and Disability Discrimination Ordinance No. 71 of 1997, Hong Kong Government Gazette, Legal Supplement No. 1, Part I, 1997-06-27, pp. A2444-2455.

| China (Taiwan only) | The Constitution provides for equality of citizens before the law "irrespective of sex, religion, race, class, or party affiliation." It also provides for the rights of persons with disabilities. While the authorities are committed to protecting these rights, discrimination against some groups continues.

The law prohibits discrimination against persons with disabilities and sets minimum fines at approximately $2,400 (NT $73,800) for violators. New public buildings, facilities, and transportation equipment must be accessible to the persons with disabilities, and they appear to meet the requirements. Existing public buildings were to be brought into conformity by 1995; however, there does not as yet appear to be a substantial effort aimed at refitting older buildings to accommodate persons with disabilities.

According to MOI statistics, as of March there were 724,224 persons with disabilities. One-third of the total are severely disabled and receive shelter or nursing care from the authorities. The Disabled Welfare Law requires large public and private organizations to hire persons with disabilities equal to 2 and 1 percent of their work forces respectively. Organizations failing to do so must pay, for each person with disabilities not hired, the basic monthly salary (approximately $570 (NT $18,880)) into the Disabled Welfare Fund, which supports institutions involved in welfare for persons with disabilities. Many organizations complain that it is difficult to find qualified workers with disabilities, and they appear to prefer to pay the fines involved. Another law requires that, to compete for government contracts, a firm with at least 100 employees must include among its employees a minimum of 2 percent of either persons with disabilities or Aborigines. Both the central and local governments have established committees for the protection of persons with disabilities.

Specific Legislation:
(a) Taiwan Const. of 1947, art. 9 (amended 1999), <http://www.oefre.unibe.ch/law/icl/tw00000_.html> (last visited on August 14, 2003)
(b) Disability Welfare Law, 1980, art. 23. |
| **East Timor** | Although the Constitution protects the rights of the disabled, the Government has not enacted legislation or otherwise mandated a provision of accessibility to buildings for persons with disabilities, nor does the law prohibit discrimination against persons with disabilities. Nonetheless there were no reports of discrimination against persons with disabilities in employment, in education, or in the provision of other state services.

Specific Legislation:
E. Timor Const. of 2002, §§ 11 (3) & 21, <http://www.etan.org/etanpdf/pdf2/constfnen.pdf> (last visited on August 14, 2003) |

Fiji	The Constitution provides for the equality before the law of all persons, including persons with disabilities, and discrimination against the physically disabled in employment, education, and the provision of state services is illegal. However, there is no legislation or mandated provision for accessibility for the disabled. There is little or no enforcement of laws protecting persons with disabilities. *Specific Legislation*: Fiji Const. of 1988, § 38 (amended 1997), <http://www.oefre.unibe.ch/law/icl/fj00000_.html> (last visited on August 14, 2003)
Indonesia	There is some discrimination against persons with disabilities in employment, education, and in the provision of other state services. The law mandates access to buildings for persons with disabilities; however, the Government generally does not enforce these provisions in practice. Precise statistics on the number of persons with disabilities in the country are not available. In 1999 the U.N. estimated that about 5.43 percent of the population (about 10 million persons) were persons with disabilities, while the Government estimated that 3 percent of the population (6 million persons) were persons with disabilities. The Constitution requires that the Government provide care for orphans and persons with disabilities; however, it does not specify the definition of the term "care", and the provision of education to all children with mental and physical disabilities never has been inferred from the requirement. Regulations require the Government to establish and regulate a national curriculum for special education by stipulating that the community should provide special education services to its children. According to a 2000 UNICEF report, there are approximately 2 million children with disabilities between the ages of 10 and 14. Law No. 4/1997 on Disability and Government Regulation No. 72 on Special Education stipulate that every child with disabilities has the right to access to all levels and types of education and rehabilitative treatment as necessary. However, this does not occur in practice. NGOs are the primary providers of education for children with disabilities. The Disability Law was designed to provide access to education, employment, and assistance for persons with disabilities. It requires companies employing over 100 persons to give 1 percent of their positions to persons with disabilities. However, persons with disabilities face considerable discrimination in employment, although some factories have made special efforts to hire workers with disabilities. The law mandates accessibility to public facilities for persons with disabilities; however, virtually no buildings or public transportation provide such accessibility. *Specific Legislation:* Social Welfare for the Disabled No. 36, 1980, Labour Legislation in Indonesia, 1986, Vol. 3, p. 70-74 (Elucidatio).

| Japan | There are an estimated 2.9 million persons with physical disabilities and roughly 2 million persons with mental disabilities. Although not generally subject to overt discrimination in employment, education, or in the provision of other state services, persons with disabilities face limited access to public transportation, "mainstream" public education, and other facilities. The Deliberation Panel on the Employment of the Handicapped, which operates within the Ministry of Labor, mandated that private companies with 300 or more employees hire a fixed minimum proportion of persons with disabilities. The penalty for noncompliance was a fine. A 1998 cabinet directive ordered private companies to raise the proportion of persons with physical disabilities in their work force from 1.6 to 1.8 percent and raised the percentage of persons with disabilities among civil servants from 2 to 2.1 percent. Some prefectural governments provided subsidies to companies that employed persons who used wheelchairs. In June the Diet passed legislation amending 27 laws that previously had banned the blind, deaf and those with mental disabilities from working as doctors, dentists, nurses, and pharmacists. The Health, Labor, and Welfare Ministry started awarding licenses for these professions on a case-by-case basis in July.

The law does not mandate accessibility to buildings for persons with disabilities; however, the law on construction standards for public facilities allows operators of hospitals, theaters, hotels, and similar enterprises to receive low-interest loans and tax breaks if they build wider entrances and elevators to accommodate persons with disabilities. In 2000 the barrier-free transportation law took effect, requiring public transport systems to take measures to make their facilities more accessible to persons with disabilities as well as to the elderly.

The Law to Promote the Employment of the Handicapped includes those with mental disabilities. The law also loosened the licensing requirements for community support centers that promote employment for persons with disabilities, and it introduced government subsidies for the employment of persons with mental disabilities in part-time jobs.

The Headquarters for Promoting the Welfare of Disabled Persons, set up by the Prime Minister's Office, in previous years recommended that municipalities draw up formal plans for the care of citizens with disabilities. The Ministry of Health and Welfare also has instructed local governments to set numerical targets for the number of home help providers and care facilities allocated to the disabled.

Specific Legislation:
(a) Human Resources Development Promotion, Law No. 64 of 1969, as amended through Law No. 38 of 1994, <http://natlex.ilo.org/txt/E69JPN01.htm> (last visited on August 26, 2003) |

Japan (cont'd)	(b) Transportation Accessibility Improvement Law, 2000. (c) Promoting the Welfare of Disabled Persons, 1995. (d) Law No. 38 of 1994 to amend the Employment Promotion for the Disabled Law No. 123 of 1960, <http://natlex.ilo.org/txt/E60JPN01.htm> (last visited on August 26, 2003) (e) Ordinance of the Ministry of Health, Labour and Welfare determining degrees of disability in accordance with Law on Welfare of Physically Disabled Persons No. 98, 2002. (f) Ordinance of the Ministry of Health, Labour and Welfare determining degrees of disability in accordance with Law on Welfare of Mentally Disabled Persons No. 99 of 2002.
Kiribati	The law does not prohibit specifically discrimination against persons with disabilities; however, there were no complaints of discrimination in employment, education, or in the provision of other state services for persons with mental or physical disabilities. Accessibility for persons with disabilities has not been mandated; accommodations for persons with disabilities are basically nonexistent. The central hospital on Tarawa has a wing for persons with mental disabilities. There is a foreign national psychiatrist working in Tarawa. Foreign-based aid workers and the World Health Organization cooperate with the Ministry of Health to conduct outer island workshops for health workers.
Korea, Democratic People's Republic of	Traditional social norms condone discrimination against persons with physical disabilities. Apart from veterans with disabilities, persons with disabilities almost never are seen within the city limits of Pyongyang, and several defectors and other former residents report that persons with disabilities are assigned to the rural areas routinely. According to one report, authorities check every 2 to 3 years in the capital for persons with deformities and relocate them to special facilities in the countryside. There are no legally mandated provisions for accessibility to buildings or government services for persons with disabilities. In a 1998 statement, the UN Committee on the Rights of the Child criticized "de facto discrimination" in the country against children with disabilities. *Specific legislation:* (a) N. Korea Const. of 1948, art. 72 & 76 (amended 1998), <http://www.korea-np.co.jp/pk/061st_issue/98091708.htm> (last visited on August 15, 2003)

Korea, Republic of	The Constitution and law forbid discrimination on the basis of race, sex, religion, disability, or social status, and the Government respects these provisions. However, traditional attitudes limit opportunities for women and the disabled. The law states that "no one shall be discriminated against in all areas of political, economic, social, and cultural life on the grounds of disability." In 1995 the Government expanded job training programs, medical benefits, and welfare facilities for disabled citizens. Firms with over 300 employees are required by law either to hire persons with disabilities or pay a fine. Surveys indicate that most companies either pay the fine or evade the law, with one 1999 survey indicating that 9 out of 10 firms with more than 300 employees failed to meet the mandated 2 percent job quota for persons with disabilities; the hiring of the persons with disabilities remains significantly below target levels. Persons with disabilities make up less than 1 percent of the work force. New public buildings are required to include facilities for persons with disabilities, such as ramp access to entrances, a wheelchair lift, and special parking spaces. The Health and Welfare Ministry has announced that existing government buildings must be retrofitted with these facilities, and, as of late 1998, 47.4 percent of public buildings and facilities had facilities for the persons with disabilities. In 1999 the Constitutional Court ruled that government agencies' preferential hiring practices for those who have performed military service discriminated against persons with disabilities and were unconstitutional. *Specific Legislation*: (a)Welfare of Disabled Persons Act No. 6460, 2001, Statutes of The Republic of Korea, Vol. 17, p. 861-879 (10). (b) Employment Promotion of The Handicapped Act No. 4219, 1990, <http://www.dredf.org/symposium/korea2.html> (last visited on August 19, 2003) (c) Promotion of Education For the Handicapped Act No. 6400, 2001, Statutes of The Republic of Korea, Vol. 7, p. 581-606 (~610).
Laos	With donor assistance, the Government is implementing limited programs for persons with disabilities, especially amputees. The law does not mandate accessibility to buildings or government services for persons with disabilities, but the Labor and Social Welfare Ministry has established some regulations regarding building access and some sidewalk ramps in Vientiane. The Lao National Commission for the Disabled (LNCD) has promulgated regulations to protect the rights of persons with disabilities, and in 2000 the Lao Disabled Persons Association set up offices in Champassak and Xieng Khouang provinces to assist with the rehabilitation, job skills training, and social integration of persons with disabilities. *Specific Legislation:* Laos Const. of 1991, art. 20 & 26, <http://www.laoembassy.com/news/constitution/body.htm> (last visited on August 15, 2003)

| Malaysia | The Government does not discriminate against persons with disabilities in employment, education, and provision of other state services. However, few public facilities are adapted to the needs of persons with disabilities, and the Government has not mandated accessibility to transportation or public buildings for persons with disabilities. In August 1999, former Minister of National Unity and Social Development Zaleha said that only 10 percent of residential and commercial buildings were "disabled-friendly." In September 1999, Zaleha announced a cabinet decision to require that 10 percent of houses in all new housing projects be accessible to persons with disabilities. In December 1999, Zaleha reportedly stated that "all buildings" would be made accessible to persons with disabilities within 2 years, although it is not possible to verify that all buildings are accessible to persons with disabilities.

The Government continued to implement efforts made to address the needs of persons with disabilities. In October 2000, the Ministry of Housing and Local Government announced that the uniform building by-laws would be amended to ensure that all newly constructed buildings include a full range of facilities for persons with disabilities, including special parking lots, elevators, and restrooms. By year's end, it was not possible to verify whether building by-laws had been amended. In November 2000, the Human Resources Ministry announced plans to draft a code of ethics for employers to address the needs of persons with disabilities including additional employment opportunities, job discrimination, and disabled-friendly work environments. In November, the Ministry of Human Resources published the code of ethics. In addition the federal budget for the year included several provisions to ease financial burdens on persons with disabilities and improve work, education, and training opportunities. In November 2000, the Human Rights Commission recommended amending the Constitution's antidiscrimination provision to include legal protection for persons with disabilities, but no amendments have been introduced.

Provisions for persons with disabilities in the 2001 budget include several allowances for tax relief for working spouses of persons with disabilities, full exemption for all medical fees at government hospitals, and full exemption on fees for travel documents. All equipment designed specifically for use by persons with disabilities would also be exempt from all import duties and sales taxes. Recognizing that public transportation is not disabled-friendly, the Government is reducing the excise duty for persons with disabilities on locally made cars and motorcycles by 50 percent.

Specific Legislation:
(a) National Welfare Policy, 1990.
(b) Uniform Building By-Laws, 1991. |

Marshall Islands	There is no apparent discrimination against persons with disabilities in employment, education, or in the provision of other state services. There are no building codes, and there is no legislation mandating access for persons with disabilities. There are approximately 50 persons who could be medically defined as psychotic. When these individuals demonstrate dangerous behavior, they are imprisoned and visited by a doctor. There were no reports of discrimination against persons with mental disabilities.
Micronesia, Federated States of	The law prohibits discrimination in public service employment against persons with disabilities. Children with physical or mental disabilities are provided with special education, including instruction at home if necessary. Neither laws nor regulations mandate accessibility to public buildings and services for persons with disabilities. The school system has established special education classes to address problems encountered by those who exhibit learning disabilities, although such classes are completely dependent on nongovernmental funding. Some private businesses provide special parking spaces and wheelchair ramps for the disabled.

Mongolia	The 1999 Labor Law prohibits discrimination against disabled persons in employment and education, and requires the Government to provide benefits according to the nature and severity of the disability, which it does. In practice, however, society shuns the disabled and most cannot find jobs. During the year the Government began implementing a section of the 1999 Labor Law that requires companies employing more than 50 persons to hire at least 3 disabled persons. Those who have been injured in industrial accidents have the right to be reemployed when ready to resume work, and the Government offers free retraining in 6 fields at a central technical school. There are several specialized schools for disabled youths, but they are free to attend regular schools. The Government also provides tax benefits to enterprises that hire the disabled, and some firms hire the disabled exclusively. There is no law mandating access for the disabled and, therefore, it is difficult for the disabled to participate fully in public life. However, during the year, the Government set aside a small sum to begin building wheelchair access ramps to public buildings. Disabled citizens' groups have demonstrated for higher government subsidies. Government pensions for the disabled are approximately 40,000 tugrik ($40) per month. Estimates vary, but there are an estimated 40,000 disabled persons in the country. Approximately 30 NGOs participate in activities assisting the disabled. *Specific Legislation:* (a) Mong. Const. of 1992, art. 16 (amended 2001), <http://www.oefre.unibe.ch/law/icl/mg00000_.html> (last visited on August 15, 2003) (b) Labour Code, 1999, ch. 8 & 15, <http://natlex.ilo.org/txt/E99MNG01.htm#c8> (last visited on August 19, 2003)
Nauru	There is no reported discrimination in employment, education, and the provision of state services to persons with disabilities. However, no legislation mandates access to public buildings and services for persons with disabilities. Upon application to the Health Department, the Government will assist persons with disabilities by building access ramps to homes and workplaces.

New Zealand	The law prohibits discrimination against persons with disabilities in employment, education, access to places and facilities, and the provision of goods, services, and accommodation. Compliance with access laws varies. The Human Rights Amendment Act passed in 1999 introduced a new standard for government compliance to replace the exemption for government that expired during the year. The Government is prohibited from discrimination on the basis of disability, mental or physical, unless such discrimination can be "demonstrably justified in a free, democratic society." The Human Rights Commission reported during the year that it received more complaints of discrimination based on disability than any other type of discrimination. *Specific Legislation:* (a) Human Rights Amendment Act No. 100, 1999, The Statutes of New Zealand 1999, Vol. II. (b) Disabled Persons Employment Promotion Amendment Act 1960 amended by Act 1985. (c) Disabled Community Welfare Amendment Act No. 69, 1997. (d) New Zealand Public Health and Disability Act No. 91, 2000, The Statutes of New Zealand 2000, Vol. II.
Palau	The National Code includes a Disabled Persons Antidiscrimination Act and a Handicapped Children Act, and the Government enforces the provisions of these acts. No instances of discrimination against persons with disabilities were reported. The law requires building access for persons with disabilities, and most government and business buildings have access for such persons. The public schools have established special education programs to address problems encountered by persons with disabilities. *Specific Legislation:* (a) Disabled Person's Antidiscrimination Act, 30 PNCA § 501 (1998). (b) Handicapped Children Act, 22 PNCA § 401 (1998).
Papua New Guinea	Through the National Board for the Disabled, the Government provides funds to a number of NGOs that provide services to persons with disabilities. The Government does not provide programs or services directly. Services and health care for persons with disabilities, except for those provided by the traditional clan/family system, do not exist in several of the country's provinces. There is no legislation mandating accessibility. Persons with disabilities face discrimination in education, training, and employment. Most persons with disabilities do not find training or work outside the clan/family structure; however, the traditional structure remains the likelihood for most Papua New Guineans. The Government provides free consultation and treatment for persons with mental disabilities; however, such services are rarely available outside major cities.

Philippines	The law provides for equal physical access for persons with disabilities to all public buildings and establishments and for "the rehabilitation, self development, and self-reliance of disabled persons and their integration into the mainstream of society." The law applies to both those with physical disabilities and persons with mental disabilities. The Department of Labor and Employment's (DOLE) Bureau of Local Employment (BLE) maintains registers of persons with disabilities indicating their skills and abilities. However, advocates for the rights of persons with disabilities contend that the law has been ineffective because implementing regulations are weak, funding is inadequate, and government programs are palliative rather than focused on integration. Among other things they have called for more government jobs and more positions at public universities for persons with disabilities. Reportedly only about 2 percent of an estimated 3.5 million citizens with disabilities receive access to services. *Specific Legislation*: (a) Magna Carta for Disabled Persons, R.A. 7277, 1992, Vital Legal Documents (Second Series): Book 2 p.8239-8422, <http://disabled.hotusa.org/documents/THE%20MAGNA%20CARTA %20FOR%20DISABLED%20PERSONS.doc> (last visited on August 19, 2003) (b) Social Security Act, R.A. 8282, 1997, Vital Legal Documents (Second Series): Book 7, p. 61-95.
Samoa	The Constitution prohibits discrimination based on race, sex, religion, disability, language, or social status. The Government has passed no legislation pertaining to the status of persons with disabilities or regarding accessibility for them. Tradition dictates that families care for persons with disabilities, and this custom is observed widely in practice. There are no reports of societal discrimination against persons with physical or mental disabilities. *Specific Legislation:* Samoa Const. of 1962, art. 14, § 1, <http://www.vanuatu.usp.ac.fj/paclawmat/Samoa_legislation/Samoa _Constitution.html> (last visited on August 15, 2003)

Singapore	The Government maintains a comprehensive code on barrier-free accessibility, which establishes standards for facilities for the physically disabled in all new buildings and mandated the progressive upgrading of older structures. Although there is no legislation that addresses the issue of equal opportunities for persons with disabilities in education or employment, the National Council of Social Services, in conjunction with various voluntary associations, provides an extensive job training and placement program for the disabled. Informal provisions in education have permitted university matriculation for visually impaired, deaf, and physically disabled students. The Government allows a tax deduction of up to $1,900 (SD 3,500) per individual for families with a disabled family member. Mental and physically disabilities are treated in the same way. Press coverage of the activities and achievements of the disabled is extensive, and discrimination or abuse of persons with disabilities does not appear to be a problem. *Specific Legislation:* Code on Barrier-Free Accessibility, 1995, ch. II, <http://www.dpa.org.sg/DPA/access/95toc.htm> (last visited on August 19, 2003)
Solomon Islands	There is no law or national policy on persons with disabilities, and no legislation mandates access for such individuals. Their protection and care are left to the traditional extended family and nongovernmental organizations. With high unemployment countrywide and few jobs available in the formal sector, most persons with disabilities, particularly those in rural areas, do not find work outside of the family structure. Persons with mental disabilities are cared for within the family structure; there are no government facilities for such persons.

Thailand	The Constitution provides for equal treatment under the law without respect to race, sex, religion, disability, language, or social status; however, in practice some discrimination exists, and government enforcement of equal protection statutes is uneven. The law provides for access to public facilities and prohibits employment and education discrimination against persons with disabilities; however, the Government has not enforced these laws effectively. An estimated 145,000 children with disabilities attend school, with approximately 130,000 enrolled in about 4,000 regular public schools equipped to accommodate students with physical disabilities. Nationwide, there are 8 government-operated and 15 NGO-operated training centers for persons with disabilities. However, with little education, very few adults with disabilities are able to find employment. Many of those who do find employment are subjected to wage discrimination. The law requires that private firms hire 1 person with a disability for every 200 other workers or contribute to a fund that benefits persons with disabilities, but this provision has not been enforced since it came into effect in 1991. Government officials estimated that 30 percent of firms disregard the law. Some state enterprises have discriminatory hiring policies. The Constitution mandates access to public buildings for persons with disabilities, but laws implementing the provisions have not yet been enacted. Persons with disabilities who register with the Government are entitled to free medical examinations, wheelchairs, and crutches. *Specific Legislation*: (a) Thail. Const. of 1997, §§ 55 & 80, <http://www.oefre.unibe.ch/law/icl/th00000_.html> (last visited on August 15, 2003) (b) Rehabilitation of Disabled Persons Act (B.E. 2534), 1991, Labour Law Documents 1992/1: Treaties and legislation on labour and social security, p. 100-104, <http://www.dredf.org/symposium/thailand.html> (last visited on August 19, 2003)
Tonga	There are no mandated provisions for accessibility to buildings and services for persons with disabilities. There were no reported complaints of discrimination in employment, education, or provision of other government services. The education of children with special needs has been a longstanding priority of the Queen.
Tuvalu	There were no known reports of discrimination against persons with disabilities in employment, education, or in the provision of other state services. There are no mandated accessibility provisions for persons with disabilities.

Vanuatu	There is no governmental or national policy on persons with disabilities and no legislation mandating access to buildings for them. Their protection and care is left to the traditional extended family and to voluntary NGOs. Due to high rates of unemployment, there were few jobs available for persons with disabilities. Persons with mental illness typically do not receive specialized care; usually they are attended by members of their extended families.
Vietnam	There is no official discrimination against persons with disabilities in employment, education, or in the provision of other state services. Government provision of services to assist persons with disabilities, however, is limited, and the Government provides little official protection or effective support to persons with disabilities. The law requires the State to protect the rights and encourage the employment of the persons with disabilities. It includes provisions for preferential treatment of firms that recruit persons with disabilities for training or apprenticeship and a special levy on firms that do not employ workers with disabilities. The extent to which the Government enforces these provisions is unknown. There are no laws mandating physical access to buildings, but international groups are working with the Government to provide increased accessibility. International groups also are assisting the Government in implementing programs to increase access by persons with disabilities to education and employment. *Specific Legislation:* Labour Code of 1994 the Socialist Republic of VietNam, as amended up to 2002, <http://natlex.ilo.org/txt/E94VNM01.htm> (last visited on August 26, 2003)

	EUROPE & EURASIA
Albania	There is some discrimination against persons with disabilities in employment, education, and the provision of other state services. Widespread poverty, unregulated working conditions, and poor medical care pose significant problems for many persons with disabilities. They are eligible for various forms of public assistance, but budgetary constraints mean the amounts that they receive are very low. No law mandates accessibility to public buildings for persons with disabilities, and little has been done in this regard.
Andorra	The law prohibits discrimination against persons with disabilities in employment, education, or in the provision of other state service, and there were no reports that it occurred. Societal discrimination does exist on a small scale. The law mandates access to new buildings for persons with disabilities, and the Government generally enforces these provisions in practice.
Armenia	The Constitution prohibits discrimination based on race, gender, religion, disability, language, or social status; however, cultural and economic factors prevent women, ethnic and religious minorities, and persons with disabilities from participating fully in public life. The Constitution provides for the right to social security in the event of disability, and the law provides for the social, political, and individual rights of persons with disabilities; however, the Government's enforcement of the rights of persons with disabilities remained rudimentary. Legal safeguards for those with psychiatric problems are inadequate to protect patients' rights. Hospitals, residential care, and other facilities for serious disabilities are substandard. There were unsubstantiated reports in 2000 that security authorities used confinement in mental institutions as an alternative form of detention (see Sections 1.c. and 1.d.). There is societal discrimination against persons with disabilities. The law and a government decree have special provisions that mandate accessibility in buildings for persons with disabilities; however, in practice very few buildings and other facilities are accessible. *Specific Legislation:* Arm. Const. of 1995, art. 33, <http://www.oefre.unibe.ch/law/icl/am00000_.html> (last visited on August 15, 2003)

Austria	The law protects persons with disabilities from discrimination in housing, education, and employment. A 1997 amendment to the law explicitly requires the State to provide for equal rights for the disabled "in all areas of everyday life." The law requires all private enterprises and state and federal government offices to employ one person with disabilities for every 25 to 40 employees, depending on the type of work. Employers who do not meet this requirement must pay a fee to the Government, and the proceeds help finance services for the disabled such as training programs, wage subsidies, and workplace adaptations. Federal law mandates access for the physically disabled; however, low fines and insufficient enforcement resulted in the inaccessibility of many public buildings to persons with disabilities. On January 1, an omnibus bill on child custody went into effect that prohibits the sterilization of minors, particularly mentally handicapped girls below the age of 18. Those 18 and older may only be sterilized in life-threatening instances. Previously, mentally retarded minor girls could be sterilized involuntarily at the request of parents, and mentally retarded women could be sterilized involuntarily at the request of the responsible family member or by court order. *Specific Legislation:* (a) Aus. Const. of 1929, art. 7 (amended 1995), <http://www.oefre.unibe.ch/law/icl/au00000_.html> (last visited on August 8, 2003) (b) Act amending the Act on Disabled Persons, the Act on Hiring Disabled Persons, and the Finance Act 2001 (No. 60 of 2001).
Azerbaijan	The law prescribes priority for persons with disabilities in obtaining housing, as well as discounts for public transport and pension supplements. The Government does not have the means to fulfill these commitments. In January and February, following a demonstration and hunger strike by Nagorno-Karabakh war veterans and persons with disabilities (see Section 2.b.), the Government promised to increase the special subsidies provided to those groups, but had not done so by year's end. There are no special provisions in the law mandating accessibility to public or other buildings for the disabled; this was not a government priority. *Specific Legislation:* (a) Azer. Const. of 1995, art. 34 & 38, <http://www.oefre.unibe.ch/law/icl/aj00000_.html> (last visited on August 15, 2003) (b) Social Protection of Invalids Act No. 284, 1992.

Belarus	Discrimination against persons with disabilities in the provision of employment, education, and other state services is a problem, as is social discrimination. A 1992 law mandates accessibility to transport, residences, businesses, and offices for persons with disabilities; however, facilities, including transport and office buildings, often were not accessible to persons with disabilities. The country's continued difficult financial condition makes it especially difficult for local governments to budget sufficient funds to implement the 1992 law. *Specific Legislation:* (a) Belr. Const. of 1994, art. 47, <http://www.oefre.unibe.ch/law/icl/bo00000_.html> (last visited on August 15, 2003) (b) Act No. 418, 2000 (Consolidation) to amend and supplement The Social Protection of the Disabled Act No. 1224-XII, 1991. (c) Act No. 564 (3317-XII), 1994 On the Prevention of Disablement and Rehabilitation of Invalids, <http://ncpi.gov.by/eng/legal/V19403317.htm> (last visited on August 26, 2003)
Belgium	The law provides for the protection of persons with disabilities from discrimination in employment, education, and in the provision of other state services. There were no reports of societal discrimination against persons with disabilities. The Government mandates that public buildings erected since 1970 be accessible to such persons and offers subsidies to encourage the owners of other buildings to make necessary modifications. However, many older buildings are not accessible. The Government provides financial assistance for persons with disabilities. It gives special aid to parents of children with disabilities and to parents with disabilities. *Specific Legislation:* Social Rehabilitation Act, 1963.
Bosnia and Herzegovina	The Federation Government is required by law to assist persons with disabilities to find employment and to protect them against discrimination. In the RS, the law also prohibits discrimination against persons with disabilities. There are no legal provisions mandating that buildings be made accessible to persons with physical disabilities, and in practice buildings rarely are accessible to persons with disabilities.

Bulgaria	The law provides for a range of financial assistance for persons with disabilities, including free public transportation, reduced prices on modified automobiles, and free equipment such as wheelchairs; however, budgetary constraints mean that such assistance occasionally is not given. Societal discrimination against persons with disabilities persists. Disabled individuals have access to university training (students with disabilities must pay the university's initial application fee but are exempt from semester fees if accepted), to housing, and to employment; however, architectural barriers are a great hindrance in most older buildings, including schools and universities. Conditions in institutions for the mentally disabled are poor. In October Amnesty International and the Bulgarian Helsinki Committee published a report on their visit to the Sanadinovo Home for Mentally Disabled Women and cited overcrowding, lack of proper hygiene, clothing, and access to medical care as serious problems. For example, as punishment, women were held in a cage made of iron bars and wire; the NGO observers noted that the cage floor was dirty with human excrement. Labor laws intended to protect the interests of persons with disabilities and create greater employment opportunity have had a mixed effect. On the one hand, the law provides incentives for small firms to hire persons with disabilities; for example, the Bureau of Labor pays the first year's salary of a disabled employee. On the other hand, workers with disabilities are entitled to shorter working hours, which often leads to discrimination against them in hiring practices. According to the law, any enterprise employing more than 50 persons must hire a certain number of disabled workers (between 3 and 10 percent, depending on the industry). Those who fail to do so must pay a fine, the proceeds of which go to a fund for persons with disabilities. Nevertheless due to low fines and delays in the judicial system, compliance rates are extremely low. The law requires improved structural access for the disabled, and public works have taken the needs of persons with disabilities into account, for example, Sofia's new subway system was designed with wheelchair access to stations. However, enforcement of this law has lagged in existing, unrenovated buildings. *Specific Legislation* (a) Decree No. 168, 2002 of the Council of Ministers to amend and supplement the Regulations governing the activities of the national council for rehabilitation and social integration and the criteria for membership. (b) Labor code, Prom. SG 1996, <http://www.bild.net/legislation/> (last visited on August 20, 2003)

Croatia	The Constitution ensures "special care for the protection of disabled persons and their inclusion in social life." While persons with disabilities face no openly discriminatory measures, job opportunities generally are limited. Special education also is limited and poorly funded. The Law on Social Welfare and the Law on Construction specify access to public services and buildings for persons with disabilities; however, the construction rules are not always enforced and they do not mandate that facilities be retro-filled. As a result, access to public facilities often is difficult. *Specific Legislation* (a) Croat. Const. of 1990, art. 57 & 64 (amended 2001), <http://www.oefre.unibe.ch/law/icl/hr00000_.html> (last visited on August 15, 2003) (b) Law on Social Welfare. (c) Pension and Disability Insurance Act, 1983 (amended 1994). (d) Act No. 22, 2002 on Vocational Rehabilitation and Employment of Disabled Persons. (e) Law on Construction. (f) Act No. 20, 2002 to amend and supplement The Protection of Mentally Disabled Persons Act No. 19, 1997.
Cyprus	In Cyprus generally, persons with disabilities do not appear to face discrimination in education or the provision of state services. In the Greek Cypriot community, persons with disabilities who apply for a public sector position are entitled to preference if they are deemed able to perform the required duties and their qualifications equal those of other applicants. In October 2000, the Government passed a law based on a 1993 U.N. General Assembly resolution on equal opportunities for persons with disabilities, which includes regulations promoting equal opportunities for them in the areas of employment, transportation, and recreation. In the Turkish Cypriot community, regulations require businesses to employ 1 person with disabilities for every 25 positions they fill, although enforcement is inconsistent. The law in the Greek Cypriot community mandates that new public buildings and tourist facilities be accessible, although little has been done to enforce the law, despite the enactment in 2000 of relevant regulations. *Specific Legislation:* (a) Equalization of Opportunities for Persons with Disabilities Act No. 127 (I), 2000. (b) Education and Culture of Children with Special Needs Act No. 113 (I), 1999.

Czech Republic	The law prohibits discrimination against persons with disabilities in employment, education, or in the provision of other state services, and there were no reports of such discrimination; however, persons with disabilities suffer disproportionately from unemployment. Businesses in which 60 percent or more of the employees are disabled qualify for special tax breaks and the Government provides transportation subsidies to disabled citizens. Regulations and the Construction Code require architects to ensure adequate access for the disabled in all new building projects, as well as in older buildings undergoing restoration; these regulations are applied in practice. However, many buildings and means of public transportation remained inaccessible to those in wheelchairs, although access is improving. In Prague 24 of 50 metro stations are wheelchair accessible; however, most of these stations are in the outskirts of the city, and the majority of stations in the city center remain inaccessible. There are a growing number of bus lines that are accessible to persons with disabilities; tram lines in Plzen are wheelchair accessible. Due to the lack of barrier-free access to public schools, access to education can be a problem, although there is at least one barrier-free school in each district. *Specific Legislation:* (a) Coll. Retirement Pensions No. 438/2000. (b) Labor Laws Act No. 1/1991, as amended by 436/2001. (c) Order No. 228/2000 on the obligatory number of persons with diminished working capacity to be employed by an employer.
Denmark	Building regulations require special facilities for the disabled in public buildings built or renovated after 1977 and in older buildings that come into public use. The Government generally enforces these provisions in practice. *Specific Legislation:* Respecting Individual Assistance to Disabled Persons in Employment Act No. 928, 1991 amended.

Estonia	While the Constitution provides for the protection of persons with disabilities against discrimination, and both the Government and some private organizations provide them with financial assistance, little has been done to enable persons with disabilities to participate normally in public life. There is no public access law, but some effort has been made to accommodate persons with disabilities; for example, ramps were installed at curbs on new sidewalk construction, and public transportation firms have acquired some vehicles that are accessible, as have some taxi companies. The law allows for persons with serious sight, hearing, or speech impediments to become naturalized citizens without having to pass an examination on the Estonian Constitution and language. *Specific Legislation:* (a) Est. Const. of 1992, art. 28, <http://www.oefre.unibe.ch/law/icl/en00000_.html> (last visited on August 15, 2003) (b) Decree No. 195, 1996 to establish conditions and procedure of the education of the disabled in vocational institutes. (c) Social Benefits for Disabled Persons Act, 1999 (amended 2002), <http://www.legaltext.ee/text/en/X30031K6.htm> (last visited on August 21, 2003)
Finland	The Constitution prohibits discrimination based on sex, age, origin, language, religion, conviction, opinion, or disability, and the Government effectively enforces these provisions. The deaf and the mute are provided interpretation services ranging from 120 to 240 hours annually. The Government provides subsidized public housing to persons with severe disabilities. Although the law requires that new public buildings be accessible to persons with physical disabilities, many older buildings remained inaccessible. No such law applies to public transportation, but each municipality subsidizes measures to improve accessibility to public vehicles. *Specific Legislation:* (a) Fin. Const. of 1999, §§ 6, 17 & 19, <http://www.oefre.unibe.ch/law/icl/fi00000_.html> (last visited on August 15, 2003) (b) Status and Rights of Patients Act No. 785 of 1992. (c) Penal Code Act No. 578 of 1995 amended by Act No. 72 of 2001. (d) Workers' Pension Act No. 395 of 1961 amended by Act No. 188 of 2003.

France	A 1991 law requires new public buildings to be accessible to persons with disabilities, and the Government generally enforces these provisions in practice; however, many older buildings and public transportation are not accessible. *Specific Legislation*: <http://www.legifrance.gouv.fr/> [French legislation (text only in French) can be found on this comprehensive government site]. (a) Labor Code of 1973 amended. (b) Law No. 90-602 of 12 July 1990, (c) Law No 91-663 of July 13, 1991 carrying various measures intended to support accessibility for handicapped people in buildings, dwellings, the places of work and the installations receiving of the public. (d) Penal Code of 1993 amended. (e) Decree no. 98-543. (f) Decree no. 99-756. (g) Decree no. 99-757.
Georgia	There is no legislated or otherwise mandated provision requiring access for persons with disabilities; however, the law mandates that the State ensure appropriate conditions for persons with disabilities to use freely the social infrastructure and to ensure proper protection and support. The law includes a provision of special discounts and favorable social policies for persons with disabilities, especially veterans with disabilities; however, many facilities for persons with disabilities remained closed due to lack of funding.

Germany	The law prohibits the denial of access to housing, health care, or education on the basis of race, religion, disability, sex, ethnic background, political opinion, or citizenship.
	The Basic Law specifically prohibits discrimination against persons with disabilities, and there were no reports of discrimination against persons with disabilities in employment, education, or in the provision of other state services. The law mandates several special services for persons with disabilities; they are entitled to assistance to avert, eliminate, or alleviate the consequences of their disabilities and to secure employment commensurate with their abilities. The Government offers vocational training and grants for employers who hire the disabled. Persons with severe disabilities may be granted special benefits, such as tax relief, free public transport, special parking facilities, and exemption from radio and television fees.
	The Government has set guidelines for the attainment of "barrier-free" public buildings and for modifications of streets and pedestrian traffic walks to accommodate persons with disabilities. All 16 states have incorporated the federal guidelines into their building codes, and 98 percent of federal public buildings follow the guidelines for a "barrier-free environment." There were no reports of societal discrimination against persons with disabilities
	Specific Legislation: (a) F.R.G. Const., (Basic Law of the Federal Republic of Germany, 1949), art. 74 (amended in 2000), <http://www.oefre.unibe.ch/law/the_basic_law.pdf > (last visited on August 25, 2003) (b) Severely Disabled Persons Act 1986. (c) Equality for Disabled Persons Act 2002.

| Greece | Legislation mandates the hiring of persons with disabilities in public and private enterprises that employ more than 50 persons; however, the law reportedly is enforced poorly, particularly in the private sector. The law states that persons with disabilities should account for 3 percent of employees in private enterprises. In the civil service, 5 percent of administrative staff and 80 percent of telephone operator positions are reserved for persons with disabilities. Recent legislation mandates the hiring of persons with disabilities in the public sector from a priority list. They are exempt from the civil service exam, and some have been appointed to important positions in the civil service. There is no societal discrimination against persons with disabilities.

The Construction Code mandates physical access for persons with disabilities to private and public buildings, but this law, also, is enforced poorly. Many public buildings had not complied with the proposals of the interministerial committee on accessibility by year's end. A 1997 survey showed that over 60 percent of public buildings were not accessible. Ramps and special curbs for persons with disabilities were constructed on some Athens streets and at some public buildings, and sound signals have been installed at some city street crossings. During the year, the Ministry of Public Works installed special sound equipment for 200 traffic lights in Attika that were selected by the Association for the Blind. The Government continued to replace old city buses with new accessible buses. Athens subway lines provide full accessibility.

Specific Legislation:
(a) Greece Const. of 1975, art. 21 (amended 2001), <http://www.oefre.unibe.ch/law/icl/gr00c___.pdf > (last visited on August 18, 2003)
(b) Law 2643/98, relating to the "employment of persons in special categories and other provisions." |

Hungary	Government sources estimated that there were between 600,000 and 1 million persons with disabilities (6 to 10 percent of the population). Of these persons, 300,000 to 350,000 were considered seriously disabled and receive increased government benefits. Persons with disabilities faced societal discrimination and prejudice. A Council for the Disabled was established in 1999 under the chairmanship of the Minister of Social and Family Affairs. The Council serves as an advisory board to the Government. A 1997 decree requires all companies that employ more than 20 persons to reserve 5 percent of their jobs for persons with physical or mental disabilities, with fines of up to 75 percent of the average monthly salary for noncompliance. In 1999 such fines yielded $6 million (approximately 1.77 billion HUF) for rehabilitation funds for the disabled. The foreign NGO Mental Disability Rights International (MDRI) and the local NGO Hungarian Mental Health Interest Forum (PEF) noted that no procedures exist to oversee the treatment and care of persons with disabilities who are under guardianship. The MDRI and the PEF also criticize the use of cages in government facilities for persons with mental disabilities. The law mandates access to buildings for persons with disabilities; however, services for persons with disabilities are limited, and most buildings are not wheelchair accessible. *Specific Legislation*: (a) Hung. Const. of 1949, art. 70E (amended 1997), <http://www.oefre.unibe.ch/law/icl/hu00000_.html> (last visited on August 18, 2003) (b) Equalization Opportunity Law Act No. XXVI of 1998, <http://www.dredf.org/symposium/hungary2.html> (last visited on August 20, 2003)

Iceland	The law provides that persons with disabilities persons have the right to "all common national and municipal services" and provides that they be given assistance to "make it possible for them to live and work in normal society with others." The law also provides that persons with disabilities should receive preference for a government job when they are qualified equally, or more qualified, than regular applicants.
	Building regulations updated in 1998 call for public accommodations—such as hotels, restaurants, banks, and stores—as well as government buildings to be accessible so that persons in wheelchairs have access without assistance. Building regulations also specify that elevators in such buildings should be large enough to accommodate wheelchairs and that 1 percent of parking spaces (a minimum of one space) should be reserved for disabled use.
	In 2000 the Supreme Court ruled that the extent to which the State was reducing social security payments to persons with disabilities based on the income of their able-bodied spouses was unconstitutional. The Court stated that the significant cuts in social security payments as a result of means testing violated constitutional protections regarding equality and support for persons with disabilities

| Ireland | The Government Commission on the Status of People with Disabilities estimated that approximately 10 percent of the population have a disability. Under the 1998 Employment Equality Act, it is unlawful to discriminate against anyone on the basis of disability in relation to employment. Nongovernmental organizations (NGOs) claim that there is societal discrimination against persons with disabilities.

The 1991 Building Regulations Act established minimum criteria to ensure access for persons with disabilities to all public and private buildings constructed or significantly altered after 1992; however, enforcement is uneven.

A National Disability Authority, with an annual budget of $2.6 million (1.75 million Irish Punt) has responsibility for setting disability standards, monitoring the implementation of these standards, and research and the formulation of disability policy. The authority's strategic plan, which was issued during the year, has three priorities: The development of policies to promote the equal status of persons with disabilities, influencing societal attitudes, and ensuring services for the disabled.

Specific Legislation:
(a) Disability Discrimination Regulations Act, No. 13, 1996, <http://www.dredf.org/symposium/uk3.html> (last visited on August 20, 2003)

(b) Employment Equality Act, No. 21, 1998, Ir. Acts (1-27), 1998, <http://www.dredf.org/symposium/EmployAct.pdf> (last visited on August 20, 2003)

(c) National Disability Authority Act, No. 14, 1999, Ir. Acts (1-27), 1999, <http://www.dredf.org/symposium/NationAct.pdf> (last visited on August 20, 2003)

(d) Equal Status Act, No. 8, 2000, <http://www.dredf.org/symposium/EqualAct.pdf> (last visited on August 20, 2003)

(e) Comhairle Act, No. 1, 2000, <http://www.bailii.org/ie/legis/num_act/2000/2000-1.html> (last visited on August 20, 2003)

(g) Pending legislation: Education for Persons with Disabilities Bill, 2003, <http://www.education.ie/servlet/blobservlet/bill_disabilities_2003.pdf> (last visited on August 20, 2003) |

| Italy | The law prohibits discrimination on the basis of race, sex (except with regard to hazardous work), religion, ethnic background, or political opinion, and provides some protection against discrimination based on disability, language, or social status; however, some societal discrimination against women, persons with disabilities, and Roma persisted.

A January 2000 law replaced previous legislation that prohibited discrimination against persons with disabilities in employment, education, or the provision of state services. The 2000 law requires companies having 15 or more employees to hire one or more disabled workers: Those with 15 to 35 employees must hire 1 disabled worker, those with 35 to 50 must hire 2, and in larger companies 7 percent of the work force must consist of persons with disabilities. Companies hiring persons with disabilities are granted certain benefits, including lower social security contributions, while the Government pays the cost of worker training. The 2000 law also provides for more severe sanctions against violators.

The law mandates access to buildings for persons with disabilities, and the Government generally enforces these provisions in practice; however, persons with disabilities occasionally encounter situations, particularly in public transport, in which mechanical barriers leave them at a disadvantage.

Specific Legislation:
(a) Italy Const. of 1947, art. 38 (amended 2003), <http://www.oefre.unibe.ch/law/icl/it00000_.html> (last visited on August 13, 2003)
(b) Law No. 162/98 of 21 May 1998, The Support Measures in Favour of People Having Serious Handicaps.
(c) Law No. 68/99 of 12 March 1999, The Right to Work for Handicapped People. |

Kazakhstan	Citizens with disabilities are entitled by law to assistance from the Government and there is no legal discrimination against persons with disabilities; however, in practice employers do not give them equal consideration. Assisting persons with disabilities is a low priority for the Government. There are laws mandating the provision of accessibility to public buildings and commercial establishments for persons with disabilities; however, the Government does not enforce these laws. Mentally ill and mentally retarded citizens can be committed to institutions run by the State; these institutions are poorly run and inadequately funded. The NGO, Kazakhstan International Bureau for Human Rights, observed that the Government provides almost no care for the mentally ill and mentally retarded due to a lack of funds. *Specific Legislation:* (a) Kaz. Const. of 1995, art. 28, <http://www.ecostan.org/laws/kaz/kazakhconst.html> (last visited on August 18, 2003) (b) Regulations of 2001 on the Program for the Rehabilitation of the Disabled for the years 2002-2005.
Kyrgyz Republic	The laws provide for convenient access to public transportation and parking for persons with disabilities, for subsidies to mass media sources that make their services available to the hearing or visually impaired, and for free plots of land for the construction of a home. In practice few special provisions were in place to allow persons with disabilities access to transportation, public buildings, and mass media. In addition persons with disabilities often had difficulty finding employment because of negative societal attitudes and high unemployment among the general population. The lack of resources made it difficult for persons with disabilities to receive adequate education. Social facilities for persons with mental disabilities were strained severely, because budgets have fallen and workloads remained heavy. In one program facilitated by foreign volunteers, local high school students began to visit special institutions such as those for persons with mental disabilities. *Specific Legislation:* Kyrg. Const. of 1993, art. 27 (amended 1996), <http://www.kyrgyzstan.org/Law/constitution.htm> (last visited on August 18, 2003)

Latvia	According to the Constitution, all citizens are equal under the law. Amendments to the Constitution passed by Parliament in 1998 provide for the protection from discrimination due to race, sex, religion, language, or disability; however, discrimination against women in the workplace is a problem. The Constitution provides for the protection of persons with disabilities against discrimination; the law provides for their right of access to public facilities. Provisions in the Labor Law and other laws aim to protect persons with disabilities from bias in the workplace and from job discrimination. There is no governmental or societal bias against persons with disabilities. In 1998 the Cabinet adopted a framework document entitled "Equal Opportunity for Everyone," which was designed to coordinate the efforts of all branches of Government in assisting persons with disabilities; however, lack of funding has limited its effectiveness. The Government supports special schools for persons with disabilities. The law requires buildings to be accessible to wheelchairs; however, the Government does not enforce the law uniformly and most buildings are not wheelchair accessible. *Specific Legislation:* (a) Lat. Const. of 1922, art. 109 & 110 (amended 1998), <http://www.oefre.unibe.ch/law/icl/lg00000_.html> (last visited on August 18, 2003) (b) Labor Law 2002, <http://www.ttc.lv/New/lv/tulkojumi/E0223.doc> (last visited on August 21, 2003)
Liechtenstein	Although the law does not prohibit expressly discrimination against persons with disabilities, complaints of such discrimination may be pursued in the courts. In December 2000, Parliament amended the law to provide for compensatory payments by the Government to companies that employ persons with disabilities. The new law increases opportunities for their integration into the workforce and promotes their right to be self-dependent. Persons with disabilities are not subject to discrimination in the provision of state services; nor is there societal discrimination against them. The Government requires that buildings and government services be made accessible, and new public buildings generally meet these provisions; however, some older buildings do not yet fulfill these requirements. *Specific Legislation:* Liech. Const. of 1921, art. 26, (In German) <http://www.gesetze.li/r2000/html/get_lgbl_from_lr.xsql?LGBl=1921015> (last visited on August 26, 2003)

Lithuania	The Constitution prohibits discrimination based on race, sex, religion, disability, or ethnic background; however, discrimination against women in employment and other areas persisted.
	The Law on Integrating Disabled People provides for a broad category of rights and public benefits for persons with disabilities. The Law on Support for the Unemployed provides additional job security for such persons, while the Law on Special Upbringing gives children with disabilities access to regular schools and universities. However, the implementation of this law for the unemployed was restricted due to a lack of money.
	During 2000 there were 205,890 adults and 13,857 children with disabilities. Many of them live in poverty because the state pension for a person with disabilities is lower than the minimum wage. Every local government runs home help services for persons with disabilities, and the central Government finances a network of facilities for them, including daycare centers, state children care houses, and residential care homes for mentally ill adults. The Disabled Persons' Affairs Council, composed of members of disabled persons' organizations and the Government, grants government money to NGOs for various employment, education, rehabilitation, and other programs ($5 million during the year).
	Legal provisions for access to buildings for the disabled are in place but are not enforced widely; the vast majority of public buildings remain inaccessible.
	Specific Legislation: (a) Lith. Const of 1992, art. 52, <http://www.oefre.unibe.ch/law/icl/lh00000_.html> (last visited on August 18, 2003) (b) Law on the Social Integration of the Disabled No. I-2044, 1991, <http://natlex.ilo.org/txt/E91LTU04.htm> (last visited on August 21, 2003) (c) Law on Support for the Unemployed No. I-864, 1990 amended by Act No. VIII-608, 1998. (d) Law on Special Upbringing (e) Vocational Education and Training Act No. VIII-450, 1997, § 4, <http://natlex.ilo.org/txt/E97LTU01.htm> (last visited on August 21, 2003)

Luxembourg	The law prohibits discrimination against persons with disabilities in employment, education, and the provision of other state services. The Government helps persons with disabilities obtain employment and professional education. Businesses and enterprises with at least 25 employees by law must fill a quota for hiring workers with disabilities and must pay them prevailing wages. The quotas are fixed according to the total number of employees; employers who do not fulfill them are subject to sizable monthly fines. The Government provides subsidies and tax breaks for employers who hire persons with disabilities. There have been no known complaints of noncompliance with the disability laws. However, despite strong legal protections, the Government acknowledged that laws establishing quotas for businesses that employ over 25 persons are not applied or enforced consistently, and there is a particular problem in the case of persons with mental disabilities. The law does not directly mandate accessibility for persons with disabilities, but the Government pays subsidies to builders to construct "disabled-friendly" structures. Despite government incentives, only a small proportion of buildings and public transportation vehicles are modified to accommodate persons with disabilities *Specific Legislation*: (a) Penal Code of July 29, 1997, §§ 444 & 453-57. (b) Labor Law on Handicapped, 1991, <http://www.dredf.org/symposium/lux1.html> (last visited on August 26, 2003)
Macedonia, The Former Yugoslav Republic of	The law prohibits discrimination on the basis of disability; however, in practice this provision is not enforced. Social programs to meet the needs of persons with disabilities exist to the extent that government resources allow. No laws or regulations mandate accessibility to buildings for disabled persons. There is societal discrimination against persons with disabilities.

Malta	The law provides for rights for persons with disabilities. The 2000 Persons with Disabilities Act built on provisions in the public employment and accessibility laws and requires the private sector to apply equal employment guarantees already in place in the public sector. For example, private development project plans must include access for persons with disabilities. Efforts continued during the year to provide children with disabilities with access to mainstream schools as opposed to segregated schools. The Employment Training Corporation has responsibility for registering unemployed persons with disabilities to insure compliance with the law, which requires that every company employing more than 20 persons hire at least 2 percent of its workforce from the Register for Unemployed Disabled Persons. *Specific Legislation*: (a) Malta Const of 1964, art. 17 (amended 1974), <http://www.oefre.unibe.ch/law/icl/mt00000_.html> (last visited on August 18, 2003) (b) Equal Opportunities (Persons with Disabilities) Act I of 2000, <http://natlex.ilo.org/txt/E00MLT01.htm> (last visited on August 21, 2003)
Moldova	The Constitution states that persons are equal before the law regardless of race, sex, disability, religion, or social origin. The law prohibits discrimination against persons with disabilities; however, there are no laws providing for access to buildings, and there are few government resources devoted to training persons with disabilities. The Government provides tax advantages to charitable groups that assist persons with disabilities. *Specific Legislation:* Mold. Const. of 1994, art. 47, 50 & 51, <http://oncampus.richmond.edu/~jjones/confinder/moldova3.htm> (last visited on August 18, 2003)
Monaco	There is no governmental or societal discrimination against persons with disabilities. The Government mandated that public buildings provide access for persons with disabilities, and this goal largely has been accomplished.
Netherlands, The	According to the Dutch Council for Chronic Patients and the Handicapped, persons with disabilities suffer from discrimination in public access. For example, public buildings and public transport often are not easily accessible. *Specific Legislation:* Disabled Worker Reintegration Act (Wet REA) (Stb. 290).

Norway	The Constitution prohibits discrimination based on race, sex, religion, disability, language, or social status, and the Government generally enforced this prohibition in practice. The law mandates access to public buildings for persons with disabilities, and the Government generally enforces these provisions in practice. *Specific Legislation:* (a) Nor. Const. of 1814, (amended 1995), <http://www.oefre.unibe.ch/law/icl/no00000_.html> (last visited on August 18, 2003) (b) Worker Protection and Working Environment Act, 1977.
Poland	There were approximately 5.5 million persons with disabilities in the country by year's end, and the number is expected to reach 6 million by the year 2010. In 2000 the Central Bureau of Statistics (GUS) reported that 17 percent of persons with disabilities able to work are unemployed, roughly equivalent to the national unemployment rate. Advocacy groups have claimed that the percentage is much higher. The law allows individuals from certain disability groups to take up gainful employment without the risk of losing their disability benefits. Statistics show that 48.7 percent of the persons with disabilities have no more than an elementary school education, compared with 33.7 percent of those without disabilities, and that only 4.2 percent have a university education, compared with 8.2 percent of persons without disabilities. The law creates a state fund for the rehabilitation of persons with disabilities that derives its assets from a tax on employers of over 50 persons, unless 6 percent of the employer's work force are persons with disabilities. While the fund has adequate resources--in 2000 it had more than $400 million (1.8 billion PLN) at its disposal--its management has encountered difficulties, including frequent changes in leadership. According to press reports, the fund had 4,000 grant applications pending at year's end. In addition, by law the fund cannot be used to assist children with disabilities under 16 years of age. The law mandates access to buildings for persons with disabilities; however, public buildings and transportation generally are not accessible to persons with disabilities. Implementation falls short of rights set forth in the legislation since the law provides only that buildings "should be accessible." *Specific Legislation:* (a) Pol. Const. of 1997, art. 69, <http://www.oefre.unibe.ch/law/icl/no00000_.html> (last visited on August 18, 2003) (b) Vocational and Social Rehabilitation and Employment of Disabled Persons Act of 1997, amended by Act No. 1019 of 1998.

Portugal	The law mandates access to public buildings for such persons, and the Government enforces these provisions in practice; however, no such legislation covers private businesses or other facilities. *Specific Legislation:* (a) Port. Const. of 1976, art. 58, 59, 63 & 71 (amended 1997), ttp://www.oefre.unibe.ch/law/icl/po00000_.html> (last visited on August 18, 2003) (b) Decree-Law No. 247/89. (c) Decree-Law No. 170/80. (d) Decree-Law No. 8/98. (e) National Initiative for Citizens with Special Needs in the Information Society, 1999.
Romania	Difficult economic conditions and serious budgetary constraints contributed to very difficult living conditions for those with physical or mental disabilities. Outside of large institutions, social services for persons with disabilities are almost nonexistent. Many persons with disabilities cannot make use of government-provided transportation discounts because public transport does not have facilitated access. The law does not mandate accessibility for persons with disabilities to buildings and public transportation. According to official statistics, there were 3,500 disabled children living in state institutions; conditions in these institutions ranged from adequate to harsh. *Specific Legislation:* (a) Rom. Const of 1991, art. 45 & 46, ttp://www.oefre.unibe.ch/law/icl/ro00000_.html> (last visited on August 18, 2003) (b) Labor Law Code 53/2003.

Russia	The Constitution does not address directly the issue of discrimination against persons with disabilities. Although laws exist that prohibit discrimination, the Government has not enforced these laws. The meager resources that the Government can devote to assisting persons with disabilities are provided to veterans of World War II and other conflicts. The law requires that firms with more than 30 employees either reserve 3 percent of their positions for persons with disabilities or contribute to a government fund to create job opportunities for them. The law also removed language defining an "invalid" as a person unable to work; however, the Government has not implemented this law. Some persons with disabilities find work within factories run by the All-Russian Society for the Disabled; however, the majority are unable to find employment, frequently are discouraged from working, and are forced to subsist on social benefits. Special institutions exist for children with various disabilities but do not serve their needs adequately due to a lack of finances. Being a child with disabilities still is a serious social stigma in the country, an attitude that profoundly influences how institutionalized children are treated. Many children with physical or mental disabilities are considered uneducable, even those with only minor birth defects. Parents wishing to enroll a child in an ordinary secondary school in Moscow must produce a medical certificate affirming that the child is in perfect health. Families with children with disabilities received extremely low state subsidies that have not changed to reflect inflation since the Soviet era. According to a 1998 Human Rights Watch report, many children with disabilities in institutions are confined to beds around the clock or to rooms that are lit, heated, and furnished inadequately. The children are given only minimal care by low-paid unskilled workers with no training in the care of the disabled. In November the President issued a decree designating several programs for children with disabilities. Reportedly the designation is an honorary one and does not affect those programs' budgets. The Government does not mandate special access to buildings for persons with disabilities, and access to buildings was a problem. *Specific Legislation:* Russ. Const. of 1993, art. 7, <http://www.oefre.unibe.ch/law/icl/rs00000_.html> (last visited on August 13, 2003)
San Marino	A 1992 law established guidelines for easier access to public buildings, but it never has been implemented fully.

Slovak Republic	The Constitution and implementing legislation provide for health protection and special working conditions for persons with mental and physical disabilities, including special protection in employment relations and special assistance in training. A 1994 decree provides incentives to employers to create a "sheltered" workplace (i.e., a certain percentage of jobs set aside for persons with disabilities). The law also prohibits discrimination against persons with physical disabilities individuals in employment, education, and the provision of other state services; however, experts have reported that discrimination in the accessibility of premises and access to education (particularly higher education) is a problem, and in 1998 the quotas for mandatory hiring of persons with disabilities were lowered in accordance with employers' wishes. Although not required specifically by law, a government decree mandates accessibility for new public building construction. The decree provides for sanctions but lacks a mechanism to enforce them. *Specific Legislation:* (a) Slovk. Const. of 1992, art. 39 (amended 2001), <http://www.oefre.unibe.ch/law/icl/lo00000_.html> (last visited on August 18, 2003) (b) Labor Relations Act No. 95/2000 Coll.
Slovenia	The Constitution provides for equality before the law regardless of race, sex, religion, disability, language, or social status, and the Government generally observed this provision in practice. The law prohibits discrimination against persons with disabilities and in practice the Government does not discriminate against disabled persons in employment, education, or in the provision of other state services. There is some societal discrimination. The law mandates access to buildings for the disabled, and the Government generally enforces these provisions in practice. Modifications of public and private structures to ease access by the disabled continued, although at a slow pace. *Specific Legislation:* Slovn. Const. of 1991, art. 50 & 52 (amended 2000), <http://www.oefre.unibe.ch/law/icl/si00000_.html> (last visited on August 18, 2003)

| Spain | The Constitution provides for equal rights for all citizens, and discrimination on the basis of sex, race, ethnicity, nationality, disability, ideology, or religious beliefs is illegal.

The Constitution calls for the State to provide for the adequate treatment and care of persons with disabilities, ensuring that they are not deprived of the basic rights that apply to all citizens. The law aims to ensure fair access to public employment, prevent discrimination, and facilitate access to public facilities and transportation. The national law serves as a guide for regional laws.

The law continued to permit parents or legal representatives of a mentally disabled person to petition a judge to obtain permission for the sterilization of that person. In 1994 the Constitutional Court held that sterilization of the mentally infirm does not constitute a violation of the Constitution. In practice many courts in the past have authorized such surgery.

The Government subsidizes companies that employ persons with mental or physical disabilities. The Government mandates that all businesses that employ more than 50 persons either hire such persons for at least 2 percent of their workforce or subcontract a portion of their work to special centers that employ them.

Specific Legislation:
(a) Spain Const. of 1978, art. 49 (amended 1992), <http://www.oefre.unibe.ch/law/icl/sp00000_.html> (last visited on August 13, 2003)
(b) Workers' Charter Act No. 8, 1980.
(c) Disabled Persons Social Integration Act No. 13, 1982.
(d) Law on Infringements and Penalties of a Social Nature, 1988.
(e) Royal Decrees Law 55/1999. |
| --- | --- |

| Sweden | The law prohibits discrimination against persons with disabilities in the workplace, but there are no other specific laws that prohibit discrimination against persons with disabilities, although considerable efforts are made to ensure that they enjoy equal opportunities. In 2000 the Parliament adopted and implemented a national plan on disability policy that provides for freedom of access and social support as basic rights for citizens with disabilities. There is an Ombudsman for disability issues. The Government provides persons with disabilities with assistance, which may include a personal assistant for persons with severe disabilities, or improvements in the workplace's accessibility to wheelchairs. Government assistance also includes services such as home care or group living. Regulations for new buildings require full accessibility, but the Government has no such requirement for existing public buildings. Many buildings and some public transportation remain inaccessible. Deaf children have the right to education in sign language. The parents of children with disabilities and workers with disabilities under the age of 65 receive financial assistance every 7 years to buy a car adapted to the person's disability.

In 2000 the Government began paying damages to thousands of persons that it forcibly sterilized between 1934 and 1976, the majority of whom were disabled either mentally or physically (see Section 1.f.).

Specific Legislation:
(a) Act Concerning Support & Service for Persons with Certain Functional Impairments, SFS No: 1993- 387.

(b) Law on a Ban Against Discrimination Disabled Persons in Working Life, SFS No: 1999-132, <http://natlex.ilo.org/txt/E99SWE02.htm> (last visited on August 20, 2003)

(c) Employment Protection Act, SFS No: 1982-80 amended by Act, SFS No: 2002-195.

(d) Work Environment Act, SFS No: 1977-1160 amended by Act, SFS No: 2002-585.

(e) Social Insurance Act, SFS No: 1999-799 amended by Act, SFS No: 2001-497. |
|---|---|

Switzerland	The law prohibits discrimination directed at persons with disabilities in employment, education, and the provision of other state services. The total number of persons with disabilities is estimated to be 700,000 (10 percent of the population). Most cantons already have implemented some provisions for persons with disabilities, but there is no countrywide standard. Advocates for persons with disabilities have called for new measures to ensure greater protection for their rights. Article 8.4 of the new Constitution (in effect as of January 1, 2000) provides for equal opportunities for persons with disabilities. An initiative called "Equal Rights for People with Disabilities" was launched in 1999 that would change the law and grant all persons with disabilities access to all public facilities and services, to the extent that the costs were within government means. Claiming that the financial consequences of the proposed change in law would have a negative impact on the economy, the Federal Council submitted an alternative draft law to Parliament in October. Parliament extended the period for debate of the bill until October 2002. Neither the Government nor the Constitution mandates that buildings or transportation facilities be made accessible, and advocates for persons with disabilities have called for easier access to buildings and public transportation. *Specific Legislation*: Switz. Const. of 1999, art. 8, <http://www.oefre.unibe.ch/law/icl/sz00000_.html> (last visited on August 13, 2003)
Tajikistan	The law stipulates the right of persons with disabilities to employment and adequate medical care; however, in practice the Government does not require employers to provide physical access for persons with disabilities. Persons with disabilities suffer from high unemployment and widespread discrimination as a result of financial constraints and the absence of basic technology to assist. There is no law mandating accessibility for persons with disabilities. There are facilities for persons with disabilities; however, funding is limited and the facilities are in poor condition. Several international NGOs provided limited assistance to persons with disabilities. *Specific Legislation:* Taj. Constitution of 1994, art. 39 (amended 2003), <http://www.geocities.com/Paris/9305/constitution.index.html> (last visited on August 18, 2003)

Turkey	According to a 2000 UNICEF report on women and children in the country, welfare institutions "provide limited financial, employment and educational support to the handicapped." According to the report, the number of persons with disabilities is unknown. The Ministry of Education reports that there are 1.1 million children with disabilities in the country. Although there are many Government institutions for persons with disabilities, most attention to persons with disabilities remained at the individual and family level. The Government established an "Administration of Disabilities" office under the Prime Ministry in 1997, with the mandate of developing cooperation and coordination among national and international institutions, and to conduct research into issues such as delivery of services. Companies who employ more than 50 employees are required to hire persons with disabilities as 2 percent of their employee pool, although there is no penalty for failure to comply. The law does not mandate accessibility to buildings and public transportation for the disabled.
	Specific Legislation: (a) Turk. Const. of 1982, art. 50 & 61 (amended 2001), <http://www.byegm.gov.tr/constitution.htm> (last visited on August 18, 2003) (b) Decree No. 8880 of 26 November 1996 amending the decree concerning the employment of the disabled. (c) Ministry of Labour and Social Security Regulation concerning the employment of disabled persons in the public sector. No.24064, 2000.
Turkmenistan	There is some discrimination against persons with disabilities in employment, education, and the provisions of state services. The Government does little for persons with disabilities.
	According to existing legislation, facilities to allow access by the disabled must be included in new construction projects; however, compliance with the legislation is inconsistent and most older buildings are not so equipped.
	Specific Legislation: Turkm. Constitution of 1992, art. 34, <http://www.ecostan.org/laws/turkm/turkmenistancon.html> (last visited on August 18, 2003)

| Ukraine | The law prohibits discrimination against persons with disabilities; however, the Government did little to support programs targeted at increasing opportunities for persons with disabilities. Legally mandated levels of employment of persons with disabilities at state enterprises were not observed. There were only five special vocational schools for persons with disabilities. As a result, according to one NGO, approximately 7,000 children with disabilities received an incomplete secondary education. Advocacy groups for persons with disabilities maintain that there is societal discrimination against persons with disabilities.

The law mandates access to buildings and other public facilities for the disabled; however, the law is enforced poorly.

Specific Legislation:
(a) Ukr. Const. of 1996, art. 46, <http://www.rada.kiev.ua/const/conengl.htm> (last visited on August 18, 2003)
(b) Labor Code, 1971, art. 36. |

United Kingdom	The Disability Discrimination Act (DDA) prohibits discrimination against persons with disabilities in the provision of access to public facilities by employers of more than 15 workers, service providers (apart from those providing education or running transport vehicles), and anyone selling or renting property. In addition all businesses are required to accommodate customers with disabilities. Adaptations must be "reasonable," bearing in mind the circumstances and size of the business. The Education Act requires local education authorities to make provision for the special educational needs of children with disabilities. However, one in seven persons in Britain has a disability, according to the Disability Rights Commission (DRC), which reported that approximately 8.5 million persons with disabilities faced discrimination in work, housing, health, and social care. In March the Government responded to a disability rights task force report by announcing new measures to cover nearly 7 million jobs previously excluded from the DDA, such as police, firefighters, and prison officers. In May the Government passed the Special Educational Needs and Disability Act, which enhances civil rights for persons with disabilities in education. Government regulations require that all new buildings meet the access requirements of all persons with impaired mobility and that all taxis be wheelchair accessible; similar regulations are in force for sensory-impaired persons. Access to many buildings, especially older buildings, including transportation centers, remains inadequate. New measures introduced in March require all businesses to make "reasonable" modifications for persons with disabilities by 2004. *Specific Legislation:* (a) Disability Discrimination Act (DDA), 1995, c. 50, <http://www.dredf.org/symposium/uk1.html> (last visited on August 21, 2003) (b) Disability Rights Commission (DRC) Act, 1999, c. 17, <http://www.dredf.org/symposium/uk2.html> (last visited on August 21, 2003)
Uzbekistan	The law provides for support for persons with disabilities and is aimed at ensuring that these persons have the same rights as other citizens; however, little effort is made to bring persons with disabilities into the mainstream. There is some societal discrimination against persons with disabilities. Children with disabilities generally are segregated into separate schools. The State cares for the mentally disabled in special homes. The Government has not mandated access to public places for the disabled; however, there is some wheelchair access throughout the country.

Federal Republic of Yugoslavia	Although the law prohibits discrimination against persons with disabilities in employment, education, or in the provision of state services, inadequate facilities and the level of unemployment posed obstacles to the employment of the disabled. The law mandates access to new official buildings; however, it was not enforced in practice. *Specific Legislation:* F.R.Y. Const of 1992, art. 56 & 59, <http://www.oefre.unibe.ch/law/icl/sr00000_.html> (last visited on August 18, 2003)

	WESTERN HEMISPHERE
Antigua and Barbuda	No specific laws mandate accessibility for persons with disabilities, but constitutional provisions prohibit discrimination against the physically disabled in employment and education. There is no evidence of widespread discrimination against persons with disabilities, although the Government does not enforce the constitutional antidiscrimination provisions. *Specific Legislation:* Ant. & Barb. Const. of 1981, art. 14, <http://www.georgetown.edu/pdba/Constitutions/Antigua/ab81.html> (last visited on August 18, 2003)
Argentina	The Constitution and law provide for equal treatment for all citizens, and the law provides for prison terms of up to 3 years for discrimination based on race, religion, nationality, ideology, political opinion, sex, economic position, social class, or physical characteristics. The law prohibits discrimination against persons with disabilities in employment, education, and the provision of other state services, and mandates access to buildings for persons with disabilities. There has been some progress in these areas. The National Advisory Commission on the Integration of People with Disabilities--a governmental office--and numerous NGOs actively defend the rights of persons with disabilities and help them to find employment. A 1994 law intended to eliminate barriers for persons with disabilities mandates standards regarding access to public buildings, parks, plazas, stairs, and pedestrian areas. Street curbs, commuter train stations, and some buildings in Buenos Aires have been modified to accommodate wheelchairs, but many public buildings and lavatories are still inaccessible to persons with disabilities. *Specific Legislation:* (a) Arg. Const. of 1853, § 75 (amended 1994), <http://www.oefre.unibe.ch/law/icl/ar00000_.html> (last visited on August 8, 2003) (b) 1994 Barrier-Free Law. (c) Law No. 22431, Mar. 16, 1981, as amended., A System of Integration and Protection of Disabled People.

Bahamas	Other than constitutional provisions of equality for all, there are no laws that specifically prohibit discrimination against persons with disabilities in employment, education, or the provision of other state services. However, the Ministry of Social Transformation established the Disabilities Unit to address the concerns of persons with disabilities and created an advisory committee on disabilities. The Labor Department, a unit within the Ministry that finds jobs for the disabled, has long advocated the introduction of legislation prohibiting discrimination. In September the Government issued a White Paper on Persons with Disabilities outlining policies to facilitate the full integration and participation in society of persons with disabilities.

While there is no legislation mandating provision of accessibility to public thoroughfares or public or private buildings, the Town and Country Planning Department set provisions for all public buildings to include accessibility to persons with disabilities. As a result, the majority of new buildings had ramps, reserved parking, and special sanitary facilities for such persons. |
| **Barbados** | The law does not prohibit discrimination against the physically disabled in employment, education, or the provision of other state services. However, the Ministry of Labor established the Disabilities Unit to address the concerns of persons with disabilities and created an advisory committee on disabilities. The Labor Department, a unit within the Ministry that finds jobs for the disabled, has long advocated the introduction of legislation prohibiting discrimination. In 2000 the Government, labor leaders, and the private sector jointly announced an agreement to promote a code of practice for the employment of persons with disabilities, as part of these groups' continuing social partnership. They also agreed to establish targets and time frames for the employment of persons with disabilities in the private and public sectors. At year's end, the unit met its target of finding employment for 25 persons; however, only 8 had been hired on a full-time basis. While there is no legislation mandating provision of accessibility to public thoroughfares or public or private buildings, the Town and Country Planning Department sets provisions for all public buildings to include accessibility to persons with disabilities. As a result, the majority of new buildings have ramps, reserved parking, and special sanitary facilities for such persons. |
| **Belize** | The law does not provide specifically for accessibility for persons with disabilities or prohibit job discrimination against them. The Government's Disability Services Unit, as well as a number of NGOs, such as the Belize Association of and for Persons with Disabilities and the Belize Center for the Visually Impaired, provide assistance to such persons. Children with disabilities have access to government special education facilities, although the requirements to enter such programs are strict. |

Bolivia	The Law on Disabilities requires wheelchair access to all public and private buildings, duty free import of orthopedic devices, a 50 percent reduction in public transportation fares, and expanded teaching of sign language and Braille. A National Committee for Incapacitated Persons oversees the law's enforcement, conducts studies, and channels and supervises programs and donations for the persons with disabilities; however, there is little information on its effectiveness. The electoral law makes arrangements for blind voters. However, in general there are no special services or infrastructure to accommodate persons with disabilities. A lack of adequate resources impedes full implementation of the law. Societal discrimination keeps many persons with disabilities at home from an early age, limiting their integration into society. *Specific Legislation*: Law No. 1678, Persons with Disability, 1995, <http://www.dredf.org/symposium/bolivia.html> (last visited on August 26, 2003)
Brazil	The Constitution contains several provisions for persons with disabilities, stipulating a minimum wage, educational opportunities, and access to public buildings and public transportation. However, groups that work with persons with disabilities report that state governments failed to meet the legally mandated targets for educational opportunities and work placement. A 1991 law stipulates that all businesses with over 200 employees must reserve 2 percent of their vacancies for persons with disabilities. In 1999 labor officials in the Federal District launched an information campaign to encourage firms to comply with the law and warned that non-complying firms could be fined; the campaign remains ongoing. *Specific Legislation*: (a) Braz. Const. (Federative Republic of Brazil, 1988), art. 70 & 201 (amended 1995), <http://www.oefre.unibe.ch/law/icl/br00000_.html> (last visited on August 8, 2003) (b) Decree No. 3298, 20 Dec. 1999 pursuant to Penal Code Law No. 7853, 24 October 1989, Integration of people with disabilities.

| Canada | The Charter of Rights and Freedoms provides for equal benefits and protection of the law regardless of race, national or ethnic origin, color, religion, sex, age, or mental or physical disability.

There is no legal discrimination against persons with disabilities in employment, education, or in the provision of other state services. Nevertheless, the Government continued to receive numerous complaints regarding societal discrimination against persons with disabilities and has instituted programs to discourage such discrimination. Persons with disabilities are underrepresented in the work force; they make up 2.7 percent of the federally regulated private sector work force, while those capable of working total 6.5 percent of the population. The law mandates access to buildings for persons with disabilities, and for the most part the Government enforces these provisions.

The law provides a variety of protections and rights for the disabled and specifically prohibits discrimination against persons with disabilities in employment, education, or in the provision of public services. Sexual exploitation of persons with disabilities in situations of dependency is a criminal offense. The law requires employers and service providers to accommodate special needs of persons with disabilities, unless it constitutes an undue hardship, and mandates access to buildings for the disabled. The Government has instituted programs to help the persons with disabilities join the work force, but they continued to experience more difficulties in getting and retaining employment than those without disabilities.

Specific Legislation:
(a) Can. Const. (Constitution Act, 1982) , (Canadian Charter of Human Rights and Freedoms), § 15, <http://www.oefre.unibe.ch/law/icl/ca02000_.html> (last visited on August 8, 2003)
(b) Canadian Human Rights Act, R.S.C., ch. H-6, (1985), <http://www.dredf.org/symposium/canada2.html> [August 21, 2003]
(c) Employment Equity Act, S.C, ch. 44, (1995), <http://natlex.ilo.org/txt/E95CAN01.htm> (last visited on August 21, 2003)
(e) Workers' Compensation Act, ch. 10, § 1 (1994-1995). <http://www.canlii.org/ns/sta/csns/20030618/s.n.s.1994-95c.10/whole.html> (last visited on August 12, 2003) |

Chile	A 1994 law promotes the integration of persons with disabilities into society; the Government's National Fund for the Handicapped has a small budget to encourage such integration. The 1992 census found that 288,000 citizens said that they had some form of disability. Persons with disabilities still suffer some forms of legal discrimination; for example, blind persons cannot become teachers or tutors. Although a 1994 law requires that new public buildings provide access for persons with disabilities, the public transportation system does not make provision for wheelchair access, and subway lines in the Santiago metropolitan area provide facilitated access for persons with disabilities only in some areas.
	Specific Legislation: Law No. 19284, 5 of Jan. 1994, Social Integration of People with Disabilities, <http://www.dredf.org/symposium/chile1.html> (last visited on August 26, 2003)
Colombia	The Constitution specifically prohibits discrimination based on race, sex, religion, disability, language, or social status; however, in practice, many of these provisions are not enforced.
	The Constitution enumerates the fundamental social, economic, and cultural rights of the persons with physical disabilities; however, serious practical impediments exist that prevent the full participation of persons with disabilities in society. There is no legislation that specifically mandates access for persons with disabilities. (Most public buildings and public transport are not accessible to persons with disabilities.) According to the Constitutional Court, persons with physical disabilities must have access to, or if they so request, receive assistance at, voting stations. The Court also has ruled that the social security fund for public employees cannot refuse to provide services for the children of its members who have disabilities, regardless of the cost involved.
	Specific Legislation: (a) Colom. Const. of 1991, art. 54 (amended 2001), <http://www.georgetown.edu/pdba/Constitutions/Colombia/col91.html> (last visited on August 26, 2003) (b) Law No. 361 of 1997.

Costa Rica	The 1996 Equal Opportunity for Persons with Disabilities Law prohibits discrimination, provides for health care services, and mandates provision of access to buildings for persons with disabilities. This law is not enforced widely, and many buildings remain inaccessible to persons with disabilities. In July 2000, a government study concluded that only 35 percent of the law's stated goals had been implemented.
	The Ministry of Education operates a Program for Persons with Disabilities, and in November President Rodriguez's wife received an award from Goodwill Industries for her efforts to support it. The program includes a national resource center that provides parents, students, and teachers with advanced counseling, training, and information services.
	Specific Legislation: (a) Law No. 7600, 18 of April 1996, Equal Opportunities for Persons with Disabilities, <http://www.dredf.org/symposium/costaeng.html> (last visited on August 21, 2003) (b) Decree No. 19101-S-MEP-TSS-PLAN, 12 of July 1989.
Cuba	The law prohibits discrimination based on disability, and there have been few complaints of such discrimination.
	There are no laws that mandate accessibility to buildings for persons with disabilities. In practice buildings and transportation rarely are accessible to persons with disabilities.
Dominica	Beyond the general protection of the Constitution, there is no specific legislation to address problems facing persons with disabilities. However, the labor laws permit authorization of employment of a person with disabilities for less than the minimum wage, in order to increase opportunities for employment of such persons (see Section 6.e.). There is no requirement mandating access for those with disabilities.

Dominican Republic	Persons with disabilities encounter discrimination in employment and in the provision of other services. Although the law provides for physical access for persons with disabilities to all new public and private buildings, the authorities have not enforced this law uniformly. The Dominican Rehabilitation Association (ADR) has 17 affiliates throughout the country and provides services for 2,500 persons daily. The Government provides about 30 percent of the ADR's budget. Discrimination against persons with mental illness is common, and there are few resources dedicated to the mentally ill. *Specific Legislation:* General Law on Disabilities, 2000.
Ecuador	There is no official discrimination against persons with disabilities in employment, education, or the provision of other state services. However, there are no laws to ensure persons with disabilities access to public buildings or services, nor are they provided any other special government assistance. In June 2000, the city of Guayaquil began a modest program to give persons with disabilities better access to public buildings. *Specific Legislation:* Law No. 180, 7 of August 1992, Law on Disabilities, <http://www.dredf.org/symposium/ecuador.html> (last visited on August 26, 2003)

El Salvador	The majority of the country's population of persons with disabilities consists of former combatants and civilians wounded during the conflict. Government and international funding provide rehabilitation programs for these persons. Efforts to combat discrimination and increase opportunities for those whose disabilities are unrelated to the war are growing but remain inadequate. A 2000 law mandates that new or renovated public buildings be accessible to the persons with disabilities, and requires businesses to employ 1 person with a disability for every 25 employees, an increase from the preexisting requirement of 1 to 50. Although the Government had not enforced the previous law's employment quota, it brought together dozens of government agencies and NGOs to discuss ways to implement the new law effectively.
	Access by persons with disabilities to basic education was limited due to lack of facilities and appropriate transportation. There was no provision of state services for persons with physical disabilities. Only a few of the Government's community-based health promoters have been trained to treat persons with disabilities, and they rarely provided such service. The Ministry of Health estimated that 10 percent of the population is afflicted by some form of disability. Many disabilities are directly attributable to the civil war.
	Specific Legislation: El Sal. Const. of 1982, art. 37 & 38 (amended 2000), <http://www.georgetown.edu/pdba/Constitutions/ElSal/ElSal83.html> (last visited on August 26, 2003)
Grenada	The law does not protect job seekers with disabilities from discrimination in employment, nor does it mandate provision of accessibility to public buildings or services. The National Council for the Disabled and the National Children's Home assist the Government in placing students with disabilities into community schools. The Council also seeks assistance from architects and builders in the construction of ramps at hotels and public buildings, and ramps have been installed at some hotels and government buildings.

Guatemala	The Constitution provides that the State should protect persons with disabilities; however, persons with physical disabilities suffer discrimination in education and employment practices, and few resources are devoted to combat this problem or to assist persons with disabilities. In 1996 Congress passed the Law on Protection of the Elderly and the Law on Attention to Disabled Persons, which mandates equal access to public facilities, prohibits discrimination based on disability, and provides other legal protections. The law defines a person with disabilities as one whose physical, mental, or emotional deficiencies limit performance of normal activities. It stipulates equal opportunity for persons with disabilities in health, education, work, recreation, sports, and cultural activities. It also provides that all persons with disabilities receive the benefits of labor laws and social security and have the right to work. In addition, the law establishes equal education opportunities, the requirement that buildings meet access codes, and the right to equal pay. Government efforts to implement the legislation have been weak. *Specific Legislation*: (a) Guat. Const. of 1986, art. 102 (amended 1993), (In Spanish) <http://www.georgetown.edu/pdba/Constitutions/Guate/guate93.html> (last visited on August 26, 2003) (b) Decree No. 135-1996, c. 487, § 2, Disability Discrimination Ordinance, <http://www.dredf.org/symposium/guatemala.html> (last visited on August 21, 2003)
Guyana	There is no law mandating provision of access for persons with disabilities, and the lack of appropriate infrastructure to provide access to both public and private facilities makes it very difficult to employ persons with disabilities outside their homes. In 1997 Parliament passed a law establishing a council for persons with disabilities, which functioned throughout the year. There are several special schools and training centers for persons with disabilities, but the facilities lack trained staff and are in disrepair. *Specific Legislation:* Guy. Const. of 1980, art. 24 (amended 1996), <http://www.georgetown.edu/pdba/Constitutions/Guyana/guyana96.html> (last visited on August 18, 2003)
Haiti	The Constitution provides that persons with disabilities shall have the means to ensure their autonomy, education, and independence. However, there is no legislation to implement these constitutional provisions or to mandate provision of access to buildings for persons with disabilities. Although they do not face overt mistreatment, given the severe poverty in which most citizens live, those with disabilities face a particularly harsh existence. Disabled beggars are common on the streets of Port-au-Prince and other towns.

Honduras	There are no formal barriers to participation by an estimated 700,000 persons with disabilities in employment, education, or health care; however, there is no specific statutory or constitutional protection for them. There is no legislation that requires access by persons with disabilities to government buildings or commercial establishments. In 2000 the Government reactivated the National Council for the Treatment of the Disabled Minor to coordinate assistance to youths with disabilities and appropriated about $1.3 million (20 million lempiras) to fund its activities. In September the National University initiated the first classes to train sign language interpreters in Honduran Sign Language.
Jamaica	No laws mandate accessibility for persons with disabilities, and they have encountered discrimination in employment and denial of access to schools. Several government agencies and NGOs provide services and employment to various groups of persons with disabilities. In 1998 the Prime Minister appointed the first blind member of the Senate. In November the Prime Minister appointed this senator to be Minister of State for Labor. The Government trains persons with disabilities for jobs within the information technology sector, and added two buses equipped with hydraulic lifts for wheelchairs during the year. In July 1999, an incident in which police rounded up a number of persons (many of whom reportedly were mentally ill) led to a national debate over the police action (see Section 1.d.). In January it was reported that numerous persons declared unfit to plead remained in prison without trial (see Section 1.d.).

| Mexico | Estimates of the number of persons with disabilities range from 2 to 10 million. In the 2000 census, 1.8 million persons identified themselves as having a disability, although 2.2 million persons chose not to specify whether or not they had a disability. In Mexico City alone, 124 NGOs address problems affecting persons with physical disabilities.

On September 18, 2002, the President unveiled a federal program, the National Public Access Program, designed to provide equal access and rights to persons with disabilities. He also urged state and local governments to follow his lead in developing such measures. The President ordered Cabinet members to evaluate and improve accessibility for more than 4,000 federal buildings, including offices, hospitals, airports, and bus stations.

A total of 27 of the 31 states have laws protecting persons with disabilities. Local law requires access for persons with disabilities to public facilities in Mexico City, but not elsewhere in the country. However, in practice most public buildings and facilities in Mexico City do not comply with the law. The Federal District also mandated access for children with physical disabilities to all public and private schools. The Mexico City Secretary of Education, Health, and Social Development stated previously that 78 percent of these children received some schooling. In August 2000, the President's Office announced that 90,000 children with disabilities were integrated into a regular education system between 1994 and 2000.

In December 2000, the President established the Citizen's Commission Against Discrimination to be headed by former Social Democracy Party presidential candidate Rincon Gallardo. The Commission's objectives include ensuring equal opportunities and access for persons with disabilities and codifying these rights in a legal framework.

Specific Legislation:
(a) Mex. Const. of 1917, art. 123, <http://www.ilstu.edu/class/hist263/docs/1917const.html> (last visited on August 13, 2003)
(b) Official Norm Mexican NOM-173-ssa 1-1998, for The Integral Attention to People with Disabilities. |

Nicaragua	In 1998 the Ministry of Health created a National Council for Rehabilitation to address the needs of the 600,000 citizens with some type of disability, only 3 percent of whom receive medical treatment. Through its clinics and hospitals, the Government provides care to war veterans and other disabled persons, but the quality of care is generally poor. However, with assistance from international NGOs, foreign governments, and the public health care system, the Government has procured thousands of prostheses and other medical equipment for veterans and former resistance members. Despite some efforts, the Government's past role in helping the disabled is minimal and often has been criticized. It has not legislated or otherwise mandated accessibility to buildings for the disabled. In the spring of 2000, the Ministry of the Family announced that it would cut a considerable amount of financial support for the Blue Bird Protection Association that shelters about 100 persons with disabilities, aged from 10 months to 40 years old, who are considered unable to care for themselves. The 1995 Law to Protect Disabled People states that companies are obligated to contract persons with disabilities, that such disabilities cannot affect their salaries, and that disabled persons must be considered equal to other workers. However, representatives of the Danish Association of Disability have noted that this law rarely is put into practice. In the past 2 years, this organization has implemented a program called Prodinic, with the objective of strengthening the country's disabled associations by assisting 20 different groups in Managua, Masaya, Leon, Juigalpa, and Esteli. This group is lobbying for easier access to transportation and travel for the disabled throughout the country. *Specific Legislation*: (a) Law No. 202, 1995, Law for the Prevention, Rehabilitation and Equalization of Opportunities for Persons with Disabilities in Nicaragua, <http://www.dredf.org/symposium/nicar1.html> (last visited on August 26, 2003) (b) Decree No. 50-97, Regulations and Policies for Law No. 202.

Panama	The Ministry of Education is responsible for educating and training minors with disabilities, while the Ministry of Youth, Women, Children, and Family Affairs protects the rights of adults with disabilities. Children with disabilities traditionally have been separated from the general population; however, in February 2000, the Legislative Assembly passed a law that requires schools to integrate children with special needs into the student body, and this law generally is enforced.
	The Department of Labor is responsible for placing workers with disabilities in suitable jobs. Placement remains difficult despite a 1993 executive order granting tax incentives to firms that hire disabled employees. Persons with disabilities also tend to be paid less than employees without disabilities for performing the same job.
	The 1998 municipal building code for Panama City requires that all new construction projects be accessible to persons with disabilities with fines from $100 to $500 for noncompliance. A 1999 national law with similar requirements for new construction projects generally is enforced. Awareness of disability issues has increased, and commercial establishments increasingly provide and enforce handicapped parking spaces. However, basic services such as handicapped-accessible sidewalks and bathrooms are largely unavailable.
	In July the Electoral Tribunal began a voting program to allow persons with physical disabilities or illnesses that prevent them from traveling to polling places to vote from home, with reportedly positive results.
	Specific Legislation: (a) Pan. Const. of 1972, art. 109 (amended 1994). (b) Family Law Code Law No. 3, 1994. (c) Panama City Building Code (1998) (d) Integration Into Schools For Children With Special Needs, 2000.

Paraguay	The Constitution and other laws prohibit discrimination on race, sex, religion, disability, language, or social status.
	The Constitution provides for equal opportunity for persons with disabilities and mandates that the State provide them with health care, education, recreation, and professional training. It further requires that the State formulate a policy for the treatment, rehabilitation, and integration into society of persons with disabilities. However, the Congress never has enacted legislation to establish such programs or provide funding for them. Many persons with disabilities face significant discrimination in employment; others are unable to seek employment because of a lack of accessible public transportation. The law does not mandate accessibility for the persons with disabilities, and the vast majority of the country's buildings, both public and private, are inaccessible.
	Conditions at the Neuropsychiatric Hospital are substandard, and some patients reportedly are kept unclothed in cells and are not treated for their mental illnesses. The physical facilities of the hospital lack running water, electricity, or even roofs, and the hospital is severely understaffed. Children are housed with adults in the facility and have been subject to sexual assaults from older patients. In April a 14-year-old inmate died amid allegations of neglect and mistreatment (see Section 1.a.). No information is available on the Government's response to problems at this facility.
	Specific Legislation: (a) Para. Const. (Political Constitution of 1992), art. 6 & 58, <http://www.oefre.unibe.ch/law/icl/pa00000_.html> (last visited on August 18, 2003) (b) Social Security (Law 431/73). (c) Labour Code Law No. 213, 1993 amended and extended by Law No. 496, 1995.

Peru	The Constitution provides that persons with severe disabilities have "the right to have their dignity respected and to be provided by law with protection, care, rehabilitation, and security." Legislation that established the National Council for the Integration of People with Disabilities specifies rights, allowances, programs, and services. The law prohibits discrimination, mandates that public spaces be barrier-free and that buildings be architecturally accessible, and provides for the appointment of a disability rights specialist in the Human Rights Ombudsman's office. However, in practice the Government devotes little attention and resources to persons with disabilities, and they remain economically and socially marginalized.

The Government does not allocate sufficient funds to make genuine integration of persons with disabilities into the economy possible.

The 1993 census counted 288,526 persons with disabilities, or 1.3 percent of the population; however, during the year, the Ministry of Health and the Pan American Health Organization estimated that the actual number of persons with disabilities could be as high as 3 million, or 13.8 percent of the population.

Although construction regulations mandate barrier-free access by persons with physical disabilities to public service buildings, no effort has been made to implement this provision. There are no accommodations, such as interpreters for the deaf in government service offices and Braille or recorded versions of the Constitution, which would facilitate the participation of persons with disabilities in the basic processes of democracy and citizenship. However, the Human Rights Ombudsman reported that a program to facilitate voter education and access for persons with disabilities during the elections was successful.

According to officials of the Institute for Social Security, less than 1 percent of persons with severe disabilities actually work. Among those who do, many have been channeled into occupations traditionally assumed to be "suitable" for persons with disabilities, such as telephone switchboard operation and massage, in the case of the blind. Some private companies have initiated programs to hire and train persons with disabilities, and a private foundation provides small loans to persons with disabilities to start up businesses. Nevertheless, such persons faced discrimination by potential employers. For example, the statute governing the policies and procedures of the judicial branch specifically prohibits the blind from serving as judges or prosecutors, a provision that the National Judiciary Council has interpreted to apply to all persons with disabilities.

Specific Legislation:
(a) Peru Const. of 1993, art. 7, <http://www.georgetown.edu/pdba/Constitutions/Peru/per93.html> (last visited on August 26, 2003)
(b) Law No. 27050, 18 of Dec. 1998. |

Saint Kitts and Nevis	Although there is no legislation to protect persons with disabilities or to mandate accessibility for them, the Constitution and the Government prohibit discrimination in employment, education, and other state services.
Saint Lucia	No specific legislation protects the rights of persons with disabilities, nor mandates provision of access to buildings or government services for them. There is no rehabilitation facility for persons with physical disabilities, although the Health Ministry operates a community-based rehabilitation program in residents' homes. There are schools for the deaf and for the blind up to the secondary level. There is also a school for persons with mental disabilities.
Saint Vincent and the Grenadines	There is no specific legislation addressing persons with disabilities, and the circumstances for such persons are generally difficult. Most persons with severe disabilities rarely leave their homes because of the poor road system and lack of affordable wheelchairs. The Government partially supports a school for persons with disabilities which has two branches. A separate, small rehabilitation center treats about five persons daily.
Suriname	There are no laws concerning persons with disabilities and no provisions for making private or public buildings accessible to them. There are also no laws mandating that they be given equal consideration when seeking jobs or housing. However, there are some training programs for the blind and others with disabilities. In practice persons with disabilities suffer from discrimination when applying for jobs and services.
Trinidad and Tobago	There is no legislation that specifically enumerates or protects the rights of persons with disabilities or mandates the provision of access to buildings or services. The lack of access to transportation, buildings, and sidewalks is a major obstacle for persons with disabilities. The Government provides some public assistance and partial funding to a variety of NGOs, which in turn provide direct services to disabled members or clients.

Uruguay	The Constitution and the law prohibit discrimination based on race, sex, religion, or disability. Despite these provisions, discrimination against some groups exists. A national disabilities commission oversees implementation of a law on the rights of persons with disabilities. Although the law mandates accessibility for persons with disabilities only to new buildings or public services, the Government provides access to a number of existing buildings. The law reserves 4 percent of public sector jobs for persons with disabilities. There is no governmental discrimination against disabled persons in employment, education, or in the provision of other state services. The country has a generally excellent mental health system and an interest in the rights of persons with mental disabilities. *Specific Legislation:* Uru. Const. of 1967, art. 115 (amended 1996), (In Spanish) <http://www.georgetown.edu/pdba/Constitutions/Uruguay/uruguay96.html> (last visited on August 26, 2003)
Venezuela	The Constitution expressly prohibits discrimination on the basis of politics, age, race, sex, creed, or any other condition, and the law prohibits discrimination based on ethnic origin, sex, or disability. Persons with disabilities have minimal access to public transportation, and ramps are practically nonexistent, even in government buildings. According to local advocates, persons with disabilities are discriminated against in many sectors, including education, health care, and employment. A comprehensive 1993 law to protect the rights of persons with disabilities requires that all newly constructed or renovated public parks and buildings provide access. The law also forbids discrimination in employment practices and in the provision of public services. However, the Government has not made a significant effort to implement the law, to inform the public of it, or to try to change societal prejudice against persons with disabilities. *Specific Legislation:* (a) Venez. Const of 1999, art. 81, <http://www.asambleanacional.gov.ve/ns2/PaginasPlanas/CONSTITUCION99.doc> [accessed August 27, 2003] (b) Law for the Integration of the Disabled People, 15 of Aug. 1993, <http://www.dredf.org/symposium/venez.html> (last visited on August 26, 2003)

	NEAR EAST & NORTH AFRICA
Algeria	The Government does not mandate accessibility to buildings or government services for persons with disabilities. Public enterprises, in downsizing the work force, generally ignore a law that requires that they reserve 1 percent of their jobs for persons with disabilities. Social security provides for payments for orthopedic equipment, and some NGOs receive limited government financial support. The Government also attempts to finance specialized training, but this initiative remains rudimentary.
Bahrain	The law protects the rights of persons with disabilities and a variety of governmental, quasi-governmental, and religious institutions are mandated to support and protect persons with disabilities. The regional (Persian Gulf) Center for the Treatment of the Blind is headquartered in the country, and a similar Center for the Education of Deaf Children was established in 1994. Society tends to view persons with disabilities as special cases in need of protection rather than as fully functioning members of society. Nonetheless, the Government is required by law to provide vocational training for persons with disabilities who wish to work, and maintains a list of certified, trained persons with disabilities.
	The Labor Law of 1976 also requires that any employer of more than 100 persons must hire at least 2 percent of its employees from the Government's list of workers with disabilities; however, the Government does not monitor compliance. The Ministry of Labor and Social Affairs works actively to place persons with disabilities in public sector jobs, such as in the public telephone exchanges. The Government's housing regulations require that access be provided to persons with disabilities. Greater emphasis has been given in recent years to public building design that incorporates access for persons with disabilities; however, the law does not mandate access to buildings for persons with disabilities.
	Specific Legislation: Legislative Decree No. 14 of 1993 amending the labour law for the private sector, Decree No. 23 of 1976, <http://www.bah-molsa.com/english/index.htm> (last visited on August 21, 2003)

Egypt	There are no laws specifically prohibiting discrimination against persons with physical or mental disabilities, but the Government makes serious efforts to address their rights. It works closely with U.N. agencies and other international aid donors to design job-training programs for persons with disabilities. The Government also seeks to increase the public's awareness of the capabilities of persons with disabilities in television programming, the print media, and in educational material in public schools. There are approximately 5.7 million persons with disabilities, of whom 1.5 million are disabled severely. By law all businesses must designate 5 percent of their jobs for persons with disabilities, who are exempt from normal literacy requirements. Although there is no legislation mandating access to public accommodations and transportation, persons with disabilities may ride government-owned mass transit buses free of charge, are given priority in obtaining telephones, and receive reductions on customs duties for private vehicles. A number of NGOs are active in efforts to train and assist persons with disabilities. *Specific Legislation:* Decree by the Ministry of Social Affairs (Department of Associations and Institutions) No. 221, 2000. Based on Law No. 32 of 1964 which regulates private associations and institutions.
Iran	There is no available information regarding whether the Government has legislated or otherwise mandated accessibility for persons with disabilities, or whether discrimination against persons with disabilities is prohibited. However, the Cable News Network reported in 1996 on the harsh conditions in an institution for children with mental retardation who had been abandoned by their parents. Film clips showed children tied or chained to their beds, in filthy conditions, and without appropriate care. It is not known to what extent this represents the typical treatment of persons with disabilities. *Specific Legislation:* Iran Const. of 1979, art. 29 (amended 1989), <http://www.oefre.unibe.ch/law/icl/ir00000_.html> (last visited on August 18, 2003)
Iraq	No information was available regarding the Government's policy towards persons with disabilities.

Israel and occupied territories	There is no mandated accessibility to public facilities in the occupied territories under either Israeli law or Palestinian authority. Many Palestinians with disabilities are segregated and isolated from Palestinian society; they are discriminated against in most spheres, including education, employment, transportation, and access to public buildings and facilities. There were approximately 130,000 Palestinians with disabilities in the West Bank and Gaza prior to the outbreak of the current Intifada. The Health, Development, Information, and Policy Institute estimates that approximately one-tenth of the Palestinians injured in the Intifada will have permanent disabilities. Some Palestinian institutions care for and train persons with disabilities; however, their efforts are consistently under-funded. *Specific Legislation*: Equal Rights for Persons with Disabilities Law No. 5758, 1998, <http://www.dredf.org/symposium/israel.html> (last visited on August 21, 2003)
Jordan	High unemployment in the general population restricts job opportunities for persons with disabilities, estimated by the Ministry of Social Development to number 220,000. Thirteen percent of citizens with disabilities receive monetary assistance from the Government. The Government passed legislation in 1993 requiring future public buildings to accommodate the needs of persons with disabilities and to retro-fit existing public buildings; however, implementation has been slow. In 2000 the Greater Amman Municipality established a new Special Buildings Codes Department for Special Needs Citizens to enforce the implementation of the 1993 law. Since 1993 the Special Education Department of the Ministry of Social Development has enrolled approximately 11,000 persons with mental and physical disabilities in public and private sector training courses. It has placed approximately 3,660 persons with disabilities in public and private sector jobs. The law requires that 2 percent of the available jobs be reserved for persons with physical disabilities. Private organizations and members of the royal family actively promote programs to protect and advance the interests of persons with disabilities. *Specific Legislation*: Protection of the Disabled (Welfare) Act No. 12, 1993, <http://www.dredf.org/symposium/jordan.html> (last visited on August 21, 2003)

Kuwait	There is no institutionalized discrimination against persons with disabilities in employment, education, or in the provision of state services. Legislation passed by the National Assembly in 1996 mandated accessibility for persons with disabilities to all public facilities, and provides an affirmative action employment program for persons with disabilities. However, this law has not been implemented fully. The law prohibits discrimination against persons with disabilities and imposes penalties against employers who refrain from hiring persons with disabilities without reasonable cause. The Government pays extensive stipends to persons with disabilities, which cover transportation, housing, job training, and social welfare.
Lebanon	More than 100,000 persons became disabled during the civil war. Families generally perform care of persons with disabilities. Most efforts to secure education, independence, health, and shelter for persons with disabilities are made by approximately 100 private organizations. These organizations are relatively active, although poorly funded.
	There are few accommodations for persons with disabilities in the cities. The Government does not mandate building-code requirements for nongovernmental buildings for ease of access by persons with disabilities, although in its rebuilding projects the Government has constructed sidewalks in some parts of Beirut that allow access for persons with disabilities. The private "Solider" project for the reconstruction of downtown Beirut has self-imposed requirements for access by persons with disabilities. This project is considered to be a model for construction efforts around the country.
	During 2000 Parliament passed amendments to the law on persons with disabilities which stipulate that at least 3 percent of all government and private sector positions should be filled by persons with disabilities, provided that such persons fulfill the qualifications of the position. The amendments provide the private sector with tax-reduction benefits if the number of persons with disabilities who are hired exceed the number specified in the law. The amendments also impose a new building code for all government buildings and require that public transportation be accessible for persons with disabilities. Implementing regulations have not yet been adopted.
Libya	No information is available on the Government's efforts, if any, to assist persons with disabilities.

Morocco	A high incidence of disabling disease, especially polio, has resulted in a correspondingly high number of persons with disabilities. The latest statistics from the Government estimate the number of persons with disabilities at 2.2 million, or 7 percent of the population. However, other estimates are as high as 3 million. While the Ministry of Social Affairs attempts to integrate persons with disabilities into society, in practice integration largely is left to private charities. The annual budget for the ministerial department in charge of affairs concerning persons with disabilities is only .01 percent of the overall annual budget. Even nonprofit special-education programs are priced beyond the reach of most families. Typically, their families support persons with disabilities; some survive by begging. There are no laws assisting persons with disabilities in housing, transportation, access to government services, or access to buildings.
	The Government continued a pilot training program for the visually impaired sponsored in part by a member of the royal family. In 2000, the Government created a special commission for the integration of persons with disabilities, presided over by Prime Minister Youssoufi. The commission is responsible for developing programs that facilitate their societal integration. Also in 2000, the Government instituted an annual "National Day of the Disabled," which is aimed at increasing public awareness of issues affecting persons with disabilities. On October 31, Member of Parliament and President of the Moroccan Association of SOS Children's Villages, Amine Demnati, announced that construction had begun south of Casablanca for a center for persons with disabilities adjacent to the Children's Village.
	On November 16, after the fourth annual "handisports" games for athletes with disabilities, the King hosted a reception in their honor at the royal palace in Rabat to increases awareness and acceptance of persons with disabilities.
	On December 5, the International Day of Handicapped Persons, the Ministry for the Condition of Women, Protection of the Family and Children, and Integration of the Handicapped, sponsored a 2-day workshop with NGOs to promote self-employment of the handicapped. The program included micro-financing for persons with disabilities.
Oman	There are no laws prohibiting discrimination against persons with disabilities. The Government has mandated parking spaces and some ramps for wheelchair access in private and government office buildings and shopping centers. Compliance is voluntary, yet widely observed. Students in wheelchairs have easy access to Sultan Qaboos University. The Government has established several rehabilitation centers for children with disabilities. Persons with disabilities, including blind persons, work in government offices. While the Government may charge a small fee to citizens seeking government health care, persons with disabilities generally are not charged for physical therapy and prosthetics support.

Qatar	The law does not address the question of discrimination against persons with disabilities. The Government has not enacted legislation or otherwise mandated provision of accessibility for persons with disabilities, who also face societal discrimination. The Government maintains a hospital and schools that provide high-quality, free services to persons, including non-citizens, with mental and physical disabilities.
Saudi Arabia	The provision of government social services increasingly has brought persons with disabilities into the public mainstream. The media carry features highlighting the accomplishments of persons with disabilities and sharply criticizing parents who neglect children with disabilities. The Government and private charitable organizations cooperate in education, employment, and other services for persons with disabilities. The law provides hiring quotas for persons with disabilities. There is no legislation that mandates public accessibility; however, newer commercial buildings often include such access, as do some newer government buildings. *Specific Legislation:* Saudi Arabia Const. of 1992, art. 27, <http://www.oefre.unibe.ch/law/icl/sa00000_.html> (last visited on August 18, 2003)
Syria	The law prohibits discrimination against persons with disabilities and seeks to integrate them into the public sector work force. However, implementation is inconsistent. Regulations reserving 4 percent of government and public sector jobs for persons with disabilities are not implemented rigorously. Persons with disabilities may not legally challenge alleged instances of discrimination. There are no laws that mandate access to public buildings for persons with disabilities. *Specific Legislation:* Syria Const. of 1973, art. 46, <http://www.oefre.unibe.ch/law/icl/sy00000_.html> (last visited on August 18, 2003)

Tunisia	The law prohibits discrimination based on disability and mandates that at least 1 percent of the public and private sector jobs be reserved for persons with disabilities. All public buildings constructed since 1991 must be accessible to persons with physical disabilities. Many cities, including the capital, have begun to install wheelchair access ramps on city sidewalks. There is a general trend toward making public transportation more accessible to persons with disabilities. The Government issues special cards to persons with disabilities for benefits such as unrestricted parking, priority medical services, preferential seating on public transportation, and consumer discounts. The Government provides tax incentives to companies to encourage the hiring of persons with physical disabilities. The law includes provisions prohibiting discrimination against persons with mental disabilities. Several active NGOs provide educational, vocational, and recreational assistance to children and young adults with mental disabilities. Some are funded by the Government and international organizations. *Specific Legislation:* Decree No. 2002-888, 2002 modifying the decree No. 90-2061, 1990, bearing organization of the institute of promotion of the handicapped people.
United Arab Emirates	There is no federal legislation requiring accessibility for persons with disabilities. However, the Ministry of Labor and Social Affairs sponsors centers that provide facilities and services to persons with physical or mental disabilities. Initiatives range from monthly social aid funds, special education, and transportation assistance, to sending a team to the Special Olympics. The Government and quasi-government entities also provide a significant amount of nongovernmental financial assistance, services, and emotional support to persons with disabilities.
Western Sahara	N/A

Yemen	Persons with mental and physical disabilities face distinct social prejudices, as well as discrimination in education and employment. In 1998 the Government mandated the acceptance of persons with disabilities in universities, exempted them from paying tuition, and required that schools be made more accessible to persons with disabilities; however, it is unclear to what extent these laws have been implemented. There is no national law mandating the accessibility of buildings for persons with disabilities. Some persons with disabilities are reduced to begging to support themselves. Patients with mental illness, particularly those who commit crimes, are imprisoned and even shackled when there is no one to care for them. In some instances, authorities arrest persons with mental illness without charge and place them in prisons alongside criminals (see Section 1.c.). The ICRC, in cooperation with the Yemeni Red Crescent Society, built and now staffs separate detention facilities for prisoners with mental illness. These facilities are located in Sana'a, Ibb, and Taiz, and collectively are able to care for a population of about 300 persons.

	South Asia
Afghanistan	No measures had been taken to protect the rights of persons with mental and physical disabilities, or to mandate accessibility for them. Victims of landmines continued to be a major focus of international humanitarian relief organizations, which devoted resources to providing prostheses, medical treatment, and rehabilitation therapy to amputees. There reportedly has been increased public acceptance of persons with disabilities because of their increasing prevalence due to landmines or other war-related injuries. There are reports that women, who needed prostheses or other aids to walk, virtually were homebound because they were unable to wear the burqa over the prosthesis or other aid. An estimated 3 to 4 percent of the population suffered from disabilities requiring at least some form of assistance. Although community-based health and rehabilitation committees provided services to approximately 100,000 persons, their activities were restricted to 60 out of 330 districts, and they were able to assist only a small number of those in need.
Bangladesh	The law provides for equal treatment and freedom from discrimination for persons with disabilities; however, in practice, the disabled face social and economic discrimination. The Government has not enacted specific legislation or otherwise mandated accessibility for persons with disabilities. Government facilities for treating the mentally ill or the retarded are inadequate. Unless a family has money to pay for private service, a mentally ill person can find little treatment in the country. *Specific Legislation:.* Bangladesh Disability Welfare Act, 2001, <http://www.din.or.jp/~yukin/BanglaLawEng.html> (last visited on August 26, 2003)
Bhutan	There is no evidence of official discrimination toward persons with disabilities, but the Government has not passed legislation mandating accessibility for persons with disabilities. Societal discrimination against persons with disabilities remains a problem.

India	According to regional NGOs, there are over 50 million disabled persons in the country. According to the Blind Foundation for India, there are more than 2 million blind children in the country, and only 5 percent of them receive an education. According to Javed Abidi of the National Center for Promotion of Employment for Disabled People (NCPEDP), the census taken during the year failed to include categories of disability, thus making an accurate estimate of the needs of persons with disabilities impossible. Neither law nor regulations require accessibility for persons with disabilities. With the adoption of the Persons with Disability Act, a nascent disabled rights movement slowly is raising public awareness of the rights of the disabled. Although the act provides equal rights to all persons with disabilities, advocacy organizations admit that its practical effects so far have been minimal in part due to a clause that makes the implementation of programs dependent on the "economic capacity" of the Government. For example, government buildings, educational establishments, and public spaces in New Delhi have almost no provisions for wheelchair access. To a large degree, physical impediments still limit mobility, legislation prevents equality, and societal discrimination maintains the status quo of persons with disabilities. The Disabled Division of the Ministry of Welfare had a budget of more than $50 million (2.3 billion Rs) for the 2000-01 fiscal year for a number of organizations and committees at the national, regional, and local levels. The Ministry delivers rehabilitation services to the rural population through 16 district centers. A national rehabilitation plan commits the Government to putting a rehabilitation center in each of more than 400 districts, but services still are concentrated in urban areas. Moreover, the impact of government programs has been limited. Significant funding is provided to a few government organizations such as the Artificial Limbs Manufacturing Corporation of India, the National Handicapped Finance and Development Corporation, and the Rehabilitation Council of India. Each entity provides specific services or training, including producing aids and prosthetics, promoting disabled-oriented economic development activities, offering training to health-care professionals and vocational instructors concerning disabled-related issues, and providing comprehensive rehabilitation services to the rural disabled. Two significant programs to benefit the disabled are the National Project to Integrate Mentally Retarded in Family and Community and the National Institute for the Multiple Disabilities. The first project, launched in six states in 1998, primarily focuses on children from the economically weaker sectors and promotes awareness concerning the mentally disabled, their problems, and their rights. The second is the Ministry of Welfare, which provides rehabilitation services to the disabled and is fostering greater awareness among communities throughout the country. As a result of the passage of the Persons with Disability Act, there is a Disabilities Commissioner who oversees implementation of the act and its protections for persons with disabilities. In addition, the NHRC formed a group of seven experts in August to identify issues affecting persons with disabilities, to review government policies, and to protect the rights of persons with disabilities. According to the Persons with Disability Act, 3 percent of positions in government offices and state-owned enterprises must be reserved for persons with visual, hearing, or orthopedic disabilities. The act

India (cont'd)	mandates that 5 percent of employees in both the private and public sector eventually should consist of persons with disabilities. *Specific Legislation:* C.I.S Part II-A (1996), Persons with Disabilities (Equal Opportunities, Protection of Rights & Full Participation) Act, 1995 (No. 1 of 1996), <http://natlex.ilo.org/txt/E96IND01.htm> (last visited on August 21, 2003)
Maldives	There is no law that specifically addresses the rights of persons with physical or mental disabilities. In 1999 the Government initiated a survey that identified 30,000 persons with disabilities in the country (primarily hearing and visually impaired). The Government has established programs and provided services for persons with disabilities. Persons with disabilities usually are cared for by their families. When family care is unavailable, persons with disabilities are kept in the Institute for Needy People, which also assists elderly persons. The Government provides free medication for all mentally ill persons in the islands, and mobile teams regularly visit mentally ill patients. In 1999 the Government enacted a new building code, which mandated that all new government buildings and jetties must be accessible to persons with disabilities. This law was being implemented at year's end.
Nepal	Persons with disabilities face widespread societal discrimination. Families often are stigmatized by and ashamed of family members with disabilities, who may be hidden away or neglected. Economic integration is further hampered by the general view that persons with disabilities are unproductive. The mentally retarded are associated with the mentally ill. Sometimes mentally ill and retarded persons are placed in prisons due to the lack of facilities or support. The Government long has been involved in providing for persons with disabilities, but limited resources have kept the level of government assistance insufficient to meet their needs. The Disabled Persons Protection and Welfare Act and additional 1994 rules mandate accessibility to buildings, transportation, employment, education, and other state services. The Government has begun developing a policy on equal access for persons with disabilities to public buildings and transportation. However, despite government funding for special education programs, the Government does not implement effectively or enforce laws regarding persons with disabilities. *Specific Legislation:* Disabled Persons Protection and Welfare Rules, 1994, Nepal Recorder, 1994-12-22, Vol. 18, No. 27, pp. 220-226; promulgated under the Disabled Persons Protection and Welfare Act 1982.

| Pakistan | There are no laws requiring equal accessibility to public buildings for persons with disabilities. The vast majority of persons with physical and mental disabilities are cared for by their families. However, in some cases these individuals are forced into begging; organized criminal "beggarmasters" skim off much of the proceeds. Parents reportedly have given children as offerings to Baba Shah Dola, a shrine in Punjab where the children reportedly are deformed intentionally by clamping a metal form on the head that induces microcephalitis. Some human rights organizations asked local authorities to investigate this practice; however, there have been no investigations. There is a legal provision requiring public and private organizations to reserve at least 2 percent of their jobs for qualified persons with disabilities. Organizations that do not wish to hire persons with disabilities instead can give a certain amount of money to the government treasury, which goes into a fund for persons with disabilities. This obligation rarely is enforced. The National Council for the Rehabilitation of the Disabled provides some job placement and loan facilities.

Mentally ill prisoners normally lack adequate care and are not segregated from the general prison population (see Section 1.c.).

Specific Legislation:
National Council for the Rehabilitation of Disabled Persons (General) Rules, 1983 (S.R.O. 713) promulgated under the Disabled Peoples (Employment and Rehabilitation) Ordinance No. 15, 1981. |
|---|---|
| Sri Lanka | The law does not mandate accessibility to buildings or government services for persons with disabilities. The World Health Organization estimates that 7 percent of the population is persons with disabilities. Most persons with disabilities, who are unable to work, are cared for by their families. The Department of Social Services operates eight vocational training schools for persons with physical and mental disabilities and sponsors a program of job training and placement for graduates. The Government also provides some financial support to NGOs that assist persons with disabilities; subsidizes prosthetic devices and other medical aids for persons with disabilities; makes some purchases from suppliers with disabilities; and has registered 74 schools and training institutions for persons with disabilities run by NGOs. The Social Services Ministry has selected job placement officers to help the estimated 200,000 work-eligible persons with disabilities find jobs. In spite of these efforts, persons with disabilities still face difficulties because of negative attitudes and societal discrimination. In 1996 Parliament passed legislation forbidding discrimination against any person on the grounds of disability. No cases are known to have been filed under this law.

Specific Legislation:
Protection of the Rights of Persons with Disabilities Act No. 28, 1996. |

APPENDIX 7

ELEMENTS FOR A FUTURE UNITED NATIONS COMPREHENSIVE AND INTEGRAL CONVENTION TO PROMOTE AND PROTECT THE RIGHTS AND DIGNITY OF PERSONS WITH DISABILITIES
(Proposal of Mexico)[2]

Preamble

The States Parties to this Convention:

a) Reaffirming the purposes and principles of the Charter of the United Nations;

b) Considering that the Charter of the United Nations reaffirms the value of the human person based on the principles of dignity and equality inherent to human beings and resolves to promote the social progress and better standards of living of all peoples within a broader concept of freedom;

c) Recognizing that the United Nations has proclaimed and agreed accorded in the Universal Declaration of Human Rights and in the International Covenants on Human Rights that everyone is entitled to all rights and freedoms set forth therein without distinction of any kind, such as race, color, sex, language, religion, political or other opinion, national or social origin, property, birth, or other status;

d) Recognizing also that discrimination against all persons for reasons of any disability is a violation of the principles of equality of rights and respect for human dignity and hinders the participation - under equality of conditions - of persons with disabilities in civil, social, economic, political, and cultural life;

e) Taking into consideration the international and regional instruments, declarations, norms, and programs adopted to promote human rights and non-discrimination against persons with disabilities, such as: the 1982 World Program of Action for Persons with Disabilities; the 1971

---

[2]   http://www.sre.gob.mx/discapacidad/elementsproposal.htm [accessed June 1, 2003]. There is a different version at http://www.sre.gob.mx/discapacidad/elements.htm#top [accessed June 1, 2003].

Declaration on the Rights of Mentally Retarded Persons; the 1975 Declaration of Rights of Disabled Persons; the 1991 Principles for the Protection of Persons with Mental Illness and the Improvement of Mental Healthcare; the 1993 Standard Rules on the Equalization of Opportunities for Persons with Disabilities; the 1999 Inter-American Convention on the Elimination of All Forms of Discrimination against Persons with Disabilities; and the statutes and pertinent instruments from specialized agencies such as the 1983 International Labor Organization's Convention no. 159 on the Vocational Rehabilitation and Employment of Persons with Disabilities;

f) Reaffirming the outcomes of the major United Nations Conferences and Summits and their respective follow-up reviews, particular as they pertain to the promotion of the rights and well-being of persons with disabilities, on an equal and participatory basis;

g) Noting with great satisfaction that the Standard Rules on the Equalization of Opportunities for Persons with Disabilities have played an important role in influencing the promotion, formulation, and evaluation of the policies, plans, programs, and actions at the national, regional, and international levels to further the equalization of opportunities by, for and with persons with disabilities;

h) Stressing the relationship that exists between the present Convention and the Covenants on Human Rights and other human rights instruments, as well as the usefulness of the Standard Rules for implementing the content of this international instrument;

i) Recognizing that, despite the numerous efforts made by governments, bodies and relevant organizations within the United Nations system and non-governmental organizations aimed at increasing cooperation and integration, as well as raising awareness about questions regarding disability since the adoption of the World Program of Action (1983-1992), these efforts have not been enough to eradicate violations and discrimination against persons with disabilities in different parts of the world;

j) Recognizing that in order to achieve equality of opportunities for persons with disabilities, the exercise of all political, civil, economic, social, and cultural rights established in the International Covenants and other instruments of Human Rights, must be guaranteed, as well as their accessibility to the physical environment;

k) Emphasizing the responsibility of States to eliminate obstacles and barriers for the full integration and participation in all spheres of social, economic, cultural, and political life - under conditions of equality - for persons with disabilities and vulnerable to multiple or aggravated discrimination;

l) Concerned over the fact of the existence of social circumstances that contribute to increase the incidence of disability, which include extreme poverty, lack of healthcare attention, violence inside and outside the home, accidents, alcohol and drug abuse, inadequate administration in medical treatment, systematic violation of human rights, lack of proper care during the ageing process, and armed conflicts;

m) Committed to take the necessary steps to reduce the causes that originate or worsen certain disabilities;

n) Bearing in mind the importance of raising the development levels and quality of life of the world's population and working toward the strengthening of international peace and security;

o) Conscious of the world movement in favor of persons with disabilities and the efforts undertaken by these organizations and their representatives in raising awareness and recognition of the rights of persons with disabilities;

p) Motivated by the principles of dignity and equality intrinsic to human beings and the values of dignity, independence, equality of opportunities, and solidarity with persons with disabilities;

Have agreed to the following:

Article 1

The object of this Convention is to:

a) Recognize, guarantee, promote, and protect the rights of persons with disabilities;

b) Eliminate all forms of discrimination against persons with disabilities in public and private spheres;

c) Promote the autonomy and independent lives of persons with disabilities and achieve their full participation in economic, social, cultural, civil, and political life, under conditions of equality;

d) Promote new forms of international cooperation to support national efforts in the benefit of persons with disabilities, and achieve the objectives of this Convention.

Article 2

For the purposes of this Convention, the following definitions shall apply:

a) "Disability" means a physical, mental (psychic), or sensory impairment, whether permanent or temporary, that limits the capacity to perform one or more essential activities of daily life, and which can be caused or aggravated by the economic and social environment.

b) Discrimination against persons with disabilities means any distinction, exclusion, or restriction based on a disability, record of disability, condition resulting from a previous disability, or perception of disability, whether present or past, which has the effect or objective of impairing or nullifying the recognition, enjoyment or exercise by a person with a disability of his or her human rights and fundamental freedoms.

Article 3

States Parties agree to adopt legislative, judicial, administrative, and any other kind of measures aimed at achieving the objectives of this Convention. To this end, they shall:

1. Include in their legislation, policies and programs aimed at promoting the full participation of persons with disabilities.

2. Adopt the necessary measures to eliminate all forms of discrimination against persons with disabilities and promote and protect the exercise of their rights. Among others, these measures shall include the following:

a) Incorporate in their national legislations the principle of equality and non-discrimination for all people and abolish or amend any legislation that permits the contrary.

b) Establish measures to prevent and sanction any practice which constitutes discrimination against persons with disabilities.

c) Ensure that the rights contained in this Convention and other related international instruments have the legal protection of the competent national courts.

d) Establish in their national legislations the necessary positive actions to promote the autonomy and independent lives of persons with disabilities and to achieve their full participation, under conditions of equality, in all activities of economic, social, cultural, civil, and political life.

3. In the elaboration and evaluation of legislation and policies adopted for persons with disabilities, special circumstances and needs of persons with disabilities, shall be taken into account and shall secure their participation and that of their families.

4. Promote the elaboration national census-taking of the population with disabilities and their access to public services, rehabilitation, education, and employment.

Article 4

1. In order to guarantee equality of rights and opportunities for persons with disabilities, States Parties shall promote, among others, positive or compensatory measures.

2. States Parties shall adopt specific measures to protect persons with disabilities who are in special situations of vulnerability.

Article 5

States Parties shall promote the changing of stereotypes, socio-cultural patterns, customary practices, or of any other nature which constitute an obstacle for persons with disabilities or their families in the exercise of their rights. To this end, States Parties shall:

a) Adopt measures to raise society's awareness regarding the rights and needs of persons with disabilities, including the creation of awareness programs at all levels of formal education.

b) Encourage the mass media to project a positive and non-stereotype image of persons with disabilities and their families.

c) Guarantee the participation of disabled people's organizations in the execution of these measures.

d) Promote dissemination campaigns to raise the awareness of society and training courses for public officials regarding the rights contained in this Convention.

Article 6

States Parties recognize the right of persons with disabilities to freedom of movement and to have an accessible environment to guarantee their autonomy, independence, and full participation in all activities.

States Parties shall legislate or take steps to ensure that:

a) Urban outfitting and public services and facilities for public use have the adaptations necessary to facilitate access, use, and circulation for persons with disabilities.

b) Vehicles and public transport services allow the access and mobility of persons with disabilities.

c) The existence of adaptations, signposting, and basic forms of communication for the freedom of movement and access to all public services and those available to the public.

d) The construction and adaptation of housing comply with regulations governing accessibility for persons with disabilities.

Article 7

States Parties shall promote access to different forms of alternative communication for persons with sensorial disabilities, as well as promoting the linguistic rights of persons who use such forms.

Article 8

States Parties shall guarantee the right to information of persons with different kinds of disabilities. To this end, they shall adopt, among others, the following measures:

a) Ensure that public information services are accessible, using appropriate technologies.

b) Encourage the mass media to make their services accessible to persons with disabilities.

c) Promote through information campaigns, awareness of the rights intrinsic to persons with disabilities and the means by which to enforce these rights.

Article 9

States Parties recognize that persons with disabilities are particularly vulnerable to different forms of violence, as well as torture and other cruel, inhumane or degrading treatment or punishment, in public and private spheres. Therefore, States shall guarantee respect for the dignity and integrity of persons with disabilities.

Article 10

1. States Parties shall promote respect for the human rights of persons with disabilities in all legal proceedings and, therefore, likewise commit to:

a) Provide legal counsel and interpretation or translation services, free of charge, to all persons with disabilities.

b) Prohibit all forms of discrimination during legal proceedings or the serving of a prison sentence.

c) Consider or categorize such discrimination as aggravated criminal behavior when committed against persons with disabilities.

d) Ensure that protection services are offered and compensation measures are established in favor of persons with disabilities who have become victims of crime.

2. States Parties shall adopt measures to comply with these dispositions, which, among other things, shall include the sensitizing and training of public officials responsible for law enforcement and administration, with regard to the rights contained in this Convention.

Article 11

States Parties to this Convention recognize the political rights of persons with disabilities and pledge to take steps to guarantee their full participation in political life, adopting, among others, the following measures:

a) Guarantee exercise of the right to universal and secret suffrage of all persons with disabilities and, for that purpose, include in election mechanisms the use of instruments and specialized technologies for each type of disability.

b) Guarantee the right to information of persons with disabilities so as to assist them in the decision-making process and in participating in political affairs.

c) Promote the participation, under conditions of equality, of persons with disabilities in positions of popular election, political parties, social organizations, and in public administration.

d) Guarantee the right of persons with disabilities to freedom of association and to form their own organizations.

e) Promote the participation of persons with disabilities and their organizations in the design of government policies relating to disability.

Article 12

1. States Parties recognize that persons with disabilities have the right to receive an education of quality that furthers their integral development, independence, and participation, under conditions of equality, in public and private spheres.

2. States Parties shall include the specific educational needs of persons with disabilities in national education policies, plans, and programs and shall provide the resources needed to allow their inclusion in the formal education system.

3. States Parties shall guarantee the presence of other methods of quality teaching, with curricula common to formal education, solely for persons with disabilities who choose to enter another educational system such as integrated, special, and open schools, as well as interactive learning systems.

In order to attain the above-mentioned objectives, States Parties shall:

a) Ensure that students with disabilities have access to information regarding the education options available so they may exercise their right to select the appropriate teaching model.

b) Guarantee that persons with disabilities will receive a public education, free of charge, in all education methods and levels, giving priority to those living in situations of extreme vulnerability.

c) Ensure the provision and ongoing training of specialized human resources that support the teaching process of persons with disabilities in formal and other education methods, promoting the training and hiring of teachers, instructors, and specialists with disabilities.

d) Include information and communications technologies in learning processes.

e) Ensure that regular programs with the necessary adaptations are the referent for the education of persons with disabilities in other education methods, and, that specialists and persons with disabilities and their families are involved.

f) Ensure that students with disabilities receive the equipment, technical assistance, and teaching and learning materials that will enable them to access and participate in curricular and extracurricular activities.

g) Promote access for students with disabilities to scholarships and financing resources.

Article 13

States Parties shall promote access for persons with disabilities to the medical and rehabilitation services they require so as to guarantee their right to health and to foster their autonomy and independent lives. To this end, States Parties shall:

a) Ensure that all medical and nursing staff, as well as other healthcare professionals, are properly qualified and have access to the appropriate technologies and methods for the treatment of persons with disabilities.

b) Ensure that persons with disabilities are able to decide on their treatment by providing them with the information necessary to do so.

c) Guarantee that persons with disabilities, especially breastfeeding mothers, children, and the elderly, receive quality medical attention within state healthcare systems.

d) Ensure that persons with disabilities give their consent prior to being subjected to any kind of research or medical or scientific experiment and likewise ensure that the genetic research and the biomedical and biotechnological advances are intended for their improvement.

e) Adopt all measures necessary to guarantee that the medical, rehabilitation, and assistance services provided to persons with disabilities include the following:

1. Opportune detection, diagnosis, and treatment.

2. Modern medical assistance and treatment that include the use of new technologies.

3. Counseling, as well as social, psychological and other assistance for persons with disabilities and their families.

4. Training in self-care activities, including aspects of mobility, communication, and skills for everyday living.

5. The provision of medication, technical assistance with mobility, and other special devices they may require.

f) Ensure that public as well as private healthcare institutions, particularly psychiatric ones, are monitored by the health and human rights authorities to ensure that the living conditions and treatment administered therein to persons with disabilities grant respect for their human rights and dignity.

Article 14

States Parties recognize the right of persons with disabilities to work and to freely choose their professions and jobs, and will adopt all measures necessary for their participation, under conditions of equality, in the labor market. For this purpose, States Parties shall:

a) Guarantee that individual and collective labor agreements and regulations protect persons with disabilities in regard with employment, job promotion, and working conditions, and, ensure the exercise of their labor rights.

b) Prohibit and abolish any discriminatory regulations and practices which restrict or deny persons with disabilities access to, and continuance and promotion within the labor market.

c) Guarantee the right of persons with disabilities to an equal wage for work of equal value.

d) Promote the adoption of positive measures that allow persons with disabilities access to and continuance in employment.

e) Promote workplace training, instruction, and updating for persons with disabilities.

f) Promote the adaptation of workplaces, work instruments, and working hours to make them accessible for persons with disabilities.

g) Grant incentives for companies that hire persons with disabilities and facilitate their freedom to attend medical appointments and undergo therapy.

h) Implement awareness campaigns to overcome negative attitudes and prejudices that affect persons with disabilities in the workplace.

Article 15

States Parties pledge to eliminate all norms and practices which restrict access for persons with disabilities to the benefits of social security and to this end, they shall adopt the following measures:

a) Guarantee that social security systems and other social welfare programs for the public in general do not exclude persons with disabilities, particularly in cases of unemployment, pregnancy, illness, elderly, and retirement.

b) Develop social security programs and measures that cater to the specific needs of persons with disabilities.

c) Take steps to facilitate access for persons with disabilities to the technical equipment and assistance necessary to raise their level of independence and the exercise of their rights.

d) Ensure that the lack of formal or permanent employment on the part of persons with disabilities does not curtail their access to social security services.

e) Promote the establishment, under governmental housing programs, of specific percentages of housing to be earmarked for persons with disabilities and their families.

f) Ensure that people who assist or look after persons with disabilities, including their relatives, have adequate training support and financial assistance, particularly in the case of persons with low incomes.

g) Establish norms whereby persons with disabilities are not discriminated against regarding the access to social security and public and private medical insurance.

Article 16

States Parties shall ensure that persons with disabilities have access to and the enjoyment of:

a) Recreational, cultural, and sports activities through adaptations which facilitate them the use of related facilities and services.

b) Their integration into routine sports activities and national as well as international competitions.

c) A system of scholarships or special incentives for cultural, artistic, and sports activities.

Article 17

In accordance with their legal systems, States Parties shall promote the establishment and strengthening of national institutions responsible for safeguarding the rights and dignity of persons with disabilities.

Article 18

States Parties agree to consult and collaborate with each other, regarding the putting into practice the content of this Convention, as well as to work together in a spirit of cooperation to achieve its objectives. To this end, they commit to:

a) Design programs which facilitate the implementation of the Convention, based on the Standard Rules on the Equalization of Opportunities for Persons with Disabilities and other instruments which promote their human rights and dignity.

b) Exchange the latest advances in scientific research and the development of technology pertaining to the treatment and rehabilitation of persons with disabilities and the elimination of obstacles that restrain their autonomy, independent life, and full enjoyment of their rights, as well as the development of national capacities.

c) Exchange information and best practices on measures and legislation for persons with disabilities.

d) Encourage the study of issues and research of common interest, including the problems and special needs of States Parties.

e) Promote courses, seminars, and workshops for training and research.

f) Promote the harmonization of criteria regarding alternative forms of communication used by persons with visual or hearing disabilities.

g) Incorporate the rights of persons with disabilities into the mandates of the bodies and relevant organizations of the United Nations, as well as in the elaboration of programs to take care of their needs.

h) Promote the elimination of import duties on technical equipment and aid materials for persons with disabilities.

Article 19

1. The object of the Conference of States Parties (hereinafter, "the Conference") shall be to:

a) Evaluate the operation and status of this Convention.

b) Promote international cooperation and assistance, as provided for in the previous Article.

c) Consider the recommendations and suggestions put forward by the Committee of Experts.

d) Elaborate a final report on the agreements reached at the Conference and submit it to the Secretary General of the United Nations.

2. The first Conference shall be convened by the Secretary General within a period of one year following the entry into force of this Convention. Subsequent meetings shall be convened by the Secretary General every three years, or whenever he deems necessary, and shall be held at the headquarters of the United Nations.

3. The Conference shall establish its own rules of procedure which, among

other, shall stipulate that:

a) Two thirds of the States Parties shall constitute quorum.

b) Conference decisions shall be adopted by a majority of votes from the members present.

4. States not Party to this Convention, specialized bodies and competent agencies of the United Nations system, and regional and non-governmental organizations may be invited to attend these meetings as observers, in accordance with the agreed rules of procedure.

5. The Secretary General shall provide the resources, personnel, and services required to hold the Conferences of States Parties.

Article 20

In order to monitor the implementation of this Convention, a Committee of Experts on the Rights of Persons with Disabilities (hereinafter, "the Committee") shall be established, the functions of which shall be as follows:

a) Evaluate the national reports submitted periodically by States Parties on the progress and problems encountered in implementing this Convention.

b) Make recommendations of a general nature to States Parties to further advance the implementation of this Convention.

c) Invite specialized bodies, other competent agencies, and non-governmental organizations to participate in studying the implementation of this Convention.

d) The Committee may invite specialized bodies and other agencies of the United Nations to submit reports on the implementation of the provisions of this Convention which apply to their particular sphere of competence.

e) Identify areas of cooperation among States Parties, and between these and specialized bodies and competent agencies that facilitate implementation of this Convention. To this end, the Committee shall submit its recommendations to the Conference.

f) The Committee may recommend technical assistance from United Nations agencies at any stage of the report evaluation process or during the implementation of its final recommendations.

g) Submit an annual report to the United Nations General Assembly on its activities pursuant to this Convention and make suggestions and recommendations based on the study of the reports and data provided by States Parties.

Article 21

1. States Parties undertake to submit to the Secretary General of the United Nations, to be examined by the Committee, a report on the legislative, judicial, administrative, or any other measures they have adopted to give effect to the provisions of this Convention.

2. Reports submitted by States Parties must specify advances as well as limitations affecting the degree of fulfillment of the obligations under the present Convention. They must likewise contain sufficient information regarding difficulties encountered in its implementation.

3. In their periodic reports, States Parties commit to include a chapter on the situation of persons with multiple disabilities and groups of disabled persons that are vulnerable to multiple or aggravated discrimination. They must also specify steps taken by the State Party to deal with their particular situation.

4. States Parties shall submit their reports for evaluation by the Committee within a term of two years following the entry into effect of this Convention for the State Party in question, and, thereafter, every four years, or whenever requested by the Committee.

Article 22

1. The Committee shall consist of 12 experts (men and women) chosen from among prominent national leaders of organizations of persons with disabilities, scholars, specialists, scientists, and doctors of recognized high moral integrity and competence in the protection and promotion of the rights and dignity of persons with disabilities and who shall serve in their personal capacity. These experts shall be elected by States Parties, taking into consideration an equitable geographic distribution and specialization in the different types of disabilities.

2. Members of the Committee shall be elected by secret ballot from a list of persons nominated by States Parties. Each State Party may propose one person from among its own nationals.

3. Committee members shall be elected at biennial meetings of the States Parties convened by the Secretary General of the United Nations and held at the latter's headquarters. At these meetings, quorum for which shall be constituted by the attendance of two thirds of the States Parties, candidates to the Committee shall be considered elected based on the

highest number of votes and on absolute majority of votes from States Parties' representatives present and voting.

4. The initial election shall be held, at the latest, six months following the date of the first Conference and, thereafter, every two years. At least four months prior to the date of each election, the Secretary General of the United Nations shall address a letter to the States Parties inviting them to submit their nominations within a period of three months. The Secretary General shall then prepare a list, in alphabetical order, of the persons nominated, indicating the States Parties they were proposed by, and notifying States Parties to the present Convention.

5. Committee members shall be elected for a period of four years. They may be reelected, if their candidatures are put forward once again. Notwithstanding, the mandate of six of the members elected in the first round shall expire after a period of two years. Immediately following the initial elections, the Committee chairperson shall chose the names of these six persons by lot.

6. In order to cover unexpected vacancies, the State Party whose expert has terminated his/her functions as a Committee member may appoint another expert from among its own nationals, subject to the approval of the Committee.

Article 23

1. The Committee shall elect its Board for a period of two years. Members of the Board may be reelected for a like period.

2. The Committee shall establish its own rules of procedure.

3. The Committee shall normally meet annually at United Nations headquarters for a period not to exceed two weeks to evaluate reports submitted in compliance with the previous Article. The duration of these meetings shall be determined and, if necessary, subject to review by the Conference of the Parties.

4. The Secretary General of the United Nations shall provide the resources, personnel, and services necessary for the effective performance of the functions of the Committee, under the present Convention.

5. Mindful of the importance of the functions of the Committee and subject to prior approval of the United Nations General Assembly, the members of the Committee shall receive emoluments from United Nations resources on such terms and conditions determined by the Assembly.

Article 24

A State Party to this Convention may, at any time, declare that it recognizes the competence of the Committee to receive and consider communications submitted by persons subject to its jurisdiction or, on their behalf, claiming to be victims of a violation by the State Party of any of the rights set forth in this Convention. The Committee will not accept any communication relating to a State Party which has not made this declaration.

Article 25

All States Parties to this Convention may propose an amendment and deposit it with the Secretary General of the United Nations. In such case:

a) The Secretary General shall inform States Parties regarding the proposed amendment, asking them to notify him should they wish to convene a Conference of States Parties to examine the proposal and put it to a vote.

b) If within the four months following receipt of this notification at least one third of the Party States come out in favor of convening, then the Secretary General shall convene an amendment conference, under the auspices of the United Nations.

c) Any amendment adopted by a majority of the States Parties present and voting at the conference shall be submitted by the Secretary General to the United Nations General Assembly for its approval.

d) Any amendment adopted pursuant to paragraph 1 of this Article shall come into force once it has been approved by the United Nations General Assembly and accepted by a two-thirds majority of the States Parties.

e) When amendments come into force, they shall be obligatory for the States Parties that have accepted them, in as much as the other States Parties shall be bound by the dispositions of this Convention.

f) States not Party to this Convention, as well as specialized bodies, non-governmental organizations, and other competent agencies may be invited to attend the Amendment Conference as observers, in accordance with the agreed rules of procedure.

Article 26

1. The Secretary General of the United Nations shall receive and circulate to all States the text of reservations formulated by States at the time of ratification or accession.

2. A reservation incompatible with the object and purpose of this

Convention shall not be permitted.

3. Reservations may be withdrawn at any time by virtue of notification to the Secretary General of the United Nations who shall, in turn, notify all States to the same effect. The notification shall take effect as of the date of its reception.

Article 27

Any dispute arising between two or more States Parties with respect to the interpretation or implementation of this Convention that is not settled by negotiation, shall, be referred to arbitration at the request of one of the parties to the dispute. If the parties fail to reach an agreement on the form of arbitration within a term of six months following the request, any of the parties may put the dispute before the International Court of Justice, in conformity with its statutes.

Article 28

Each State Party commits to widely disseminate this Convention and its periodic reports, and publicize them.

Article 29

1. The Secretary General of the United Nations is designated as the depository of this Convention.

2. This Convention shall be open for signature to all United Nations Member States.

3. This Convention shall be open for ratification or accession to all United Nations Member States.

4. The Secretary General shall periodically deliver information on the number of signatures, ratifications, and accessions to this Convention, as well as on the efforts made and steps taken for its promotion and dissemination.

Article 30

This Convention shall enter into force on the thirtieth day after the date the tenth instrument of ratification or accession has been deposited with the Secretary General of the United Nations.

For each State ratifying or acceding to this Convention after the tenth instrument of ratification or accession has been deposited, the Convention shall enter into force on the thirtieth day following the date on which the

State in question has deposited its own instrument of ratification or accession.

Article 31

1. This convention, whose texts in Arabic, Chinese, Spanish, French, English, and Russian are equally authentic, shall be deposited in the archives of the United Nations.

2. The Secretary General of the United Nations shall send certified copies of this Convention to all States Parties.

C

D

W